'There can surely be very few books about economics which make one's hair stand on end. Yet this is the effect of Bernard Connolly's *The Rotten Heart of Europe* . . . The author is the top official within the European Commission directly responsible for EMS affairs. [His] account combines extraordinary attention to detail, a broad and rigorous analysis of the effects of the ERM on Europe's economies, and a rare understanding of monetary theory.' *Wall Street Journal Europe*

'*The Rotten Heart of Europe* must surely now be on the reading list of any politician who wishes to argue about Britain's European future . . . The days when Europe's statesmen could build currency grids and integration treaties over the heads of voters have gone for good. Mr Connolly has given vivid expression to an unease previously voiced by only a few others but widely felt by many . . . The more people like Mr Connolly who speak that plain truth the better it will be for the Europe of the next century.' *The Times*

'One of the most important books ever written about Europe.' *Knack*

'The Brussels Commission has just suspended its senior economist, Bernard Connolly, for writing a book savaging the prospects for a common currency. There are many who now believe he should have been lauded as a prophet.' Editorial, 1 October 1995, *Observer*

'We need to ponder how our whole ruling class has turned so flabby since the fall of Margaret Thatcher . . . the story has now been bravely told by the head of Brussels' own Unit of the European Monetary System. Connolly details how the ERM was devised in their own interests by élite French bureaucrats.' Norman Macrae, *Sunday Times*

'Connolly has spun a surprisingly gripping yarn.' *Financial Times*

Bernard Connolly was born in Manchester in 1949, and studied at Oxford. He has worked on Wall Street, and for six years from 1989 was the head of the European Commission responsible for analysis of the European Monetary System and national and Community money policies. On publication of the hardback edition of this book he was suspended from his job and subsequently sacked. He is widely regarded by academics and bankers as the foremost practical expert on the interaction of politics and economics in European monetary affairs. Now an economic consultant influential in both London and New York, he is in constant demand for articles, press, TV and radio interviews and speeches throughout Europe and North America.

# The Rotten Heart
# of Europe

*The Dirty War for Europe's Money*

## BERNARD CONNOLLY

*faber and faber*

LONDON · BOSTON

First published in Great Britain in 1995
by Faber and Faber Limited
3 Queen Square London WC1N 3AU
This paperback edition first published in 1996

Phototypeset by Wilmaset Ltd, Wirral
Printed in England by Clays Ltd, St Ives plc

*A CIP record for this book
is available from the British Library*

ISBN 0-571-17521-X

2 4 6 8 10 9 7 5 3

# Contents

# Preface to paperback edition

The opportunity to write this preface to the paperback edition was granted to me by the forbearance of Faber and Faber and the lack of forbearance shown by my former employer, the European Commission. The role of my publisher is straightforward enough; but the role of the Commission perhaps needs some explaining. Even before the hardback edition was officially released, the Commission had made clear its decision to get rid of me. My crime, apparently, was serious indeed: I harboured fears that the European Monetary Union project was not quite the Heavenly City that relentless propaganda had made it out to be. 'If I had fears like that', said Jacques Santer's spokesman, 'I would resign this afternoon.'

At any rate, the Commission, after suspending me from my job as head of the Commission Unit responsible for the EMS and monetary policies, countenancing a smear campaign against me, denying me access to Commission buildings, posting photos of me at entrances to buildings and garages as if I were a dangerous terrorist bearing semtex and armalites, 'inviting' me not to leave Brussels, communicating with me through night-time visits from its little-known Security Service, and engaging in a disciplinary procedure that disregarded all the rules of natural justice, inflicted the penalty it had in effect decided five months earlier. At the end of January 1996, I was sacked.

The Commission made it plain in the formal sacking decision that it would not have granted permission for the publication of the book had I sought it. The book was, so the Commission said, a synthesis of the economic analysis I had been doing for several years as the senior official responsible for analysing – and to anyone with the Community interest at heart that must inevitably mean criticizing – the dreaded ERM and its advertised transmogrification into monetary union. In saying this, the Commission not only disregarded the duty placed on it to allow the publication of any book that did not damage the interests of the Community (how could analysis possibly do damage?) but unwittingly posed the question of what on earth it thought I was supposed to have been doing in my job. Perhaps my sacking took on the nature of an exorcism, a ritual chasing-away of the evil forces of inquiry and discussion. At any rate, it freed me to have this preface published – something that would not otherwise have been possible, given the Commission's self-proclaimed ban on analysis. It also freed me to respond to a huge number of invitations, coming from practically every Community country and from many outside, to speak and write on the subjects the Commission most wants people to keep quiet about.

Normal people in the Community countries are clearly thirsting for knowledge about what their leaders are doing and why they are doing it; they fear they are having the wool pulled over their eyes; they suspect that hidden agendas are being implemented; they are fed up with the establishment sloganizing that has replaced analysis; they are coming to understand that the myths propagated by the supporters of EMU have no foundation; above all, they now realize that monetary union is a political project – an attempt to create a European superstate.

There are reasons for believing that the publication of this book in September 1995 played a part in opening people's eyes to the realities of European monetary politics. And it is certainly the case that events since last September have validated the book's theses and predictions. For one, the idea of monetary union as a barrier against the 'Anglo-Saxon' world has been made more explicit than ever before: in March 1996, for example, the Belgian Finance Minister said baldly that monetary union was about 'preventing the encroachment of Anglo-Saxon values' in Europe. And when it became clear even to the wilfully blind that the economic policies followed in the pursuit of monetary union were destroying jobs, not creating them, ravaging the public finances, not restoring them, devastating confidence, not fostering it, a whole slew of European politicians changed tack and proclaimed the essentially political, not economic, ambition underlying the single currency idea.

Moreover, the divisiveness of the monetary union project can no longer be hidden. There will be a European political and economic 'hard core'. Its members will be those existing countries, present and future members of the Community, that together made up the empire of Charlemagne. The southern, western and northern 'peripheries' of the Community will be tributaries of the hard core. In economic terms, they will be expected to join a new ERM, one in which they will face only burdens and responsibilities, expected to manage their policies (under surveillance) not in their own interests, nor even in the interests of the Community, but in the interests of the hard core – to all intents and purposes in the interests of France and Germany. If they jib at this, they will be reminded that they must do as they are told. President Chirac expressed it clearly in March 1996: the union (that is, the hard core) must give itself means of 'punishing' those countries outside the hard core that 'do not respect the common discipline'.

Even within the so-called hard core (whose underlying economic performance is now, as was predicted in this book, clearly deteriorating relative to other Community countries and the world as a whole) the atmosphere of mutual distrust and suspicion has become palpable. French politicians make it clear that they fear German dominance; certain German politicians, and most of all Helmut Kohl himself, warn of a return to Balance of Power politics and war in Europe if their ideas on monetary and political union are not accepted lock, stock and barrel. Yet European union can only enshrine German dominance, whether voluntary or – much more likely as far as the German people are concerned – involuntary. That is something the French élite currently seem prepared to accept, in the name of giving 'Europe' greater muscle against the Anglo-Saxon, Asian and Latin-American worlds. But once economic and geopolitical developments make it clearer even to French technocrats that 'the European model' will bring nothing more than continued economic decline and a further deterioration in the quality of political and democratic life, the new empire of Charlemagne will split asunder – and much more rapidly than its eighth-century forerunner and model.

In sum, the mask of European 'solidarity' has been slipping. This book shows how the reality behind the mask was always one of political and bureaucratic infighting, of national and sectional powerplays and of a 'devil take the hindmost' attitude far removed from the Euromyths.

During the forty years of the Pax Americana in Europe, the western half of the continent enjoyed unparalleled prosperity, stability and democratic legitimacy. In these conditions, our countries felt more at ease with one another than ever before in history. But in the ten years in which the drive to recreate the empire of Charlemagne has gathered pace, the foundations of European amity have been eroded. Europe – continental Europe, at least – is in economic disarray; political legitimacy, based on feelings of cohesion – of nationhood – within states and on the principle of 'live and let live' among states, is in clear and present danger; the trust between people and rulers that must underly democracy, and the trust among countries that must underly peace and stability, are both disappearing. None of this can be repaired if discussion and reasoned argument about European problems are treated as disloyalty and lunacy. Both those accusations have been levelled against me, usually by people who have not read the book. I leave it to readers to judge whether those charges are justified.

# Preface to the first edition

The idea for this book was born in December 1991, in Maastricht, just a few days after the name of that very agreeable, and agreeably cosmopolitan, town was besmirched by the meeting of the European Council that unwittingly spelled the end of the European Communities. I was attending a conference, at the European Institute of Public Affairs, on Europe after Maastricht. In one of the sessions, a Euroenthusiast academic gave a conventional interpretation of the history of the ERM, presenting the mechanism as a 'glidepath' to monetary union. My critical comments on this thesis apparently impressed Professor Klaus Gretschman, the Director of the EIPA. He suggested that I should write a chapter on the ERM for a book based on the conference discussions. I agreed, and submitted a draft to the Commission authorities for clearance (I was head of the EMS, National and Community Monetary Policies Unit in the Commission). I was told that permission would not be forthcoming: evidently, any analysis that challenged the ERM orthodoxy was to be suppressed.

There the matter might have lain, but for the influence of Keith Middlemass, professor of Contemporary History at Sussex University. He was leading a multinational team researching a major work on the informal politics of the Community. Someone in the Commission hierarchy had suggested that he should consult me on the workings of the ERM. During the course of our long and enjoyable discussions, it occurred to both of us that it would be worthwhile for me to work up my draft chapter for the EIPA into a book in its own right.

This book is the final outcome of the promptings and encouragement of Klaus Gretschman and Keith Middlemass, even if they may have expected it to be rather more academic and less political in tone. The book does have an analytical economic core. My way of thinking about economics and my confidence in the face of criticism owe a great deal to Rudi Dornbusch and Olivier Blanchard, both of MIT, the first of them German in origin, the second French. I worked very closely with them in 1983–5, when I was secretary of the Commission's Macroeconomic Advisory Group, of which Rudi was the first Chairman and Olivier an outstandingly creative member. At that time, the Commission was more open to analysis and intellectual debate than it became once Jacques Delors had got his feet firmly under the table. Rudi and Olivier stimulated a taste for analytical rigour and intellectual adventure that I have retained even through the stifling years that began with Delors. I am sure they will enjoy the attempt in this book to make economic analysis accessible and even pleasurable to the general reader.

My interest in the *political* economy of 'Europe' was first sparked in the mid-1980s by Herbert Giersch, an immensely wise economist who was then President of the Kiel Institute for World Economics and also a member (subsequently Chairman) of the Macroeconomic Advisory Group. He was also very influential in helping me begin to get a feeling for the distinctively German way of approaching monetary questions.

Analysis need not crowd out passion: they can go very happily together, even if this combination is too often seen as 'not the done thing'. I want to thank two more distinguished economists, Alan Walters and Patrick Minford, for the determination they have shown, not without personal cost, in insisting that the endeavours of economists, even official ones, are better directed to getting things right than to doing the right thing.

So much for the origins and principles of the book. I have a great many people to thank for helping me put flesh on the bones. Not all of them can be named individually, or would want to be. I should mention, among central bankers and officials, my friends and colleagues from the Economic Unit and the Monetary Policy and Foreign Exchange Policy Sub-Committees of the Committee of Central Bank Governors of the European Communities, from the OECD's Ad Hoc Group of High Level Monetary Experts, and from the EC-EFTA Economic Council. Years of discussion, debate and argument with them, much of it over glasses of beer, have sharpened and solidified my understanding of the issues involved in what I have called the dirty war for Europe's money. In this book there are many severe criticisms of 'bureaucrats' and 'central bankers' as a caste. I want to record that many of them, as individuals, are both exceptionally able and exceptionally likeable. That judgement certainly applies to the twenty or so dear friends, whether full-time Commission officials or people on second-ment from central banks or national administrations, who have worked with me in my time as head of the EMS unit in the Commission. Without their unstinting and unselfish support, the sometimes difficult personal circumstances of my job in an environment hostile to thought might have become impossible. While I am not necessarily sure that any of this score of people would share all the very personal political views expressed in this book, I know that practically without exception they agree with its essential economic analysis. I hope that my saying so here will not cause them harm.

Officials and politicians – again viewed as a caste – would no doubt like to have had the battlefield to themselves in their dirty war. Financial markets have had a habit of taking their ball away. My own insights into financial markets began to be developed during the time I spent with J.P. Morgan in New York. They have since been sharpened, I hope, by discussions with financial market economists and analysts too numerous to name exhaustively. But there is a certain number of them with whom I have had a particularly close relationship over a number of years. They have made me constantly challenge, re-examine and refine my own thinking. None of them is responsible for my opinions, and if I have still made mistakes – and no doubt I have – it is my fault, not theirs. I am thinking particularly of Derek Scott of BZW, David Bowers and John Lomax of Smith New Court, Dominique Georges of J.P. Morgan, Paris, Ignacio Ruperez of Banco Santander, Mark Brett of Capital International, Larry Kantor of Liberty Capital, Giles Keating and Sean Shepley of CS First Boston and – perhaps above all – Jonathan Wilmot, also of CS First Boston.

My agent, Bill Hamilton of A. M. Heath, my copy-editor Steve Cox and Julian Loose, commissioning editor at Faber and Faber, have, through their wise advice and friendly criticism, made this book better than it would otherwise have been.

# Introduction

This book tells the true story of the Exchange-Rate Mechanism, the ERM. It is about why the mechanism is a bad thing – economically perverse and politically perverted – and why so many politicians, bureaucrats and commentators have fought so hard to hide this reality. The story of the ERM tells us a great deal about the motivation of the proponents of European monetary and political union – the European superstate. It tells us much they would prefer to keep quiet, for almost every one of the many misconceptions about Europe is embedded in the monetary mechanism that has done so much harm to us all. Even after the ERM ceased, after the market triumph of July 1993, to be a functioning economic mechanism, 'the authorities' did not want its true story to be told, for the myths, misconceptions and taboos that sustained the ERM are exactly those that underpin the relentless drive towards monetary union and a federal superstate in Europe.

I was once prey to some of those misconceptions. I became an official of the EC Commission in August 1978, at almost exactly the time that Helmut Schmidt and Valéry Giscard d'Estaing were finalizing the Franco-German deal that brought the ERM into being. I did not join the Commission out of any desire to 'build Europe', but I did believe that the Community was a useful forum for cooperation, helping to buttress friendly relations among European countries. In particular, I believed that economic coordination would bring real material benefits.

Like most mainstream economists at that time, I was sceptical about the new ERM and did not expect it to survive for long. When it did, I paid little attention, for I was not at first working on specifically monetary affairs. When I did switch to the monetary side of the Commission, in late 1986, I was responsible among other things for analysing and making recommendations about the British monetary scene. It was then, as I studied the slowly unfolding tragedy of Nigel Lawson's obsession with the ERM, an obsession that led directly to the fall of Mrs Thatcher, that I began to understand just how damaging the ERM was to the economies in its clutches. And I came to realize that the mechanism was part of a programme to subvert the independence – political as well as economic – of Europe's countries. Anyone who stood in the way of the European superstate had to be cut down. Mrs Thatcher was a prime target of the Eurofederalists; this book knits together strands of evidence that she was the victim of a Continental conspiracy abetted by some of her own earlier comrades-in-arms in the battle against British economic decline.

The struggle to unseat Mrs Thatcher coincided with the rebirth of plans for European Monetary Union (EMU). That period thus inevitably saw an intensification of the monetary warfare, presented as cooperation, between France and Germany that has been a persistent feature of the ERM since its inception. By the time, in late 1989, that I became head of the Commission division dealing with the ERM and monetary policy affairs, I was convinced that the mechanism, together with the EMU it was intended to produce, was a massive lie.

In one way this is an 'inside' book. I have lived the ERM for many years. In dozens of academic conferences, hundreds of meetings and thousands of hours of discussion involving central bankers and Treasury officials I have heard every conventional argument about the ERM and EMU made and contested a dozen times. I think I can say I know what makes the ERM actors think and act as they do, both as individuals with a wide variety of faces and as faceless bureaucrats. But there is no individual 'fact' in the book that is not available to anyone with the patience to read the newspapers of this and other countries, to fillet the content of speeches and articles, to plough through official reports and publications, to gaze at the financial market screens and endure the rubber-chicken-and-warm-champagne circuit in a town like Brussels, where journalists, diplomats and officials mix and talk so freely. Indeed, it is one of the astonishing things about the ERM and EMU that what needs to be revealed is not 'the facts' but their manipulation and distortion. The more blatantly obvious the falsehood, the more insistently its perpetrators repeat it. My own decision to write this book in the way I have done was born first of incredulity at the hundreds of 'black is white' statements made about the ERM, and then of anger at the treatment given to anyone who tried to point out the lies.

The proponents of the ERM and EMU have understood perfectly well what propaganda is. To quote the political scientist and philosopher Leonard Schapiro, writing of Stalin, 'the true object of propaganda is neither to convince nor even to persuade, but to produce a uniform pattern of public utterance in which the first trace of unorthodox thought reveals itself as a jarring dissonance.' The fanaticism of some such proponents, expressed in language akin to that of the Bolshevik cells of immediately pre-revolutionary Russia, is captured in the thoughts of John Pinder in his contribution to a conference marking the fiftieth anniversary of the Movimento Federalista Europeo:

The European federation will be created in the 1990s. It is necessary. It is possible. It is our task to ensure that it is done. Thanks to the efforts of the federalists, Europe is already in a preconstituent situation: structurally, the conditions exist for establishing the federal constitution when the political conjuncture enables the process to begin . . . Above all, we must be grateful for the historic contribution of the score of federalist pioneers who met fifty years ago in the house of the Rolliers in via Poerio 37, in order to start our struggle.

It is surely not irrelevant that for many left-wing, middle-class Britons, 'Europe' exercises a grip on the imagination similar to that of the Soviet Union on the Philby generation at Cambridge in the 1930s. Nor is it illegitimate to seek a parallel between the apologias for the Soviet Union issued by the British intelligentsia in the 1920s and 1930s, and today's wilful closing of intellectual eyes to the realities of 'Europe'. The left-wing fellow travellers of the 1930s constantly made unfavourable comparisons between Britain and the supposed paradise to the east. Today, the same is true of the British Euroenthusiasts. The head of the Commission's representative office in Britain, for instance, seems to view ceaseless denigration of his own country as the most effective way of selling 'Europe' to his fellow Britons.

Nor is it only Britain's intelligentsia that is fascinated by the secular religion of 'Europe'. Gabriel Robin, a retired French ambassador formerly close to Giscard d'Estaing and the inner circle of 'committed' French Euroenthusiasts, has recently dared to make the point in France. He writes:

The two ideologies, of Communism and of Europe, have much more in common than they [Euroenthusiasts] like to admit . . . One had its apparatchiks, the other its Eurocrats . . . Their respective credos come together [in many respects including their belief in] the inevitable withering-away of the nation-state . . . Initiates in the secrets of History, the two schools are equally convinced that they know where History is leading – towards the Promised Land. For the first, its name is the classless society, for the second, it is Europe without borders.

The techniques and modes of thought of twentieth-century secular religions have marked the attitudes of the European Establishment to the ERM 'common good' and to the 'historic inevitability' of monetary and political union. Only the International Olympic Committee's ban on political demonstrations prevented the European Commission from spending taxpayers' money to turn the Barcelona and Albertville Olympics into flag-waving propaganda rallies. 'Europe' has been promoted, again most notably by Delors, almost as synonymous with Christendom, a counter to the supposedly pagan Anglo-Saxon worship of markets and a bulwark against decadent Anglo-Saxon culture.

A senior official of the Bank for International Settlements once accused the Commission's Directorate-General for Economic and Financial Affairs of publishing propaganda in the guise of analysis. Apparently, this is what is now expected of Commission staff – they are missionaries, soldiers in the crusade for a European superstate. Every Commission official has received a blue, 'European Commission' diary (even the name is a piece of propaganda: all staff are ordered to use it even though legally the institution is still 'The Commission of the European Communities'). With the diary comes a message in three languages. It is so sacred that it is printed on a plastic insert, that it may not become crumpled or dog-eared. The plastic carries the words of João de Deus Pinheiro, member of the last Delors Commission responsible for 'information' and personnel. Combining his two areas of responsibility, Pinheiro reminds his fifteen thousand knights that: 'It is clear that staff will be more effective and enthusiastic communicators if they feel a strong sense of commitment to the goals of the Community.' Professional conscience? Remember the *auto da fé*.

Senior Commission officials have complained that 'intellectual terrorism' employed by Delors and his associates stifled any attempt at serious, open-minded discussion of European monetary issues. Even the Secretary-General of the Commission, David Williamson, in theory the most senior of all Commission officials, complained of 'the KGB [members of Delors's *cabinet*, or private office] looking over his shoulder' during the Maastricht negotiations and preventing him from doing his job professionally.

In Stalinist Russia, dissent was regarded as evidence of lunacy. In the present-day European Community, dissent does not yet warrant incarceration in brutal mental hospitals, but unorthodox thought is still a dissonance. In Britain, Enoch Powell very quickly saw the subversion of democracy implied by the ERM, yet his perspicacity was treated by enlightened opinion as further evidence of what John Major might call 'barmy' thinking. Equally early, Alan Walters saw and proclaimed the economic contradictions of the mechanism. This was an offence so heinous that even the patronage of Mrs Thatcher could not save him from the revenge of the outraged media Establishment, led by Sam Brittan (created Chevalier de la Légion d'Honneur by a French government grateful for his enthusiastically pro-ERM stance) in the *Financial Times* and the unnamed editorialists of *The Economist* who infamously attempted to ridicule him by referring to him as 'one of the world's top three hundred transport economists'.

As we shall see, in France the long arm of the authoritarian state has pressurized dissident economists and bankers, deployed financial information programmes on international TV channels, threatened securities houses with loss of business if they questioned the official economic line, and shamelessly used state-owned and even private-sector banks, in complete contradiction with their shareholders' interests and Community law, to support official policy. French officials have bemoaned the need for elections as creating problems for the ERM. In Italy, securities houses have been 'punished' by the state for publishing accurate economic analysis that made life difficult for the lira within the system. In Denmark the central bank acted illegitimately to 'punish' banks who might conceivably have defied the Prime Minister's warnings not to finance sales of the Danish currency. In Britain the minister supposedly responsible for open government ruled that exchange-rate parities were a subject about which the government could legitimately lie to Parliament. In Germany it seems that implicit exchange controls were covertly introduced to hide the truth of the ERM's impact. In Ireland, Church leaders denounced market attacks on Ireland's ERM parity as 'unbelievably immoral'. The economics profession in Europe organized literally hundreds of conferences, seminars and colloquia to which only conformist speakers were invited; and the Commission's 'research' programmes financed large numbers of economic studies to provide the right results from known 'believers'.

In the face of this relentless and overbearing propaganda and worse, this book will attempt to expose the double myth of the ERM: that it was economically rational and beneficial, and that it was politically a symbol of friendship and cooperation. I will argue instead that the mechanism was a major reason for economic failure, for impaired political legitimacy, and for the unhappy state of affairs recently described by a German newspaper as 'the pitch-black distrust with which European Union members today regard each other'. The newspaper continues: 'This distrust is greater than when the European Community was founded 37 years ago – that is no basis for an enlarged union.'

This book treats the ERM as the field on which three battles have been waged simultaneously. The first of those battles is between politics and economics, the expression of a bureaucratic way of thinking, an attempt to stem the tide of market forces that threatened to engulf corporatist Europe in the 1980s and 1990s. The second is between the Bundesbank, the redoubtable, unaccountable and extremely powerful German central bank, and the forces aiming to take it down a peg: France, the German government, and financial markets. The battle-ground, after a decade and a half of strife, is littered with dead and wounded: Tory radicalism; national sovereignty; capital liberalization, the Single Market in Europe, and an open trading system in the world as a whole; hundreds of thousands of firms and millions of jobs; the Italian state; trust in governments and even in the democratic system of government; the rule of law in some countries; the idea of central-bank independence as something worthwhile and practicable; the hope of economic convergence and self-reliance in the poorer members of the European Community; and the economic integration and development of Eastern Europe. And even now, when the battle of the ERM might appear to have been won by markets, for democracy and for freedom, the battle of EMU still has to be fought.

The third battle is even more titanic; it has gained in intensity since the fall of the Berlin Wall and the longed-for collapse of the Yalta carve-up of Europe. It is the battle for control of the European superstate, in which French technocrats confront German federalists, both sides claiming to fight under the banner of Charlemagne. The 'collateral damage' from this battle lies mainly in the future, but it could be ghastly. Whether Britain can avoid it is a major question of the final section of this book.

My central thesis is that the ERM and EMU are not only inefficient but also undemocratic: a danger not only to our wealth but to our freedoms and, ultimately, our peace. The villains of the story – some more culpable than others – are bureaucrats and self-aggrandizing politicians. The ERM is a mechanism for subordinating the economic welfare, democratic rights and national freedom of citizens of the European countries to the will of political and bureaucratic élites whose power-lust, cynicism and delusions underlie the actions of the vast majority of those who now strive to create a European superstate. The ERM has been their chosen instrument, and they have used it cleverly.

The first part of this book analyses the history of the ERM from its inception to the signing of the Maastricht Treaty. It describes how the ERM confidence-trick worked for so long, and how – despite the economic damage it was inflicting on most of its members – it came to be hailed as a motor of economic progress and political reconciliation. The analysis stresses the paradox that, while the ERM during that period was increasingly seen as outstandingly successful, giving impetus to the forces that produced the treaty, it in fact was running counter to all the economic objectives of the Community: monetary stability, a levelling up of productivity and living standards, high employment, sound public finance, free trade and the Single Market, the liberalization of capital movements and a harmoniously competitive world economic order. To mask this paradox, the champions of the mechanism ingeniously invented a series of superficially attractive economic fallacies. These fallacies will be exposed.

The first part also describes how the cloak of ERM 'cooperation' masked ferocious political in-fighting within and between the countries participating, or thinking of participating, in the mechanism. Particular attention is given to the combination of economic mismanagement by the Treasury and the Bank of England and conspiracy within the Tory party and European Establishments that ultimately toppled Mrs Thatcher. I also emphasize the growing divergence during this period about monetary issues – all appearances to the contrary – between France and Germany that now threatens the whole future of the European Community.

The second part of the book chronicles the collapse of the narrow-band ERM between Maastricht and the great market assault of July 1993. The emphasis here is on explaining how the interplay of economic forces, political events and personal motivations laid bare the economic contradictions and political hypocrisy of the mechanism, allowing markets to discover, after fourteen years of succumbing to illusionism, that the Emperor indeed had no clothes. I explore the role of Helmut Schlesinger, Bundesbank President in the critical 1991–93 period and one of the very few heroes in a landscape overpopulated by villains. A central argument of this part of the book is that Schlesinger was able to manoeuvre German monetary policy, aided by economic developments and market power, until ultimately the monetary pretensions of France were laid bare with such starkness that Helmut Kohl could no longer resist German popular indignation with the French assault on Germany's monetary sovereignty.

The final part of the book describes the remarkable tenacity with which the proponents of EMU have clung to their ambitions despite the collapse of the ERM and a lack of popular support that even the Commission has had to admit to. How great is the danger that EMU will go ahead? And what damage would it do to Britain, Europe and the world? Those are the questions with which the book ends. But if answers are to be given, the book must begin with an exploration of the motives of the proponents of the ERM. 'L'Europe se fera par la monnaie, ou elle ne se fera pas' – 'Europe will be created via a currency or not at all' – wrote Jacques Rueff in the 1950s. As we shall see, that maxim motivated the fathers of the ERM, Valéry Giscard d'Estaing and Helmut Schmidt. Why?

# PART ONE

# I

# Genesis

## The history men

The making in 1978 of the European Monetary System (EMS), the formal shell containing the exchange-rate mechanism, was a personal initiative of two men, Helmut Schmidt, the German Chancellor, and Valéry Giscard d'Estaing, the French President, aided by a third, Roy Jenkins, President of the European Commission. The making in 1990 of a plan for monetary and political union in Europe (EMU) was also largely the work of two men, Helmut Kohl, the German Chancellor, and François Mitterrand, the French President, aided by a third, Jacques Delors, President of the European Commission. What were these Chancellors and Presidents doing, and why were they doing it? Would they succeed? Why did other politicians in other countries go along with them?

Even after seventeen years, and the publication of politicians' memoirs, official reports, academic analyses and journalistic investigations, the questions about 1978 remain controversial. Yet answers must be attempted if we are to have any chance of understanding the even more controversial and burningly relevant questions of 1990.

The ERM, although largely political in inspiration, is an economic mechanism. The politics and economics of the ERM have interacted with the personal quirks and motivations of its managers in a dirty war for the control of Europe's money. In the recurring patterns of history, the battleground today looks very much like that of 1978 – a salient here, a hill retaken there, but the main trenches are where they were seventeen years ago. One might say they remain where they have been for more than a thousand years – running down the spine of the 'middle kingdom' of Lothar. Can a currency recreate the empire of Charlemagne? Can the *franc fort* take over *Francfort*? Or will *Frankreich* become incorporated into a new *Frankenreich*? At the heart of Europe lie those two conflicting interpretations of what monetary union is about. Yet the subtle differences of emphasis between French and German desires, differences expressed in the startlingly apt wordplays in the two languages, have given a central role

3

to an extraordinary institution, one in which politics and monetary economics successively ally and conflict with each other – the Bundesbank. For the French élite, money is not the lubricant of the economy but the most important lever of power. Capture of the Bundesbank is thus, for them, the great prize in the European monetary war. To secure it, they have been willing to tempt Germany with the lure of political union, while never intending to deliver it.

Across the Rhine, successive German governments have, in their pursuit of a 'European' cloak for German ambitions, been prepared to accept an apparent cession of national monetary authority – as long as the new European monetary authority looks, sounds, smells and acts exactly as the German monetary authority now does. The Bundesbank has, as the intended sacrificial victim in this power-play, been the most determinedly outspoken proponent of the view that monetary union, as desired by the French élite, cannot be contemplated without simultaneous, preferably prior, political union, the goal of German governments. The Bundesbank was the missing partner in the genesis of the ERM in 1978. For fifteen years, under three presidents, it fought, with varying degrees of conviction and intensity, to free itself from the constraints the ERM imposed on it. Ultimately, in the last weeks of Helmut Schlesinger's tenure of office, it succeeded – only for Schlesinger's formidable successor, Hans Tietmeyer, to start his self-appointed task of rebuilding the ERM. But this time the architecture would be Tietmeyer's own, not that of hostile politicians.

Where does the Commission fit in? Individual commissioners seek, with greater or lesser energy and success, to advance national interests. The Commission staff engine has always been tuned to support French interests in particular. But there is no doubt that the Commission has given the federalizing process a momentum of its own, by constantly seeking to invent and exploit 'spillovers' from one area of policy to another. The myths assiduously propagated by the Commission – myths of 'solidarity', the benefits of economic 'coordination', the need for fixed exchange rates to sustain a common market, the evils of 'competitive devaluation' – have provided important cover for the ambitions, whether collusive or conflictual, of France and Germany. It was so in 1990. It was so in 1978, where our story begins.

4

# Dynastic alliances

In 1978, the political geography of Europe had been frozen for three decades. Another decade was to pass before the Yalta settlement crumbled. But the monetary geography of the Western part of the Continent already reflected the breakdown, at the beginning of the decade, of the Bretton Woods system of fixed exchange rates among the non-communist industrial countries. With the United States no longer the monetary hegemon, Western Europe was split into two camps. The first was a group of countries clustered around Germany in an arrangement known as the 'snake'. The countries involved (Germany itself, Benelux, Denmark, Norway and Sweden) had agreed to restrict movements of their exchange rates against each other (their 'bilateral rates') within a margin of plus or minus 0.75%.[1]

From the point of view of the German government of the day, the snake played a role in protecting German competitiveness when the dollar was weak, as it unmistakably was in the first half of the Carter presidency: the snake prevented a number of other currencies important for German trade from falling in sympathy with the greenback. But the role was a limited one, since the three biggest economies in Europe, excluding Germany, were not part of it.

France, Britain and Italy had all briefly been members of the snake. It had initially been intended to cover all Community countries in the belief that the Common Market (as it was still called in those days) could not work if the currencies of member states fluctuated widely against one another. This belief is erroneous, as we shall see later. But it was widely held at the time.[2] When it came into operation in 1972, it included all existing members as well as the four, Britain, Ireland, Denmark and Norway, that were supposed to join the Community in 1973.[3] But when economic policies and inflation rates diverged after the 1973 commodity price shocks, Britain, France and Italy all withdrew as the system's obligations began to threaten their national policy-making autonomy.

1 Suppose, for instance, that the central rate of the DM was set at 20 Belgian francs (BEF). Then the permitted range of fluctuation between the two currencies would be BEF 20 (0.9925) to BEF 20 (1.0075), i.e. between BEF 19.85 and BEF 20.15.

2 It is still held, or at least espoused, by the intellectually lazy. On 16 January 1995, Kenneth Clarke opined that exchange-rate stability was necessary for the Single Market to work: trade could be endangered by currency fluctuations, he said.

3 The snake was thus seen as a step on the path towards monetary union – a concept embraced enthusiastically by Edward Heath from the start.

Helmut Schmidt viewed this monetary division of Europe as deeply unsatisfactory. First, it left Germany too exposed to weakness in the dollar, which could be expected to drag the franc, sterling and the lira down with it.[4] Second, fluctuations in exchange rates caused enormous complications in the Community's Byzantine Common Agricultural Policy (CAP), threatening to make it unworkable. This might have been counted a blessing, not a bane, since the CAP was even then notoriously wasteful, illogical and inefficient. But it was a *common* policy, and therefore dear to the hearts of European federalists, of whom Schmidt was, for whatever reason, certainly one.

These economic arguments – or, at least, arguments couched in terms of economics – were secondary to explicitly political ones. Schmidt wanted European union, and saw some symbolic return to the path of monetary union as an essential political precondition. One of his reasons, perhaps the main one, for wanting European union was that Germany was hamstrung by its Wilhelmine and Nazi past in pursuing its diplomatic interests in the world, and particularly in Eastern Europe. Totally out of sympathy with Jimmy Carter and exasperated with the feebleness of American 'leadership' in the free world, Schmidt was developing a determined *Ostpolitik* independent of the United States in key respects. But Germany was still politically punching less than its economic weight.

A major priority for Schmidt in adjusting this balance was to secure the cooperation of the French President, Giscard d'Estaing. France's diplomatic problems were in a sense the mirror image of Germany's. Its high-profile political activity, permanent seat in the UN Security Council and independent nuclear *force de frappe* were not enough, it seemed, to provide international monetary clout. The breakdown of the Bretton Woods system and the end of unquestioned US monetary hegemony might have given France the opportunity to play a bigger role on the world economic stage. A similar opportunity had seemed to present itself in 1932, when most of the world, including the two most important financial powers, the US and Britain, left the Gold Standard. France had clung to gold, as the centre of the '*bloc or*' that included its small neighbours, in the hope of re-establishing the financial prestige it had lost after 1918. The decision was a costly one: the French franc became massively overvalued, the French

---

4 Since Britain's rather humiliating application to the IMF for a balance-of-payments loan in 1976, the form of monetarism instituted as one of the loan conditions had in fact led to a stabilization and then strengthening of sterling against the weak dollar.

economy was devastated, social and political tensions, culminating in the Popular Front government of Léon Blum, threatened to tear the country apart. France admitted defeat in 1936, finally going off gold, but not before so much damage had been done that French diplomacy and military capacity were enfeebled in the face of Hitler's Germany.

With this unhappy experience behind it, France followed a different path in the 1970s, concentrating on international monetary diplomacy in its pursuit of '*grandeur*'. But this time excessively lax policies in response to the oil-price shocks of 1973–74 combined with trade-union militancy and recourse to interventionism and controls, as in Britain and Italy, to reduce the country's standing in the world. By 1978, however, Giscard was politically more secure: the alliance of Socialists and Communists had unexpectedly been beaten off in parliamentary elections that spring, and an economic stabilization programme introduced.

The European Monetary System proposed by Schmidt was an attractive option – *if* its operation could be differentiated from that of the 'snake', from which France had twice had to withdraw. Specifically, the increase in France's weight in international monetary diplomacy, hoped for from a monetary alliance with Germany and its satellites, must not be undermined, as the '*bloc or*' had been, by the demands of a monetary régime tighter than the French economy could bear. If the EMS could ensure this, and if in addition it could be presented as leading to a strengthening of the European union process – a process France instinctively felt able to control and shape to its own advantage – then it could be supported enthusiastically.

But the EMS *did* have to be different from the snake. In the snake, it was economic weight and reputation that mattered – Germany had much more of that. What Giscard needed, and what Schmidt was prepared to offer, was a monetary arrangement that could be brought within the ambit of the Community institutions. An institutionalized arrangement would make exchange rates part of the Community horse-trading game, allowing France's political weight to come to bear. Just as Germany wanted European cooperation and, ultimately union, to help it bring its economic weight to bear diplomatically, so France wanted it to give economic muscle to *its* diplomatic ambitions. As De Gaulle had once said, 'The EEC is a horse and carriage: Germany is the horse and France is the coachman.'[5]

5 He once expressed this same thought rather differently, in conversation with Henry Kissinger. When Kissinger asked how France would prevent German dominance of the European Community, the French President replied: '*Par la guerre.*'

So the EMS looked like a match made in heaven. In fact, it was the consummation not of selfless mutual love but of cold calculation of self-interest. No sooner had Schmidt and Giscard plighted their troth than quarrels began about the details of the marriage contract. And there was an aggrieved third party in what was to become an eternal triangle. There was Bonn, there was Paris . . . and there was the Bundesbank, which feared that it was being offered by Schmidt as dowry. It is time to make the acquaintance of this redoubtable institution.

## Nemo me impune lacessit

The Bundesbank had been set up in 1958, inheriting the functions of the Bank deutscher Länder. The latter had been created in 1948 not, at least formally, by the West German government – none existed at the time – but by the Allied Control Commission. Its regionalized structure and autonomy from governmental control had deliberately been designed as part of an embryonic political framework in which central government power would be carefully limited: the aim was to reduce the likelihood of a Fourth Reich. In 1958, the West German state slightly modified the structure of the central bank, increasing the weight of its central Directorate, appointed by the Bonn government, vis-à-vis the Chairman of the *Länder* central banks (organizations whose economic significance was minimal, almost non-existent), the latter being nominated by *Land* governments.

The 1957 law instituting the Bundesbank retained the feature of its independence of government in the key area of interest-rate decisions. But the government retained the right to make decisions on exchange rates within formal international agreements. In addition the Bundesbank was mandated to 'safeguard the value of the currency' while supporting 'the general economic policy of the government'. In 1958, with Germany part of the hegemonic Bretton Woods fixed-exchange-rate system, these provisions seemed to leave the central bank little room for manoeuvre. 'Safeguarding the value of the currency', when the government decided on possible revaluations or devaluations of the DM, subject to the agreement of the IMF, seemed to imply using interest rate and other monetary instruments simply to carry out the government's wishes.

But as the 1960s progressed, the bank began to flex its muscles, choosing more and more explicitly to interpret 'the value of the currency' in terms of its *internal*, not its external value. The independent central bank's mandate gave it the opportunity to criticize, harangue and even threaten other actors

8

– governments, employers and unions – in the economy. The Bundesbank began to use this opportunity to the full, overturning its obligation to 'support the general economic policy of the government'. In 1966, it deliberately engineered a recession that dethroned the Chancellor, Ludwig Erhard, who, as Finance Minister, had overridden Bundesbank objections to DM revaluation in 1961. The Bundesbank President of the time, Karl Blessing, commented with evident satisfaction that 'we had to use brute force to put things in order' – a formula not very different from those used by leaders of the military in Third World countries who summarily depose an uppity civilian leader before returning to barracks. It did not go unnoticed that the man who replaced Erhard, Georg Kiesinger, was, like many prominent figures in the Bundesbank at that time, a former Nazi Party member, however much or little significance that fact may have.[6]

When the Bretton Woods system fell apart in 1971–72, the relative power of the Bundesbank vis-à-vis the government increased dramatically. Decisions on exchange-rate changes within the 'snake' still belonged to the government, but as the snake evolved into a system of unilateral pegs against the DM, the Bundesbank was little constrained by this. *Its* monetary policy determined the monetary policy of the snake as an area, and the snake floated against the dollar and all other currencies. The Bundesbank reigned supreme: its freedom to set interest rates, free from electoral or other forms of political accountability, allowed it to crack the whip at the government and unions. Its position would be under grave threat from a multilateral exchange-rate system under the management of politicians – and it feared that the proposed EMS would be just that. Worse, the politicians in charge would not be exclusively German. Within Germany, the strong desire of the population to avoid inflation gave the Bundesbank a potent weapon in any conflict with the government. But an exchange-rate system designed to meet the political desires of other countries – France in particular – would lack this safeguard.

The fact that the Bundesbank was bound to be suspicious of anything like an EMS was one reason for Schmidt to conduct his initial negotiations

6 Kiesinger was himself subsequently to fall out of favour with the Bundesbank Council, whose political composition shifted more to the left in the late 1960s as the SPD gained control of a number of *Länder* and were, in time, able to appoint supporters to *Land* central bank chairmanships.

with Giscard in secret, bypassing the normal route.[7] The idea of the EMS was sprung on the European Council (the gathering of heads of state and government, formalized only in 1974 and still without a legally clear role in the Community set-up) by the French and German leaders at the Copenhagen meeting in April 1978.[8] At that level, Franco-German initiatives are not resisted (or at least were not resisted before Mrs Thatcher came on the scene).

## But me no buts

The Franco-German axis *is* the Community, and the role of the other members of the European Council is to give a ceremonial benediction to what the French and German leaders want to do. This is what happened at Copenhagen, where the principle of the EMS was accepted. Thereafter, outright opposition to the EMS would automatically be branded 'anti-communautaire', a label that connoted a mixture of heresy, blasphemy and treason. The details of the scheme would henceforth have to be worked out in the 'competent bodies' and any necessary legislation passed by the Ecofin, but it would not be possible for any of these bodies simply to say 'no'. Any opposition to the idea would have to be expressed as, 'yes, but'. Something called the EMS would see the light of day. Giscard and Schmidt had ordained that it should, and that was that. But the work of the 'competent bodies' could be used to try to extract the maximum national advantage – or sectional safeguard – from the rather vague ideas initially put forward by Schmidt and Giscard.

The fiercest battle raged over the precise extent to which the EMS would differ from the snake. After Copenhagen, Schmidt and Giscard invited Jim Callaghan, the British Prime Minister, to join a troika whose personal representatives would work on the broad architecture of the new

7 In principle, the Community institution responsible for overseeing the process of economic integration and for considering measures thought likely to advance that process was the Council of Ministers for Economic and Financial Affairs (Ecofin). In the monetary field, the Ecofin was advised by the so-called 'competent bodies', the Monetary Committee and the Committee of Central Bank Governors. The membership of the second of these bodies reflected its name. The first was made up of the top Treasury official (or the top official on the international side) from each country and the deputy governor (or equivalent) of each central bank, together with two representatives from the Commission. The Bundesbank thus had a say in both Committees and was in a position to block or water down most initiatives that displeased it.

8 When the European Council had been instituted in 1974, it was seen as strengthening the inter-governmental approach to the Community, precisely because it somewhat downgraded the established Community institutions.

system before presenting it to the 'competent bodies'. But the realities of international and domestic politics and of economics soon made it clear that 'yes, but' was, for Britain, no substitute for 'no'. The complementarity of French and German geopolitical interests did not extend to Britain, especially in the monetary field, where Britain favoured a global, cooperative approach rather than the power-play against the US involved in Franco-German views. British public opinion did not want European union, towards which the EMS was an explicit step, and Britain's economic woes, if unremedied, would not allow the country to live with a DM link, but the process of treating those woes would – as later experience showed all too clearly – of itself require monetary policy to be framed solely with domestic needs in mind.

From a rather early stage, it became clear that Callaghan, despite his personal leaning towards the aims and aspirations of the EMS, would have to go for a 'halfway house', as it was called in the jargon of the time: Britain would enter the formal shell of the EMS,[9] but would not, at least initially, participate in its operational core, the exchange-rate mechanism. Callaghan's compromise uncannily prefigures John Major's 'opt-out' from the Single Currency decided at Maastricht. Major's predecessor, Mrs Thatcher, had actually said 'no' (in fact, 'no, no, no'!). For the rest of the Community, and for the Euroenthusiasts in her own country, she had committed a political capital offence. She had to be executed, and executed she was. A year of 'yes, but' in the subsequent negotiations for Maastricht got Major nowhere. All that was left to him, despite his personal leaning towards the aims and aspirations of EMU, was to follow the path first trodden by Callaghan: accept the principle, but stand aside from the operational core, Stage Three, until 'the time is ripe'.

In another prefiguring of the Maastricht line-up, Ireland and Italy both agreed to participate in the ERM despite the obvious inappropriateness for them of a link to the DM. Ireland's trade was heavily involved with Britain. There was very considerable mobility of labour between Ireland and Britain. Ireland was, in fact, part of a monetary union with Britain, the Irish pound locked at par with sterling, and British banknotes circulated freely in Ireland alongside Irish notes. While it might make sense for a country such as the Netherlands, with its very strong trading links with Germany, to link its currency to the DM, it did not make economic sense for Ireland to do so.

9  This meant nothing more, in practice, than relabelling 20% of exchange reserves as 'European Currency Units (ECUs), and ensuring a seat in meetings of the 'competent bodies' dealing with the operation of the system.

Politically, however, things were very different. For Jack Lynch, the Irish Prime Minister, the ERM offered an opportunity for a final, symbolic shaking-off of British influence. Community membership had in itself increased Ireland's national self-confidence, since it put the country, formally speaking at any rate, on the same footing as Britain. It also promised a 'Community dimension' to the Northern Ireland question, a dimension that Ireland and the Commission were to exploit assiduously. Further, the Catholic élite in Ireland had long maintained a network of contacts with similar élites in Continental countries, and Community membership was a way of formalizing those contacts. Helmut Schmidt, the main paymaster of the Community, was prepared to defray part of the economic cost to Ireland of achieving a political ambition that he himself eagerly supported. He was prepared to offer – and the French to accept – Community handouts to Ireland to offset part of the expected economic costs of ERM entry.

Italy did not have to contend with the predominance of UK trade links, but it had more than enough problems of its own – double-digit inflation, an extremely fragile balance of payments and the emergence of budget deficits of a size that would ultimately bring a threat of financial collapse. These problems made an ERM flirtation extremely unwise, but the wisdom of the time had it that Italy's political needs dictated ever closer links with the rest of Western Europe. Italy's political system had been ossified by the growing electoral strength of the Communists. In the early years after the war, the then new Christian Democratic party had seemed the only bulwark against the risk of a Communist takeover. Once in power, however, it took such a tight grip on the reigns of power and patronage that it exercised what seemed a perpetual domination of Italian political life, despite the giddying speed of the revolving doors to the prime ministerial palace. In the late 1970s, the rottenness and inadaptability of the political system had allowed political conflict to degenerate into terrorist violence – some of it, it is widely believed, orchestrated from within the state system. Towards the end of the decade, there seemed a real prospect that Communists might be brought into the government – a prospect that dismayed Schmidt, in particular. A strengthening of Community ties via the ERM might, he reasoned, be one way of keeping Italy on the non-Communist track.

Giulio Andreotti, then enjoying one of his several periods of office as Italian Prime Minister, had additional reason to favour closer European monetary and political integration. The Euroenthusiasm of Christian

Democracy gave it a cloak of political respectability: 'Europe' could be associated with 'Christendom'[10] and with liberal democracy. This helps explain the apparent paradox in which so many Italians have said: 'Better to be ruled from Brussels than from Rome' while the Roman politicians have been the most enthusiastic proponents of such a transfer of power. The resolution is that for many years the mirage of 'Europe' deflected what would otherwise have been demands for a thoroughgoing reform of the Italian political system; and if 'Europe' ever materialized, it would almost inevitably replicate the Italian political system, providing a safe haven and happy hunting ground for veterans of the Italian scene.[11]

## Funding the ECU

Thus there was never really any doubt that Italy and Ireland would join the EMS and participate in the ERM. Italy, too, managed to use the work of the 'competent bodies' to extract handouts from the Community; it also obtained the consent of the other countries to enter the ERM with wider bands than the others. It was in such technical areas of the operation of the proposed new mechanism that the Bundesbank was to seek to repair some of the damage it might suffer from the Giscard–Schmidt initiative.

The Bundesbank was worried, with reason, that the EMS was an attempt to do a number of things that were anathema to it: institutionalize exchange-rate arrangements, thus increasing the role of politicians – including foreign politicians, not least French; make realignments more difficult and more politicized than in the snake; lead to a common 'dollar

10 The connection between Euroenthusiasm and the idea of 'Christendom' was a significant one in several countries. Interestingly, it was less strong in France, where Christian Democracy has never taken a strong hold. It has been seen as a German notion, and the 'Lotharingian' origins of the Christian Democrat trio of Robert Schuman, Konrad Adenauer and Alcide de Gasperi were remarked on unfavourably in the French Catholic debate on Europe. Many French Catholics are really 'Gallicans' rather than Roman Catholics – although Delors himself has always attempted to ascribe to the European Community a moral significance and identity that it does not possess: playing the 'Catholic card' has sometimes been useful to him. Among many genuine Roman Catholics in France and, even more, in Britain, there has been a reluctance to subscribe to the selfish, exclusive, inward-looking view of the Community as 'Christendom'. A Catholic is literally a universalist, and attempts to create a 'European' Catholic identity have been abhorrent, smacking of the division of the Church into ethnic cults that was such a problem for the first Pope, St Peter. French Catholic thinking has also tended to see German Catholicism, in particular, as 'medieval', corporatist and selfish, untouched by the 'contractual' aspects introduced into French religion by the Revolution and by the missionary force of the postwar French Church.
11 We shall return to these questions in chapter 10.

policy' and therefore in effect to a common monetary policy dictated by governments;[12] and shift the burden of adjustment to exchange-rate pressures, placing more of it on the strong currencies and less on the weak. Some of its fears were shared by the German opposition party, the CDU-CSU. Franz-Josef Strauss, the hardline anti-Communist CSU leader,[13] who particularly disliked Schmidt's *Ostpolitik*, warned that the EMS would produce 'a Community of Inflation'. Helmut Kohl, the CDU leader, agreed with Strauss that the Bundestag must not be presented with a *fait accompli*: it must be consulted before any decision was made. The CDU, the Kohl/Strauss statement declared, had always been committed to the political and economic unity of Free Europe, but the conditions did not exist for the creation of a viable EMS.

Thus, it seemed, Schmidt would have political difficulty in giving Giscard everything he wanted in the technical construction of the EMS. In one more striking parallel with the later Maastricht negotiations, a compromise was struck that left everything up for grabs.

First, the French had insisted on the creation of a new institution, the European Monetary Fund. The EMF would provide a forum in which the redoubtable French technocrats would gradually come to gain control of monetary policy for Europe as a whole. The proposal for an EMF had first been made public, in fact, by Schmidt (just as the first worked-out proposals for a European Central Bank would also come from within Germany – from Hans-Dietrich Genscher, the Foreign Minister, in 1988[14]). But the obvious beneficiary would be France. The point was made with the greatest bluntness by Dr Klasen, recently retired President of the Bundesbank. He began in ritual fashion, inescapable for a 'respectable' German of that epoch, by welcoming the idea of 'real progress towards currency union'. But he then warned that Germans would have to make absolutely certain that 'Eurofanaticism' (*Europa Begeisterung*) did not lead to a loss of control over their own money. The EMF was a major threat: if it were once established, then 'we would not be dealing with M. Giscard d'Estaing but with the French bureaucracy. And if there is one thing I admire it is the French bureaucracy: it has been trained to the highest level

---

12 Fifteen years later, Helmut Schlesinger's fears on this score would be revived by Mitterrand during the French referendum debate – with consequences we shall explore later in this book.

13 The CSU is the Bavarian sister-party of the Christian Democrats (CDU). Its separate existence is a token of the strength of regional identity in Bavaria.

14 See chapter 5 below.

by centuries of experience and is vastly superior to us in the diplomatic pursuit of national interest.'[15]

The compromise finally worked out between the French and Germans and incorporated in the Resolution of the Brussels European Council was that there would be a two-stage EMS: a first stage without a new institution; and a second stage, at most two years after the inception of the system, which would be equipped with an EMF of undefined role. Once again, there is a parallel with Maastricht, in which the legal framework for the move to a single currency was laid down, but the question of whether or not that move actually takes place was left subject to the outcome of several years of Franco-German jousting for political advantage.

Second, fierce battles raged over the role in the new system of the ECU, the new name given to the European Unit of Account (EUA). The EUA was what its name implied, and no more: the unit in which Community financial calculations were expressed. The ECU was intended to be more than that. To begin with it was, from the first, written in French as *écu*, the name of a medieval French coin. Schmidt, when introducing the Franco-German proposals, said of it that it could ultimately become a single European currency – an ambition relaunched the previous autumn by the Commission President, Roy Jenkins.

The importance of Jenkins's 1977 initiative was to revive and reinforce the romantic, as opposed to national *Realpolitik*, vision of a single currency. His own proposals were regarded by most finance ministry and central bank officials as impracticable, but his speech recreated a psychological atmosphere in which the Schmidt–Giscard scheme bore the 'communautaire' stamp.

In immediately practical terms, expressing exchange-rate obligations in the new EMS in terms of the ECU rather than in terms of exchange rates against the DM would downplay Bundesbank leadership in the system. Naturally, German finance and central bank officials, as opposed to the German Chancellor, were aghast at such an idea, as were their Dutch partners (the guilder was widely regarded as being in a *de facto* fixed link with the DM). Their objections were expressed so strongly that it was ultimately agreed, in a Franco-German summit at Aachen, that compulsory intervention would be triggered, as in the snake, only if the *bilateral* limits between two currencies were reached (to take account of the divergences in

---

15 The role of the *crème de la crème* of the French administrative élite, the graduates of the Ecole Nationale d'Administration (ENA), commonly known in France as *énarques*, is discussed in several later chapters.

inflation rates between snake and non-snake countries, the margins were set at $+/-2.25\%$ rather than $+/-0.75\%$).[16] But, in yet another compromise, the ECU would, as already agreed at a European Council meeting in July, be described as the 'centre of the system': all central rates would be expressed in terms of ECU (a feature that was meaningless in practical terms but important symbolically for the French).

## Ghostly visions

The compromise between the bilateral parity grid and ECU-based approaches to adjustment within the system had initially been proposed by the Belgians. The Belgian franc was a member of the snake. But its geographical, economic, cultural and linguistic position between the Latin and Germanic worlds had always posed problems – most obviously in terms of the notorious proclivity, for more than a thousand years, of the larger kingdoms and powers to fight their battles on the soil of what is now Belgium. The disappearance of the 'middle kingdom' of Lothar in 870 had left the territory of the modern country straddling the great divide. To this day, Belgium is an uneasy amalgamation of two different linguistic and cultural traditions. At the formation of the modern state in 1830, and for a century thereafter, political, economic and cultural dominance was exercised by the French-speakers, the Walloons. Belgium was part of the so-called Latin Monetary Union, led by France, before the First World War and also part of the disastrous French-led '*bloc or*' in the 1930s. Changed economic circumstances after the war and the signing of the Benelux treaty on economic union, however, put Belgium economically in the Germanic camp, a development paralleled by the rise of Dutch speakers – Flemings – to economic and political influence within the country. To the Belgian authorities, it seemed that the conflict between traditional and modern poles of attraction could only be resolved, in the end, by the association of Belgium, monetarily, economically and politically, with *both* France and Germany. The answer was to reverse the divisions of Verdun in 843 and Mersen in 870 and recreate the empire of Charlemagne. It was no

16 Interestingly, the conclusions of the Bremen European Council in September declared that the EMS would not affect the snake, which would continue in operation. The final agreement on the EMS (concluded at the European Council in Brussels in December) contained no such provision: the snake lapsed (though in yet another prefiguring of later events – see chapter 12 – the Dutch and German authorities agreed among themselves to maintain tighter margins between their two currencies).

coincidence that the Belgian government housed the offices and meeting-rooms of the EC Council of Ministers in the Charlemagne building in Brussels.

It was no coincidence, either, that Giscard and Schmidt agreed to accept the Belgian compromise proposal at a bilateral summit in September 1978 at Aachen, principal seat and burial place of Charlemagne. The symbolism was heavily underlined in both France and Germany; the two leaders paid a special visit to the throne of Charlemagne and a special service was held in the cathedral; at the end of the summit, Giscard remarked that: 'Perhaps when we discussed monetary problems, the spirit of Charlemagne brooded over us.'[17]

Such Euro-claptrap ignored the awkward fact that the empire of Charlemagne did not long survive Charlemagne (any more than the empires of Napoleon and Hitler, other would-be inheritors of the mantle of Charlemagne, long survived them). Nonetheless, the Aachen agreement was subsequently endorsed by the European Council held in Brussels – as all such agreements are endorsed by prime ministers who want to be permitted to stay in office.[18] But like the compromise later reached at Maastricht (just a few kilometres down the road from Aachen), it was a formula so designed that it could be given very different interpretations for the sake of domestic opinion in France and Germany. Did it represent a major change in the German-dominated snake (as claimed in France), or an extension of the domain of the snake to France and Italy (as claimed in Germany)? In the new empire of Charlemagne, who would play Charlemagne? Exactly the same question was implicit, and left unanswered, at Maastricht.

Both Schmidt and Giscard seemed determined, for their different reasons, to ignore the warnings of history, preferring instead the supposed allure of 'History'. There had been thirty years of peace, legitimacy, amity and growing prosperity within Western Europe. That happy state of affairs had in part been the result of a common purpose, shared with the United States in NATO, of resisting the potential threat from the Soviet Union. The great feature of the Western Alliance was that it respected the right of

17 Could it be, one wonders, that ghostly visions of emperors past also informed monetary discussions in the close relationship between Giscard and Bokassa which resulted in the acquisition by the poverty-stricken former Central African Republic of an emperor and imperial throne of its own, and by Giscard of a collection of extremely valuable diamonds?
18 John Major's veto of Jean-Luc Dehaene as Commission President in June 1994 was a purely cosmetic exception.

each Western European country to order its own domestic affairs without interference either from any other or from the institutions of the Alliance itself. The Eurofederalists instead wanted – and still want – to fence and wrestle with each other to decide which shall have the greatest success both in meddling in the internal affairs of the others and in challenging and confronting the United States, the country that has protected Western Europe militarily and nourished it economically since the war.

The history of the ERM (as I shall henceforth call it) gives one clue to understanding this perplexing and disturbing compulsion. That story is one of a struggle to maintain an outmoded conception of the interaction between politics and economics in the modern world. In that conception, economics – and monetary economics in particular – is the instrument of political hegemony, whether for a state or for a caste; currencies are an expression of state or caste power, and the wider the currency's domain, the greater the power of those who control it. How this power-struggle developed, and how economic logic was distorted, is what we shall now explore.

# 2

# Creating the Illusion

When the idea of the ERM was sprung on the Bundesbank in 1978, one of Frankfurt's greatest fears was that the ERM would operate in such a way as to undermine its control of German monetary conditions. It had expressed its opposition to the EMS so forcefully that Schmidt actually threatened to revoke its independence if it did not bow. That threat was probably an empty one (fifteen years later, as we shall see, Helmut Schlesinger would have put himself in a position to ignore a similar threat from Helmut Kohl and thereby put an end, to all intents and purposes, to the ERM). Indeed, it was subsequently revealed to monetary diplomats that in correspondence between Schmidt and Otmar Emminger, Bundesbank President at the time (the so-called Emminger Letter, which will assume considerable importance in this narrative), the bank had obtained the right to ask the Federal government for a realignment if intervention was swamping the German money market. As we shall see, a combination of political circumstances ensured that this right did not need to be invoked until January 1987, eight years after the system's inception. When it finally did, the struggle for control of the ERM between France and Germany entered a new, more intense phase. But in the course of those eight years, the ERM operated increasingly to the satisfaction of the Bundesbank, to the extent that its current President looks back to the 'old' ERM with nostalgia and harbours a desire to recreate that system. Understanding how those first eight years masked the initial, geopolitical purpose of the system and gave rise instead to the myth of the ERM as a beneficent economic mechanism is what this chapter is about.

## Absent father

The first two years of the system's operation look rather uneventful on the surface. The expected battles between French politicians and the Bundesbank failed to materialize. So too did the EMF. Yet another absentee was the convergence of inflation performance among the main Community countries touted as one of the economic benefits of the system. Almost from the first, the presumptions around which the ERM debate had turned were shown to be irrelevant.

First, the dollar began to recover on the back of a package of economic measures introduced by the Carter administration in November 1978. From October 1979 recovery became sturdy advance as the Federal Reserve (the American central bank) under Paul Volcker tightened monetary policy drastically; with the election of Ronald Reagan at the end of 1980 market hopes of business-friendly supply-side improvements turned advance into cavalry charge. On the other side of the Atlantic, the arrival of Mrs Thatcher in 10 Downing Street, armed with a similar combination of monetarist and supply-side policies, sent sterling shooting skywards. This unheralded ascension of the Anglo-Saxon currencies meant that Germany, far from using the ERM to shield its competitiveness from a weak dollar, found its own currency slipping in the ERM band as its partners basked in the warm glow of depreciation against major non-ERM currencies.

Weakness in the DM was compounded by the economic policy course chosen by Schmidt in the autumn of 1978. The Carter team in the US had for some time been pressing the European countries to reflate their sluggishly growing economies, hoping that increased European demand would spur world growth while simultaneously improving the American current account. Germany was the designated 'locomotive'. Schmidt agreed at the Bonn summit of world industrial leaders, in July 1978, to increase Germany's budget deficit. The Bonn summit was a classic example of international economic 'coordination': one country agrees to do something that is bad for it on condition that another country does something equally bad for *it*. The world economy suffers, a diplomatic triumph is proclaimed, and the bureaucratic policy-making establishment on all sides comes away with a mandate for increased misdirected interference in economic life. At Bonn, the maleficent tradeoff between the US and Germany was a further access of interventionist measures in America combined with US support for the EMS,[1]

1 The US State Department favoured the EMS more or less unconditionally as a step towards the European Union that the Ivy Leaguers of Foggy Bottom had promoted ever since the end of the war – the State Department in its views on Europe seems to play the role in the US of the Foreign Office in Britain: favouring foreigners at the expense of domestic interests. The US Treasury and the Federal Reserve were privately realistic, and thence hostile to the EMS. The

and a Keynesian fiscal stimulus in Germany.[2]

In fact, the sluggishness of European growth in the period after the first oil-price shock in 1973–74 was the result of deteriorating supply-side conditions as governments and unions strove to maintain both real wages and employment in the face of increased import prices. The net result was to rigidify the economy, make production unprofitable and convert attempts at stimulating demand into accelerated inflation. Before 1978, although Germany had suffered a deterioration of profitability and employment, it had largely resisted the siren voices of 'internationally coordinated demand management', but in 1978 Schmidt needed international approval in the economic field to support his diplomatic ambitions.

The German fiscal expansion took effect just as the Iranian revolution caused a further savage hike in oil prices. In Britain, a newly elected Conservative government was determined to avoid the mistakes of the 1970s: reducing the budget deficit, not stimulating demand, came first. In France, the austerity-minded Prime Minister, Raymond Barre, reversed France's planned contribution to the world 'growth initiative'. But Schmidt ploughed on. With potential supply in the German economy weakened by the oil-price shock, the demand stimulus pushed inflation up to an uncomfortable peak of close to 7%. And, with other large European countries putting fiscal expansion into reverse, Germany's go-it-alone demand push not only worsened the budget deficit but produced the almost unheard-of situation of a current-account deficit. Ironically, while in France Barre's austerity was a major factor in Giscard's defeat in the

---

Euroenthusiasm of the WASPish State Department is disregarded by Continentals who, as we shall see in this book, rail about supposed 'Anglo-Saxon' plots against 'Europe'. For some of these Continentals, 'Anglo-Saxon' is in fact a euphemism for 'Jew financier'. Before the war, they did not bother with euphemisms. Some of them still don't. The 'post-Fascist' Minister of Labour in the Italian government, for instance, openly accused 'New York Jews' of a conspiracy against the lira in the autumn of 1993.

At any rate, the Treasury Assistant Secretary for International Affairs, Anthony Solomon, a 'moderate' in Treasury terms, commented in the spring of 1978 that: 'Experience of the past decade had demonstrated repeatedly that exchange-rate stability cannot be imposed on the system but must be the result of sound economic policies.' It took the Europeans another decade-and-a-half of experience to come to the same conclusion, finally expressed by a temporarily chastened EC Commission in its 'convergence report' at the end of 1993.

2 A 'Keynesian' fiscal stimulus involves increasing government spending relative to tax receipts in the hope that this additional spending in the home economy will stimulate output and employment both in the country concerned and – particularly important in the context of 'coordination' – in other countries that supply the home economy with imports. The name 'Keynesian' is somewhat misleading in that Keynes would certainly not have recommended fiscal stimulus in Germany in 1978.

presidential elections of 1981, in Germany the opposing course steered by Schmidt had a similar destination – the political rocks – as Germans worried that their economic virtue was being betrayed.[3] Within the ERM, however, the German fiscal expansion and growing market disenchantment with Schmidt combined with the strength of sterling and the dollar to boost other currencies against the DM (dollar strength, in particular, has always tended to draw funds away from the DM, the main international investment currency in Europe, weakening it against other European currencies). Indeed, the DM was even the weakest currency in the system for a few months in 1980.[4]

By early 1981, the weakness of the DM, both within the ERM and against the dollar and sterling, together with mounting inflation pressure at home, forced the hand of the Bundesbank Council. Schmidt's political fortunes were already in decline, and in those economic and political circumstances the SPD supporters on the Council would have been accused of political bias if they had resisted a tightening of policy.[5] The opportunity was grasped with both hands by Helmut Schlesinger,[6] recently promoted to Vice-President, whose authority was instrumental in getting the Council to engineer a sharp rise in interest rates.[7]

At around the same time, fears about rising public debt levels forced Schmidt – under pressure from his FDP coalition partners – into a change of course on budgetary policy.[8] That year, measures to reduce the budget deficit already had a slightly negative impact on demand in the German economy. By 1982, that impact was much larger. The fiscal tightening,

3 By the time of the election campaign in Germany at the end of 1982, the Catholic hierarchy expressed the view that rising public debt was a loss of virtue *tout court*. Although the West German parties were not strictly speaking 'confessional', the Catholic Church had tended to favour the CDU–CSU, strongest in Catholic regions of the country, against the SPD, which garnered most support in Protestant areas.

4 In 1979 there had been two realignments, the first involving, in line with prior expectations, a revaluation of the DM, together with a devaluation of the Danish krone, and the second a unilateral devaluation of the krone.

5 The Bundesbank had already begun tightening policy in January 1989 immediately after the EMS agreement was concluded, despite the publicly expressed opposition of the government, and carried on increasing interest rates over the next eighteen months. But the savage move came only in early 1981.

6 We shall see much more of Schlesinger in this book. He is sketched in chapter 4.

7 The normal ceiling on money-market rates, the Lombard rate, was suspended, and very short-term rates soared for a time to around 30%.

8 Net public debt was only 17.5% of GDP in 1981 (compared with 48.2% in Britain). But for nearly all West Germany's history the government had actually had net assets. And West German debt was now higher than in France – a troubling phenomenon for most Germans.

combined with the turning of the monetary screw by the Bundesbank, sent the German economy into recession. GDP actually fell slightly in both 1981 and 1982, and unemployment doubled in two years. Schmidt was in serious political trouble – attacked on the right for economic mismanagement, outflanked on the left by the emergent Greens, about to be left in the lurch by the FDP. He was in no position to push for the establishment of an EMF, all the more so as German lawyers and officials – unhappy about the way they had been bypassed in 1978 – made it clear that such an institution would require a revision of the Treaty of Rome, with all the attendant difficulties of parliamentary ratification.

The French were furious. So too was Tommaso Padoa-Schioppa, Director-General for Economic Affairs at the Commission. Both these parties pointed to the agreement of the European Council in December 1978: the establishment of the EMF was there in black and white. But Schmidt was now powerless against Bundesbank opposition. Horst Schulman, the key German negotiator of the 1978 agreement and by now Chairman of the Monetary Committee, knew which way the wind was blowing. He developed a diplomatic 'flu at the moment the Commission attempted to force the issue in the Committee. The field was left open to Leonhard Gleske, member of the Bundesbank Directorate responsible for international affairs (the Bundesbank's 'Foreign Minister'), and thus its representative in the Monetary Committee. A subsequent Chairman of that Committee described Gleske's office as being that of 'the Bundesbank's ambassador to the Monetary Committee, but also the Monetary Committee's ambassador to the Bundesbank'. Gleske himself, unlike at least one of his successors, was not at all receptive to this description of his role as Janus-like. Not noted for his subtlety, he dismissed the EMF in four words: '*Wir wollen das nich.*' The Bundesbank had spoken. Padoa-Schioppa was to remember the lesson. By the end of the decade he thought he had his revenge when a different German Chancellor agreed, at Maastricht, to a legally binding treaty that reflected Padoa-Schioppa's ideas more than anyone's. The old proponents of the EMF hoped that it would mean the end of the Bundesbank.

## Clean break

All that was in the future. In 1981, while Schmidt's political grave was being dug by the Bundesbank, using the shovels provided by the misguided 1978 exercise in coordination, the removal men were turning up at the Elysée to

23

cart away Giscard and his diamonds – in part because of Barre's austerity. The victor in the May presidential elections was François Mitterrand – former supporter of the extreme Right, former Pétainist, former minister in Fourth Republic governments, former centrist, now Socialist and partner of the Communists, always opportunist. In the run-up to the election, Mitterrand had spoken of 'making a clean break with capitalism'. Capital immediately decided to make a clean break with him: funds flowed out of France at a dizzy rate in the days following his triumph.[9]

Mitterrand's programme had been agreed jointly with the Communists, and he included four of them in his government. The government rapidly implemented cuts in the working week, an increase in the minimum wage, far-reaching nationalization and increases in government transfers, dressed up as salaries, to Socialist supporters in the public administration and the education system. Together, these measures reduced the productive capacity of the French economy, while in the short-run increasing the demand for goods and services. The French balance of payments inevitably swung into deficit: there were insufficient sources of French supply to meet the increased demand, so imports rose and exports fell back. To add to this, foreign capital continued flowing out of France, partly to take advantage of German interest rates that had rocketed after the Bundesbank strike at Schmidt, partly out of fear of the Socialist/Communist joint programme. The stock market fell sharply after Mitterrand's election. The franc, too, would have fallen sharply but for intervention by the Banque de France and a tightening of France's already extensive exchange controls.[10] But France's foreign exchange reserves were seeping away: a devaluation had to come.

The incoming Socialists had in fact discussed among themselves whether they should devalue the franc immediately on taking power. Mitterrand had vetoed the idea. Even though in France devaluation did not

9 Two days after his election victory, a letter of fulsome congratulation, complete with protestations of lifetime devotion to the Socialist cause, appeared in the left-wing newspaper *Libération*. It was signed by a large number of French officials of the Economics and Financial Affairs Directorate of the European Commission, few of whom had manifested Socialist leanings previously. The letter was a flagrant breach of Commission staff regulations. Naturally, no action was taken against the signatories. Instead, their careers prospered mightily, upward movement accelerating, of course, when Jacques Delors became Commission President at the beginning of 1985. One wonders if the Commission authorities would have remained silent if – pigs might fly – any non-Socialist French Commission officials had written to, say, *Le Figaro* to voice their *disapproval* of Mitterrand's victory.

10 According to the Treaty of Rome, all exchange controls in the Community should have been abolished by 1961.

then have quite the stigma it was later to acquire, he did not want the glorious sun of electoral triumph to be clouded, even partly, by an acceptance in advance that the French economy was going to be devastated by his policies. So devaluation was postponed until the autumn, by which time it could be blamed on 'foreign speculators' – a refrain that was to be taken up with increasing enthusiasm and violence by successive French governments as the ERM story unfolded.

The October 1981 devaluation gave pointers to the future of the ERM. Mitterrand and Jacques Delors, his Finance Minister, wanted to have the realignment presented less as a negative verdict on the French government's policies than as a general reordering of the ERM in the face of imbalances in Germany – a large budget deficit and inordinately high interest rates. Appearance has always been more important than reality in ERM politics – indeed, the ERM is a means of distorting reality. So it was that when Delors asked for an 8.5% downward realignment of the franc, he asked not the body supposedly responsible for managing realignments – a meeting of finance ministers and central bank governors of the EMS countries, which usually delegates decisions to the Monetary Committee, whose members then meet as the personal representatives of their principals – but the German government. The point of this démarche – like the Schmidt–Giscard démarche of 1978 and like most things of importance affecting the Community – was for France and Germany to be able to tell the others what they must do.

On this occasion, what Delors wanted, in an eerie prefiguring of his attitude in July 1993, was twofold. First, the realignment must be presented as primarily a DM revaluation. He quickly got the agreement of the German government to announce a 5.5% revaluation of the DM and a 3% devaluation of the French franc. Schmidt, increasingly floundering in German politics, undoubtedly hoped that a DM revaluation would help the public forget the shame of the current-account deficits and DM weakness his 'locomotive' policies had brought on Germany – in the event, the public blamed him for these sins and gave the Bundesbank the credit for the DM's ascension from purgatory. The markets, of course, gave their own verdict, as unfavourable to the franc as that of German public opinion was to Schmidt: the DM remained unchanged against non-ERM currencies, and the franc fell by the full 8.5%, give or take some temporary upward movement in its new band. Second, Delors insisted that the French franc must not be singled out for devaluation. When the Monetary Committee was finally convened, the Italians learnt that they had been designated as the partner of France in the devaluation foxtrot. They made it clear that they preferred to sit this one out, still feeling the effects of a solo performance of a few months earlier, when the lira had devalued without either fuss or discussion. But, in the time-dishonoured tradition of the Community, a lady was in the end always prepared to sell her favours. The Italian government, needing to maintain an alliance with France in matters such as the CAP and the Community budget, told its Monetary Committee members to agree – thereby strengthening a reputation for opportunism that a decade or so later was to colour the attitudes both of the financial markets and of the Bundesbank.

The other members were somewhat miffed that France and Germany had also decided what should happen to *their* currencies. The Dutch guilder, it was ordained, would follow the DM, while the others (the Belgo-Luxembourg franc, the Danish krone and the Irish pound) would be used as 'pivots', their central rates unchanged but devaluing slightly in weighted-average terms. The Dutch had no great economic objection to following Germany – indeed they plugged the guilder as a sort of substitute DM. However, the Benelux Treaty of 1947, which had created an economic union among its three signatories, specified that no party would make a decision affecting its exchange rate without the agreement of the other two. The Monetary Committee discussions, since they involved all three countries, provided the formal cover for such a decision. But the Franco-German diktat, when reluctantly obeyed by the Netherlands, in effect spelled the abrogation of the Benelux Treaty for all practical monetary purposes. The Netherlands had all but accepted the role of a monetary appendage of Germany, thereby shifting the monetary geopolitics of the Continent in a way that Delors, at least, evidently failed to recognize. Over the previous thousand years, buffer zones between France and Germany had been created, destroyed, resurrected, destroyed again. Now, the effective dissolution of the monetary buffer created by the Benelux Treaty meant that there was bound to be competition for satellites between the two great stars of the European firmament. France, in 1981 as in 1993, was prepared to see the Netherlands as a German satellite. In 1981 as in 1993, she wanted Belgium, as well as Italy, to remain part of a group clustered around her. But such was the perversity of the economic policies pursued by Delors, by Pierre Mauroy, the French Prime Minister, and by Mitterrand, that France would first have to suffer the humiliation of a monetary Vichy.

The route to that humiliation was via Socialism. The banking sector was almost entirely nationalized, credit controls, exchange controls (strengthened in June 1981) and price controls were pervasive. The 'Auroux laws' enlarged the statutory role of unions. Further measures continued the trend of the 1970s (under Giscard) of reducing the ability of employers to dismiss redundant workers or to resort to part-time and temporary employment.[11] Throughout French industry and business, the remaining 'freedom of managers to manage' was in any case only a freedom to follow the wishes of the government. Much of large-scale industry was under state control, and the *nomenklatura* formed by the graduates of the *'grandes écoles'*, the training-ground of the French political, administrative, industrial, commercial and media élite, was everywhere.

Naturally, the French economy continued to deteriorate. Employment, supposedly the key target of the Socialist–Communist policy strategy, suffered. The unemployment rate rose inexorably, even if not yet quite as rapidly as in Germany or Britain (in the latter country, the economy was undergoing the painful but necessary process of being reclaimed from the East-Europeanization of the 1970s). But, for the mercantilist French mind, the most worrying manifestation of problems was the ongoing worsening of the current account. In subsequent chapters, we shall see how a current-account deficit can be a symptom of economic renascence. But in the case of France in the early 1980s, the deficit was an accurate reflection of the structural decline of an over-regulated economy, a reflection that worried the authorities to distraction far more than did the mess that caused it. Their instinctive reaction was to multiply the controls and distortions that were at the root of the problem. Of course, 'control' of the exchange rate was an essential element in this benighted strategy. The ERM was essential to Mitterrandism. But, with the balance of payments deteriorating at a rate to have Colbert spinning in his grave, a second devaluation was having to be 'prepared' during the spring of 1982.

## Recidivist Delors

During the spring, the French franc drifted down in the ERM band, despite a 3-percentage-point increase in the differential between French

---

11 Jacques Chirac, as Prime Minister in 1975, made it impossible for firms to declare collective redundancies without administrative approval. As Prime Minister again in 1986, during his brief period as an economic liberal, he abolished the rules, only for Edouard Balladur to reintroduce something similar in 1993.

and German Euro-market rates.[12] Given the attitudes expressed by the Bundesbank and the unhelpful political situation in Germany, there was no way of avoiding a French franc devaluation. Once again, there were prior Franco-German bilateral negotiations. The Germans insisted that a freeze on prices in France, already in effect, should be extended to wages. This was a shocking demand in the minds of most French Socialists – but the government accepted it and committed itself to keep the budget deficit to 3% of GDP, in return for a 10% devaluation which, once again, would be presented as a joint move, with the DM and the guilder 'revaluing' by slightly more than the French franc devalued.

Germany was now in a position vis-à-vis France even stronger than it had been vis-à-vis the small countries in the old 'snake'. It was deciding the 'when' and the 'how much' of franc devaluations. In addition, it was dictating the domestic policies the French government must follow. From the French side, things seemed very clear indeed. The combination of the ERM and the out-and-out Socialist phase of Mitterrand's government had led to almost total French monetary subjugation to Germany. But even worse was to come.

By September 1982, the French franc was again under pressure, as the futility of Keynesianism-Socialism in an ossified, sclerotic economy became ever more visible. Delors fulminated about speculators, the constant refrain of French finance ministers since the early 1920s. 'There is an international conspiracy against France,' he declared. 'They want to smash our experiment and make us devalue a third time.'

At the beginning of 1983, pressure mounted again, prompting substantial interventions by the ERM central banks. In February, the dollar's stellar progress temporarily paused, strengthening the DM against other ERM currencies. On 7 March, general elections in Germany confirmed the CDU/FDP coalition in office, giving the DM a further boost. On 13 March, the first round of local elections in France inflicted substantial losses on the Socialists – the result of the disenchantment of Socialist voters with the 'austerity' measures of the previous summer. When forex markets reopened at the beginning of the next week, the franc immediately

12 France's exchange controls meant that domestic interest rates could be insulated in some measure from Euromarket rates, the rates for borrowing and lending French francs among banks outside France. In addition, credit controls and extensive state subsidies to credit – at this time, more than half the loans extended by the nationalized banking system attracted a state subsidy – meant that Euro-rates could be pushed up for quite some time before French domestic borrowers felt any pain.

fell to its ERM floor. The Belgian franc and the Irish pound were also under heavy pressure. On 15 March, the German, Dutch and Swiss central banks lowered interest rates by a full point (the Bundesbank cut its discount rate from 5% to 4%) and the French authorities again pushed Eurofranc rates up to 25%. But heavy selling of the weak currencies continued, forcing unprecedentedly large amounts – for that period of the ERM's history – of obligatory intervention by the central banks, including the Bundesbank.

German willingness to help the franc had much to do with the ongoing German economic stagnation. The previous October, the Swedish authorities, who had already devalued the krona very substantially in late 1981, produced a further massive devaluation – 16% against a basket of currencies – out of the blue. German fears of a round of 'competitive devaluations', damaging to German industry, increased. Schulman, soon to depart the political stage as his master fell, railed against Sweden. His successor as State Secretary in the Finance Ministry and Monetary Committee member, Hans Tietmeyer,[13] held very different political views, but shared Schulman's view of the EMS as a safeguard of German competitiveness. Ten years later, Tietmeyer – by then Vice-President of the Bundesbank – was again, during the final crisis of the ERM, to argue in favour of a German interest-rate cut to defend the franc. As we shall see in chapter 12, he was overruled in 1993. But in 1983, things were different.

The pressures on the franc were stoking a titanic political battle in Paris. On one side stood the left wing of the Socialists, who wanted to return to the policies of 1981, leave the EMS and introduce protectionist measures – if necessary 'suspending' EC trade rules. The Industry Minister, Jean-Pierre Chevènement, and Mitterrand's Chief of Staff, Pierre Bérégovoy (who, ten years later, would be defending – literally to the death – a diametrically opposed set of policies), were the standard-bearers of the Left. Against them were ranged the 'modernizers', Delors chief among them, who wanted to remain in the EMS and impose further 'austerity'.

Chancellor Kohl was determined that Delors should win the battle in Paris. A victory for the rival Chevènement faction could have damaging consequences for German trade and, by damaging the EC, greatly weaken Germany's diplomatic position in the world. But Delors was not

---

13 Tietmeyer will dominate the later stages of this book. His personality is sketched in chapter 4 below.

an easy customer. Yet again, Franco-German negotiations began on the details of a devaluation package. Delors could not be seen by French public opinion as simply caving in to German demands. And the Germans had to convince their own public opinion that the ERM was exporting German financial 'virtue' to France, not importing French 'vice' into Germany – after all, the ejection of the SPD, admittedly very different animals from the French Socialists, was attributed in part to Schmidt's loss of control of the German budgetary reins in 1978–80. And while a French withdrawal from the ERM was to be avoided if possible, German industry would not be happy if the price of maintaining the ERM were too large a franc devaluation.

Delors gave full rein to his capacity for histrionics. On two occasions he flew back from Brussels to Paris to consult the French 'war Cabinet'. He attacked Germany bitterly on every front – interest rates, intervention, the size and attribution of the devaluation under negotiation. He even expostulated to his fellow Finance Ministers, after Stoltenberg had initially rejected a DM revaluation, that: 'Before such arrogant and uncomprehending people [as the Germans], what can I do?' At one point in the negotiations, the French produced the idea of a widening of the permitted ERM margins (as we shall see in chapter 12, the same suggestion would be made on the *German* side in the great confrontation of July 1993), in an attempt to blackmail Germany into accepting a substantial franc devaluation dressed up as a DM revaluation. Delors's antics disgusted German and Dutch central bankers as well as Tietmeyer. Even the Governor of the Banque de France talked to other central bankers about the 'psychodramas' of a realignment *à la Delors*.[14]

In the end, Delors got his way on the appearances. The franc was devalued by 8% against the DM, though the cosmetic presentation was of a 5.5% DM 'revaluation' and a franc devaluation of only 2.5%. The reality was that the franc had been devalued in total by 30% against the DM in less than eighteen months. French wage and budget policy had already ended up being set by Germany. Now, as part of the March 1983 devaluation package, the Mitterrand government had to agree to targets for the French current account. The humiliation for the French Socialist government was near total, a sort of monetary 1940.

14 It is symptomatic of the distorted logic of the ERM/EMU that, according to some accounts, first discussions of EMU between Kohl and Mitterrand took place at this time.

## Corporatism in one continent

The psychological reaction of the French élite was not that the country had to change its ways and learn to stand on its own feet. In Britain, Mrs Thatcher was cajoling her country into doing just that after the even greater economic humiliations suffered in the 1970s under the Heath, Wilson and Callaghan governments. But whereas in Britain June 1940 is remembered for Dunkirk and a determination to fight on alone, in France it is associated with total capitulation and the establishment of the collaborationist Vichy régime. In May 1983, the French government believed it had no choice between autarky and subservience to the German model. Being French and Socialist, it never even considered the alternative of economic liberalism, the only way of combining national sovereignty with openness to the rest of an interdependent world. Instead, it chose the route of June 1940, echoing the view that (to quote a recent brilliant chronicler of the Mitterrand catastrophe) France 'was doomed to defeat, and it would be forced to change for the better only by being under the tutelage of the victorious Nazis.'

Kohl, of course, is no Nazi, and the German model is not Nazism. It is something that the French call 'Rhenish capitalism', in contrast with the 'Anglo-Saxon capitalism' so detested by the Nazis, by Vichy and by French 'Christian Socialists' such as Delors. The essential element of 'Rhenish capitalism' is corporatism. The French decision of May 1983 to embrace it was to destroy politics in France. The associated decision to embrace the cross of the '*franc fort*', as if in atonement for French degradation, was to destroy the French economy. Together, the two decisions led the French political élite inevitably to its present obsession with 'Europe'.

The EMS had been designed as an instrument of geopolitics, of history, from the start. But the ensuing political weakness of Schmidt and Giscard, together with the emergence of divergent economic policies in France and Germany, soon reduced it to little more than a mechanism for creating sporadic financial market turbulence and retarding inevitable exchange-rate movements. It did little or nothing to promote the 'convergence' that the Brussels European Council had looked forward to. Instead, it was already a vehicle for political unaccountability, buck-passing and irre-sponsibility – to that extent it was already creating the political conditions for acceptance of the same phenomena in 'Europe'. But the first four years of its existence had disappointed those who saw in it the route to, as well as from, Aachen. The new phase in the history of the ERM ushered in by the climacteric of March 1983 was more intensely geopolitical in nature than the first – though its historical resonance was much more to do, in economic terms, with the Third Reich than with the First Reich, the empire of Charlemagne. The devaluation of March 1983 marked the acceptance by Mitterrand and Delors that, in the modern world economic order, 'Socialism in One Country' was economically impossible. Instead, they set their sights on the creation of 'Corporatism in One Continent', along lines similar, as it happens, to those envisaged by Nazi and Vichy theorists, to confront the 'Anglo-Saxon' world.[15] A little less than nine years later, the Maastricht Treaty seemed to have brought that vision within reach.

Yet mysticism, quasi-religiosity and something approaching Aryanism are only one element in the French élite's approach to 'Europe'. Hard-nosed technocracy is the other. For the *énarques* whom Klasen had so feared in 1978, the *franc fort* was not just a painful penance for past sins: it was to be the route to wresting monetary leadership from Germany. '*Il faut reculer pour mieux sauter.*' The only way to gain German respect for France sufficient to gull Germany into handing over monetary sovereignty was to reduce French inflation to German levels and to maintain a strong currency. With a brief and timorous interruption in 1986 (an interruption that had a certain historical appropriateness, since it occurred under the 'cohabitation' government led by the Gaullist, Jacques Chirac), French monetary and economic policy would thereafter be directed towards maintaining the franc–DM link. But French monetary diplomacy would also continue the efforts begun in 1978 by Giscard to ease the rigours of German monetary leadership and ultimately to replace it.

## Regat Bundesbankia!

There is more than one side to every story. Seen from Frankfurt, the period of French economic self-abnegation from 1983 to 1986 looked like evidence that initial Bundesbank misgivings about the ERM had perhaps been mistaken. After the change of budgetary and monetary course in 1981, the German economy had performed to the bank's satisfaction. By the final year, 1986, of the second phase of the ERM's history, German inflation was actually negative. A current-account surplus had been re-established. The government's budget was back in something like reason-

---

15 Nazi views on the new world economic order are sketched in chapter 9 below.

able order. Monetary targets had been met for several years in succession (1986 itself was an exception, but an overshoot was tolerable given the inflation outlook and the fact that the dollar's vertiginous rise between 1981 and 1985 was now being succeeded by what was to turn out to be an equally steep fall).

Perhaps even more satisfying to the German mind, the ERM had, since March 1983, turned into an undeclared DM-zone, thus enabling the benefits of German price stability to be exported to other members of the system – along with economic stagnation and unemployment. In Germany itself, the disappearance of inflation had been brought about only by five years of increasing under-utilization of resources. Unemployment had risen steadily. From 1983 to 1986 it also rose steadily in France, Italy and Ireland. In Belgium and the Netherlands, only embellishment of the unemployment statistics prevented a similar rise from showing up. Denmark was the only real – but sadly temporary – exception. The years of undisputed Bundesbank domination of the ERM were also the years of the most concentrated 'Europessimism'. In Britain the fruits of the Thatcherite revolution, the antithesis of Rhenish capitalism, were beginning to ripen in the sunnier climate outside the ERM. In the next chapter we shall look in some detail at the strange intellectual derangement that attracted Nigel Lawson, with such terrible consequences, to the ERM, the 'modern-day Gold Standard with the DM as the anchor' (as John Major was later to call it, misguidedly). In this chapter, we shall look more briefly at how it actually worked. This is a subject of more than historical interest (in the pejorative sense so often given to the word 'historical'), since it seems to be the intention of the current monetary tsar of Europe, Hans Tietmeyer, to recreate certain aspects of the conditions of 1983–86.

It is time to confront certain dragons in their lair. The words 'symmetry', 'asymmetry' and 'anchor' will recur repeatedly. They need to be explained. The ERM is formally symmetrical in that, as we saw, its main feature is a bilateral parity grid. If one currency reaches a margin of $+2.25\%$ (the biggest possible in the original narrow band) against another, the second has by definition reached a margin of $-2.25\%$ against the first. The duties, rights and obligations of the 'strong' currency are formally identical with those of the weak. In practice, however, the strong currency is under much less pressure to react than is the weak currency: the system works *asymmetrically*.

The Bundesbank was fairly clearly the leader of an asymmetric ERM in 1983–86. Another way of putting this is to say that the ERM was a DM-zone in this period: the other countries simply pegged their currencies to the DM. The Bundesbank thus provided the monetary policy 'anchor' of the system: someone, somewhere had to set the monetary policy of the countries in the system, and that someone was the Bundesbank.

Why were the other countries prepared to go along with this? For the old snake members, of course, there was nothing new in accepting Bundesbank leadership. What was new for Belgium and Denmark – though not the Netherlands – was a determination to eschew devaluing against the anchor country. Whatever the internal political motivations for this, some intellectual cover was provided by the 'death of macroeconomics' school that reigned throughout the world in the mid-1980s. One relatively thoughtful and, in some respects, accurate version of this was represented by the Medium Term Financial Strategy in Thatcher's Britain – we shall see in the next chapter how things nonetheless started going wrong. But the bastardized version current on the Continent was just another expression of Europessimism: the structure of European economies, and especially their labour markets, was so bad that any attempt to stimulate growth by budgetary or monetary policy would, it was argued, create nothing but inflation. Excessive real wages were seen – even in Mitterrand Mark II France – as the problem, and they had to be reduced through de-indexation, wage freezes and 'social dialogue'. There were indeed major structural problems in Continental Europe. But they had most to do with excessive government regulation, too large a state-controlled sector, inadequate competition, too big a role in policy-making for trade unions, tax rates too high for enterprise and initiative to be rewarded, minimum-wage rules, barriers to new firms, restrictions on firing workers, social security benefits that provided disincentives to work and social security costs that provided disincentives to offering work. The 'social dialogue' and 'incomes policy' routes set many of these deficiencies even more firmly in concrete. And whatever genuine 'structural' unemployment there was, it could only be made worse by a failure of aggregate demand in the economy to take up even the restricted amount of profitable and willing supply. Yet sticking to the Bundesbank *did* tend to impose monetary policies too tight for demand to match available supply.

France itself strayed once from the penitential route laid out in 1983. In April 1986, the pursuit of Socialist austerity and the Vichyite *franc fort* had had a predictable electoral result (just as it was to do again in March 1993): the Socialists lost the parliamentary elections. The incoming centre-right coalition, led by the Gaullist Jacques Chirac, had two sets of reasons for questioning the Mitterrand–Delors exchange-rate policy. First, a Gaullist could hardly be expected to look with favour on Vichyite monetary obeisance to Germany. Second, given that both Mitterrand Mark I Socialism and Mitterrand Mark II corporatism, or at least their unemployment consequences, seemed to have been rejected by the electorate, it might reasonably be thought that different policies were in order. (Here, the analogy with 1993 breaks down: by then, democratic politics had been so thoroughly banished from France that the policies of Mitterrand's Socialist Prime Minister, Bérégovoy, were quite simply taken over by his new, supposedly Gaullist, Prime Minister, Edouard Balladur.)

Chirac, almost as much a political chameleon as Mitterrand himself, plumped for a degree of economic liberalism unwonted in France. Exchange controls would be abolished. Financial markets would be deregulated and modernized, modelled explicitly on New York. Privatization would be introduced. Tax rates would be cut. Restrictive labour market regulations would be eliminated. But Chirac did not want this programme to be stymied by an immediate loss of competitiveness and surge in unemployment as had happened in the early years of Thatcher's rule. He had no time to be patient. His real objective had much less to do with reforming the French economy than with becoming the French President, and the presidential elections were only two years away. His revolution would have to be a gentle one, and must proceed without cutting away any of the dead wood built up over the previous twelve years. Thus immediately on taking office he instructed his new Finance Minister, Balladur, to negotiate a devaluation.

The excuse was the loss of competitiveness ('the cumulated divergence of costs and prices' in Bundesbank-speak) built up over the three years since the last devaluation – France's inflation rate had been coming down, but prices and wages had nonetheless risen significantly more than Germany's over the past three years as a whole. This was the sort of realignment of which Tietmeyer, already clearly the dominant force in German economic policy-making, approved, or would at least accept, even though an improvement in French competitiveness implied some smaller worsening of German competitiveness. It did not come in response to speculative pressure, and would give no profits to speculators; it put no political pressure on Germany and there were no public arguments about whether Germany should revalue; the Bundesbank was not involved through rows about intervention or interest rates, and so could not stick its oar in the negotiations; it remedied rather than created movements in real exchange rates (nominal exchange rates corrected for movements in relative costs and prices); and it followed a period of satisfactory (because German-dicated) domestic stabilization efforts. The negotiations took a little time, but went off smoothly. The realignment was a model of what, for Tietmeyer, a realignment should be.

Nonetheless, from the French point of view the realignment hardly represented a brandishing of the Cross of Lorraine. Chirac was still a monetary collaborator rather than a resistance fighter. By following the rules of the ERM game as laid down by Germany, he was confirming German supremacy in the system. He was not yet in a position to challenge German leadership, and the alternative of floating never seemed to have occurred to anyone – Chirac's cloak of economic liberalism could not hide his statist attachment to fixed rates. But the costs of following the Bundesbank would soon force him to contest its leadership. It is time to see how and why Bundesbank leadership came to be contested.

## All that glitters

By the end of 1986, many changes were in the offing, not least in France. Together, they would make the question of the anchor a highly conflictual one. The Chirac government was relaxing exchange controls. The Banque de France had already switched from credit controls to market methods of monetary control in 1994. Financial markets were being deregulated and modernized. All this meant that any increases in interest rates to defend the franc would have much more immediate and pervasive effects on the French economy. The Single Market might bring greater competition. And using the exchange rate as a shock-absorber was not obviously consistent with the rediscovered goal of monetary union. Of more immediate domestic political importance, the April 1986 devaluation could be blamed on the outgoing Socialists. But Chirac himself would have to take the blame for any subsequent devaluation (in the Vichy-like atmosphere created by and for the political élite since 1983, devaluation was increasingly regarded as a national disgrace), unless someone else – the US? Germany? – could be blamed instead. Moreover, the patience of ordinary French people was becoming strained. In 1986, French inflation was down to 2.7%. There had been some political benefits in getting it down to that level from the double figures of the early 1980s – but not enough to prevent the Socialists losing their parliamentary majority. There would almost certainly be no political benefit whatsoever to Chirac in reducing inflation further. If he was to become President in 1988, the emphasis would have to shift to reducing the unemployment rate, which had swapped places with inflation and was now itself in double figures.

All these concerns came to a head in January 1987. There was a wave of strikes and industrial unrest in France, inevitable in an 'incomes policy' economy. It was equally inevitable that these strikes should have a political character and that Mitterrand should exploit them to undermine his Prime Minister. On the international monetary scene, the dollar lurched further down. As always dollar weakness provoked flows into DM and created tensions within the ERM.[16] In the new framework of liberalized French financial markets, there were large outflows from France. The franc was pushed to the bottom of its band. Both the Banque de France and the Bundesbank had to intervene in unprecedented volume, and French interest rates were forced up with much more immediately painful impact than in the past. For two weeks, there were bitter public recriminations between France and Germany. German interest rates were already at historical lows: there was no prospect of a further reduction to save the franc. There had to be a realignment. Germany insisted that the franc must devalue, Chirac that the DM must revalue. Mitterrand sat in the Elysée Palace and smiled. Politically, it was no contest. The asymmetry of the ERM prevailed, and Chirac had to give in. The franc was devalued, and the Chirac government could be branded by the Socialists as 'devaluationist', as twice besmirching the good name of France after the three years of Socialist 'virtue' from March 1983.

## Louvred doors

Chirac was furious. Mitterrand was freezing him out from Franco-German relations at the highest level and indeed from foreign affairs and defence matters – the natural area for a Gaullist prime minister to try to make his mark – in general. Chirac and Balladur clearly resolved to make use of the opportunities for *monetary* diplomacy left to them by 'cohabitation'. In a reversal – forced by circumstances – of the Schmidt–Giscard approach in 1978, they used whatever doors were still open to them at ministerial and official level to get round their exclusion from the highest levels of power.

Their first opportunity came almost immediately. In February 1987, the finance ministers of the G-7 industrial countries (the United States,

16 As we shall see in later chapters, there developed another mechanism through which strains that had their origin *within* the ERM produced dollar *strength*.

Germany, Japan, France, Britain, Italy and Canada) met at the Louvre, at that time still the home of the French Finance Ministry.[17] There they concluded an agreement to 'stabilize' the weak dollar, which, by falling sharply, had done everything that the finance ministers had enjoined it to do at the time of the Plaza Agreement less than eighteen months before.[18] The Louvre Accords, a classic example of the misdirected interference known as 'coordination', allowed Balladur and Chirac to present themselves to French opinion in a favourable light. The agreements concluded at French initiative and in the ornate magnificence of the Louvre appeared to show France as contributing to decisive action to counter the factor – dollar weakness – that could be blamed for the January franc devaluation. And it showed France as a significant player on the larger stage of the G-7 even if she was clearly a follower within the ERM.

By the same token, some members of the Bundesbank Council were very unhappy about the agreements. Over the past eight years Frankfurt had turned the ERM round to its own advantage: the creation of a DM-zone wider than the old snake meant that the Bundesbank had to worry less about monetary events in the rest of the world, notably changes in the value of the dollar, and could concentrate on domestic monetary targeting – with all the room that gave for domestic politicking, free from overtly political control. The Louvre Accords potentially brought some benefit if, by stabilizing the dollar, they avoided pressures on the French franc of the sort that had forced the Bundesbank into January's massive, unwelcome intervention. But they had the great disadvantage that the setting of target zones for exchange rates among the leading world currencies, in a forum where decisions were taken by politicians, including French and Italian politicians, could undermine the Bundesbank's own leadership within the ERM. Still, there was little it could do: the Bundesbank Law gave the Federal government the right to decide international agreements of this kind.

In these circumstances, the *enragés* in the Bundesbank Council had to grit their teeth. Further trials awaited them, however, as France pressed in the Committee of Central Bank Governors and the Monetary Committee

---

17 At different stages in the proceedings, the first five of these countries, then Canada and then Italy got in on the act. There is some confusion, therefore, about whether one should speak of the meeting as being one of the G-5, the G-6 or the G-7. I refer to the G-7 for consistency with current practice, even though the term was not widely used at the time.

18 In fact, the Plaza ageement was simply taking advantage of a turn in the dollar trend that had already happened in the market several months before.

for technical 'improvements' in the ERM in the light of the January events. The increased volume of speculative movements, French officials argued, meant that the resources of the central banks available for countering speculation had to be increased. And, drawing on the theoretical need for monetary policy coordination in a fixed-rate system, they insisted that there should be regular monitoring of exchange-rate *and* interest-rate and other economic policies and developments in Europe and the world both in the Governors Committee and the Monetary Committee. The French demands were accepted by and large, in both 'competent bodies'.[19]

Karl Otto Pöhl, the Bundesbank President, played an ambiguous role in the Governors Committee, as he was later to do in the Delors Committee. He may have realized that the Bundesbank's apparently dominant position in the ERM in fact made it highly vulnerable. It was simply not conceivable, he might well have thought at the time, that other countries, France in particular, would accept Bundesbank leadership for ever; if the Bundesbank did not accept some gesture of 'coordination' now, manageable within the reasonably friendly and clubby 'competent bodies', then irresistible pressures for a more political, Euro-institutional solution might be created.

At any rate, the technical changes were agreed by the Governors Committee in Basle and approved by an informal Ecofin (which governors attend) in Nyborg, in September 1987.[20] These changes somewhat reduced, in principle, the asymmetry of the system. France could thus claim a victory for its way of thinking. But the agreement also established a presumption that movements of currencies within the band should be used first when a currency came under attack,[21] to be followed, if need be, by adjustment of interest-rate differentials and only then by intervention. (Movements within the band, management of interest-rate differentials and intervention became known as the 'Basle–Nyborg instruments'.) This agreement allowed the Bundesbank to present the deal as a whole as a move in the direction *it* favoured. The two conflicting interpretations given to the

19 Similar suggestions for the 'non-institutional strengthening' of the ERM were put forward in 1981–82 after the idea of the EMF had been buried. But at that time the Bundesbank's position of political strength had enabled it to reject them.
20 The Very Short Term Financing facility in the EMS had hitherto been available for weak-currency central banks to draw on to finance only obligatory intervention at the lower permitted ERM margin. Now there was to be a 'presumption' that strong-currency central banks would allow borrowing of their currency within the VSTF for intramarginal interventions – but not in unlimited amounts. The repayment period was also extended, and repayment 100% in ECU, rather than in the strong currency, was also allowed, subject to certain conditions.
21 The point of this was to try to establish so-called 'two-way risk' for speculators, a concept subsequently appealed to in August 1993.

Basle–Nyborg compromise recalled those attached to the compromise involved in the EMS itself, and prefigured the conflict, still unresolved today, over the 'correct' interpretation of the Maastricht compromise. After 1978, the Bundesbank was able to impose its interpretation, despite the 'psychodramas' of 1981–83, and the others were, in the end, prepared to accept it. After Basle–Nyborg, the ERM entered a more conflictual phase, despite the appearance of calm and stability given by a five-and-a-half year absence of realignments. There was to be a trial of strength between the Bundesbank and those, notably the French, who were determined to get their hands on the levers of monetary power.

## Wall Street crashed, Louvre smashed

The first conflict to erupt, however, was provoked by the Louvre Accords rather than directly by the ERM. During the summer and early autumn of 1987, the Federal Reserve, in keeping with the aims of the Accords, put the dollar's exchange rate top of the list of factors affecting its monetary policy decisions – for the first time since before the breakdown of the Bretton Woods system. The Bundesbank, it turned out, was not prepared to do the same. The 'target zones' established by the Accords had no leader. There was therefore no monetary policy 'anchor'. From the Bundesbank's point of view, the great danger was that calls would arise to establish an anchor through joint management, in some undesirable form or other, for world monetary policy. To forestall that danger, the Bundesbank Council – undoubtedly worked up by Helmut Schlesinger – decided to insist on maintaining its own anchor, the German money supply. Early in October, the Bundesbank raised its official rates, for the first time since 1981, with the announced aim of steering the money supply back into the target range from which it was straying.

The impact on the other side of the Atlantic was immediate. James Baker denounced Schlesinger for, in his view, jeopardizing the world recovery. Schlesinger replied that German price stability could not be put at risk. US financial markets feared that American interest rates might rise, or at least be prevented from falling. The stock market had been booming while long-term interest rates had been rising, a vulnerable combination. Now, the open conflict between Baker and Schlesinger and the prospect of a long period of high long rates shattered the fragile, misplaced confidence on which the stock-market boom had reposed. On Friday, 16 October, Wall Street fell sharply, prompting Baker into even more urgent denunciations of the Bundesbank. On Monday, 19 October, the market crashed completely, sending shock-waves around the world. For several hours, the US financial system was threatened with total meltdown. The Federal Reserve immediately and wholly justifiably pumped huge amounts of liquidity into the markets, in effect saying the dollar could go hang, which it promptly did.[22] To all intents and purposes, the Louvre Accords were dustbinned.[23] Schlesinger had won.

His triumph did not come without a price, however. The fall of the dollar and the initial fears – soon shown to be unfounded – of a relapse into world recession in the wake of stock-market crashes fed into strong downward pressure on the franc. This confronted the Bundesbank with an awkward dilemma. It had just raised interest rates; to have to lower them now to defend the franc would be embarrassing. But the alternative of being forced into massive intervention, in the face of what would certainly be ferocious determination on the part of Chirac and Balladur not to devalue, would also be painful. The Bundesbank's sanguine interpretation of Basle–Nyborg would be put immediately to the test. From the moment Giscard and Schmidt had first pulled the EMS rabbit out of a hat in 1978, the Bundesbank had dreaded being forced into massive, unlimited intervention that would destroy its control over German monetary developments more openly and dramatically than a cut in official interest rates. January 1987 had been a nasty experience, reawakening fears that had lain dormant for several years.

Intriguingly, there may also have been a dramatic geopolitical element in the Bundesbank's attitude. According to some analysts, Kohl and Gorbachev had already come to an agreement, in the autumn of 1987, on German reunification in return for Western acceptance, to be brokered by Germany, that the Baltic States, the Ukraine and Byelorussia would remain within the Soviet sphere of influence. The agreement could not be made public, it is suggested, until the missing link of the INF treaty was in place, leading inexorably to American disengagement from Europe and giving Germany the chance to resume its traditional dominance of central and eastern Europe. To allay French fears and prevent the re-emergence of the

22 The massive liquidity injection was temporary – a classic example of the 'lender of last resort' function of a responsible central bank. But the deliberate downplaying of the exchange rate was a lasting benefit to the US of the Wall Street crash.

23 Academics and some market participants have ever since argued about whether or not undeclared Louvre-type target zones for the three major world currencies still exist, supported by concerted intervention. But it is clear that the subordination of US interest-rate policy to the dollar ended on 19 October 1987.

'Rapallo complex' in France, a monetary bone would have to be tossed to Mitterrand.

So in early November 1987, for whatever reason, the Bundesbank chose to play the game the Basle–Nyborg way. Rather than face a prolonged period of obligatory intervention, it reached an agreement with the French authorities on the use of the second Basle–Nyborg instrument: the Bundesbank reduced its interest rates and the French increased theirs. The markets were impressed with this early example of coordinated Basle–Nyborg management of interest differentials, and the franc recovered sharply. The Bundesbank could justify the move in domestic terms as a reaction to the DM's effective appreciation as the dollar fell. But there was no getting away from the fact that in fending off the threat of the Louvre Accords it had put itself in a dilemma that showed its undisputed leadership of the ERM to be over. If proof were needed, it came in the form of Kohl's agreeing, at the urging of Chirac and Balladur and in the face of the direst Bundesbank misgivings, to set up a Franco–German Economic and Finance Council at which the two countries' finance ministers *and central bank governors* would meet twice a year to discuss matters of common concern.

Worse, Chirac and Balladur, having been given an inch, were about to try to take much more than a yard. Genscher was soon to appear to give them even more. Whether he was compensating for the reported Kohl–Gorbachev Pact or exploiting it as a preparatory move to extending German dominion westwards as well as eastwards remains an open question, one that France – and the rest of Europe – will soon have to find an answer to. At the time, however, it was a question that clearly never entered French heads. Two months after the November operation, Balladur would present the Ecofin with a proposal for a European Central Bank – in effect, in French thinking, for the replacement of Bundesbank leadership with a joint (essentially Franco–German) central bank council with powers of decision going far beyond the consultative role of the Franco–German Economic and Finance Council. From that moment on, the ERM would be turned on its head by the political drive to monetary union. We shall see the impact of this sea-change in the next chapter but one. But first we must cross the Channel to Britain, where a Greek tragedy was unfolding – all the more ironic since the French revolt against Bundesbank supremacy smashed the underlying assumptions (without his noticing it) of the main and fatally misguided protagonist in the tragedy: Nigel Lawson.

# 3

# Lawson, the ERM and the Strange Death of Tory Radicalism

Sterling was to enter the ERM on 5 October 1990. The decision was certainly a reprehensible act of economic and political mismanagement, the first of many, by John Major, the Chancellor at the time. Yet in some ways, the worst damage had already been done – by Nigel Lawson between 1985 and 1989, in his campaign of defiance of Mrs Thatcher's veto on ERM entry. When the Prime Minister finally did bend before the massed forces of the ERM's supporters, she had not overcome her well founded opposition to the system. Her reasons for accepting entry were entirely political. The story of how she was forced by her enemies, both abroad and at home, into this abandonment of British monetary sovereignty is one of a strange blend of political miscalculation, betrayal, ambush and conspiracy.

A sad irony of the affair is that two of Mrs Thatcher's most powerful and persistent tormentors were Nigel Lawson and Geoffrey Howe, important figures in implementing the economic strategy of the early Thatcher years. The sacrifices of jobs, homes, firms demanded by the ERM's denial of economic logic – these were antithetical to that early strategy, the strategy that formed an important part of Tory radicalism. Lawson subtitled his account of his part in the Thatcher government 'The Memoirs of a Tory Radical'. Yet it was Lawson, through what he did, and Howe, through what he said, who killed Tory radicalism. Howe's motives in forsaking his own early work are clear enough: his increasingly overt Euroenthusiasm and his belief that he was better fitted to guide European policy than Mrs Thatcher. But why did Lawson, 'my <u>brilliant</u> Chancellor', as Mrs Thatcher called him with deliberate underlining, go off the rails? Why did so many businessmen, financiers, commentators and opinion-formers, even – to their shame – economists, follow him? To understand the dirty politics of British ERM entry, one first has to understand the murky economic reasoning of its protagonists, and why it was so totally wrong.

43

## Flawed diamond

The decision of James Callaghan at the end of 1978 not to enter the ERM had been the result of his fear of the political hostility of most of the Labour Party to manifestations of 'Europe' and of a presumption that sterling would be a weak currency in a system biased in favour of the strong. Mrs Thatcher's guarded criticism of that decision had stemmed from her fear of the political enthusiasm of much of the Conservative Party for manifestations of 'Europe'. On taking office, one of her government's first steps was to be to submit sterling to the judgement of the market by abolishing exchange controls, one of the most daring and important steps taken in the whole of her premiership. The decision was an unmistakable indication of the determination of the Prime Minister and her immediate circle to break with the regulatory mania that had gripped Britain ever since 1940. It was an affirmation of faith in the capacity of the British economy to stand on its own feet. It was also a declaration that *markets*, not governments, must determine the value of the currency. To join the ERM would have been blatantly in contradiction with the principles of the new government – or at least of its leader and her most trusted allies and advisers. Britain, like Germany and the Netherlands, would also be at a disadvantage in a system in which all the other countries maintained extensive exchange controls – but this point was secondary to the philosophical argument for staying out. Nonetheless, the Euroenthusiasm of much of the Establishment was such that the official government position was that sterling would join the ERM 'when the time is ripe'. By the autumn of 1985 Nigel Lawson, as Chancellor, had decided that the time was now indeed ripe.

No one who has read Lawson's account of his years at Number 11 can fail to be impressed by his brilliance. He combined a penetrating philosophical vision with an unrivalled grasp of technical detail. He had been a member of the team that put together the Medium Term Financial Strategy (MTFS), the keystone of the government's strategy, and helped to implement it as Financial Secretary to the Treasury under the Chancellorship of Geoffrey Howe. The strategy (whose origins can even be traced back to the Chancellorship of Denis Healey) was based on a number of admirable principles. First among these was a stress on the importance of sound public finances and a belief that budgetary policy should be concerned with medium-term structural objectives, with providing the correct, neutral environment for national saving and with encouraging a more innovative, responsive and entrepreneurial supply side. In that respect as in so many others, Lawson was a true exponent of 'Tory radicalism'. And a necessary corollary of these views was the eschewal of budgetary policy as a tool of demand-management. Lawson was also quite right to stress the importance of what he called 'a nominal framework'. The idea was that macroeconomic policy[1] could not determine the breakdown of a given amount of nominal growth – as determined by, say, a given rate of growth of the money supply – between real output growth and inflation. Only the institutions of the market, and in particular the mechanisms of wage-bargaining and price-setting, could do that. Here, too, Lawson was a genuine Tory radical, and his support for Mrs Thatcher and Norman Tebbit in their battles to reform the trade unions was important, as was his ceaseless advocacy of privatization.

The great tragedy of Nigel Lawson was that he did not think through the *macroeconomic* implications of the *microeconomic* reforms he either implemented himself in the field of taxation, capital liberalization and financial deregulation, or encouraged others to implement in union reform and privatization. A subsequent section of this chapter will show just how badly, in 1987–88, he failed to cope with 'the problems of success'. But we need first to deal with his initial, failed attempt to join the ERM in late 1985. The episode will reveal much about his misunderstanding of the true economic and political nature of the mechanism.

## Money can't buy me love

By late 1985, Lawson was having serious doubts about how his nominal framework should be defined. The original Medium Term Financial Strategy of the Thatcher government had had no such doubts. It postulated a stable relationship between the demand for money and nominal GDP, the level of output in the economy expressed in money terms, that is, at the prices of the period concerned. If a stable growth path for the money

---

1 Macroeconomics concerns the movements, and the forces governing them, of output, demand, inflation, unemployment and so on in the economy as a whole; questions of *stabilization* of output, employment and inflation are prominent in macroeconomics. Microeconomics, in contrast, studies things such as the output decisions of a single firm, the way a single household allocates its spending among different goods, the determination of the relative prices of different goods and services and so on; questions of the efficient *allocation* of resources among different uses are at the heart of microeconomics. The border between macroeconomics and microeconomics is rather fuzzy. For instance, exchange rates, the central concern of this book, have an important influence on macroeconomic variables, and can contribute to their stabilization or destablization, but have an equally important influence on the relative prices of different goods and services, and can contribute to efficient or inefficient allocation of resources.

supply[2] was maintained, then nominal GDP would in the long run grow by a similar amount, depending on the stability of velocity. Money targets thus became the centrepiece of the MTFS. Unfortunately, they did not work as they were supposed to. In the early years, money supply rocketed: the high interest rates enforced to try to keep it within its target range simply depressed the economy in 1980–81. Institutional change – the abolition of credit controls and a more competitive environment in the banking industry, with depositors offered more favourable terms – had increased the demand for money. Over the next four years, the Treasury attempted to do better by adding targets for different measures of the money supply, but all of them seemed to suffer from 'Goodhart's Law',[3] which stated that any aggregate given the status of a target underwent a change in its relationship with nominal GDP.

Thus, by the autumn of 1985 Lawson decided that his nominal framework needed a new buttress. In October of that year, he effectively abandoned monetary targeting, giving emphasis instead to the monitoring of nominal GDP directly and, most significantly, to the exchange rate as an indicator. For Lawson this was an unsatisfactory halfway house. He had come to the conclusion that, given the difficulties of monetary targeting, the only clear, transparent and reliable nominal variable that could guide and discipline expectations in the British economy was the exchange rate. What he wanted to do was to replace a money-supply target with an exchange-rate target. The most visible exchange-rate target, and therefore the one most likely to be binding on the government, was represented by the ERM. It was also thought – how wrongly we shall see in later chapters – to guarantee support in a crisis, for both Germany and France had been exerting considerable pressure for Britain to enter the mechanism. And Howe, who favoured ERM entry because of his Eurofanaticism, was constantly whispering in Lawson's ear, urging him to take sterling into the mechanism.

Fortunately for the British economy, Mrs Thatcher, advised at a distance by Sir Alan Walters,[4] was not at all happy with Lawson's arguments. In late 1985 Lawson nonetheless campaigned strongly for ERM entry, detailing

2 Money supply can be defined in various ways, but the ways relevant to the discussion of this chapter will involve cash in circulation plus some measure of bank deposits.
3 Named after its author, Charles Goodhart, for many years a senior economist in the Bank of England. Goodhart is now a professor at the London School of Economics.
4 Walters had been Mrs Thatcher's personal economic adviser in 10 Downing Street in 1981–84. Convinced that policy was on the right track, he left in 1984 to join the World Bank. But he remained in contact with Mrs Thatcher.

his manoeuvring in his memoirs. The matter clearly became an obsession with him, and the tunnel vision he developed was to send the British economy, the Thatcher government and Tory radicalism slamming into the buffers of real-world economics. Lawson simply could not understand the political significance of the ERM: for him, it was a question of one nominal target versus another. Money targets had been performing badly, so why not use the exchange rate instead? Having narrowed the question down, in his own mind, to this technicality, it became obvious to him that it fell entirely within the competence of the Chancellor of the Exchequer to decide it.

Lawson, then, was enraged when Mrs Thatcher rejected his recommendation to join the ERM. She was rightly suspicious of the attempts of Delors and others to include a commitment to EMU in the Single European Act. The Foreign Office had told her not to worry – the reference was meaningless and harmless. Mrs Thatcher had not yet realized the extent of what must have been either treachery or incompetence from the Foreign Office, and she accepted their bland reassurances, to put sterling in the ERM just after she had agreed to the Single European Act would be seen as a clear signal of British acquiescence in a conveyor belt towards EMU. That, of course, is why Howe was so much in favour of entry in the autumn of 1985. But it was too much for Mrs Thatcher. More than that, with her larger vision she intuitively felt that what Lawson wanted would prove fatal to 'Thatcherism' even in domestic terms. Why should a British economy on the verge of rebirth, thanks to six years of struggle against the Socialism, corporatism and defeatism bequeathed by Heath, Wilson and Callaghan, shackle itself to Continental economies almost universally regarded in 1985–86 as suffering from 'Eurosclerosis'?[5]

## Oil on troubled waters

At all events, Mrs Thatcher was able to frustrate Lawson in the autumn of 1985. Outside events had begun to play an important role. For some time, the oil price had been sliding. At the end of 1985 and the beginning of 1986

5 This was a term coined by the respected German economist, Herbert Giersch, to denote the economic under-performance of the Continental European economies, relative to the rest of the industrialized world, as a result of rigid and poorly performing markets, excessive governmental interference and regulation and the excessive political and economic power of the so-called 'social partners', that is, trade unions and employer organizations.

the slide became something like a free fall. For the industrial world as a whole, this was marvellously good news. For Britain the picture was more mixed. As Britain was a (small) net exporter of oil and oil products, the fall in prices was a minor negative factor for the economy as a whole. But for the non-oil sector, it was a major boon, reducing costs and therefore making supply potentially more profitable – the same was true for other industrialized economies as a whole. But those other economies also received a boost to their real incomes as a result of the oil-price fall, so that people could spend more, taking up the increased supply of goods and services that improved profitability made possible. In Britain, for the economy as a whole there was no improvement in real incomes from the oil-price fall,[6] so less chance of increased spending. That meant that for the (increased) potential output of the British non-oil sector to be taken up, there would have to be a switch in demand from foreign to British goods. In other words, there would have to be a depreciation of the real exchange rate, a fall in the level of British costs and prices relative to foreign costs and prices, all expressed in the same currency.

There are two routes through which a real depreciation, inevitable in such circumstances, can be reached. The first is straightforward: a depreciation of the nominal exchange rate. The second involves relative disinflation: depressing the rate of increase of costs and prices below the rates of increase in competitor countries. The first route is quick and effectively painless. The second is slow and painful at the best of times – the required cumulative undershooting of costs and prices tends to take several years and to be produced only via recession and increased unemployment.[7]

6 Some of the impact of falling oil prices was felt in reduced profitability of foreign-owned companies operating in the North Sea; but it remains true that British real incomes fell relative to real incomes in other industrial countries, and particularly European countries.

7 It is sometimes claimed that relative disinflation can also be achieved fairly quickly and painlessly through 'incomes policy', some form of centralized setting of wages or 'social dialogue' that pushes wage increases down without the need for any intervening rise in unemployment. Both theory and evidence, however, suggest that this is not in fact possible. Centralized wage-setting and government-sponsored 'social dialogue' contribute to rigidities and inefficiencies in labour markets that ultimately must *increase* structural unemployment. It is no coincidence that the Community countries that have gone furthest and most persistently down the 'incomes policy' road – France, Ireland and Spain – now have the highest rates of unemployment. In any case, in circumstances where a real depreciation is inevitable, nominal depreciation is the route that causes the least disturbance to prices throughout the economy. Relative disinflation, whether produced directly by unemployment or by 'incomes policy' and subsequent unemployment, disturbs the aggregate price level in a way that economists usually consider damaging to economic efficiency and to welfare.

In the particular circumstances of 1986, with inflation in industrial countries already low and being pushed down further by the oil-price fall, it would have been particularly difficult. Germany, for instance, actually had slightly *negative* inflation – falling prices – in 1986.

Fortunately for Britain, sterling was floating rather freely, and, although there was some 'smoothing' intervention, between October 1985 – the time when Lawson said more weight would be given to the exchange rate as an indicator – and October 1986 the currency fell by 16% against the DM and by 12% in trade-weighted terms. The UK authorities did not prevent the fall. As a result, the British economy continued growing, and by October 1986 unemployment actually started to decline, while inflation – under the influence of falling oil prices – carried on falling (just as it did after the big depreciation of 1981–82 and again after sterling's ejection from the ERM in September 1992), but there was not the deflation that would have been required for some years in the absence of the exchange-rate depreciation.

What would have happened if Lawson had got his way in the autumn of 1985 and put sterling in the ERM? The markets, seeing the need for real depreciation, would have sold sterling. To try to maintain the parity, the government would have had to increase interest rates, thereby intensifying recessionary trends and sending unemployment up sharply. The 'Walters Critique' would have been immediately relevant and, ultimately, the government would have had to admit defeat, just as it had to in 1992.

Lawson claims in his memoirs that the oil-price fall would have been a classic reason for an ERM realignment – such 'rational' realignments, he says, were still possible in 1986, and the ERM only became unworkable when the politics of EMU 'hijacked' it in 1989 and made realignments politically impossible. But does he really believe that, the decision to join the ERM once having been taken, it would be easy for any government, even Mrs Thatcher's, to ask for a major realignment within weeks? Mrs Thatcher would certainly not want to repeat the humiliating experience of the Heath government in 1972, when sterling had to be withdrawn from the 'snake' after just six weeks. And who would have decided just how big a realignment was appropriate? The mandarins of the EC's Monetary Committee, whose dubious role, motivation and collective competence we shall investigate in some detail in later chapters? The finance ministers of the foreign countries that were members of the ERM? What price would these gentlemen demand in the good old Community game, where you get nothing without crossing a great many palms with political silver? In any case, in ERM practice as opposed to Lawson's ERM theory, rational alignments decided by the government concerned to cope with a genuine change of economic circumstances rather than simply to *restore* competitiveness, had *always* been frowned on. They constituted, in the eyes of the ERM High Priests, 'competitive devaluations' and were therefore not 'communautaire'. For many of the ERM's most fervent admirers in those early years, the whole point of the ERM was to *prevent* movements in real exchange rates. Once you were in the ERM club, you just had to suffer, to the profit of your 'partners', if your economy was hit by some unavoidable shock.

Lawson had simply failed to understand what the ERM was all about. It was *not* a rational economic mechanism. It was an instrument for advancing the political objectives of a generation of French and German leaders. Might they not instead simply decide that Britain, as a 'petrocurrency', was a disruptive element in their system and demand sterling's withdrawal? Even if, *par impossible* (as French lawyers write when making belt-and-braces submissions to courts), the ERM managers had somehow been willing and able to get it right about the amount of sterling devaluation needed in late 1985 or early 1986, what would have happened subsequently when optimism about the supply-side improvements in Britain led the market to start buying sterling heavily (as it was to do in the real world, as opposed to this counterfactual hypothetical world, from late 1987 onwards)? Sterling would then have needed to realign upwards in order to avoid inflationary pressures. While *downward* realignments of currencies other than the DM might still be politically possible in 1985–86, an *upward* realignment of any currency against the DM had *never* been politically possible.

Whatever he may say in his memoirs, Lawson was probably heartily glad, with hindsight, that Mrs Thatcher had said 'no' in 1985. If he had prevailed then, in all probability the Conservatives would have lost office in the next election. If the government had hung on by the skin of its teeth, Lawson would have almost certainly have been moved from the Exchequer, instead of surviving to destroy everything Mrs Thatcher – and he himself – had worked to do in improving the structure of the British economy.

## Working miracles

October 1986 saw a remarkable conjunction of four events: sterling stopped depreciating against the DM for the first time (apart from a few blips) since 1981, unemployment started falling for the first time since

1979, the ruling Conservatives overtook Labour in the opinion polls for the first time since 1984, and the City of London undertook the 'Big Bang' modernization of its financial markets and practices that would enable it to challenge for world financial leadership for the first time since 1914. The conjunction was no coincidence. Once it had come about, a self-fulfilling process of optimism began. With the oil-price fall and the associated depreciation out of the way, sterling looked a 'low-risk' currency for all sorts of reasons. Mrs Thatcher, lionized by Reagan and Gorbachev, was at the height of her powers. She now seemed likely to win a third successive election victory, one that would force Labour to accelerate its conversion into a party somewhat more reconciled to markets and much more reconciled to big-business interests (the two are not the same, of course, as Christian Democrats know well). 'Popular capitalism' was all the rage in Britain, as council house sales and privatizations were turning traditional working-class Labour voters into Thatcher Tories. The unions had been tamed, and foreign – particularly Japanese – direct investment in new factories was starting to flood in. So too was Japanese, Swiss and American investment in City stockbroking and jobbing firms, as part of the rush to create new, integrated 'securities houses' on the New York model after 'Big Bang'.[8] In industry, productivity was beginning to rise as working practices were reformed; the more enlightened unions saw the potential wage advantages of improved productivity, after a century of believing that defying productivity improvement and thereby condemning 'outsiders' to unemployment was the best way of 'defending' wages. Even where unions were still unenlightened and uncooperative, the combination of the new union laws and the increasingly 'go-for-it' *Zeitgeist* had given the freedom to manage back to managers. Britain actually started *exporting* volume cars again, even if for some time longer it was to have a negative balance in car trade.[9] Most important of all, in public finance the years of grind in the early 1980s were now bearing fruit in a sharp improvement in the underlying budgetary position. The door to the long-awaited, long-delayed

8 It is worth noting that this rush of foreign investment came when Britain was outside the ERM and before anyone had really started to get excited about the European Single Market.

9 Whether or not there is a negative or positive balance in trade in a particular sector – or indeed overall – is not necessarily an indicator of economic efficiency or well-being (and recently concerns have been expressed about the competitiveness of Britain's motor component supply firms). But the symbolic significance of British car factories actually being able to export to willing and enthusiastic foreign buyers after the catastrophic 1970s decade of Marxist-inspired disruption and decline was considerable.

radical cuts in income tax was now open. With unemployment finally falling, consumer and business confidence – and with it the confidence of the markets in sterling's prospects – blossomed like a tropical plant.

By May 1987, after the tax cuts in the budget and the Conservatives' election victory (the most 'Thatcher-specific' of their three victories under her leadership), the casual visitor could literally see, hear, taste – and almost literally smell and feel – the bullishness in the country. There was a feeling, perhaps for the first time since before Lloyd George's 'People's Budget' in 1909, that there was some point in Britain in trying to stand on one's own feet; that wealth-creation would attract approbation, not opprobrium; that there would be incentives to effort, enterprise and initiative; that the government would get out of the hair of people trying to make their way in the world. Everywhere, there were new entrepreneurs, eagerly searching for new markets and new niches. By 1988, a staggering one hundred thousand new firms a year were being registered.

From the vantage point of 1995, many observers are tempted to see the vibrant optimism of 1987–88 as a false dawn for the British economy. The rest of this chapter will try to show that the reason why things went wrong economically was not primarily that the 'feel-good factor' got out of hand but simply that Lawson's mismanagement of monetary policy ensured that everything would end in tears. The hard work of 1979–85 was wasted, the hopes of 1986 unfulfilled, the euphoria of 1987–88 shattered, all because Lawson got it irredeemably wrong.

Put at its simplest, Lawson's post-1986 theory of economic management was based on the apparently straightforward logic that Germany had a relatively stable price-level record. Tying sterling to the DM, as a sort of 'shadow member' of the ERM, would mean that Britain's own inflation experience would be brought into line with Germany's. Behind Germany's (relatively) good inflation record lay both an apparently stable relationship between German money supply and German nominal income and a supposedly independent central bank. The problems of unstable British money demand that had so perturbed Lawson in the 1980s, and of a Prime Minister who rightly viewed monetary policy as something to be considered and acted on in a wider context and by accountable politicians, could both be circumvented by ERM-shadowing.

The flaws in Lawson's thinking can usefully be grouped under three heads. The first concerns what he thought happened in Germany, how it happened and why it happened. Much of this book is devoted to giving what I hope is a more rounded view of German monetary policy; the question need not be gone into in this chapter. The second error was more narrowly economic. Lawson simply did not understand the new macroeconomic challenges created by structural improvement. The third error was perhaps the most reprehensible. Any Chancellor can – and does – make mistakes of economic judgement (and so, it might be said and will be said at every possible opportunity in this book, can central bank governors). But Lawson also made the catastrophic error of political judgement of thinking he could seek to confront and undermine his Prime Minister without doing serious damage to the credibility of the government as a whole and of economic policy in particular. By feuding with Mrs Thatcher, Lawson made it impossible for himself to admit his economic errors without a loss of face that he – or his office, as he would no doubt prefer to put it – could not accept. The rest of this chapter will seek to explain how economic folly and political hubris intertwined to make Lawson, intellectually the best-equipped of modern Chancellors, as much a disaster as his immediate successor, John Major.

## The feel-good factor[10]

In 1987 and much of 1988, the feeling that Britain was undergoing an economic renaissance was tangible. The 'feel-good factor', to whose extinction Kenneth Clarke was subsequently to devote his energy, or at least his attention, affected producers and consumers alike. In the past, the exuberance of 'animal spirits' might not of itself have produced an explosive boom, but now the globalization, deregulation and modernization of financial markets in general and of British money-lending institutions in particular produced fireworks. To use the language of economics for a moment, one can stylize what happened in Britain over this period as a perceived favourable supply shock. Entrepreneurs believed that the rate of return they might be able to earn had gone up; consumers believed that improved productivity would bring permanently higher real incomes. Rising stock-market values (in most of 1987) and house prices (throughout 1987 and 1988) made people feel wealthier; falling unemployment made them less cautious. Entrepreneurs invested in new factories, offices and

10 The material in this section may prove difficult for non-economists (although not as difficult as it seems to have proved for some supposed economists), but it is essential to an understanding not only of Lawson's mistakes but also of the total incompatibility of the ERM with the goals announced for it in 1978 and with the subsequent establishment of the Single Market and capital liberalization. I have tried to make it as non-technical as possible.

vehicles (business investment rose by a massive 20% in 1988). Households were able to borrow from eager-to-lend banks on the strength of their optimistic real income expectations; they could spend part of their stock-market gains; or they could 'withdraw equity', borrowing against the apparent security of their suddenly more valuable houses.

Were those optimistic expectations justified? Even with hindsight it is impossible to say. But if monetary policy had reacted more rationally, the initial boom in output (*not* demand – a point to be explained below) would have been moderated. The sharp rise in inflation, the loss of confidence and credibility would have been avoided. In all probability, ERM entry would not have happened. There would certainly not have been the devastating recession that in fact took place. Output, productivity and employment would indeed have been substantially higher than the levels we now observe. Investment would not be held back, in the way it now is despite a reasonably strongly-growing economy, by the fears of firms of getting burnt again in another subsequent economic 'bust'. In short, the whole economic landscape of Britain would now look better and the optimism of 1987–88 would look much more soundly based.

There can be little doubt that consumer spending did, nonetheless, become frenzied at that time, but the primary reason for that appears to have been the 'bubble' in the housing market to which inappropriate monetary policy (and, in the final phase of the boom, an inappropriately timed announcement on the ending of double tax-relief on mortgages for couples) contributed most. In essence, the investment and consumption boom initially sparked by optimism about supply-side improvement was perfectly sound and healthy. It was natural for firms and households, in those circumstances, to borrow to finance investment purchases – obvious enough in the case of firms, but no less rational in *consumer* investment in durable goods, from houses through furniture and cars to home entertainment equipment. But the macroeconomic impact of all this was, in the short run, to increase *demand* for goods and services in the economy without commensurately increasing their *supply*. New investment takes time to come onstream: in the interim, it uses up resources (those required to build and install it) without adding to potential output. Thus these healthy, optimistic private-sector reactions, so necessary if an economic transformation really was to take place, created excess pressure on resources in the economy.

How should policy have reacted? It is quite clear that there should have been a substantial monetary tightening, beginning as soon as the strength of 'animal spirits' – so evident to the casual visitor and observer from early 1987 onwards – became apparent to the authorities. Britain was experiencing what is known to economists as an 'asymmetric real shock', that is, an event or series of events, previously unanticipated, perceived as affecting real variables (output and productivity) in the economy concerned to a greater extent than other countries. There would have been no need for Britain's main competitor countries to tighten *their* monetary policies. So the desirable and appropriate monetary tightening in Britain would have produced a sharp appreciation of sterling. Indeed, even without a tightening of monetary policy, sterling was appreciating in the foreign exchange markets from October 1986 onwards, for the reasons set out earlier in this chapter: the world wanted its share of the action in the new Thatcherite Britain and was buying sterling-denominated assets to get that share.

Appreciation of sterling switches demand away from British goods towards foreign ones, as a rising currency reduces foreign costs and prices relative to those in Britain. It thus prevents excess demand in Britain – in circumstances of the sort we are discussing here – from leading to excessive strains on resources that give a tight labour market and rising inflation. Later, as investment projects are completed, demand falls back (as firms and households reach their desired levels of holdings of factories, office equipment, houses, cars, furniture, videos, and so on), while at the same time the economy's potential output increases as the new factories start producing. When that happens, the right thing for the authorities to do is to loosen monetary policy, cutting interest rates and allowing the currency to slide back down. In this way, the adjustment to the new, improved supply-side conditions can take place without a 'boom-bust' cycle in output, employment and inflation – even though the 'feel-good factor' is given free rein.

## Britannia smooths the waves

One inevitable consequence of, and indeed requirement for, this desirable set of macroeconomic developments is that the current account of the balance of payments swings very substantially towards deficit in the phase of strongly rising demand. In the initial phase of strong demand provoked by 'animal spirits', it was natural and appropriate for Britain's imports of goods and services to rise relative to its exports – in other words, for the current account of the balance of payments to show a deficit. This was the mechanism that, had it been strengthened by an earlier appreciation of sterling, would have prevented the strength of demand in Britain from placing an excessive strain on the productive resources available in the short run. But, even if policy had been got right, the emergence of a substantial, persistent, current-account deficit would have been a sign that, at some point in the future, sterling would have to depreciate again.

Understanding why this is so is central to understanding the inconsistency of the ERM with the successful modernization of the economy – not just in Britain but in a series of other European countries. As we saw above, in a world of integrated and liberalized financial markets, improved economic prospects in one country (let us say it is Britain) lead its residents to spend more, in advance and anticipation of higher profits and wages in the future. The world capital market is willing and eager to provide the necessary lending. So the increased spending on imports by British residents (a current-account deficit) is matched by willing lending to the private sector by the rest of the world. The lending from abroad constitutes a capital inflow into the borrowing country, or in other words creates a surplus on the capital account to balance the deficit on the current account of the balance of payments.

However, if all goes well, the anticipated improvements in productivity and potential output in Britain eventually take place, as new investment comes onstream, new firms get into their stride and new working practices bear fruit. But, by the same time, the anticipatory spending (on investment goods by firms, on houses and other consumer durables by households) will have been completed. Thus domestic *demand* is likely to be falling back just at the time potential domestic *output* is rising. In the first phase of the cycle imports must rise relative to exports (the current account must move in the direction of deficit) to fill the 'inflationary gap' between strong demand and static supply. But in the subsequent phase, exports must rise relative to imports (the current account must move in the direction of surplus): this is to ensure that there is sufficient total demand to take up all the potential increase in available output and prevent a 'deflationary gap' developing.

Monetary policy can perform the function of smoothing the path of demand relative to supply. In a closed economy, this has to mean restraining domestic demand (which is, of course, equal to total demand in a closed economy) in the initial phase and stimulating it in the subsequent phase. This happens through initial increases in interest rates, which make firms and households hold back some purchases of producer and consumer durables until output actually rises, at which point falling interest rates stimulate additional spending. Of course, because investment by firms is initially somewhat restrained, it takes longer for the process of increasing potential to be completed.

In an open economy in a world of liberalized capital movements, a tightening of monetary policy in the initial phase has rather different effects. As interest rates rise, the currency appreciates. The currency appreciation does two rather wonderful things. First, it shifts demand from domestic to foreign sources of supply, reducing the pressure on domestic resources. But it also allows investment and purchases of consumer durables to adjust much faster to the new, optimistic supply-side expectations than would be possible in a closed economy. Domestic interest rates still go up (a factor restraining purchases of producer and consumer durables), but the appreciation of the currency reduces the price, in domestic terms, of foreign durable goods (a factor stimulating purchases).

How do things look from the foreign point of view? International investors rush, when British interest rates initially go up, to lend to Britain, since they get higher interest rates in Britain than elsewhere. This rush is what produces the appreciation of sterling (if the British authorities are not intervening by selling sterling). But we and international investors know (we are still assuming sensible behaviour by the authorities) that the appreciation of sterling will not be permanent: once domestic demand in Britain subsides and new output comes onstream, there will need to be a depreciation. It is precisely this expectation of future depreciation that allows interest rates in Britain to be higher, at a time when they need to be higher, than interest rates in the rest of the world (if people expect sterling to fall in value against other currencies, they will not hold it unless they are compensated by higher interest rates on sterling than on other currencies). Later, as the coming-onstream of new supply proceeds, both sterling and British interest rates will drift back down.[11]

The obvious conclusion is that the whole point of capital liberalization, by allowing capital to flow where the return is highest, thus aiding economic development and integration, requires flexibility in nominal exchange rates. This is fully recognized in the North American Free Trade Area

---

11 Professional economists reading this account might be tempted to dismiss it as a fable unrelated to what actually happens in the real world: in the jargon, interest-rate differentials are poor predictors of future spot exchange rates and uncovered interest parity does not hold. I agree with them! The point is to describe what *would* happen *if* the authorities behaved appropriately. The failure of uncovered parity is not (or at least is not primarily) a failure of financial markets, but a failure of transparency, consistency and rationality on the part of the economic policy authorities.

(NAFTA), for instance, where no one has ever thought that free trade and free capital movements require fixed exchange rates as a complement.

In Europe, unfortunately, contrary ideas have come to the fore: the notion that the Single Market requires a single currency has been assiduously peddled by the Commission (Leon Brittan in the van)[12] and by the industrial associations who fear economic dynamism. Such associations are made up mainly of large, senescent firms who devote much of their remaining energy to lobbying governments for privileges, subsidies and protection. Their leading executives, already rich, feel a desire for power and influence, as well as a need to protect the positions of their companies. Corporatist governments need interlocutors, and the captains of industry want to be among those interlocutors. The Commission is the most corporatist 'government', or would-be government, of the lot; it wants a single currency for its own ends, and it suits industrialists to pander to it. After all, it is the oldest, largest, heaviest and most decaying trees that are most at risk of being uprooted by 'the gale of creative destruction', as the great Austrian-American economist Joseph Schumpeter described the process of change in capitalist economies. The new firms and the enterprising characters who might found more new firms, seeds blown by the same capitalist gale, have no voice in the Councils of the CBI or UNICE, no access to the Commission to plead for the flexibility and adaptability of exchange rates that alone can combine macroeconomic stability with microeconomic dynamism and structural change.

A single currency in Europe would be consistent with integration, economic convergence, with the drawing of full advantage from capital

12 It is sad to see Leon Brittan, once a Cabinet Minister of undoubted intellect, taking his cue from Roy Jenkins and behaving like the 'Fat Boy' in *Pickwick* by telling tales to make the flesh creep. He bemoans the fate of innocent travellers who, setting off from Britain with £100 in their pockets, make a tour of the Community countries. They arrive in France, change their sterling into French francs, thereby losing 2 or 3% at the tourist exchange rates. Then they move on to Belgium, changing French francs into Belgian francs and losing another 2 or 3%. They repeat this strange manoeuvre in each of the other eight countries that have separate currencies. Finally, they arrive back in Britain, change their remaining money back into sterling and, without having spent a penny anywhere (a remarkable feature of their horror story journey in more ways than one), they discover that they have less than half of the £100 with which they set off. Anyone stupid enough to behave in this way (instead of taking a credit card or a cash card) might also be stupid enough to listen to what Leon Brittan or Roy Jenkins had to say about EMU and the Single Currency; surely no one else would. And even the tortures inflicted by money-changers on such mythical hapless souls would amount, in the aggregate, to utter insignificance compared with the undoubted costs – in unstable inflation, cyclical variations in unemployment, permanently reduced productivity, employment and real incomes – that a single currency would bring.

liberalization and with a successful Single Market *only* if asymmetric real shocks were of minimal importance. For this to happen, the process of levelling-up of productivity and income standards would have had to be completed – for the changes that trigger such levelling-up are themselves asymmetric real shocks. Even that would not be enough: the whole 'economic culture' would have had to become totally uniform across countries, to rule out the possibility of future divergence. The relative sizes of the public and private sectors, the degree of government regulation and subsidy, the role of corporatist institutions versus free markets, the scope and direction of social security systems, the cast of education – all these would first have had to be 'harmonized'. What is more, there would have to be complete certainty that no country in the monetary union could ever move away from this state of conformity in the future. That list of conditions amounts, in effect, to the prior existence of a single government – complete political union. But of course, if all these prior conditions were satisfied, exchange rates would be stable in any case. There would be no need for a single currency – its only benefit would be the elimination of exchange transactions costs. But these are already piffling (even the Commission itself in 1990 estimated them at less than 0.5% of Community GDP – hardly more than the amount of CAP fraud that is publicly admitted to and a very great deal less than the economic costs of existing Community common policies). And in future, these costs will fall to negligible amounts as financial technology and the 'cashless economy' make further strides. In short, there is *no* meaningful economic argument for a single currency in Europe – now or ever.[13]

A currency has meaning because it expresses national monetary sovereignty.[14] The circumstances that might make a country want to give up its national monetary sovereignty irrevocably can never have anything rationally to do with economics – though the connection is often falsely made. A reason can be found only in politics or, more accurately, in the desire of certain groups of people to create, extend or buttress power for themselves at the expense of the electorates they are supposed to serve. We shall see many, many examples of this throughout this book.

13  This does not rule out, of course, the option of unilateral monetary union with a larger country for very small economies whose external transactions are a very large share of total transactions and are predominantly denominated in the currency of the larger economy: Luxembourg's monetary union with Belgium is one example – but even that is potentially subject to strain.

14  This would not be true of *private* currencies issued by private banks. Those who find national monetary sovereignty offensive yet still claim to favour a market economy should, logically, advocate private money, not European government money.

## Bucking the market

To return to our narrative, Lawson was, unhappily, not willing to operate monetary policy in the appropriate way: it would have meant accepting significant, and more or less continuous, movements in sterling. He wanted to avoid that, because his new theory of economic management required sterling to remain stable against the DM. Howe, as Foreign Secretary, supported Lawson because he seemed more interested in forcing Britain into European union than in advancing the country's economic interests. Between them, they ensured that what should have been the fruits of Thatcherism – a high-wage, high-productivity, high-employment economy – became a cancer of frenetic consumption and inflation, inevitably followed by an economic and political crash.

The result was stark and unpleasant. While the strength of demand in the British economy should have elicited *higher* interest rates from early 1987 onwards, Lawson was so fixated with his DM-shadowing policy that he not only refused to raise rates but actually cut them, first in October 1987 and then again in February and May 1988. In an atmosphere in which consumer confidence was already buoyant, inappropriately and unsustainably low rates of interest drew more and more families into a frenzy of buying, accentuating the demand boom. Lawson compounded his errors when in the 1988 budget he announced the ending – to take effect four months later – of double mortgage relief available to joint purchasers of houses. This announcement not unnaturally created a huge rush to buy houses before the change took effect. In turn, this gave a further twist to the upward spiral of house prices, which by late 1988 were rising at an annual rate of almost 30%. The housing market boom gave the impression of making people rich overnight – and families proved eager to borrow against the 'security' of their overpriced houses.

Even before Lawson's mistake on the timing of mortgage relief changes, it was becoming clear that the situation was getting out of hand. By the early spring of 1988, Mrs Thatcher was growing increasingly worried about Lawson's attempts to hold sterling down. A row erupted in March, when the Prime Minister rightly criticized Lawson's intervention tactics, saying at Prime Minister's Question Time in the Commons that 'you can't buck the market.' With the weight of foreign buying growing ever greater, and his Prime Minister by now very much alive to the problem, a reluctant Lawson was forced to call a halt to intervention. Sterling surged through the top of the range of DM2.90 to DM3.00 that he had imposed. In mid-

May, in an effort to stem the rise in the pound without again resorting to intervention, the Chancellor cut interest rates one last time (the Labour Party, one should not forget, was pressing for even bigger cuts). But even Lawson could no longer ignore the mounting evidence of inflationary pressure (in the form of rapid increases in demand and output, in house prices and – as unemployment fell very rapidly – in wages and labour costs).[15] Having reduced interest rates to 7.5% in mid-May to restrain sterling, at the end of May he *raised* them to restrain inflation, apparently unwilling to recognize that the inflationary pressure was the result of his DM-shadowing policy. Sir Alan Walters, in a radio interview, presciently remarked that the Chancellor, by having delayed far too long in tightening policy, had condemned Britain to much bigger increases in interest rates in the future. We shall soon see how right he was, and what damaging economic and political consequences were to follow.

The upshot of Lawson's strategy in 1987 and early 1988 was that an unsustainable inflationary boom took hold in Britain. The worst of it was tempered by Mrs Thatcher's insistence on uncapping the pound in the spring of 1988, but by then the damage had been done. Inflation was out of control: the increase in the retail price index shot up from a low of 2.7% at the beginning of 1987 to almost 11% in late 1990.[16] As Walters had predicted, the inflationary outburst necessitated a much more brutal tightening of monetary policy than if appropriate steps had been taken in time. Bank base lending rates were raised from 7.5% in May 1988 to 15% in October 1989 (the last percentage point of this increase coming shortly before Lawson's departure). By early 1989 the tightening of monetary policy was accompanied by weakness in sterling as market confidence in the credibility of British economic policy was eroded.

To the genuine problem of inflation was added market concern about the

15 It should be emphasized that the problems of overheating were *not* caused by the big cuts in marginal tax rates in the 1988 budget. Tax cuts were more than balanced by reductions in the share of public expenditure in national income. The budget deficit turned into a substantial surplus, and budgetary policy was contractionary, in mechanical terms, in 1987–88 even if one takes full account of the automatic impact of strong growth in improving the budgetary position. It is true that the tax cuts had a powerful impact on consumer and entrepreneurial confidence: but this was exactly what they were intended to do. They represented Lawson's greatest triumph. But his failure to counteract the resulting strong pressure on resources with higher interest rates sufficiently early was his greatest disaster.

16 This comparison is admittedly distorted by the inclusion of mortgage interest costs in the RPI. When interest rates doubled from 7.5% in May 1988 to 15% by October 1989, this component of the index exploded. But the increase in the 'underlying' index was nonetheless dramatic: from around 3% in mid-1986 and most of 1987 to 7.5% in late 1990.

balance of payments. Lawson quite rightly insisted that the current account was not an independent source of concern and should certainly not be a target of policy. He was also right to argue that a current-account imbalance would be self-righting. But he failed to realize, indeed denied, that the current-account deficit made it clear that there would have to be future real depreciation of sterling and that this would best be brought about through a future decline in the value of sterling in the foreign-exchange market.

By the autumn of 1989, the demand boom had already peaked. But for the inflation problem, it would have been time for monetary policy to start *easing*, for interest rates and sterling to start drifting down. But the inflation problem created by Lawson's earlier insistence on preventing sterling from rising now ruled out reductions in interest rates. With the economy so badly out of control, both international investors and domestic firms and households lost confidence. Policy lost credibility. Sterling was weakening from the spring of 1989 onwards; interest rates were raised further in an attempt to restore 'credibility', put a floor under sterling and make a start on dealing with the inflation problem. A sharp recession, long inevitable, came closer: not only was there no chance of easing monetary policy as domestic demand subsided, it was actually being tightened. Once inflation had got a hold, it could be squeezed out *only* by recession. How that recession would unfold, how it would be aggravated by the ERM and what damaging effects it would have on the public finances, on the confidence of entrepreneurs and on the belief of the public in general in the efficacy of radical, supply-side measures will be told in a later chapter.

## Toothless tigers, tearful clowns

It is undeniably Lawson who must bear most of the blame for the exchange-rate folly of 1987–88 and thus some of the miseries of 1990–92. Can anything be said in his defence? The former Chancellor himself has recently claimed that, in a modern, dynamic, deregulated capitalist economy, macroeconomic fluctuations simply cannot be avoided. He has thus distanced himself from the present incumbent at the Treasury, Kenneth Clarke, who has made known his view that preventing a recrudescence of the 'feel-good factor' can ensure that the economy stays on an even keel. Both men are wrong, but they are wrong in characteristically different ways. It is instructive and important to see *how* they are wrong. Lawson's argument is rooted in a strong belief in economic freedom, capitalism and radicalism – it is marred only by faulty macroeconomics. Clarke's reflects an illiberal, 'nanny-knows-best' and essentially anti-capitalist view of the world.

Lawson, a brilliant thinker with a firm historical grasp, comes close to saying that the modern world has in the past decade or so returned to conditions similar to those of the late nineteenth century. There was reasonably free trade, there were free capital movements, there was no fiscal policy as such, there was great innovative activity in business and technology and there was an international monetary framework, the Gold Standard, that ensured price stability in a long-run time-frame. But successive waves of bullish and bearish animal spirits, often triggered by the exploitation of new technological advances, led to sharp trade cycles in output, prices and employment and to rapid changes in market structure, trade patterns, the comparative advantage of nations, and the relative prosperity of industrial sectors and individual firms.

Lawson's view inclines towards saying that the booms and slumps just have to be lived with as the price of a capitalist system that nonetheless delivers great benefits. A greater risk to the capitalist system, in his view, would be persistent inflation created by attempts to avoid unemployment. Some apolitical, rules-based monetary system would be the best means of avoiding persistent, long-term inflation. The ERM, he claims, was – from a *British* point of view – such a system until it was 'hijacked' by Delors and other federalist politicians from 1989 onwards.[17]

Clarke's view is very different, and appears to be much less consonant with the capitalist, free-market philosophy that the Conservative Party has continued to claim as its own even though it deposed the only leader this century actually prepared to implement it. Clarke is unhappy, it would seem, with the restlessness of the untamed capitalist tiger, its inbuilt tendency towards 'permanent revolution', its waywardness, its disregard of existing patterns and structures, its 'gale of creative destruction'. Capitalism devours the politicians and bureaucrats who would ride it. It is dangerous, and has to be tamed. Macroeconomic fluctuations *can* be avoided, as long as the state keeps the unruly private sector in check. There must be no surge of positive 'animal spirits', no 'feel-good factor' leading to

---

17 As Alan Walters has emphasized to me, Lawson not only confused the anonymous, apolitical and market-driven Gold Standard with the highly political, German-dominated ERM, but also neglected the automatic specie-flow mechanism of the genuinely fixed-rate Gold Standard which, whatever the system's faults, did at least spare it from the perverse real-interest-rate movements of the pegged-but-adjustable rate ERM identified in the 'Walters Critique'.

unsustainable spurts of spending. If the private sector behaves itself, and if the budget deficit stays within fixed limits – as set by the Maastricht Treaty, for example – then all like-minded countries can move harmoniously together, their economies – and their currencies – in lock-step.

The Clarke strategy is indeed a profoundly conservative one, totally at odds with the combination of economic liberalism and support for the nation that defines Tory radicalism. It is also a profoundly mistaken strategy. Western capitalism contained is Western capitalism destroyed. Toothless and drugged, the caged tiger is prey to lethargy, disease, premature senility. Worse, only the bars of his cage protect him from the new, fierce and powerful capitalist animals of Asia. If he stays inside with the door locked he will rot. If he opens the door, the new cats will leap in and maul him to death. To turn from metaphor to unadorned language, only the private sector can provide the initiative, the enterprise, the energy and the dynamism to maintain the West's economic well-being. And the private sector, if it is to behave as capitalism requires, *must* be allowed to 'feel good', even if from time to time the optimism is overdone. For without optimism, *nothing* will be done. Lawson himself expressed it persuasively in his memoirs:

It may well be that optimism had become so unfamiliar to the British that they inevitably became intoxicated by it and threw prudence and caution to the winds. But I remain unrepentant in the belief that a climate of optimism was what Britain needed in the 1980s and what it continues to need today. The debilitating pall of defeatism which characterized the Britain we inherited in 1979 had to be swept aside. Not only was it infinitely depressing, but it had become self-fulfilling and made economic success impossible. For too long the British had been learning to live with decline and defeat.

Lawson's buccaneering approach would be preferable to Clarke's embrace of decline and defeat if there were no other choice. The British electorate is now not offered even that unsatisfactory choice – after narrowly surviving Butskell in the early 1950s, we have to cope in the mid-1990s with the tears of a Clown, as the Chancellor and his lugubrious Shadow, Gordon Brown, compete to rend the hearts of the British taxpayer. Clarke and Brown are both 'Europeans'. They need to peddle the inevitability of 'defeat and decline' to prepare Britons for the loss of national independence the European Union wants to inflict.

Yet even a Lawson/Clarke choice would still be unsatisfactory. The problem remains: how can one prevent the capitalist boom-bust cycles that plagued the Gold Standard era and have plagued Britain – and, as we shall see later – Spain, Portugal, Denmark, Sweden, Finland, Norway and

Germany (and as a result France and the Benelux) among European countries? What this list of latter-day unfortunates has in common with the Gold Standard era is, of course, fixed exchange rates.[18] The essential similarity between the Gold Standard and the European attempts at exchange-rate fixing in the 1980s and early 1990s is that the inherent dynamism of capitalism was transformed into destructiveness by monetary policies that were simply not good enough.

Here, perhaps, lies part of the attraction of fixed exchange rates to bureaucrats, industrial federations and cartels, unions, Socialists, Continental (and Clarkeite) Conservatives, Christian Democrats, corporatists and anti-liberals of all persuasions (and here too lies the mystifying nature of Lawson's attraction to the ERM – for he was a man who excoriated the Delorsian view of 'Europe' with greater articulacy and penetration than anyone). Fix the exchange rate, neuter monetary policy, and then use the fear of macroeconomic instability as an excuse to stifle the dynamism of the capitalist process. As an enfeebled Europe then stumbles into economic decline, make use of 'Europe's' supposedly greater might, as a Union, in the world monetary and trading systems to cajole or bully other regions of the world into the same terminal torpor. This is not, of course, how the drive to European monetary union has been presented by its priests. The rest of this book will detail how the truth was hidden – and is still being hidden – by the sect leaders.

## Get Thatcher!

While the recession rendered inevitable by Lawson's mistakes still lay ahead, those mistakes had immediate political implications. The rise in inflation and interest rates, the loss of foreign confidence, the dawning inevitability of recession and of a housing-market crash and, not least, the spectacle of bitter conflict between the Prime Minister and her two most senior ministers, Howe and Lawson, was already fatally weakening Mrs Thatcher's political authority. As early as the autumn of 1988, Eurofanatical Tories and those who saw her as an obstacle to their own advancement were plotting their leader's downfall. There was talk of a 'stalking-horse' candidate in a leadership election even then. But, less than eighteen months after a third successive election victory, and with the opinion polls still favourable to the Tories and Mrs Thatcher, the rebels had to bide their time.

18 They also exhibited important differences from the Gold Standard, as indicated in footnote 17.

By the beginning of 1989, the debate had reached Brussels. At a dinner in the home of Peter Ludlow, a self-styled 'federalist and functionalist' and Director of the Brussels-based Centre for Economic Policy Studies, the new economics Commissioner, Henning Christophersen, was brought into the discussion. Michael Emerson, the Director in the Commission responsible for turning dubious analysis to EMU-propaganda advantage and formerly economic adviser to Roy Jenkins when Britain's leading Eurofanatic had been Commission President, was there. So too were Conservative MEPs and a number of academic advisers to the Commission. The talk was of the chances of Mrs Thatcher being overthrown on the ERM question.

The circumstances looked propitious. 'Informed opinion' in Britain, orchestrated by Sam Brittan in the *Financial Times*, the *Economist* magazine, the CBI and the BBC, was witlessly – if hardly guilelessly – blaming Britain's worsening economic woes on Mrs Thatcher's 'stubborn' refusal to turn a difficult situation into outright calamity by joining the mechanism. In a few months' time (as we shall see in the next chapter), the Delors Committee would produce its report on European Monetary Union, promising diplomatic isolation for Mrs Thatcher in Europe and division within her Cabinet. Howe – subsequently identified in Charles Grant's recent biography of Delors as having been an important behind-the-scenes ally, along with Kohl, Mitterrand, Andreotti and Gonzalez, of the Commission President – was likely to make trouble for Mrs Thatcher, as would the vast majority of the Tory MEPs. At Westminster, the split between Thatcher and Lawson was making even loyalists uneasy.

Time was thus on the side of those who saw Mrs Thatcher as the greatest obstacle to their ambition of a European superstate. Late in 1988, Roy Jenkins, in a Brussels speech on EMU listened to very carefully by a number of senior Commission officials, argued that only Mrs Thatcher's personal conviction and prestige stood between Britain and EMU: no other political leader would have the courage and authority to keep Britain out. And, he might have added, without a British refusal to acquiesce there seemed nothing else in 1989 to prevent the EMU juggernaut from rolling over Europe. It is often argued (Nigel Lawson is among those who do so) that Mrs Thatcher's confrontational style united other European leaders in a sort of Euro-crusade in reaction to her. But Mrs Thatcher's European opponents, at home and abroad, did not base their strategy on pique. If they were angry with her, it was because they knew she could confound their plans. Getting rid of her became a major priority.

## The road to Madrid

In mid-May, Mrs Thatcher, for the first and only time as Prime Minister, made a direct public criticism of Lawson. In a radio interview with the BBC World Service, the suggestion was made, illogically but inevitably, by her interlocutor that ERM entry would have avoided the problems being faced by the British economy. Exasperated, she made the economically unobjectionable point that the inflation problem had in fact been caused by Lawson's ERM shadowing. A Prime Minister cannot, however, criticize a leading colleague without hurting herself unless she is able and willing to dispense with that colleague's services. With so much of the British political, media and business Establishment now happy to support Lawson, a radical whose views on most issues they detested, against Mrs Thatcher, she could not take the risk of provoking his resignation. Instead, she had to apologize to Lawson in private, thereby making it very clear to him that he was in a position to engage in political blackmail against her.

An occasion to do so soon presented itself. The Delors Report, advocating a three-stage progress to a single European currency, had just been published (its significance in the overall European monetary context will be analysed in the next chapter). The report would be discussed by the European Council under Spanish chairmanship in Madrid at the end of June. In early June, the Spanish government, wishing to display its Euro-credentials ahead of the meeting, put the peseta in the ERM. It was a decision that, as we shall see in subsequent chapters, was to cost the Spanish people very dear. For Lawson, however, it provided an opportunity to reopen his campaign for British entry.

Howe also re-entered the fray. He certainly used the conjunction of the vital forthcoming meeting and the self-immolating Spanish decision to enter the ERM to good Eurofanatic effect. Delors himself, always terrified by the prospect of being told a few – or a good many – home truths by Mrs Thatcher, was very apprehensive about the Madrid meeting, confiding to his staff that he expected to be badly 'handbagged', with damaging effects for his scheme. Howe may have been told of these fears; he may have been disposed to help his ally, Delors, overcome the threat posed to Euroenthu-siast aspirations by his own country's leader.

What is certain is that he proposed to Lawson that the two of them should submit a joint memorandum to the Prime Minister on the politics and economics of the ERM. According to Lawson in his memoirs, Howe told him that he had had intimations from Spain that Gonzalez was prepared to go along with a strategy of accepting Stage One of EMU as set out in the Delors Report (in which all Community countries would be enjoined to enter the ERM). The aim was supposedly to help forestall an Inter-Governmental Conference (IGC) and a new treaty: Britain should do the same and follow the Spanish lead on the ERM.

According to Lawson, Gonzalez himself, perhaps aware of Howe's thinking, said as much to Mrs Thatcher on 19 June. Perhaps he simply wanted to avoid a confrontation between Mrs Thatcher and the other leaders that would tarnish 'his' European Council in Madrid. At any rate, anyone with the slightest insight into Spanish Euroenthusiasm would have been astonished. Spanish strategy on Europe was mainly concerned with ensuring that the country should not be 'left behind' in European union and with squeezing as much money as possible out of other countries' taxpayers. Either Howe and the Foreign Office were falling down on the job they were supposed to be doing – that of analysing the positions of other countries so as to prepare tactics for advancing British interests – or, more likely, they were doing the job they seem to prefer of advancing the interests of their chums in the European diplomatic 'community'.

Lawson also reports that the Foreign Office produced, apparently for the first time, the canard that a British refusal to 'cooperate' in monetary union would be met with a decision by their 'partners' to steam ahead with a two-speed Europe. This argument was put forward by a Foreign Secretary who three years earlier had persuaded Mrs Thatcher that the references to EMU in the Single European Act were empty, meaningless and innocuous. And it was put forward by a man whose sympathy with Eurofederalism, constantly expressed in the tired metaphors of 'missing the bus', 'trains leaving the platform', and 'being in the slow lane', was made increasingly explicit after he left the government.

Howe, it seems, was now doing to Lawson what he had done to Mrs Thatcher in 1985–86, telling him that joining the ERM was a way to avoid EMU. Just as Mrs Thatcher had swallowed Howe's line on the Single European Act because she genuinely wanted the market-opening impact she saw in it, so Lawson, it seems from his own account, was prepared to believe the incredible things Howe was telling him because he desperately wanted ERM entry. What is particularly ironic is that Lawson, who was subsequently to claim that the ERM went wrong *only* because it was 'hijacked' by the EMU enthusiasts, was now prepared to make an EMU-political argument for bringing forward British entry to the mechanism.

Unfortunately, he was 180° wrong in his assessment of the political connection between the ERM and EMU.

At all events, the joint paper was submitted to the Prime Minister the day *after* Lawson had, in evidence to a House of Commons Committee, set out conditions for ERM entry. It was clear that a determined attempt was being made to bounce Mrs Thatcher. A few days later, after she had sought to add further, perfectly sensible conditions to the convergence of UK inflation and complete abolition of exchange controls by others that Lawson had mentioned to the Parliamentary Committee, Howe told Lawson that he would resign if Mrs Thatcher did not behave more 'constructively'. Lawson pledged that if Howe went, he would go too. On the morning of the Sunday when Mrs Thatcher and Howe were to fly to Madrid for the European Council meeting, the Foreign Secretary and the Chancellor issued a threat to Mrs Thatcher: agree to our demand for 'movement' on the ERM, or lose us both.

The Prime Minister made a semi-capitulation. At the Madrid Council, while making clear her opposition to the conveyor-belt of the Delors Report, she made no attempt to kill it: a relieved Delors did not get the handbagging he had so feared. And she went along with the others in accepting the so-called Stage One of the Delors process, in which all Community countries were enjoined to enter the ERM. She laid down certain conditions for sterling's entry, but they were not as stringent as those she had proposed in her reply to Howe and Lawson. They had got the 'movement' they both wanted. Howe was demoted a few weeks later – and four years too late; but he had won – by failing to block the Delors Report, Mrs Thatcher was now entangled in the European union process. The Establishment propaganda machine could turn up the volume on 'isolation', 'slow lanes' and 'missing the bus' – even the distinctly un-English 'historic inevitability'. Lawson might feel pleased that the prospect of ERM entry had been brought nearer. But he had been ill-advised to go along with Howe. By letting himself be involved in pressurizing Mrs Thatcher he had advanced, not damaged, the cause of the European monetary and political union that he regarded as the most dangerous folly in Europe since Munich.

Perhaps it would have been better for Mrs Thatcher to have taken up the challenge. But Howe and Lawson were not 'wets'. As Lawson constantly reminds the world in his memoirs, he and his partner in political blackmail were more royalist than the queen in the realm of 'Thatcherism'. If their resignations had been accepted, they would have lost no time in arguing, in

Parliament, in the Conservative Party and in the media – as they were subsequently to do – that Mrs Thatcher was someone who was prepared to ditch her closest political allies for the sake of a ludicrous personal obsession, a wanton refusal to accept a perfectly sensible improvement in the economic policy framework and at the same time to improve Britain's negotiating position in 'Europe'. She would have been depicted – as she subsequently was – as arrogant, out of touch, a Prime Minister who stayed on beyond her sell-by date. She would have been increasingly isolated in the Cabinet, derided in the Party, reviled in the Press and on the BBC – as she subsequently was.

The reality was different. Between them, Howe and Lawson were destroying Tory radicalism. Howe's fault seems to be the greater, for he – who had recently seen Mrs Thatcher reject an opportunity to retire on her tenth anniversary in power, thereby denying him the succession he presumably sought – was striving to force his Prime Minister onto the conveyor belt of 'Europe', while Lawson believed he was helping to keep her off it. The Chancellor, as well as the Prime Minister, was taken for a ride by the Foreign Office, the sort of ride you don't come back from. But Lawson's dismissal of Mrs Thatcher's additional conditions for ERM membership confirms that he, not his boss, was the one who was obsessed, arrogant, out of touch with reality. Unwittingly, he put himself in the camp of those 'neo-functionalists' against whom he rightly inveighs for the folly of the Delors EMU project.

Mrs Thatcher's desired additional condition for ERM entry was that the Single Market programme should first have been completed (completion was scheduled for the end of 1992) and that sufficient time should subsequently have elapsed for the effects of the programme to be considered. Lawson, seeing this simply as a delaying tactic, thereby displayed a lack of economic perception in a vital area. Worse, he was in effect giving credence to the 'One Market, One Money' brigade in the Commission and elsewhere who had never cared about the Single Market as anything but a back door to monetary and political union.[19]

The point is that the Single Market programme constituted a major real shock, potentially positive to the Community countries. In a British view, at

19 'One Market, One Money' is the title of a Commission propaganda tome, supposedly a research study, on the alleged necessity of a monetary union for the full benefits of the Single Market to be realized. As we shall see in the next chapter, the publication of this shameless piece of anti-scientific empiricism was brought forward to coincide with the Rome Ambush of October 1990, the proximate cause of Mrs Thatcher's fall.

least, the programme aimed at eliminating non-tariff barriers, such as government procurement practices favouring domestic suppliers, non-mutual-recognition of standards and a host of others, that prevented labour, goods, services and capital flowing as freely between the Community countries as they would do within any one of them. There were academic arguments – still unresolved today – about whether the various measures in the programme would increase the rate of return in any particular country (by, for instance, permitting economies of scale and reductions in costs) or reduce it (by reducing barriers to competition). Socialists and trade unions feared the former, seeing the Single Market as a 'businessmen's charter' that needed to be offset by the introduction of a 'Social Charter'.[20] Others, notably protected firms in the more regulated member states, feared the latter. Mrs Thatcher, by nature optimistic, had enthusiastically supported the measures in the programme (she had been misled by the Foreign Office about its political significance, and quite simply lied to by the other members of the European Council and by Delors about the use of majority voting).[21]

At the time, the safest thing one could predict was that different countries, depending on their initial economic structures, would experience different movements in the rate of return. As a result, real rates of interest would need to diverge temporarily while differential rate-of-return disturbances worked themselves out. In a world of increasingly free capital movements, temporary divergences among countries in the real rate of interest would be possible only if there were expected movements in real exchange rates. But if nominal exchange-rate movements were constrained by the ERM, especially an ERM conceived as a 'glidepath' to monetary union, movements in real exchange rates could come about only through relative inflation or disinflation in the member states. Such variability in the inflation rate is generally considered by economists to be bad (welfare-reducing) in itself, on account of its distributive effects and because it reduces the efficiency of price signals and thereby worsens the allocation of resources. And, of course, it would only appear as a result of unnecessary 'boom-bust' cycles. These are injurious to supply-side improvement and

20 Space limitations prevent me from pursuing this attractive quarry, one of the more odious examples of the clothing of abhorrent, unfair and anti-economic maxims in the Delorsian language of 'solidarity'.
21 The European Council that approved the Single European Act assuaged Mrs Thatcher's institutional fears by issuing a formal, but legally non-binding 'declaration' that the majority voting provisions would be used *only* to introduce the measures necessary for the completion of the Single Market. She believed it; the others have never provided any evidence they meant it.

provide the worst political backdrop for market-liberalizing measures. In short, the Single Market programme would inevitably lead to asymmetric real shocks in Community countries. Just as the potential supply-side improvements of Thatcherism were being put at risk by the macroeconomic instability Lawson's obsession made inevitable, so too the benefits to Britain of the Single Market programme could be jeopardized by ERM membership.

By mid-1989, Mrs Thatcher had fully grasped this analysis. Whereas in 1985, and even in 1987–88, she had intuitively grasped the incompatibility of the ERM with Tory radicalism without being able to give formal economic expression to her objections, she was now able to articulate the argument. As Sir Alan Walters subsequently said: 'Nigel Lawson was a very clever man. His problem was that he came up against someone cleverer than he was: Mrs Thatcher.'

Sadly for Mrs Thatcher, in the 'Stupid Party' cleverness was no guarantee of survival. She was losing the propaganda war. Many of the tabloids might be on her side – as were their readers. But the broadsheets – read by Tory MPs – were increasingly against her. Lawson, a former financial journalist himself, was treated very favourably by them. And the Foreign Office/Commission view of 'Europe' was eagerly swallowed and regurgitated by 'serious' journalists and the BBC. To make things worse, the doubling of interest rates since May 1988 was having the most painful effects on precisely those people who were doing what Tory radicalism wanted them to do – start up new businesses, buy their own homes, stand on their own feet. By mid-1989, the crash in the housing market had not yet come, but it was obvious that it was coming. With it would come financial distress and hardship for many traditional – and many new – Tory supporters. The political and economic conditions could hardly have been worse for the introduction of the poll tax.

By mid-1989, many of Mrs Thatcher's supporters knew in their hearts that she was politically dead. Tory radicalism would die with her. So too, there was reason to fear, might British independence. So too – a matter of considerably less importance – might the Tory Party as it had existed since the 1860s. The cause of death: misadventure by Mrs Thatcher? Surely the more reasonable answer involves murderous intent by the Commission and Britain's 'partners' in Europe, a clear, determined and totally wrong-headed political strategy from Howe, and suicidal tactical miscalculation and economic misunderstanding by Lawson.

# 4

# The World Turned Upside Down

## Corporate functions

We had left the story of Franco-German ERM politics in late 1987, after the Wall Street crash had had the effect, evidently desired by Schlesinger, of breaking any possible constraint on the Bundesbank imposed by the Louvre Accords. The Basle–Nyborg agreements remained in place, of course, but, from the French point of view these technical impediments to unfettered Bundesbank power were not enough. A political approach was necessary. The Louvre Accords had clearly not been binding enough. In November 1987 the Franco-German Economic Council had already been agreed. In January 1988, then, Edouard Balladur, the French Finance Minister, went a step further when he made the proposal of a European Central Bank to control monetary policy for the whole of the Community. Germany would, like all the other countries, be represented on the governing body of such a bank, but it would no longer have a preponderant role. Indeed, the French might hope for exactly what Klasen had feared when the EMS was set up: that cunning, crafty and fiercely nationalistic *énarques* would end up running the show as a result of their superior manipulative and bureaucratic skills.

The proposal for a European Central Bank necessarily implied a monetary union. It went far beyond the projected second institutional stage of the EMS. The Bundesbank had been able to scotch that idea with a minimum of effort. But their task had been made easy by the political weakness of Helmut Schmidt, one of the founding fathers of the EMS (that political weakness owed something, as we have seen, to the effects of the Bundesbank's own actions). Now, at the beginning of 1988, the situation was different. Hans-Dietrich Genscher, the German Foreign Minister, as wily and determined as any *énarque*, had his own reasons for supporting the idea. He wanted to change the perception of Germany as 'an economic giant but a political pygmy'. Whether or not there really had been a Kohl–Gorbachev Pact, the task of increasing Germany's political weight in the world, and especially in relations with the Communist states of

Eastern and Central Europe – the GDR above all – would need to be handled carefully, however, given the sensitivities arising from Germany's historical record. Closer Western European 'cooperation', culminating in some form of political union, would provide a convenient shell for German diplomatic action. The neo-functionalists' theory, emphasizing the doctrine of 'spillovers' (or the conveyor belt to federalism, as Mrs Thatcher rightly called it), suggested that the time was ripe for an initiative aimed at an eventual political union. The programme of measures to institute a Single Market in the Community had been drawn up. The majority voting rules established by the Single European Act were an important breach of national defences within the Community. The combination of the measures and the institutional provisions for implementing them created a forward momentum. And, it was being claimed, the 'spillovers' from the Single Market would make the necessity of a single currency apparent to everyone.[1] The step from a single currency to a federal political union would be the shortest of all, as recognized by innumerable participants in the debate[2] – indeed the 'spillovers' might require a political union to be established even before a single currency came into being. Thus Genscher was prepared to offer France the bait of a diminution of German national sovereignty in monetary policy, an area that did not interest him a great deal, in order to increase Germany's diplomatic weight.

The Bundesbank, the institution that looked to have most to lose from the creation of a European Central Bank, was strangely passive in the face of the Balladur–Genscher initiatives. Plans for a European Monetary Union, it felt, were pie-in-the-sky. Foreign ministers like Genscher – even finance ministers like Balladur – might produce plans, but nothing would ever come of them. For, the Bundesbank had proclaimed time and again, monetary union implied political union. When push came to shove, France would not abolish itself for the sake of having a seat on the board of a European Central Bank.

The Bundesbank had reckoned without Jacques Delors. The Frenchman is a deeply ambivalent person with a double driving force. Part of it is an intense antipathy to America and Japan. He has never made any secret of

1 As I have suggested in the previous chapter, people who rejected this linkage were treated as non-persons.
2 Nonetheless, when Michael Portillo made the point in Britain in 1994, he was immediately reprimanded by John Major: government policy was, officially at least, against a federal union, but did not rule out British participation in a single currency. Portillo's comments showed up the illogicality of Major's position, and were therefore objectionable.

his desire to construct an economic, political and military union in 'Europe'. His Euronationalism, if one can call it that, is a particularly clear example of the construction of an 'imagined community' based on hostility to some 'other' which is often regarded as suggesting a dubious and fragile origin of the nation-state. But at least nation-states have some internal coherence – problems arise when the border of the 'nation' is not equivalent to that of the 'state'. What constitutes a nation is one of the most fiercely contested questions in political science. No one has yet suggested that 'Europe' (of twelve? fifteen? twenty? thirty-two?) constitutes a nation. Delors himself was to ask his staff for reading material, for his 1991 summer holidays, ahead of the Maastricht Council, on a European cultural identity. They were unable to provide him with any.[3] In a series of articles and interviews immediately before Maastricht, Delors was thrown back on generalizations about the 'destiny' of 'Europe' empty of anything but antagonism to the 'Anglo-Saxon' world and to Japan. While political scientists see 'Europe' either as a new form of political structure, having little in common with the nation-state, or as a structure for advancing the interests of existing nation-states, Delors wants to create a new state, 'Europe', and to create with it a new 'nation' based on some supposed cultural identity that can be defined only in terms of what it is not, what it is antithetical to.

Delors is a French nationalist as well as a Euronationalist. How is this contradiction resolved? He sees the creation of 'Europe' as the best way of extending French influence. In his ten years in Brussels he assiduously packed the Commission with French Socialists: the Commission became, to a large extent, a French Socialist machine. His hope, rather clearly, was that 'Europe' would be run by the Commission and thus dominated by France. The 'regionalization' of Europe would help to achieve this aim, since the process, French politicians and bureaucrats have traditionally felt, would be far more likely to lead to the dissolution of Germany and the United Kingdom than of France. That would return Europe to, in effect, its configuration during the reign of Louis XIV, the era which saw the longest period of French domination of the Continent.

Nationalism, whether French or Euro-style, is just one aspect of Delors's makeup. He is also a corporatist. As Finance Minister in France during Mitterrand's attempt to create Socialism in one country, he

---

3 A recent study notes that the idea of 'Europe' in cultural or ideological terms is simply absent from post-1945 literature – perhaps in revulsion from the Aryanism of the Third Reich.

devalued the franc three times in two years and presided over a sharp deterioration of the public finances in his charge. The experience convinced him that France could not 'go it alone' in defying 'Anglo-Saxon economics'. Socialism in one country might be impossible, corporatism in one continent might just work. It was initially his corporatism that won him most friends in Germany and, in particular, his biggest friend, Helmut Kohl. Equally suspicious of traditional state Socialism and of Anglo-Saxon liberalism, Kohl saw in Delors a fellow champion of so-called 'Rhenish capitalism', the capitalism of the big battalions, the industrial-financial complex, the banking cartels, the big business associations, the trade unions. Both men saw the Single Market, proposed by Delors on his arrival in the Commission, as a way of creating European industrial 'champions' (in the courtly medieval sense, not the sporting sense). Combined with the 'social dimension' (which Delors had hidden from Mrs Thatcher), the Single Market would buttress the dominant positions of the largest French and German companies, enabling them at once to 'stand up to' the Americans and Japanese and to make it that much harder for new firms, whether indigenous or foreign, to muscle in.

Large Continental firms immediately understood the implications of the Single Market as conceived by Delors and Kohl, and began showering the Commission President with fulsome praise. For them, the Single Market indeed seemed a 'businessmen's charter'. The 'social dimension' made things even better for them, for the Social Charter that gave expression to this idea was unambiguously aimed at stifling competition from the low-cost countries of the Community's periphery. The countries concerned – except Britain, whose Community budget rebate so hard-won by Mrs Thatcher went only a small way towards righting the disastrously unfair EC entry terms conceded by Edward Heath – would have to be paid off with Community transfers. But taxpayers and consumers would have to foot the bill for the 'social dimension', not big firms and trade unions.[4]

Profiting from the example of the Single Market/social dimension, West German industry and West German trade unions were soon to join forces to impose West German unions and labour costs on East Germany after

---

4 An obvious question to ask is why people wearing the hats of industrial executives or trade union members would follow a strategy that benefited them in that guise but penalized them as taxpayers or consumers. Part of the answer, of course, is that they gained at the expense of *other* firms and other workers (or would-be workers, since the biggest losers from this kind of trade-off are the unemployed). But the main answer must be that industrial and trade union leaders gain power and prestige through such strategies.

unification. The consequence was massive unemployment in East Germany, compensated by huge handouts from the West German public purse. The combination destroyed any possibility, however remote it might have been, of effective competition from indigenous East German firms. It left the East more or less virgin industrial territory that could be colonized by West German firms. West German unions were spared competition from East German migrants, who instead became welfare dependants. Big business and the unions gained; taxpayers, consumers and the dignity of Germany's new citizens were the losers.

The parallels between the Delors/Kohl plan for strengthening 'Rhenish capitalism' and German reunification do not end there. As we saw in the previous chapter, 'disorderly' liberal capitalism, of the sort favoured by Reagan and Thatcher, required exchange-rate flexibility. 'Rhenish capitalism', on the other hand, required exchange-rate fixity, whose ultimate form is monetary union, if it was properly to impose the ossification that would keep the same families and castes in political and economic power from one generation to the next. The forward-looking, dynamic and aggressive view of the Single Market programme embraced by Mrs Thatcher could never succeed if exchange rates were not allowed to move to absorb shocks. The Single Market as viewed by Delors and Kohl was intended precisely to protect established dinosaurs in the hard core from shocks by making them bigger and less vulnerable to new competitors. Exchange-rate fixity was an obvious corollary of this static, backward-looking and defensive view.

Thus it was that the might of the German industrial-financial and union complex swung behind the idea of monetary union. German public opinion – the private opinion of the man and woman in the street, as opposed to the manipulated opinion of 'experts' and public figures – might worry about the loss of national sovereignty that would go with the loss of the DM.[5] But 'correct' opinion had an even greater monopoly of public expression in Germany than it had in Britain. It was not to be until the day after (quite literally) the signing of the Maastricht agreement that the German press – in the shape of the 'vulgar' tabloid, *Bild* – spilled the beans.

---

5 As we shall see later, the events of 1992–93 were to open many German eyes to the nationalistic nature of French aims in Europe; but, as 'neo-functionalists' would predict, perceived *sectional* interests are in conflict with everyone else's *national* interests. The propaganda alliance between the Commission, big business and the unions has been a major factor in hiding this truth from European voters, promoting instead a mythical Community interest.

## The club is mightier than the handbag

It was against this background that the European Council, under German presidency, met in Hanover in June 1988 to discuss proposals for establishing monetary union. The twelve countries had committed themselves to the goal of monetary union in the Single European Act. As we have seen, Mrs Thatcher reluctantly went along with that because she wanted the Single Market and had been misled, not for the first time and not for the last, by the Foreign Office. But she became alarmed when the agenda for Hanover was being prepared. As usual on these issues, she wanted to avoid open confrontation with Britain's European 'partners'.[6] At that stage, Mrs Thatcher tended to see Delors as something of a Trojan Horse of capitalism in the citadel of French Socialism – a false impression reinforced, perhaps, by Howe, who in reality seems to have seen the Frenchman as a welcome Trojan Horse of Eurofederalism. At Hanover, she agreed to the idea of a study group, made up of the governors of the Community central banks, supplemented by three 'independent experts' and chaired by Delors.

In accepting the Delors Committee, Mrs Thatcher hoped that hard-headed central bankers would scotch plans for a single currency and a European Central Bank. Sadly, she was wrong. Delors realized from the start he could play on two features of the governors: their egos and their clubbiness. He turned their heads with the prospect of a new Super-Bundesbank at European level, totally independent of governments and consequently able to exercise a degree of power beyond the wildest dreams of many heads of government. The Bundesbank, of course, would lose power, so many observers expected Pöhl to block proposals for an ECB. To their surprise, and to the dismay of Mrs Thatcher and Nigel Lawson, he did not.

Pöhl may have thought he could see the way the wind was blowing. France was demanding a greater say in the framing of the monetary policy of the 'anchor' and Kohl and Genscher were prepared to support it. The Bundesbank risked being subject to continual political interference, French and German, within the ERM. Might it not be better to go along with Balladur and Genscher in planning a new institution – as long as the

6 After many episodes of reluctantly going along with European initiatives, always told by the Foreign Office that this was the only way to prevent something much worse happening, Mrs Thatcher was finally to say 'no' at the infamous Rome Council in October 1990 – and 'no, no, no' in the Commons immediately afterwards. It was then that Howe struck her down.

78

conditions for its actual creation were so tough that probably nothing would come of the scheme, and in the unlikely event that it did get off the ground, the new institution would conform to the Bundesbank model and philosophy? At all events, Pöhl, instead of trying to block the monetary union plan in the Delors Committee, insisted instead on the fulfilment of certain conditions for the creation of an ECB: a commitment that the ECB could not 'bail out' Community governments in financial difficulties; tight limits on the size of budget deficits that countries could run if they wanted to join the monetary union; and the granting of independent status to all national central banks before monetary union started.

It was at this point that Delors's tactical astuteness in suggesting a committee composed essentially of central bankers became most apparent. The conditions laid down by Pöhl were hardly likely to deter his fellow governors. They all wanted independence from government control, and most of them seemed already to devote most of their time and energy to berating governments for running excessive budget deficits. They quickly agreed to Pöhl's conditions. Whether he had really believed that his conditions would prove unacceptable within the Committee – which would imply a crass misreading of the personal and political motivation of his fellow governors – was putting up a smokescreen to avoid criticism from within the Bundesbank, or expected the 'Jacobin' French government to recoil from central bank independence and the Italian government to be scared off by the budgetary conditions, is not clear. At any rate, he agreed to sign the Committee's report, forwarded to the Ecofin in May 1989.

Lawson, in his memoirs, evinces a degree of disgust with Pöhl, calling him 'a broken reed' and implying that he was the sort of man who would always let you down in the end. Surprisingly, he has no such words of criticism for 'Robin' (Leigh-Pemberton, the Governor of the Bank of England), who signed the report on the lame excuse that he did not want to be the odd one out. Leigh-Pemberton was not a member of the government and was therefore not subject to collective responsibility. His desire to be part of the central bankers' club could therefore overcome any reticence he might or might not feel. If Leigh-Pemberton had refused to sign and had instead submitted a minority report, it is unlikely that the others would have been deflected from their goal – the Committee was an advisory one, and Leigh-Pemberton had no veto, unlike Mrs Thatcher in the European Council. But the fact that he *did* sign did much to undermine Mrs Thatcher at home in her opposition to monetary union. Once again, Mrs Thatcher's sense of having been betrayed was far from illusory. In conflict with her

Chancellor, let down by her Governor, increasingly suspicious about the intentions of her Foreign Secretary, plotted against by Eurofanatic MPs and MEPs, bereft of the support of Ronald Reagan, badgered by the new Bush administration on 'Europe', by now seeing Delors for what he really was, it is hardly surprising that her attitudes became more aggressive, her tone more strident, her defiance of a hostile world an ever more predominant reflex. And the Madrid arm-twisting was still to come.

The European Council meeting in Madrid in June 1989 duly agreed, outvoting Mrs Thatcher, that an Inter-Governmental Conference (IGC) to discuss a revision of the Treaty of Rome, necessary if the institutional proposals of the Delors Report were to be implemented, should be convened when initial preparatory work by officials had been done.[7] A further result of the Council was that all the member states except Britain accepted the view that the Delors Stage One – whose main element was the participation of all Community currencies in the ERM – would inevitably be followed by monetary union. Thus was engendered the fallacy, soon current among politicians and many officials, that the ERM was a 'glidepath' to monetary union and that realignments were no longer a feature of the system.[8] There is little doubt that the Spanish authorities' desire to be on the 'glidepath' was the key factor in their decision in June 1989, a couple of weeks before the Madrid Council, to put the peseta into the ERM, with the +/–6% bands then enjoyed by the lira. It is to the consequences of that decision that we now turn.

## Welfare dependency

The Europolitical motivation for ERM entry overrode economic self-interest. In economic terms, putting the peseta in the system was a catastrophically perverse response to a period of economic renascence. Spain's economy was growing fast – the result of household and entre-

---

7 A proposal to *convene* an IGC could not, under the Treaty of Rome, be vetoed. A country cannot be compelled to participate in an IGC, however: it can pursue an 'empty-chair' policy. Since the revision of the treaty requires unanimity (at least in principle!), refusing to participate in an IGC implies blocking its recommendations. But, as we saw in the previous chapter, Mrs Thatcher did not feel politically secure enough at home to pursue such a policy. Nonetheless, Britain's 'partners' were still to feel, in late 1990, a need to unseat Mrs Thatcher as Prime Minister to ensure British compliance with their wishes.

8 This attitude was expressed totally unambiguously by the French Socialist Director of Monetary Affairs in the EC Commission, Jean-François Pons, in 1991 when he was asked whether a realignment would be appropriate. His reply was: '*Réalignements? Il n'y en aura plus!*'

preneurial optimism about the future engendered by the market-opening impact of EC entry in a low-cost economy and by policy moves, however hesitant, to reduce the rigidities of the corporatist labour market and primitive and uncompetitive financial system inherited from the Franco era. As in Britain, the fast growth was associated with inflationary pressure only partly mitigated by a rapidly widening current-account deficit.

In the year or so before March 1989, the peseta had appreciated quite significantly, by around 12% in trade-weighted terms. But in an effort to 'prepare' ERM entry, the Finance Minister, Carlos Solchaga, attempted, with some success, to 'talk the peseta down'. So that when the peseta entered the system in June, its level was clearly too low to counter the inflationary pressures in the Spanish economy. In the year after entry, inflation actually rose slightly, and thereafter there was no clear downward trend until after the peseta's 1992–93 devaluations (whose circumstances will be described in subsequent chapters). The Spanish authorities were afraid of allowing the peseta to rise to a level that would be appropriate in the short run because they feared that the competitive losses thereby incurred would be unsustainable in the longer term; but they did not want to be seen to be programming a future devaluation.

It was therefore far from clear what the Spanish authorities thought they were going to get, in economic terms, from the system. Spain's inflation rate when it joined the system was close to 7%, significantly higher than the average of other ERM members. 'Talking the peseta down' before entry produced, to begin with, a stronger competitiveness position than otherwise – too strong, in fact, given Spain's overheating. The choice of entry rate simply changed the route through which Spain lost competitiveness: inflation stayed high, making Spanish goods and services expensive relative to those of competitor countries in Europe. Getting Spanish inflation down to the levels of competitor countries – the ostensible economic reason for ERM entry – could only happen via recession. The higher the inflation rate in the period after entry, the deeper the recession would have to be. In this sense, the entry rate is irrelevant. In an economy in which the balance of supply and demand is changing, *no* rate can be the right rate both for today's conditions and for tomorrow's conditions. And *whatever* the entry rate, a high-inflation country that enters a quasi-fixed-rate exchange-rate system will, if it stays in, ultimately have to have its inflation rate forced *below* the rates in competitor countries, for initial competitiveness losses to be recouped.

The ultimate inevitability of a recession in Spain – with all its negative consequences on unemployment, the public finances, the willingness of firms, whether native or foreign, to undertake investment projects, and on the political acceptability of structural reform – was ensured from the moment Spain entered the ERM. It was therefore no wonder that Gonzalez's decision should have been greeted with glee by French and German industry: they could see perfectly well that the ERM was a mechanism for keeping the poorer countries poor and shielding rich ones from the more competitive environment that the Single Market was, at least for liberals such as Mrs Thatcher, supposed to bring. By the same token, a future peseta crisis in an ERM regarded as a fixed-rate system also became inevitable. At that point, as we shall see, the hypocritical cry would arise in France and Germany that Spain was engaging in 'disloyal competitive devaluation'.

Did the Spanish authorities realize all this? Did they believe the impact of the ERM was going to be politically sustainable? Was it something not to be worried about because elections were a long way off, and it was more important for Felipe Gonzalez to cut a good 'European' figure? Did they make a cynical choice of welfare-dependency via the Structural Funds handouts from Germany and – willy-nilly – Britain rather than the embrace of progress towards productivity and real income convergence through pursuing market liberalization? Or did the Spanish authorities always intend a massive devaluation? Whatever the answer, the double myth of the ERM – its supposed economic benefits and its supposed expression of 'solidarity' and cooperation – was to be cruelly exposed by subsequent events. Once again, however, the cruelty would be inflicted on the Spanish people, not on the perpetrators of the calamity.

## ERM paradox

The ERM was to have a painful impact on Spain. There is, perhaps, some ironic satisfaction to be gained from the peseta's disruptive impact on the ERM.

For most of the system's life to 1989, the currencies of high-inflation countries had been weak in the system. The reason was simple enough: high inflation meant worsening competitiveness, and worsening competitiveness led to expectations that the currency concerned would have to realign downwards – devalue, in other words. Because markets expected the currency to be devalued at some point in the near future, it was weak within the ERM bands. As corollary, the 'virtuous' countries with low inflation (Germany and its satellite the Netherlands, to all intents and purposes) tended to be the strongest in the ERM. Indeed, this tendency was quasi-institutionalized: it was quite clear that Germany could never allow the DM to be devalued within the system. It was also to become clear that the others would never want the DM to devalue, and that if, for whatever reason, the DM became weak in the forex markets, the governments of the other ERM countries would be perfectly content to let such DM weakness drag all their currencies down against the rest of the world.[9]

In consequence, German interest rates set the floor for interest rates in other ERM countries. If the DM could never devalue, but only revalue upwards, other ERM countries could not have significantly lower interest rates than in Germany. There was, of course, some possibility of temporary upward movements of other currencies against the DM *within* the ERM bands, and as a result short-term money-market interest rates in other countries could be marginally lower than German rates at times, if some upward movement within the band was expected. But it remained the case that Germany was 'leader' in the system. Central banks in the other countries could not set their official short-term rates lower than corresponding rates set by the Bundesbank without challenging Germany's leadership role. As we shall see in chapter 12, the collapse of the ERM in its original form was precipitated by just such a challenge by France in the summer of 1993. In the summer of 1989, the natural order of things reigned in the ERM, but the entry of the peseta was to make people think again, earning Spain the enmity of an affronted Bundesbank.

As we have seen, the Spanish economy was overheating at the time of ERM entry and the logical response would have been a monetary policy tightening. The Banco de España indeed kept interest rates as high as the ERM constraint would permit. Yet that was not high enough. Spain really needed a bigger interest-rate differential with its ERM 'partners'. But if Spanish short-term interest rates had gone up further, foreigners would have rushed to buy pesetas, pushing the currency through its permitted margin against other ERM currencies unless the Banco de España intervened to *sell* pesetas. In fact, it was a struggle not to allow interest rates to fall, so strong was foreign demand for pesetas. The Banco de España had

9  It would not quite be true to describe the Dutch as being 'content' in such circumstances. But they *never* voiced any public criticism of German economic policy or concern about German economic developments.

to intervene even more massively than Lawson had let the Bank of England do in the 1987–88. Spain's domestic demand boom certainly produced a current-account deficit, but not one big enough to offset inflationary pressures, and because the peseta could not rise far enough to clear the market, the Banco de España had to do it instead by creating as many pesetas as the market wanted to buy at the pegged ERM price. That price was pegged because the peseta, very soon after ERM entry, had gone to the top of its permitted ERM band and had no room to go up further.

Thus the ERM theorists were confronted with the spectacle of a country with high inflation, high interest rates (even if not high enough), a large current-account deficit and no record of 'credibility' at the top of the ERM, muscling the traditional top dogs out of the way. Surely, they complained, such a country should be at the *bottom* of the ERM, with its currency under *downward*, not upward pressure, and its central bank should be having to intervene to *support* the currency, not restrain it. They quickly invented a label for this phenomenon, a slogan lest people might start wondering if the ERM was really a flawed mechanism. 'The ERM paradox' was what the system's acolytes, many of them *soi-disant* Catholics, came up with, a comforting notion of revealing significance. The 'paradox' could be seen as being like the mysteries of religion – beyond human comprehension, a test of Faith, not Reason.[10] Yet just as in every pilgrim's spiritual journey the test of Faith may be made more anguished by a test of Morals, so too would the ERM have to cope not only with the Spanish 'paradox' but, almost simultaneously, with a Germany that seemed to want to kick over the traces of good behaviour. The temptations of German reunification were about to entice the ERM's leader and exemplar away from the straight and narrow path of fiscal rectitude and price stability.

10 The tendency of many ERM/EMU supporters, the duped rather than the cynical, to see their views as having a religious foundation, has caused concern not only among Protestants but among those Catholics – including, it would seem, the present Pope – who find the deification of European Union almost blasphemous. Non-believers had another name for what was happening: the 'Walters critique' of the ERM. Mrs Thatcher's adviser had predicted the state of affairs now instantiated by Spain as early as 1986. Strangely, City analysts and economists were to write, after seeing what was happening to the peseta, such bromides as: 'The Walters critique is alive and well and living in Spain.' Yet they were loath to apply the critique to their own country. The problem in Britain was not the Continental tendency to confuse religion and economic logic, but the much more Anglo-Saxon failing of Political Correctness. Until about ten minutes before sterling's ejection from the system in September 1992, it was politically highly incorrect to question the ERM's merits.

## Let no man put asunder

In the second half of 1989, the Bundesbank's main worry was not so much the peseta as the Delors Report. Pöhl's stock, never enormously high within the Bank, fell as a result of his putting his signature, however reluctantly, to the Report.[11] Other Council members, seeing the Report's view of the ERM as now being a no-realignment 'glidepath' to EMU, began a very public campaign of speeches, interviews and articles in favour of a DM realignment. That autumn Helmut Schlesinger, in pep-talks to Bundesbank staff members departing on secondment to international organizations, impressed on his young missionaries the need to campaign for a DM realignment in the pagan countries they were being sent to.

Not for the first time, and not for the last, however, the German government took a different view. German diplomacy had, throughout the summer of 1989, been aiming at the collapse of the Communist régime in the GDR. By the autumn, the strategy was coming increasingly near to success – and some of Germany's neighbours in Western Europe were starting to worry. Among those anxious about the geopolitical implications of the meltdown of Communism in Central and Eastern Europe as a whole was François Mitterrand. To reassure him that Germany was not going to strike out on its own as the great Central European power, Kohl pointed to the Delors Report and its plan for monetary union. And it must have been at this time that the German Chancellor first issued an edict to the Bundesbank: whatever else might happen in the ERM, there must be no realignment of the DM against the French franc.

The economic argument underlying Schlesinger's 'open-mouth' campaign had centred on current accounts and competitiveness. The Bundesbank had begun tightening monetary policy in the summer of 1988. Now, on 5 October 1989, it raised its key interest rates by a full point. In the past, such an increase might have sparked ERM tensions and paved the way for a realignment. Indeed, the very next day Pöhl himself, in a speech to a banking association in Bonn, declared that the Bundesbank saw a realignment as desirable from a stability-policy point of view. But, in the

---

11 Plucked out of journalism and installed in public life as an adviser in the Finance Ministry by Helmut Schmidt, Pöhl had subsequently been appointed Bundesbank President by the Socialist Chancellor. Though regarded by the international media as the incarnation of the Bundesbank, Pöhl was regarded by cynical Bundesbank staff as more interested in being in the glare of TV cameras ('Is that how he keeps his year-round tan?' they asked).

very next sentence of his oration, he acknowledged that Germany's 'most important partners' in the ERM had ruled out the use of the exchange rate as an instrument of external adjustment. His use of the plural fooled no one – nor was it intended to. Pöhl was talking about France. And the external adjustment that was being blocked was Germany's, not France's. In effect, he was acknowledging that France, backed by Kohl, had forbidden a DM revaluation. The French Finance Minister, Pierre Bérégovoy, confirmed French obduracy in a speech of his own a few days later. But Pöhl went even further. Germany's 'most important partners' (that is, France) were behaving, he said, as if there were already a monetary union, defined as a zone of fixed exchange rates and free capital movements. And, speaking for the first time of a 'hard core', he claimed that things had gone further in that direction than, in all probability, people were conscious of. Perhaps people were intended to interpret the speech (echoed in the following months by certain other Council members), as putting forward an alternative to the institutional approach to EMU set out in the Delors Report: namely that there was a monetary union already in being.[12] (As we shall see in later chapters, it was to become an endlessly reiterated theme of the Bundesbank, when the political and market climate subsequently shifted in its favour, that the idea that a *de facto* monetary union existed was a dangerous illusion.)

The problem, from the point of view of the hawks in the Bundesbank Council, was that other ERM countries were also growing strongly, could follow the Bundesbank's interest-rate rise with equanimity[13] and showed no interest in a devaluation of their currencies (indeed, as we have seen, Britain and Spain had unwisely been restraining *upward* movements in their currencies for much of the previous three years). Only the Danish krone showed signs of weakness. The Danish economy was in recession as a

12 Pöhl, whatever his reasoning at the time he signed the Delors Report, later considered that he had been mistaken.

13 The UK, although still outside the ERM at this time, was one of the countries that followed the rate rise. Lawson found the precise timing somewhat unfortunate, since it occurred during a Tory Party Conference, but he wanted British rates to rise and it suited him to pretend that Britain had to follow whatever Germany did and might therefore just as well join the ERM. Alan Walters opposed the British rate rise and Mrs Thatcher acceded to it only very reluctantly. In his memoirs, Lawson omits to mention – perhaps no one ever told him – that Pöhl in his speech the next day directly contradicted the Lawson argument, speaking of the existence of a 'European exchange-rate union' of fixed exchange rates and free capital movements. Such a set of arrangements, he said, inevitably implied a loss of national autonomy in economic, fiscal and monetary policy, and that was the main reason why Britain had not joined the 'exchange-rate union'.

result of ERM membership – a story we shall look at in some detail in chapter 11 – but in the general Europhoric atmosphere of late 1989, speculative pressure never really mounted, and the Danish authorities were able to eliminate exchange-rate pressure through a small rise in interest rates.

In November, however, the picture changed dramatically. The fall of the Berlin Wall was a shock to the geopolitical structure of the whole of Europe. It was also, as we shall see later, a shock to 'Europe'. But its most immediate consequences were economic. The opening of the borders between the two parts of Germany constituted an asymmetric real shock, as we defined it in the previous chapter. Freedom of movement would be likely to bring a huge influx of East German workers and their families into the West, attracted not only by political freedom but also by Bonn's 'welcome money' and by the prospect of sharing in the West's high living standards. The migrants would have to be housed. They would want to acquire Western cars and consumer durables. Their children would need schools, their families medical services. All this would increase the pressure of demand on resources in West Germany, already stretched by two years of relatively strong economic growth. More than that, the arrival of very large numbers of new workers – Germans, well-educated, accustomed to the discipline of industrial work, mostly young, mostly the more enterprising – would be a welcome infusion into West Germany's sclerotic labour market. Labour costs would be forced down and working practices improved by the competition from the new arrivals. All this – increased consumer demand for goods and services, improved labour supply – would increase the rate of return on physical capital in West Germany and lead to an investment boom, further adding to the pressure on available resources in the short run. Rather like Britain in 1986–87, if for rather different reasons, West Germany's currency, the DM, was bound to appreciate in real terms.[14] If that was not to come about through inflation in West Germany, which the Bundesbank, it was firmly believed, would not countenance, there would have to be a nominal appreciation – a revaluation – of the DM. And that revaluation would have to be against European currencies as well as against the dollar and the yen.

14 In the circumstances as they appeared in November 1989, the only way to prevent a real appreciation would have been through a fiscal tightening – a reduction in the already tiny budget deficit. That would have been entirely inappropriate economically. More to the point, it would have been quite simply impossible politically, especially given the foreseeable increased need for state spending in education, health, social services, industrial training and so on.

The financial markets responded immediately. German long-term interest rates rose and the DM strengthened against the dollar – a combination that clearly indicated a perceived rise in the rate of return on capital and a need for real appreciation. Whereas in October the Bundesbank hawks had been pushing on a string in their realignment campaign, now they seemed to be pushing at a financial market door opened for them by the East German frontier police. Within a few days, however, that door was slammed firmly shut – by the West German government.

The politicians in Bonn reacted to the opening of the Wall with a mixture of delight and alarm. Both emotions pointed policy in the same direction: German reunification. The delight needs no explanation; nor does the desire to make use of a historic 'window' to reunite Germany. The alarm was sparked by the prospect of social and political strains if the mass migration whose prospect was delighting the forex market actually came to pass. A way of keeping East Germans in East Germany had to be found – the plans for a monetary union with the East and massive budgetary transfers from West to East could not be far away. But, as German politicians, officials and bankers have always insisted, a monetary union, whether within Germany or in 'Europe', cannot work without a political union. The political reunification of Germany would reawaken visceral French fears of German domination of the Continent. To square Mitterrand, Germany would have to promise monetary union in 'Europe', and such a promise would lack any credibility if it coincided with a realignment of the DM against the franc at the behest of the Bundesbank. Thus, just six days after the Wall crumbled, Hans Tietmeyer, State Secretary at the German Finance Ministry, stated quite categorically that there would be no ERM realignment – at least not within the narrow band.

Tietmeyer will play a particularly important part in the rest of the book, and it is worthwhile to introduce him here. A Westphalian Catholic, Tietmeyer was in his youth a theological student before turning to government employment. Serving in the Economics Ministry, he was part of the German team involved in negotiating the 1970 Werner plan, an ill-starred predecessor of the Delors Report. When the FDP switched horses in 1982, ushering Kohl and the Christian Democrats into power, Tietmeyer was appointed to the post of State Secretary to Finance Minister Gerhard Stoltenberg. There is no equivalent in the British system of the role of State Secretary, one which combines the functions of a permanent secretary in a civil service department with those of a junior minister. The holder of the post is not an elected politician but plays a political role. Tietmeyer was particularly close to Kohl.

His post gave him a seat in the Monetary Committee, where he soon became the dominant member (in addition to chairing the Committee in 1985–87). He combined tremendous intellectual power with a fearsome physical presence and great ruthlessness in debate. He would give other speakers a remorseless hammering. Before the kill, he would arrange his features into a half-smile, half-snarl, his bared upper gums looking for all the world like the gumshield of a heavyweight boxer about to deliver the knockout blow to an opponent trapped already near-senseless on the ropes.

He was no respecter of position or reputation. Nigel Lawson, while recording his brilliance, found him 'something of a rough diamond for an official'. A German diplomat (married, like so many in Kohl's immediate circle of foreign policy advisers, to a Frenchwoman) once described him as a 'typical Boche'. Tietmeyer seemed to take particular delight in baiting Treasury knights (presumably 'smooth' in Lawson's terms), placing malicious and dismissive emphasis on the 'Sir' when he pronounced their names. Knights apart, he rarely descended into the chummy use of first names in meetings so favoured by other members of the international monetary and financial circus and seen by Bundesbank officials as a mark of Pöhl's 'unsoundness'.[15] But a counterpart of his scant respect for the position or reputation of others was a total absence of 'side': he was down-to-earth as well as earthy.

By November 1989, Tietmeyer had already been designated to join the Bundesbank Directorate (from the beginning of 1990) as the member responsible for international monetary affairs, replacing the recently retired Leonhard Gleske.[16] The appointment was not greeted with enthusiasm in Frankfurt, where it was viewed as an attempt by Kohl to put 'his' man in. But Tietmeyer's dual position in November 1989 – State Secretary and confidant of Kohl, and soon-to-be Bundesbank Directorate member –

15 Helmut Hesse, a member of the Bundesbank Council, is quoted in David Marsh's book on the Bundesbank as follows: 'The monetary masters of the world meet regularly, they become personally close to one another. They call themselves not "Mr President", but "Karl Otto". This is a good thing, but it is also a form of straitjacket which can be constrictive, because you have to take into account the personal interests of other people you meet.'

16 Gleske had been the man whose four words, '*Wir wollen das nicht*', had killed the proposed EMF in the early 1980s (see chapter 2). A few years later, over lunch in a New York bank, he had dismissed Lawson's ambitions for UK ERM entry. 'Not even with 6% bands?' he was asked. He replied, with a would-be joke: 'The British won't want to be in the same boat as the Italians', but was nonplussed and uncomprehending when an Englishman present immediately added 'with all its turrets facing aft'.

gave his words particular authority. And, after all, the German government retained the right to decide parity changes, whatever the Bundesbank might think, and subject only to the Emminger Letter.

Not for the last time, Tietmeyer's words might be comforting to France but distinctly unsettling for certain other ERM member countries. By saying there would not be a realignment 'at least in the narrow band', he was turning the spotlight on the two countries, Spain and Italy, whose currencies operated with 6% bands (although the Italian government was, a mere six weeks later, to display typical and ultimately self-destructive craftiness by joining the narrow band). He clearly did not mean that the peseta and the lira should realign upwards against the DM: that would break the most important unwritten rule of the ERM – that no currency could ever revalue against the DM. Instead, he was implying that these two currencies should *de*value – an irresponsible and mischievous suggestion to countries whose inflation rates were too high and, in the case of Spain at least, edging higher precisely because neither the ERM nor the government wanted to allow revaluation.

Tietmeyer made the amazing accusation that Spain and Italy – and also the United Kingdom – were 'exporting inflation' to a helpless Germany via an aberrant mix of high interest rates and – according to Tietmeyer – 'expansionary' budgetary policies.[17] It is true that investment booms in these countries and others were boosting exports in Germany and thus contributing to incipient inflationary pressures there. But Tietmeyer, like most other apostles of 'Europe', fell into the trap of denying the logic of the Single Market: that logic required that if domestic demand in Britain, Spain or Italy spilled over into Germany, it was no more the responsibility of the governments of those three countries to restrain demand than it would have been their responsibility to offset, through their own budgetary policies, the output impact in Germany of an overheating of *German* domestic demand. The responsibility of each government was, while ensuring sound public finance, to take the *monetary* policy actions necessary to stabilize output, employment and prices in its own economy. Instead, Tietmeyer was demanding that other governments should tailor their

---

17 There was clearly a case at the time for the Italian government to use the opportunity of a period of relatively strong growth to cut into its huge budget deficit. The reasons it did not do so were connected with the Euro-illusions infecting Italian political life – in addition to its endemic problems. Chapter 10 below reflects on this experience. But Italian budgetary policy was certainly not 'expansionary' in demand terms in 1989. Nor was budgetary policy in Spain and Britain.

policies to suit Germany, since Germany could not stabilize its own economy because of Kohl's political commitment not to allow a DM revaluation against the franc.

Schlesinger has often been described as acting in Germany's selfish interest by attempting to steer monetary policy with domestic objectives in mind. But to the extent Schlesinger was indeed doing that, he was doing exactly what was required – both from Germany's point of view and from that of everyone else's economies (if not necessarily everyone else's political and bureaucratic classes). The position genuinely damaging to an understanding of economic well-being – not to mention the myth of ERM 'solidarity' – was Tietmeyer's. Less than three and a half years after his November 1989 speech, he was to accuse Britain and Italy (illogically and falsely) of 'competitive devaluation' and thereby risking *importing* inflation into their own economies (and he warned Spain that it risked the same charge). We shall meet this example of Tietmeyerian double-talk in chapter 10. There will be others.

Within a few months, the boot would be on the other foot, and by a piquant irony the Bundesbank – with Tietmeyer now installed – would find itself severely embarrassed by the doctrine he enunciated on 17 November. The more immediate impact of his speech was ironic in a different way: it ruled out a realignment just at the moment the previously uninterested markets saw a genuine reason for having one.[18] Politics, as always in the ERM, prevailed over economic logic in the motivation of the system's managers; and fallacious economic doctrines had to be invented on the hoof to hide the fact. The masquerade fooled many credulous spectators who should have known better. Among the most damagingly influential of these were those pre-eminently 'Anglo-Saxon' organs of enlightened opinion, *The Economist* (the pen presumably held by Rupert Pennant-Rea, an ERM enthusiast subsequently installed – no doubt on the say-so of his former colleague Sarah Hogg, who became head of John Major's policy staff in 10 Downing Street – as Deputy Governor of the Bank of England, before being carpeted) and the *Financial Times*, in the person of Sam Brittan. The former pontificated on 2 December 1989 that 'a realignment ought to be not merely avoidable, but avoided'; the latter complained sanctimoniously on 15 January 1990 that: 'the Bundesbank's sotto voce

18 On 11 December, Schlesinger said in a speech that stability policy was 'possible only if the exchange-rate instrument is available' (another comment neither noted by Lawson in his memoirs nor reported by the ERM-besotted, anti-Thatcher 'quality' British press), but reluctantly admitted that, for the time being, realignments were 'politically refused'.

campaign for an EMS realignment[19] is irresponsible, damaging to European integration and represents a time warp in the institution's thinking'.

## Frankfurt versus Bonn

By December, Kohl had already produced a ten-point plan for German reunification. The pace of change suddenly increased again in early February 1990, when Kohl, alarmed by reports of three million East Germans 'sitting on their suitcases' and preparing to flood into West Germany, surprised the Bundesbank with a plan for rapid monetary union between East and West. The DM would become the currency of the whole of Germany, replacing the inconvertible ostmark in the GDR.

The Bundesbank was appalled. At the end of January, Pöhl had described the idea of monetary union as 'fantastic' and Schlesinger as 'very unrealistic'. On the very day, 6 February, that Kohl announced his intention, Pöhl had spoken of the idea as very premature. At a stroke, practically the whole of the East German economy would be made uncompetitive, whatever the conversion rate for wages from ostmarks into DM. There would either have to be massive subsidies from the West German government to keep East German firms in operation, or equally massive transfers to unemployed East German workers. In either case, the cost to the West German budget would be enormous.[20] At the same time, since East German wages expressed in inconvertible ostmarks would be converted into DM at a decreed rate of one to one (the unofficial exchange rate at the time was about seven to one), East German families, suddenly finding their wages (or welfare payments) worth seven times as much in terms of West German goods and services as they previously had been, would be likely to go on a spending spree – in West Germany.[21] All in all, there was likely to be a further surge in the demand for goods and services in the new German monetary union as a whole, yet the output of the union as a whole would fall as East German firms became even more uncompeti-

19 In effect, the campaign was Schlesinger's.
20 Some budgetary costs were inevitable whatever the chosen conversion rate. With the labour markets of East and West Germany now linked by potentially massive migration, there was bound to be a rapid process of convergence of disposable incomes, expressed in DM, by one route or another.
21 Savings were converted at an average rate of about 1.6 to one, thus increasing the purchasing power of East German financial wealth, as well as current incomes, in terms of West German goods and services.

tive than before on world markets (and as previously guaranteed markets in Eastern Europe and the Soviet Union collapsed).

The net impact of all this would be substantial inflationary pressure in unified Germany as a whole. Normally, the response to this would be a DM appreciation, to switch demand away from overstretched German sources of supply to foreign sources. Yet Bonn was ruling out an ERM realignment even more firmly than ever, for reasons of keeping Mitterrand sweet. So the inevitable *real* appreciation of the DM[22] would have to take place through a rise in German inflation above inflation rates in the economies of the country's trading partners – a quite horrific prospect for the Bundesbank, whose prestige and political power depended on its reputation as being the most resolutely anti-inflation monetary authority in the world (except for the Swiss National Bank, which needed neither Bundesbank leadership nor the ERM to take the palm).

To make things worse, the government's overriding of the Bundesbank – both on the very idea of monetary union and on its terms – had been very public. Pöhl himself had thought of resigning, and some members of the Bundesbank Council made outspoken public statements attacking Kohl for 'acting as if the autonomy of the Bundesbank has been set aside for the process of unification' in a way that could 'start to damage the credibility of the Bundesbank' by 'stripping it of monetary leadership'.

The financial markets again reacted quickly. As in the previous November, German long-term interest rates moved up sharply after the unification announcement on 6 February. But this time the DM, rather than strengthening further, *weakened* significantly. The combination clearly expressed both a weakening of Bundesbank credibility and fears of increased German inflation.[23]

Tietmeyer, by now a Bundesbank Council member, began to play the ambiguous role that his new functions seemed to require of most who fulfilled them. As early as March he sharply criticized the EC Commission

---

22 The initial real appreciation would, appropriately, overshoot the new long-run equilibrium real rate, which would itself probably be below its pre-unification level, implying a future real depreciation of the DM to correct the initial overshoot.

23 It is worth stressing that the real macroeconomic problem was not the ostmark conversion terms – Kohl simply had to find some way to raise East German real incomes immediately, ahead of productivity movements, and it was democratically unacceptable to challenge those terms – but the refusal to contemplate a realignment, combined with an attempt to mislead the West German public about the budgetary cost of unification. The great *structural* mistake was to let West German unions, with the connivance of West German firms, colonize the East and extend the 'German social model' across the Elbe.

for publishing estimates of the budgetary cost of German unification as 3%
of West German GDP for three or four years. Such ludicrous and
irresponsible estimates, he said, were the reason for the rise in German
long-term interest rates. In fact, such estimates turned out to be very low.[24]
But Tietmeyer's patron, Kohl, was telling the German people that
reunification would be a costless affair. At the beginning of April,
Tietmeyer, while retaining his Bundesbank responsibilities, was appointed
Kohl's special adviser on German monetary union – an appointment that
increased suspicion of him in Frankfurt, and even more so in the
headquarters of the regional central banks. Throughout 1990 Tietmeyer
insisted that unification posed no inflationary threat. His stance can most
plausibly be explained by a desire not to discountenance Kohl's Christian
Democrats in the period leading up to the first pan-German elections in
October 1990[25] but it was also a reflection of the importance Tietmeyer
attributed to the ERM as a guarantor of German competitiveness – as well
as illustrating the Bundesbank's temporary impotence.[26]

For many months after its February defeat, the Bundesbank lay licking
its wounds. Kohl had simply brushed its objections aside. The Bundesbank
would take its revenge in the end, but it would have to bide its time. Kohl
was riding the crest of a popular wave. However much the Bundesbank was
respected in Germany, it could not hope to come out on top in any direct
confrontation with 'the Chancellor of German Unity'. To enter into such a

24 In fact, transfers have, from 1991 onwards, been around 5–6% of pan-German GDP (and
  around 6.5% of West German GDP) a year. It is now widely expected that transfers on
  something like this scale will have to continue for another ten years. Pessimistic observers fear
  the creation of a German 'Mezzogiorno', a permanent welfare-dependency, in the East.
25 Once a monetary union between West and East Germany was accepted (it came into being on
  1 July 1990), political union clearly had to follow immediately. As the Bundesbank has
  consistently and rightly agreed, monetary unions necessarily imply political union if they are not
  to collapse.
26 There is a further factor which might, if it had been recognized at the time, have affected
  Tietmeyer's stance. There is no direct evidence that he was in fact aware of it, though his
  apparent conviction that the strength of the peseta and the pound in the face of asymmetric
  demand shocks would prove to be only temporary is indirect evidence that he might have been.
  The point is that any initial DM appreciation, though it would have been entirely appropriate in
  the absence of ERM constraints, would have overshot the real long-run equilibrium level of
  the currency. Since the whole ERM reposed on a 'no-DM-devaluation' assumption, a
  correction, at some future time, of the overshoot would have required either the abandonment
  of the ERM or relative disinflation in Germany. The latter in turn would have implied either a
  German recession much deeper and longer than the one that actually took place in 1992–93, or
  a rise in absolute inflation in Germany's ERM partners, thus all too clearly invalidating the
  ERM's claim to be a tool of inflation convergence.

confrontation and lose would be even more damaging to its monetary credibility and to its political influence than to accept the inevitable. Kohl's powerful tactical position, and his firm promise to Mitterrand to preserve the franc–DM link as an earnest of his commitment to EMU, meant that the Bundesbank could not indulge in its usual expression of disapproval of government action – a sharp rise in interest rates. Yet if the Bundesbank did nothing, the markets' fear of inflation as a result of unification would *weaken* the DM just when the demands of the German domestic situation required it to strengthen. It is against this background that Tietmeyer's behaviour in 1990 should be judged. If it was politically impossible, at least before the October elections, for the Bundesbank to take action to forestall inflation, it would be best to reassure the markets as much as possible by playing down the inflation risks. Tietmeyer could hardly be expected to issue jeremiads about overheating and inflationary pressures if his institution was prevented from doing anything about it – unless he wanted to undermine Kohl politically, which he very obviously did not want to do. Nor could he admit to the scale of the budgetary deterioration that unification must imply. Not only was there an immediate electoral imperative for Tietmeyer in playing down the costs, there was also the unfortunate matter of his speech on 17 November the previous year, when he had castigated 'certain countries' for using high interest rates to offset expansionary budgetary policies. As we have seen, the countries concerned were not actually pursuing expansionary budgetary policies at the time. But Germany certainly now was, and this must be hidden if Tietmeyer's own critique were not now to be turned against the DM.

As it was, in the months following the February announcement of unification, the DM wobbled against non-ERM currencies but did not collapse. The markets were torn between a fear that the Bundesbank would be forced to allow inflation to rise (a fear that tended to weaken the DM) and a residual belief that at some time it would react, whatever unkind things Tietmeyer might have said about Britain and Spain, by sharply tightening monetary policy (a belief that supported the DM). Within the ERM, the DM weakened slightly. Its weakness did not primarily take the form, however, of a downward movement in the ERM band. Instead, it was manifested in the increased ability of other ERM countries to reduce the spread of their interest rates over German rates.

## Anchors aweigh

The French monetary authorities initially took – or affected to take – a very relaxed view of German monetary reunification. Like Tietmeyer (who was soon accorded by financial markets the sobriquet of 'the representative of the Banque de France in the Bundesbank Council'), they pooh-poohed fears about inflation in Germany. Bundesbank inaction on interest rates suited them down to the ground, for financial market worries about the credibility of the German central bank allowed other countries actually to reduce their interest-rate differentials with Germany.

By May 1990, indeed, French officials were beginning to question whether Germany could still be regarded as the 'anchor' of the ERM. But this questioning could not go too far: if German monetary policy was no longer the anchor, then what was? For hawks such as Schlesinger, there was no conceivable alternative: the ERM would cease to exist if Germany were no longer the anchor.

Some more naive souls were prepared to believe that France – whose inflation rate was, as a result of a rising trend of unemployment, by now lower than Germany's[27] – could take over the anchor role. But this would have to imply that markets believed French policy to be committed to low inflation for its own sake. Very few people, in the markets or in the governments and central banks of other ERM countries, were prepared to believe that. France was pursuing a policy of '*désinflation compétitive*' (competitive disinflation), reducing its inflation rate below Germany's in order to improve its competitive position without a devaluation against the DM. If German inflation went up, it would be easier for France to gain competitiveness without having to squeeze its own inflation down. And the weakness of the DM engendered by higher German inflation would allow French differentials in interest rates to fall, so that French *real* interest rates (nominal interest rates less inflation expectations) could be lower than otherwise. As there was no evidence whatsoever that France would continue a policy of low inflation if German inflation went up, there was no way that France could perform the anchor role in a system whose *raison d'être* was proclaimed as 'price stability through discipline'. But if Germany no longer seemed able to play this role, and France was

27 At around this time, many British commentators, notably Sam Brittan, pointed to French experience as the model that Britain should follow – by joining the ERM.

unwilling to, what was the point of the system, other than as a piece of political symbolism?

The author of the policy of '*désinflation compétitive*' was Jean-Claude Trichet, since 1988 the Directeur du Trésor, the permanent head of the French Treasury, a post more powerful than those of most ministers in the French system. Like most of his kind, he was a graduate of the Ecole Nationale de l'Administration (ENA), and like so many members of the ENA caste he was endowed with a self-importance that would be comical if its owner did not have so much power over other people.[28] Trichet is legendary for the volume of his outpourings. Listeners bored to distraction by his streams of empty maxims take to recording his verbal mannerisms. A favourite pastime is counting the number of times in a particular soliloquy the words *méditation*, *méditer* and their various declensions and conjugations give expression to his transcendental wisdom. Trichet regularly invests Delphic phrases with great significance. In May 1990, he outoracled the oracle. Faced with the question of where the ERM anchor resided after the DM's unification-induced weakness, he replied: '*L'ancre du système, c'est le système lui-même*' ('the anchor of the system is the system itself'), pronouncing the words slowly and deliberately and then repeating them for good measure. No one asked him to explain himself. The supposedly self-anchoring properties of the ERM were, like the 'ERM paradox', incapable of explanation by Believers, and analyses by infidels were anathematized.

Thus, by mid-1990 the ERM was in considerable disarray. First, the currencies of the two member countries with the highest inflation rates (Spain and Italy) were the strongest in the system. Second, while the economic rationale of the system had often been described in terms of allowing other countries to 'borrow the credibility' of the Bundesbank, the Bundesbank's own credibility was now questioned. Third, German inflation was rising, and would soon be the highest in any member of the ERM narrow band. Fourth, the policy of '*désinflation compétitive*' followed by France meant that rising German inflation was welcomed. Fifth, the doctrine that '*l'ancre du système, c'est le système lui-même*' made it very clear that, for better or for worse, there was *no* anchor in the system and that France was not interested in providing one.

Clearly, not everyone saw the position as depressing. The proponents of early monetary union were in fact delighted. The new relative weakness of

28 See chapter 12.

the Bundesbank and the relatively poor performance of German inflation were taken by them as indicating that a major obstacle to monetary union – the understandable reluctance of the German people to give up national monetary independence and throw in their lot with high-inflation, weak-currency countries – looked as though it might tumble. EMU's backers were not interested in the price stability that the Delors Report had proclaimed – and the Maastricht Treaty was to proclaim even more fraudulently – as its aim and justification. Price stability was never desired for its own sake – not even by the Bundesbank, as we shall see later. Those outside the Bundesbank who paid lip-service to the goal of price stability did so as a way of furthering the pursuit of EMU, and they sought EMU as a way of furthering the pursuit of their own power. Wilhelm Nölling, Chairman of the Hamburg Landeszentralbank and a Bundesbank Council Member, put it very clearly at the beginning of 1991, saying: 'We should be under no illusion – the present controversy over the new European monetary order is about power, influence and the pursuit of national interests.'

Towards the end of 1990, something quite remarkable happened. The European Commission produced a piece of analysis, as opposed to propaganda, about the workings of the ERM and the implications of EMU. Needless to say, this analysis was not published. Its existence was revealed only in 1993, in an article in a Brussels-based review, *De Pecunia*, well known for its 'commitment' to EMU and the ECU (or 'écu', as the review always refers to it). The Commission analysis made it clear that the anchorless situation so beloved of Trichet could not continue. And if the ERM really was to be the 'glidepath' to EMU as well as a guarantor of price stability, some collective anchor would have to be established. Otherwise, speculative attacks would lead to a breakdown either of the system itself or of monetary control in the anchor country. This was an uncannily accurate prediction of the dilemma – and the Franco-German conflict about how to resolve it – that was to destroy the ERM in the summer of 1993.

The suggested solution was entirely in line with the reasoning of the Delors Report: that there should be a sort of 'trial period' before full EMU in which monetary policy would be coordinated. Instead of the Bundesbank targeting the German money supply and the other ERM members simply targeting, in effect, their exchange rates against the DM, *all* ERM members would target the domestic components of their money supplies with the aim of achieving a commonly agreed monetary target for the ERM area as a whole.[29] The implication of such a procedure was clear: if the aim was to produce a commonly agreed target for the area-wide money supply, there must also be agreement in each participating country that what mattered was inflation, output and employment in the ERM as a whole, not in each individual country.

The Commission analysis was saying, in somewhat different form, what the Bundesbank had said a couple of months earlier in its first full, considered and formal response to the Delors Report: 'A monetary union is an irrevocably sworn co-fraternity – "all for one and one for all".' Yet, the article in *De Pecunia* implies, the member states dismissed the scheme more or less with one voice. Why? The answer points both to the Bundesbank's desire to retain its own supremacy and to the hypocritical posturing by the EMU fanatics. The Bundesbank statement on EMU had warned that 'an early irrevocable fixing of exchange rates and the transfer of monetary policy powers to Community institutions would involve considerable risks to monetary stability'. Putting together the two Bundesbank quotations would lead to the conclusion that aspirant members of EMU should demonstrate their commitment to 'a sworn co-fraternity – "all for one and one for all" ' *in advance of* full monetary union. The Commission scheme would have allowed such a test: the target for the ERM-wide money supply would be agreed by the monetary authorities of the participating countries, not imposed by a Community institution – and any country could withdraw from the scheme and adjust its exchange rate if it wanted to. No new institution would be required, and the main change would be to give the monetary authorities of the other countries an equal role with the Bundesbank.

So the reason for Bundesbank opposition was straightforward: the German central bank did not want to have to share responsibility for monetary conditions in Germany whether in EMU or before EMU. Moreover, the Bundesbank had no reason whatsoever to believe that the other countries would play the game according to price-stability rules.

If the attitude of the Bundesbank was unsurprising, the reported dismissal of the Commission scheme by other countries was revealing. Such countries were evidently not prepared to accept 'all for one and one

---

29 The technical merits and demerits of this scheme should not detain us unnecessarily. The basic idea, for those who may be interested, was that if the ERM currencies as a bloc floated against the rest of the world, and if all interventions within the system were unsterilized, the domestic money supply components in the individual members would together produce the desired result for the ERM-wide money supply.

for all'. As Nölling points out, EMU was all about power and about *national* interests, not about a mythical *Community* interest. If countries were ever to engage themselves in an exercise that so explicitly gave priority to the Community interest (whatever that might be) over national interests, then the whole EMU project would be put in jeopardy. Ideas of 'solidarity', 'community', 'fraternity' and the rest were fine as cover for the power-play of European monetary politics, but heaven forfend that anyone should ever try to put them into practice!

In rejecting the Commission's scheme, the monetary mandarins made three things perfectly clear: that they were not interested in price stability for its own sake; that the ERM would be anchorless unless the Bundesbank regained its authority and unstable if it did; and that EMU would fail, would be nothing more than a source of economic instability and nationalistic conflict within the Community. Could those have been the conclusions that the anonymous authors of the Commission paper, knowing the reception it would have, *wanted* to provoke? Perhaps. But logic, transparency and openness played no part in the ERM and EMU game. It was no wonder the Commission's scheme and the reaction to it were not made public: at almost exactly the same time, Continental politicians were laying and implementing the plans for the imposition of EMU and for the political liquidation of the one figure prepared to tell the truth about it: Margaret Thatcher.

## Liquidation

In chapter 3 we left the story of Lawson's and Howe's efforts to undermine Mrs Thatcher at the point at which conditions for sterling's ERM entry had been laid down, at the Madrid summit. A few months later, in late October 1989, Lawson, feeling the intellectual pressure from Mrs Thatcher and Walters, whose analysis was being proved ever more right each day, resigned. The resignation provided an excuse for a 'stalking-horse' to challenge Mrs Thatcher's leadership of the Conservative Party. About 80 MPs voted against her or abstained, enough to cause severe political damage. The party's Eurofanatics, and their allies in Brussels, Strasbourg, Bonn and Rome, as well as in the CBI, the bulk of the British media and the Labour, Liberal and Socialist Workers parties, were confident that the job would soon be finished and Mrs Thatcher unseated. With grim satisfaction they watched as 15% interest rates – Lawson's parting gift – throttled small businesses, particularly the new firms set up by a whole new class of Thatcher-inspired entrepreneurs, and devastated the family finances of home-buyers. In such conditions the poll tax was simply unacceptable to the middle classes and the Tory-voting working-class council-house buyers. The opinion polls and by-election results in 1990 were disastrous for the Tories.

Mrs Thatcher's position became weaker and weaker. Her opposition to the ERM and to EMU was reviled and derided. Soon, John Major, Lawson's successor as Chancellor, had redefined the key ERM entry conditions accepted at Madrid – convergence of Britain's inflation rate with European rates – to 'proximation' of inflation in a forward-looking perspective. And by the spring of 1990 he was making it clear to the press that ERM entry was imminent. Why? Could it be that Major, traumatized by his unhappy three months in the hands of the Foreign Office, was displaying the classic symptoms of 'hostage syndrome': irrational feelings of devotion towards the terrorists who had captured and humiliated him, sympathy for their position, an eager willingness to do anything that might gain their favour, and pathetic gratitude for the smallest mitigation of brutality?

Whatever was going on in Major's mind, it was clearly politically impossible for Mrs Thatcher to restrain him so soon after losing his predecessor. Like it or not – and she most definitely did not like it – she was going to have to let Major take sterling into the ERM. Making the best of a horribly bad job would have to be the primary concern. Thus the timing of entry was dictated entirely by political considerations.

In the end it came immediately before the start of the Tory Party Conference in early October. The hope must have been that it would be a gesture that, while not enough to satisfy the Tory Eurofanatics, would calm the mass of Tory backbenchers persuaded by the Establishment that Britain needed the ERM. It would help if entry was coupled with a reduction in interest rates. The financial markets had persuaded themselves that ERM entry would be good for sterling. The hints from the Treasury, combined with the DM's post-unification softness, had taken sterling back up from a low of DM 2.70 at the end of 1989 to almost DM 3 by the summer, where it remained, give or take a pfennig or two, until the autumn. During the first half of 1990, the British economy had still been growing at around its trend rate – the recession had not yet started. In these circumstances, and with the government committed to maintain monetary conditions tight enough to push inflation back down, it was a common expectation, both in Britain and on the Continent, that an 'ERM honeymoon' effect would take sterling to the top of its band when it entered the system – as had happened with the peseta – thus permitting a cut in interest rates.

On Friday, 4 October, sterling was trading at DM 2.95, a level that corresponded to the middle of Lawson's DM 2.90 to DM 3.00 target range during his 'shadowing' folly. The Treasury, as far as one can see, believed this to be an 'appropriate' level for sterling. The combination of ERM entry (which, on the evidence of sterling's response to several months of hinting, they believed would push sterling up) and a substantial cut in interest rates (which would tend to push sterling down) would keep the currency at this 'right' level while relieving the political pressure coming from mortgage payers and indebted firms.

A variety of myths has subsequently grown up around the choice of the entry rate. For example, Nigel Lawson berates those who claim that DM 2.95 was an unsustainably high rate for sterling: 'I could not help noticing that those who castigated John Major for having joined at the excessively high rate of DM 2.95 to the pound were the same as those who had earlier castigated me for having shadowed the Deutschmark at the excessively low sterling rate of DM 3 to the pound . . . there is no way that it can seriously be maintained both that DM 3 was significantly too low in 1988 and DM 2.95 significantly too high in 1990.' What Lawson fails to recognize is that it is precisely because the appropriate real exchange rate can move very significantly over a two-and-a-half year period that there is no such thing as the 'right' rate in the ERM. For the reasons we saw in chapter 3, the rate that is 'right' for today may not be 'right' for tomorrow, and the rate that would be 'right' for tomorrow might not be 'right' for today. Yet the whole point of the ERM is that today's rate should be the same (give or take movement within the bands) as tomorrow's. The ERM is a system fit only for static, sclerotic economies. In the British economy in the late 1980s, sclerosis was avoided by Tory radicalism but the attempt to find a single 'right' exchange rate induced a near-fatal stroke. DM 3 *was* too low a rate to prevent overheating and inflation in 1987–88. By the summer of 1990, the British economy was just on the cusp: it is possible that DM 2.95 to DM 3 was the 'right' rate for that time. But if it was, it was clearly too high for the period of sharp recession that was just beginning. We shall review the consequences of the decision in more detail in chapter 6.

The most persistent entry myth is that the Bundesbank would have preferred a lower interest rate for sterling, believing DM 2.95 to be unsustainable, and because its wishes were not accommodated eventually took it out on Britain in September 1992. As we shall see, the Bundesbank was indeed unforgiving of British hubris, but the sins it perceived were not those they are commonly supposed to be. The Bundesbank certainly believed DM 2.95 to be an unsustainable rate,[30] but what the Bundesbank really objected to was that Britain entered the system at all. Its fear – or at least the fear of its Monetary Committee member, Tietmeyer – was that the 'ERM paradox' created when the peseta entered the system would be aggravated by sterling entry. Britain's high interest rates (even after the 1 point reduction announced on entry) would, within the ERM, attract capital flows into the country, pushing sterling to the top of its band and creating pressure for British interest rates to fall or for French interest rates to rise.[31] This was not how the ERM was, in Bundesbank eyes, supposed to work. The ERM, they felt, if it was to be tolerable at all would have to operate as in 1983–86, with undisputed German leadership imposing a discipline on other countries and forcing their inflation rates down. The last thing the Bundesbank wanted was another high-inflation, large-current-account-deficit country (a double sinner) coming in to sit at the top of the ERM system in defiance of all principles of good German order. It would be all the more embarrassing that Germany itself was becoming just such a sinner, even if one that could not yet resort as freely as it might have liked to the high-interest-rate medicine.[32]

British negotiators knew this to be the likely Bundesbank reaction and, according to press accounts of the Monetary Committee meeting convened to consider sterling's entry, went armed with graphs and tables showing that the British economy had, after its resilience until the summer, just fallen off the cliff. What they were trying to show was that the ERM would

30 Pöhl had said so shortly before the decision was announced. Lawson subsequently criticized John Major for not having consulted the Bundesbank about the entry rate, emphasizing that *he* had done so, sending *his* officials to Frankfurt, when he had been trying to put sterling in the system in 1985. In 1926 the choice of the rate at which Britain would rejoin the Gold Standard had been that of the Chancellor, Winston Churchill; in 1985 the choice of an ERM entry rate would have been Lawson's; in 1990 the choice of a rate in the middle of Lawson's shadowing range, still favoured by the Treasury, was John Major's.

31 The one grain of truth in the assertion that the Bundesbank wanted a lower entry rate is that, if Britain was determined to enter the system, there would initially be less risk, in Tietmeyer's eyes, of its 'exporting inflation' to Germany if it came in with, in effect, a devaluation of sterling.

32 By early 1993, as we shall see, it suited the Bundesbank's changed circumstances to tell a different story – or at least for Tietmeyer to tell a different story. In this story, a build-up of previous competitiveness losses had forced an inevitable depreciation on sterling, but depreciation had now gone too far, constituting the even more serious sin of 'competitive devaluation' – a charge that will be discussed and rebutted later in this book.

not be a 'soft option' for the British economy preventing a sufficient degree of disinflationary rigour from being imposed, that DM 2.95 was not too *low* a rate.

Recently, an even sillier hare has been set running in Charles Grant's biography of Delors. There, it is claimed that Delors felt DM 2.95 to be too high a rate, one that would eventually lead to pressure on sterling within the ERM and thus turbulence for the system as a whole. The truth is rather different. Delors's main concern was to get rid of his most formidable enemy, Mrs Thatcher.[33] The announcement of British ERM entry angered him precisely because it might offer her a political lifeline, however tenuous. In one of his characteristic explosions of petulance, he had two stormy telephone conversations with Major that Friday afternoon. Delors's pretext for anger was that Britain had not followed the rules – it had announced the entry rate it wanted (DM 2.95) and the bands it wanted (+/−6%) to the markets as a *fait accompli*, instead of asking permission from its 'partners' first. In fact, no one has ever been sure what rules are supposed to apply when a new member seeks admission to the ERM. And Delors himself had shown the utmost contempt for the ERM and the other finance ministers and governors in his prima donna performances during French franc devaluations. But none of that mattered. He did not care *what* the entry rate was, he told his officials, as long as it was not the one announced by the British (and as long as it was expressed in ECU rather than DM);[34] because the request had been for 6% bands, the Commission must insist on 2.25%; and because Britain had already made an announcement, there would have to be a meeting of ministers and governors which would humiliate Britain by forcing it to accede to the Commission demands. Officials were horrified: the Commission would look even sillier than usual if it argued along such lines in the Monetary Committee. But Delors was adamant, telling his top monetary official: *'J'ai déjà liquidé un Directeur-Général qui n'a pas suivi mes ordres; je suis tout-à-fait disposé à en liquider un deuxième.'*[35]

The political consequences of sterling's ERM entry were to be felt much sooner than the economic ones. Mrs Thatcher had to be got rid of quickly.

33 It was not surprising that, in what turned out to be a valedictory utterance in December 1994, he was concerned to make the dubious claim that he had defeated Reagan and Thatcher by installing Socialism as the guiding principle in the European Union.

34 Indeed, it is said that the Commission representative argued in the Monetary Committee for a *higher* entry rate.

35 'I've already liquidated one Director-General who didn't follow my orders; I'm quite prepared to liquidate a second.'

An ideal opportunity was at hand. A European Council was scheduled for late October, under Italian presidency. It was supposed to clear the decks of other business, notably on the GATT talks, so that the normal end-of-presidency summit in December could tackle what were seen as the really big issues relating to the aims and organization of the forthcoming IGCs on political and economic union.[36]

To keen observers, however, it became clear that something was in the air when, for instance, orders were given within the Commission that at all costs the publication of *One Market, One Money*, programmed for just before the December Council, must be advanced: it should now appear immediately before the October Council. *One Market, One Money* was a piece of blatant neo-functionalist propaganda, a set of specious anti-economic arguments and rigged model simulation results intended to give support to the idea – which we saw in chapter 3 to be totally false – that the Single Market in the Community required a single currency if it was to work properly. The document was long, heavy, deliberately technical and abstruse in order both to mask its twisted logic and to impress 'opinion-formers' with its 'scientific' authority.[37] It achieved its aims – at least in the short term, which was what mattered politically – with dismaying completeness.

The something in the air began to smell even nastier when the Christian Democrat cabal met immediately before the Council began. The doyen of Christian Democrats, Andreotti, then Italian Prime Minister and President of the European Council, now in disgrace and undergoing trial on criminal charges including Mafia contacts and complicity in murder, won the agreement of his fellows for an ambush of Mrs Thatcher: the Council would deal with monetary union and would declare that the final phase

36 Mrs Thatcher had been outvoted on the establishment of an IGC on economic union at Madrid in June 1989. Kohl and Mitterrand had produced political union out of a hat in April 1990 (Kohl persuading Mitterrand that he needed some elements of political union if Germany were to accept the monetary union that France had demanded in return for its acceptance of German reunification). The Franco-German diktat had had to be accepted by Mrs Thatcher, given her political difficulties at home, in the Dublin Council in June.

37 The work on the publication was masterminded by Michael Emerson, whom we met briefly in chapter 4. Richard Portes, Director of the Centre for Economic Policy Research and an old chum of Emerson from Balliol days (Jenkins, Emerson's patron, was also a Balliol man), notes that the research project, in which he was invited to join, was originally entitled 'The Costs and Benefits of EMU'; but as time went on, costs disappeared and benefits were played up. Propaganda outweighed analysis. The economics of the publication were immediately demolished by Patrick Minford, a long-time critic of the ERM, but of course that did not deflect Euroenthusiast 'opinion-formers' from giving it a delirious welcome.

would begin on 1 January 1993. Mrs Thatcher, having made so many equivocal concessions under domestic political pressure so often in the past, would be forced out into the open: either she would agree, conceding game, set and match to her foreign enemies, or, more likely, she would have to refuse, leaving the door open for a strike by her British opponents.[38]

The ambush had the expected result. Mrs Thatcher refused to accept that the result of the IGC's would be a foregone conclusion and that EMU would begin, willy-nilly, at an early fixed date.

On the Monday morning following the Rome Council, Jean-François Pons was debriefing his staff.[39] One naive soul asked if the Council had not been a failure, since unanimity had not been achieved. On the contrary, affirmed Pons, the Council had been an outstanding success, since it had re-established an eleven-to-one situation in the Community and would destabilize Mrs Thatcher at home! That afternoon, Mrs Thatcher made her famous and impassioned 'no, no, no' report to the Commons on the Rome ambush, criticizing Delors particularly severely. Two days later, Howe – identified approvingly by Charles Grant as a potent Delors ally – resigned, setting in motion the sequence of events that was to end three weeks later in Mrs Thatcher's tearful departure from Downing Street.[40]

For some weeks after Mrs Thatcher's political execution Delors was even more puffed up and pumped up than usual. In December, John Major, not wishing to be too quick to disillusion the Thatcherite MPs who had just voted for him, made some querulous remark about the size or colour of the hoops that the Commission President was now confidently expecting him to jump through. Delors metaphorically (and perhaps literally) stamped his foot on the ground, threatening that if 'domestic political difficulties' in Britain got in the way of his appointment with Euro-destiny then he would 'not hesitate to provoke a crisis'. The implied

---

38 The leading Westminster Conservative most openly in thrall to Christian Democracy is David Hunt. In December 1994 he told Eurofanatic Conservatives in a private meeting that he was proud that the party had been ridded of Thatcherism. 'Conservative' Euro-MPs, of course, are locked in a passionate embrace with Christian Democrats in Strasbourg. There are undoubtedly many fellow-travellers in Westminster.

39 Pons was an *énarque*. He had previously worked in Pierre Bérégovoy's cabinet in Paris and then in the French Treasury, until his bosses decided French interests would be better suited by moving him to Brussels.

40 For some time afterwards, rumours circulated in the Commission that Howe's wounding resignation speech had its origins in Brussels. This seems unlikely, and most observers claim to detect the hand of his wife; but consultation with Brussels about the timing and content of the speech would not be a surprise.

message was clear: '*J'ai déjà liquidé un premier ministre qui n'a pas suivi mes ordres; je suis tout-à-fait disposé à en liquider un deuxième.*'

## The empire strikes back

By the end of 1990, the Bundesbank was beginning to emerge from the immmediate post-unification quiescence that had raised so many questions about the ERM anchor. Both the need and the opportunity for action were becoming more evident. The opportunity was concerned with domestic politics: the general elections were out of the way, with Kohl back in the driving seat; it was 'tell-the-truth' time about the costs of unification, and Finance Minister Theo Waigel started making it clear how much the budget deficit was going to increase. And the unions' opening wage demands for 1991 were pointing to a sharp increase in West German inflation.

The Bundesbank would have no shortage of domestic excuses for a tightening of monetary policy. The need for action came both from its embarrassment at relative DM weakness in the ERM and from its fears that EMU might soon become unstoppable after the Rome and December European Councils. The two were linked, of course. Towards the end of 1989 both Pöhl and Tietmeyer had been peddling the line that the ERM already constituted a monetary union, and one that – since it was led by the Bundesbank – would be better than the Delors version. Events in 1990, both in the German economy and in Europolitics, had since made it much less likely that a Bundesbank-dominated quasi-union via the ERM could hold the line against the institutional approach of a revised Treaty of Rome and the creation of a European Central Bank and a single currency. If the ERM was now the 'glidepath' to EMU rather than an alternative to it, perhaps, some Council members seemed to think, a little turbulence was called for. It was time for the Bundesbank to reassert its authority. The asymmetric real shock of unification implied a real appreciation of the DM. Germany's 'partners' would not allow a nominal appreciation within the ERM (and would not be happy if the whole ERM as a bloc moved up against third currencies such as the dollar). So German inflation would instead have to rise relative to inflation elsewhere. The behaviour of the French authorities had made it plain that France would be happy to follow German inflation upwards. Yet, with domestic political constraints now loosened, the Bundesbank was rightly determined that the *absolute* rise in German inflation that was now in train must go no further and must indeed be reversed. The only remaining route that Germany's real appreciation could follow was an absolute reduction in the inflation rate of its main trading partners, notably France. If the French would not allow a DM revaluation, then they would have to endure the recession that would reduce their inflation rate.

These distressing implications for France applied *a fortiori* to countries whose need was now or was soon to be to *improve* their own competitiveness – countries such as Britain and Spain (for reasons we have seen), Portugal (whose circumstances were very similar to Spain's), Italy and Denmark (whose problems we shall investigate in a subsequent chapter). In short, the other ERM countries were going to have to pay very dear for their membership, and the federalist aspirations of Delors, Mitterrand, Kohl, Gonzalez, Andreotti, Haughey, Schluter, Martens, Lubbers, Hurd and Cavaço Silva.

At all events, Bundesbank determination to regain top-dog status in the ERM, repay Bonn for the unification humiliation and force other countries, France in particular, to lie on the bed of nails they had made for themselves, was increased in mid-1991 by the resignation of Karl Otto Pöhl. The Bundesbank President's relations with Bonn, difficult ever since the announcement of monetary unification plans, deteriorated sharply in March 1991 when he described unification as a 'disaster'. Two months later, apparently for a mix of personal and professional reasons, he decided he had had enough and announced he was quitting, three-and-a-half-years early.

The consequent hardening of the Bundesbank's attitude was not the result of the institution's desire to avenge a fallen leader. (Pöhl had never had a particularly close relationship either with his staff or with his Council colleagues.) Instead, it was the elevation of Helmut Schlesinger to succeed him that had a profound effect on the bank's actions. Schlesinger has been described – ambivalently – as 'the boy scout of central banking' by David Marsh, chronicler of the Bundesbank, and – disapprovingly – as 'a German nationalist' by Helmut Schmidt. He spent his whole career in the Bundesbank, working his way up the hierarchical ladder and gaining a place on the Directorate in 1972. He is widely regarded as the soul of the Bundesbank and, from the time that Pöhl took over the President's role from Otmar Emminger in 1980, as the main force in the bank's decision-making. His devotion and loyalty to his institution was rewarded with a similar devotion and loyalty from his staff. Unlike Pöhl and Tietmeyer, he never felt more at home with 'the monetary masters of the world' than with the Bundesbank's own officials and with ordinary Germans (this is presumably what Schmidt – who had reason to dislike him after the 1981 interest rates episode[41] – meant by calling him a 'nationalist'). He certainly had a remarkable feel for the concerns of the German public. In particular, he had no desire to see his own institution sacrificed, along with the DM, to satisfy the aspirations of Eurofederalists, whether in Germany or else-where. A Bavarian, he is a conservative, close to the thinking of the CDU's Bavarian sister party, the CSU, but not personally committed to Kohl in the way Tietmeyer is. In appearance, he fits everyone's image of the kindly grandfather. His voice is attractive, sonorous and reassuring. Unfortun-ately, although he speaks excellent English, the slight additional strain of expressing himself in a foreign language often produces a rather fixed, nervous-seeming smile and a verbal tic. That may have led non-German-speakers to underestimate his toughness, as well as the extent to which he was in tune with, and could influence, German public opinion.

Marsh, writing in 1992, rather surprisingly says of him that: 'He was not . . . equipped with the political capacity to confront and master the extraordinary challenge suddenly confronting the institution which he had made his life.' We shall see that in fact Schlesinger possessed political skills of a very high order: by the time he retired in the early autumn of 1993, the Bundesbank was once again – in appearance at least – lord of all it surveyed. No doubt most satisfying of all, from Schlesinger's point of view, the French challenge to the German anchor role in European exchange-rate relations (to all intents and purposes the ERM would no longer be in existence) would have been resoundingly defeated.

The very first meeting of the Bundesbank Council under Schlesinger's presidency, at the beginning of September 1991, gave due warning of the shape of things to come by increasing key interest rates by half a point. The screw was slowly being turned – on the German government, on the unions and on the narrow-band ERM, France in particular. Among these objects of unfriendly Bundesbank attention, the German government was to be the first to make the mistake of engaging in public recrimination, as we shall soon see. The French, for their part, had been doing their best not to antagonize the Bundesbank too openly during 1991. One reason for this most unaccustomed emollience was the need to smooth the path to Maastricht and the treaty revision that would, they hoped, mean the end of the Bundesbank. They did not want to make life difficult for Kohl by giving

41 See chapter 2.

the bank the chance to stir up German public opinion against the EMU project. But a second reason had been created in the first half of the year by short-term tactical needs within the ERM. German interest rates were not of themselves a major problem for France in 1991. Differentials were still coming down as Europhoria about prospects for a single currency – and thus complete interest-rate convergence – increasingly gripped the markets. Germany's demand boom meant strong French exports and the French economy was growing reasonably rapidly.[42] The bigger problem was that the nudging upwards of German interest rates, combined with a continued decline in French differentials vis-à-vis Germany and its Benelux satellites, had left the French franc the lowest-placed currency in the ERM.

## Peseta pest

The gap between the French franc and the other narrow-band currencies was not large. Annoyingly, however, the peseta was making a nuisance of itself, jammed up against the top of its wide 6% band as foreign capital continued to flood into Spain. The upward pressure took the peseta to the very limit of its permitted fluctuation margin against the lowest currency, the French franc – and, by the formal symmetry of the system, the French franc was at the very limit of its fluctuation margin against the peseta. In the technical jargon of the system, the two currencies were 'in opposition'; and in plain language, the two countries were in opposition about what should be done.

Such a situation was unprecedented in the ERM. There had been many times in the past when the French franc (or the lira, the Belgian franc or the Danish krone) had been 'in opposition' with the DM or its Dutch surrogate. In the 1979–83 period, the answer had been clear: the weak currency had to devalue, even if spin doctors such as Delors tried to package the realignments as revaluations of the strong currencies. In the March 1983–January 1987 period, the answer was equally clear: the weak-currency country had to grit its teeth, introduce austerity measures and try to become more 'virtuous' – and then devalue nonetheless. Such outcomes

---

42 It was not growing fast enough to ameliorate the increasingly menacing unemployment problem, but the measures that would in 1991 at least, have been necessary to stimulate growth and employment were Thatcherite – unlikely to appeal to the Delorsian French Prime Minister, Edith Cresson, at a time when farmers were rioting and ministers were forbidden to leave Paris because their safety could not be guaranteed in provincial France.

were wholly in line with the prevailing 'philosophy' of the ERM in those two periods, as we discovered it in chapter 2.

But now, the bottom currency in the ERM was that of an officially 'virtuous' country, France, with low inflation, a healthy budgetary position (in those far-off, happy days) and a balanced current account. The top country, in contrast, had high inflation and a large current-account deficit, even if its budget seemed (in those days) under reasonable control.

A realignment was out of the question. For one thing, it would damage the 'glidepath' illusion; but even without that constraint, there was no way that a peseta–franc realignment would be possible. A French devaluation would be unthinkable: so much political capital had been invested in proclaiming the *'franc fort'* and in getting the Germans to accept it that France would exert every one of the many means of political blackmail against Spain available to it in the Community to prevent one. A peseta revaluation was also out, for the unwritten rules of the ERM meant that no currency was allowed to realign upwards against the DM, least of all a 'bad' currency such as the peseta. This feature of the system was self-reinforcing: if a currency other than the DM could not revalue when necessary, inflation would develop, there would be a loss of confidence and an economic 'bust' ultimately necessitating *devaluation*. Devaluation of other currencies reinforced market, political and public perceptions of the DM as the strongest currency and thus strengthened the interdiction or revaluations against it. The most important thing, economically, that a country gives up in the ERM (and *a fortiori* in monetary union) is not, as claimed by Euroenthusiasts, its right to devalue but its right to *revalue* and thus to *avoid* boom-busts and, in the ERM, subsequent devaluations.

In the Spanish case, how were the tensions in the ERM to be resolved without a realignment? There would have to be a change in relative interest rates. Should the French raise their interest rates to strengthen the franc or should the Spanish reduce theirs to weaken the peseta? The Spanish authorities, or at least the Banco de España, had no desire to reduce Spanish rates. Spanish inflation had edged up after ERM entry, to the embarrassment of the authorities, whose flimsy economic cover for the political decision to enter had been that expectations would be 'disciplined' by the ERM, smoothing the convergence of Spanish inflation with the rest of the Community.

From the point of view of the ERM as a whole, or at least of its advertised goal of price stability, the outcome should have been a rise in French rates, since this would move the ERM-area *as a whole* towards price stability, while a cut in Spanish rates would have moved the area *as a whole* away from price stability. If – as the Commission analysis at the end of 1990 had uncomfortably made clear – the ERM was to act as a 'glidepath' to EMU, then countries must take monetary policy decisions on the basis of what was right for the area as a whole rather than for them individually.

From the French point of view, raising interest rates to 'defend' the franc against the peseta was not an option. Most Frenchmen regard Spain as being halfway to the Third World, and such an outcome would have been an unbearable humiliation, one that could have turned public opinion – and even some political opinion – against the ERM. At a deeper level, if the ERM situation had forced a rise in French rates, then the whole idea of EMU would have come into question from one angle or another. In French eyes, the point of EMU, in monetary terms at least, was to get French hands on the Bundesbank. But what would happen in EMU if the needs of a collection of tin-pot countries such as Spain had an influence on monetary policy in the area as a whole? To give way now in the game of 'opposition' with the peseta would imply that, in EMU, specifically French interests would continue to be submerged: getting hands on the Bundes-bank would be an illusory victory. The needs of the system as a whole? Price stability in the Community? *'Je m'en fiche.'*

If French hypocrisy about the ERM and EMU was only to be expected, the Bundesbank's position may have disappointed those who saw it as a missionary intent on exporting the good news of price stability to pagan neighbours. The Bundesbank, in the hulking shape of Tietmeyer, sided with the French.[43] He did not want to upset France during the Maastricht negotiations, any more than the French wanted to upset Tietmeyer's more Germanocentric colleagues on the Bundesbank Council. But more than that, he had specific reasons for not supporting Spain. Recall that in November 1989 he had meted out harsh criticism of Spain's 'excessively high' interest rates and 'expansionary' budgetary policy. Tietmeyer was more affronted by the 'ERM paradox' than anyone. If anything, his distaste for what was happening had increased since then as a result of German unification. The last thing he wanted was to give his benediction to a Spanish use of monetary policy to combat inflation. What lessons might be applied to Germany? The hawks in the Bundesbank Council might start to

43 Tietmeyer had pretty much a free run on ERM matters under Pöhl. As Directorate member responsible for international monetary affairs, he represented the Bundesbank not only in the Monetary Committee but also in the Committee of Alternates of the Central Bank Governors, the body that had the greatest influence in the technical running of the EMS (see chapter 1).

believe that *they* could rid Germany of its post-unification inflationary hangover with the pill of sharply higher interest rates. What lessons might be applied to the rest of Europe? That domestically oriented monetary decisions, rather than simply following the Bundesbank, might be the best anti-inflationary path.

In Tietmeyer's book, the main job of a central bank was to moan at delinquent governments and trade unions, always threatening a tough monetary policy if good behaviour were not restored, but never actually implementing one for fear of engendering political and economic conflict. We shall have opportunities later in this narrative to reflect on the merits and demerits of Tietmeyer's approach to central banking. But its practical application to the ERM in 1991 was directly at odds with the Bundesbank's 1990 declaration – drafted by Tietmeyer himself – on EMU. The doctrine of 'all for one and one for all' should, in the conditions of 1991, have implied Bundesbank support for Spain against France. Instead, Tietmeyer sniped at the 'ERM paradox': the peseta's position at the top of the system was an aberration, and it was the job of the Spanish authorities, no one else, to get it down.

That is what in fact happened. With France and Germany standing together, Spain had no choice but to toe the line that had been drawn for it. The Banco de España, with extreme reluctance, several times trimmed Spanish interest rates, solely to relieve pressure on the French franc.

By the second half of 1991, sterling had joined, and ultimately replaced, the franc 'in opposition' with the peseta. Indeed, in the period between October 1991 and April 1992, the sterling/peseta exchange rate was almost constant, with a gap close to the maximum 6%. Some academic commentators have interpreted this in absurd fashion, claiming that the peseta, not the DM, was the constraint on an easing in British monetary conditions. This is simply not so. Cuts in British interest rates continued during this period. It was only when British rates hit the floor constituted by German rates that the process stopped, and, as we shall see later, that the ERM constraint became unbearable. It is more accurate to say that, as in the case of the French franc, sterling was the main influence on Spanish monetary policy, which faithfully accommodated successive British loosenings. 'Influence' is a better word here than 'constraint', for by late 1991 and early 1992 the Spanish authorities were becoming concerned about the slowdown in their own economy. A gradual loosening of Spanish monetary policy was by now not unwelcome to them – to the government, at least.

All the same, if British monetary policy was not constrained by the peseta, it is very likely that policy in *other* areas – on reactions to Spain's demands for additional handouts at Maastricht at the end of 1991 and subsequently in the negotiations on the 'Delors 2' package of transfers;[44] on fishing questions; on the CAP; the position of Gibraltar, and in particular, fraud in Spain relating to milk quotas – was shaped by the perceived need to maintain Spain's 'accommodating' attitude on the sterling/peseta rate.[45]

In sum, the ERM had been in disarray in 1990. It had prevented the DM appreciation so necessary for economic stability not only in Germany but elsewhere in Europe. Its economic *raison d'être*, always dubious at best, had collapsed. Yet three new currencies were lured into joining the system or pegging to its notional cornerstone, the ECU, despite economic circumstances that made the decision suicidal.[46] By 1991 the operation of the system was unambiguously perverse. Its contradictions had been exposed: yet the managers of the system closed their eyes. The limping, discredited mechanism was clung to with greater tenacity than ever, its praises sung by just about all 'respectable' politicians and commentators, the markets gulled by falling differentials into thinking it stronger and more stable than ever. Discussion of the system's faults was prohibited; it was nothing more than a receptacle for great torrents of cant and doubletalk. The reason for maintaining the Big Lie of the ERM was the Even Bigger Lie of EMU: and Maastricht was now on the doorstep.

44 'Delors 2' was the Community budget package agreed by the European Council, largely in line with Delors's proposals, to increase transfer payments to the poorer member states. 'Delors 1' was a similar but smaller package to accompany the Single European Act.

45 Two of the foremost academic apologists for the ERM and EMU, Nils Thygesen (himself a member of the Delors Committee) and Daniel Gros, writing in March 1992, make the doubly preposterous assertion that: 'The present arrangements [in the ERM] have kept monetary policy largely in the hands of central bankers and thus [sic] free of direct political interference, at least in the EMS.'

46 Between November 1990 and the summer of 1991 Norway, Sweden and Finland all pegged to the ECU, hoping that this gesture would soften the opposition of France, Italy and Spain, the main proponents of the ECU, to the Nordic countries' membership of the Community. In so doing, they were to earn the displeasure of many in the Bundesbank who would, at this delicate time for the German currency, have preferred a vote of confidence in the form of pegs to the DM.

# PART TWO

# 5

# Gambling at Maastricht

## Chalk and cheese

By late 1991, the Bundesbank had tried a variety of stratagems to head off the threat of EMU. It had made a severe political miscalculation over German monetary union. By criticizing and, implicitly, opposing the government on an issue where Bonn had overwhelming public support, the bank had damaged its own credibility. It could not afford to make the same mistake twice. And the Bonn government had, ever since the foundation of the Federal Republic, been able to count on unthinking support for greater European integration. Naturally, the public enthusiasm for giving up the DM was very much less, but monetary union was never presented in such terms by the government. Rather, the official message was hardly different from that propagated by the Reichsbank during the early years of the Second World War: Germany was exporting monetary order to the rest of Europe. Even the Delors Report was represented in such a way in Germany. Pöhl, a signatory of the Report, said in an interview shortly after its publication that: 'If the idea spread and the German population understood what it [European Monetary Union] is about – namely, that it centres on their money, and that decisions on it would be taken not by the Bundesbank, but by a new institution – then I would imagine that considerable resistance might arise.' Yet the Bundesbank made no public effort to tell the German public what EMU meant: the taboo against criticism of European integration was so strong that the bank remained silent. Instead of telling the German people what would be involved for them – the loss of the DM – the Bundesbank instead concentrated on the conditions that, in its view, would be necessary for EMU to represent the extension of the DM's domain to the rest of Europe.

Several members of the Council were aghast when the Maastricht agreement was finally revealed. What was agreed to was an apparently clever but in reality destructive compromise between the two traditionally opposed views of monetary union. The so-called 'economist view', traditionally espoused in Germany and the Netherlands, was that economic convergence must precede monetary union, which would otherwise be damaging and unsustainable. The so-called 'monetarist' view (which had nothing to do with the 'monetarism' of Milton Friedman and his followers), held most strongly in France and Italy, claimed on the contrary that monetary union would *produce* economic convergence. In the first view, monetary union was a distant *goal*; in the second, an *instrument*, to be used immediately, to achieve the supposed goal of convergence. The Maastricht agreement made a bow to the 'monetarist' view by specifying fixed dates for monetary union, but also acknowledged the 'economist' arguments by laying down criteria, in terms of inflation convergence and budgetary good behaviour, for entry to the union. All the twelve countries could sign the agreement, but there were very divergent views about what it meant. What would happen if too few countries had met the convergence criteria by the set dates (an absolute majority of countries by 1997, or a minimum of two countries by 1999)? Which would prevail? If the date took priority, then the 'monetarist' view had won; if it was the criteria, then the 'economists' would be the victors.

The unhappiness of many Bundesbank Council members sprang from the realization that several of the signatory countries did not have a hope in hell of respecting all the criteria by 1997. Yet those were precisely the countries that did not want 'to miss the bus', or 'find themselves in the slow lane'. The obvious implication was that the convergence criteria were a sham which could be 'interpreted' into innocuousness by the Commission and national politicians. There was a strong feeling that Germany, or at least the Bundesbank, had been 'had'. Their fears were increased when, immediately after Maastricht, Kohl told the Bundestag: 'I repeat: this Europe [of Maastricht] will have a common currency in 1997 or 1999. One has to think about what that means: a common currency from Copenhagen to Madrid, from The Hague to Rome.' Kohl's *ex cathedra* statement seemed to indicate that the convergence criteria were merely ornamental: a political decision had been taken on which countries would take part in EMU (not Britain, Ireland, Portugal and Greece – or was Kohl's geography rather vague?). What would happen, asked Nölling, if only France and Denmark fulfilled the criteria by 1999? Could anyone believe that the politicians would not nonetheless go ahead? The fact that the supposed irreversibility of the Maastricht process, inserted at the last moment by Mitterrand and Kohl, had found its way into the Maastricht agreement would, said Nölling, make people rub their eyes in disbelief.[1]

Yet still the Bundesbank was strangely reluctant to come out openly and say that Maastricht, if applied, quite unambiguously meant the demise of the DM. Schlesinger himself was conscious that the Bundesbank's conditions had been met, formally at least, and he was, as a central banker, in no position to brand the heads of government or foreign ministers of other Community countries as liars and cheats (in the cases of certain of them, that was subsequently to be the task of the press or magistrates in their own countries). Instead he had to content himself with an indirect strategy – drawing to the attention of the German public statements by others that the Bundesbank could not make itself. The chosen vehicle was the *Auszüge*, the Bundesbank's weekly publication comprising reprints of selected articles and speeches on monetary matters. Just before Maastricht, Schlesinger had personally ordered a German translation, to appear in the *Auszüge*, of a paper given at a somewhat obscure academic conference in America by Martin Feldstein, a very distinguished American economist, former Chairman of the Council of Economic Advisers under Ronald Reagan and a constant scourge of the proponents of international economic 'coordination'. The paper was a scathing, root-and-branch attack on monetary union, predicting not only economic but also political calamity in Europe if it came to pass. Normally, papers reprinted in the *Auszüge* appear in their original language. Schlesinger's desire to see Feldstein's arguments made publicly available in Germany was a telling sign of his own deeply felt worries.

Shortly after Maastricht, the *Auszüge* carried, again translated into German for the benefit of German public opinion, an interview given to a French newspaper by Jacques de Larosière, Governor of the Banque de France. In it, he emphasized the view that Maastricht meant a *strengthening*, not a weakening, of French monetary sovereignty. He made it as clear as he possibly could, without actually using the words 'getting our hands on the Bundesbank', that in his eyes Maastricht represented a triumph for the strategy launched by Balladur in January 1988, De Larosière went on to point out that, according to Maastricht, national currencies would disap-

1 According to one academic account of the Maastrict conference, Kohl's agreement to the 'irrevocable' final date of 1999 came at the last moment in response to wheedling from Andreotti and created great consternation in the German delegation – consternation shared by the Finance Minister, Theo Waigel.

pear 'very quickly' once Stage Three of EMU began, to be replaced by 'the écu'. Yet the German government was trying to give the impression that somehow EMU did not endanger the DM.[2]

In short, Maastricht, and the spin doctors' efforts to present it, was a papering over of very deep political cracks – within Germany, within the Bundesbank, between Germany and the southern countries and, most important of all, between Germany and France. These fissures were not to be brought fully into the open even in the French Maastricht referendum campaign in 1992. It was only in the autumn of 1994, when the CDU published plans for a 'hard-core' union in Europe, that a furore was created in Spain and Italy and that the true nature of the choice confronting France began to be realized there, leading to, among other things, the withdrawal of Delors from the presidential election race.[3]

## The Maastricht Handicap Hurdle

If the instability of the Maastricht compromise in political terms was not to become generally apparent at once, the economic instability it generated was to make itself felt much more rapidly. One of the treaty's convergence criteria specified that for a country to enter Stage Three of EMU (membership of a single currency area managed by a European Central Bank), its currency must have participated for at least two years in the 'normal bands' of the ERM[4] without capital controls, 'severe tensions' or

2 Few members of the Council were much impressed when Tietmeyer's successor as State Secretary at the Finance Ministry, Horst Köhler, said in April 1992 that through EMU 'a good piece of German identity' was, far from being abandoned, exported to other countries. 'We should not fear that the others are taking away the D-Mark and our stability.' It was partly in response to such statements that, for six months after Maastricht, one Council member after another, in speeches, articles or interviews, stressed the primacy of the criteria over the dates, emphasizing the vast amount of work that certain other countries had to do if they were to pre-establish the *Kultur* of low inflation so necessary for EMU to work, and redoubling the emphasis on the political union implications of EMU.

3 The journalist Paul Fabra, writing in *Le Monde* on 13 December 1991, saw this much sooner than most others: 'Each of the two main protagonists, Germany and France, has acted in such a way that the most difficult decisions, the breaks with long-established habits, have been pushed back as far as possible. But at the same time they have fixed a rendezvous – before the year 2000 – close enough to give their enterprise the character of a major challenge . . . The combination is so unstable that all bets on the outcome remain open.'

4 At the time the treaty was written, everyone knew that 'normal bands' meant 'narrow bands'. Subsequently the meaning has become open to interpretation – something that could give the German Constitutional Court a justification for declaring any decision to proceed to Stage Three unconstitutional and invalid under German law.

requesting a devaluation. The treaty thus enshrined the concept of the ERM as a 'glidepath' to EMU – or at least it did so in the eyes of most countries. However, the Bundesbank had, during the course of the Maastricht negotiations, succeeded in fighting off French proposals to codify the rules and practices of the ERM as part of the treaty. If the ERM had become a treaty instrument then the 'Emminger Letter' would be overruled by Community law. Worse, the new Stage Two institution[5] – the European Monetary Institute, which the Bundesbank was determined to restrict to a brass-plate role – would have a legal justification for intervening in interest-rate and intervention decisions.

Now, after Maastricht, many Bundesbank Council members were determined to show that the ERM was still a voluntary mechanism and Germany still its anchor. Just before the Maastricht meeting, the Bundesbank set an impossibly tight money target for 1992. On 19 December, the first Council meeting after the agreement on the treaty, the Bundesbank raised both its official rates, the discount rate and the Lombard rate, by half a point, taking the Lombard rate to a postwar record of 9.75%[6] If other countries wanted to follow, that was up to them. If they did not, they would have to take the consequences on their exchange rate. Of course, a few days after agreeing the Maastricht Treaty, those countries that thirsted after the taming of the Bundesbank that EMU would bring had no real choice but to accept that the Bundesbank was master *now*. But they did it with an ill grace. The Italian press spoke of the rate rise as 'a German hatchet-job' on Maastricht. Bérégovoy, after a long period of verbal self-restraint while the treaty was being negotiated, now felt moved – with the agreement in the bag – to brand the Bundesbank decision 'a victory of German selfishness over international solidarity'. Revealingly, one Bundesbank Council member, Lothar Müller, spoke gleefully of these reactions in a speech just a few days later. If the French and Italians, he seemed to be saying, who had seduced Kohl thought they had now got their hands on the Bundesbank, then the Bundesbank would prove them wrong!

5 'Stage Two' as defined by the Delors Report and the Rome Council of October 1990 – Padoa-Schioppa heavily influencing both – would see the European Central Bank (ECB) already in existence before the final locking (that is, disappearance) of national currencies. The Stage Two ECB would already play the role of coordinating monetary policies and preparing the single monetary policy of Stage Three. This was somewhat watered down in Maastricht, the EMI – with very limited functions – being ordained instead. Padoa-Schioppa himself has expressed disgust in print at this move away from his blueprint.

6 As we saw in chapter 2, however, the Lombard rate was suspended in 1981–82 and the rate at which the Bundesbank provided emergency liquidity to the market reached 13%.

To the chagrin of Frankfurt, the first financial market reactions to Maastricht seemed to mark an intensification of 'Europhoria'. Most galling of all, both prices and the volume of new issues in the ECU bond market rose smartly in the first month or two following the agreement. The implication was that markets expected a single currency to emerge. 'Convergence plays' were being made. To cut through the technical detail, this meant that funds were being put into the high-interest-rate currencies, including the ECU (which, before Stage Three, was in effect a weighted basket of the Community currencies), in the expectation that Maastricht-style convergence along a no-realignment 'glidepath' to EMU would produce capital gains on bonds, with no risk of currency depreciation. Nonetheless, these 'convergence plays' did not eliminate differentials in long-term interest rates. Indeed, differentials remained high enough on the lira, peseta and escudo to indicate that holders of bonds in these currencies required compensation for the risk of substantial devaluations. The nature of the financial market gamble in the Maastricht compromise between 'economists' and 'monetarists' should have been clear: it was a race against time. *If* countries such as Spain and Italy made sufficient progress on meeting the EMU entry criteria,[7] the risk of devaluation would be seen by markets as diminishing, and bond prices would indeed rise. But if they did not, markets would bring forward the prospect of devaluation, and even short-term interest-rate differentials would have to rise. There would be a crisis, an exchange-rate realignment, and the country concerned would find itself excluded from the first, 1997, 'rendezvous'. However, such a prospect could be expected to be so horrible, given the known predilections of the governments in power in the relevant countries at the time, that those governments would perform whatever 'convergence' was necessary to avoid it: they would win the race against time.

The success of this Maastricht strategy depended on three conditions.

7  These involved convergence in inflation rates and long-term interest rates; limiting government deficits to no more than 3% of GDP, except on a 'temporary' or 'exceptional' basis; limiting public debt to no more than 60% unless the ratio was declining at a 'satisfactory' pace; membership of the 'normal' band of the ERM for a period of at least two years before the beginning of Stage Three while avoiding, without capital controls or 'severe tensions', a devaluation at the initiative of the country concerned within that 'normal' band. The various qualifications and ambiguities in the criteria, together with the fact that they are not, strictly speaking, *conditions* at all but merely a guide for the political judgement of the members of the European Council, means that, even in mid-1995, no one knows exactly how they will be interpreted or even how much attention will be paid to them when the time comes to make a decision on Stage Three.

First, the 'prize' to be won at the end of the race – participation in a single currency from 1997 onwards – must always be on offer. So anything that threatened to derail the Maastricht timetable would reduce the incentives for the authorities to go through the pain barrier in striving for the prize. Second, the authorities must continue to lust after the prize – or be allowed to by their electorates. Any doubts about their commitment to the single currency might lower their convergence 'pain threshold'. So the prospect of a change of government might, if a potential successor government were believed to be less committed to EMU, unsettle market expectations. Third, the pain of convergence within the ERM must not become unbearable. If it did, then however great the prize might seem, the markets might expect the runner to retire from the race. In other words, factors such as recession and unemployment might be considered by the markets as more important 'fundamentals' than the Maastricht convergence criteria. As we shall see in later chapters, all three conditions were very soon to come into question, with dramatic results. But in the spring of 1992 the odds in the race appeared attractive enough to tempt one of the most heavily handicapped runners, Portugal, into attempting the hurdle of ERM membership.

## Last huzzah

The Portuguese bond market is hardly one of the world's most developed. Indeed, it had been so thin and illiquid, especially in the fixed-rate sector, that Portuguese negotiators in the Maastricht preparations had had some doubts about agreeing to the Stage Three convergence criterion relating to long-term interest rates. Sharp, erratic price movements are not uncommon in such markets – a single large buy or sell order can upset the balance of the market quite significantly. Nonetheless, there seemed something rather odd when, in the middle of the first week in April, Portuguese bond prices started moving up, then up again, then up further still, for no apparent reason. Such movements are often associated with rumours about important events said to be impending. But the gossip that week was as thin as the market itself. Some market players, it seems, must have been reading the political runes and making guesses about an event that would change the relationship between bond prices and the exchange rate.

On the evening of Friday, after the markets had closed, rumours started to fly. They were confirmed next morning by an official announcement from the Finance Ministry: the escudo was going to enter the ERM; a meeting of the Monetary Committee had been convened for that afternoon in Brussels. Whoever had been buying bonds had guessed right. In the last weeks, as it turned out, of Europhoria, commitment to the ERM was seen as locking on to the EMU 'glidepath' with all that was fondly believed to imply in terms of long-term interest-rate convergence. For a 'high-yielder' like Portugal, that meant falling long-term rates, rising bond prices.

Yet there was grim foreboding in the Bank of Portugal. Its Vice-Governor, Antonio Borges (whose acquaintance we shall make more fully later), probably had clearer ideas about the ERM than any other central banker – and certainly than any minister or Treasury official – in Europe. He had absorbed the lessons of experience in Denmark, Britain and – most significant of all, from a Portuguese perspective – Spain. He was convinced that Portugal, with its high inflation rate (almost 13% in 1990) and relatively dynamic growth (more than 10% over the years 1989–90), needed the freedom to pursue its own monetary policies until the economy was on a more even keel. He had, in fact, been a partisan of an appreciating escudo during the boom. In October 1990, Borges managed to persuade the government to allow a modest appreciation of the escudo. He would have liked a stronger appreciation, not only to bear down on inflation but also to squeeze low-productivity sectors, thus releasing resources for the modern, higher-productivity activities that foreigners wanted to invest in – but traditional exporters, in textiles and leather in particular, exerted a disproportionate influence on the government. Nonetheless, the somewhat more rational policy gave the monetary authorities better control over liquidity in the economy, and inflation started to subside a little.

Yet controls on inward investment still had to be maintained – if they were removed, the escudo would appreciate more than the traditional exporters could allow the government to countenance, and there would be severe political pressure on the Bank of Portugal to reduce interest rates. The controls were unfortunate in that they helped insulate not only the escudo but also the archaic, protected and inefficient Portuguese banking and financial systems. Indeed, much of the capital inflow from abroad was aimed at buying into the banking system – the large spread of lending rates over money market rates that the uncompetitive structure allowed was a honeypot for foreign banks, who were sure their modern management and technology could wipe the floor with the indigenous houses.

The Finance Minister, Jorge Braga de Macedo, who came to office in October 1991, replacing his old school classmate, Miguel Beleza, was very much in favour of improving the efficiency of the Portuguese financial system. A former academic, he had been a Director in the EC Commission's economics Directorate-General before returning to Portugal to claim the parliamentary seat and ministerial office that his family background and his personal contacts made almost a right. Braga de Macedo was a man prone to being enraptured by buzz-words. He railed against 'financial repression' in Portugal and advocated a 'régime change'. He was quite right in thinking that financial and other structural reforms would be very important in Portugal's development – just as Lawson had been wholly right in his advocacy of radical structural reform in Britain. Unlike Lawson, he had been made well aware of the destabilizing effects of pegged exchange rates in such circumstances. But he was unlike Lawson in another respect, too. Like his Prime Minister, Anibal Cavaço Silva, he was a fervent supporter of EMU.

He was determined both to remove exchange controls *and* put the escudo in the ERM, a combination that was bound, it seemed, to give a perfect ERM-based excuse for lower interest rates. The Bank of Portugal, and Borges in particular, continued to fight hard against this. By early 1992, much of earlier demand exuberance in Portugal was petering out, but inflation remained at above 10% at the beginning of the year. Braga de Macedo recited the usual mantra of 'régime change' and 'credibility' in favour of ERM entry: Borges riposted with the need to maintain a tighter monetary policy than the ERM would allow in the short run. Braga grew impatient: Portugal could not afford politically to stay much longer as the only Community country, apart from the clearly hopeless case of Greece, not to be a member of the ERM.

The Portuguese government had also observed the 'opposition' between the peseta and sterling. They may well have suspected that Spain was doing very nicely, thank you, out of this, being able to twist British arms in the Community horse-trading game. In mid-March the British Parliament was dissolved, with elections due early in April. The received wisdom was that there would be a hung Parliament in Britain and sterling was likely to be particularly weak. The escudo, if it entered the ERM, would be in a position that would allow Portugal to blackmail Britain at a particularly delicate and sensitive time in British politics. This consideration appears to have been the clincher in deciding the timing of the escudo's entry application.

There were two remaining questions: the choice of bands and the entry rate. On the first, Braga had no option but to ask for wide 6% bands. The Bank of Portugal, in the shape of Borges, its Monetary Committee member, might show open dissent if asked to swallow narrow bands. The Spanish would have their noses put severely out of joint if Portugal leapfrogged them straight into the 'normal' band. Most important of all, if the escudo entered the narrow band it would find itself 'in opposition' not with the currency of a country led by the weak-kneed Major and Hurd, but with the French franc or even, at times, the DM itself. Portugal could not expect to exert political pressure on France and Germany. Whatever the situation had been between France and Spain in 1991 ahead of Maastricht, the French would kick Portugal very hard where it hurt most if the escudo started causing trouble for the French franc. In any case, the narrow-band countries would simply send Portuguese representatives away with a flea in their ear if there was any mention of narrow bands.

The entry rate appeared to give more scope for political manoeuvring. Braga tried to use it to the full. He announced to the world before the Monetary Committee meeting started that the escudo's central rate on entry would be below the prevailing market rate. Now the experience of both peseta and (initially) sterling entry had been a move towards the top of the band. Putting the escudo in the system at a rate weaker than the market rate would, if this previous experience were repeated, help turn the trick of establishing the escudo at the top of its band (and thus the Portuguese government in a position to exert pressure on Britain) without the sharp appreciation in the market that would otherwise upset the traditional exporters (particularly strongly represented in the region of Oporto, Braga's home town and his parliamentary constituency).

Braga's announcement did not go down well with the Monetary Committee.[8] Press reports of the meeting, in Portugal and elsewhere, confirm what was going to be obvious. First, to combine the entry of a new currency with what would be, in effect, a devaluation, whatever happened in the market thereafter, would give the impression that the ERM was being used as a 'soft option'. None of the existing members wanted that sort of message to be sent, no matter how much some of them – Britain and France – were trying to soften the ERM constraints as much as they possibly could. Might the example of a 'technical' escudo devaluation lead markets to think that other devaluations might be possible? Second, the prospect of a reinforcement of the 'ERM paradox' if, as expected, the

8 Although there is, not surprisingly, no indication that Delors repeated the instructions he had given to his Director-General when Britain announced the proposed terms of sterling's entry.

escudo quickly appreciated within its ERM band, was clearly going to be abhorrent not only to Britain, the likely victim, but also to Germany, for the same reasons as in the peseta story (that this objection might go in the opposite direction from the first was not likely to deter its use in the hands of people as blithely unsubtle as Köhler or as craftily subtle as Tietmeyer).

After many hours of wrangling, the Monetary Committee had clearly not been able to agree to the requested entry rate. Braga then attempted to play the second card he had been dealt by political events in Britain and also Italy. General elections were to be held in Italy the very next day, and in Britain the following Thursday. The finance ministers of both countries were thus otherwise engaged and would not at all welcome a summons to Brussels to participate in a meeting of finance ministers and central bank governors to sort out the escudo mess. It is thus easy to imagine the horror of the British and Italian members when Braga ordered his representative in the Monetary Committee to suggest just that. Braga may have been bluffing: he was unlikely to get a sympathetic hearing the next day from Norman Lamont, for instance. But he probably calculated that his antagonists would do anything to avoid being embroiled in a major Brussels row that particular weekend. The upshot was a fudge. The Committee eventually offered, and Braga deigned to accept, an entry rate equivalent to the notional ECU rate of the escudo when it had entered the EMS. This happened to be about halfway between the market rate and Braga's original request.

Seven months later, when the escudo devalued in the midst of the ERM turbulence that had by then been unleashed, Braga told the Portuguese press that the escudo was now near the central rate he had requested in April but had been refused because of worries that there might be problems for sterling. In fact, as we shall see later, the November devaluation took the escudo's central rate below what had been asked for in April. But Braga's emphasis on the sterling question surely confirms what he had had in mind. The outcome of the Monetary Committee meeting also gives the lie to suggestions that anyone could have argued in the Monetary Committee for a *lower* sterling entry rate in October 1990. Portugal in April 1992 was in a very similar position in key respects – notably the inflation rate – to Britain's at the time of sterling entry. If there were doubts about the sustainability of sterling's entry rate, there should have been similar doubts about the escudo. Yet the Monetary Committee insisted on a *higher* rate for the escudo than the Portuguese government had asked for. Sure enough, the escudo appreciated slightly immediately after entering the mechanism:

the 'new' ERM of no realignments was still sending the currencies of high-inflation countries to the top of the band. But all that would soon change. The ERM bubble was about to burst.

# 6

# Pricking the Bubble

*Nej!*

The Danes do not like Germans.[1] They are wary of Catholicism and have little patience with Brussels bureaucrats. They were not founder members of the 'Common Market', and agreed, in 1972, to join the Community only very reluctantly, when Edward Heath sabotaged the European Free Trade Area by taking Britain into what he clearly hoped would become a federal state. The clinching factor then had not been any positive attraction exercised by the Community, but rather the fear that the selfish members of the European club, now to include Britain, the biggest market for Danish agricultural products, would squeeze Danish exports out via the Common Agricultural Policy and the common external tariff on manufactured goods. Things were to be little different two decades later.

In Denmark, ratification of the Maastricht Treaty required a referendum. In keeping with the tradition of (relative) openness of government in the Scandinavian countries, the government distributed hundreds of thousands of copies of the treaty through the post. Not surprisingly, the Dane in the street was terrified by this terrifying document. Shortly before their referendum, they were shocked when Delors's plans to limit the rights of small countries and increase the powers of the Commission were revealed in the press.

But the Danish government was in favour of Maastricht. As twenty years earlier, industrial interests and the large farming concerns were afraid of punitive measures of exclusion if Danish voters defied the European Leviathan. And, as in most other European countries, the politicians, bureaucrats, big businessmen, lawyers, journalists and lobbyists *qua* caste were solidly in favour of the corporatist, élitist Community. With the usual arrogance of their caste they, and their counterparts in other Community

[1] They were so worried about being swamped by Germans that, in an attempt to assuage them, their government had managed to insert a special protocol in the Maastricht Treaty allowing the prohibition of purchases of holiday homes by foreigners: Germans were very fond of the Jutland beaches, a short Mercedes-drive from Germany.

countries, simply did not believe that the referendum could possibly produce anything other than a 'yes' vote. The opinion polls said otherwise – but they simply reflected the little people's futile expression of their feelings; when the time came to vote, the proles would do what the great and good told them, just as they had done in 1972 and just as 'neo-functionalist' theory predicted they should do again.

Thus the narrow rejection of the treaty on Sunday, 2 June 1992, left Euroenthusiasts everywhere shocked and momentarily speechless. But it did not take long for threats and recriminations to begin. João de Deus Pinheiro, the Satanic-featured Portuguese Foreign Minister, could see his own country's 'seat at the top table' disappearing up the Swanee, along with the billions of ECUs of EC handouts sucked out of his partners, if Maastricht failed. He was particularly savage. His Spanish colleague, Carlos Westerdorp, European Affairs Minister, opined, in cod-Shakespearean mode, that: 'Something is rotten in the state of Denmark.' But French and German politicians, too, were refusing to accept the referendum verdict. The Treaty of Rome be damned, they said in effect, a few thousand Danish votes one way or the other could not be allowed to stop the March of History, to frustrate the General Will as decided by the political bosses in the countries that really counted. Was there a crisis for the Community? No, they implied, there was a crisis for Denmark! A judge of the European Court, supposedly one of the guardians of the Treaty of Rome, joined in the chorus. According to news-wire reports, Paul Kapteyn, writing in a Dutch legal periodical, came close to saying that Denmark must get out of the Community: it could not presume to prevent what the other countries' politicians wanted. And, while in Britain the Danish Embassy was showered with messages of congratulation, in the corridors of Brussels the atmosphere was sinister and unpleasant. Sheepish and embarrassed Danish Eurocrats were berated by angry 'colleagues' from Continental countries for the sins of their countrymen and countrywomen.

As ever, the financial markets were politically neutral. Every piece of political news, wherever it came from and whatever it meant, brought opportunities for profit and the risk of loss. The Danish 'no' shattered the assumptions of a smooth, trouble-free glidepath. EMU might be sunk completely; or the 'core' countries might instead go off and form their own mini-union outside the Maastricht framework.[2] In either hypothesis, the

2 As careful analysis at the time would have predicted, and as events were to show, such a mini-union was not a practicable legal, technical or political possibility. But it weighed on market sentiment nonetheless.

'high-yielders' would be out. The markets repositioned themselves instant-aneously. Psychologically, the ERM bubble had been burst. The dynamics of the process were to prove irreversible and self-reinforcing.

As convergence plays were unwound, huge amounts of money began to flow out of Spain and Italy. Investors had bet on falling long-term interest rates and firm exchange rates in the less virtuous countries. Now, in telling comment on the Emperor's clothes of the supposed European consensus that inflation convergence, budgetary retrenchment and the embrace of the ERM straitjacket were all good things in their own right, they found themselves having to get out in a hurry.

Both Spain and Italy had accumulated large stocks of reserves during the period in which their currencies were camped at or near the top of the ERM bands. Now they started spending them. But the authorities also used the width of the bands. All this was well and good. In form at least, they were employing two of the three so-called Basle–Nyborg instruments. But, for the peseta at least, the slide down through the 6% band looked much more like a change of philosophy. For three years the peseta had been persistently strong in the ERM and the Spanish authorities had been prepared to *cut* interest rates to restrain currency movements. Now, at the first sign of a loss of investor confidence, they were letting currency movement take most of the strain, with no attempt made to brake the fall by using the third of the Basle–Nyborg instruments, interest rates.[3] If the authorities were so willing to let the peseta fall within the band without *any* increase in interest rates, was it reasonable for the markets to believe that when it reached the bottom of the band those same authorities would suddenly raise interest rates by whatever it took – perhaps by tens of per cent rather than tens of basis points – to prevent a breach of the band? Could such a belief, if it existed at all, be held strongly enough for the market to stop selling pesetas as the currency approached the lower limit? The speed of the peseta's fall through the bands, with relatively little fundamental 'news' about the Spanish economy, suggested that a previous strategy was quite simply being jettisoned. The Spanish horse, it seemed, was being pulled up even before the first fence in the Maastricht Handicap Hurdle. It was only a matter of time before the massive peseta devaluations discounted by long-term interest rates became fact.

3  During July, the Bank of Spain did on one occasion let its repo rate rise by a mere 13 basis points (0.13%); but given the measures that Sweden had taken the previous November and Italy was now taking, this merely served to emphasize that significant interest-rate increases had been ruled out.

In Italy, the reaction to the unwinding of convergence plays was very different. The need for EMU and the ERM had become part of an unthinking credo of political life in the Italian system. To prevent the whole edifice of bribery, political corruption and governmental unaccountability and irresponsibility from tumbling down, the political class had had to hold out the prospect that – rather like a Western in which homesteaders in some wild, lawless territory vote for statehood so that US marshals can ride in, liberate them from the rule of gangsters and give them the benefit of the American Constitution – the European Community would somehow solve all Italy's problems for it. Jim Callaghan could, if he had chosen, have pointed out the implausibility of this scenario. Turkeys don't vote for Christmas. Yet the near-gangsters in Italian politics were depicted as spearheading a drive to deprive themselves of power. Probably much nearer to reality is the hypothesis that people such as Andreotti were pulling the wool over the eyes of the Italian public, knowing that any attempt by the country to solve its own problems would mean political demise – and perhaps worse – for the old ruling class. If such people had got their way, then the Wild West would have taken over the Community, not the other way round.

Thus it was that, once convergence plays started unwinding and capital flowed out of Italy, massive cuts in the budget deficit and a final, formal abolition of the wage-indexation system came to be seen by the Banca d'Italia and by international bureaucrats as the only way to 'save the lira' and thus save the ERM. As an example of putting the cart before the horse in economic reasoning, this took some beating,[4] for reasons we shall reflect on in a later chapter. The government that finally emerged, in June, from the traditionally inconclusive general election, in April, was headed by the Socialist, Giulio Amato, who announced a package of huge cuts in the budget (or, rather, cuts in the projections for the budget deficit, which would otherwise have hugely increased) and formalized the abolition of wage-indexation.

At first, the market was 'impressed'. The lira stabilized for a time. But those spirits in the market and elsewhere who had best resisted the ERM indoctrination asked themselves one or two awkward questions. Would not the budgetary measures, necessary and desirable as they were, have more

4 Sam Brittan had, many, many years earlier, used this particular metaphor to describe the idiocy, as he had then seen it, of fixed-exchange-rate systems, at a time when opposition to the ERM had not become so closely identified with opposition to the policies of Mrs Thatcher.

chance of actually working if the economy were growing? Might this not suggest a need for a relaxation of monetary policy and for improved competitiveness via a lower exchange rate? And might not the abolition of wage-indexation increase the chance that devaluation would actually improve competitiveness instead of just increasing inflation? Before the Danish 'no', such thinking would have had little chance of influencing the market. After the 'no', it could not be ignored.

During the course of the summer, a very influential article by David Walton, currency economist of Goldman Sachs, articulated the doubts. The article infuriated the Italian authorities who, according to market gossip, 'punished' Goldman Sachs by cutting them out of prospective privatization business and generally making life difficult for them in Milan. But there was another actor about to take the stage, one who possessed far more power than an 'Anglo-Saxon' securities house and had every reason to use that power to 'punish' the Italian government and the Banca d'Italia, the peddlers of EMU. In this Spaghetti Western, it was not a US marshal who came riding into town, but an elderly, implacable vigilante with Helmut Schmidt and the Louvre Accords already notches on his gunbelt.

## Too much money is bad for you

Throughout the first half of 1992, the time bomb of the Bundesbank M3 target for the year had been ticking away. For several years, M3 targets had been missed and the concept downplayed. Tietmeyer only paid lip-service to monetary targets. At one meeting, when reminded by a veteran monetary official that the Bundesbank had begun using them in 1959,[5] he growled: '1959 was a very bad year.' Later, when his concept of room for political manoeuvre by central banks began to be threatened by the adoption of explicit inflation targets in a number of countries, he was able to muster considerable enthusiasm for monetary targets. But in 1992, he appears to have been ruefully aware of one of the laidback Pöhl's throwaway lines: 'They [his colleagues on the Bundesbank Council] only look at the money supply if they can't think of any other excuses for raising interest rates.' By July, there were, it is true, other excuses. Inflation in Germany stood at around 4% and, although lower than earlier in the year, was bound to rise again at the beginning of 1993 when a planned rise in VAT came into

5 The Bundesbank began publishing formal monetary targets only in 1974, but had been giving weight to them in its internal policy-making since Germany lifted exchange controls in 1959.

effect. On the other hand, given the usual long lags in monetary policy, it could be expected that the hike in interest rates the previous December, the seventh in just over two years, would eventually start to push inflation back down again. The post-unification demand boom had come to an end, and industrial output was already falling. Yet, inevitably, the money supply was growing above the top of its target range. If the Bundesbank ignored its chosen indicator once again, the monetarists could argue, it would look as though the bank was either submitting to international pressure – raising more, unwelcome questions about the ERM anchor – or indulging in cyclical fine-tuning – in which case you might as well let the politicians run monetary policy.

And now, of course, the arch-monetarist Helmut Schlesinger was President, supported by another keeper of the monetarist flame, Otmar Issing.[6] For seven months, since the December hike, Schlesinger had been keeping his power dry. The market, forward-looking as ever, seeing the turnaround in the German economic cycle and becoming accustomed to disregarding M3, was wondering when the Bundesbank would begin to *reduce* interest rates. But in July, the M3 time bomb carefully primed the previous December was about to explode, growing way outside its target range and, if anything, accelerating.

There were, it seemed, only two choices. The Bundesbank traditionally conducted a mid-year review of its target. But, equally traditionally, it abstained from adjusting the target, for fear of seeming to indulge in 'fine-tuning.'[7] To change the target now would mean that it had been got wrong the previous December. That was unthinkable. But if the target set in December was to have any chance of being met, interest rates would have to

6 Issing, formerly a professor of economics, is the member of the Bundesbank Directorate responsible for its economics and statistics department. Journalists often refer to him as the bank's chief economist. But officials find this usage a solecism: the chief economist is a senior staff member, not a member of the Directorate. For them, the Bundesbank's chief economist is the head of the economics department, Dr Reinmut König. A few months later, a Bundesbanker reacted with mirth to a speech by the Bank of England's chief economist, Mervyn King, in which the Old Lady and the Bundesbank were depicted as essentially similar institutions (successive drafts were sent to the Bundesbank for vetting before King lost patience with the nit-picking responses and went ahead). 'The only similarity', chortled one Bundesbank staffer, 'is that their chief economists are both misnamed: in every central bank, *politics* is king.'

7 The only exception had been in 1991, when the target had been adjusted *downwards* in mid-year. This was ostensibly because the uncertainty about the money demand of East Germans was dissipating: residents in the East were said to be running down the DM money balances with which they had been presented a year earlier and converting them into financial assets of other forms. But there was no such excuse – or at least none was sought – in 1991.

rise – as had been obvious from the start – with every chance of blowing the ERM apart.

That was the dilemma with which the Bundesbank Council had to wrestle. There is no doubt that for many members of the Council – probably including Schlesinger – it was no dilemma at all: the target could not be disregarded. Some wanted to chastise the government and tame the unions, but for others – certainly including Tietmeyer – the international political constraints were of primary importance. If the ERM fell apart, so might the Maastricht process. And while the Bundesbank's powers might then be safe from transfer to a body *outside* Germany, there was nothing in the German constitution to stop the government amending the existing Bundesbank law to take away its independence of the *German* politicians.[8] Whatever Schlesinger might think, Kohl could see an interest-rate rise as an intolerable provocation by the Bundesbank.

In the end, a compromise emerged from the heated discussions in the Bundesbank Council on 16 July. The discount rate would be raised, but the Lombard rate would be left unchanged. The discount rate forms the floor of the corridor within which the Bundesbank guides money market rates,[9]

8 This safeguard was put at risk in the autumn of 1992 during the process of parliamentary ratification of Maastricht in Germany. The constitutional change proposed by the government during this process would have given it a general right to transfer the Bundesbank's functions to a supranational body. Schlesinger sensed that the government might be preparing a threat to create a Franco-German central bank council, something totally anathema to him and most of his colleagues, if the Bundesbank created trouble for the Maastricht approach to monetary union. He rushed to Bonn, where he deployed his formidable prestige, intellectual powers and political nous to persuade the parliamentary committee in charge of the ratification legislation to make a key change in the government's proposal. The legislation that finally passed laid down that the government could transfer the Bundesbank's prerogatives abroad *only* within the framework of European Monetary Union as defined in the Maastricht Treaty. Since the constitutional changes also involved provisions to make any future constitutional change more difficult, Schlesinger could feel that his intervention had very considerably strengthened his bargaining position vis-à-vis the government. Schlesinger's position on this issue was most certainly different from that of his predecessor, Pöhl, or his successor, Tietmeyer.

9 Within this corridor, money-market rates are influenced by the so-called repo rate, the rate at which the Bundesbank agrees to 'buy' securities from the banking system (thus increasing the liquid reserves of the banks) for a fixed period (usually 14, 21 or 28 days) at the end of which the banks have to buy them back. In practice, the Bundesbank is lending to the banks against the security of their portfolios of bills and bonds. Often, when the Bundesbank wishes to give a clear signal to the market about the money-market rate it wishes to see established, it announces the interest rate at which it will accept bids from the banks for sale-and-repurchase agreements (a 'fixed-rate tender'). At other times, when it suits the Bundesbank to seem to be simply reflecting a market-determined rate, it invites the banks to bid at an interest rate of their choosing and then decides how much liquidity to allocate at the various rates bid by the banks. Since the *Directorate* decides the terms and conditions of repo agreements, usually once a week, while the *Council*

the Lombard rate the ceiling. When money market rates are moving up, the Lombard rate is usually the more important; when the trend is downwards the discount rate attracts the greater interest. This normal pattern can change, however, when a turning-point in the path of interest rates is thought to be imminent.

This is exactly what happened in July 1992. The foreign reaction to the rise in the discount rate was one of shock. Discount rate, Lombard rate, repo rate – who cared? The Bundesbank had *raised* one of its key official rates when the authorities in several other ERM countries were in desperate need of reductions in their own interest rates. The foreign exchange markets smelt panic: there were all the signs of the kind of breakdown in monetary 'coordination' that had preceded the Wall Street Crash and the demise of the Louvre Accords. Those foreign funds that still held large amounts of Spanish and Italian assets as a result of previous 'convergence plays' became more and more nervous. The leak of money out of the two countries started again.

As the lira once more came under pressure, the Banca d'Italia decided that a show of resoluteness was required to calm the markets. In mid-July, it raised its own discount rate by a substantial 1.25%. To its dismay, the hoped-for strengthening of the lira in response never came. The markets were doing some rapid sums. Most Italian government debt was short-term and had to be rolled over rather frequently. If the new higher level of interest rates persisted, the additional budgetary cost of debt service would wipe out many of the budgetary gains programmed in the Amato plan – even before taking into account the depressing effect of higher interest rates on the economy and thence on tax revenues. The budgetary package was supposedly necessary to save the lira. But now it looked as though defending the lira would wreck the budgetary package.

Once the market started to think in such terms, the lira's ERM parity was doomed. In their hearts, the men at the top of the Banca d'Italia knew it. For the next month, they could do little but buy lire in the market, using up foreign exchange reserves at a worryingly rapid rate. Their only hope was that when the Bundesbank Council came back from its summer break at the end of August market psychology might be reversed by a cut in German interest rates.

---

decides the levels of the discount and Lombard rates, the regional central bank presidents, members of the Council but not the Directorate, generally like to keep the corridor between discount and Lombard rates rather narrow, so as to limit the discretion of the Directorate.

To their despair, events in the German money markets in August pointed in precisely the opposite direction, with talk of a suspension of the Lombard rate and, in consequence, a sharp rise in the market rates.

At this point, the German government became thoroughly alarmed. According to an article entitled 'Sabotage gegen Bonn' the following week in *Der Spiegel*,[10] the government had had to issue the direst of warnings to the Bundesbank – there would be full-scale political conflict if the bank provoked a sharp rise in money-market interest rates. The article spoke of divisions in Frankfurt even within the Directorate and, without naming names, implied that certain members of the Directorate had warned the rest of disaster ahead for the bank if there were no change of course. At all events, there was suddenly an obvious change of tack from the Bundesbank, as its money-market desk began feeding the market with liquidity and pushing money-market rates back below – just below – the Lombard rate. But the threat of a rise in the Lombard rate still hung very heavy over the markets.

Towards the end of the month, the selling of lire and pesetas intensified. In late August, the lira touched the lower limit of its permitted band.

In Britain, Major's unexpected election victory in April, dispelling market nightmares of 'that old removal van' turning up at 10 Downing Street and installing Neil Kinnock, had frustrated Portuguese hopes of putting a half-Nelson on the country. It also allowed Major to display his uncanny ability to proclaim victory while nemesis was already tapping on his window. Flushed with sterling's post-election honeymoon strength, and ignoring the increasingly loud grindings of the tectonic plates beneath his feet after the Danish referendum at the beginning of June,[11] Major made a quite staggering statement at the beginning of July. Sterling, he piped, was going to become the strongest currency in the ERM, even the anchor of the system.

---

10 *Der Spiegel* generally supports the SPD. It certainly did not like Kohl, and neither did it like Maastricht, complaining of an imbalance between the political and economic fronts in the treaty. But it also did not like the Bundesbank, and particularly not Schlesinger, whom it tended to hold responsible for Schmidt's downfall a decade earlier. The article may have been intended to kill three birds with one stone: embarrassing Kohl, by insinuating that his government's financial mistakes were so serious that even the CDU-friendly Bundesbank Directorate felt impelled to whack Bonn across the knuckles; at the same time to imply that the Bundesbank was behaving in a constitutionally improper fashion; and to buttress its criticisms of Maastricht by suggesting that the Bundesbank was going to drive a coach and horses through it.

11 The implications of the Danish vote are looked at in the following chapter.

Instead it became increasingly obvious that the intense deflationary squeeze imposed on the British economy by the ERM was becoming unbearable, particularly in the shell-shocked housing market. At the beginning of August, the government cut interest rates on national savings in an attempt to avert an economically, politically and socially disastrous rise in mortgage rates. This distress signal led markets to doubt that the government could raise money-market rates if sterling got into serious trouble.[12]

## No zone is an island

Meanwhile, anger about the Bundesbank's money-market tactics had not been confined to Europe. In the United States, the Federal Reserve had for two years been pursuing a policy of cutting interest rates in an effort to haul the economy out of recession[13] and to restore the battered balance sheets of the banking system after a commercial property crisis. Just below the surface, the economy was stirring, and in the final quarter of the year would spring into life. But in August the signs of recovery were not evident. The Fed signalled one more cut in the key Fed funds interest rate, bringing it down to 3%, and dragging three-month rates down to 4.1%. With German three-month rates actually slightly above the 9.75% Lombard rate, the gap between US and German rates was at an unheard-of size of almost 6 percentage points.

The dollar, which had been weakening all summer, plunged. From the Fed's point of view, a falling dollar was an integral part of the easing of monetary conditions it sought when it guided interest rates down. But the Bush administration, while welcoming lower interest rates, was uneasy. A lower dollar would improve competitiveness and that should boost growth and employment in a year or two, but that timescale was politically irrelevant – the presidential elections were less than three months away. Administration officials feared that a sharp plunge in the dollar might

12 A similar distress signal had been sent out by the French authorities in May, when they announced a cut in the banks' reserve requirements, allowing them to reduce retail lending rates without affecting the interbank rates directly relevant to the franc's attractiveness versus the DM. The signal turned out to be more important than the action itself, and the franc began weakening slightly in the ERM band.

13 A recession that was relatively mild in comparison with that then afflicting, or about to afflict, European economies. But the Fed is responsive to popular (not just political) opinion in the United States, and Americans do not like unemployment.

frighten Japanese investors out of US stock and bond markets.[14] A stock-market crisis, even a mini-crisis, was what they wanted least in the election run-up. As the talk of increases in the Lombard rate filled the pages of the world's financial press, the dollar crumbled. The Bush administration ordered the Fed to intervene to support it, and drummed up support from other central banks. On 21 August, eighteen central banks entered the market to buy dollars. All they succeeded in doing was, for the first time in several years, to give the commercial banks' forex traders an easy profit as intervention failed to hold the line.

The dollar's plunge against the DM (to DM 1.40) took it to $2 against the pound, a level not seen for a decade. With US trade far more important for the British economy than for the Continental countries, the falling dollar put considerable pressure on sterling's parity against the DM. In fact, sterling hit the bottom of its permitted ERM band, forcing the Bank of England to intervene to support it.

In addition to hitting its bilateral floor against the DM, sterling's 'divergence indicator' (a measure of the extent to which it had moved away from the average of other currencies in the system) reached a level that, in theory, created a 'presumption' of action by the UK authorities. Having already resorted to movements within the band and then heavy intervention at the margin, the next step, according to the rules, should have been an increase in British interest rates. But an increase in interest rates, when sterling was strengthening sharply against the dollar bloc, Britain's single most important trading area, when the economy was in deep, deep recession, and when the distress in the housing market was a major economic, social and political preoccupation, would have been simply crazy. Instead, the government resorted to the tried, tested and failed methods of the 1960s and 1970s: bravado, declarations of undying and irrevocable commitment to the parity, insinuations that sterling would soon enter narrow bands, sneering denunciations of anyone who suggested a change of policy on the exchange rate – all the 'over my dead body' rhetoric that immediately had forex traders dreaming about how they were going to spend their bonuses and subsequently ensured that vast swathes of the

14 This fear was unfounded. Instances in which markets react perversely to rational moves by monetary authorities are very hard to find. 'Crashes' of one kind or another tend to occur when markets feel that the policy assumptions on which market scenarios have been based are no longer tenable. In particular, 'crashes' tend to be associated with attempts by the authorities to peg or otherwise manipulate exchange rates – the 1987 Wall Street crash was one example, the ERM crisis itself another, the bond market crash of early 1994 a third, the crash of all Mexican financial markets at the end of 1994 and beginning of 1995 yet another.

electorate would never again believe a single word John Major said on any subject whatsoever.

On 26 August, it was announced that the Chancellor, Norman Lamont, would make an early-morning statement, shortly before the markets opened, from the steps of the Treasury. The market expectation was that he would announce a rise in interest rates. Instead, he made a brief statement that the parity would be maintained using all necessary means – a clear indication to markets that interest rates would *not* be raised, one that was immediately taken on board in the interest-rate futures market, where the interest rate expected to prevail in three months' time was revised down. The statement was followed by aggressive intervention to buy sterling by the Bank of England. However, the impact on sterling was undermined by the advance release of a speech to be made by Reimut Jochimsen, a Bundesbank Council member, which spoke of the potential for a realignment.[15] Sterling remained dangerously close to its ERM floor.

Two days later, 28 August, the spotlight was back on the lira. Significantly, late that Friday afternoon the DM rose to the top of the ERM band for the first time since the German government stifled the Bundesbank's realignment campaign in October 1989. As a result, the Bundesbank would now be first in line to have to engage in obligatory intervention, under the ERM rules, if the lira remained at its floor. Past experience suggested that this would prompt the bank to ask Bonn for a DM revaluation. After the ERM intervention obligations lapsed for the day (at 5 pm Brussels time), the lira slipped below its floor. In response, the EC finance ministers issued a statement via the Chairman of the Monetary Committee, Trichet, ruling out a realignment. This was to be the first of several such declarations that left the market cold. The pretence that the ERM was a commonly managed mechanism leading to a monetary union was being exposed as a cruel farce. From now on, only nods and winks from the Bundesbank would have the power to move markets.

Thursday, 3 September, turned out to be a particularly significant day. It began with a smug announcement from the British Treasury that arrangements had been made for the government to borrow what seemed a very large amount, the equivalent of 10 billion ECU ($14.5 billion) in foreign currencies, mostly DM, from an international syndicate of banks and to sell them for sterling. The Treasury claimed in a press release that 'these

---

15 When the speech was actually delivered, this phrase was cut out, allowing the Bundesbank to claim it was not advocating a realignment. Schlesinger himself was to use a similar trick two weeks later.

arrangements demonstrate once again the government's clear determination and ability to maintain sterling's position in the ERM at the existing central rate regardless of the outcome of the French referendum on the Maastricht Treaty'. Sterling rose back above DM 2.80 for the first time in the fortnight as the more credulous analysts proclaimed the borrowing as evidence that 'the government is putting its money where its mouth is'. The stock market took a rather different view, rising 2.5% in value as traders interpreted the borrowing as evidence that the government would do whatever was necessary, not to avoid devaluation but to avoid increases in interest rates. By the close of London trading, the lira was significantly below its permitted limit against the DM – promising fireworks the next day when ERM intervention obligations resumed.

## Porkies

The most significant event that Thursday, however, came late in the evening in the Sorbonne, during the course of an elaborately rigged French telethon on the referendum campaign. The show included a live appearance (in Bonn) by Kohl, who made a plea for a 'yes' vote. This was followed up by a 'debate' between Mitterrand and Philippe Séguin, the leading 'no' campaigner, who had that morning criticized the invitation to Kohl as 'perfectly scandalous'. The programme's stage managers put Séguin in a weak position from the start, scheduling the debate immediately after Kohl's message and after almost two hours of rambling conversation with Mitterrand interspersed with loaded commentaries on selected texts from the treaty.

But it was Mitterrand's own performance during the debate that was to have the most far-reaching consequences, contributing mightily to the destruction of the ERM and perhaps even to that of the plans for EMU. Séguin criticized the treaty for giving control of the key elements of economic policy to an unelected, democratically unaccountable bunch of 'technocrats' in the ECB. In reply, Mitterrand provided an interpretation of the treaty so diametrically opposed to the Bundesbank's that, from that moment on, there could be no possibility of Helmut Schlesinger's becoming reconciled to any French influence in the shaping of the ECB. What the treaty meant, said Mitterrand, was that 'the technicians of the [European] Central Bank are charged with applying in the monetary domain the decisions of the European Council . . . One hears it said that the European Central Bank will be the master of the decisions. It's not true!

Economic policy belongs to the European Council and the application of monetary policy is the task of the [European] Central Bank, in the framework of the decisions of the European Council . . . The people who decide economic policy, of which monetary policy is no more than a means of implementation, are the politicians . . . [The members of the ECB would be like members of the Commission who] no doubt cannot help feeling a certain tenderness for the interests of their country.'

The scale of the Bundesbank indignation aroused by this barefaced rewriting of the treaty can be gauged from the next edition of the *Auszüge*. It was largely devoted to articles (no fewer than eight were reprinted) provoked by Mitterrand's comments. The lead item, entitled (in German) 'Paris Calls ECB Independence into Question', was an excerpt from an article in a Stuttgart newspaper[16] that consisted mainly of a translation into German of what Mitterrand had said. Then came, verbatim, the relevant section of the offending remarks, this time in French, as if to convince people who simply did not believe that what they had read in German could be true. The Bundesbank was sparing no effort to get home to German public opinion that Mitterrand was going back on his word.

As in so many other ways, the cat had been let out of the bag in the French referendum campaign. German newspapers (and even Martin Bangemann, one of the two German Commissioners) had been complaining about the anti-German tone of the 'yes' campaign. Leading French Socialists in particular – Bérégovoy, the Prime Minister, Fabius, former Prime Minister and someone close to both Mitterrand and Delors, and Rocard, also a former Prime Minister and now leader of the Socialist Party – had all implied that only the Maastricht Treaty could hold the 'old demons' of the German character in check. Now Mitterrand himself was stating without any ambiguity whatsoever that the Bundesbank had had the wool pulled over its eyes: the independence of the European Central Bank, the key requirement for Bundesbank acquiescence in Maastricht, was a sham. This should have been obvious from the start. The idea that French chauvinists such as Mitterrand and Delors would devote themselves to the creation of a monetary union and then hand control of it to a conclave of central bankers was always incredible. Yet Schlesinger, a man in whose personal myth honour, correctness and reliability were all of overriding importance, had believed it; his belief had helped other members of the

16 The editors of the *Auszüge* had clearly combed through the regional press to find the headline that best conveyed the shock-horror message they were looking for.

Council to swallow the treaty.[17] Now faced with irrefutable evidence of Mitterrand's treachery, many members of the Council, say Bundesbank insiders, determined to have their revenge.[18]

The day after Mitterrand's interview, fears of a weekend devaluation again prompted massive sales of lira assets by the markets. The day had begun irritatingly from a Bundesbank point of view when Italian banks, companies and funds that had brought lire the previous evening at a rate *below* the ERM floor presented themselves at the Bundesbank's (electronic) door and demanded to have the lire bought off them, as the ERM rules required, *at* the ERM floor. They consequently made a tidy profit, leaving the Bundesbank dealers and their bosses gnashing their teeth at the injustice of it all. The lira remained close to its floor all day, despite continued intervention and an announcement from the Banca d'Italia that it was drawing on the theoretically unlimited VSTF borrowing available under the ERM rules. At the beginning of the European afternoon, the announcement of weak US employment figures for August created expectations of further American interest-rate cuts. The DM strengthened against the dollar, pushing the lira against its lower ERM limit and reversing most of the gain sterling had made after the borrowing announcement. A desperate Banca d'Italia raised its discount rate by 1.75% to 15%. Short-term market rates rose to 18%, prompting Gianni Agnelli, head of Fiat, to comment that: 'Interest rates are at unbearable levels for industry.' And what was unbearable for industry was also going to be unbearable for Italian public finances.

All the Italians could do now was to hope to hang on until the French referendum on 20 September. If there was a 'yes' vote, then the markets' faith in EMU and 'convergence' might be restored, 'saving' the lira. If the vote was 'no', then the whole ERM might disintegrate: at least Italy would not be singled out as the black sheep. What would be regarded as disastrous by Rome would be an isolated lira devaluation. But Italy could no longer maintain the lira's parity by itself: there had to be a gesture by the Bundesbank implying commitment, at least for two more weeks, to the

17 In one of his speeches shortly after Maastricht, Schlesinger had referred to the Bundesbank's fears before Maastricht about the independence of a future ECB vis-à-vis the Council of Ministers, particularly in the field of exchange-rate policy, but stated that independence 'appears to be assured by the formulation of the treaty approved in Maastricht'.

18 Schlesinger made his own feelings plain in a speech a few weeks later. Referring directly to Mitterrand's television comments, he expressed doubts about whether the eleven Community countries other than Germany would appoint genuinely independent figures to the board of an ECB.

'glidepath' view of the ERM. The rise in the Italian discount rate, a rise that in normal times would have been considered swingeing, was intended to show that Italy was abiding totally by the ERM rules. Now it was the turn of the others – that is, the Bundesbank – to act.

Relations between the Banca d'Italia and the Bundesbank were not good, at any level. A direct appeal had no chance of bearing fruit. Instead, the Italian central bank tried whatever roundabout methods were to hand. Padoa-Schioppa, *éminence grise* of the Delors Report, contacted Delors, warning him that only a 'political' solution to the lira crisis was now possible. Delors, he urged, should emphasize the gravity of the situation to Mitterrand, asking the French President to use his special relationship with Kohl to have pressure put on the Bundesbank from Bonn.

For its part, the Italian government was pinning its hopes on the 'informal' Ecofin that would take place that weekend, under British chairmanship, in Bath. An informal Ecofin, which takes place once in each member country's six-month presidency, differs from normal meetings of the Finance Ministers' Council in several respects. It does not take votes on items of legislative business. It is intended to provide a forum for discussion, in some congenial setting. Most important, the 'informal' is attended by the governors of central banks and their deputies. All the managers of the EMS (and all the members of the Monetary Committee) are present. At Bath, this provided an opportunity to mount concerted political pressure on the Bundesbank.

There was indeed a concerted attempt by the British, Italian, French and other ministers to put pressure on Schlesinger. The scheduled business was forgotten. Nine hours of heated argument about the ERM took place. Lamont, as Chairman, pleaded with Schlesinger for a cut in German interest rates. In all, he put the demand directly four times, slimming down his request from an initial one of a cut in the discount rate to, finally, a 'signal' of the future direction of rates – even 10 basis points (0.1%) off the repo rate would do. On each occasion, Schlesinger, growing increasingly angry, refused. His Council had met only two days earlier and had fixed the Bundesbank's interest-rate orientations. He had no authority to change those orientations, and the Bundesbank Council would not do so unless there were some significant change in circumstances.

It was clear to the participants in the 'informal' that the only significant change in circumstances that was possible that weekend was an ERM realignment. There has been persistent speculation that the Bundesbank floated the idea of a general realignment 'in the margins' of the 'informal', but Schlesinger cannot have raised the matter directly in the official meeting: the German government was responsible for decisions about the DM's parity within the ERM. What is clear is that there were no takers for the idea of a realignment that weekend. A 'general' realignment would have had to include the French franc, which was wobbly as a result of the referendum campaign and the increasingly evident recessionary trends in France. But ten years of the *franc fort* policy in France had been sold to the population almost entirely on the argument that it was necessary if ever Germany was going to be finagled into a European Central Bank. To devalue the franc now would be a failure of that policy: the French electorate would be confronted, two weeks before the Maastricht referendum, with the dominance of the DM, and would believe that the treaty would simply buttress and formalize that dominance. A devaluation was therefore totally unacceptable to the French authorities.

Italy would not willingly devalue if France did not, for fear of ruling itself out of EMU. For Britain, the constraints were somewhat different. There were undoubtedly some Cabinet ministers, led by Clarke and Heseltine, whose view of the situation was directly comparable to Italian thinking. Major appears to have been against a devaluation to avoid the personal loss of face that would have been involved.[19] Lamont and his officials were also conscious of the arguments that devaluation would still not allow British interest rates to fall significantly below German rates. This too had political as well as economic significance. Accepting a devaluation would imply that Britain's competitive position, not the level of interest rates imposed in the system by the Bundesbank, was the major reason for Britain's terrible recession and everything that flowed from it. Major was responsible for the chosen ERM parity, but not for the Bundesbank's interest rates. Since he wanted to be able to blame the Bundesbank, not himself, for what was going wrong, he was against a devaluation.[20] Thus the unfortunate Lamont was under firm instructions to get 'movement' from Schlesinger at Bath.

By the time Lamont had put his request for the fourth time, Schlesinger had had just about enough. What was happening was confirmation, on the

19 David Mellor had a particular interest in the ERM drama. Major had given him a vote of confidence after the disclosure of evidence of the enthusiasm with which the 'Minister for Fun' attacked his briefs. If Major caved in to pressure to sack Mellor, his 'credibility' on the exchange rate might suffer. Mellor's job was therefore safe as long as sterling was being held in the ERM. His ejection from the Cabinet was to follow hard on the heels of sterling's ejection from the ERM.
20 As we shall see, the Bundesbank played the same game from the opposing court when the time came for attributing 'blame' for sterling's withdrawal from the system.

first possible occasion, that not just Mitterrand but politicians throughout the Community had been lying at Maastricht. He slammed his folders shut and made to rise from his chair. Waigel, who had been sitting beside him in evident discomfort, conscious of the charged relations between Bonn and Frankfurt, grabbed his arm and persuaded him to stay put. If Schlesinger had left the room, it is made clear by central bankers that the other governors would have had to leave too. During the long hours in which Lamont and other ministers had harangued Schlesinger, not one of them – not even Carlo Ciampi – had said a word in their support. They, at least, were behaving as good 'neo-functionalist' members of a supranational club. Their greatest desire might be to find themselves in a position where *they* could overrule Schlesinger, or rather his successors, but they would only ever get there if, in the meantime, the central bankers' club did not break ranks. Yet a mass exodus of governors from the room would, coming two days after Mitterrand's declarations on the primacy of the Council of Ministers over the central bankers, have ensured a French 'no' to Maastricht. It was only the strong grip of Swabian fingers on a Bavarian arm that prevented the world from being able to consign the treaty to the dustbin of history.

One can only sigh for what might have been. As it was, sufficient decorum was restored for a communiqué to be cobbled together. It had two important elements, both of which were to cause their authors far more trouble than they were worth. The first was a declaration that the finance ministers' statement, issued by Trichet a week earlier, on the rejection of any realignment was 'confirmed'. Five minutes before it was issued to the press, the communiqué said that the previous statement had been 'unanimously confirmed'. The word 'unanimously' must be taken out, insisted Schlesinger: the previous statement had been issued in the names of the finance ministers and of the finance ministers alone. Governors were now present; the word 'unanimously' would associate them with the statement, and Schlesinger did not wish to be associated with it. The second element was a welcoming of 'the fact that the Bundesbank has in present circumstances no intention to increase rates and is watching the further development of the economy'. Since the Bundesbank Council had, two days earlier, decided not to change its rates 'in present circumstances', Schlesinger was saying nothing new or significant whatsoever. Yet, as they staggered wearily out of the meeting-room, several finance ministers perked up at the sight of the waiting microphones and TV cameras. Lamont claimed that it was 'the first time' that the Bundesbank had committed itself 'openly and publicly' not to raise rates. Michel Sapin, the *énarque* technocrat appointed Finance Minister when Bérégovoy had moved to the Matignon in April, gurgled that there had been 'a new spirit' in the meeting. 'The outlook is for lower interest rates. The Bundesbank is no longer in a frame of mind to raise rates,' he said. Both Lamont and Sapin were talking nonsense.[21] Schlesinger had *not* committed the Bundesbank not to raise rates. And there was no 'new spirit' in the talks. Schlesinger was simply playing by the rules – or, at least, he was reading out the rulebook.

The folly of the communiqué was soon made evident. The very next day, in a BBC radio interview, Schlesinger declined to support the ministers' no-realignment declaration. The question, he said, went to his heart and the answer was therefore something which he would not make public. And over the next two or three days, Bundesbank press briefings emphasized that Schlesinger had said nothing more on interest rates than to repeat the Bundesbank's official statement after the previous Thursday's Council meeting.

Monday saw the usual post-weekend lira recovery, but sterling weakened on Schlesinger's radio interview and Lamont's failure to extract a cut in interest rates. The following day, Tuesday, was another tumultuous one. The Finnish government finally accepted the inevitable and floated the markka, fifteen months after pegging it to the ECU. The currency instantaneously fell by 13% against the DM. The Finnish decision immediately put pressure on the Swedish krona. The Swedish central bank pushed overnight rates up to 24%. The British and Italians were horrified. The markets had won on the markka (so too had the Finnish economy – but that was a matter of no concern to ministers and central bankers), and the Swedes had had to do horrible things to defend their rate. Mortgage rates in Sweden were going up by 5 percentage points in a week!

On Wednesday, the slide towards the ERM exit chute accelerated. The

21 It is just possible that this interpretation does not do Lamont justice. Precisely what his motivation was at Bath will probably be revealed only in his own memoirs. Certainly, his reactions immediately after sterling's exit from the system, described below, suggest that the ultimate outcome of Bath may have pleased him more than 'success' there would have done. It is already clear from Lamont himself that Britain has him to thank for deflecting Major and Hurd, during the Maastricht negotiations in December 1991, from a sinister plan to have ERM membership made a legally binding obligation on Britain even if the country remained outside Stage Three. Such an obligation would subsequently have made it very easy for those two devious personages to have argued that it was much better for Britain to join the Single Currency and have a seat in the ECB than to be tied to the ECB's interest-rate policies via the ERM with no input into its decisions. The importance of Lamont's blocking role here cannot be overestimated.

Swedes were forced to increase overnight rates to 75%, while expressing rather pathetic and deluded hopes of an 'association' with the ERM that would give them access to intervention support from the Bundesbank. But the Swedes had made their own bed when they chose to peg to the ECU; the Bundesbank was now happy to make them lie on it. In any case, the Bundesbank's most pressing concern was to *rid* itself of obligations to help Italy, not to take on new ones. In pursuit of this aim, Bundesbank sources again downplayed the significance of the Bath communiqué, and, to press home the point, the bank unexpectedly tightened money-market conditions in Frankfurt, pushing call-money rates back up to the Lombard rate and sparking fears that the Lombard rate itself would be raised at the following week's Council meeting. The UK Treasury and the Banca d'Italia were both obliged to issue further statements denying that there would be a realignment, but the market inevitably paid much less attention to these statements than to comments from a Bundesbank source that the lira, sterling and the peseta were all 'candidates for devaluation'.

On Thursday, the lira came under massive pressure and closed in London below its floor. Traders in Milan complained that Bundesbank intervention had been too small (not, presumably, to 'save the lira' but to provide a sucker-buyer for all the lire that traders wanted to sell at an increasingly certain profit). The Bundesbank, indeed, was telling some important market players that, 'there are some problems, some technical hitches, with our credit lines to the Banca d'Italia.' In other words, it was making it quite clear that it was not intervening as unreservedly as the Banca d'Italia would have liked. The writing was more visibly on the wall than ever when in response an angry Ciampi defied the rules of central banking freemasonry by declaring that German interest rates were 'excessively high and needed to be brought down'.

Sterling was under slightly less pressure than the previous day: Major's ERM commitment was seen as less tied to the survival of the Maastricht Treaty than was Italy's. Nonetheless, it remained very close to its floor. That evening, Major made the speech that, together with the pre-election promise not to raise VAT, was to destroy his credibility with the British electorate. He dismissed the idea of a realignment as 'the soft option, the devaluer's option that would be a betrayal of our future and our children's future'. Major might have Faith in the ERM, but there was certainly no Charity in his clinging to the ERM wreckage. He was prepared to condemn more firms to closure, more workers to unemployment, more families to homelessness, in the pursuit of 'his' ERM conviction.

While Major was indulging in squeaky rhetoric that Thursday evening, caring only about his political face, so soon to correspond with his own, unnecessarily self-deprecating assessment of the image in his shaving mirror as 'plug-ugly', the Bundesbank had come to its own conclusions about the lira.

## Dirty work at the crossrates

Friday began as the previous Friday had done – with the usual array of Italian banks, corporates and funds benefiting from arbitrage opportunities and dumping large amounts of lire with the Bundesbank. During the course of the day, the Bundesbank and the Banca d'Italia intervened in unprecedented volume. But there was no further rise in the Banca d'Italia's discount rate. Again, the lira closed below its permitted ERM floor. Everything pointed to a realignment. A meeting of the Monetary Committee could surely be expected the next day, Saturday, to sort out all the details before the markets reopened after the weekend. Yet none came. There was indeed a realignment, but only after two days of murky deals, plots and deceits that were to blow the cover of the 'common good' of the ERM, as Trichet in particular liked to call it.

Trichet's role that weekend would be an ambiguous one, and subsequently much criticized. Previous accounts of the weekend's events portray him as having misled German emissaries about his intentions, receiving information from them in the guise of Monetary Committee Chairman but using it as a French official. In fact, there can be little doubt that he and Köhler and Tietmeyer, the German members of the Monetary Committee, were consorting closely together.[22]

The formal side of the story was publicly recounted the following Monday by Schlesinger. In fulfilling its intervention obligations the previous week, Schlesinger said, the Bundesbank had had to take in the equivalent of DM 24 billion, twice the amount involved in intervention before the January 1987 realignment. The German monetary base had been swollen in a single week by as much as would have been appropriate for the whole year. The EMS agreements were, said Schlesinger, quite clear about what should happen in such circumstances: after unsuccessful

---

22  The most serious, but incomplete, attempt to fit together the pieces of the weekend jigsaw is by Peter Norman and Lionel Barber, 'Behind the ERM Crisis', *Financial Times*, 11 December 1992.

*intramarginal*[23] intervention and a rise in interest rates in the weak-currency country, there had to be a realignment – 'That is an element of agreement.' As we shall see in chapter 12, that interpretation of the ERM rules was certainly not one with which France, at least, would agree. Schlesinger was in all likelihood referring to the agreement between the Bundesbank and the German government, when the EMS was set up, contained in the 'Emminger Letter'. He went on to say: 'The Bundesbank had, however, to turn to the responsible partner in the negotiations, the Federal government, which, together with Italy, the currency in opposition, came to an agreement that produced the result, as is known, of a revaluation of the DM and the other EMS currencies [*sic*][24] and a devaluation of the lira.'

On Friday, 11 September, Kohl had paid a secret visit to the Bundesbank. Schlesinger had clearly invoked the 'Emminger Letter' and had asked the government to initiate a realignment. As he said the following Monday, 'the solution to the exchange-rate trap lay in the hands of the governments; we have the Federal government to thank for extricating us'. The events of the next ten-and-a-half months were to make it clear what conditions Kohl must have imposed before agreeing. The first, clearly, was that the Bundesbank must, for that day at least, fulfil its intervention obligations to the letter. Second, there would have to be some 'signal' on interest rates. Third, most onerous of all, the 'solution' to the exchange-rate trap must not endanger the French franc – in any circumstances![25] If those conditions were fulfilled, the two German Monetary Committee representatives, Köhler (from the Finance Ministry) and Tietmeyer (from the Bundesbank, even if only nominally in this instance), could negotiate a realignment with the Italians.

On Saturday, Köhler and Tietmeyer flew down to Rome. But their journey was not a direct one. First, they travelled to Paris to meet Sapin and Trichet at the French Finance Ministry.[26] The reasons for that detour have never been admitted. A little more than two weeks later Schlesinger, in a

23 My emphasis.
24 Following Continental practice, Schlesinger did not differentiate between the EMS and the ERM. The drachma, a member of the EMS but not the ERM, was not involved in the realignment.
25 Wilhelm Nölling, shortly after retiring from the Bundesbank Council, reported that France had initially opposed a lira devaluation. Tietmeyer had obviously made this known to his fellow Council members. What is not clear is whether he told them the nature of the conditions under which the French dropped their objections.
26 By now housed, much to the displeasure of its officials, in a new brutalist building in the unfashionable Bercy quarter.

PRICKING THE BUBBLE

document that fuelled a bitter row with the British Treasury, implied that the Bundesbank had asked the German government to negotiate a realignment, 'among the group of EMS partners', involving more than just the lira. Trichet, of course, was Chairman of the Monetary Committee, and his duties involved sounding out the members in advance of a realignment meeting. He was a natural starting-point for 'negotiations among the group of EMS partners'. But he could have been consulted over the phone. And why was Sapin involved? If Trichet was being consulted as Chairman of the Monetary Committee, why had not Lamont, as Chairman of Ecofin, and Wim Duisenberg,[27] as Chairman of the Governors' Committee, also been informed? But if Trichet was *not* greeting the two Germans in his *Community* role, why was he, along with Sapin, being made privy to what Germany was up to when other ERM countries were not?

There can be little doubt about the answers to these questions. Whatever Schlesinger might have believed, Köhler and Tietmeyer were in Paris to discuss how to put a 'ringfence' around the lira and prevent or, if need be, repulse attacks on the French franc. The 'sweetheart deal' (a term first coined some months later by Bertie Ahern, the Irish Finance Minister) was conceived that Saturday morning. The strategy that was thrashed out was twofold.

First, the realignment must be 'dedramatized' and confined to the lira. It would be possible to depict Italy as being at fault on account of its public debt problems. Trichet, as Chairman, would not convene a meeting of the Monetary Committee. A meeting would open a Pandora's box in which questions of a general realignment would be raised and further attacks on the Bundesbank's interest-rate policy might be made: Tietmeyer, in particular, would find himself in a difficult position, since everyone knew that for some time the Bundesbank had been dropping hints about trading off interest-rate cuts for a general realignment. Instead, Trichet would wait until Köhler and Tietmeyer had cut a bilateral deal in Rome and would then simply inform other members of the Committee of the details over the phone, asking for their agreement without giving them any time for reflection. The apparent ambiguity of Trichet's position vis-à-vis Köhler and Tietmeyer that morning is resolved: he didn't appear to be acting as 'honest broker' as required by his Monetary Committee role. Nor was he misleading the Germans. He was part of a Franco-German alliance against the supposed 'common good' of the ERM – and against the Bundesbank.

27 Governor of the Nederlandsche Bank, the Dutch central bank.

Second, if things went wrong, ERM turbulence spread and the franc came under attack, the Bundesbank would have to commit itself to special arrangements, outside the formal ERM rules, to provide unlimited support to the franc and the franc alone – the sweetheart deal. The magic incantation of the 'Emminger Letter' that the Bundesbank had used to protect itself from the evil eye of the ERM would lose its potency.

Arrived in Rome, Köhler and Tietmeyer got down to the business of negotiating a realignment with the Italians. Tietmeyer, in particular, knew he had little room for manoeuvre. Too small a lira devaluation, and he and Schlesinger would have difficulty in persuading the rest of the Bundesbank Council to agree to anything more than a derisory cut in German interest rates. Too large a devaluation, and the French would complain about the competitive advantage Italy would derive. The Italians themselves had always been clear that if they were forced into a devaluation at all, then they would go for a big one, probably 15%. There was no point in half-measures. Politically, any devaluation, however small, would be seen as a defeat for the 'European' strategy Italy had been pursuing; one might as well bow to economic logic and restore the competitive position, or else the markets would just come back for more.

The compromise reached in Rome – a 7.1% devaluation[28] – satisfied no one but was, it seemed, acceptable to the two governments involved. When Trichet was given the news on Saturday evening, he set about presenting other members of the Monetary Committee with a *fait accompli*, simply asking them over the phone if they would agree to the deal, one including an unspecified cut in German rates. He stressed the need for a quick agreement: the Bundesbank Council would have to be 'squared' the next day before markets reopened on Monday. The one calculated risk that Trichet had to take was with the Spanish. Their actions since June indicated that they would not fight hard against a peseta devaluation, especially if the taboo against realignments had already been broken by the lira. They might ask for a meeting of the Monetary Committee, whose outcome could easily be a devaluation of the lira, peseta and sterling. That would put severe competitive pressure on the French franc as well as muddying the referendum waters still further. To forestall this possibility Trichet asked outright: 'Do you want to devalue the peseta?' His

28  The official communiqué subsequently issued in the names of ministers and governors of the EMS countries referred to a lira devaluation of 3.5% and a similar revaluation of the other ERM currencies. This was merely a presentational device to provide some cover for a cut in Bundesbank interest rates.

interlocutor, seeing no opportunity to negotiate a general settlement but merely the dangers for Spain in upsetting a Franco-German applecart, said 'No.'

Late on Saturday evening, the deal was in the bag. By six o'clock next morning, newspaper placards in Rome were announcing a lira devaluation and a cut in German interest rates – before most members of the Bundesbank Council knew anything about what was going on. For much of Sunday, Schlesinger took soundings among his Council members, feeling them out on how big a cut in rates would be acceptable. By Sunday evening, the authorities in other countries had, it seems, been informed of the results, which would be confirmed by a specially convened meeting of the Council the next morning. On Sunday evening, the news of the lira devaluation, and of accompanying interest-rate moves by the Bundesbank, was officially released.

The next morning, markets initially reacted favourably. The lira shot briefly to the top of its new band as market operators who had held short positions in the lira took their profits, buying lire at the new rate in order to repay their lira borrowings. The news that the Bundesbank was going to reduce interest rates produced a 99-point rise in the Footsie when the London market opened. Stock exchanges across Europe powered ahead, and bond prices surged. In mid-morning, the results of the Bundesbank Council meeting were announced: the Lombard rate would be cut by 0.25%, the discount rate by 0.5%. Markets, which had got used to concentrating on the Lombard rate when the trend of interest rates was upward, were disappointed by the size of the cut in this rate, and stock markets trimmed their early gains. But, by and large, the 'monetary masters of the world' in Europe could feel generally relieved: their ambitions were still intact.

Within Germany, however, the rate reductions, while welcomed by business, caused shock in the banking community. Fears were expressed by many commentators that the Bundesbank had, by caving in to external political pressure, again weakened the role of the DM as ERM anchor and given credence to those – not least Mitterrand – who claimed that a future ECB would not in practice be independent. Schlesinger did his best to rebut the accusations. In the Bundesbank press conference he spoke of an 'advance concession' in expectation of better future behaviour on the German budgetary and wage fronts. In his speech on Monday evening, he emphasized that it was the Bundesbank that had asked the government for a realignment and that past realignments had often been followed by a cut in Bundesbank rates. This was important: in effect he was saying that while the Bundesbank might cut rates after a realignment, because a revaluation of the DM of itself *tightened* monetary conditions in Germany, the Bundesbank would not cut its rates to *avoid* a realignment, since this would produce a net *easing* of monetary conditions in Germany, purely for external political reasons. The distinction between the two sets of circumstances was a fundamental one. Schlesinger can hardly have foreseen how quickly the Bundesbank would be forced into purely 'foreign policy' reductions in interest rates. But, even sooner, all the three 'candidates for devaluation' identified by the Bundesbank the previous week would be back in the firing line.

## White Wednesday

The lira devaluation sounded the death-knell for sterling's ERM membership. It showed that realignments were still part of the system (something that Schlesinger was at pains to point out in his Monday night speech, one sentence after referring to 'cumulated cost and price divergences' in a number of countries easily identifiable as Italy, Britain, Spain and Portugal). It showed that there were profits to be made out of the central banks. The scale of the previous week's intervention for the lira – DM 24 billion – put the UK government's borrowing of DM 5 billion, announced with such fanfares ten days earlier, into perspective. And the fact that the Bundesbank had been able to call a halt to intervention was highly significant.

The odds looked juicily attractive to people with strong nerves. George Soros, managing Quantum, the largest of the hedge funds, certainly had strong nerves. According to the hedge-fund community, he contacted four or five other large players, suggesting that they should together commit themselves to leveraged borrowing of the staggering sum of $18 billion[29] to finance short positions in sterling (some of the others blanched; in the end, a war-chest of a 'mere' £10 billion was put together). With sterling so close to its lower limit, sterling sales of only a small fraction of that amount would push the pound to the point at which the Bundesbank would be forced to intervene by the ERM rules. On the evidence of the previous week, the British would not be able to count on Bundesbank assistance for long enough to fight off the attacks – and following the Swedish path of sky-high interest rates would be both politically suicidal and financially catastrophic.

29 For comparison, this was an amount similar to the UK government's borrowing, to cover the budget deficit, for the whole of 1991.

The storm-clouds grew even darker on Tuesday when it was announced that John Major had cancelled a trip to Spain at the last minute. Veterans in the market recalled Denis Healey's embarrassment when he had to be recalled from an IMF meeting to deal with a sterling crisis in the autumn of 1976: Major was staying in London to avoid the same humiliation, they reckoned. The same day, Whitehall was full of rumours that the Cabinet could not reach agreement on the following year's public spending round: government borrowing was going through the roof, and the dramatic rise in unemployment benefits and slump in tax receipts as a result of the recession would have to mean big cuts in other ministers' budgets, cuts that were being fiercely resisted. Sterling closed in London at its lowest ever rate since joining the ERM, a mere $\frac{1}{5}$ of a pfenning above its DM floor of 2.7780.

The lira too, was again falling fast after the initial burst of profit-taking on Monday. The Milan stock exchange also plummeted. Most market calculations of the lira's overvaluation against the DM before the weekend devaluation were in the region of 15 to 20%. A few months previously, the forex market – if not the bond market – had given no thought to such considerations. But once the ERM bubble was pricked, the traditional 'fundamentals' of exchange-rate behaviour came back into play. A 7% devaluation was not enough.

Many of the large investment funds that had poured money into Italy in 'convergence plays' now panicked, telling their banks to get them out of lire at any price. Large Italian companies, who had performed their own 'convergence plays' by doing much of their borrowing in the DM and the Swiss franc to profit from lower rates of interest than in Italy – amounts up to $180 billion according to one market estimate – were falling over themselves to buy foreign currencies to cover part of their borrowings before those currencies became even more expensive. The lira plunged through the central rate of its new bands, with no attempt by the Banca d'Italia to stop it. The Italian central bank, it was thought, simply had no reserves left. At some point it would actually have to *sell* lire for DM so that it could pay back its borrowings from the Bundesbank. And a new element in the Tuesday chaos was a slide in the peseta below its ERM central rate, a rate that the Banca de España had spent part of its massive reserves to defend for several weeks past.

But it was after the close of the European markets that sterling ran into a firestorm of selling – in New York. The trigger had been German news agency reports that Schlesinger, in a newspaper interview to be published the next day, had said that the weekend's realignment had been insufficient – other currencies should have been involved. Shocked British ministers ordered Leigh-Pemberton to contact the Bundesbank immediately to demand an immediate denial. The answer he got served only to aggravate the wounding nature of the report: Schlesinger's remarks had 'not yet been cleared for publication'.

Sterling plunged below its ERM limit in New York trading, forcing the Bank of England to intervene there. The ERM rules did not oblige it to do so, but if it did not then there would be massive arbitrage as soon as the European markets opened next morning and formal intervention obligations resumed. In the event, the bank's operations in New York were too small to have the desired effect. Wednesday morning in Europe began in the worst possible way for the Bank when it had large packets of sterling bought by market operators in New York below the lower limit presented for sale *at* that limit. From the first seconds, quite literally, of the trading day, the Bank of England was leaking reserves at a catastrophic rate – and sterling remained nailed to its ERM floor. Lamont authorized round after round of intervention, but with no effect whatsoever on the sterling rate.

By mid-morning the decision that the government had done everything to avoid could no longer, in the lunatic world of the ERM, be shirked: Major and Lamont ordered the Bank of England to announce an immediate rise in minimum lending rate to 12%, implying a rise of 2 percentage points in base lending rates and, inevitably if with a lag, in mortgage rates. There was absolutely no response from sterling, and only continued massive intervention prevented a clear break through the ERM floor. At two o'clock in the afternoon came the message that the markets had been hoping for: minimum lending rate was to be raised by a further 3 percentage points, to 15%, with effect the next day. The stock market leapt for joy: every trader in the market interpreted the unprecedented second rise as meaning the game was up – sterling was going to have to leave the ERM.[30] If anything, the volume of sterling selling increased. Within

30 One of the most telling comments on what was happening was made the next day by Ruth Lea, chief economist of Mitsubishi Bank in London: 'The ironic thing is that we may get an economic recovery because the government's economic policies failed.' Perhaps the crassest comment – competition much stiffer here – and perhaps also the least surprising given its source at the heart of the consensus that had campaigned so vociferously for ERM membership, came from Sir Michael Angus, President of the CBI. On 16 September he had said, in reaction to the day's second rise in base rates: 'We need 15% base rates like we need a hole in the head. But if it is a choice between that and devaluation then I suppose it will have to be.'

minutes of the announcement, UK officials began to contact monetary officials in other ERM countries: Britain wished to convene a meeting of the Monetary Committee for that night, and in all probability would be suspending its membership of the system. The second announcement of a rise in interest rates can never have been intended to stick – whatever panic there may have been among Treasury and bank officials that day, the terror that would have struck Lamont, at least, if sterling *had* moved off its floor would have been even greater. 'Living with 15% base rates' – the title of a spread FT journalists were feverishly putting together late that afternoon – would be quite simply impossible. The rise was simply a gesture by 'caring' John Major to his 'partners' that Britain had fully complied with the rules of the ERM game. How many suicides, heart attacks and mental breakdowns the interest-rate announcement provoked in struggling firms and families, less alive to its meaning than the stock market, is not recorded. It was Major himself, according to accounts clearly inspired by Downing Street, who constantly wanted reassurance during the day that Britain's ERM obligations were being fulfilled to the letter. The 'caring' Prime Minister seems not to have cared that his re-election five months earlier brought with it much more important responsibilities – to the people of Britain.

Even when intervention obligations lapsed for the day, at 5 pm Brussels time, and the Bank of England gave up the ghost, letting sterling fall four pfennigs below the ERM floor, there was no announcement from the government. People returning home from work, unaware of what had been happening all day, were greeted only with the news that they would very soon be paying half as much again in interest on mortgages and bank borrowings. Not until mid-evening was Lamont allowed to announce that sterling's membership of the ERM would be suspended. At the same time, he stated that the second of the day's two rises in interest rates would be withdrawn: next day's minimum lending rate would be 12%.

Meanwhile, the Italian lira had also fallen through its new floor after a crisis meeting between the top Banca d'Italia officials and the Prime Minister sparked rumours that Italy, too, would have to withdraw from the system. The peseta also dropped close to its ERM floor, having entered the lower half of the band for the first time the previous day. The Banco de España intervened, but there was no hint from the authorities that interest rates would be raised. The ERM was in tatters.

## Black suspenders

The Monetary Committee meeting that began that night at 11 pm Brussels time was a surprisingly low-key affair, and its results predictable. There were no recriminations among the officials involved – although there might well have been if everyone had fully realized the role played the previous Saturday by Trichet, who was now exuding the Gallic charm, courtesy and diplomacy befitting the official persona of Monetary Committee Chairman.

The aims of the various countries were clear enough. The main concern of the British officials present – or at least the Treasury officials – was to save as much political face as possible for Major. The most attractive – but least realistic – way of doing so was to get the whole ERM suspended, using the upcoming French referendum as an excuse. François Mitterrand, who had called the referendum, could then be represented as the real culprit for ERM turbulence. This would be preferable to trying to pin the blame on Germany, given the importance Major attached to his illusory friendship with Kohl.[31] The one surprising facet of the suspension call is that, according to diplomats, Treasury officials plucked up the courage to suggest it only after the Commission representative had done so first.

The Italians, with practically no reserves left and lumbered with mountainous short-term debts to the Bundesbank, were clearly in no position to defend *any* parity for the lira. But, unlike the British, they were unwilling to announce a suspension of their membership: the psychological shock to the 'European' strategy would be too great. Instead, they argued that they would remain in the ERM but would 'temporarily abstain from intervention' in the light of the British decision to suspend sterling membership (the next day, the Italian authorities announced that they would rejoin the system the following Tuesday, after the markets had had time to react to the French referendum result).

For Spain, the objectives were to remain in the ERM (they saw their chances of satisfactory handouts from the 'Delors 2' package of Community transfers, to be decided at the Edinburgh summit three months later, as being linked to ERM membership) while avoiding a rise in interest rates. In

---

31 When the ploy did not work, Major did indeed find himself having to try to save his own face by, on 18 September, blaming Germany, backing Lamont's explicit condemnation of German economic policy. Tietmeyer, who was subsequently to have no qualms about attacking British policy, replied to Lamont in a way that justified Lawson's description of the German as 'something of a rough diamond for an official': Lamont's comments, he haughtily declared, were 'inappropriate for a minister'.

June, they had absorbed pressure mainly by letting the peseta drift down from the top of the band. Subsequently, they had intervened aggressively to hold the peseta above its central rate. Once that strategy had been overwhelmed, on Tuesday, the need for a devaluation became obvious. Spain had already been fingered by the Bundesbank as a 'candidate'; if it did not take advantage of the opportunity presented that night, renewed pressure on the currency would certainly find the Bundesbank asking the German government for another realignment the next weekend, when all the relevant officials, ministers and governors gathered in Washington for the annual IMF meetings.

That left the question of French and German attitudes. The position of the French government, fortified by the recently conceived sweetheart deal, was clear: there could be no going back on the *franc fort*, or on the 'glidepath' view of the ERM. The attitude of the German government was identical. As for the Bundesbank, its representative in the Monetary Committee was Tietmeyer. While Schlesinger would have seen attractions in a suspension of the ERM, Tietmeyer did not, for two reasons. The more important, in the short run, was that Kohl and the rest of the government were against the idea. There was no point whatsoever in disagreeing – especially as Tietmeyer had himself been involved in the secret deal with France. The second reason was to do with Tietmeyer's longer-run strategy. What he wanted was to get back to the ERM of 1983–86, a period of undisputed Bundesbank leadership, and also a period when the German central bank was not in practice troubled by intervention: other countries did the decent thing and devalued if they got into difficulty. The ERM had, in his view, been exporting price stability to the other members of the system during that period. If a 1983–86 mechanism could be resurrected, and its membership confined to countries prepared to give priority to price stability and possessing economic characteristics similar to Germany's, then the Bundesbank could – once Tietmeyer had succeeded Schlesinger as President – take account of the needs of the system as a whole in reaching its monetary policy decisions. This 'benevolent dictatorship' in monetary affairs would, in his view, be much preferable to the 'symmetry' suggested by the Commission in 1990. It could also be a means of holding things together if Maastricht failed, as he suspected it must in the absence of the kind and degree of political union that France could not accept. So Tietmeyer was playing the mirror-image of the game the French had been playing for so long. They had been prepared to go along with the German-dominated ERM if it led to their 'getting their hands on the Bundesbank' via the ECB. Tietmeyer was prepared to swallow the 'sweetheart deal' if it kept in being an ERM that would still be German-led and could provide an *alternative* to Maastricht, or at any rate a safety net if Maastricht toppled.

On interest rates, Tietmeyer's private advice to the French must already have been what he was consistently to reiterate over the next fifteen months: be patient, keep quiet, don't antagonize the hawks on the Bundesbank Council, and the recession in Germany will bring interest rates down, whatever the money-supply figures show. It seems that during the early hours of 17 September, the French were prepared to heed that advice, and the rest of the would-be 'hard core' took their cue from France. Given all this (nearly all of which will naturally have gone unspoken),[32] it seems rather surprising that the Monetary Committee took more than six hours to announce the results of its deliberations to a waiting world. Perhaps the members of the Committee felt that the gravitas of the occasion required that the impression of deep discussion be conveyed. When the British delegation emerged, sleepless and downcast, they were rather unkindly filmed first failing to find taxis and wandering around in some degree of confusion and then, having finally reached the airport, having to sit around in grim embarrassment as flight schedules were disturbed by technical problems at, of all places, Frankfurt airport.

## Counting the cost

The absence of contingency plans for getting to the airport and then the difficulties created at Frankfurt was a facile metaphor for the circumstances of Britain's ERM exit. It was certainly one that was exploited by the British press. But what was the true balance-sheet of the ERM experience, and who should really be blamed for, or credited with, its ending? What was going to replace it as the cornerstone of British economic policy?

John Major once said: 'If it isn't hurting, it isn't working.' The ERM certainly hurt. During the two years of ERM membership, Britain suffered its worst postwar recession. Unemployment climbed to record heights. Thousands of firms, tens of thousands of homes, hundreds of thousands, even millions, of jobs were lost. Lost too, was the entrepreneurial confidence of the late 1980s, the radicalism of government policy, and the

32 The Bundesbank's official comment the next day said that the decisions were 'an appropriate response to the previous tensions'. This formula was a direct, and clearly deliberate, ex post contradiction of the finance ministers' statement of 26 August which had said that a realignment would *not* be an appropriate response to the tensions then evident in the system.

healthy position of public-sector finance that Howe and Lawson had striven to achieve. Much of this ground has been gone over in earlier chapters, where it was argued that a recession was made inevitable once Lawson's failure to control the earlier boom had sparked inflation. What the ERM did was to convert a recession, necessary to bring inflation back under control, into a slump that threatened the whole economic, financial and social structure of the country.

When John Major took sterling into the ERM in October 1990, the economy had just, in the words of Treasury officials at the time, 'gone off the edge of the cliff', for reasons spelt out in earlier chapters. Unemployment rose, inflation fell in response. By the time Britain was booted out of the ERM, it was back down to 3.6%, roughly where it had been before Lawson's mistakes lost control of the economy.

There were many financial market economists, even in September 1992, who argued that this showed the ERM experience to have been necessary and that there should be no 'dash for growth' with the formal constraint removed. There were dire predictions that, within a year, inflation would be back at 6 or 7% if policy were to be eased significantly.[33] These jeremiahs had totally failed to recognize the severity and the nature of the squeeze that the ERM had imposed on the economy. The government machine itself had been more perceptive, for once. From the very start, the authorities did everything they could to make the 'discipline' of the ERM less binding, cutting interest rates at every opportunity (from 15% immediately before entry to 10% by May 1992). But this was not enough. The loss of competitiveness in the boom years had been inevitable, but now had to be unwound. Domestic demand was depressed, over and beyond the natural cyclical down-phase after earlier exuberance, by falling house prices, high interest rates, rising unemployment, banking sector problems, the apparently illusory nature of the Thatcherite revolution and a generalized loss of confidence in the government's ability to manage the economy. There could be no durable recovery unless competitiveness improved, boosting exports relative to imports. But, throughout the ERM period, British competitiveness actually carried on getting *worse*, not better. British price and wage increases would have had to be forced down *below* those in

---

33 Perhaps significantly, most of those who had been most attached to the ERM and were now prophesying doom and disaster worked for English securities houses and banks. The analyses produced by American houses in London tended to be much more balanced and, as it turned out, much more accurate.

competitor countries before net exports could even start to slowly fill the gap left by depressed domestic demand.

By mid-1992, Treasury and Bank of England economists had gloomily come to the conclusion, without of course sharing their thoughts with the world at large, that prices would actually be *falling* in 1993, with worse to come in 1994, recalling the pre-war depression. Denmark had been trying to follow the path of 'competitive disinflation' for six years, and unemployment was still rising. France had been doing something similar for almost ten years, with much the same effect. In Britain, things were a lot worse, akin to the state of affairs in the Nordic countries. The British financial and political system would never be able to take such strain. The financial system was already in trouble after the Lawson boom went sour. Prolonged deflation and unemployment would destroy it. In America, similar risks were averted by a determined Fed policy of monetary ease, low interest rates and a depreciating dollar (something that itself increased Britain's ERM woes). In the Nordic countries, nailed to their ECU pegs, the risks had become unpleasant fact, with near-bankrupt banking systems forcing governments into bail-outs (and budget deficits) and semi-nationalization.

Politically, too, the ERM was never a credible option in these circumstances. However much the electorate might have felt unhappy about the burst of inflation in 1988–90, there was never going to be the slightest support for a policy that would certainly have required outright *deflation* and constantly rising unemployment. In France, the technocratic/political élite had been able to get away with such an outcome because nearly the whole of the traditional political class saw it as a necessary evil – necessary to pursue the goal of taming Germany and confronting the Americans and Japanese. In Britain, that obsessive fear of Germany and hatred of America and Japan was just not there (except perhaps in the left wing of the Conservative Party). Murdering the economy would never find popular support on 'geopolitical' grounds.

By the autumn of 1991, Major, personally tied to the ERM, was grimly aware of the political bind he had got himself into. The official forecasts that had been produced at that time predicted some sluggish growth the next year, but only with the assistance of a massive relaxation of public spending. The ERM had brought Keynesian deficit-financing back with a vengeance, as the government sought to offset the monetary squeeze with fiscal largesse. As Treasury officials admitted in private, it also led to damaging backtracking on supply-side policies and strengthened the hand of the more interventionist members of the Cabinet. Yet even the government was too optimistic, and by the time of the 1992 budget it was apparent to official forecasters that yet more Keynesian pump-priming would be needed, so fiercely was the country being throttled by the ERM constraint. In addition, the 'automatic' effects of recession were inexorably forcing the budget deficit ever upwards via reduced tax receipts and swollen unemployment payments.

The path of public finances was becoming unsustainable. If Britain had stayed in the ERM, the country would soon have been in the position of Italy, Sweden, Finland and Belgium – all of them countries in which exchange-rate 'discipline' had led to fiscal irresponsibility on a grand scale. As it was, Britain was pushed out in time to avoid irretrievable fiscal catastrophe. The easing of monetary policy and early economic recovery that ERM exit allowed meant that steps could be taken to restore order to the public finances vandalized by the mechanism. Those steps, inevitably painful in political terms, would have had to be taken at some stage if financial and economic chaos was to be averted. But only the freedom to manage monetary policy with *domestic* considerations in mind made it possible to take them in conditions of economic growth instead of catastrophic slump. Both sharply lower interest rates *and* a sharply lower pound were needed. White Wednesday made them possible.

It is little wonder, then, that Norman Lamont, directly responsible for managing the public finances, was happy to tell the world that he had been 'singing in the bath' after White Wednesday. Nor is it surprising that he soon found himself kept in office only as 'an air-raid shelter', to use his own words again, to protect the true author of the public finance calamity, John Major. But it was to the newly cheerful Lamont that there fell the task of reconstructing economic policy after White Wednesday. The Euroenthusiasts in the Cabinet were in no mood to make life easy for him. On the evening of White Wednesday, Lamont said in his statement (toeing the official line one last time) that it was hoped to take sterling back into the ERM 'as soon as market conditions permitted'. The next day, commenting on this contingency, Major noted: 'Clearly, it is not imminent.' But both Clarke and Heseltine, leading the 'Rhenish capitalists' (that is, anticapitalists) in the Cabinet, left no doubt about their desire to see sterling back in the mechanism very quickly indeed. So strong was their desire that it was undoubtedly they who counselled against going any further than to rescind – as was in fact done on 18 September – the 2% rise in interest rates remaining from the White Wednesday panic. Why? They may have been worried that the beneficial results of a more rational, independent monetary policy might kill any chance of Britain's agreeing to monetary union. And in the shorter term it was apparent that big cuts in British interest rates, taking them significantly below German rates, would rule out an early return to the ERM. It would not be possible to maintain sub-German rates in the ERM – and Germany would probably block re-entry in such circumstances anyway. But if rates were cut outside the ERM it would be politically impossible to raise them again for the sole purpose of going back in. Better, then, the ERMomaniacs thought, not to cut interest rates in the first place. They may also have used another argument likely to weigh heavy in the Prime Minister's calculations: Major and Lamont had claimed in the period before White Wednesday that leaving the system would bring *higher* rates, not lower, as well as higher inflation.[34]

Fortunately for Britain, the political timing of White Wednesday could not have been worse for Clarke and Heseltine or better for Lamont, whose tactical repositioning was rapid and radical.[35] It came just two weeks before a Tory Party Conference that, to judge from the constituency resolutions submitted to it, was going to be distinctly rebellious on the ERM and on Maastricht. The sole fact of Major's appearance, in flesh and blood, would be reminder enough of all the broken 'over-my-dead-body' promises to stay in the ERM. Better to brass-neck it, cut interest rates and stay out of the ERM to please the rabble. Otherwise, both the Maastricht Treaty and Major himself might suffer the same fate as sterling – summary dismissal.[36]

34 Long-term rates did briefly rise in *nominal* terms immediately after White Wednesday: it was inevitable that British inflation would be higher with sterling depreciation than without it. This was seized on gleefully by the ERMomaniacs, who could still see no further than the end of their out-of-joint noses. Sam Brittan, for instance, declared: 'Forget further early interest-rate cuts over and above the foolish reductions made after ERM departure. The government will be lucky to avoid a base rate increase before the Tory conference is over.' But since the prospect without depreciation was for outright deflation, an offsetting of deflationary forces was no bad thing, as Eddie George was later to point out when he became Governor. *Real* long-term rates of interest, as proxied by the yield on index-linked gilts, fell dramatically as a result of White Wednesday, just as the economy needed.

35 According to one contemporary account, in the few days after White Wednesday Lamont unilaterally changed the line on the ERM that had been agreed by the Cabinet on 17 September. His success, in political if not in personal terms, could be judged from Kenneth Clarke's subsequently having to put some tactical distance between himself and the ERM while the ousting of Lamont from the Exchequer was being prepared.

36 This book is primarily about what did happen and why it happened, not about what did not happen. But it would be wrong not to wonder what might have taken place if the expected Labour victory in the April 1992 election had actually happened. If a Labour government had been in office to be confronted with the inevitable sterling crisis, everything suggests that it would have learnt nothing either from the disaster created by Philip Snowden in 1929–31 or from the Mitterrand/Delors/Bérégovoy Socialist misery in France. As recently pointed out by

Thus, bit by bit, Lamont obtained clearance for his new policy framework – one, as he said with justifiable satisfaction and emphasis, that would allow for a *British* monetary policy with *British* economic interests in mind.[37] The philosophy of the new framework is discussed in chapter 10 below; its practical results were, over the first few months following White Wednesday, a succession of cuts in interest rates and a downward adjustment of sterling. By the early spring of 1993, the markets believed that both interest rates and sterling had reached levels appropriate to the government's aims of economic recovery, necessary budgetary retrenchment and the stabilization of inflation in a range of 1% to 4%. At that point, the low level of British interest rates relative to German rates was consistent with expectations of a sterling appreciation. During the course of 1993, the British recovery was seen to be firmly established, yet inflation carried on

Anatole Kaletsky, a Labour government in September 1992 would, to judge from the pronouncements of John Smith at the time, have tried to devalue within the ERM. This would have been the worst possible option, requiring *higher*, not lower, interest rates, as well as the reintroduction of exchange controls, to 'defend' the new parity. It would have devastated private-sector confidence, hammered the already battered housing market and worsened, not relieved, the recession. The economic, fiscal and social consequences would have been so ghastly as to raise doubts even about the future of democratic politics in Britain. But in this game of might-have-been, one should also remember the role of London's financial markets. As we shall see, such a combination of devaluation, high interest rates and exchange controls was to have very damaging effects even for Spain's infant financial markets. In London's highly developed markets, dependent on liquidity, the impact would have been cataclysmic. There would have been a financial market collapse so dangerous as to sweep Britain out of the ERM even under a government as stupid as Labour would have been (and shows signs of still aspiring to be).

In this sense, London's financial markets would have been the best guarantors of liberal democracy in Britain. The same cannot be said of all the City's financial market dignitaries. Sir Michael Butler was British Permanent Representative in Brussels when the Foreign Office was trying to pull the wool over Mrs Thatcher's eyes about the federalist intentions of Britain's 'partners' and is now a leading light in the campaign by those City figures who want to see their country in EMU. During the course of White Wednesday he argued for a macho policy like that – involving 500% overnight rates – then being pursued by the Swedish central bank (as we shall see, the bank ultimately came to recognize it as futile and damaging). As quoted by a heartily approving Sam Brittan, himself writing as the events of 16 September were still unfolding, Butler said that the only losers from very high day-to-day rates were the speculators. As Butler was speaking, the interest-rate options market in London was on the verge of a collapse that could have produced financial meltdown.

37  As we shall see, Continental politicians and banker/politicians were soon to attack such a policy philosophy because it was too successful. The initial reaction of ERM-consensus-defenders in Britain, however, was to deny that it was even possible. The political editor of the *Financial Times*, for instance, referred to 'Lamont's appeal to the spurious notion that there can be something akin to a uniquely British economic strategy'. More ominously, Kohl told the Bundestag on 25 September, in his usual bullying way: 'No one in Europe – and I repeat, no one – should labour under the illusion that he is in a position to go it alone.'

gently declining to the middle of the target range. The pound did indeed start moving upwards against the DM. From a low of DM 2.37 in February 1993, it had risen back to DM 2.65 (against its old ERM central rate of DM 2.95) by early 1994 before, first, the embarrassing collapse of 'back to basics' led to renewed turmoil in the Conservative Party and, subsequently, signs of German economic recovery stiffened the DM.

As we shall see in subsequent chapters, the increasingly evident success story of British monetary policy outside the ERM led to vituperation from those who felt most threatened by it – the Commission, the French government and, not least, Tietmeyer. It threatened to expose the theatre of cruel deceit in which the ERM story was still playing. Somehow, the ERM myth had to be maintained.

# 7

# Some Are More Equal Than Others

## Snookered at the Crucible

As politicians, bureaucrats, economists and 'opinion-formers' across Europe surveyed the wreckage of the ERM on the morning following White Wednesday they began an intellectual damage-limitation exercise. For close on six years the proponents of the system had been walking on water: all the economic theories had said that fixed exchange rates were not consistent with free capital movements and imperfectly coordinated monetary policies. Yet the ERM had had fixed exchange rates, in effect, since 1987. After the publication of the Delors Report in May 1989 was followed by the German government's slapping down of a Bundesbank realignment campaign in October 1989, the doctrine became current, notably among French politicians and officials in Paris and Brussels, that: '*Réalignements? Il n'y en aura plus*' – no more realignments. After the beginning of 1990, only Ireland, Portugal and Spain among ERM members maintained residual controls on capital movements. As the Commission analysis at the end of 1990 had pointed out, coordination of monetary policies was far from perfect. How had the system held together? The apparently mystifying stability of the ERM after January 1987, and especially after May 1989, was the result of an enormous confidence trick in which, sadly, not only politicians and bureaucrats but also journalists and many economists were implicated.

The *locus classicus* of glib enthusiasm for the 'glidepath' view of the ERM is perhaps found in the book by Daniel Gros (one of the authors of the Commission's propaganda tract 'One Market, One Money') and Nils Thygesen (one of the independent members of the Delors Committee), *European Monetary Integration: from the European Monetary System to European Monetary Union*. Writing in March 1992, the two authors concluded that: 'overall, there is therefore little reason to believe that the EMS would be destabilized by random self-fulfilling attacks in the 1990s . . . the basic ingredient for exchange-rate stability [is] a firm and credible commitment to subordinate domestic policy goals to the defence of the exchange rate.' But why should *any* country *ever* 'subordinate domestic policy goals to the defence of the exchange rate'? There are two possible answers: one is that domestic policy goals other than the purely *economic* might be furthered by defending the exchange rate. The second is that *domestic* goals, even broadly defined, might be subordinated to the exchange rate if that somehow advanced the goals of some wider political entity.

One can label these two possibilities 'political selfishness' and 'political altruism,' respectively.[1] In the Community context, the dismissive rejection by the member countries, at the end of 1990, of the Commission proposal for a symmetric anchoring of the EMS showed the second possibility to be a non-starter: *no one* gave a hoot about the interests of the Community as such. That leaves the 'political selfishness' argument for defending the ERM, as the 'glidepath' to EMU, in line with 'neo-functionalist' theory. The implications of this for the politics of EMU in the future are something the final chapter will reflect on. In understanding the collapse of the ERM, however, what is important is that to subordinate domestic (that is, national) *economic* considerations to national foreign policy goals almost always corresponds to subordinating the preferences of the population at large to those of a political élite, and can never be unconditional, except – possibly – in the most ruthlessly efficient totalitarian state.

The story of the ERM from the morrow of White Wednesday to the climactic struggle of July 1993 will show how some Community countries indeed suppressed dissent, spread disinformation, using black propaganda, issued dire threats of fearful retribution, disregarded the rule of law and operated 'class punishment'. But all these countries had to have some regard for domestic economic interests, whether those of the nation as a whole or of particular interest groups within the nation. Nonetheless, in the years from the Delors Report to the Danish 'no', the apostles of European Union had managed to gull markets into thinking that the sacrifice of economic interest in following the EMU path was small and even that there were economic gains to be had. As we saw in chapter 5, the Maastricht compromise represented a bet by the politicians that this illusion could be maintained long enough for the dates fixed for EMU to be realizable. The

1  The second of these labels is perhaps over-generous as long as the wider entity is not the world as a whole: even if one believed that Delors, for instance, had abandoned *French* nationalism, his enthusiasm for European Union would still be based on a *Euro*nationalism defined by antipathy towards Americans and Japanese, among others.

period from June 1992 to 16 September 1992 marked the growing recognition of the markets that for Italy, Britain and Spain at least, the ERM was nothing more than illusion: it was apparent that the economic costs of defending the exchange rate were far greater than the nebulous benefits, including those of preserving political face, attached to the 'glidepath'. Once that recognition took hold, nothing could prevent the market forces of risk-management and self-protection (Soros just gave the final push) from smashing the ERM fixity of the lira, sterling and the peseta and the ERM fixation of those currencies' managers.

The markets' hasty, defensive repositioning as they unwound 'convergence plays' in June–September 1992 was matched by a rapid revision of philosophy among European politicians after 16 September. 'Solidarity' broke down. For Britain – immediately – and for Spain and Italy – with more hesitation and reluctance, but inescapably – the call came for 'reform' of the ERM. The 'fault lines' in the system that John Major belatedly discovered two days after White Wednesday had to be repaired to make the ERM workable again: it was the system that was wrong. But for the other countries, it was time to cast the three losers as sinners who had abused the system and then got their just deserts: there was nothing wrong with the system itself, if countries played by the rules. Both camps, of course, were indulging in political cant. But the rift pointed to the impossibility of a 'single-speed' monetary Europe. From then onwards, the story of the ERM would revolve around the frantic efforts of non-German would-be members of the 'hard core' to prove their virtue by undergoing a trial by ordeal – while within Germany the battle raged for the right to determine who would be judge in that trial.

The ordeal began the day after White Wednesday, as the Irish pound – guilty, unless proved otherwise, of association with sterling – was pushed close to its ERM floor, as were the Danish krone and the French franc. To the true believers in the ERM, this was alarming, suspicious, unnatural: the ERM paradox in reverse. For Ireland, Denmark and France were the goody-goodies of the ERM class: countries with sub-German inflation, current-account surpluses and low budget deficits. It could be claimed – and Tietmeyer seized every opportunity to do so – that the lira, sterling and the peseta were not right for the system. But if the Justified as well as the Sinners were now to be forced into a painful defence of their ERM parities, then the pagans might find ready ears for their jibes that the system itself was at fault. There were three ways for the *soi-disant* believers to respond to the new challenge to Faith: the Jesuitical, the Calvinistic and the

Superstitious.[2] The first would attempt to finesse the problem, to prove every proposition and its contrary as the occasion demanded, often with little regard to consistency with positions previously held. The Calvinistic would rely on drawing the circle of the Elect ever tighter, until those who were left would achieve salvation through Faith alone, and find sustenance in the desert through the manna showered down by a beneficent German deity.

Fittingly, Tietmeyer, a former student in a Jesuit theological college and a son of Westphalia, with all the historic resonances of that name, was to take on the task of combining the Jesuitical and Calvinist reactions to the ERM crisis. Equally fittingly, the superstitious reflex was most evident among the French Socialists in power in Paris and Brussels. For them, there were dark, malevolent forces at work in the travails of the ERM. The Devil and his fallen angels had had an easy task in enticing decadent Britain and Italy into the outer darkness and trapping Spain in a semi-detached Purgatory. Now they were deploying all their wiles to ensnare the virtuous.

Who were these agents of darkness? The financial markets of course, inhabited by speculators and controlled by some sinister Anglo-Saxon cabal.[3] It is not surprising that men who spent much of their working lives in hatching convoluted plots saw plots everywhere they looked. There was nothing new about this culture. As long ago as 1924, Keynes could write:

Each time the franc loses value, the Minister of Finance is convinced that the fact arises from everything but economic causes. He attributes it to the presence of foreigners in the corridors of the Bourse, to unwholesome and malign forces of speculation. The attitude is rather close to that of the witch doctor who attributes the illness of cattle to the 'evil eye', and the storm to an insufficient quantity of sacrifices made before some idol.

2  The Secretary of the Monetary Committee at the time, Andreas Kees, was a man with a keen interest in theological questions. A German Protestant, he often expressed great admiration for John-Paul II. The Pope was a figure, he told colleagues, of great historical religious importance: what a pity that he was theologically in error on the question of women priests. 'So you mean', enquired one of those colleagues, 'that it is good to have a Pope but it would be better if the Pope were Protestant?'

3  Even the term 'financial markets' itself was enough to have some énarques gritting their teeth. Did not the highest of the high in the ENA caste bear the title 'Inspecteur des Finances'? Finance was an area for the bureaucratic élite to preside over, not one to be dominated by vulgar little men with multicoloured jackets screaming and bawling and waving their arms in 'pits' (evocative words) in London and Chicago of all places. One very senior French monetary official in Brussels was greatly annoyed whenever his aides told him that such-and-such was unwise because of the likely reaction of financial markets. Finally he exploded: 'Je m'en fous de ces marchés financiers et leurs huitièmes de pour cent' (I don't give a damn about these financial markets and their eighths of a per cent).

Now of course what is needed to turn ancestral dislike of markets into a superstitious willingness to impute to them all the ills of the world is ignorance. That was to be had in plenty. Delors himself was astonished by the violence of the market storm that had blasted sterling out of the ERM. How could it be, he asked his aides, that a foreign exchange crisis could blow up in a market as liquid as London? Presumably, someone had once told him, perhaps excusing the remodelling of French financial markets in the image of New York during the Chirac government's brief flirtation with economic liberalism, that in liquid markets large movements of funds can be absorbed with only small movements in prices. London was a liquid market, so why had the price of sterling not remained stable? There had obviously been a politically inspired Anglo-Saxon plot to take sterling out of the system and engage in a 'competitive devaluation' at the expense of the rest, all with the aim of wounding the EMU project.[4]

## Liquid gold

Before we resume the narrative of ERM events, it is worthwhile to look at the two elements of Delors's anti-economic notion of what was happening, since his misunderstanding and prejudice was typical of so many of the monetary policy bigwigs in Europe (Kenneth Clarke included).[5]

Liquidity first. It is true that in a liquid market, it is possible for someone who wishes to make a large sale to find a buyer without 'turning the market against himself', that is, without having to accept a considerably lower price than the one prevailing when he starts trying to sell. In fact, that is one definition of a liquid market. But if *all* the participants in a market believe that a price is 'wrong', out of line with underlying fundamentals, then there will be *no* buyers at the original price, and market-makers will mark the price down precisely to prevent themselves being swamped with 'sell' orders when there is no sign of corresponding 'buy' orders. Markets will generate massive flows of *quantities* in such situations, rather than movements in prices, only if some market participant is willing to meet all

4 As it happened, White Wednesday coincided almost to the day with the three hundredth anniversary of the hanging in Salem, Massachusetts, of seven people wrongly accused of witchcraft. The parallels with the Salem witch hunts, in which accusations of Satanic possession and devil worship were used by one group of families against another against a background of economic and political rivalry, are fascinating.
5 An entertaining, if also sometimes chilling, account of the propagation of the 'Anglo-Saxon conspiracy' myth is given by Lionel Barber, Brussels correspondent of the FT, in the *Washington Post* of 28 February 1993.

the 'sell' orders and hold ever-increasing amounts of the asset that everyone else wants to sell. The rules of the ERM required the central banks to perform this role. Mrs Thatcher had a clear grasp of these basic dynamics of markets: either the exchange rate is fundamentally 'wrong', in which case trying to buck the market and defend it will fail, or the rate is 'right', in which case there is no need of all the paraphernalia of the ERM to 'defend' it.[6] In fact, pegging an exchange rate that was 'right' (for the moment), could in itself *provoke* market turbulence. Schlesinger, too, as we shall soon see, grasped this basic fact, confounding those who believed he did not understand markets. Delors and his acolytes never really understood them, and perhaps never really tried to.

Where do the notorious 'hedge funds' managed by such figures as George Soros fit into this story? Hedge funds manage investment portfolios on behalf of, in the main, large private investors. They are not subject to the reporting requirements imposed on public investment management funds. As a result, they are less constrained by 'short-termism'. They are thus able to perform an important role of 'stabilizing speculation' in financial markets, taking advantage of any movements in prices away from underlying equilibrium, and thus helping to restore equilibrium. They can, of course, like anyone else, be wrong about what the underlying equilibrium of the market really is. The hedge funds were conspicuous among those who had succumbed to the Maastricht illusion and moved heavily into sterling, lira and the peseta in the run-up to Maastricht and immediately thereafter. The distinctive contribution of Hungarian-born George Soros, once a London railway porter and now the brain behind Quantum, reputedly the largest hedge fund, was to see the risks involved. The 'convergence plays' had seen heavy purchases of gilts (British government bonds) on the expectation that the interest-rate

6 There are two other possibilities, but they do not invalidate Mrs Thatcher's basic insight. One is that the monetary authorities give financial markets to believe that they are following a particular policy rule when that rule is not compatible with the needs of stabilizing the economy. The result can then be an exchange rate that is also out of line with the real needs of the economy. For instance, putting emphasis on the role of the exchange rate as a trigger for interest-rate decisions can, even outside a formal exchange-rate arrangement, itself distort market perceptions and lead to a vicious circle of inappropriate interest-rate decisions and exchange-rate movements. But the problem is one of faulty conception or communication of monetary policy, not one caused by floating exchange rates. Exchange-rate movements can also play a potentially ambiguous role if there is a conflict between the stances of fiscal and monetary policies that lead markets to protect themselves against the possibility of future changes in monetary policy. But such problems cannot be avoided – indeed they are likely to be created or aggravated by attempts to fix the exchange rate.

convergence promised by EMU would bring capital gains (British long-term interest rates were higher than German rates; convergence would mean falling British long-term rates and thus rising gilts prices). It is believed that when Soros was asked to review his clients' portfolios, he very quickly began 'hedging' their holdings of gilts – that is, he borrowed sterling at short-term, against the security of the bond holdings, and converted it into DM, thus covering the sterling 'exposure' represented by the bond holdings. Since, by this time, British *short*-term rates had already fallen practically to the German level, so that the interest costs of short-term sterling borrowing was almost completely compensated by the return available on short-term holdings of DM, this hedging operation was virtually costless.

A key feature was the liquidity of UK financial markets in general, which allowed people like Soros to borrow large amounts of sterling without difficulty and without having to pay exorbitant rates of interest. In a number of other countries, as we shall see, it was easier for central banks to resist pressure on the exchange rate, at least for a time, because the under-developed nature of their domestic financial markets and the existence of exchange controls – which prevented linkages with world financial markets – allowed them to restrict liquidity. In Britain, as in New York and, increasingly, in Paris, the financial markets operated on the assumption that liquidity would always be sufficient. Complicated pyramids of highly-leveraged deals in derivatives allowed a more efficient management of financial risk – *as long as* there was sufficient liquidity. In countries like Ireland, Spain, Portugal and even to some extent Sweden, the authorities could for a time restrict liquidity, forcing up the cost of borrowing to astronomical levels, without risking a total collapse of financial markets. In London, and even in Paris, such a course would be unthinkable.

Thus Delors was totally wrong: it was the liquidity of London markets, and the need to maintain that liquidity, that made the defence of sterling's ERM bands impossible as well as undesirable. In the end, when it became clear that the *only* buyers of sterling at the ERM floor were the central banks, there were opportunities for the hedge funds, Soros included, to go beyond hedging. They could, as we have seen, put together a war-chest of leveraged borrowing that could be used to overwhelm the authorities' defences. But what they were attacking was the indefensible as well as the undefendable. If John Major had any sense either of humour or of justice, Soros would have been granted an honorary knighthood in the New Year's Honours of 1993. He was the White Knight who, on White Wednesday, administered the *coup de grâce* to the ERM dragon that was destroying the British economy.

## Beggaring belief

It did not take long after White Wednesday for the defenders of the ERM to switch from insisting that membership brought untold benefits to every member country to insisting that countries that left the mechanism were gaining an unfair competitive advantage. From 17 September onwards, portentous utterances warned Britain and Italy that they must eschew 'competitive devaluation'. Most of the warnings came from Paris and from the Commission (but as we shall see in a later chapter, it would be Tietmeyer who made one of the most brazen attacks on British and Italian monetary policy). Britain in particular, it was claimed, was pursuing a beggar-thy-neighbour policy by letting sterling slide, improving British competitiveness and boosting Britain's economic growth at the expense of its trading partners.

As usual, such accusations were a mix of hypocrisy and economic illiteracy. They were hypocritical because France, at least, had quite deliberately been pursuing a policy of 'competitive disinflation'. In chapter 8 we shall discover how damaging this policy was to the French economy. But if it had succeeded it would have had exactly the same beggar-thy-neighbour impact as a depreciation of the currency, by improving French competitiveness against its trading partners. The difference was that competitive disinflation had its effects only over a period of years, not more or less overnight as with exchange-rate depreciation. And it produced those effects only by forcing the French economy into recession, contracting the market for France's partners. Clearly, anyone genuinely interested in the economic well-being of the world as a whole, or even of a region of the world such as the Community, should prefer countries that needed real depreciations to obtain them through nominal depreciation rather than through 'competitive disinflation'.

But suppose that there was a generalized problem of inadequate demand in the world (or in the Community economy). Would it not then be the case that a country that devalued its currency just to grab a bigger share of an inadequate world market was behaving selfishly and destructively? Would it not provoke others to defend themselves by devaluing their own currencies, setting off a whole round of individually futile but collectively disruptive 'competitive devaluations' and stoking up protectionist sentiment? Those who argued in this way often pointed to the 1930s, when depression conditions were associated with 'competitive devaluations' by many countries. The truth, however, is that such competitive devaluations, by together amounting to a loosening of world monetary policy, were an important factor in boosting economic activity in the world as a whole, thereby leading the way out of depression.

Of course, in the 1930s the countries in the '*bloc or*' centred upon France that refused to join in the general monetary loosening involved in going off gold lost out. France remained tied to gold until 1936, and the economic, political and social tensions, culminating in the Popular Front government of Léon Blum, created by that curmudgeonly stubbornness were an important cause of France's perceived need to appease Nazi Germany. The historical parallels with the 1990s are striking. France was, for misguided geopolitical reasons, determined to stick to the DM, but French officials were terrified that a weakening of France's competitive position might evoke memories of the 1930s and stir up popular and industrial pressure, making a rerun of 1936 hard to avoid.

Those officials, instinctively jealous of state power, had another motive for decrying 'competitive devaluation', as had all the 'monetary masters of the world' to some degree. If the pressure of national economic self-interest really did, through forcing a general round of 'competitive devaluations' and a world monetary loosening, improve *everyone's* welfare,[7] then there would be a triumph for market forces. 'The masters of the world' inevitably much preferred 'coordination' to competition as a way of arriving at the desired result, simply because the processes of international 'coordination' increased their own influence, prestige and insulation from political accountability. In addition, each nation hoped (the French most of all) that in the bargaining process involved in 'coordination' they would gain bureaucratically an advantage that market forces would deny them. Whereas the struggle for national self-interest expressed in a round of 'competitive devaluation' is a *positive*-sum game for the world as a whole, the bureaucratic struggle in a 'coordination' setting has a *negative* sum: the bureaucrats use the process to justify distortions, controls, inefficiency and 'targets' for inappropriate variables such as current-account balances that *reduce* world economic welfare. What applies to the bureaucrats of individual G-7 countries applies with equal or greater force to bureaucrats

7  The same reasoning would apply to 'competitive *re*valuations' and a world monetary *tightening* if the problem faced by the world macroeconomy were inflation.

whose whole rationale is 'coordination'. Thus not only the protectionist, regulatory, illiberal Commission, but also the free-trading, deregulatory, generally liberal OECD were loud in their condemnation of 'competitive devaluation'.

## French leave?

When markets make mistakes, it is often through giving 'the authorities' too much credit for rational economic behaviour. After being deluded so totally by the official propaganda touting Maastricht, the markets after White Wednesday appear to have assumed that, the illusion once shattered, governments and central banks would start copying Lamont and frame policy in the economic best interests of their populations. They immediately started selling Irish pounds and Danish kroner, currencies whose economies looked particularly vulnerable to the competitive impact of the September exchange-rate movements. They also sold the French franc: a climate of black economic gloom was gripping firms and families in France, as they waited despairingly for the recovery that '*désinflation compétitive*' had been fraudulently advertised as assuring. The gloom was becoming self-feeding: the French media wrote and spoke constantly about '*morosité*' and the risks of deflation.[8] There must be a strong chance, the markets reasoned, that anything other than a resounding 'yes' in the Maastricht referendum would lead to a change in the *franc fort* policy.

The resounding 'yes' never came. Instead, there was a '*petit oui*', a wafer-thin margin in favour of the treaty. Despite yet more declarations from the Monetary Committee and from the finance ministers and – this time – governors, all of them gathered in Washington for the autumn IMF meetings, the three days following the referendum saw massive outflows from France. The franc was pushed perilously close to the ERM floor.

But France was not Britain, nor even Italy or Spain. The ruling caste reacted ferociously to what its members saw as an attack on their whole concept of '*l'état*'. The power of the French state still extends much further in the financial area than does that of the British government, and it was

---

8 We shall see more of this in subsequent chapters. Deflation, with its echoes of the 1930s, was the French economic nightmare, comparable to German horror of inflation and memories of the 1920s. At around this time, the Bundesbank reprinted a German newspaper article that derided French fears of deflation and portrayed the French, in effect, as wimps.

used to the full. The Banque de France was able to force overnight money market rates up to high levels, increasing the cost of borrowing to finance short positions in francs, without provoking an immediate rise in banks' lending rates. Their ability to do this came in part from the nationalized status of many of the largest French banks. As for the 'privatized' banks, most still run by people who were *énarques* or other members of the ruling caste, their attitude to the '*pouvoir public*' was deferential. In practice, the banks would not dare raise their lending rates without permission from the government. Even so, the government had to tread carefully, for the banks' balance-sheets were not in good shape after a rash of ill-advised lending, much of it in the now-moribund Paris commercial property market and some of it, notably by Crédit Lyonnais, to finance Mitterrand's architectural follies and murky cronies. So the pain of keeping their lending rates unchanged when overnight rates were so high had to be eased by offering them special lending facilities, unavailable to foreign-owned banks, with the Banque de France. The quid pro quo was undoubtedly that the French banks would not use these facilities either to short the franc themselves or to lend to anyone wanting to do so. These measures constituted an implicit breach of Community law on the freedom of capital movements reinforced by the Single Market rules. Naturally, the Commission – responsible for monitoring capital movements – averted its eyes:[9] one more example of the hypocrisy of the 'One Market, One Money' slogans.

Even more important to the French authorities than their internal power was their external ally. The 'sweetheart deal' was about to be activated. The signs were already there immediately after White Wednesday when Tietmeyer told Agence France Presse on 18 September, in his first public comment since the turbulence began, that: 'The franc is a very strong currency that has achieved inherent stability.' Schlesinger too, in Washington for the Annual IMF meetings, made a speech describing the French franc as a 'stable and healthy currency'. And in Washington, in marked contrast to his attitude at Bath, he concurred in a finance ministers' and governors' declaration of confidence in the ERM parity grid. He must have known that Kohl would in no circumstances agree to a Bundesbank request for a DM revaluation against the French franc. Hence he had every reason to fear a massive market assault on the franc's parity, for he would be forced

9 It is hard to believe that French monetary officials in the Commission, with their exceptionally close links with fellow-*énarque* cadres in the French Treasury, the Banque de France and the commercial banks, did not know what was going on.

to provide unlimited support, entailing a loss of control of German money markets, with no way to call a halt. Much better then, to support the franc verbally in the hope of forestalling the onslaught.

But, two days of battering on the Monday and Tuesday following the referendum had the franc pinned on the ropes by the morning of Wednesday, 23 September. Repeated intervention by the Banque de France had kept it away from its absolute floor, but to do that foreign exchange reserves had had to be used up at a profligate rate. Now, there were hardly any left.

During Monday and Tuesday, heavy sales of DM by the Banque de France were already creating a wave of liquidity in DM money markets, pushing down very short-term German interest rates. The Bundesbank faced problems: a week before, Schlesinger had explained that it was precisely this kind of situation, as a result of intervention in the lira, that had prompted the bank to ask the German government for a realignment. Now, however, the Bundesbank knew that such a request would be turned down. But simply to accept that German interest rates could be determined by market movements, outside the bank's control, would be devastating for credibility, a victory for those who believed that the Bundesbank could be overwhelmed by inflows. So the bank used every weapon it could to counteract the impact of the inflows on money-market rates.

On Wednesday, one of its weapons was to give a clue to the gravity of the situation. The Bundesbank offered to sell Treasury bills to the market for a two-day maturity, at a rate of 8.9% (Lombard rate was at 9.50%, discount rate at 8.25%). In theory, that should have put a floor under money-market rates: banks would bid up the rate on available funds if it was lower than the Treasury bill rate, competing to acquire funds and buy bills carrying 8.9%. But by Tuesday evening the stock of Treasury bills was running out. Thus, by that evening, both the Bundesbank and the Banque de France were showing signs of distress. If market attacks continued unabated, then continued defence of the franc would force one or the other of the two central banks to do something it desperately wanted to avoid: acquiesce in a collapse of interest rates in Germany, for the Bundesbank, or follow a Swedish-style policy of pushing interest rates to astronomical levels, for the Banque de France.

The sharpness of the dilemma was worsened by two pieces of news, one in Germany, the other in France. The German M3 figures for August showed a rise at an annual rate of 9% since the previous year – so far out of the target range that Schlesinger had to admit the target for 1992 would not be met. That made it the most embarrassing time possible for the Bundesbank to let German interest rates be forced down. In France, Crédit Lyonnais, the giant, state-owned socialist banking fiefdom, announced shockingly bad profits figures, the result of writing-off bad debts. This served to emphasize the risks of a financial crisis if the Banque de France tried to tread the Swedish path. Something had to be done.

Early the next morning, the French and German authorities put in place a three-pronged defence plan. Before the markets opened, the Banque de France raised its repo rate from 10.5 to 13%, forcing overnight rates up to 30% and raising the cost of speculative positions; but it kept its intervention rate unchanged, enabling the banks to hold their base rates. This was not an interest-rate constellation that could hold for very long. The 'moral suasion' already in effect was intensified: a significant gap opened up between short-term rates in the domestic markets and the Euromarkets,[10] indicating the presence of implicit exchange controls.

Next, shortly after the rise in the repo rate, the French and German governments, together with the two central banks, issued a joint communiqué stating that no change in the franc/DM parity was justified. This was not the Eurowaffle of the Monetary Committee or the Ecofin: the statement had real political clout, and produced cold feet in some market players. Finally, the Bundesbank announced that it was intervening intramarginally to support the franc. This was the first time in the whole history of the ERM that the Bundesbank had intervened to support a currency other than when obliged to so because the weak currency had reached the lower permitted margin. Clearly, Wednesday, 23 September, was going to be different from Wednesday, 16 September. To ram home the message, Michel Sapin issued bloodthirsty warnings to speculators that they would be hit hard and recalled that during the French Revolution speculators had been beheaded. Speculation, he implied, was akin to treason – a crime against the state, and for an *énarque*, no crime can be worse.

Apart from the determined, almost crazed *joint* defence of the parity, one difference from the previous week was the attitude of Soros. It was soon made known (by the French authorities, market observers suspect) that Soros was betting *against* a franc devaluation. He saw the balance of

10 The Euromarket for French francs is the interbank market for franc deposits held outside France.

arguments as very different from the one he had applied to sterling. The *economic* case for a franc devaluation, he believed, was weak, and the political determination of the authorities not to devalue was intense, almost fanatical. Soros was, perhaps, impressed by the strength of this political will because he himself aspired to European Union – even if not in precisely the form France might like. Thus the central banks were *not* the only people buying francs.

So the forces on 23 September were much more evenly matched than a week earlier. Even so, the battle raged fiercely throughout the day, with repeated rounds of heavy intervention required to keep the franc off its floor. Surprisingly, almost miraculously it seemed, the Bundesbank managed to maintain a floor of 8.9% for short-term rates in the German domestic money market despite the massive creation of DM liquidity as a result of that week's intervention. Rumours circulated that the Bundesbank had had to ask the German banks to restrict their purchases of the Treasury bills it was offering.[11] But if that was so, why were money-market rates not falling? The state of affairs seemed even more puzzling in the Euromarket for DM, where rates for DM deposits of up to two days fell to 0.5%. At one point, *negative* interest rates were being offered on such deposits. How could there be such a huge gap between domestic rates and Euro-rates? What on earth was happening? Schlesinger is reported by Bundesbank insiders to have asked exactly that question as he stood watching the trading screens. The answer, according to employees of German banks in Luxembourg, is once again 'moral suasion'. All the German banks in the Grand Duchy, the centre of the Euro-DM market, had received requests from the Bundesbank not to transfer DM from the Euromarket to the domestic market. 'None of our clients wants to hold anything but DM,' said one banker. 'Luxembourg is just awash with marks, and we are being prevented from depositing them in Germany.' In other words, the Bundesbank was operating covert exchange controls. Who had given the orders? No one is prepared to say. The only clue is Schlesinger's reported puzzlement and perplexity. Someone, it seems, may have been going behind his back.

---

11 One Bundesbank official was asked why the requirement for the minimum reserves the German banks were obliged to hold with the Bundesbank could not be raised to help mop up liquidity. 'Because if we did that,' he replied grimly, 'the sky would be dark with the squadrons of Mirages coming across the Rhine to bomb us.'

Whoever was the culprit in this breach of Community and German rules, it helped to produce the desired effect in the poker game being played, for the highest stakes ever, in the forex market. The French authorities were in a state of out-and-out terror, but managed not to let it show. The nerve of the market operators cracked first. The franc survived Wednesday, strengthened a little on Thursday, and on Friday bounced back towards its highest level for some months. The Banque de France was able to restore the pre-crisis level of interest rates rather quickly yet still replenish its stock of reserves and, presumably, repay whatever loans the Bundesbank had made it (subsequently estimated by market sources at 130–140 billion francs, out of total intervention of 160 billion francs, significantly more than the £10 billion of futile intervention in the battle for sterling the week before).

The authorities had won the September battle for the franc. But the ERM had been weakened further. Both France and Germany had had to use covert exchange controls and other forms of moral suasion. Those critics of the ERM who had always maintained that the system could not work without exchange controls had been proved right. Once again, the Commission had stood aside. The damage to the principles of monetary and financial integration in Europe was greater than any that a devaluation might have caused. The Bundesbank had been humbled, forced to do what it had always feared that the ERM would make it do – give absolute priority to the exchange rate at the expense of its domestic targets, money supply above all. Over the next few weeks, the Bundesbank would be forced to validate the non-sterilization of inflows, and a desire to prevent a recurrence of that painful week in September would be one factor leading it to reduce its interest rates despite a wide and unfinesse-able overshooting of the money-supply target. By mid-November, since France was able to follow those cuts in interest rates, French rates were lower than before the crisis, and German M3 bloated and uncontrolled. The franc parity had been held, but it had become harder, not easier, than before 23 September to justify the continued existence of the ERM. With Germany seen, once the dust had settled, to have borne all the adjustment to the exchange market movements, for the first time ever, it was hard to see where the anchor of the ERM was to be found. What was the system *for*?

That question was already in some people's minds in the week of 21–25 September. Delors had insinuated that week that if certain countries continued to be difficult about the Maastricht Treaty, the rest might accelerate into a mini-union.[12] Alfons Verplaetse, the highly political Governor of the National Bank of Belgium, went further: Germany, the Benelux and France could form a monetary mini-union *immediately*. Part of the reason for this kite-flying, at least Verplaetse's, derived from the war of nerves going on in the foreign exchanges. If markets believed that an irrevocable monetary union involving France and Germany was going to happen soon, with the two currencies converted at the central rate of FF 3.35 to the DM, it was distinctly risky to bet on the franc being driven below its ERM floor.

At the end of the week, both Kohl's office and the Elysée denied that such a mini-union was imminent: by then, the franc had fought off the market attacks. But once the genie of a 'mini-union', an early two-speed Europe, had been let out of the bottle for short-term tactical reasons, it proved impossible to stuff it back in again. The idea of a monetary union covering the whole Community was seriously wounded on 16 September. By 23 September it had been killed stone-dead. The 'peripheral' countries – Spain, Portugal, Italy, Denmark (despite its referendum result), Ireland and Greece – still clung desperately to the notion. The Irish Prime Minister, Albert Reynolds, for instance, wasted no time in responding to the comments from Delors and Verplaetse; in fact, seeing the way the wind was likely to blow, he attempted to get his retaliation in first, telling a largely unimpressed world on 23 September: 'The single currency is more necessary than ever. If there is to be a fast-track to monetary union, we will be part of it.' From then on, the tactics of all these countries, and of unreconstructed Euroenthusiasts in the British government, would be determined by calculations about whether trying to get into the hard core would pay greater or smaller dividends than trying to disrupt it. And within the hard core itself, the great questions remained unresolved. Would France and Germany be part of the same monetary union? If they did, who would have the upper hand? Could a narrow union happen outside the Maastricht framework? How would the countries in between, most of all Belgium, be affected? How would such a union affect monetary relations

12 He also put the boot into opponents of Maastricht once again. Having displayed a contempt for democratic pluralism during the French referendum campaign by declaring that: 'There is no place in a democracy for people who call for a *Non*, for the sorcerer's apprentices, for those who awaken phantoms. I will say to them they should get out of politics' (what should the man-in-the-street opponent of Maastricht do – get out of the country?), he now refined his concept of a General Will – presumably as divined by himself – by intoning that politicians in the Community who were against Maastricht were interested only in 'the short-term satisfaction of their public opinion and their personal vanity . . . leading to decline and ridicule.'

with countries in Scandinavia and in Eastern and Central Europe? How tight would be the relations between monetary union and political union?

Yet in November 1992 the ERM was a system with a membership wider than that of any foreseeable early union. Events affecting 'peripheral' countries could not be ignored – they were to sting Schlesinger into outright, if sotto voce, opposition to the ERM and usher in a long battle of wits and of wills between him and his deputy at the Bundesbank. It is to the 'peripheral' currencies that we now return.

# 8

# Unravelling the ERM

On 16 September, Britain had finally found itself in the same boat as Italy, one with all its popguns facing aft. But after the two countries had abandoned their capsized ERM craft, their courses rapidly diverged. In Britain, the happy timing of the Tory conference ensured that a decision was taken to undercut German interest rates and let sterling find its own level. Even before the dirty work at the crossroads in France and Germany on 23 September, Lamont had succeeded in ditching the formula that sterling would re-enter the system 'as soon as market conditions permitted'.

The Italian authorities, not benefiting from the services of a finance minister who was actually jolly pleased not to be in the ERM any more – or at least not one who could admit as much – found it much harder to plot a new course. Indeed, they were finding it hard to keep afloat at all. Like Britain, they let their currency float more or less freely: they had no choice. Substantial Banca d'Italia debts to the Bundesbank had to be repaid by mid-December, and for some time the markets were worried that it might simply be impossible to do so. In principle, the Banca d'Italia could buy all the DM it wanted to – it could never run out of lire to pay for them (since it had the power to create lire) – but only at the cost of a large fall in the lira exchange rate and a sharp increase in the Italian money supply. That would, in the opinion of many economists, including Italian government and central bank economists, send Italian inflation shooting up.

To add to Italy's financial woes, there was substantial political trade union opposition to the massive package of budgetary measures (93 *trillion* lire, or 6–7% of GDP) identified by the government as necessary just to keep the budget deficit and public debt ratio in check.[1] The appalling state

---

1 Italian governments always show the deficit as moving inexorably upwards from one year to the next by very large amounts on a 'trend' basis. This practice is undoubtedly intended to allow some credit to be claimed for 'effort' (which, in Community financial affairs, is regarded by the Ecofin as much more important than results) if the deficit actually increases by a somewhat smaller amount.

of Italian public finance owed much to the EMU illusion (as will be explained in chapter 10 below). But it was hardly surprising, when financial markets had been fed – and had fed on – the message that the 'glidepath' to EMU could guarantee a solution of those problems, that there was a degree of panic after the deception was laid bare. The combination of near-despair about public finance and worry that repaying the Bundesbank might lead to a plunging lira made government financing very difficult during late September and early October. Long-term interest rates rose to around 14%. At the same time, even though the bulk of government debt was short-term the Banca d'Italia was reluctant to cut interest rates below German levels, for three reasons. First, success would be embarrassing. Why had the central bank persisted for so long with a dear-money, 'hard lira' policy, to the detriment of public finance? people might ask. Since the Banca d'Italia did not have a party conference to encourage it to see the error of its ways, this consideration probably carried great weight. Second, it was still believed by many people at that time that cutting interest rates would take away any remaining floor under the currency, thus stoking inflation. In fact, as experience in a number of countries was to show over the next few years, exchange rates may react 'perversely' to interest-rate changes in countries where markets are scared that, if monetary policy remains too tight, the government will end up defaulting on its debt in one way or another.[2] But to admit to this possibility would have destroyed another illusion fostered by the Banca d'Italia, that the monetary policy of an 'independent' central bank could ever be independent of what the government did in public finance. Third, undercutting German interest rates would, as in the British case, rule out early ERM re-entry.

The Italian government had already, on 22 September, announced that it would not, as previously advertised, be seeing immediate re-entry to the system. The same day, Schlesinger made it clear that re-entry terms would have to be negotiated, that is, dictated by the Bundesbank. In retaliation, the Italian authorities started making noises about the need for 'reform' of the system in a more symmetrical direction. But they did not want to be

---

2 This possibility was recognized by Keynes in the 1920s, and the experience of German hyperinflation in 1923, the year after the Reichsbank, predecessor of the Bundesbank, had been granted total legal independence, served to show that central banks cannot prevent inflation in the face of an unsustainable position in the public finances. The possibility was rediscovered, and expressed in elegant mathematical form, in an article in 1981 by the renowned American economists, Thomas Sargent and Neil Wallace. Central bankers shiver whenever they hear the names of Sargent and Wallace.

seen as pursuing, like Britain, an explicitly domestically oriented policy that 'partners' would brand as 'anti-European'.

A combination of a sinking currency and high, and even rising rates, is severely damaging to industrial and consumer confidence. Such was the case in Italy, where domestic demand remained depressed. It was bound to be weighed down by the prospect of the promised – or threatened – budgetary cutbacks, but the monetary-policy stance made things worse. As a result, the output recovery in Italy, necessary if an improvement in the budgetary situation was actually going to happen, had to rely almost entirely on improved net exports. That, in turn, meant that the lira had to keep falling, exposing Italy to charges by its 'partners' that it was opening a beggar-thy-neighbour policy of 'competitive devaluation'. To make things even worse, the refusal to cut interest rates as much as common sense would have dictated meant missing an opportunity to reduce government debt service costs. As a result, market worries about the risks of a future default were not assuaged, leading to further downward pressure on the lira.

In the midst of this policy mess, the Italian authorities indicated to the press in October that they would request a very large medium-term balance-of-payments loan from the Community. A number of other countries were unhappy about both procedures and substance. Tietmeyer, for instance, must have had reason to suspect that there were negotiations between Italy and the Commission to present the Monetary Committee and the Ecofin (formally responsible for deciding on such loans) with a *fait accompli*. Memories of the way he, Tietmeyer, had been 'bounced' by Delors into a dubious balance-of-payments loan to Greece in 1985 may still have rankled. And what, countries might ask, was a balance-of-payments loan *for*? With the lira floating, the balance of payments always balanced without any need for official intervention. The Bundesbank suspected that the loan would be used to repay debts incurred in September, thus converting a very short-term support mechanism into a medium-term one.[3] Such a conversion operation would, to the alarm and disgust of the Bundesbank, make other potential recipients of intervention support more likely to request it instead of opting for an early realignment. Nonetheless, most of Italy's partners were worried that a financial crisis in

3  It was precisely the mix of central banking functions (including the administration of the VSTF) with a governmental role (deciding on medium-term balance of payments assistance and its associated conditionality) proposed for the EMF in the planned 'institutional' stage of the ERM that had so stiffened Bundesbank resistance in 1980 – see chapter 1.

Italy might spill over into other countries, and they were prepared to do just about anything to stem the falls in the lira that threatened their own competitiveness.[4] So, since ERM 'solidarity' forbade them from advising Italy to make sharp cuts in interest rates, they instead accepted the principle of a loan.

As seen by Italian bureaucrats, the point of the loan, which came with budgetary conditions attached, was not so much the money (in the event, only a part of the loan eventually granted was drawn down) as the reaffirmation of Community 'solidarity' with, and Community-imposed constraints on, Italy. Not surprisingly, given the history of Community loans, the constraints on budgetary policy turned out to be largely fictional; but the markets were given a partial substitute for the 'glidepath' to EMU and convergence supposedly represented by the ERM. The talk of the loan, together with the growing realization that lira depreciation *would* help the Italian economy to recover from recession, calmed the markets, temporarily at least. But still denuded of reserves and with the lira vulnerable to the increasingly rapid crumbling of the old political order and the uncertain prospects for its replacement, the authorities were not foolhardy enough to want to risk a repeat performance of early September. Staying out of the ERM was still, at this stage, an expression of fear rather than of Lamont-like optimism that something much better could replace it as the cornerstone of economic policy.

The four 'peripheral' currencies still in the ERM all took a buffeting in the week following the French referendum. The Spanish authorities were soon made to realize that the markets now regarded them as a soft touch. The slide through the top half of the band and the formal 5% devaluation soon after the currency went through its central rate were intended to maintain a 'comfortable' position for the peseta in the ERM without a rise in interest rates. But the markets immediately came back for more. On 23 September, the Banco de España shocked the market by reintroducing tough exchange controls to 'burn' operators with short positions in pesetas.[5] But the controls

---

4 In fact, by the spring of 1995, the lira's total depreciation against the DM, compared with its pre-September 1992 parity, was about 65%, big enough to make the stabilization of Italy's public debt ratio feasible, temporarily at any rate, but much bigger than would have been necessary if Italy had followed a 'British' policy from September 1992 onwards.
5 Spain had abolished exchange controls, to conform with Community rules, only eight months previously. That the new measures were illegal no one doubted – except the Commission, which, after two days' agonizing, issued a two-sentence statement giving provisional clearance. The 'in-depth study' promised by the Commission never saw the light of day, if it ever took place at all.

devastated liquidity in the Madrid stock and bond markets: they slumped instantaneously. The international financial community warned that Spanish efforts to integrate its financial markets with the rest of the world would suffer lasting damage and that international banks and financial institutions would be very wary of doing business in Madrid. But the controls did their misdirected job for a couple of days, by which time the peseta was comforted by the markets' retreat in the battle for the French franc.

At the end of that week, the chastened Spanish Finance Minister, Carlos Solchaga, called for 'an urgent reordering of exchange rates within the ERM'. This was to be the first of several increasingly broad hints dropped by the Spanish authorities over the next few weeks that they would not be averse to a second devaluation. In the deceptively calm atmosphere after the survival of the French franc they were not, however, willing to incur the wrath of other countries, most of all France, by demanding a *'réalignement à froid'*. This would be seen as an unfriendly act, putting competitive pressure on France. Instead, Spain began insinuating that lira re-entry into the ERM might provide an occasion for a more general 'reordering' of exchange rates.

Not unnaturally, these insinuations were resented by Ireland, Portugal and Denmark, seen by the markets as candidates for such a 'reordering' of parities. All three of these currencies had come under intense pressure after White Wednesday. Ireland and Portugal reactivated exchange controls. (This was legal, in their cases, since they had maintained a 'derogation' from Community legislation on capital movements.) In the rather thin and illiquid Irish and Portuguese financial markets, the controls made speculation difficult and expensive: overnight rates were at times quoted at thousands of per cent.

But in Ireland the September turbulence brought a sharp rise in bank lending rates and mortgage rates. And looming up was Ireland's commitment to abolish its remaining controls by the end of the year. Ireland faced two big problems, both related to the link, in market minds at least, between the Irish pound and sterling. The first was political and related to Ireland's desire to be part of whatever European 'hard core' might develop. Sterling's detachment from the 'hard core' threatened Irish objectives – of which we shall see much more later in this chapter. The economic problem was that sterling's fall against the DM since White Wednesday was also a fall against the Irish pound, one that threatened Ireland's trading competitiveness. In response, the Irish authorities introduced extensive subsidies to those industrial sectors most directly in competition with Britain – a clearly discriminatory measure inconsistent with Single Market legislation. It was the ERM, not sterling's depreciation, that induced this step back from the Single Market. And almost from the first, it was clear that the strains and distortions created by the authorities' obsession with maintaining the parity would make its defence unsustainable for long. As we shall see, events in the British economy would eventually put paid to that obsession. But the trigger for a renewed assault on the ERM, after the relative calm of October, was the spectacular collapse of what had been an even stronger commitment to fixed exchange rates – Sweden's.

In September 1992, the Swedish economy was in a catastrophic state, facing its third year of recession, trying to cope with a banking crisis and speeding towards a crisis of public finance. The staggeringly harsh interest-rate measures introduced in early September, including, on 16 September, a 500% marginal rate for lending from the central bank to the banking system, had stemmed the tide of krona selling – for a time, and at a cost that could not be borne for long. During the September crisis, the Swedish authorities had, whistling in the dark, spoken of ERM 'association' – but nothing had come of it. Countries such as France did not want to welcome a new unstable currency into the ERM when the existing currencies had problems enough. The Bundesbank did not relish having to take on new intervention obligations, and was permitting itself a certain *Schadenfreude* as the Swedes struggled and suffered to maintain the ECU peg that they had chosen in preference to the DM.[6]

By November, the strains on Sweden were becoming intolerable. ERM 'association' would probably have done little to relieve them, but any market belief that Swedish overtures had been rebuffed by the ERM countries would prove fatal. Exactly such a belief arose – or, more precisely, was created. In mid-November, rumours swept the forex market that the

---

6 As early as January 1993 the Swedish Finance Minister, Mrs Anne Wibble, had asked the EMS countries for intervention support, without receiving a favourable response. A few days later Schlesinger, who happened to be giving a lecture in Stockholm, went out of his way, at the beginning of his remarks, to draw attention to the fact that Sweden had chosen of its own free will to peg to the ECU rather than the DM (he also drew attention to the fact that whereas the great Swedish economist, Knut Wicksell, had written his major works in German, he himself was delivering his lecture in English, which 'shows how much the world had changed'). In November, during the krona crisis, he was able to comment, no doubt gleefully, that the trouble with Swedish policy was that it was linked to 'a currency that doesn't really exist'. Swedish central bank officials apparently expressed agreement with Schlesinger. It is not inconceivable that the central bank, squeezed between a banking system in serious danger of collapsing completely as a result of the 'defence' of the currency and a prime minister determined not to give in, had an interest in spreading rumours that would spark massive outflows, thereby giving itself an excuse to throw in the towel.

Monetary Committee had turned down an urgent Swedish request for help. And on Thursday 19 September Sapin told the *Financial Times* in an interview that Sweden had been told – not specifying by whom – that it could not have the associate status it had been pleading for because it was not a Community country. Indeed, although Sapin claimed in the interview that France was now favourable to EC enlargement (as a way of trying to persuade Danish voters not to feel afraid of Maastricht) he may well have been trying to create trouble for the Swedish currency. The reason was that a few days earlier Bundesbank Council member Otmar Issing had raised the spectre of scrapping Maastricht and substituting for it a mini-union including certain EFTA countries grouped around the DM. Sapin must have known, presumably from Tietmeyer via Trichet, that the Bundesbank had no intention of coming immediately to the rescue of the krona, whatever place Sweden might have had in the strategic plans of certain people in Frankfurt.

At all events, the day of the publication of the FT article saw further 'repositioning' by corporates and investment managers, fearful of a krona devaluation. The move out of the krona suddenly gathered pace. After a brief struggle, in which it intervened massively, the Riksbank threw in the towel the same day. It gave only ten minutes' notice to the dumbfounded Prime Minister, Carl Bildt, that it was going to abandon the ECU peg and float the currency. The krona fell immediately, losing 10% against the ECU that day. The shock-waves soon spread. The Swedish defence of the currency in September had been the most determined yet seen, and came in a country where a supposed 'national consensus' behind a fixed exchange rate was taken for granted. The fact that the Riksbank then had to succumb to renewed market pressure, eschewing the reintroduction of exchange controls, abolished only in 1988, made the successful unilateral defence of any other parity look impossible.

The ERM currency most immediately affected by the krona float was the Danish krone (outside the system, the Norwegian krone's ECU peg also came under pressure), for it added to the competitiveness losses that Denmark had already suffered since the ERM crisis began. The Danish central bank immediately signalled its intention to stick to its ERM parity, raising its discount rate by a painful 5 percentage points. But the peseta, escudo and Irish pound also came under renewed attack. The excuse Spain had been looking for had arrived. On Friday, 20 November, the Spanish authorities convened a meeting of the Monetary Committee for the next day to approve a devaluation of the peseta.

## Rooks and pawns, Rioja and prawns

The Spanish request for a devaluation had none of the dramatic appurtenances of 'Black Wednesday'. As we have seen, the Spanish authorities had for some weeks been dropping hints that they would seek a second downward step in the peseta's parity. The realignment, when it came, lacked the Manichean quality of the battle between markets and mandarins that had made September's events seem so cataclysmic. Yet 21/22 November was a crucially important step in the unravelling of the ERM, and the weekend was to have far-reaching consequences.

In Italy, the lira's September expulsion from the ERM challenged all the assumptions that had underpinned the country's rotten political system. The old strategy of attempting to hand over Italy's problems to a European superstate had always been logically contradictory as well as morally pernicious. But it was not until after Black Wednesday that it started to dawn on the Italian public that the country was going to have to put its own house in order. The plea for a balance-of-payments loan from the Community in response to the October financial crisis nonetheless showed that recognition of Italy's true needs was not complete. The results of the 21/22 November meeting were to remove scales from a few more important pairs of eyes.

In Spain, the process of reappraisal had gone less far than in Italy. Indeed, their tactics on 16 September had in some ways suggested that the Spanish authorities, unlike the British and Italians, felt their initial assumptions were being justified by what happened to the ERM that day. Their officials were beginning to voice the claim that the ERM had become something very different from the system they had entered in 1989. They insinuated what Nigel Lawson, adding an epilogue to his memoirs, was trumpeting: that the ERM had been hijacked to become a 'glidepath' to EMU. But, unlike Lawson, the Spanish still had no qualms about the chosen landing area. Rather, they now implied, the Spanish aircraft was going to crash into a jagged mountain range if monetary policy remained set by the ERM on autopilot. These arguments smelled strongly of revisionism. But they enabled the Spanish government to avoid either the admission of a Major-style U-turn or a collective neurosis of the political class as in Italy: the ERM was being reclaimed from French-inspired determinism.

Thus Spain's decision to devalue the peseta on 16 September rather than withdraw from the system had been presented as entirely consistent with a distinctively Spanish and clear-headed approach to the ERM: yes, the ERM continued to have political resonance as the token of a commitment to the *goal* of monetary union, but the system's managers had to realize that it was not *itself* a monetary union. So the peseta was to remain in the system, with a devaluation that would serve the triple purpose of defusing speculative pressures, improving Spanish competitiveness as recessionary clouds darkened, and reintroducing the notion of fixed but *adjustable* rates into the system.

Unfortunately for the Spanish authorities, the long period of quasi-fixity in the ERM had veiled the hard fact of life that was to emerge: in a world of massively increased capital mobility and of enormously powerful but nervous markets, a quasi-monetary union might well be premature and unwise for Spain, but a system of fixed but adjustable exchange rates was simply impossible. The experience of the peseta, the escudo, the Irish pound and the Scandinavian currencies between 16 September and late November had made that clear to many market actors in the ERM game. After the chicanery of 24 September, the 'hard core' had been relatively untroubled, the markets conned into believing that quasi-union between its currencies was still in place. But the potential 'adjusters' had been receiving an unrelenting battering from the markets. Spain's request for a second realignment meeting showed that the lesson had not yet been fully absorbed in Madrid: a bit more competitiveness, the chance to restore a more comfortable place for the peseta in its new, lowered band – and the markets might calm down. Thus, in Spanish government eyes, the 21/22 November meeting would be rather anticlimactic, 'shooting the fox' being hounded by the markets.

For their part, most of Spain's fellow contestants in the ERM game gave the impression of thinking the realignment request an indication of rather poor sportsmanship, a piece of sneaky Iberian goalpost-shifting. This was especially true of the French, who were becoming ever more worried about the competitive advantage being gained by the British, Italian and Spanish economies. And, of course, Portugal could hardly remain unmoved. But few of the men (and two women) making their way to Brussels to ponder the Spanish request were fully aware of the damage that their much-cherished 'common good' mechanism was about to suffer. And only one man saw the opportunity.

## Relegation dogfight

According to Irish accounts, the most important concrete decision was taken before the meeting even started. Things did not get off to a good start when the Portuguese Treasury member of the Committee, Jose Braz, told reporters waiting at the entrance of the Borschette building that the Irish pound, as well as the peseta and the escudo, would come under discussion. Then the Irish delegation, having fought their own tight-lipped way through the scrum of reporters and cameramen, found themselves confronted with the even more formidable presence of Tietmeyer, his bodyguards in attendance,[7] once they got inside. On the escalators taking them up to the third-floor meeting-room, Tietmeyer bluntly asked the Irish to devalue by 4% – the amount he calculated would restore an 'appropriate' level of competitiveness. The Irish refused: whatever Spain's decision to seek a realignment might imply about that country's attitude to the ERM philosophy that had prevailed since 1989, Ireland wanted to be considered part of the 'hard core' of the ERM, a monetary quasi-union in which the use of the exchange rate as an instrument for regulating competitiveness was ruled out absolutely. Devaluing on competitiveness grounds would risk tying the Irish pound, in the eyes of the markets, to sterling, as sterling's slide since 16 September had been the most important factor in Ireland's loss of competitiveness. Indeed, the Irish suspected that Tietmeyer was deliberately trying to trap them into admitting a dependence on sterling, one which could subsequently be used against them as a reason for exclusion from EMU. There has been no suggestion that Tietmeyer renewed his invitation to the Irish to devalue during the course of the meeting.[8] The reason for his silence on the issue would become clear enough when the world had had time to digest the results of the meeting.

But first the members of the Commitee, most of them unaware of the twenty-second interchange between Tietmeyer and the Irish, had to endure eleven hours of wrangling between Spain and Portugal. The issues seemed insubstantial to most observers of the squabble: nothing more than intra-Iberian sensibilities was at stake. But for the two participants, both of

7 Tietmeyer had been the object of an assassination attempt by left-wing terrorists when he had been State Secretary at the German Finance Ministry. Thereafter he was always accompanied by bodyguards.
8 Italian newspaper accounts of the weekend's events wrote of pressure on both Ireland and Denmark to devalue, but the authoritative Irish account makes it clear that there was no discussion of this in the meeting proper, while Danish sources insist there was no pressure, formal or informal, on Denmark.

them countries in the forefront of the political drive to create 'Europe', ancient rivalries and mutual disdain came to the fore. According to Spanish and Portuguese newspaper accounts, the Portuguese opening gambit was, for cosmetic purposes, to oppose any devaluation by Spain. But once the inevitable had happened and Tietmeyer had given his *nihil obstat* to a peseta devaluation, Portugal too asked for a downward realignment of its currency.

The impact on Portuguese competitiveness of the substantial fall in the peseta over the previous six months was to be cited as the reason. This had some plausibility: before the two Iberian countries joined the Community, they had maintained arm's-length economic relations with one another, but since accession trade between them had grown rapidly, to the extent that by 1992 Spain was, on some measures, Portugal's biggest trading partner. But Portugal was in effect freely stating, and indeed claiming, what both Ireland and Denmark were struggling desperately not to admit: that exchange-rate relationships with the 'hard core' could be put under strain by movements in the exchange rate of geographically close trading partners that had shown themselves *not* to be part of the core – the UK in Ireland's case, the other Nordic countries in Denmark's. Thus Portugal was accepting its exclusion from the 'hard core' and condemning itself, in market perceptions, to a shared exchange-rate future with Spain, whether 'the fundamentals' made that appropriate or not. But 'short-termism' prevailed.

The Portuguese Finance Minister, Jorge Braga de Macedo, was in constant telephone contact with his officials in the Borschette. His primary concern was to make sure the official communiqué castigated Spain for a failure of internal adjustment and blamed that country for forcing a supposedly unwelcome devaluation on Portugal. Not unnaturally, the Spanish delegation was unwilling to oblige. Braga de Macedo, as he had done the previous April, threatened to convene a meeting of finance ministers and governors for the next day, Sunday, if he did not get his way. Such a meeting would probably not have advanced his cause greatly. Braga de Macedo had no friends among his fellow finance ministers. He was a man with a well-developed – if somewhat solitary – sense of his own intellectual pre-eminence among his peers. While still a Commission official, before stepping openly into the political arena, he had disparaged the members of the Monetary Committee as 'overworked and not very intelligent'. Subsequently he had, when Chairman of Ecofin, reportedly annoyed other ministers by commenting critically on their contributions to

Ecofin discussions rather in the manner of a professor grading economics students in a graduate seminar.[9] But he must have been hoping that the members of the Committee would not want to have to confess to their ministers and governors that they had been unable to sort out a spat among Iberians, thereby causing those august personages to be torn away from memoir-writing, from rounds of golf or from whatever other Sunday pursuits they found most expedient or enticing.

Trichet, the Chairman, had a particular desire to settle the matter there and then in the Borschette. Suspicious both of elected politicians and of the 'Anglo-Saxon' markets, he feared that a hurried meeting of ministers the next day would widen the discussion: even the French franc might be speculated about and against. Unbriefed ministers tend to make unguarded comments. Who was to know what they might say, and how the Reuters, Knight-Ridder, Blomberg and AP-Dow Jones headline-writers might misinterpret those statements to the waiting financial markets?[10]

At all events, boredom (most participants in the realignment meeting apparently spent most of their time standing around in the bleak, unfurnished antechamber of the Committee meeting-room, eating open prawn sandwiches and drinking Rioja), as well as a desire not to disturb their bosses' Sunday diversions, must have dulled the warning antennae of the guardians of European finance. In contrast with the chaotic night of 16/17 September, many of them had had the foresight to book Brussels hotel rooms. They had a bed to go to when the meeting ended and so did not need to use the Borschette as an all-night shelter from the November cold.[11] When Trichet at last produced a concession from the Portuguese as the Spanish held firm and the threat that Braga's bluff would be called loomed increasingly large, there must have been relief among the non-belligerents. The question of how the communiqué should attribute blame and virtue had apparently been settled.

9 The Spaniards in particular found it hard to take him seriously. One top Spanish official described Braga as 'one of those people who talk a lot and say nothing'. It was unfortunate for Braga that his name forms a Spanish word meaning 'knickers'.
10 In moments of crisis, French officials tended to lash out at the 'Anglo-Saxon' news media without any qualification. But in their occasional moods of sweet reasonableness, they would concede that the main texts of stories on the financial newswires were reasonably accurate – after all, they merely quoted what had been said. But the *headlines* – they were wicked and malicious distortion!
11 In contrast, the journalists and TV crews spent the bitter night standing on the pavement outside the Borschette. They were so unhappy with their treatment that, subsequently, a delegation was sent to complain to Trichet. During the next realignment meeting, at the end of the following January, the journalists were allowed into the front lobby of the building.

## Self-help without smiles

Yet those tired men and women let one of their number – it can only have been Tietmeyer – slip in an apparently platitudinous but in fact explosive last sentence: 'Member states whose currencies are in the exchange rate mechanism will implement their economic and monetary policies in such a way as to improve their convergence and ensure the stability of their currencies within the parity grid.' That sentence explained why the Bundesbank Vice-President had not, it seems, raised the matter of an Irish devaluation in the formal session of the meeting: he had not wanted to provoke a *communal* discussion of a parity when the country concerned had not asked for a realignment. Such a discussion would have opened a can of worms from Tietmeyer's point of view. First, other countries might have raised the question of other parities – perhaps even the French franc's. There could have been recriminations about 'sweetheart deals'. The Bundesbank might have been accused of being at the root of the problems of the ERM. Second, even if none of this happened, a communal discussion of one parity might then be taken to imply that all parities within the system were the subject of mutual agreement. Those that were discussed, but without agreement that there was need for a change, would presumably be regarded as mutually agreed. The same conclusion might attach to those parities that were not discussed at all. That might in turn lead to an implication that such parities should be mutually supported. Such a result would have been pleasing indeed to the Italians, whose constant refrain had been the need for more symmetery and for the unreserved acceptance of *mutual* obligations in the system – matters on which anathema had always been pronounced by the Bundesbank (here Tietmeyer was at one with Schlesinger, at least as far as *formal* obligations involving ERM members were concerned).

The 'Tietmeyer sentence' implied – and was no doubt meant to imply – the acceptance of an ERM philosophy diametrically opposed to one of mutual decision and mutual obligation. When the Banca d'Italia's usual Monetary Committee member, Lamberto Dini, absent from the meeting, saw the communiqué, he exploded: Tietmeyer was changing the rules of the game, and once the market analysts realized it, then the ERM was in danger of total collapse. They realized it very quickly. On the first working day after the meeting, a *Financial Times* report on the realignment quoted one analyst as arguing that the communiqué in effect rejected the idea of mutual support of the parity *grid*. When Dini read the report, his anger deepened. He complained bitterly to his aides, waving the salmon-pink sheets, that the ERM could not be made workable when its managers in the Monetary Committee were incapable of interpreting the situation and the communiqué with the same ease as an anonymous market analyst.

Rome's boiling anger at the communiqué soon set into a cold disillusion-ment with the ERM as a whole. The prospect of Italian re-entry was deferred; Italian politicians and officials increasingly put the emphasis on need for systemic reform, as much as or even more than an improvement in Italy's own financial performance, as a precondition for the lira's re-entry. On 23 November, Treasury Minister Piero Barucci made it clear that the weekend's events had put back the lira's re-entry into the system. He argued that Italy had every interest in restoring a 'solid and credible' parity grid in the ERM, thereby indicating his belief that the outcome of the meeting was *not* a solid and credible ERM. Next day's Italian newspapers carried comments from unnamed Banca d'Italia officials complaining that they regarded the communiqué as a clear step towards a 'two-speed Europe' involving the DM, the Benelux currencies and the French franc in the fast lane, and all the rest outside.

Thus that pregnant final sentence in the Monetary Committee com-muniqué had scotched any threat – as the Bundesbank saw it – that the ERM would find itself burdened by having to support a bail-out of Italy's debt. And that same sentence served as a further warning – if one was needed after Tietmeyer's private 'invitation' to devalue the Irish pound – that Ireland was on its own. Ireland was the most virtuous country in the EMU class, the one that had followed the self-flagellating Maastricht principles to the letter. The country had achieved the 'best' results in terms of virtually eliminating a previously enormous budget deficit. It was maintaining an inflation rate among the lowest and most stable in the Community (even if it shared with Spain the dubious distinction of having created the highest unemployment rate in the whole of the Western world). Yet Tietmeyer had made it crystal-clear that Ireland was not part of the hard core – a privileged group defined, it seemed, not by common agreement within the ERM, but by himself at the behest of the German government.

## Dive aid

The realization that Tietmeyer was thinking in these terms was a sickening one for the Irish authorities. Exclusion from the ERM's inner circle might very well be a prelude to exclusion from EMU. Ireland had been willing to do *anything* to ensure its entry into monetary union – even to the extent of allowing Maastricht ratification to become enmeshed with the embarrassing and divisive issue of abortion. The country's masters were prepared to risk sociological as well as economic disintegration in their country – all for the sake of obeisance to the Golden Calf of the Structural Funds. Like one of Ireland's most famous sons, but with motives much less praiseworthy, they bawled: 'Put your hand in your pocket! Give us your money! I want your money! Now!'

For Irish politicians, influence over the allocation of money from the Structural Funds meant keeping a grip on the levers of influence, patronage and power in Ireland's parish-pump political world. For them, EMU and Maastricht were all about maximizing the flow of largesse from Brussels (more accurately, from taxpayers in Britain and Germany – a detail glossed over in the Community propaganda hoardings that adorn every new bridge from nowhere to nowhere in Portugal, every plant for irrigating fictitious olive groves in Greece, and every new 'education and training facility' for creating highly skilled unemployed in Ireland). On 9 November 1991, the Irish, Spanish, Portuguese and Greek foreign ministers had left a secret meeting with Jacques Delors in which he had promised fabulous amounts (6 billion ECUs to Ireland) of other people's money if they pledged to support his federalist, corporatist ambitions in the final Maastricht negotiations. The Irish government had sold the country's soul to Delors.

But after 22 November 1992, things suddenly started looking scary to the Irish bigwigs: the Bundesbank, it seemed, was not only intent on exorcizing the spectre of taking over Italy's public debt, but also wanted to avoid the burden of supporting indigent Irish, Spaniards, Portuguese and Greeks in an unworkable, broad monetary union. The Irish reluctantly decided that they would have to bear the costs of a *unilateral* defence of the Irish pound's ERM parity if they wanted to proclaim Ireland's status as an EMU front-liner: the Bundesbank must not be allowed to nullify the commitments made by the German and other governments, as well as the Commission President, in the Maastricht compromises.

But the Irish authorities knew they were in for a hard time, and their difficulties would be compounded by their obligation to abolish the remaining controls on short-term capital movements by 31 December 1992. To renege on it would mark Ireland as unfit for membership of the 'hard core' just as much as – perhaps even more than – a devaluation. Yet abolishing controls would mean that there was no longer any buffer between downward pressure on the exchange rate and upward pressure on short-term lending rates in the Irish economy. With the Irish population even more enamoured of the joys of home-ownership than their English neighbours and with mortgage rates determined – as in Britain – by short-term money-market rates, ongoing pressure on the Irish pound could not be resisted for long. To be more precise, it could be resisted only as long as a further rise in mortgage rates could be staved off. Otherwise, there would be political ructions. One Irish official, with one of those glorious celebrations of the subtleties of the English language so often misprized in Britain as 'Irishisms', expressed it thus: 'The surest way to get them out on the streets is to put them out on the street.'

## Franc talking

Irish strategy after 22 November thus became one of hoping for something to turn up. The likeliest candidate for rescuing the Irish Micawber from financial embarrassment was a successful, *generalized* assault by the market on the ERM parities. In paticular, if the French franc went under, Irish bacon would be saved: the pound would no longer be isolated and Ireland could not be singled out for exclusion from EMU. As early as a few days after the November realignment, Irish officials were reacting with grim satisfaction to the news that the French franc was indeed under pressure again. One senior Irish monetary official at a meeting in Brussels spotted the worried looks of French officials, their toing and froing in and out of the meeting-room, and left the room to phone his office. Told that the Banque de France was having to intervene heavily, he replied with a single word, 'Good!', put the phone down and walked back into the meeting with a spring in his step.

The trigger for the markets to have a second bite at the cherry, despite their losses on 24 September, was the fateful 'Tietmeyer sentence'. Tietmeyer, it seemed, had fallen foul of the 'Law of Unintended Consequences'. He can certainly have had no desire to pull the rug out from under the franc. Indeed, rumours were circulating at around this time that Kohl had told Tietmeyer that he would not succeed Schlesinger as Bundesbank President unless he was able to preserve the mark–franc link,[12] and in the New York hedge-fund community Tietmeyer was commonly referred to as 'the representative of the Banque de France in the Bundesbank Council'. He probably genuinely believed what had been said

12 These rumours were subsequently reported in the *Financial Times* of 16 August 1993.

in the Franco-German communiqué of 23 September: that the 'fundamentals' did not justify a change in the parity. If the French government behaved as the Dutch had for so long (and the Belgians had since 1990) in absolutely and completely avoiding any suggestion of unhappiness with the level of interest rates resulting from Bundesbank policy, then the system could hold together. The problem was that, as shown by the events of 23–24 September, the markets believed that profits could be made from attacking the *system*, whatever the 'fundamentals', if Bundesbank support for it was not unconditional, unreserved and unlimited.[13] As we have seen, an important reason for the markets' cold feet at the crucial moment in September had been the fear of an immediate Franco-German monetary union, or at least of overwhelming Bundesbank support for the franc. But the November realignment communiqué might suggest that the 'sweetheart deal' had gone sour. If the French really did have to defend the franc all on their own, then the markets could swamp them.

Unlike the September flood, however, the late-November pressure on the franc took the form of a moderate but persistent leak. Several factors accounted for this. First, fingers had been burnt in the first attack on the franc. Second, the hedge funds, taking their lead from Soros, did not take the plunge. Third, and more mundanely, as year-end approached, the traders in the inter-bank market became, as always, more and more reluctant to take positions: markets were becoming thinner, the risks in backing a losing position were commensurately greater – why take too many chances when fat year-end bonuses were already in the bag? Fourth, there were easier targets than the franc – as we shall see when we pick up the story of the Irish pound in the next chapter.

## Paean of pain

In fact, the main haemorrhaging out of francs in the final weeks of 1992 came from French corporates who, sooner than anyone else – and certainly sooner than the French government, sticking to predictions of 2.5% GDP growth in 1993 – could see and feel the depth of the recession the French economy had slid into. The emerging recession was a particularly bitter pill for Trichet. Just a month before the November realignment he had published a paean of praise, 'Dix ans de désinflation compétitive en

---

13 This certainly does not imply that countries with supposedly good 'fundamentals' would be better off in a monetary union with a single currency. It means instead that they would be better off – would experience less exchange-rate instability – if they let their currencies float.

France', for the '*franc fort*' strategy pursued since March 1983. This document was a piece of quite astoundingly bad economic writing – a compound of crass errors in elementary economic reasoning, flagrant contradictions, cant and misrepresentations of the experience of other economies. Trichet's many claims for 'competitive disinflation' included those that the strategy enabled France's economy to grow faster than those of other G-7 and Community countries, that it 'rewarded virtue' within a fixed but adjustable rate system, led to the lowest possible interest rates in the system and went hand in hand with successful control over public finance. In truth, however, 'competitive disinflation' in the ERM was a recession-creating juggernaut that imposed crushingly high real interest rates on low-inflation ('virtuous') countries and inevitably led to an explosion of the budget deficit.

The key element in this doomsday machine was the key element of the ERM itself: the markets' absolute conviction that the DM would never be formally devalued within the system. It was from this conviction that everything flowed: the DM's role as anchor of the system, the impossibility for nominal rates on other currencies in the system to be substantially lower than German rates and, ultimately, the inability of the system to survive speculative attack (although in late 1992 the markets had not yet worked out how to place the right each-way bet that would destroy the narrow bands).

A country, such as France, that initially fixed its exchange rate with Germany when its inflation rate was higher than Germany's was bound to suffer losses of competitiveness at first. As time went by the resulting squeeze on the economy forced inflation down to the German level. But this was not good enough. To recoup the initial loss of competitiveness, French inflation would actually have to dip below the German rate by a significant amount and for a substantial period. But German interest rates effectively formed the floor for nominal rates in the ERM, so relatively low French inflation could only mean that real interest rates in France had to be higher than in Germany. Even worse, this was at a time when German real rates were themselves being kept high by the Bundesbank to counter Germany's reunification-induced inflation headache. High real interest rates in France depressed consumer and business confidence – already knocked back as unemployment crept upwards under the impact of earlier competitiveness losses – and reduced domestic demand. The shortfall in domestic demand meant that overall economic activity could be restored only if net exports were spurred by competitiveness gains. But, with the nominal exchange rate fixed, competitiveness could improve only through yet more relative deflation. That, in turn, could be achieved only through recession – keeping confidence depressed – and, once achieved, translated into even higher real interest rates.

In effect, France – in common with the other 'virtuous' low-inflation countries, Ireland and Denmark[14] – was facing the ERM equivalent of a Keynesian liquidity trap: real interest rates were forced above their equilibrium level, not because there was an absolute floor of zero to nominal interest rates, but because there was an ERM floor constituted by German rates. Ireland – as we shall see – was soon to escape, as Britain had recently done, by courtesy of beneficent (if not necessarily benevolent) speculators. But France and Denmark had only the remedy recommended by Keynes himself – fiscal expansion. France succumbed first, and by the time Trichet was writing his article, a massive deterioration of the French public finances was taking shape. On every count, then, Trichet was proved dramatically wrong by events.

Trichet did not like to be proved wrong, by events or by anything else. His worries about 'Anglo-Saxon' conspiracies increased: Anglo-Saxon economics, as well as Anglo-Saxon markets, were out to get the franc. And while Dini was unhappy about the analytical exploits of the system's managers, Trichet doubted their political backbone. He grew more and more critical of what he saw as faint-heartedness among his peers (or at any rate, his 'homologues') in other countries: if they expressed a lack of confidence in the ERM and a sense of powerlessness vis-à-vis predatory markets, how could renewed market attacks be forestalled?

Trichet's desperation reflected the accelerating collapse of the strategy he had maintained ever since the beginning of September. His attempt to dedramatize and isolate the lira devaluation had backfired, contributing to 'Black Wednesday' and the subsequent attack on the French franc, an attack that scared the wits out of the French authorities. His doctrine of 'competitive disinflation' in the ERM has been shown to be unworkable for Britain, Italy, Sweden and now Spain and Portugal. With the French economy sliding into deep recession and the government almost certain to

---

14 The Trichet article was most preposterous in its allusions to these two countries sharing France's perilous boat. It claimed that, in Ireland and Denmark, the discipline imposed by fixed exchange rates had allowed adjustment programmes to eliminate inflation without any consequences for employment ('*sans conséquences pour l'emploi*'). Yet between 1981 and 1991, the period of Ireland's budgetary adjustment effort, Irish unemployment had risen from 11% to 23%. During Denmark's adjustment phase (1987–92), unemployment had risen from 6 to 11%. Unemployment was still rising in both countries as Trichet wrote.

change within a few months, would Paris be the next apostate? Britain and Italy were openly criticizing the functioning of the ERM from outside; even worse, Spain and Portugal, while remaining in the system, had destroyed the myth of the 'glidepath'. Ireland was feeling lonely and betrayed, and was unlikely to survive for long without devaluation. Tietmeyer's rejection of mutual support mechanisms drew a sharp line between the ERM reality and the 'all friends together' Maastricht lie. The French franc was itself again under attack.

Trichet's only consolation was that Kohl was determined to maintain the DM–FF link come what may, and that Tietmeyer would have to support him. And Schlesinger could not openly defy Kohl and abandon the franc; nor was it politically possible for him to engineer the rise in German interest rates that would smash the ERM. But Schlesinger was playing a long game. Frustrated by the events of 24 September, he was, it seems, painstakingly putting the bricks together, one by one, of a strategy that would ultimately enable him to invoke the 'Emminger Letter' and free the Bundesbank from the ERM intervention burden he so detested. Trichet's apprehension as November drew to a tense and, for him, depressing close was justified: Schlesinger was about to make his next move. The ascetic professor, Bundesbank President only by accident, was widely regarded as out of touch with market psychology and as a political *ingénu*, but he was to demonstrate a strategical profundity and tactical awareness against which none of his Florentine opponents – not Mitterrand, not Kohl, certainly not Trichet, not even Tietmeyer – could prevail.

# 9

# War of Attrition

*Herrschaftswissenschaft*

Schlesinger had been appalled by the events of 23–24 September. The fear that had haunted him ever since the EMS was imposed on a reluctant Bundesbank in 1978 had been realized. Massive, unlimited interventions in support of the French franc had swamped the possibilities of sterilization. The Bundesbank had lost control of the money market. For those two crucial days, it had to all intents and purposes covertly operated exchange controls. If that was without Schlesinger's approval, it represented an abandonment of Schlesinger by his own colleagues; if it was with his approval, it represented a departure from his own principles. Worse had followed, as even after the crisis German M3 remained bloated yet the Bundesbank was constrained to reduce short-term interest rates further. In France, in contrast, once the speculative attack had been repulsed, the money supply and interest rates had returned to their pre-crisis path. The post-crisis world was one in which *all* the impact of the speculative attack had, in monetary policy terms, been borne by the Bundesbank, with France untouched. In short, the Bundesbank might still be the anchor of the system, but it was no longer the leader. It had become the prisoner of an exchange-rate constraint forced on it by Mitterrand and Kohl. The constraint chafed even more than the formal rules of the EMS: the interventions to save the franc had been intramarginal and 'voluntary', and the massive credits extended to the Banque de France ad hoc and bilateral, with settlement terms that were never disclosed but were almost certainly even more favourable to France than the formal terms of the EMS.

What could Schlesinger do about this? The Bundesbank Law obliged it to support the general economic policy of the government, while safeguarding the value of the currency. The 'unbreakable' DM–franc parity was an imperative of German foreign policy rather than economic policy, so Schlesinger need feel no ethical or constitutional qualms if he chose not to support it, but politically it would have been impossible for the

Bundesbank to pursue a course of action totally in contradiction with the central element of a still-powerful Chancellor's world view. Public opinion in Germany was not yet quite ready for that. And, in any case, the Federal government retained the sole right to determine parity changes. In the case of the September crisis even the 'Emminger Letter' had not been available to the Bundesbank as an option: the intervention had been intramarginal and ad hoc: it had not, strictly speaking, been *required* by the rules of the ERM, so the 'Emminger Letter' override of those rules could not be invoked.

In the summer of that year, the Bundesbank had twice cocked the interest-rate gun whose discharge would have left the ERM a bloody, shattered corpse, but it had twice pulled back, under the most intense and threatening pressure from Bonn. Since then, in an attempt to preserve its own credibility, the Bundesbank had had to explain the September and October interest-rate reductions in terms of domestic economic needs. It would now, in market, political and public relations terms, be impossible to reverse the downward trend in rates. Indeed, Schlesinger was under constant pressure from Kohl to reduce them further, for domestic political reasons as much as for exchange-rate reasons.

The key to Schlesinger's strategy in response to the straitjacket in which he seemed to find himself was found in the communiqué of 23 September, reread in the light of events at the end of November and early December. That joint Franco-German declaration had stated that the economic fundamentals did not justify any change in the DM–franc parity. Yet if that was so, why then had the market been betting so heavily on a franc devaluation? From the French side the response had been clear: there was a politically inspired Anglo-Saxon conspiracy to break the ERM and forestall the creation of a European Union that could challenge the economic and political assumptions of Anglo-Saxon 'liberalism'. This view was expressed at almost every level – Mitterrand, Bérégovoy, Sapin, Trichet, Delors, French monetary officials in the Commission, the politically subservient and stridently anglophobe French press. On the German side, Schlesinger, despite his reputation as an ivory-tower academic out of touch with the vulgar markets, possessed more powerful insight into the problem than the earthy Tietmeyer. The latter believed, and continues to believe, that if the ERM could somehow return to its 1983–87 form, it would not incite speculative attacks. For that earlier incarnation to reappear, countries must make serious domestic adjustment efforts, be prepared to realign when their competitiveness got out of line and follow Bundesbank leadership without question – or at least without public question. In return, Tietmeyer would try to steer Bundesbank Council decisions in a direction that the other ERM members could live with. Thus Tietmeyer, who had been so irked by the 'ERM paradox' experience, had gladly given his blessing to the peseta and escudo devaluations and had pressed the Irish to realign their currency. And as long as the French kept their own counsel and waited for Tietmeyer and Kohl to manoeuvre German interest rates down, the franc would not come under attack. Like every Bundesbank office-holder, he could not publicly accept that his institution should be expected to bail out currencies in trouble (hence the final sentence of the 22 November communiqué), but if the favoured countries behaved according to the rules as he saw them, then the system could survive as a 'hard core' and currencies would not get into trouble in the first place.

Schlesinger's interpretation was more radical, and, to the despair of the French, particularly of Trichet, he made his thoughts public. On 1 December, he launched a scathing attack on the whole concept of the ERM, describing it as, in essence, a machine for enriching speculators that would create wave after wave of instability in foreign exchange markets, leading, in the absence of parity changes, to unbearable disturbances to monetary control in Germany. The implication, supported by the renewed drain on French reserves, was that fundamentals did not matter in the ERM. Instead, the system provided a one-way bet to speculators as long as the DM was perceived as the anchor of the system – yet no other anchor was conceivable.

As events the following summer were to show, Schlesinger's analysis was correct. But, in the short run, his public statement had ambivalent effects. It was certainly an expression of no confidence in the ERM as such, but did not in itself seem to provide a trigger for a renewed all-out assault by the markets on the French franc. With sterling and the lira now out of the system, and the smaller peripheral countries apparently abandoned by the 'Tietmeyer sentence', massive intervention could only be needed in support of the franc. By complaining about it, Schlesinger appeared to be confirming that France would indeed continue to receive ad hoc bilateral support from Germany of a sort that was not available to others through the ERM.

## Beyond the pale

The initial pleasure of the Irish authorities at the problems of the French franc at the end of November thus soon dimmed when it became clear that a major, generalized assault on the ERM would not come, at the earliest, before the New Year. True, with the help of exchange controls, they could hold the line until then, but every week that went by increased the risk that the Irish banks (the main housing lenders in Ireland) would have to raise mortgage rates, thus signing the death warrant for the parity. But the authorities were determined not to give in: while there was life, there was hope. The Central Bank of Ireland maintained a stranglehold on the money market. It suspended its Short-Term Facility rate, which formed the usual upper bound to money-market rates. It replaced it with a one-week rate of 30%, but applied that only to marginal borrowing by the banks. The aim was to discourage speculative borrowing of Irish pounds to finance short sales of the currency, while insulating the bank's funding of existing mortgage lending. The combination of measures had the desired effect, making it very difficult for foreign banks to find Irish pounds to borrow. But the Central Bank of Ireland knew the line could not be held for long. As soon as some seasonal or technical factor came to increase the domestic bank's need for liquidity, the 'marginal' 30% interest rate would affect the banks' funding of mortgage lending.

Irish hopes rested, then, on a market onslaught against other ERM currencies when the markets reopened after the Christmas and New Year break. The franc–DM link was the undisputed core of the ERM and the French–German axis the obvious centre of gravity of European integration. The Irish hope was that pressure on the Irish pound would, perhaps via the Danish krone, spill over into further attacks on the franc. These would be seen as undermining the system as a whole, forcing the Bundesbank to act (or the German government to constrain it to act) as guarantor of the whole ERM parity grid. If the worst came to the worst, and sufficient Bundesbank assistance was not forthcoming, then there would be a *general* realignment in which the Irish pound could quite happily devalue along with the franc.

If the Irish pound had to be devalued alone the whole of Ireland would find itself beyond the EMU pale. The country would be chaff, not wheat; it would be cast into the ulterior darkness – and great would be the wailing and the gnashing of Ballsbridge teeth were that to happen; for just as Irish politicians felt their careers depended on the European pork barrel, so the personal myth of the Irish élite as a whole – with a few very honourable exceptions – depended on its members being able to strut their stuff on a Brussels stage as equal partners with the big boys. Unfortunately for the *amour propre* of the Establishment – but fortunately for almost everyone else in Ireland – assumptions about the respective motivations of the Bundesbank and the German government, and thus about the underlying dynamics of the Maastricht process, were about to be proved entirely wrong.

## Scotch mist

Throughout December, market pressure on the Irish pound, the Danish krone and the French franc continued, but everyone expected the main assault to come on the first business day of 1993. December proved more significant on the political front. The Edinburgh summit approved a declaration (with no legal standing, as pointed out with his usual bluntness by Helmut Kohl in a *Financial Times* article on 4 January 1993) allowing Denmark to opt out of those features of the Maastricht Treaty most disliked by the Danish electorate: the single currency, citizenship of the 'union', immigration policy, and defence and security policy. It seemed likely that a second referendum would approve Denmark's ratification of the treaty on these conditions. Now the Danish government had been telling the electorate that failure to ratify would mean having to leave the Community, with disastrous effects on the country's economic well-being. These propositions were extremely dubious: rejecting the treaty again would certainly not have implied a need to leave the Community,[1] and leaving the Community would arguably not have done any economic harm. But the propaganda campaign – aided by some Danish companies with close links with Prime Minister Poul Schlüter's Christian Democrats – had frightened many Danes, as well as some foreign investors. Thus Edinburgh's apparent resolution of the crisis produced a degree of relief for the Danish krone, which moved off its ERM floor.

Revealingly, the French franc did *not* gain from the improved prospects for Maastricht ratification. Instead, it weakened further on the news from Edinburgh. The reaffirmation of the Maastricht process by Kohl and Mitterrand meant that the chances of an early Franco-German monetary union outside the treaty framework were very much reduced. And since market fears of, or hopes for, such a union had been a major factor in

1 It would clearly have provoked a political crisis in the Community, one that would have put the ambiguous role of the European Court into sharp relief.

dissuading players from pressing home their earlier attacks, it seemed that the French currency would inevitably come under pressure as soon as forex traders returned to their desks from the Christmas celebrations of an unusually profitable year.

The first trading day of the New Year was Monday, 4 January. Within minutes of the opening of the European exchanges, massive sell orders had pushed the franc to the level of 3.42 against the DM (compared with a formal limit of 3.4305) at which the Banque de France had intervened massively in September. The pattern of the previous crisis swiftly repeated itself: early the next morning the Banque de France temporarily suspended its money market window and increased its official emergency lending rate by two points to 12%. Overnight rates in the Paris money market climbed to $13\frac{1}{2}$%, and three-month rates neared $12\frac{1}{2}$%. Once again, a communiqué was issued jointly by the finance ministries of France and Germany and by the two countries' central banks. The Banque de France intervened massively, and the Bundesbank confirmed that it was intervening continuously and intramarginally (i.e. voluntarily, since the ERM rules imposed obligatory intervention only when a bilateral parity touched the permitted margins). In other words, the sweetheart deal was still in place. The Edinburgh summit might have put paid to hopes or fears of an early Franco-German monetary union in a formal sense, but it remained clear that Kohl was requiring the Bundesbank to do whatever was necessary to support the franc. The following day, Tuesday, the Bundesbank announced its first tender of the year, offering repos at a fixed rate of 6.7%, down from 6.85%. The market had not attacked early enough, *before* the Christmas break, to take advantage of the Bundesbank's pre-announced one-month freeze in the repo rate from 11 December. By the close of European trading on 5 January, the attack on the franc had, to all appearances, failed. Where did this leave Bundesbank thinking?

## Eyes on the prize

Behind Schlesinger's strategy lay the knowledge that, while the French authorities had succeeded in maintaining the franc within its ERM bands, the cost was high and increasingly hard to bear. The French economy was entering into its deepest postwar recession, unemployment had hit 12 per cent; even more worryingly in some respects, youth unemployment was double that rate, and higher still in the bleak, high-rise North African ghettos surrounding France's cities. In an attempt to offset the monetary squeeze imposed by the ERM, the government was having to loosen the budgetary reins, undoing – as in Britain – a decade of hard work to restore healthy public finances after experiments with state Socialism.

For France, and not just for the Socialists, maintaining the franc's DM parity had a double political significance. The government's leading figures had invested a great deal of political capital in keeping their monetary virility symbol as rigid as possible: they preferred to impose the pain of economic deflation on the French people rather than suffer themselves the ignominy of political detumescence.[2] This desire not to be seen as merely piss-proud was felt as keenly by senior officials as by elected politicians. Trichet in particular was – as we have seen and shall soon see further – prepared to go to quite extraordinary lengths to hide the impact of his policy of 'competitive disinflation'. And, at a deeper level, not only the economics but also the politics of post-1983 French strategy risked exposure as fundamentally misconceived if the franc were devalued. The Maastricht Treaty had seemed to bring the goal of getting French hands on the Bundesbank within sight, since one hand had already been gripping Frankfurt since September 1992. If the grip was now relaxed, the prize might be torn away for ever. If that happened, more than just 'monetary Europe' could be lost to France's corporatist *fonctionnaire*, industrialist and financier class: 'Europe' itself, with its promise of 'Corporatism in One Continent' in which bureaucrats, indigenous multinationals and trade unions could hold at bay the tide of the Anglo-Saxon market economy, would be at risk if ERM superstition had to give way to economic rationality.

The managers of the smart money in the markets were aware of all this. Some of them – such as Soros – even approved of what the French ruling class thought that they were doing. The Bundesbank had for a second time been obliged to defend the franc, acting as the agent of the Kohl–Mitterrand axis. As long as the Socialists remained in power, the big market players reckoned, there was little chance that the parity would succumb to an all-out attack. But everything could change when the Socialists lost control of the government, as everyone expected they would, in the second half of March. And it soon became clear that a large proportion of the market bets taken out against the French franc at the turn of the year were three-month positions, timed to expire shortly after the formation of a new

---

2 At around this time, the word 'deflation' was effectively banned from economic discourse in France (perhaps, to avoid the charge of anachronism – the Toubon Law still lay eighteen months ahead at this point – I should write that the word '*déflation*' was banned).

government: if an incoming conservative administration was going to change course and float the franc, they would surely do it immediately. The prospects for this were mixed, with Alain Madelin the only 'respectable' opposition figure of any standing openly advocating such a policy. But he might expect to become Finance Minister or at least Industry Minister, and his views would thereby carry weight. Moreover, a conservative government, it was wrongly believed, would be more sensitive to the views of small and medium-sized companies – suffering particularly severely from the recession and from cripplingly high real rates of interest – than to the giant nationalized or semi-state firms run by highly political members of the ENA caste or the Socialist mafia or both.[3]

## Heads I win, tails you lose

Of course, even if the franc were floated at the end of March, that would not guarantee a profit to speculators. If, as was claimed by the French and German governments and central banks – and for that matter by some journalists and many financial market economists – the franc was at a fundamental equilibrium against the DM and was under attack only because of politically inspired Anglo-Saxon attacks on the ERM and EMU, floating the franc would not lead to any change in its market value. But many market operators believed that France's unemployment fundamentals were in fact so bad that a franc float would have to be accompanied by a deliberate policy of cutting French short-term interest rates below German levels. Such a policy would indeed produce a franc depreciation, at least initially. So, all in all, it seemed worthwhile to maintain positions aimed at profiting from franc depreciation (or, in market jargon, 'short' positions in francs).

The Banque de France thus had little opportunity to rebuild the reserves in January. Reflows into France simply did not take place on the scale seen the previous October: operators were not taking out new positions against the franc, but they were maintaining existing ones, many of them timed to expire only after the March elections. This made for a very uncomfortable period for the French authorities: the weekly statements of the Banque de France showed how exiguous were the accretions of reserves. The markets suspected, rightly or wrongly, that some rebuilding of reserves would be necessary to repay borrowings from the Bundesbank (recall again that the precise terms of the sweetheart deal were never made public). In conditions

3 As we shall see, the Brahmins of the *grandes écoles* were to prove just as able to maintain a united front against the lower castes under Balladur as under Bérégovoy

in which large short franc positions were being maintained, the need to rebuild reserves would have to mean continuing to bear the pain of high short-term rates of interest. Relief could come only if the Bundesbank hastened the pace of its own interest-rate reductions.

It was precisely this that Schlesinger showed no sign of wanting to do, despite the increasing parlous state of the German economy and the growing volume of criticism of Bundesbank caution from within the country. Schlesinger also had domestic reasons for maintaining a tight monetary course: during January, the German inflation rate rose yet again, to 4.4%. He himself was going to retire in September and he did not want his reputation as the high priest of price stability to be supplanted by the historical remembrance of a Bundesbank President unable to restore disinflationary order after the unification shock. Schlesinger thus declared in January that inflation would be no more than 3% by the end of the year – a prediction that many observers felt it would be impossible to realize. Whatever his domestic hopes and fears might have been, however, some Bundesbank insiders claim Schlesinger had another very strong motivation, that of putting pressure on France, keeping his finger in the wound of high interest rates in the hope that the pain and haemorrhaging would induce a new French government to float the franc at the end of March.

## Friends like that

Across the Rhine, Trichet, like a boxer trying to hide from his opponent how close he had come to being knocked out by a series of sickening blows, was doing everything he could, not to lessen the pain, for he was powerless to do so, but to mask it. His response to the September attacks on the franc, and to the risk that unenlightened *hoi polloi* in France might press for an independent policy, *à l'anglaise*, to be pursued, was to publish his fatuous paean of praise to his own policy of '*désinflation compétitive*'. But French inflation was already below 2% and likely to fall further. Many French analysts considered that, if statistical biases in the official figures were taken into account, the general level of prices in France was in fact *falling*. It was hard to doubt that, especially with Schlesinger determined to stuff the inflationary genie back in the bottle in Germany, further competitive disinflation would bring outright deflation, a prospect that horrified French popular opinion, as traumatized by the history of the '*bloc or*' adherents to the Gold Standard in the 1930s as the Germans were by their two hyper-inflations.

Trichet must thus have been furious when a warning of French deflation came from a particularly unwelcome quarter – the Commission. According to the left-wing daily, *Libération*, the Commission services had submitted to the Monetary Committee, as part of the confidential so-called multilateral surveillance exercise in which risks to the convergence of Community countries' economies are identified and discussed in a supposedly frank atmosphere, a report which questioned whether the *franc fort* policy was sustainable, given a risk of outright deflation.[4] This was heresy indeed! The situation was made doubly difficult by the fact that French public opinion took it that every word issuing from the Commission must have had the imprimatur of Delors himself – a reason for Delors's discomfiture over GATT and for the highly ambivalent attitude towards agreement with the US that, just a few weeks earlier, had provoked the EC's trade negotiator, Ray MacSharry, to attack Delors openly and give up his portfolio in disgust. Worse still, it appeared that the leak of the purported Commission document must have come from the Banque de France. Trichet had the Treasury firmly under his thumb, but the central bank – at that time at least – harboured dissidents.[5]

## Twisting, not turning

Trichet's riposte to the growing uneasiness about the unemployment – and possible deflation – consequences of the *franc fort* was distinctly double-edged, and was probably possible only because his Socialist political 'masters' had given up hope of retaining office. The French Treasury began to give increasing prominence in its media briefings (and no doubt in the various forums of international economic discussion at official level) to the idea that all, in effect, of France's unemployment was the result of

4 'Monetary sources', probably Irish, still hoping for a franc devaluation, told reporters two weeks later that 'the EC Commission had sparked a fierce row by presenting a highly detailed report on the economic performance of each Member State' and that 'the report' which has since been deeply buried, not only upset some countries because of its unflattering view of their economic performance but also caused general anger by making specific mention of exchange rates, a touchy subject.' That mentioning exchange rates in a multilateral surveillance discussion should provoke general anger is another clear indication of the make-believe nature of the ERM under the stewardship of men like Trichet.

5 Later that year, a week after Trichet had been appointed Governor of the Banque de France, one of the bank's senior officials commented in private that things were looking up. Was that, asked his interlocutor, because of Trichet's appointment? 'No,' came the dry reply. 'It's because a week ago he had a term of seven years ahead of him; now it's only six years and fifty-one weeks.'

structural rigidities in its economy and particularly in its labour market. Thus, it was claimed, macroeconomic policy, or at least a loosening of policy, could have no impact on unemployment. This analysis could be seen as a condemnation of twelve years of Socialist rule in France.[6] That the government was prepared to let it be advanced was an indication both of their hopeless electoral prospects and of the absolute priority that Mitterrand and Bérégovoy gave to the foreign policy strategy of tying the franc to the DM.

Trichet might duck and weave to avoid analytical criticism of the effects of his policies. He could claim that unemployment had nothing to do with the *franc fort* policy. But there were other, more immediate woes that could not be divorced from the measures taken to defend the franc. In particular, the state of the French banking system was increasingly worrying. State-owned banks, most of them run by members of the omnipresent, largely *énarque* mafia of Mitterrand's cronies, had been making dubious loans, particularly but not exclusively in the property sector. As in Britain somewhat earlier, though less spectacularly, French commercial property prices were, by early 1993, under pressure from mountainously high real interest rates, a direct consequence of the *franc fort* policy. 'Asset-price deflation' looked set to continue, worsening the bad property loans of the banks. And the general *morosité* in France early in 1993 was, if nothing happened to relieve it, likely to produce an ever-rising number of bankruptcies and loan defaults.

To make things worse, the French authorities faced many of the pressures with which the Irish government was struggling. Thanks to the sweetheart deal, French money-market rates had not reached the extravagant levels recently experienced, and soon to be experienced again, in Ireland. But the war of attrition in the foreign exchanges was keeping them far above the commercial banks' base rates for lending to customers, despite a half-point rise in December. It was known that the banks were agitating to be allowed to raise base rates substantially to better reflect their marginal financing costs. Such a rise would have been very damaging for the credibility of exchange-rate policy. Trichet repeat-

---

6 Similarly, UK Chancellor Kenneth Clarke's later acceptance of the absurd Delors White Paper on employment and competitiveness could be seen – as was probably intended by Clarke – as a condemnation of Thatcherism in Britain, a convenient way of escaping a need to confront the devastating consequences of the Lawson passion for fixed exchange rates, a passion to which Clarke was even more in bondage.

edly played down the importance of short-term bank finance in France, anxious that the market should not feel that France was as constrained by interest-rate considerations as Britain had been.[7] There were, it is true, important differences between the financial structures of the two countries. In particular, the nationalized industries and the large 'private sector' firms that formed part of the web of economic and financial relations in the Mitterrand/*énarque* state either had access to international capital markets or to privileged domestic sources of finance. But the great mass of small and medium-sized firms (traditionally owned and managed by political conservatives) were heavily dependent on bank loans. Further increases in their financing costs would almost certainly force their representatives to call on the conservative government-in-waiting to follow the British lead.

So a rise in lending rates was, for Trichet, to be avoided at all costs. Yet the American credit-rating agency, Standard & Poors, had already warned about a possible downgrading of the rating of the French banks. There were also market rumours that the state-owned banks had been instructed by the Treasury to support the French bond market. If this were true, and if fading hopes of interest-rate reductions created a bear market in bonds, the already fragile banks would take another big hit. Any hint of a banking crisis would be as damaging to the *franc fort* as a loss of patience by the entrepreneurial class. In response, the authorities resorted to subterfuge. First, as was common knowledge in the markets, the Banque de France was instructed to give French banks preferential access to its lending windows. The Banque de France's own rates for lending to banks, though raised in defence of the franc, nonetheless offered cheaper finance than inter-bank rates. So differential access made life somewhat easier for French banks as opposed to the French branches of foreign banks. This measure was a *prima facie* breach of Single Market regulations (although of course the European Commission, in theory the Single Market watchdog, showed no inclination to inquire into what was going on). Next, Trichet and his Minister, Sapin, encouraged one bank, at least – Crédit Lyonnais, the greatest Socialist banking fiefdom and, not uncoincidentally, the rockiest

---

7 In March 1992, before the ERM crisis had begun, André Icard, one of the most senior economists in the Banque de France, had submitted an article to an American academic journal that in fact showed the importance of short-term finance for French industry. For some reason that appears to have been other than the usual long lags in academic publishing, the article did not see the light of day for two years, until well after the dénouement of the franc crisis and the consequent relaxation of short-term interest rates.

financially of the French banks – to hide the extent of the bad debts in its balance-sheet.[8]

*Morosité*, already mentioned, was another source of great concern to Trichet. It could be used as an argument that, whatever he, or for that matter the Bundesbank, might argue, French fundamentals were less than brilliant – the proof of the pudding was in the eating, and France did not seem interested in eating. Indeed, it seemed less and less disposed to undertake any activity that involved spending. Families were worried that breadwinners might lose their jobs, and that school-leavers and university graduates might never have jobs to lose; businessmen worried that they were going to lose their firms – all the more so as the GATT accord loomed. Trichet, an engineer by training as well as a state-knows-best bureaucrat by temperament, railed at the stupidity and faint-heartedness of the French people. If only they would get off their derrières and spend, spend, spend, everything would come right.[9]

It was undoubtedly true that if people spent more, if the economy grew in consequence and if the markets then upgraded their assessment of the sustainability of the *franc fort*, then interest rates would come down and something of a virtuous circle could be created. But Trichet's insistence on a *demand*-led way out of *morosité* sat ill with his argument that *supply*-side deficiencies were at the root of French economic problems. And while the engineer-bureaucrat could describe the desirable equations of motion of the system *if* psychology changed, he could offer no suggestions as to *how*

8  This was revealed in July 1994 by parliamentary investigations into the activities of Jean-Yves Haberer, a great friend of Mitterrand and President of the bank. Haberer's career had followed lines similar to that of Trichet. He had been *Directeur du Trésor* and Chairman of the Monetary Committee. This connection assumed greater political prominence when in March 1995 the full extent of Crédit Lyonnais's massive losses became known and a 50-billion-franc rescue plan had to be announced by the French government. Alain Juppé, Foreign Minister in the Balladur government but strong supporter of Balladur's presidential rival, Jacques Chirac, made thinly veiled criticisms not only of Trichet (now Governor of the Banque de France) but also of Hervé Hannoun, Bérégovoy's *chef de cabinet* until early 1993 and now Deputy Governor of the Banque de France) and of Jacques de Larosière, Governor of the Banque de France until October 1993 and now President of the EBRD. Juppé also said: 'You have a mighty department in the Finance Ministry – *La direction du Trésor* – that propels its best officials to the head of our big nationalized banks. How do you imagine that the controller can control someone who has emerged from its own ranks?'

9  Trichet's emphasis on the virtues of consumption will not necessarily have endeared him to Delors, for whom a society of excessive consumption is one of the worst manifestations of the American culture he so detests. Trichet's denunciation of labour-market rigidities, too, must have been anathema to Delors. It seems that personal relations between the two men – each of them confident of his own intellectual pre-eminence – were never very good.

that psychology might be changed without a prior change in the policy that had made everyone so miserable.

Trichet's attitude on this question is enormously revealing. *Les français* would have to adapt their humours to the policy decreed by the state. The idea that the state might have to adapt its policy to the humours of *les français* was anathema to the French Establishment: the suggestion was anti-republican! '*Entre l'état républicain et le désordre libéral*' – 'between the republican state and liberal disorder', the headline of a *Libération* article sometime later bemoaning the GATT agreement – only one choice was possible. The General Will was expressed by the government and implemented by the *énarchie*. *Les français* had the right – inconvenient though it might sometimes be[10] – to legitimize the General Will by voting in elections. But, once the General Will was enunciated, it was inconsistent, illogical and politically incorrect for *les français* to frustrate it through their own individual actions as economic agents.

Thus Trichet was forced into a paradox: *les français* were behaving economically like anarchic Anglo-Saxons by not consuming as much as the General Will required to give credibility to the ordained policy of the *franc fort*; yet urging them to consume would, in the eyes of such as Delors, be to give in to the supposed American cultural imperialism whose defeat was one of those prime objectives of the United States of Europe that the *franc fort* was intended to bring nearer.

All in all, Trichet's December sense of malaise was far from dispelled as the days began slowly to lengthen again. Despite the further evidence at the beginning of January of Bundesbank support for the franc, he faced long months in the trenches. If the market speculators came over the top at him a third time, and then a fourth, how long could he be sure that the Bundesbank would stand beside him?

10 At one gathering of senior international monetary officials at around this time, a French representative commented unfavourably on the need for elections as creating difficulties for policy on the franc. One of his American counterparts expostulated that such comments betrayed an unfortunate attitude towards democracy: did the French want to go back to monarchy or something? While British representatives smirked uncomfortably, Canadians examined their consciences and the Japanese pretended not to understand, it was left to a Swede to defend the idea of constitutional monarchy. At a subsequent meeting of the same group, that US representative, leaving his microphone turned on, perhaps deliberately, after his own intervention in the debate, turned to his companion and referred to their French opposite numbers as 'assholes'. Since one of the Frenchmen was speaking and most other people were listening on their headphones, the benefit of the American's aside was widely distributed. This time there was no discomfort behind the smirks around the table.

## Finger in the dyke

The French franc story, with its implications for Bundesbank strategy, will be resumed in a later section of this chapter. But our immediate concern is with the impact of the franc's New Year survival on the Irish pound. Frustrated once more in their attempts to devour the franc, the markets turned their hungry eyes back to smaller, weaker prey. The Irish pound was now all the weaker because the authorities had, at the end of 1992, had to abolish their remaining exchange controls. This was an obligation imposed by the Community's capital movement Directive of 1988. In theory, Ireland could have invoked the 'safeguard' clauses of the Directive and maintained certain controls or even have imposed new ones. But for any of Ireland's European 'partners' hoping to find an excuse to keep the country out of the EMU hard core, such backsliding on capital liberalization could be condemned just as harshly as an Irish pound devaluation. Instead, the Irish authorities chose to continue relying on increasingly Heath-Robinson 'liquidity management' gimmicks by the Central Bank of Ireland, intended to make Irish pounds difficult to borrow by speculators while avoiding increases in the key one-month inter-bank rate, the main influence on mortgage rates.[11] But it was clear that this was finger-in-the-dyke stuff: at some point the sea was going to come crashing in over the top. In the first week of January, the central bank was forced to let overnight rates rise to 100%.[12] If such rates persisted for long, no amount of ingenuity could prevent a sharp rise in one-month rates and then in mortgage rates.

11 These schemes had the effect of segmenting financial markets, contrary to the spirit of the Single Market. But, unlike the devices resorted to the previous autumn, whether openly or covertly, by France, Germany, Spain, Portugal and Ireland itself – all of which were arguably contrary to Community Law – the Irish central bank's segmentation measures now were not based on nationality or residence and therefore did not constitute infractions of the capital movements legislation.

12 The significance of Thursday was to become clear to the rueful Finance Minister, Bertie Ahern. On Thursday, 7 January, Ahern had chanced upon a gaggle of pressmen and broadcasters in Dublin. To the horror of his accompanying officials, he seized the opportunity to give the Irish media the benefit of his views on the currency situation, telling them that the Irish government was not going to devalue 'today or tomorrow'. I am assured by Irish friends that this is simply a figurative way of saying not now and not ever. But for press and markets used to thinking of Saturdays as the day for realignment meetings of the Monetary Committee, Ahern seemed to be announcing a devaluation for the coming weekend. There was a flurry of selling of Irish pounds and, more significantly, the Bundesbank could interpret his words as evidence of irresolution in the defence of the currency. It was partly as a result that the central bank had to send interest rates skywards.

The new government finally formed on 12 January, more than six weeks after the elections, was a coalition of the outgoing government party, Fianna Fail, and the Labour Party. Both partners had strong reason for wishing to avoid a devaluation. Fianna Fail had made much in the election campaign of their ability to maintain the Irish pound's ERM parity, contrasting that supposed achievement with the August 1986 devaluation accepted by the Fine Gael government that lost office shortly afterwards. The 'sin' of that ERM devaluation, and the Irish pound's even bigger fall against sterling in the following eighteen months, had, together with the UK boom in 1987–88, been an essential precondition for the period of strong growth and budgetary adjustment, between 1987 and 1990, that allowed Ireland to claim membership of the European Elect. '*O felix culpa!*', the Irish Establishment might have been expected to exclaim. But Irish political debate has, still less than in other countries, never been conducted on a high intellectual plane. The 1986 devaluation had quite simply been a defeat for Fine Gael, one that helped eject it from power. Fianna Fail, a political party as consecrated to the pursuit, retention and usufruct of office, perks and patronage as ever were the Italian Christian Democrats or the Japanese LDP, had no intention of following the example of Fine Gael and Garret Fitzgerald, the former academic economist who, as Prime Minister at the time, had sanctioned the 1986 realignment. And, of course all the political groupings in the Dail clung to the hope that Ireland's European 'partners' would come to their rescue out of the 'solidarity' so important to the Establishment's vision of a European future in a land flowing with the milk of CAP fraud and the honey of the Structural Funds.

Yet the pressures for devaluation seemed irresistible. The cries of pain from the indigenous industrial sector increased with every day that sterling's post-September slide continued and the Irish pound/sterling rate forged through and above par.

The new government determined on an intensified appeal to European, that is, Bundesbank, solidarity. After the rebuff Irish officials had received from Tietmeyer on the night of 21/22 November, they had waited expectantly for their government to make higher-level appeals. But, characteristically, all the efforts of the caretaker government in late November and December had been devoted to maximizing the amount of money Ireland could extract from other countries' taxpayers via the 'Delors 2' package of Structural Funds. The Irish government believed it had promises from the European Commission of particularly large amounts, and had been considerably put out both by the opposition of the German, British and Dutch finance ministers to the overall size of the handouts proposed by Delors[13] and by the determination of Spain to grab a bigger slice of whatever cake was available. It therefore decided to avoid trying to pressurize the Bundesbank with the attendant risk of annoying the German government. By mid-January, however, most of the money the Irish government had been looking for was in the bag: the time seemed ripe to try to play the card of the 'common good' supposedly represented by the ERM.

Subsequent Irish press reports indicated that this 'diplomatic offensive' began on 14 January, with the Irish members of the Monetary Committee making a plea for support at that day's meeting of the Committee. If such a plea was made, it can hardly have met with anything but the frostiest of receptions from Tietmeyer. Had not the communiqué of 21 November made it clear that countries had to defend their own parities? Was it not obvious that if a country had pursued the right policies, there would be no market attacks, and that if there *were* market attacks then the answer must be a realignment such as he had urged on Ireland in November? Perhaps the Irish were hoping that embarrassment at the obvious contradiction between Tietmeyer's stated philosophy and the example of the French franc would force the Bundesbank Vice-President to act. But 'the old Westphalian ox' knew what he was doing when he applied that epithet to himself: a Jesuit education had taught him how to deal with the problem of guilt, and Irish gnat-bites of mere allusion were not going to penetrate his thick hide.[14]

Schlesinger, for his part, could take a relaxed view of the Irish pound crisis. He conspicuously praised the Irish authorities for jacking overnight rates up to 100% – praise that may have misled them into believing that they were being considered good boys worthy of the Bundesbank's grace and favour. But Schlesinger's remarks fall into place much more readily if they are interpreted as a rebuke to the French, who came running to Frankfurt (via Bonn, of course: Bundesbank independence did not yet go

---

13 Not for the first time Kohl had made Euro-gestures without thinking about the financial impact, thereby creating friction with Waigel. On 12 November he had agreed to Delors's proposals and even suggested an increase in the amounts to be handed out to Ireland.

14 One member of the Irish delegation in the Monetary Committee subsequently told the Irish press that: 'We are like fair-weather friends who have been thrown together into desperate waters; there is no real coordination . . . and a mood of great cynicism.'

far enough to deny Kohl and Mitterrand what they wanted) rather than standing up for themselves and taking it on the chin. As for formal ERM obligations, the Irish pound was at its ERM limits, but against the Belgian franc and Dutch guilder, not against the DM, so the Bundesbank was not having to engage in marginal intervention to support it. Would there be a public guarantee of Bundesbank intramarginal intervention? Not on your life!

So the Irish 'diplomatic offensive' never even had the chance to be stillborn. It was simply misconceived. Nonetheless, the new government's stubborn commitment to the parity seemed to guarantee a few more weeks of suffering rather than a merciful release. The markets settled back to wait for the inevitable, and while overnight rates again eased, one-month and three-month rates continued both to reflect the market's belief that a devaluation was ultimately inevitable and to ensure, via the pressure put on mortgage lenders, that the market would be proved right.

## Plane tails from the Raj

In late January the *coup de grâce* was delivered. But it came from a most unexpected quarter: from India. The British Prime Minister, John Major, had gone there with a group of businessmen in the hope of drumming up trade. It appears that he had some success in this enterprise, but the gaggle of UK political correspondents who followed Major were not interested in contracts for electricity-generating turbines – they had gone hoping to witness prime ministerial gaffes. This was a period when Major's reputation was at a particularly low ebb: not yet recovered from the shock of 'Black Wednesday', narrowly winning a House of Commons vote on the principle of reintroducing legislation to ratify Maastricht, trailing badly in the opinion polls, struggling to convince the public that the much-heralded recovery was a reality, derided by commentators from right and left. Major's 'nerd' rating was probably then at its highest, with few observers of the political scene believing he could survive to the autumn.

Against this background, the Indian trip was something of a public relations disaster, with Major criticized for leaving Britain at all at such a difficult time. The favourite newspaper comparison was with Jim Callaghan's apocryphal 'Crisis? What crisis?' remarks on his return from a Caribbean trip during the 'winter of discontent' in 1979. Most of the journalists treated Major with something approaching contempt during the

Indian trip,[15] and the disparaging stories they filed at home proved too much for him. The Prime Minister decided to turn the headlines in his favour by overriding the caution of his Chancellor and the Bank of England to provide the voters with some mid-winter cheer. A message was sent back to London, and on 26 January markets were taken by surprise with a one-point cut in base rates.

From an economic point of view, the decision was a sound one. But Norman Lamont, who with some justification was proud of the new framework for monetary policy that White Wednesday had enabled him to put in place, was understandably put out. He seems to have expressed his anger in no uncertain terms to the man for whom he was acting as an 'air-raid shelter'. Thereafter, the writing seemed to be on the wall for Lamont. Just a few days later Kenneth Clarke, up to then the most unrepentant ERM-fanatic in the Cabinet, was to be heard on radio stating that sterling should not try to return to the ERM in the lifetime of the current Parliament (up to mid-1997). One reason for the change of heart was that British interest rates were so much lower than German ones that an early return would require a similarly early *rise* in British rates.[16] Clarke was pragmatic enough to realize that such a rise, for ERM purposes and ERM purposes only, would be politically suicidal. However, shrewd political observers discerned another motive, suspecting that Major had told him that the keys to 11 Downing Street would soon be his, but that he must first go through a period of appeasing Eurosceptics: the necessary first step was to publicly disown the idea of an early return to the ERM and to undertake to indulge in his known proclivities only in private.

At least the Chancellor and the Bank had to confine themselves to off-the-record complaints to the press. But a very public storm was about to break over Major's head from across the Irish Sea and the Channel. The surprise cut in British interest rates provoked an immediate plunge in sterling, which fell seven pfennigs, about 3 per cent, against the DM. It also pushed the Irish pound, hard against its ERM floor, up by 3% against sterling to 1.10, an unheard-of rate. This was the kiss of death for the Irish pound's ERM parity. The opposition parties in Ireland demanded an

---

15 On the flight home, the mood of the tired and tetchy press men was not improved when the Prime Minister insisted on slumming it with them in the tail of the ageing and narrow VC-10, kneeling beside a victim in the aisle and thus preventing the stewardess from advancing the much more eagerly awaited drinks trolley.

16 How skin-deep was Clarke's Damascene conversion we shall see in chapter 12.

immediate recall of Parliament. Cries of anguish from Irish exporters were the 'blood in the water' signal for the market sharks to move in. It seemed that every bank in the world wanted to borrow Irish pounds to sell them short. Overnight rates shot back up to 100%, and the Irish banks intimated that a 300 basis points rise in mortgage rates was imminent.

In desperation, Irish officials pleaded with Trichet, as Chairman of the Monetary Committee, to intercede with the Bundesbank (presumably in the form of Tietmeyer) on their behalf. On the evening of 28 January, Trichet, attempting the role of honest broker that not everyone had seen him playing in September and November, telephoned the Irish Department of Finance. He floated the idea of concerted intervention in support of the Irish pound. The Bundesbank, he said, might back the idea. However, the Governor of the Irish Central Bank, Maurice Doyle, alerted by the Finance Ministry, wanted to confirm this directly with the Bundesbank. As it happened, neither Schlesinger nor Tietmeyer was available to speak to Doyle: Schlesinger was giving a speech in Brussels[17] and Tietmeyer was said to be 'on leave'. Their private offices were apparently unable to contact either of them. This throwback to a more leisurely nineteenth-century mode of diplomatic communication, when messages back and forth between the British government and the Viceroy in India took a month in either direction, must have been particularly galling to the Irish Governor: how he might have wished that Major's instruction from India to his Chancellor were still on a P & O steamer in the Bay of Bengal! Any such wistfulness aside, it was not until the morning of Friday, 29 January, that Doyle was able to speak to a high-level official in the Bundesbank. He was told that the idea of concerted intervention was being examined. The reply seemed to indicate that no help would be forthcoming before the weekend.

## Bell, book and vandal

At this point, with the Bundesbank remaining in its tent before the walls of Troy, there stepped into the fray Ireland's nearest equivalent as a powerful and unaccountable political force – the Church. Sapin had spoken of beheading speculators. Numerous other politicians and central bankers had warned the markets that they would get their fingers burnt. Now the

---

17 Schlesinger's remarks in Brussels that evening were hugely significant, as we shall see a little later in the narrative.

Irish Churches upped the stakes: speculators risked burning in hell for all eternity. One Catholic bishop, using words that might have been written for him by Trichet, intoned that: 'This speculative activity damages the country's future and is at the expense of the common good.' He added: 'It cannot be condoned and is contrary to any Christian principle.' The Protestant Bishop of Meath joined in: 'It is unbelievably immoral that wealthy people and corporations can make millions by holding a nation to ransom. It is appalling to see what they are doing to the lives of so many people.'

What prompted this clerical irruption into the Irish pound debate? Was it an expression of justified disgust at the elevation of Mammon? Was it a reminder of the duty of all Christians to give priority to the needs and rights of the poor? There is little doubt that that was what the Irish bishops *thought* their statements were. But such statements had about them much of the muddle-headedness and political correctness, the irreligious New Age mysticism, that characterizes the utterances on political matters of much of the Church of England – modern echoes of the secular religion of Jacobin France.[18]

'Get rich quick and don't care who suffers' is always an unsavoury philosophy. Its most blatant expression is the attitude of the Irish Establishment towards Europe. Many of the most prominent lay members of the Irish Churches are major beneficiaries – financially, politically or socially – of the government's obeisance to the Delorsian Golden Calf. But in addition, the attitude of the Irish Catholic Church, like that of the Catholic Churches in many Continental countries, was influenced by a desire to see a shadow Holy Roman Empire recreated in 'Europe'. Just as the French Establishment has never forgiven the Anglo-Saxon world for liberating the homeland from the Nazi occupation their incompetence and decadence had permitted, so also the Christian Democrat and Christian Socialist tradition in Europe has never forgiven the forces of nationalism and liberalism that in the nineteenth century seemed to have finally freed

18 The same perverted moral values were to be publicly expressed on 20 February 1995 in an article in *Le Monde* by Jean Boissonat, a member of the Banque de France Council, three days before the first round of voting in the French presidential elections. Boissonat, clearly concerned that the *franc fort* policy, the Banque de France's ticket to unaccountable and irresponsible political power, might be threatened by a Chirac victory, insisted that the currency was a moral issue. Replying in *Le Monde* next day, Chirac supporter Philippe Séguin commented that Boissonat's contentions were enough to make one's hair stand on end.

the Church from the self-imposed chains of its pretensions to temporal power.[19]

## Pound in the pond

Luckily for the people of Ireland, the country's government, deprived of the support of the Bundesbank and given little practical comfort by the Churches' animadversions against speculators, decided that Friday that the game was no longer worth the candle. Why, given that apparently the Bundesbank was stalling rather than giving an outright thumbs-down to Trichet's proposal? A clue was given a few weeks later, when official Irish sources told the press that what might or might not have been on offer from the Bundesbank was 'too little, too late'. The implication of 'too late' was clear enough: after the cut in British interest rates and the slide in sterling, the situation was close to irrecoverable. The 'too little' element of the familiar couplet is more intriguing. It suggests that while the Bundesbank might have been prepared to engage in concerted intervention, such intervention would be little more than a public relations exercise. Specifically, it seems that the Bundesbank might have accepted intervention only as *agent* of the Irish Central Bank, buying Irish pounds on that institution's behalf but without any associated credit line of the sort given to the Banque de France. Such an interpretation is given credence by market rumours about the nature of the following week's intervention in favour of the

19 These strains are combined in a particularly virulent form, of course, in the French Christian Socialist, Jacques Delors. As an aside, it is either amusing or chilling, according to taste, to note that a few years ago Delors received a letter from an English Catholic, a well-known figure in the public relations world. This luminary, presumably having noted that Delors had been responsible for promoting the 'European flag', with its unmistakable Marian symbolism of a circle of twelve stars on a blue ground, suggested that the European Community should be dedicated to the Blessed Virgin Mary. The member of Delors's private office responsible for the Commission President's relations with the Catholic Church replied that the suggestion was gratefully received. However, the President did not feel that it was within his authority to respond affirmatively. Now, anyone who knows anything of Delors might feel surprise at learning that the great man ever considered anything whatsoever to be beyond his authority. Would he really defer to the European Council, or even to a referendum on the issue? Elucidation came in the next sentence: the President, wrote the amanuensis, would make the suggestion known to the Holy Father, and if 'after prayerful consideration' the Holy Father considered it appropriate, Delors would do everything he could to implement it. The Pope is a much wiser man than Delors, and his devotion to the Blessed Virgin is great and genuine enough for him not to want her name to be sullied and ridiculed. Nothing more was heard of the idea.

Danish krone – but let us not get too far ahead of ourselves. At all events, the Irish government surrendered to the inevitable.[20]

A meeting of the Monetary Committee in Brussels was convened for Saturday, 30 January. As its members closeted themselves in the Borschette Centre, some of their political chiefs were, as usual, engaging in megaphone diplomacy. In Ireland, Ruari Quinn, the Labour Party Employment Minister in the new coalition, fulminated against Britain: the cut in British interest rates on 26 January had, he said, been 'indicative of Britain's whole attitude to the European Community'. Immediately after the weekend Michel Sapin, that great *énarque* proponent of the General Will, was even more outspoken, working himself up to such an extent that he could declare that Britain 'doesn't have the right to try to solve' its own economic problems. The sources of Irish ire and French frenzy were easy enough to divine. From Ireland's point of view, no matter that a devaluation would improve the country's economic prospects: after all its attempts to stave off the inevitable, nemesis had arrived in the most malevolent guise – the pull of the British economy, from whose orbit Ireland seemed doomed never to escape. Ireland's Establishment had seen both entry to the Common Market (as politicians in Britain and Ireland deceitfully called the Community at the time) and membership of the ERM as declarations of economic independence from Britain. Now to be forced into a course of action by events in Britain was psychologically hurtful in itself. Even worse, both the markets and the Bundesbank would see a devaluation as confirming the Irish pound's ongoing vulnerability to sterling developments, putting a baleful question-mark against Ireland's longing to be considered part of the 'hard core' in Europe.

As for Sapin, he must have smarted at the British interest-rate cut and the associated slide in sterling. First, the associated improvement in UK competitiveness was seen as having a negative impact on French growth,[21] at a time when Sapin had been clinging to an increasingly risible – and

---

20 Inevitability was taken for granted by, for instance, CNN's late-night business programme, which had recently run a five-minute lead item on the impact of the coming Irish pound devaluation. This was drawn to the attention of the French Treasury. One of CNN's other business programmes was sponsored by a heavily state-influenced French bank. No doubt it was hoped that the programme would increasingly be dominated by commentaries from analysts at French banks and securities houses who solemnly explained, night after night, why the French franc was strong and why the ERM would never be defeated.

21 This was a false perception. The debate on so-called competitive devaluations is looked at in chapter 7.

increasingly derided – forecast of around 2.5% GDP growth in 1993.[22]
Second, the British example, one of making monetary policy decisions with
the well-being of the domestic economy, rather than an exchange-rate
totem, in mind, might kindle demands from French industrialists for a
similar strategy. Why, they might well ask, must French business be
throttled by obedience to the monetary policy dictates of Germany,
supposedly France's greatest friend, ally, partner and co-adventurer in the
European enterprise, when perfidious Albion could steal marches whenever it liked? It was already bad enough that, according to Jacques Delors,
Britain's social chapter opt-out meant that the country would become 'a
paradise for foreign investment'. Next, an Irish devaluation meant more
profits for speculators, more 'blood in the water' for the market sharks
whose fins might again soon be seen circling around the French franc.
Things would be even worse if the Irish did not behave like gentlemen but
instead, feeling themselves ERM outcasts, cut up rough and made life
difficult for the countries with invitation cards to the Bundesbank's party.

For the rest, there can have been little for the Monetary Committee to do
but bemoan the uncomfortable fact that one of the most 'virtuous'
Community countries, in terms of its low inflation, dramatically improved
budget performance and large current-account surplus, had been forced to
devalue. This was certainly embarrassing. If one pointed to Ireland's high
unemployment as the reason for the currency's woes, that would imply that
the Maastricht 'fundamentals' were less relevant than domestic growth,
and the whole convergence strategy dangerously misguided. Emphasizing
the sterling link would mean confessing that the ERM, at least with Ireland
a member, was not a haven of monetary stability in a storm-tossed ocean.
Accepting that the system itself induced speculation would have been fine
for Schlesinger, but not for the Bundesbank's Monetary Committee
representative, Tietmeyer. It may also have been fine for Lamberto Dini,
the long-time Director-General of the Banca d'Italia, who on entering the
Borschette Centre had emphasized to reporters that the meeting would be
about the Irish pound, not the lira (a few days earlier Carlo Ciampi, Dini's
boss at the bank, had suggested that a lira return to the system might be
possible, something that Dini may at that time have regarded as unrealistic

22 As early as September 1992 – although it was not disclosed at the time and indeed has never
been officially admitted – the directors both of INSEE (the government agency responsible for
statistics and economic studies) and of the forecasting department within the Finance Ministry
had warned Trichet and Sapin that the growth forecast was hopelessly optimistic.

or even undesirable).[23] But Italian – or for that matter British – criticism of the working of the system would be regarded by the others as special pleading. Trichet, in particular, may well have been quite ready to stifle any attempt to discuss Major's 'fault lines'.

However reticent the Committee may or may not have been in discussing these delicate questions, the Irish pound devaluation did bring important general lessons (although, naturally, none of them were to be acknowledged in the two official reports by the ERM high priests produced a couple of months later[24]).

The most obvious lesson was that unemployment mattered a great deal. On most measures of overall competitiveness, Ireland was in a strong position, only marginally affected by sterling's slide. There were major doubts about the reliability of the precise figures, but their overall message was clear. However, no matter how good the competitive position might appear to be, it was clearly not good enough to bring down Ireland's crucifyingly high unemployment rate. *Any* worsening of the competitive position of Irish firms, however modest, would worsen labour-market prospects and threaten to exhaust any remaining margin of public acceptability of unemployment.

Second, it showed that there was *some* truth in Lawson's contention that the working of the ERM had been complicated by the drive towards EMU. The markets had never doubted what Quinn reiterated on the morning of the Monetary Committee meeting: Ireland would in no circumstances leave the ERM. Yet this conviction was not something that deterred speculation against the Irish pound. Rather, it encouraged it. Suppose that the Irish pound really had been at an appropriate level, given the country's economic requirements and political preferences. Then if the Irish government had been prepared to float the currency in response to market pressure, there would in fact have been no speculation, for the market

23 There is little love lost between Ciampi and Dini. The latter, the main internationalist in the upper reaches of the Banca d'Italia, felt excluded and threatened by the close relationship between Ciampi and his protégé, Tommaso Padoa-Schioppa, the main proponent of the defeatist 'European' strategy. When Ciampi subsequently became Prime Minister, his last days in office were marked by a bitter public attack from Dini over his failure to cut the budget deficit more vigorously. In the Berlusconi government that came to power in May 1994 – thanks in part to its more positive attitudes to solving Italy's problems by the country's own efforts – Dini became Finance Minister. Like Ciampi before him, he soon discovered that criticizing budget deficits was easier than eliminating them. But he was able to block the succession of Padoa-Schioppa to the post of Director-General left vacant by Dini's translation.
24 These reports are discussed in chapter 11.

would have no reason to expect the currency to depreciate if it were floated. Instead, the government's determination, for the reasons explained earlier, to remain in the ERM at all costs was likely to mean that if speculative pressure on the exchange rate became irresistible (because of the strain on interest rates), the only possible response would be a devaluation – and almost certainly a large one, in an attempt to buy the market off once and for all. Thus the political commitment to the ERM significantly improved the markets' chances of making a killing once some factor – such as the cut in British interest rate – acted as a trigger for speculation.

But Lawson's contention was not the whole truth, nor was it unadulterated truth. As earlier chapters have made clear, it was precisely the drive towards EMU that, in the face of clear market expectations of large medium-term depreciations of the 'peripheral' currencies, prevented a much earlier series of realignments in the ERM. Indeed, it is unlikely, with capital movements increasingly free after 1988, that the ERM could have survived at all without the belief, drummed into the markets by unremitting official propaganda in almost every EC country (and above all by Commission propaganda), that monetary union was inevitable, the ERM a smooth 'glidepath' to monetary union, and that political commitment to unchanged ERM parities was unbreakable.

## Black tie and blackshirts

Economic analysis aside, the Irish pound devaluation represented a key moment in the whole history of the European Community. On the Monday immediately following the devaluation, there went ahead in the Central Bank of Ireland a long-planned party, a party attended by several hundred guests. *Le tout Dublin* turned out in black tie. Given the circumstances, many of the guests felt that black arm-bands might have been more appropriate. Most of them were old enough to have paid off their mortgages, or rich enough never to have needed one. Their sons and daughters could benefit from the cronyism endemic in public life, and might not have to face unemployment or involuntary emigration (although many of the *jeunesse dorée*, of course, had their sights set on lucrative and – in Irish eyes – prestigious jobs in the Community circus). So the fact that the devaluation was about to set Ireland on a swift path to reduced mortgage rates, a surge in economic growth and – wonder of wonders – even a fall in unemployment did little to cheer their spirits. The Irish Establishment had suffered a major defeat.

The nature of the defeat was rubbed in by the reason for the party. It had been intended to celebrate the fiftieth anniversary of the creation of the Central Bank of Ireland in 1943. At that time, Ireland – despite its wartime neutrality – remained part of a monetary union with Britain. It therefore had no need of a fully functioning central bank of its own. Instead, its monetary affairs – essentially, the matter of note issue – were administered by a body known as the Currency Commission, which acted in essence like the currency boards the British had instituted in most of their smaller colonies. It issued Irish pound notes (their value fixed at par against sterling) one-for-one against its holdings of claims on the Bank of England. Given the overwhelming importance, at the time, of the United Kingdom in Ireland's trade, and the free and abundant labour flows to Great Britain, a monetary union with sterling was probably economically unavoidable.[25] However, the role – and more especially the name – of the Currency Commission was an unwelcome reminder of Ireland's former colonial status and of its continuing existence as an economic appendage of Britain. By the beginning of 1943, the Irish government, which for three years had lived under the threat of either a German invasion as a stepping-stone to Britain or a British takeover to forestall it, could look forward to a rather different future. The final outcome of the war was still uncertain, but America's entry and, now, the death agonies of Hitler's Sixth Army before the city of Stalingrad meant that Ireland's own political independence was certainly assured, and any postwar settlement in Europe seemed sure to increase America's role, to the detriment of Britain's. The time seemed ripe to make the symbolic gesture in the monetary field of giving the Irish monetary authority the title, if not the tasks, of an independent central bank (independent, that is, of the Bank of England, not of the Irish government).[26]

Not surprisingly, the developments in the war that gave the Irish government the green light for a declaration of (symbolic) monetary independence were having a different impact in Berlin. They required a shelving of the plans for a German-dominated European Economic Community (*sic*) that had been detailed during 1941 in a compendium of

25 In the economics jargon, Ireland probably formed part of an optimum currency area with the United Kingdom.
26 Canada had given itself the dubious present of a central bank in 1935. Students of central banking history generally consider that this decision was essentially aimed at giving Canada a stronger national identity.

papers presented by the President of the Reichsbank (predecessor of the Bundesbank) and a number of leading bankers, industrialists and economists. That blueprint bore a quite startling resemblance to the EEC of the Treaty of Rome, as modified by the Single European Act and the Treaty of Maastricht, foreshadowing the agricultural, industrial and regional policies and trans-European networks advocated by the more fervent Eurocrats.

In language redolent of the views, with their racist overtones, of European 'idealists' such as Delors, the Nazi professor charged with synthesizing the contributions wrote that:

Europe is much more than a geographical term. Its foundation will reflect its political power, and the extent of awareness of its political existence. It has been said that 'the national boundary of Europe coincides with a boundary of a way of life, of civilization'. In our own times the Führer himself has yet again pointed out that there is no geographical definition of Europe, but only one of peoples and culture ... The intellectual and political solidarity, the very community of living space, is the decisive feature of the New Europe. Another conclusion is that the only possible aim of economic cooperation must be the establishment of the European Economic Community. The decisive conclusion in terms of economic policy is that Europe is not to be what one would call a major area or market in terms of a reduced world economy, in which, moreover, the old structural laws of the Anglo-Saxon world economy apply; rather, the European Economic Community must be shaped in accordance with new political criteria and will consequently appear different from the economic structures of the past.[27]

Most interesting of all, for our purposes, was the paper on the future 'European Currency System'. The paper, an extension of a July 1940 analysis by the Reich Economics Ministry, was given by Dr Bernhard Benning, Director of the Reichs-Kredit-Gesellschaft.[28] The key features of the Reich Economics Ministry/Benning blueprint were that the Reichsmark would be the leading currency in a German 'economic area' and, with the dollar, one of the world's two reserve currencies. 'Within

27 Similar sentiments were expressed almost word for word by Delors in an interview in *Der Spiegel* on the eve of the Maastricht summit.
28 Benning had already become notable as the main proponent of the system of *geräuschlose Finanzierung* (noiseless financing) of the German war effort, which involved tapping the banking system's short-term liquidity. Ultimately, it had horrendously inflationary consequences. After the war – and after spending five years in a Russian concentration camp – Benning became a member of the Directorate of the Bank deutscher Länder, the new central bank which in 1958 was transmogrified into the Bundesbank. He remained a member of the Bundesbank Directorate until he retired, in 1972. Benning's place in the Directorate was taken by a staff member – a certain Helmut Schlesinger.

the German currency bloc', fixed exchange rates would be introduced to 'ease the way later to a currency and customs union'. There would be a Bank of Europe, but 'For political reasons it could be undesirable to damage the self-esteem of member states by eliminating their currencies'. Thus, initially at least, individual countries would maintain their own currencies, but would agree to permanently fixed exchange rates against the Reichsmark. In other words, there would be a Reichsmarkzone in the German '*Grosswirtschaftsraum*'. The members of this R-mark zone would be Germany itself (including, of course, Austria and Bohemia and Moravia), the Netherlands, Belgium (and thus presumably Luxembourg, which had been in monetary union with Belgium since 1926), Denmark, Norway, Sweden, Slovakia, Romania, Bulgaria and Hungary. Italy and Japan, the two other Axis powers, would also each lead a '*Grosswirtschaftsraum*' (including Spain, Greece and Turkey in the Italian case). Russia (in accordance with the Ribbentrop–Molotov pact) would dominate the economic affairs of Finland and the Baltic states. Britain would have an undefined '*Grosswirtschaftsraum*' (presumably involving its colonies) and the USA would dominate the whole of the Americas. The 'missing' country, interestingly, was France, which was neither included in the German currency area nor accorded a '*Grosswirtschaftsraum*' of its own.

The significance of this historical excursion is that it puts the European currency situation on the morrow of the Irish devaluation very firmly in context. Of the Community currencies, the drachma had never been part of the ERM. The lira, sterling, the peseta, the escudo and now the Irish pound had, in effect, all been shaken loose. Outside the Community, Norway and Sweden had been forced to give up their pegs to the ECU so despised and distrusted in Frankfurt; both were countries with a tradition of exchange-rate pegging and, it could be presumed, would look next to the DM after their periods of enforced floating. The economies of southeast Europe were in a state of flux after the fall of Communism, but the scission of Czechoslovakia into the Czech Republic (the provinces of Bohemia and Moravia incorporated into the German Reich in 1939) and Slovakia also held out the promise of future inclusion in a German currency bloc. Of the remaining 'hard-core' ERM members, all except France were also intended members of the German '*Grosswirtschaftsraum*'. In other words, the prospect of a DM-zone modelled on Third Reich ideas seemed a very real one, much more real than that of a European Monetary Union of Twelve (and later sixteen, twenty or twenty-four

members), each of whom would have equal one-man one-vote representation on an ECB Council.[29]

For any proponents of such a DM-zone, however, the problem was
France. The pursuit of the *franc fort* had certainly meant subordinating
French domestic monetary policy interests to the pursuit of foreign policy
aims. But those aims included precisely that of elevating France to co-
leadership status, at least, with Germany in the European Community. It
would never be possible for a French government to openly accept
membership of a DM-zone, and no one in Germany (or at any rate no one
in the Bundesbank, except possibly Tietmeyer) had the slightest intention
of imposing membership of a DM-zone on a reluctant France.[30] Thus the
ERM, and the Franco-German sweetheart deal within it, was a major
obstacle to the pursuit of a particular monetary vision. That particular
vision, it may be surmised, was Schlesinger's, but it was not Kohl's and
probably not Tietmeyer's. So how could Schlesinger detach the French
franc without running the risk of first detaching, say, the Danish krone or
the Belgian franc?

## Soft spot for a hard zone

On the evening of 28 January, Schlesinger, uncontactable by the desperate
Irish, rose to his feet to address an audience in Brussels. Adopting his

29  It should be made clear here that an idea is not *necessarily* a bad one simply because it originated
in the Third Reich. Indeed, some of the ideas expounded by Benning and the Reich economics
ministry had a parentage going back to at least 1919. '*Grosswirtschaftsräumen*' (or 'co-
prosperity zones') dominated by the Axis Powers were subjected to the utmost barbarity. That
in no way implies that a DM-zone led by today's democratic Germany would undergo even
remotely similar experiences. Hegemonic monetary systems have historically worked quite well
if the follower countries have been sufficiently economically and culturally similar to the
hegemon. The problem with a hegemonic DM-zone involving Germany's immediate
neighbours would arise if Germany were tempted to try to exercise hegemonic political
influence over those same neighbours. Would European Union create irresistible temptations
for Germany to attempt to exercise political hegemony? And over which countries? These
important questions are looked at further in chapter 14.

30  The same point has recently been made by the president of the EMI, Alexandre Lamfalussy (a
naturalized Belgian but of Hungarian origin), at a press conference in Frankfurt to present his
institution's first annual report. He argued that a 'hard-core' monetary union was likely to be
feasible: small countries might group their currencies around that of a large neighbour, but this
was unlikely to be acceptable for other large countries. Since France is the only large country
other than Germany that has ever been mentioned as a possible member of a hard core,
Lamfalussy was clearly coming to the same conclusion as the realistic (in this respect if in no
other) monetary planners of the Third Reich.

habitual air of bewildered and aggrieved innocence in the face of chicanery, Schlesinger expressed surprise at recent statements suggesting that a particular form of accelerated monetary union might be in preparation. How could this be so? The Maastricht rules were quite clear. In particular, how could the idea have got around that some sort of union could be possible 'without the Benelux countries, for example'? Schlesinger then went on, to the surprise of most of his audience, to argue that Belgium's massive debt ratio was not actually all that much of a barrier to the country's participation in a monetary union.

How should these remarks be interpreted? It seems clear that a primary aim was to quash speculation of a Franco-German monetary union outside the Maastricht framework (and the *Financial Times* headline the next morning, for instance, said exactly that).[31] This was important in itself, since Sapin had again been speaking of early measures to strengthen Franco-German monetary cooperation; and, according to the international press, unnamed diplomats and officials in Brussels had been expressing the view that some form of early monetary union between France and Germany was inevitable. Shortly before Schlesinger's speech, a 'senior French monetary official in Brussels' was quoted as saying that talk of such union was helpful since it kept the markets at bay and thus eased pressure on French interest rates. Thus one motivation for the Bundesbank President's remarks may well have been precisely to maintain such pressure.

Schlesinger was also signalling, however, that Belgium was 'in'. But in what? It would be bizarre for the President of the Bundesbank, the institution whose *nihil obstat* to Maastricht had been given only on condition that high debt ratios must be corrected, to argue that Belgium's 125% ratio was compatible with the Maastricht rules. Perhaps he wanted to encourage Belgium not to give up its *deficit*-reduction efforts simply because fulfilling the *debt* criterion seemed out of reach. More likely, he was implying that Belgium's place was in a DM-zone, not in a Maastricht EMU. The Bundesbank, not the European Council, would decide the criteria for membership; and Belgium's name had been written in the book of the Elect in 1942.

Schlesinger's remarks had recently been prefigured by Bundesbank officials in private. Belgium was already in a *de facto* monetary union with

---

31 As seen in chapter 6 above, Schlesinger had obtained a change in the wording of the Maastricht ratification law in Germany that seemed to rule out any non-Maastricht monetary union more or less absolutely.

Germany, they indicated, and the Bundesbank would allow Belgium to formalize the union, if market circumstances demanded it, by turning the Belgium National Bank into, in effect, a currency board. In other words, the Bundesbank would be happy to see Belgium do in reverse what Ireland had done vis-à-vis Britain exactly fifty years earlier. How might this work? The Belgian National Bank would give a guarantee of convertibility of Belgian francs into DM at an absolutely fixed rate, by constraining itself (or being constrained by a new law) to issue Belgian francs only one for one[32] against its holdings of DM reserves. In other words, the whole of the Belgian monetary base – the monetary *liabilities* composed essentially of banknotes and the deposits of the banking system with the central bank – would be backed by corresponding monetary *assets* exclusively in the form of DM (normally, part of a central bank's monetary liabilities are indeed backed in part by foreign exchange reserves, though in a variety of currencies, but also by its lending to the government, to the domestic banking system and to the domestic non-bank private sector). Remarkably, Bundesbank officials, it seems, went even further, indicating that the German central bank would, if the BNB were converted into a currency board, provide, via currency swaps, enough DM to back the whole of the pre-existing Belgian monetary base. Such an operation, if sterilized so as to prevent an increase in the German money supply, would mean that the Bundesbank accepted to back part of the German money supply with holdings of Belgian francs – precisely what it would *not* accept in the case of France, as the events of July were to make shatteringly clear.[33]

On Monday, 1 February, following hard on Schlesinger's remarks and the devaluation of the Irish pound, new excerpts from the Commission multilateral surveillance document, the confidential paper whose comments on France had already leaked in that country's press, appeared in the biggest-selling Francophone Belgian newspaper, *Le Soir*. According to the

---

32 Strictly speaking such a union would not necessarily involve – at least initially – the establishment of parity between the Belgian franc and the DM, but would fix the BEF/DM at a rate of 20.54 to one.

33 In fact, by January 1993 the Belgian National Bank's foreign exchange reserves already exceeded the total amount of the monetary base. Many of these reserves were already in the form of DM, and it would have been a painless matter – in technical terms if not necessarily in internal political terms – for the BNB to convert the rest of its reserves into DM. Such operations would induce a slight appreciation of the DM against the other currencies previously held by the BNB. The remarkable fact that forex reserves exceeded the monetary base was not picked up by financial market analysts outside Belgium, but provoked some comment within the country, where there was more awareness of its potential significance.

leak, the document, which had been available to the Bundesbank before Schlesinger's speech, suggested that the apparent immunity of the Belgian franc from attack within the ERM was hard to explain in terms of the Maastricht so-called 'fundamentals', given that Belgium's public debt position was so much worse than that of other 'hard-core' currencies such as the French franc and the Danish krone, both of which *had* suffered intense speculative pressure. The paper argued, according to *Le Soir*, that the Belgian franc instead benefited from a market perception that if a 'mini-union', essentially a DM-zone, were constituted, Belgium would be granted membership. Presumably the Bundesbank would play the role of St Peter standing at the Pearly Gates. But St Peter would be, for this purpose at least, a good Protestant, assessing Faith, as evidenced by Belgium's 1990 decision to peg to the DM within the ERM, rather than Works in the field of debt reduction. Indeed, he might even be Calvinist, numbering Belgium among the Elect predestined for eternal monetary union. In more earthbound terms, the suggestion might have been that the markets did not attack the Belgian franc, despite its poor fundamentals and ultra-narrow margins (and hence the virtual absence of two-way risk for speculators), because it was believed that the Bundesbank would always support it – and would do so in pursuit of its own goals rather than, as in the case of the French franc, because the German government told it to.

## Belgium for the Belgians?

These apparently esoteric matters were of major political significance for Germany, for Belgium and for all other would-be members of a 'mini-union'. But, once again, it would be a mistake to view the interests of any of the countries involved as clear-cut and uncontroversial – even domestically. The leak in *Le Soir* is a case in point. Whoever was the culprit, it set off a chain reaction that attested to the seismic nature of the issues raised. As background it can be said, at only limited risk of caricature, that Belgian membership of an explicit DM-zone would be welcomed by elements in the Flemish part of the country but resisted by the Walloons. From 1865 to 1926, when French-speakers had been socially, politically and economically dominant in Belgium, the Belgian franc had been part of a monetary union with France and with the other Low Countries; France being the dominant partner. During the 1930s, Belgium had formed part of the ill-fated '*bloc or*' with France. During the Second World War, the German occupiers had played on linguistic divisions within the country, favouring

Flemish nationalists. Much more recently, shortly after the signing of the Maastricht Treaty, Flemish nationalist politicians sent out some particularly significant campaign literature. It first denounced the impact of the Community in flooding the Flemish-speaking Brussels periphery with 'foreigners' (i.e. non-Flemings), and notably with EC officials and lobbyists, and then reproduced, with apparent approval, Nazi maps of a future European settlement along linguistic and ethnic lines. The symbolism for many Flemings was clear: '*L'Europe des régions*' would be linguistically pure. If forming part of a German *Grosswirtschaftsraum* and a DM-zone opened up the road to such apartheid within Belgium, so much the better. But for Walloons, Belgium's being part of a DM-zone would be an unbearable confirmation of the postwar reversal of the hegemonic relations between the two linguistic groups. Even the 1990 decision to peg to the DM within the ERM had caused rumblings in Wallonia.

At all events, the days immediately following the *Le Soir* article saw a flurry of statements from leading political figures in Belgium – all of them, whether coincidentally or not, with Flemish political affiliations – suggesting that a monetary 'mini-Europe' was in the offing. The statements (by the Prime Minister, Jean-Luc Dehaene, the Governor of the BNB, Alfons Verplaetse,[34] and the Belgian Commission member, Karel Van Miert) came hard on the heels of the latest in a series of suggestions from Sapin that a further significant tightening of specifically Franco-German monetary cooperation was imminent.[35] That perhaps suggests that the *Le Soir* leak was intended to make it clear that both the Commission and the markets saw Belgium as being just as much part of the hard core as was the French franc (according to Belgian sources, French officials were engaged, in this period of January, in a rather unseemly game of shouting 'our fundamentals are better than yours' at the Belgians, rather as though the two countries were squabbling for the affections of Siegfried). By the middle of the week of the article's publication, the markets seemed, for the first time since the ERM crisis began, to need such reassurance. But first we, as the markets did, must turn our attention to the Danish krone.

34 Verplaetse was the first governor of the BNB to profit from the bank's newly 'independent' status. 'Independence', of course, really meant 'unaccountability'.
35 'Franco-German cooperation is very close. It will grow deeper in the coming period; you will soon once again see some tangible signs of it.'

## Cutting up rough

Schlesinger had been kind to Belgium in his Brussels speech. But what of more apparently 'virtuous' countries, Denmark and Ireland? The Bundesbank President's addition of the words 'for example' after mentioning the Benelux countries as those not to be excluded from monetary union was an exercise in studied ambiguity – and it came on an evening when the Irish were feverishly trying to stir the Bundesbank into concrete action to support the Irish pound. Even if one believed the story that Schlesinger was unaware of this,[36] his words fell so far short of a ringing endorsement of Ireland's 'hard-core' status as to more nearly resemble the discreet, muffled tolling of a funeral bell for the currency's parity.

As it turned out, there was little immediate reaction to Schlesinger's speech. The French franc was not the first currency in the market's sights – it was trapped wriggling in the net of crippling interest rates, exhausted reserves and a creaking banking system and could be left aside for the moment – while the Irish pound was doomed, and what Schlesinger did not say about it was of little interest. But once the Irish pound devaluation was got out of the way that weekend, the ambiguity of Schlesinger's words would be probed mercilessly.

The Irish authorities had made it clear in private that: 'If we [i.e. the parity] have to go, we will not go quietly.' Irish spokesmen also intensified their explicit condemnation of sweetheart deals in the ERM. Then, most tellingly of all, the authorities showed, by their actions in the forex markets immediately after the devaluation, their readiness to bring down the whole house of cards. It rapidly became clear on the Monday following the Monetary Committee meeting that the markets were satisfied with the 10% devaluation. Instead of maintaining short positions in Irish pounds in the expectation of further depreciation, market players took their profits, buying Irish pounds at the new rate to repay their borrowing. Tensions on Irish money markets immediately disappeared, and the Irish pound rose to the top of its new ERM bands. Yet the Irish authorities carefully abstained from using all their new room for manoeuvre. They let money-market interest rates drop back to a level at which a rise in mortgage rates was no longer a threat. But they made no attempt to go further. This must to some extent have been because they wanted to avoid the stigma, both in Irish

36 Anyone who believes that will also believe that Schlesinger was unaware of the impact his remarks on 15 September 1992 would have on sterling.

psychology and in French polemics, of following the British example. But a desire, or at least a willingness, to create trouble for the rest of the ERM grid must have played a part. If one currency – the Irish pound – was at the top of its permitted bilateral band, another currency by definition had to be at the bottom. That currency was the Danish krone. By Tuesday, the pressure was clearly on. As the rules required, the Irish and Danish central banks intervened to prevent the krone from falling below its official limit against the Irish pound. The Danes appealed to the Irish central bank to buy up all the foreign currencies that the market was offering and to reduce interest rates further. The Irish declined. It seemed that the market would now pick off the Danish currency.

## Danegeld

By Wednesday morning the distress signals coming from Denmark grew more evident. When the krone had come under pressure during the previous bout of turbulence, non-residents had done practically all the selling. Now, Danish residents were starting to move heavily out of the currency and into DM, pushing the krone to its floor against the Belgian franc and Dutch guilder. This was taken by the Danish central bank as an indication that the credibility of the parity was seriously damaged. What had made the difference this time was the Irish devaluation, the first of a 'virtuous' country's currency since the ERM turbulence had begun.

At lunchtime on Wednesday, the task of the central banks in attempting to keep the krone within the ERM bands was complicated by Christophersen in Brussels. That day, by coincidence, he was speaking at a press conference, introducing the Commission's latest economic forecasts. Inevitably, he was asked for his opinion on the Irish devaluation and the continuing troubles of the ERM. No doubt keen to show that he was not under the thumb of Delors, whose critical view of Bundesbank behaviour was well known, Christophersen replied in words that echoed the 'Tietmeyer sentence' from the November communiqué: countries that had not put their own houses in order could not expect to be bailed out in the currency markets by the central banks of those countries who had. But not content with this general statement, he went on to list the countries that, in his opinion, were the good guys: Germany, France, the Netherlands and Belgium. He, a Dane, thus seemed to be resolving the ambiguity of Schlesinger's 'for example' the week before: Denmark was out.

As Christophersen's comments were flashed on to the financial news screens, the krone, already below its permitted limit against the guilder and the Belgian franc, immediately plummeted further in the London market. Profitable arbitrage possibilities were instantaneously opened up: players could enter into contracts to buy kroner in London and sell them for DM in Frankfurt, where the Bundesbank was obliged by ERM rules to buy them at the ERM limit. This the Bundesbank proceeded to do, preventing the krone from breaching its formal limit in direct trades of krone against DM in Frankfurt. At 5 pm Continental time, when the European markets closed, the intervention obligations lapsed for the day. The Bundesbank announced that its own interventions had indeed been obligatory. In other words, it had played by the rules but had done nothing more to help – no sweetheart deal for the krone.

On Wednesday evening, the Governor of the French central bank, de Larosière, decided (so it appears from French officials) that a multilateral defence of the krone would have to be mounted. If the Danish currency succumbed, the markets would view the ERM as damaged beyond repair, and the French franc itself might be overwhelmed by waves of selling. His plan was to surprise the markets with a barrage of concerted intervention, as soon as the Continent opened next morning. All the narrow-band ERM central banks would be involved. The Danish government readily agreed. That evening, the new Danish Prime Minister, Poul Rasmussen appeared on television. His party, the Social Democrats, were in favour of Maastricht, even if the majority of their voters was not. An enforced krone devaluation could put paid to the chances of a 'yes' vote in the second referendum in Denmark. Rasmussen was uncompromising in his television interview. The parity would not be changed. Those who speculated against the krone would, he threatened, be hurt badly.

Thursday morning, 4 February, began with a barrage of concerted intervention by the Danish, Dutch, Belgian, French and German central banks (pointedly, the Irish central bank did not join in). At the same time the Danish central bank announced a 2 point increase in its discount rate (to 11.5%). Together, these moves pushed the krone back within its permitted fluctuation band. Significantly, intervention, including public Bundesbank intervention, continued. Intramarginal intervention by the Bundesbank was an important signal – but the crisis was not yet over. Market analysts suspected that the Bundesbank was merely acting as agent for the Danish central bank, executing on their behalf orders to sell DM and buy kroner in Frankfurt. But the Danish central bank would have to cover those operations. If there were no reflows of foreign currency into

Denmark before the end of the day, the Danish central bank would – unless it could arrange more loans from other central banks – actually have to *sell* its own currency in order to acquire the foreign currencies it needed to reimburse the other central banks. By mid-morning, although the krone was within its bands, there were no indications of reflows.

The Bundesbank was now faced with a dilemma: if it did nothing, the krone would have to devalue and the Belgian franc would definitely be the next currency to be attacked by the markets. Yet for the bank to extend the French franc sweetheart deal to the krone would be unthinkable, as made clear by the 'Tietmeyer sentence' in November. The only way out, it seemed, was a cut in German interest rates that *might* convince the markets that the Bundesbank stood behind the krone. That would have the disadvantage, at first sight, of making it seem that Bundesbank interest-rate decisions could be swayed by ERM tensions and political pressures (German bond prices had been rising all week as markets anticipated that the Bundesbank might have to submit to the pressure for rate cuts made explicit by Köhler immediately *after* – to the chagrin of Dublin – the Irish pound devaluation). But that was preferable to the alternative – a krone devaluation, followed either by the dreaded attack on the Belgian franc in isolation or by another general assault involving the French franc, leading to a trial of strength between Kohl and Schlesinger for which the latter had not yet finished preparing the ground. In addition, an interest-rate reduction could be presented as responding to German domestic needs, with industrial output plummeting and West German unemployment starting to soar.

There were also, however, domestic factors that weighed against an interest-rate cut to save the Danish krone. Only a few days before, West German inflation had risen to 4.4%, a delicate wage round was in progress, and the German government's efforts to produce a so-called 'Solidarity Pact' of budgetary retrenchment were publicly known to be regarded with derision by certain members of the Bundesbank Council. Thus none of the conditions set by the Bundesbank for further monetary policy relaxation had yet been fulfilled.

To make things worse, the Bundesbank was again facing a counter-attack from the government. On 1 February, the influential left-leaning magazine *Der Spiegel*, one of the very few organs of opinion in Germany ever to question the use the bank made of its legal status, published an interview with Horst Köhler, State Secretary at the Finance Ministry, a protégé and disciple of Tietmeyer, his immediate predecessor. In it,

Köhler, who, it seems, had in late 1991 already warned the bank to trim what he saw as its ambitions to become a 'super-government', reacted tartly to Bundesbank doubts about the adequacy of the Solidarity Pact: their expression raised the question of whether the independence of the Bundesbank should not imply 'modesty and discipline' in commenting on political developments. For the bank to be constantly insinuating that on the one side there were the experts of the central bank, who were always right, and on the other side the politicians, always wrong, 'would be dangerous for our democracy'. Köhler also made a plea for lower interest rates and gave a clear warning that Bundesbank independence was neither absolute nor irrevocable. The European economies, he said, were so closely linked that it was impossible for Germany to ignore the situation in other countries in making economic policy – the Bundesbank could not escape this reality. Even more threateningly, he said that the law need not even be changed to clarify the central bank's legal duty to support the general economic policy of the government, because the mandate it gave the Bundesbank to ensure monetary stability 'does not contain the obligation that stability be achieved through a deep recession'.[37]

Weighing what they thought they knew of the various domestic and external considerations, the majority of market analysts were not expecting an interest-rate reduction at that time. Yet something had to be done.

That Thursday morning, the Bundesbank Council was holding its regular fortnightly meeting in Frankfurt, beginning at nine o'clock. When the bank's press office announced before the meeting that no press conference would be held afterwards, the markets had assumed that no major unexpected decisions were to be taken. Then, at a quarter past one, came an announcement that there *would* be a press conference. The impact was immediate: the dollar rose against the DM, the Danish krone began to recover sharply. Crucially, the recovery was not simply a matter of dealers changing prices for the krone with few actual trades taking place. Large reflows began, making it possible for the Danish central bank to honour the repayment obligations that, market analysts suspected, the morning's central bank interventions had entailed. Forty-five minutes later, the outcome of the Council meeting was announced: the Lombard rate, the ceiling for short-term market rates, was cut by 0.5% and the discount rate, which formed the floor for market rates and was therefore the more important indicator when the trend of market rates was downward, was cut

---

37 Köhler had made similar remarks both in December and in January.

by 0.25%. The dollar actually weakened slightly against the DM, as dealers followed the maxim: 'Buy on the rumour, sell on the fact.' But the Danish krone continued to strengthen sharply, as the markets were convinced that the German rate cuts were a clear signal that the Bundesbank was willing to throw its weight behind the defence of an ERM hard core that included Denmark.

## Tactical retreats

The krone crisis was now over. But the behind-the-scenes battle for the right to determine the future shape of 'monetary Europe' was intensifying. The reaction of commentators to the Bundesbank's interest-rates decision was virtually unanimous: the Council, and Schlesinger in particular, had caved in to pressures to save the ERM. Within Germany, there was criticism of the move, the employers' federation fearing that the pressure on unions to agree to moderate wage settlements would be reduced. German long-term interest rates rose slightly, indicating that markets saw the move as putting a question-mark against the Bundesbank's inflation-fighting credentials. But reaction from the French authorities in Paris and Brussels was little short of ecstatic. 'This is the signal we've been waiting for,' said a spokesman for Bérégovoy.[38] An aide to Mitterrand added that 'the supertanker [the Bundesbank] has changed course'. Delors went further, greeting the rate cut as 'a much-needed signal that it [the Bundesbank] recognized it had a responsibility not just to the German economy but to the rest of the Community'. The cut was a 'good political signal at a time when one was entitled to worry about the long-term monetary stability of the European Monetary System'. In other words, the Bundesbank had to act as a 'Bank for Europe', a concept totally abhorrent to most members of its Council.[39] Maastricht had been accepted by the Bundesbank with a bad grace, but the treaty had, at least to the naive,[40] seemed to offer guarantees that any European central bank would have

38 In a radio interview two days earlier, Bérégovoy, under pressure from French banks to allow a rise in base rates and from French companies not to, had urged the Bundesbank to cut rates, and the Banque de France had reinstituted lending facilities suspended during the New Year attack on the franc.

39 As we shall see in chapter 13, Tietmeyer's pubic words were in line with traditional Bundesbank thinking on this question – but once installed as President his actions were totally at odds with that thinking.

40 Among whose number the German Constitutional Court was to place itself when, later in 1993, it gave its blessing to German ratification of the treaty.

even more independence of political pressures and an even more unambiguous anti-inflation mandate than provided for in the German Bundesbank Law. The Bundesbank's acting, under foreign political instruction, as a 'Bank for Europe' would be a clear signal that Mitterrand had been right in his 3 September 1992 television interview.

Some of the more enthusiastic French officials, including those who, occupying Commission positions, were supposedly engaged in promoting Maastricht, even began to think they were pushing at an open door towards an early Franco-German union *outside* the Maastricht framework. Ignoring Schlesinger's Brussels speech of a few days earlier, they fanned rumours that they themselves inspired. The day after the Bundesbank Council meeting, a 'senior French official in Brussels' was quoted in the press as foreseeing an early locking of the DM–franc rate. Dismissing the incompatibility of such a move both with the Maastricht Treaty and with the Bundesbank's recently strengthened legal position, the official reprised Mitterrand's September television analysis: while the Bundesbank was in charge of 'day-to-day' decisions, 'the politicians have the last word'.

Such comments betrayed the total misunderstanding of Germany that underlay the disastrous French negotiating tactics in the crisis that was to come in July and that will ultimately make 'monetary Europe' impossible. The French appeared to be interpreting Schlesinger's Brussels speech simply as a reminder that some arrangement would have to be found to associate the Benelux countries with any monetary union outside Maastricht. They failed to realize that Schlesinger was instead pointing towards a DM-zone, the very antithesis of the sort of exchange-rate linking with the DM that they now appeared to be contemplating. Their vision was of a union in which the Bundesbank was subject to French political decisions; in a DM-zone, the political decisions of the members would be subject to the Bundesbank. Schlesinger knew that France could never accept a DM-zone. His comments, properly read, consistently favoured such a zone over either the ERM or the union of Twelve envisaged by Maastricht and implied that *no* form of monetary union between France and Germany was going to happen.

Kohl, for his part, was then in no position to give any encouragement to ideas of a narrow union; it was less than two months since he had gone along at Edinburgh with declarations ruling out a two-speed Europe. He had even been prepared to put his money where his mouth was, agreeing to the Delors 2 package of transfers in order to keep Spain and the other 'cohesion' countries on board. He had done so at the expense of the

German taxpayer – in the face of the strong misgivings of Waigel and the Bundesbank, and at a time when Germany had pressing internal income-distribution problems of its own, encapsulated in the government's efforts to shift the income distribution away from labour towards capital in the wages round and to cut back social security and unemployment benefits in the 'Solidarity Pact'. The Maastricht Treaty was not yet formally ratified by Germany, though already accepted by the Parliament. To accede now to French schemes so blatantly at odds with German public understanding of the Maastricht conception of monetary union would swing public and political opinion against *any* cession of German monetary independence. That, in turn, would stiffen the backbone of the German Constitutional Court sufficiently for it to declare Maastricht unconstitutional. Only the blinding arrogance of Frenchmen such as Sapin, Trichet and Delors and his Commission acolytes could prevent them from seeing what was to be made painfully clear to them at the end of July – and will have to be made clear to them again in the future.

Schlesinger himself could scarcely have been clearer in the Bundesbank press conference on 4 February: 'We hope this unfriendly game sometimes called dominoes, in which speculators pick on one currency after another, has finally come to an end.' Schlesinger, as he had consistently made clear over the previous two months, did not like the ERM. But he was not yet in a position to smash it and he certainly did not want the Belgian franc to be pushed over. It was already irksome to have to take ERM considerations into account – but the worried reaction of German industry could be used as a weapon by the Bundesbank in future. It was galling to have to listen to the crowing from Paris and Brussels, but the German man-in-the-street might as a result also become more resentful of French attitudes.[41] The time for the great battle was not yet, but the psychological ground was being prepared.

The most immediate repercussion of the Bundesbank's rescue of the Danish krone was a retreat from the bellicosity affected by the Irish authorities in the preceding few days. Bertie Ahern gave a grudging welcome to the operation, even if he could not forbear to complain that if only such assistance had been available to the Irish pound then a devaluation could have been avoided. On Friday, 5 February, the Irish central bank began the task of making the best of what it viewed as a bad

41 It was in reaction to the events of 4 February that the editor of *Handelsblatt* gave very clear expression to the fears of many Germans in an article quoted extensively in the final chapter of this book.

job. It reinstituted its normal money-market lending facility, at a rate 0.75% below the rate prevailing when the facility had been suspended the previous November. There was no point in hoping to stir things up in the parity grid now that the Bundesbank had been forced, it seemed, to underwrite the Danish krone. Thus, for the Irish authorities, things could hardly have turned out worse. They had suffered the political defeat of a devaluation; the contrast between the Bundesbank's treatment of the Irish pound and of the krone looked like a clear signal that the Irish currency was not part of a hard core whose boundaries seemed to be becoming clearer; and Ireland was again linked more strongly in the markets' eyes to sterling than to the Continental currencies.

From an economic point of view, of course, the balance-sheet of the devaluation was very different. For one thing, sterling soon began to rise as evidence of the British economic recovery sparked by 'White Wednesday' (as it was becoming known) became harder for the markets to ignore. Just as sterling's earlier slide had put the Irish pound under pressure, so now its rebound pushed the Irish currency up, to the top of its new band, in fact. Over the next few months the Irish central bank was able to cut official interest rates nine times (some of these cuts were timed to ease the Irish pound away from the top of the ERM band, thus cosmetically reducing pressure on the French franc in the hope of earning brownie points for being 'good Europeans'). Cumulatively, these reductions – which soon fed through into lower bank lending rates and, crucially, mortgage rates – together with the lifting of the atmosphere of continuous exchange-rate crisis, the sharp improvement of Irish competitiveness, especially against a strengthening sterling, and the recovery in Ireland's major export markets, Britain and the USA, gave a very strong boost to confidence and activity. Growth soon began to power ahead, home-owners were spared the trauma of repossession that had been inflicted on so many households in Britain during the ERM nightmare, and unemployment began to fall. Yet many in the Irish Establishment – government, civil service, central bank, Church, and, of course, most of the Irish contingent of passengers on the Euro-gravy train – would willingly have forsaken these unmixed blessings to ordinary Irish people.

## Raison d'état

While Paris, Brussels, Bonn and Frankfurt and even little Dublin were engaged in their games of monetary warfare cloaked as diplomacy, events of an apparently more parochial nature were taken place in Copenhagen, though what they implied about the nature of ERM and EMU politics was of major significance. On Wednesday, 3 February, the day of greatest pressure on the Danish krone, the Danish banks had lent kroner – which were subsequently 'sold short' – to anyone who was prepared to borrow at the going market interest rate influenced by the Danish central bank's operations. In doing so, they were breaching no law, regulation, guideline, convention or agreement. Denmark had abolished exchange controls many years before and operated a market-based monetary policy in which neither lending ceilings nor central bank directives played any part. Both the absence of exchange controls and a market-based monetary policy were not only applauded by monetary orthodoxy but required by Community legislation or enjoined by Community bodies. Important general articles of the Maastricht Treaty (article 3) and the treaty protocol on the statutes of the proposed European Central Bank (article 2) ordained that monetary policy (and all other economic policies) should follow such principles. Thus the actions of the Danish banks were completely above board.

Yet on Wednesday evening, the Danish Prime Minister had promised in this television address that 'speculators' would be hurt. By Thursday afternoon, the krone parity was no longer in danger. The Danish commercial banks had lent on Wednesday, as we have seen, at the short-term money-market rates in effect determined by the central bank. By Friday, they had to re-establish their liquidity position – which they expected to do, in the usual way, by borrowing from the central bank. On Friday morning, the Danish central bank took a quite breathtaking decision. It would act as executioner, 'honour' the Prime Minister's quite unconstitutional television threat, and inflict condign punishment on the banks for financing speculation. Thus it engineered a liquidity squeeze in the money market and, instead of offering overnight funds to the banks at the normal rate, required all of them to borrow for an extended period, seventeen days, at a penal rate of 40%. It was thus acting contrary to all principles of a free society governed by the rule of law, behaving with totalitarian vindictiveness against banks who had broken no law and had no legal or administrative redress.

Few people anywhere have much sympathy with banks. In nearly all countries they make fat profits when times are good and expect to be bailed out by the public purse when times are bad. In many they receive scandalously favourable tax treatment. In some they exert an undue degree of unaccountable political influence. But none of that makes it any more acceptable that, once again, as in Revolutionary France or the totalitarian dictatorships of the twentieth century, the General Will required legal and democratic niceties to be forgotten so that targeted 'classes' would not dare to engage in 'anti-social' behaviour.

The central bank apparently felt a degree of embarrassment about its actions. First, it was shooting the messengers: the 'speculators' who had actually sold kroner on the Wednesday were mostly Danish firms and households. Presumably, the Prime Minister's political future would not have been very secure if he had tried to punish all these individuals. So instead, a scapegoat class had to be designated – the banks who had lent the kroner that other people then sold. Second, some of the Danish banks were short of liquidity for reasons unrelated to Wednesday's forex activity, yet they were 'punished' along with the rest. Third, the supposedly independent central bank was hurting the banking system, and in so doing contradicting its own *raison d'être*, for unambiguously political reasons – to ensure that the Prime Minister did not look like a paper tiger.

When, a short time later, US Federal Reserve officials were briefed on what the Danish central bank had been up to, they took some convincing that they were not having their legs pulled with a central bankers' sick joke. This incident provided US monetary officials with final confirmation, in their eyes, that Continental Europeans' exchange-rate fetishism was not only irrational – they had always believed that – but, in effect, destructively psychotic. The issues raised in fact went beyond the ERM, pointing up the 'Continental', as opposed to 'Anglo-Saxon', conception of the state, of law and of authority embodied in the Maastricht design.

In Britain and the USA, the central banking function had developed (in Britain) or been explicitly instituted (in the USA) to ensure the stability of the financial system. In other words, it was intended to provide a 'public good', enabling private markets to operate more safely and effectively.[42] In Continental Europe, however, central banks have a much more political function. The form taken has differed from one country to another. In France, for instance, the role of the central bank has traditionally been that of agent of the General Will decided by the state, enforcing interventionist and discriminatory government policy in the economic arena in ways not accountable to the Parliament and only very tenuously accountable to the electorate. In Germany, the framework governing the Bundesbank obeyed

---

42 There is a lively debate among economists about whether the existence of a central bank is necessary or desirable for financial-market stability and efficiency, but that debate is tangential to the clash of concepts of the state involved in the issue discussed in the text.

a double imperative: to give legal form to an assumed precedence of price stability over accountable political choice; and to reduce the authority of central government in a federal political system.

The Maastricht Treaty, in the area of central banking philosophy as elsewhere, attempts to reconcile these two irreconcilables, but in practice there can be little doubt that, here as elsewhere, the Continental conception would hold sway if the monetary provisions of the treaty were ever implemented. The European Central Bank would be a centre of power, not a 'facilitator' for private markets. Whether that power would be exercised by politicians to neuter German monetary domination, or by central banking 'philosopher kings' to override, if need be, electoral preferences is – as the whole of this book has shown – the subject of intrigue, controversy and conflict. But there can be no doubt that a Maastricht ECB would be a very different animal from the central banks with which Anglo-Saxon financial markets have had a symbiotic relationship since the First World War. This is an important consideration in assessing the degree of damage that would be done to the City of London by British membership of an EMU. That question will be taken up later in this book.

For now, the key point is that central banks in the Maastricht philosophy – like Continental legal systems – are designed, not to protect individuals against the arbitrary exercise of coercive power, but as instruments for enforcing that power.[43] There could have been no clearer example of that than the money-market actions of the Danish central bank on Friday, 5 February 1993.

43  Wilhelm Nölling, then a member of the Bundesbank Council, was quite explicit in a lecture he gave in London shortly after the Maastricht agreement: British participation in the EMU designed by Maastricht would, he said, be inconsistent with Magna Carta.

# 10

# Wars of Religion

For the rest of the grid, February and March were relatively quiet months on the surface, but the process through which economic logic and political necessity would finally converge to destroy the old ERM pursued its tortuous course.

Once the Belgian constitutional changes were passed and the usual negotiations produced a sellable budget, the Belgian franc's brief period of shakiness came to an end. The French franc and the Danish krone remained anchored near the bottom of their permitted bands; interest rates in these two countries remained crushingly high, especially in real terms. In France the financial position of the banking system gave cause for concern; Sapin and Trichet carried on the job of hiding the gravity of the problem. For both France and Denmark, the perverse nature of the ERM economics was becoming ever clearer: 'virtue' in achieving the low inflation required for 'competitive disinflation' was not 'rewarded' (as Trichet claimed) with low nominal interest rates, since German rates determined the floor, but 'punished' with high real rates. The vicious circle described in the previous chapter was given a further violent twist when the markets suspected that the economic illogicality of the system would force a change of course: as operators covered themselves against the risk of devaluation, nominal interest rates actually had to rise to maintain the affected currency within the ERM straitjacket. The Spanish Inquisition could hardly have devised a more cruel form of torture: once heresy was suspected, protestations of innocence, even the production of evidence of innocence, could only intensify the agony.

## Do as I say, not as I do

While the true believers in France and Denmark continued to suffer, trying to stifle their screams, the High Priest of the cult was pronouncing anathema on recent apostates. At the beginning of March, Tietmeyer gave warnings to Britain and Italy. In a speech quite extraordinarily prescriptive and hectoring in its attitude to supposedly independent countries, he echoed Sapin's bile on the day of the Irish pound devaluation. This speech was particularly significant in that it prefigured the role of monetary dictator of the whole of Europe that we shall see Tietmeyer assuming in all its majesty at the beginning of August – even before he had succeeded Schlesinger in the Bundesbank presidency. On 1 March, Tietmeyer told Britain and Italy that they must not neglect exchange-rate policy now that they were no longer formally subject to ERM discipline. Unlike Sapin, of course, the Bundesbank Vice-President had to make his adjurations look compatible with the 'every man for himself' doctrine of the 'Tietmeyer sentence', but he nonetheless inserted an imputation of possible ill intent. Thus, he pontificated: 'In their own long-term interest, they [Britain and Italy] should not allow themselves to be led astray into a benign or malign neglect of exchange-rate developments.'

Tietmeyer certainly had cause for concern about British and Italian policy, but his concern was hardly philanthropic in origin. As far as Britain was concerned, Tietmeyer's grouse was unlikely to be about sterling's impact on the Irish pound. Rather, he had good reason to worry about the example being set by British monetary policy. First, he must have been aware that Britain's freedom to manage its own monetary affairs was being looked at enviously by the intellectual dissidents in France (something we shall return to in more detail in chapter 12) – hence Sapin's vituperation against Britain. Second, there was the more immediately practical point that the dramatic improvement in British – and Italian and Spanish – competitiveness was starting to hurt French industry. Industrialists' warnings that it was not possible to bear the combination of British exchange rates and French interest rates much longer must have alarmed Tietmeyer almost as much as Trichet.[1]

## Finding a better 'ole

Yet there was a deeper worry for Tietmeyer in what was happening in Britain. September 16 had been White Wednesday for the British economy and Black Wednesday for Major's political reputation; for monetary policy,

1 Tietmeyer also issued one more in a long line of warnings that German industry's own competitiveness was being damaged by DM appreciation. As we shall see later, Tietmeyer, once he became Bundesbank President, would give overriding importance to issues of German competitiveness and the need to preserve it by keeping France 'on board'.

it was Blank Wednesday. Britain's ejection from the ERM left a policy vacuum: the framework for monetary policy had simply disappeared. As the ERM experience had shown, something is not always better than nothing. Yet, among monetary authorities, only the Bundesbank gets away with passing off a succession of Delphic utterances as a consistent monetary policy. Markets, firms, workers and households (probably in that order) had to be given some indication of what, in the new world of rather daunting freedom, monetary policy was aiming at and how it was going to be operated.

For several weeks after September, confusion reigned. Sterling slid, but interest-rate cuts were initially slow in coming, for the reasons we saw in chapter 6. But for once, political constraints were fashioned by a strong popular consensus which political functionaries could not withstand. As a result, monetary policy began to follow surprisingly commonsense lines.

By the end of October, new guidelines for monetary policy with a floating currency were in place. Most important, as the much-maligned Chancellor, Norman Lamont, went out of his way to make clear, British economic policy would be determined with British interests first – hence the worries of Sapin, Trichet and Tietmeyer, and hence too the quiet rejoicing on the Continent when Lamont was replaced a few months later by the 'Europe First' Clarke. Within this context, the most important innovation was the setting of an explicit target range for inflation. Such targets were already in operation in Canada and New Zealand, and were soon also to be adopted by Sweden and Finland, countries forced to abandon an ECU peg.

In principle, the setting of an inflation target range by the British authorities was an important and welcome step away from the prevailing deflationary bias of policy-makers in Continental Europe. The target range had a lower bound (1%) as well as an upper bound (4%), so if unemployment was too high – above the non-accelerating inflation rate of unemployment (NAIRU) – inflation would fall through the bottom of the range unless there was a monetary policy loosening in good time. Before 16 September, it was clear to everyone in the Treasury and the Bank of England – and they subsequently made no bones about admitting it – that the deflationary pressure exerted on the British economy was so intense that there would almost certainly have been outright deflation – actual falls in prices – if sterling had remained in the ERM.[2] Thus the setting of an

2 These admissions also give the lie, of course, to disingenuous government claims that a sustainable recovery in the British economy was under way *before* White Wednesday.

inflation target range was consistent with, and indeed required, a significant easing of monetary conditions in the new, post-ERM, régime in which British interests could be put first.

## Shutting out the light

For Tietmeyer, this must have seemed a very dangerous precedent. The danger was not to the economies of Continental Europe, which would have benefited enormously from such a policy framework, if only the ERM allowed it. Rather, the threat was to the role of the Bundesbank and its vision of how monetary policy should operate if a European Central Bank one day came into being. The biggest problem for the Bundesbank in explicit inflation-targeting was precisely its explicitness. The Bundesbank's discretionary power and lack of political accountability – its most prized assets – depend on the vagueness of its legal mandate, even if interpreted in terms of price stability, and on the bank's leadership role in any exchange-rate system. 'Price stability' could mean anything it suited the Bundesbank to have it mean.

The Bundesbank has given indications on a number of occasions that *it* considers 'price stability' to mean measured inflation in the range of 1.5 to 2%.[3] On this basis, Bundesbank policy must be judged a failure, since in the quarter-century or so since the bank started interpreting its mandate in the inflation sense, price increases have fallen within this range in just *one* year. Nonetheless, the Bundesbank has avoided being branded as incompetent through stressing that 'price stability' is something to be achieved *in* and *over* the (undefined) medium term, rather than on a year-to-year basis. In practice, the vagueness of its mandate has spared the Bundesbank from ever being called to account for actions many of which are politically inspired in a broad sense, and even party-political in a narrow sense.

Why an unaccountable political role for such an important institution is tolerated and even welcomed within German democracy is a key question which will be taken up in the final chapter of this book – as will the question of whether the Bundesbank model either could or should survive in an EMU. But for now the important point is that the inflation-targeting framework announced in Britain was a potential challenge to an indepen-

---

3 For instance, this is the figure used in the Bundesbank's procedures for setting its money-supply targets.

dent, discretionary, unaccountable and to some extent arbitrary monetary authority such as the Bundesbank.

The British approach brought three horrors, from the Bundesbank perspective. First, the target was precise – and therefore relatively constraining. Second, it was in principle symmetrical, so there could be circumstances in which the monetary authority was constrained to loosen. Third, the target was set by the government, not by the central bank, a dangerously democratic procedure. In short, the framework was perhaps a halfway house to the New Zealand model, so much praised by economists and political scientists throughout the world and so much detested by the Bundesbank. In that model the central bank entered into a contract with the government, one which bound it to deliver inflation rates, over a three-year period, within a range determined by the government. In the pursuit of that inflation range, the central bank could take whatever monetary policy measures it thought fit, free from government interference. But if it failed to deliver the inflation rate it contracted for, the governor of the central bank would lose his job. Thus the central bank, far from being a great Estate of the realm, was in a position similar to a company supplying, say, office furniture under contract. The government would include specification in the contract, a price would be agreed, and there would be provisions for review of performance. The company could organize the production of the furniture in any way it liked (in the jargon, it would have 'functional independence'), but could not exercise any independent *political* power.

Tietmeyer's response to the British threat was twofold. First, he implied in his March speech that it would not work because it did not give enough weight to the exchange rate.[4] Second, he made a series of statements over the following two years in which he emphasized that monetary policy alone could not achieve a particular inflation outcome and that therefore the monetary authority could not be held responsible for success or failure in respect of inflation.

4 In fact, the exchange rate does play a role in any inflation-targeting framework, since it is one of the factors influencing future inflation developments. But it is only one such factor. As the Bundesbank has always emphasized in its own philosophy, placing excessive – and, *a fortiori*, exclusive – emphasis on the exchange rate will make price stability unattainable. As we shall see in chapter 13, however, the Bundesbank may have been instrumental in undermining Spain's inflation-targeting approach in early 1995 by emphasizing the role of the exchange rate. There may also be circumstances – such as supply shocks or terms-of-trade shocks (including exchange-rate shocks) – when it is not appropriate to enforce price stability: what is or is not 'appropriate' in these circumstances should be decided *only* by governments, not central banks.

Unfortunately for Tietmeyer, the Bundesbank and any future independent ECB, this last argument is distinctly double-edged. In normal circumstances, it is not strictly true that monetary policy cannot achieve a particular inflation range, at least if the target is defined over a period of a couple of years or more.[5] What Tietmeyer had in mind was the possibility of a wages explosion or a fiscal expansion. These could, at least for a time, push up inflation without any loosening of monetary policy (indeed, this is just what happened in Germany after unification). Yet, if monetary policy were tightened sufficiently drastically in response, an increase in inflation could be avoided. But of course there would be a price to pay. Monetary tightening in response to increased wage demands or fiscal expansion would (except in the circumstances of supply-side improvement and booming private-sector confidence we looked at in chapters 3 and 4) create a recession and raise unemployment.

To what extent the price of monetary restraint of inflation in these circumstances would be worth paying would be a political decision. In the New Zealand model, for instance, the government can, after obtaining parliamentary approval, adjust or override the inflation targets in its contract with the central bank if unforeseen developments threaten to make the cost of hitting the targets politically unacceptable. In Germany too, after unification, a political judgement had to be made about striking the right balance between the costs of higher inflation and the costs of preventing it through monetary tightening. Inevitably, the outcome was a halfway house: inflation *did* rise, but not as much as it would have done without monetary tightening; monetary policy *was* tightened, but not enough to forestall inflation completely. As we saw in chapter 4, the political process through which this compromise was reached involved very strained relations between Bundesbank and government, with the bank in effect exacting a degree of revenge on the government for having overridden its advice on the terms of unification. The Bundesbank used the threat of monetary tightening, and the inevitable consequences of recession, unemployment and general economic disruption, in an attempt to enforce *its* ideas about budgetary retrenchment (including the balance between expenditure cuts and tax increases, and even that between increases in different forms of tax)

5 There *are* circumstances in which monetary policy, or at any rate monetary policy run by an independent central bank, cannot guarantee price stability. They are those in which a central bank tries unsuccessfully to impose its will on the government over budgetary policy, thereby creating a risk of repudiation of government debt via inflation – a problem evoked later in this section, and one which is now painfully relevant to Sweden and Italy.

on the government, and *its* ideas about wage settlements on firms and unions.

The Bundesbank is not alone in this kind of behaviour. Central bankers throughout the world never criticize their own monetary policy stance and rarely criticize each other's – at least in public. But they all fulminate at great length and at frequent intervals about the sins of budgetary policy or wage behaviour. The satisfactory enjoyment by central bankers of an independent status in fact *requires* 'bad behaviour' on the part of other actors: it gives the central bankers an ever-present excuse for their own failures and enables them to exercise political power by threatening its authors. A corollary of this is that the 'coordination' of the various aspects of economic policy, in countries burdened with an independent, unaccountable and irresponsible central bank, is inevitably conflictual.[6] Such conflict is invariably damaging to the economy unless it is resolved. It can be resolved either by the government's assuming control of monetary policy or by the central bank's assuming effective control of, or significant influence over, government policy in other areas. Whatever the choice might be within a particular country, EMU will have to impose one choice on *all* participating countries. That does not bode well for its success.

## Borrowing time

Italy, the second target of Tietmeyer's wrath, was a striking example of the damage done by Stackelberg warfare, and a dire warning of the likely future of an EMU. From the mid-1970s onwards, the country had experienced the problems of a large budget deficit, with an upwards-spiralling ratio of government debt to national income, and relatively high inflation. The theoretical links between these two problems had been investigated by economists more exhaustively in Italy than anywhere else in the developed world (with the possible exception of Israel).

The budget deficit was clearly the primary problem. It resulted from those key structural features of the Italian state that would inevitably be replicated in a European Union. There were large disparities in incomes and productivity between the regions of the country; and a system of proportional representation in elections. The interaction of these two

6 In the economics jargon, this is known as a state of 'Stackelberg warfare' between the monetary authority and the government.

features produced a political system of 'revolving-door' governments in which prime ministers changed with dizzying frequency but Christian Democracy retained a grip on the levers of power, patronage and corruption with dulling constancy.

Christian Democracy had a particularly strong grip on the backward southern half of the country – or perhaps it would be better to say that the South had a particularly strong grip on the government via Christian Democracy. The South was a vast welfare-dependency of Christian Democrat governments, with the tab picked up by taxpayers in the dynamic North. And Christian Democracy was a vast welfare-dependency of southern Mafia bosses (and all 'respectable' parties were clients of Italian firms, for whom the cost of bribes was an unavoidable business expense). Thus government spending, particularly in the form of transfers to the South in the form of social benefits, unproductive public sector unemployment and equally unproductive industrial development projects, was uncontrollable. Tax evasion was pervasive: in the South, a large fraction of legal income passed through the hands of the Mafia and was 'laundered' long before it could appear on a tax form. In the North, the normal reluctance to pay taxes was compounded by a mixture of disgust at what tax revenues were used for and a feeling that quite enough was already being extracted in the shape of bribes.

Thus a large budget deficit developed, one that was aggravated by the growing burden of interest payments on past borrowing. Yet Italy's debt ratio, despite the enormous deficit (14% of GDP by 1991), rose less rapidly than in Belgium, and the tax burden (excluding bribes, at any rate) was lower than in Belgium. Throughout the 1980s, the Italian economy, unlike Belgium's, remained rather dynamic by sclerotic Continental standards. The difference between the two countries lay in the inflation rate, which was significantly higher in Italy, and in particular in the much less marked deceleration of inflation in Italy than in Belgium in the period from 1982–83 to the beginning of the 1990s. In the early 1980s, and indeed throughout the decade, Belgium issued large amounts of long-term bonds at high fixed rates of interest. Its government then allowed the Belgian franc to be dragged into an ERM transformed by the impact of internecine strife in the French Socialist Party in 1983 from a 'soft-currency' grouping around the French franc into a 'hard-currency' zone dominated by the Bundesbank. The ensuing sharp deceleration in inflation, however welcome in itself, vastly increased the real burden of Belgian government interest payments.

Italy, in contrast, chose to finance the bulk of its debt at short term;[7] it continued a strategy of occasional downward realignments in the ERM during the 'classical' period of 1983–86; it maintained wide ERM bands until the beginning of 1990; and, until early 1991, kept a system of exchange controls that allowed domestic interest rates to remain significantly below the Euromarket rates relevant to defending the lira within the ERM. In the late 1980s and into the beginning of the 1990s, Italy's relatively low-tax and, in the 'informal' sector, relatively flexible economy was in a good position to benefit from the general upswing in growth in the industrial world. It also benefited from the Europhoria that extended from 1988 to 1991; investors, foreign ones at any rate, believed that somehow the European magic would produce low budget deficits and low inflation in Italy, and they did not look too closely for evidence that the policies required for this miracle were actually being put in place.

## Divorce, Italian style

The reckoning arrived in the shape of central bankers determined to exercise 'monetary leadership'. In other words, instead of monetary policy having to accommodate the government's need to finance the deficit at low real rates of interest, the government would have to reduce the deficit to accommodate the central bank's policy of a fixed exchange rate and decelerating inflation. The Banca d'Italia had been agitating for such a shift of priorities ever since the early 1980s. A first step had been taken in 1981, in the so-called 'divorce' of the bank from the Treasury. Previously, the bank had undertaken to take onto its books any government paper it was unable to sell to the private sector at the interest rate set by the government. That obligation meant that the bank could not control the money supply, nor influence market interest rates, independently of the government. In 1981, the obligation was removed. Political scientists consider that the reason for the change was the likelihood, in the period preceding the change, that the Communists might have to be brought into government. The 'divorce' somewhat reduced the economic power of the government,

---

7  It might be accurate to say it was *forced* to borrow short: there has been no 'bond culture' in Italy, partly because the shortcomings of Italian financial markets meant that bonds were illiquid and therefore risky assets even in nominal terms, partly because of problems of tax treatment, and partly because of a probably justified fear that if the bulk of debt were in the form of fixed-interest bonds, the Italian government might renege on it, in real terms, through engineering a burst of inflation.

and in particular its potential power to renege on its debt obligations – an option more likely to be favoured by Communists – by forcing the Banca d'Italia to 'print money'.[8]

Nonetheless, after the 'divorce' the government retained the right to determine the Banca d'Italia's official rates, and thereby the possibility of influencing market rates. And of course, it retained the right to decide on realignments of the lira. By the late 1980s, however, the Banca d'Italia found that it could push against the open door of 'Europe' in the pursuit of its ambitions for greater economic policy power – even if that power would have to be shared with other central bankers in a European Central Bank. Tommaso Padoa-Schioppa, the Banca d'Italia's Deputy Director-General and favourite intellectual son of the Governor, Carlo Ciampi, was one of the 'rapporteurs' of the Delors Committee. Padoa-Schioppa, a charming, fearsomely intelligent and even more fearsomely hard-working man, is widely regarded as having deployed his formidable talents to become the driving force behind the Delors three-stage plan to railroad Europe into monetary union. He was also a key proponent of a 'European' strategy for Italy – a strategy based on pessimism about Italy's ability to solve its budgetary problems, to govern itself, or, ultimately, to resist the North–South regional tensions that threatened its viability as a unified nation-state. The hope of those who believed in the 'European' strategy was that the tough budget rules of the projected EMU would provide discipline on Italian governments that could not be generated within the country's internal political processes, and that inside EMU, Italian governments would be servant, not master, of a powerful central bank whose independence was guaranteed by international treaty.

The strategy was possibly over-pessimistic about Italy's ability to regenerate its political system; and it was certainly over-optimistic in failing to realize that while monetary union was, as relentlessly hammered home by Bundesbank spokesmen, impossible without political union, a 'united' Europe would exhibit an aggravated version of the problems that beset disunited Italy. Yet Padoa-Schioppa and others in the Banca d'Italia were able to see another major problem in the strategy. This concerned the transition to EMU, the 'race against time' built into the Maastricht

8 This episode brings to mind the ludicrous and illogical rumours current in Britain in 1985 and 1986 that Mrs Thatcher would join the ERM because a Labour victory in the next election was likely and the ERM constraint would prevent a Labour government from reversing the sound financial and monetary policies of the Thatcher administration. Mrs Thatcher clearly had no time for such specious arguments.

compromise. The Banca d'Italia had always taken the view that monetary union would produce convergence. It was thus diametrically opposed to the Bundesbank, which insisted that convergence must *precede* monetary union – indeed Padoa-Schioppa was something of a bogey-man within the Bundesbank because of his role in the Delors Committee. In the end, the Maastricht compromise was apparently brokered by Andreotti. He may, like the French, have misread the problem of possible German political dominance, post-unification, in Europe, and felt as anxious as the French to prevent the creation of the DM-zone presaged by the Belgian decision of 1990. (It is also far from inconceivable that Andreotti and his Foreign Minister, Gianni De Michelis, both of whom were subsequently charged with corruption, sensed the coming political upheaval in Italy and hoped that acquiring a position as fathers of a United Europe would give them a degree of personal and political protection.)

The Banca d'Italia, like the Bundesbank, was worried by the Maastricht compromise, but for very different reasons. It had hoped for an unconditional date for entry into monetary union. Padoa-Schioppa himself was the author of the phrase 'the inconsistent quartet', which posited that fixed exchange rates, free trade, free capital movements and national monetary policy autonomy could not hold simultaneously.[9] Thus the bank was strongly in favour of an early move *away* from national monetary autonomy – or, in other words, from the autonomy of the Bundesbank – towards a more coordinated and symmetrical management of monetary policy. It would have preferred early, unconditional monetary union, but as a second best would have accepted a more collective management of the ERM. It got neither. What it got instead, however, were the inflation, budgetary and ERM-stability convergence criteria of the Maastricht Treaty, together with further provisions of that treaty that required all would-be members of EMU to grant independence to their central banks in Stage Two and to forbid any form of central-bank financing of the government deficit. Taken together, these provisions appeared to give powerful reinforcement to central banks, including the Banca d'Italia, versus national governments. On the face of it, central banks would have much greater moral and practical clout in their attempts to force governments to reduce deficits, while monetary policy bore down on inflation. In other words, central banks, in all those countries that aimed at EMU membership, looked set

9 See chapter 4 above for an analysis of why the 'inconsistent quartet' did not bring a collapse of the ERM in the 1987–91 period.

fair to become 'Stackelberg leaders' in the policy game with governments, making government budgetary decisions conform to the dictates of the central banks.[10]

But the Banca d'Italia had to face the reality that, for inflation to fall as demanded by the Maastricht Treaty, there would have to be a recession in Italy. That would make it harder to reduce the deficit. And, if monetary policy tightening was going to achieve the inflation reduction, there would have to be a longish period in which short-term real interest rates rose significantly. That would impose further interest burdens on the budget, especially as most of the Italian debt was linked to short-term Treasury bills. Thus, if one started from the monetary side, attempting to fulfil the inflation criterion for EMU was going to make it more difficult to meet the budgetary criteria on deficits and debt.

The Banca d'Italia had always been aware of this dilemma, even before it was written into the Maastricht Treaty. It attempted for several years to steer a perilous course in managing interest rates – high enough to maintain the lira's ERM parity and, if possible, to nudge inflation down whenever favourable external factors permitted, but not so high as to jerk growth downwards and real interest rates upwards. During the 'Europhoria' years of 1988–90, this did not present too difficult a task. Even when German interest rates started edging up after unification, the 'convergence plays' described in chapter 5 kept Italian interest-rate differentials with Germany moving downwards. But this period brought another problem: one of sharply deteriorating Italian competitiveness. The fixity of the lira ever since January 1987,[11] combined with Italy's above-average inflation rate, meant that Italian firms were being increasingly squeezed out of export markets and were finding it harder and harder to hold the line against import penetration at home. At first, the impact on Italian growth was hidden by the strong growth of markets in the industrial world in 1988–90, but as the world economy, and in particular the European economies,

10 A striking example of the growing arrogance of central bankers was provided in the early summer of 1994 by Alfons Verplaetse, Governor of the Belgian National Bank. He appeared to order the government to announce early general elections 'to avoid uncertainty that would affect the currency'. He was rather sharply put in his place by the Prime Minister, Dehaene. But the trend towards greater interference by central bankers in explicitly political affairs, set in train by Maastricht, will be hard to arrest as long as the fools' paradise of EMU beckons, as recent events involving Trichet's role as Governor of the Banque de France show rather clearly.

11 With the minor technical adjustment involved in the move to narrow bands for the lira in January 1990.

slowed down into 1991, Italian industry began to squirm in the vice-like grip of the ERM.

## Taking Dutch courage

This was entirely predictable but its timing was particularly unhappy. For by mid-1991 it was becoming clear that drastic and painful measures would have to be imposed in the budget if Italy's EMU candidacy were to be taken seriously by its partners. The years of relatively strong growth had seen a slackening of adjustment efforts. Rising tax revenues and falling unemployment outlays reduced the deficit as long as the growth persisted, but the underlying deficit was actually getting worse. The return to only sluggish economic growth in 1991 meant that the budget shortfall started to balloon alarmingly.

By that time the Dutch, who were going to have to fashion a compromise at Maastricht, knew that the deteriorating Italian budgetary situation could produce a German veto on monetary union plans. They began exerting pressure for a 'crash programme' of budgetary austerity in Italy. The Italian government, it is said, were intensely angered by this démarche.[12] They read it as an attempt to block Italian entry into EMU, the promised land in which their budget deficit would magically disappear without any effort on their part, perhaps taken over by 'Europe'. After some tense moments, however, the row simmered down. The singling-out of Italy as a divergent country was transmuted into the idea of 'convergence programmes' for all countries whose current performance did not match the EMU entry criteria then being exhaustively – and exhaustingly – discussed. But the row brought home to the Italian government, if not at that time to the Italian people, that the prospect of EMU would not spare them painful budgetary austerity.

Now, economic theory – which is surprisingly commonsensical – predicts that if taxes have to rise, or welfare payments be cut, so that Italians

---

12 The flavour of Banca d'Italia distrust of the Dutch, and in particular of Cees Maas, who in 1991 was both Chairman of the Monetary Committee and, in the crucial second half of the year, President of the IGC on monetary union, can be tasted in an article on the negotiations leading up to Maastricht subsequently written by Padoa-Schioppa himself, Lorenzo Bini-Smaghi (the bank's Alternate [deputy] member of the Monetary Committee and a key negotiator) and Francesco Papadia, another senior official.

in the street have less in their pockets and therefore spend less,[13] or if the Italian government itself is forced to spend less on goods and services, then output and employment will fall. To prevent this, Italians must devote a greater proportion of their reduced total spending to buying Italian goods and services rather than foreign ones, and foreigners must be induced to buy more Italian goods and services. These switches in spending patterns will not take place, however, unless Italian goods and services become cheaper relative to foreign goods and services. In other words, competitiveness would have to improve. Since by mid-1991 the starting-point was one in which Italian competitiveness was already poor, the scale of the problem was huge.

Thus, by mid-1991, one could predict with almost absolute certainty that a large devaluation of the lira had to happen. So how could the Euroguardians of the Monetary Committee, the Committee of Governors and the top levels of the Commission remain so blind to the obvious? As we have seen before, convergence in the Community institutions was further advanced in a refusal to accept reality than in any aspect of the economic performance of the members' economies. There was nothing surprising in this particular manifestation of Euroblindness. Of course, the politicians and mandarins would in any case argue that they were not blind: anyone who saw problems ahead was instead experiencing hallucinations, nightmares, phantasmagorias induced by witchcraft or the malevolent incantations of the Anglo-Saxons. Once more, ERMonomics could be brought into play to confound the sceptics; once more, Ireland and Denmark – the countries whose experience was so traduced by Trichet in his defence of 'désinflation compétitive' – were hauled into court as star witnesses for the economics equivalent of the Flat Earth Society. The experience of these two countries, it was argued,[14] showed that a return to fiscal virtue would, far from depressing the economy, actually boost it, even in the short term.

---

13  To the extent that Italian citizens can foresee what is going to happen, they may start to cut their spending before the budgetary retrenchment actually takes place, but the need for improved competitiveness remains.

14  Most notably by two Italian economists. Franco Giavazzi and Marco Pagano, who in a much-remarked-on paper on Ireland and Denmark coined the phrase 'expansionary fiscal contraction'. By mid-1991, Giavazzi was installed as a Director responsible for macroeconomic analysis in the Italian Treasury.

## Potatoes two, turnips nil

Denmark in 1983–86 and Ireland in 1987–90 had, it was said by the defenders of the ERM, experienced strong growth immediately after undertaking major programmes of budgetary retrenchment. Once again, this reading of economic history, if not as blatantly distorted as Trichet's on the later occasion, was highly selective and very misleading. It is worth pausing in our narrative to review the experience of Denmark and Ireland more objectively. The lessons that *could* have been drawn from the experience, not least by Nigel Lawson in his obsessive battle to force Mrs Thatcher into the ERM, would have avoided economic hardship and political misery throughout Europe. The fact that Denmark and Ireland could instead be regarded as shining example of the benefits of ERM virtue says much about the perversion of economic analysis practised by the Eurofanatics.

In the autumn of 1982, Denmark had devalued within the ERM, restoring a strong competitive position. Shortly thereafter, the government fell. The Social Democrats, who had been in power for much of the preceding half-century and had presided over a quarter-century of current account deficits, were ejected. Growing public concern about Denmark's external indebtedness and steadily rising public debt ratio played a significant part in the travails of the Social Democrats. A new, conservative-led government pledged an entirely different strategy: a hard currency, the abolition of wage indexation, cutbacks in government expenditure and the over-generous welfare system, and a generally more 'business-friendly' approach.

The impact of this change on international confidence in the krone was immediate. (There had been just as immediate an effect on sterling when Thatcher was elected, and on the DM when Kohl replaced Schmidt; the markets in the early 1980s liked conservative governments.) Large amounts of capital flowed into Denmark, but because of the tight ERM margins the krone could not rise much in response. Instead, the money supply skyrocketed, and long-term interest rates, which had been exceptionally high, fell precipitously. The combination of a prior improvement in competitiveness, the fall in interest rates and the tonic given to consumer and, especially, business confidence by the change of government produced a remarkably strong growth surge in Denmark. The measures of budgetary restriction introduced early in 1983 were in fact relatively modest, and their potentially damping effect on output and employment was swamped by everything else that was going on. The Danish economy boomed, and it was this, more than underlying budgetary contraction, that turned the public-sector accounts round so rapidly that by 1986 the government actually had a surplus. In fact, the boom was so strong, with investment roaring ahead, that unemployment was halved and inflationary pressures began to mount, while the current-account deficit carried on widening despite the improvement in the budgetary position. Labour costs accelerated sharply, their rate of increase reaching 12% by 1986.

By late 1986, international investors began to lose confidence in the Danish economy; the krone weakened and interest rates edged up. Faced with this apparent evidence of the failure of the 1982–83 change in strategy to effect an underlying improvement in the Danish economy, households and firms also became sunk in gloom. By early 1987, then, everything was in place for a cyclical downturn in Denmark. But the government, concerned by the negative change in market sentiment towards the krone, decided that a further dose of budgetary restraint was called for – just see what miracles it had worked in 1983! This time, the budget measures had bite as well as bark, and they ripped a substantial chunk out of the Danish economy, held obligingly in bonds by the ERM constraint and weakened by the generalized loss of nerve. Inevitably, the economic cycle of 1983–86 went very precisely into reverse. With the exchange rate held fixed, investment and output fell. The current account improved. Inflation declined to below the rate in trading partners' economies, and unit labour costs actually fell – no miracle, this, but the result of a fierce labour-market squeeze.

The Danish recession continued unabated for six years – despite the pickup in world trade from late 1987 and the particular boost that German unification gave to Danish export markets. Unemployment, having fallen to 6% by 1986, doubled, reaching 12% by the end of 1992. By mid-1992 the country's unemployment-induced low rate of inflation was clawing back earlier competitiveness losses and the most painful effects of earlier budgetary austerity had been absorbed. Ten years of a boom-bust cycle had been enforced by the ERM, which prevented monetary conditions from adjusting to smooth the path of an economy hit by a succession of shocks to confidence and demand. But by mid-1992 it looked as though the economy was finally getting back on an even keel – only to be battered again by exchange-market upheaval. The depreciations of sterling and the Nordic currencies in late 1992 were thus

particularly unwelcome to Denmark. The improvement in Danish competitiveness had been illusory. A major part of it reflected the fact that
important trading partners – Britain and the Nordic countries – had
themselves suffered major losses of competitiveness through their own
unhappy experience with exchange-rate pegs. They were fortunate that,
rather than having to endure six years of recession like Denmark, the
markets blew them off those pegs, restoring their lost competitiveness at a
stroke but, in the process, thrusting Denmark's growth prospects back
below the waves and triggering the market selling of the krone described
in the previous chapter.

Long, long before 1993, the reasons for and lessons of the Danish
boom-bust should have been understood and absorbed by European
economic policy-makers. They were not.[15]

Irish experience should also have been read as clearly unfavourable
to ERMonomics. Ireland, after entering the ERM for political reasons
in 1979 (and getting a transfer sweetener whose cost fell disproportionately on Britain via its EC budget contribution), enjoyed an easy ride
for the first two and a half years of the system's existence. Sterling,
outside the system, rose to dizzying new heights. Ireland basked in the
warm glow of Continental political approval, while sterling's strength
shielded competitiveness from the ravages of high Irish inflation. But
the Fianna Fail government had been indulging itself and its supporters
in budgetary fecklessness on a grand scale.[16] By 1981, the budget
deficit had reached a massive and totally unsustainable 17% of GDP,
and the debt ratio was racing upwards. As in Denmark a year later,
there was a change of government and of budgetary tack, but instead of
a shift to a more market-oriented, business-friendly approach, taxes
were jacked up sharply, worsening supply-side incentives. The scale of

15 Not just politicians but also economists who enjoyed the favour of the Euro-élite were
blind. Significantly, an economic adviser to the Danish central bank when Christophersen
was Danish Finance Minister was Nils Thygesen. Thygesen and Gros's weighty book on
the ERM and EMU, despite its format as a history of the ERM, made no reference to
Denmark's economic instability in the years since it chose the 'hard-currency option'
within the ERM in 1982.
16 One of the most blatant examples was the decision, by Prime Minister Jack Lynch, to
abolish the extremely unpopular local property taxes, the equivalent of UK rates, in 1979.
Unlike Mrs Thatcher, who also abolished such taxes in 1990, Mr Lynch did not trouble
to replace them with anything else, nor did he make any attempt at offsetting reductions,
or even restraint, in spending.

the tax increases took households by surprise and forced them to cut back their spending. Worse still, a similarly tough budget had just been introduced by Geoffrey Howe in Britain. British interest rates, determined in Britain not Frankfurt, trended downwards (though not without temporary jerks up if domestic conditions demanded it), and sterling slid fast.

Poor Ireland, however, was trapped in the ERM. Not only could it not, from a starting-point of high inflation, improve overall competitiveness within the ERM without devaluation, it also had to watch sterling's adjustment devastate Irish bilateral competitiveness with Britain. The Irish pound rapidly became a weak currency within the ERM. It realigned downwards on a number of occasions between 1981 and 1986, but never by enough to offset economic weakness, and thus never by enough to remove market expectations of the next realignment and a consequent penalty in Irish interest rates. Throughout the period 1981–86, the Irish government was running to stand still. It made repeated efforts to trim its deficit, but the unfavourable budgetary impact of economic stagnation frustrated these efforts. Irish interest rates stayed high, yet Irish inflation fell as everywhere else, particularly in 1985–86 as oil prices collapsed. Thus the real burden of steadily growing government debt increased. A vicious circle ensued, and by late 1986 the public debt ratio, at 140% of GDP, was the highest in the developed world. International investors were becoming wary of buying Irish government debt, fearing the possibility of default. The government resorted to exceptionally heavy borrowing in foreign currencies, seeking to avoid the high rates of interest on Irish pound borrowing. Yet the private sector and the banks were moving capital out of Ireland so fast, despite exchange controls, that the Irish money supply actually fell during 1986, and interest rates reached record heights.

Despondency was palpable in Ireland, where there seemed to be two roads ahead, both involving vicious punishment for someone or other. Along one road lay a government default on its debt – either by an outright refusal to pay or, more likely, by a massive devaluation and a surge in inflation that would wipe out much of the real value of the debt. This road would plunder the savings of all those Irish people – mainly of course, the wealthier ones – who had invested in government bonds or national savings. Down the other road – and not very far down it if it was to be taken at all – lurked savage tax increases, or spending cuts, or both. Faced with these depressing alternatives, Irish households lost all appetite for spending, thus compounding the stagnation of the country's economy. Politicians looked on despairingly, and political commentators wrote, only half-jokingly, that the parties would be competing to *lose* the next election, so awful would be the responsibilities of the victors.

But the luck of the Irish had not deserted them. Indeed, it was to occupy centre-stage so dramatically that only the wilfully blind could dismiss its role. On the economic side, as we have already seen, an Irish pound devaluation in the ERM came, in August 1986, only a few months before sterling began a steep ascent reflecting radically improved British economic confidence and performance. At the same time Lawson continued steering interest rates downwards. This combination was ideal for Ireland: improved competitiveness; booming export markets; reduced pressure on the Irish pound and falling UK interest rates together induced a spectacular fall in Irish interest rates.

On the political side, there was a complete fluke. At the end of 1986, the Fine Gael government was defeated in the Dail on details of its austerity budget. The ensuing elections threw up a Fianna Fail government that needed the support of an independent MP (one who had in the past been suspected of gun-running for the IRA). Commentators initially bemoaned the result as the worst possible from the point of view of budgetary adjustment: 'independent' MPs were notoriously rapacious in their demands for budgetary favours for their constituents in return for backing the government. In fact, the new parliamentary configuration produced an overwhelming consensus for austerity. Fianna Fail were now 'in', had to face the financial music, and had no choice but to bring forward a budget that in its broad lines replicated the one that had brought Fine Gael's downfall. Fine Gael, being the slightly more reputable party in Ireland, could not reverse its stance of a couple of months earlier, and felt honour-bound to support a strategy of austerity. This consensus was vitally important, for it gave financial markets confidence that budgetary adjustment was politically feasible and would not go off at half-cock: the adjustment effort had 'credibility'. This credibility, together with the favourable economic circumstances, was an additional factor both in the fall in Irish interest rates and in the turnaround in international and domestic confidence.

## We are the masters now

Anyone who looked seriously at the examples of Denmark and Ireland could have seen that Italy in mid-1991 had no hope whatsoever of avoiding a deep recession in the wake of tough fiscal adjustment – unless there was a very substantial depreciation of the lira. Competitiveness was already poor, the US was in mild recession, and European growth was clearly slowing as the German unification boom subsided. Domestically, there was no great reawakening of confidence in the economy, no belief that a new government with new ideas and methods could create an economic renascence, no expectation of either strong leadership or a stable parliamentary consensus to give credibility to adjustment. Quite the reverse seemed to be true. The disintegration of the old political system had already begun, but with it seemed likely to come disintegration of Italy itself; in the North, the 'leagues' were at that stage openly and explicitly divisive, advocating taxpayers' strikes and secession from the Republic. In this morose political climate, no one had any belief in the supposedly confidence-restoring powers of austerity. It was thus hardly surprising that vague notions of 'Europe' had appeal in Italy: the country was incapable of solving its own problems as a country. Both the phenomenon of the Northern leagues and the widespread, if fundamentally misconceived, desire to be ruled from Brussels rather than from Rome reflected this pervasive pessimism[17] – the brief optimism of Forza Italia lay in an unrecognizable and unforeseen future.

How, then, could it be that the country's debt and deficit problems, much debated and analysed in the Italian media, did not cast the pre-adjustment pall over economic activity that it had done in Ireland in 1986–87? By far the most plausible answer is that Italians believed that the European Community would bail them out in one form or another. Even the international markets shared in this belief to some extent, as Europhoria in 1988–91 led to a growing convergence of interest rates. Official economists in Italy happily did calculations that purported to show that much of the deficit and debt problem would disappear once Italy's interest-

---

17 Fabrizio Saccomani, one of the most senior officials in the Banca d'Italia, an influential player in European monetary relations and an associate of Padoa-Schioppa, went public on this in an interview, praising the ERM as, in effect, a device for constraining a poorly functioning mode of government: '. . . we took the EMS as the foundation stone of our [i.e., Banca d'Italia] policy. The central element responsible for the changes was the desire of the political system and of public opinion for European integration. This is a reflection of the lack of confidence on the part of public opinion in the quality of our own political leaders. The Banca d'Italia exploited this.' Ironically, this interview, redolent of the assurance of 'monetary leadership', was given on 16 July 1992, the day on which the Bundesbank's decision to raise its discount rate pulled the rug out from under the ERM and with it the Banca d'Italia.

rate differential disappeared completely in monetary union.[18] And it had not occurred to the Italian in the street that the love affair with 'Europe' might be unrequited, that once the Maastricht compromise – so gloated over by Andreotti – was in the bag, Germany would simply ensure, by fair means or foul, that Italy was kept out of EMU. In 1991, the idea of a 'two-speed' Europe was not mentioned in polite diplomatic circles. But as soon as the Bundesbank began its post-Maastricht campaign to ensure that any monetary union would be on its terms – and in particular that the Bundesbank would have the loudest voice in deciding its membership – the enormity of Italian governmental misjudgement became apparent. As we have seen in chapter 5, the unstable dynamics of the 'Maastricht Handicap Hurdle' rapidly turned very unfavourable for Italy. The harsh reality of the huge austerity package introduced by the new Amato government in June 1992, shortly after the referendum on abandoning most aspects of proportional representation, knocked the stuffing out of the Italian consumer. The country was staring into the abyss of a recession so deep that the Italian state, and not just its electoral system, was in danger of being swept away.

Italy's ejection from the ERM in September 1992 was politically salutary as well as giving the chance of economic salvation. It exposed the Euro-aspirations of the élite as mere delusion; and the collapse of the 'European strategy' hastened the demise of those corruption-ridden and scandal-racked parties, the Christian Democrats and the Socialists. It opened the door for Forza Italia subsequently to generate an optimism, however self-serving in origin and short-lived in effect, about *Italy*. Economically, it ensured that the recession in Italy would be relatively mild and short-lived. It could not of itself ensure that the budgetary problems would be solved. The new political system that was soon to emerge would have to prove its ability to generate a viable consensus for budgetary adjustment. In 1995, the jury is still out on this, and the possibility of failure has led to a massive fall in the lira. But without ERM expulsion, and without a very substantial depreciation of the currency, there could have been no possibility whatever of successful adjustment. Financial crisis, default on debt, the strengthening of Northern secessionism, the collapse of Italy into chaos and possibly violence – all would have been brought frighteningly nearer, facing Italy's

---

18 In fact, the differential would not have disappeared completely even if the lira had disappeared: investors would still have required a significant risk premium to induce them to hold Italian government debt in ECU rather than German public debt in ECU once national currencies disappeared.

European 'partners' with an appalling choice. Would they simply stand and watch a financial and political collapse; or would they find some means – probably in direct contradiction of the Maastricht Treaty – of taking over the burden of Italian debt and, in counterpart, exerting direct, almost colonial, influence on Italian economic and budgetary decisions?[19] Either choice would have incalculable consequences for political legitimacy and for economic and financial stability throughout Europe. The Bundesbank could be pleased that its handiwork in August and early September 1992 had brought at least a chance that such nightmare scenarios could be averted. Italians should have been even more pleased.

Unhappily, not everyone in the Banca d'Italia was pleased. The potential, at least, for a more democratically credible political system was emerging. So too was the inescapable need for a change in monetary conditions to soften the impact of budgetary contraction. In this new political and economic landscape, the Banca d'Italia's implicit claim to exert monetary leadership looked more and more questionable. It was no surprise, then, that in the bank's imposing Palazzo-style headquarters on the Via Nazionale, fronted by a typically Mediterranean melange of palm-trees and machine-gun-toting paramilitary police, anti-Bundesbank feeling, never far from the surface, was intense.

## Pyrrhic victory?

Yet by March 1993 Tietmeyer was brooding uneasily – not for the first time and not for the last – on the consequences of his institution's success in creating upheaval in the ERM. Taken together, the dramatic changes in the economic policy situation in Britain and Italy risked being far to much of a good thing from his point of view. Explicit inflation-targeting in Britain; a questioning of 'monetary leadership' in Italy; a collapse of the exchange rate in both countries in reaction to recession or its prospect and to the need for fiscal tightening: all these posed a potential challenge to the Bundesbank's favoured model of the role, privileges and prerogatives of a central bank – and perhaps to its conception of the future ECB.

Within Germany, the Bundesbank was itself coming under fire from two directions at once. The interest-rate decisions of 4 February were resented

19 The so-called 'no bail-out' provision of the treaty was never believable – at least it seems that Jacques Delors never believed it. In February 1995, after quitting his Commission job, he told a committee of the European Parliament that, 'EMU means, for instance, that the Union acknowledges the debts of all those countries that are in EMU.'

by the partisans – and there were many in Germany, even outside the Bundesbank – of central-bank independence as long as it meant *German* independence. More insistent criticism in the opposite direction was coming from the unions, the *Länder* governments and even some of the regional central bank chairmen on the Bundesbank Council. Their fear was that the Bundesbank was engaged in overkill, keeping monetary conditions too tight in its attempts to enforce its will on the government's budget planners and on wage bargainers.

By the time Tietmeyer made his speech, however, the Bundesbank's hard line seemed to be paying off: wage settlements were starting to come in much lower than in the previous two years, and a 'Solidarity Pact' between the Federal government and the *Länder* governments on financing transfers to Eastern Germany and reducing the budget deficit looked almost in the bag. Yet the price exacted was a high one. Eastern Germany's economy was showing the first tentative and hesitant signs of recovery after the cataclysmic post-unification slump, but in the West, manufacturing production was falling at an annual rate of almost 10%, and investment was sharply down. Worse, fears were being voiced about German industry's high costs, short working hours, stagnant productivity and outdated working practices. Nerves were frayed when Mercedes decided to build cars for export to the North American market in Mexico not in Baden-Württemberg, and when BMW preferred production in the USA to relying on Bavarian workers to seduce NAFTA car buyers. In an attempt to catch up with productivity levels in Japan, the US, France, even Britain in some sectors, German industry was cutting back savagely on the workforce.

Was the DM overvalued? Did it need to fall sharply to prevent recession in Germany from turning into slump? George Soros thought so, and was soon to say so very publicly indeed. Tietmeyer, of course, disagreed in public, employing his usual heavy, almost threatening sarcasm to belittle peddlers of DM weakness, but there is every reason to believe that his public discourse hid private worries.

Schlesinger liked nothing better than a rising DM: the economy must adjust to DM strength; the DM must not respond to cyclical economic weakness; a strong DM was evidence that Germany and the Bundesbank found favour with the gods. Tietmeyer, closer to the concerns of government and of party politics, was less sure that the German economy, in the changed structural situation after unification, could stand excessive DM appreciation. The social and political climate remained tense; Kohl was unpopular; there were ugly manifestations of violent nationalism among the unemployed young, particularly in the Eastern *Länder*. Too strong a DM – even against sterling, the lira and the peseta – could deepen the recession and intensify social and political discontent. If that happened, the markets might turn on the DM with a vengeance. Schlesinger still had another seven months in office, and Tietmeyer may well have reasoned that if the DM were to show signs of weakening dramatically while he was still there, the Bavarian hardliner might do what he had always done in such circumstances – use the force of his prestige and popularity in Germany to compel the Council to slam on the monetary brakes. That would throw the ERM into chaos, topple the economy into slump, and put Kohl – and therefore the Bundesbank's independence – in the gravest danger. In fact, Schlesinger was soon to prove himself a master political tactician – though not in a way Tietmeyer would approve of. But from the perspective of early March, there is no doubt that Tietmeyer's animadversions on British and Italian exchange-rate policy were prompted by the gravest misgivings about the way they might impinge on the Bundesbank's own position. Five months later, Tietmeyer's fears were to gain substance, and he would then take the gloves off completely in his relations with other ERM members. We shall return to that story.

## The mirror crack'd from side to side

Tietmeyer's speech did not omit some words of warning for Spain and Portugal: measures of internal adjustment must not be put off, he said, or new cost and price divergences could accumulate. The Bundesbank Vice-President did not, however, see fit to reproach either of the two Iberian countries for their devaluations, even though the peseta had lost much more value than sterling since the ERM crisis began and about as much as the lira. The difference, of course, was that the Iberian devaluations had come within the ERM framework and resulted, at least in theory, from a collective decision of the Monetary Committee of which Tietmeyer himself was the most influential member. If anything the Bundesbank vice-President seemed to be forecasting further depreciation for the two currencies, even though both had been near the top of their ERM bands for most of the time since the November 1992 realignment. Problems were indeed beginning to surface again in both countries. In Portugal, their first, dramatic manifestation came in a form that – depending on whether or not one believes Tietmeyer wanted Portugal in or out of an eventual monetary union – was either deeply disturbing or cause for tactical satisfaction to him.

In Portugal, as elsewhere, recession was hitting hard, yet interest rates remained particularly high. The November devaluation had convinced markets that the level of competitiveness was the major policy indicator for the government. In fact, the Bank of Portugal had for three months managed monetary policy after the devaluation in such a way that the market value of the currency was little changed by the realignment. By mid-February, however, pressure from the government began to mount.

The Prime Minister and Finance Ministry spokesmen claimed that short-term interest rates in Portugal would decline by three percentage points in the course of the year. The Bank of Portugal, however, showed no inclination to transform these wishes into action. Its attitude was strongly influenced by the real driving-force in the bank, one of the most determined anti-inflation hawks in any central bank anywhere. This 'ayatollah of low inflation', as he was disparagingly labelled by a senior monetary official in the EC Commission (whose opinion was shared by the Governor of the Banque de France), was the young Vice-Governor, Antonio Borges. Trained in the United States, he had been professor of economics at the Institut Européen d'Administration des Affaires (Insead), the international business school at Fontainebleau, outside Paris.[20] He is a perceptive and rigorous economist. Stocky, red-haired and bespectacled, he exudes an aura of physical and intellectual vigour and has a penchant for saying exactly what he thinks. He was one of the first European monetary officials at the highest level to grasp the import of German unification for the ERM.

Arguing strongly that Germany's low-inflation record was the cornerstone of the system, one whose preservation was worth a high price to *all* ERM members, Borges praised the Bundesbank's determination to keep monetary policy tight. But the inevitable result of the initial post-unification demand boom in Germany was a real appreciation of the DM. The insistence of other countries that the DM should not revalue in nominal terms meant that the German real appreciation could come about only through *relatively* high German inflation. But with the Bundesbank committed to preventing, or at least reversing, any *absolute* increase in German inflation, the implication had to be that inflation should fall in other ERM countries. The mechanism for producing such a fall would be

20 Insead is regarded with the greatest suspicion by the French authorities despite – or perhaps because of – its success and international reputation, since it uses English as a working language as well as French and its economic and business philosophy is uncomfortably 'Anglo-Saxon'.

the need to maintain higher interest rates than would be required in the absence of the ERM, thus producing a recession. High-inflation countries should positively welcome this sequence of causes and results; but even countries with inflation starting-points as low as they desired should accept it, for the sake of the *real* 'common good' of the system – low inflation in the anchor country, Germany.

Needless to say, this analysis meant that Borges was praised to the skies by Tietmeyer, even though this gentleman had, when Kohl's personal adviser on unification in 1990, pooh-poohed the idea that there might be any risk of inflationary pressures in Germany. Equally unsurprising, Trichet's brow would furrow in perplexity when forced by circumstance to listen to the ineluctable logic of Borges's analysis. Whether, as subsequently implied by a very distinguished official economist from another country, he simply did not understand economics or was feigning puzzlement because Borges was turning the doctrine of '*désinflation compétitive*' on its head must be a matter of opinion.

More dangerous for Borges, his strongly voiced opinion that Portugal should welcome the full rigour of ERM discipline made him distinctly unpopular with the Portuguese government. That government, and in particular its Finance Minister, Braga de Macedo, had certainly not presented the ERM as a vale of tears when they took the escudo into the system less than a year before. Nor did the government enjoy the fact that it seemed, thanks to the Bank of Portugal, to have got the worst of both worlds from the November devaluation: it was tainted in the eyes of the market as competitiveness-conscious and devaluation-prone, yet the escudo had not actually declined in value, so with competitiveness unimproved, the markets suspected a second devaluation and had to be paid a substantial interest-rate premium not to provoke one. Braga's personal standing within the government and in the country had plummeted. Press articles, said by the unkind to have been inspired by the Prime Minister, depicted him as incompetent, disorganized and peripheral to economic policy-making. Braga needed a whipping-boy, and the Bank of Portugal's Vice-Governor was a tempting target for what amounted to a public humiliation of Borges.

In early March, in a formal speech in the Bank of Portugal, with Borges seated in the front row of the audience, Braga made a fierce attack on the bank's cautious attitude to interest-rate reductions, accusing it of not according enough importance to growth in the economy. Even worse, the Finance Minister reproached the Bank of Portugal for having failed to put across the intellectual arguments for the commercial banks to reduce the rates at which they lent to firms.[21] The press took this as a personal attack on the top men in the bank, and in particular on Borges, who was responsible for the Research Department. There was immediate speculation that both Borges and the Governor, Miguel Beleza, would resign. Borges had already been less than happy with the turn of events since the beginning of February, when, under pressure from the government, the Bank of Portugal had begun reducing interest rates and the escudo drifted down from the top of its ERM band. Braga's speech, rubbing salt in the wounds, proved too much for Borges, who, after several days of anguished reflection, submitted his resignation. (Beleza, a friend of Braga since childhood and his predecessor as Finance Minister, stayed on.)

There is little doubt where the personal sympathies of most of those who knew Braga and Borges lay, but personal sympathies often cloud political and economic judgement. On the substance of his argument with Borges, Braga was probably right: Borges's inexorable economic logic was simply not politically sustainable in a society whose economic renascence and political structure were still fragile after the stagnation of the long Salazar years, the savagery of recent colonial wars, the collapse of empire and the chaos of Marxist revolution. Borges was as conscious as anyone of the frailties of his own country, but he saw the greatest danger in a return to economic indiscipline and inflation. He had been opposed to, and had managed to delay, Braga's decision to take the escudo into the ERM. Spanish experience had convinced him that for a country experiencing a surge of favourable 'animal spirits' and attracting massive capital inflows, the ERM constraint detracted from monetary discipline. And he would clearly have preferred a higher entry rate for the escudo.

But once the economic cycle in Portugal began to turn down, the ERM became a fiercely contractionary and deflationary force, which Borges was determined to use to grind Portuguese inflation downwards. The problem was, as Tietmeyer had spotted and had pointed out on a number of occasions, that when a high-inflation country joins the ERM, it inevitably loses competitiveness. By the time its inflation rate has been forced down, inescapably via recession, to the rate in the 'core', substantial cumulative

21 Braga was right to attack the cosy and privileged position of the commercial banks, and indeed showed political courage in doing so: when he was finally sacked at the end of the year it was largely on the say-so of the Portuguese banks. But he was not justified in using *this* issue as a peg on which to hang an attack on the central bank.

divergences in costs and prices, as the Bundesbank calls them, have built up. In the absence of a devaluation, this loss of competitiveness prolongs and deepens the recession until inflation has actually fallen *below* that in the core by enough and for long enough to restore competitiveness. In any economy, such a policy strategy is unambiguously harmful. In Portugal, it could have destroyed the infant consensus in favour of democratic political institutions and a market economy.

Braga took the escudo into the ERM at a time when politicians, officials, central bankers – at least outside Germany – and tame economists were proclaiming it a fixed-rate system. Perhaps in the atmosphere of Euro-phoria that then still prevailed he had not grasped or had disregarded the economic dynamics of the system. He would not, of course, admit that ERM entry had been a mistake. But actions speak louder than words, and Braga's actions in the spring of 1993 make it clear that he disowned the quasi-fixed-rate system to which he had previously subscribed. The risks of continuing to pay more than lip-service to ERMonomics were too horrendous.

There is a general point here of some importance. Many central bankers are intelligent, cultured, courteous and affable: your typical central banker is quite a high class of person, much nicer, one imagines, than your average politician. But politicians have at some point to confront the consequences of their mistakes; their unaccountable central bankers do not. And politicians have to engage in trade-offs between the scores of issues, interests, disputes and conflicts that they have to deal with – or choose to create; independent central bankers are single-issue fanatics, and are beholden to one group in society – bond-holders – above all others. However admirable they may be as people, Continental central bankers in their professional role are increasingly seeking what Baldwin, speaking of the 1930s press barons, famously attacked as 'power without responsibility: the prerogative of the harlot throughout the ages'.

In the specific circumstances of Portugal in the spring of 1993, however, the markets seemed to be signalling that Borges was right. The 'credibility' of Portuguese monetary policy certainly appeared to be damaged by both the slide of the escudo in the ERM band and the resignation of the Vice-Governor. The immediate consequence of Braga's picking a quarrel was that Portuguese short-term interest rates actually had to be *increased* to prevent the escudo falling into the lower half of the band and thus engendering expectations of an early devaluation. However, no incredible policy can ever be credible (a tautology, but one that the proponents of the

ERM as credibility-enhancing were very reluctant to recognize). Interest rates rose in Portugal after Borges's resignation not because the step-by-step abandonment of the ERM route to disinflation was a mistake but because the market anticipated the next downward step in the exchange rate. But if the direction of exchange-rate policy in Portugal was clear,[22] why did the authorities, with Borges gone and Beleza fairly pliable, attempt to hold the line for a particular period of time, at the expense of higher interest rates? The answer was that everyone expected a peseta devaluation, and this would, following the example of November, provide a public-relations justification for an escudo realignment. So it is time to look further at what was going on in Spain.

## Sophistry is not enough

In many ways the Spanish situation was strikingly similar to Portugal's. As we saw in chapter 4, the initial impact of ERM membership was to reduce the ability of the authorities to prevent overheating and reduce inflation. Indeed, inflation rose slightly after entry. Thus the real appreciation of the peseta in response to the enthusiasm of households, firms and foreign investors about Spain's economic prospects took place through inflation that was high both in absolute terms and relative to the country's trading partners. As in Denmark, as in Britain, as in Portugal, recession was bound to follow. No escape was possible: once the domestic demand cycle turned round there was no route other than through massive deflation to achieve a competitiveness improvement and – slowly, painfully and uncertainly – restore balance to the economy.

Yet the Spanish authorities, like those in Denmark, Britain and Portugal, for long behaved like members of the Flat Earth Society, rejecting both the predictions of theory and the evidence of experience. It was the change in Spain's own cyclical circumstances that prompted its reassessment of ERM strategy. As we saw in chapter 4, when the economy had been booming, ERM tensions had seen the peseta at the top of the band 'in opposition' to the French franc or sterling. Germany would not have

---

22 Ironically, the escudo depreciated in almost straight-line fashion against the DM for more than a year, beginning very soon after ERM entry. That should have meant there were no profits to be made from speculation. It was during the periods of pause in this depreciation that the markets came to expect a discrete change – with associated profit opportunities – in the exchange rate.

allowed a peseta revaluation even if Spain had wanted one,[23] and France and Britain would not permit devaluations of their currencies. Neither Britain nor France (the latter with German support) would increase their interest rates, so the only remaining possibility was a reduction in Spanish interest rates. Even if the Bank of Spain was made unhappy by this necessity, the Spanish government saw no reason to kick too hard against it and was in fact probably rather pleased. But when Spain moved into its inevitable recession, and the peseta came under market attack, things were different. The symmetrical solution of a *rise* in Spanish interest rates certainly had no appeal, while one of the constraints in the earlier situation was now removed – the other countries were not in a position to prohibit a peseta realignment, this time in a downward direction. Thus while in the boom Spain thought it was at least gaining Euro-brownie points by tailoring its interest rates in the 'common good' of the ERM, in the downturn its 'cumulative cost and price divergences' gave it no alternative but to pay back any 'cumulative gush and cant convergence' credits it had previously built up.

Having twice devalued, however, the Spanish authorities found themselves in an awkward position by the end of 1992. Tietmeyer was warning that there could be no more attempts to use the ERM as a disinflation mechanism: not only was convergence a prior condition for monetary union, it was now also to be seen as a prior condition for Spain to rejoin a 'hard' ERM. Yet two weeks before Tietmeyer's speech, Delors had warned that its massive unemployment (20% at the time he spoke) might also prevent Spain from converging and thus keep it out of EMU. What then, it might be asked, was the point of the peseta's remaining in the shell of the ERM at all? Uncomfortably, with general elections in the offing, the main Spanish opposition party, the Conservatives, was indeed beginning to put that very question. Jose-Maria Aznar, its leader, was making statements about monetary and exchange-rate policy that were distinctly equivocal in their attitude to the ERM.

Meanwhile, the recession was deepening. Markets reasonably believed that, with the 'hard' ERM jettisoned by Spain – and, once overboard, no longer retrievable – recession would certainly lead the authorities to reduce

---

23  It is often said by the ERM's supporters that the only freedom a country gives up if it joins the system is the freedom to devalue and thus to run a high inflation rate. As always with the ERM, the reality is very different: the one thing unambiguously given up is the freedom to *re*value against the DM; as a result, inflationary pressures develop that make subsequent devaluations – or painful and foolish recession – inevitable.

interest rates even if this meant a lower peseta. Such expectations were in themselves enough to weaken the currency, which in mid-January began moving down from the top of the band. Market expectations about policy reactions were confirmed when interest rates were cut, by 50 basis points on 22 January and by another 25 basis points on 12 February. But short-term rates remained at 13%, even though the recession was now forcing inflation down sharply – to not much more than 4% by early 1993. It was clear that the government wanted more substantial rate reductions, and the market carried on selling the peseta. On 21 February Gonzalez had to make a television statement setting his face against devaluation and vowing not to take the peseta out of the ERM. This was not enough to prevent overnight rates in the money market from shooting up to 20% the next day. These higher rates pushed the peseta back up to the top of its band, but the market remained convinced that further, more permanent, weakness was likely.

Electoral considerations were expected to determine just when the devaluation would take place. Gonzalez was facing difficulties within his own ruling Socialist Party. The 'traditionalist' wing, led by Alfonso Guerra, was unhappy with the policies of austerity adopted, if not actually implemented, by the government. Their price for continued support of Gonzalez was rumoured to be the head of Carlos Solchaga, the Finance Minister. But Solchaga was, at that time, regarded by the markets as essential to the 'credibility' of the government.[24]

Whether the Socialists won or lost at the general election, it seemed, Spain was going to have to devalue. In September and November 1992, there had at least been the apparent excuse of restoring competitiveness previously lost in the ERM or the prior period of ERM shadowing. But a third devaluation would look like the dreaded 'competitive devaluation' stigmatized by the French government, by Delors and now by Tietmeyer himself. Would Spain's 'partners' allow it? The Governor of the Bank of Spain, Angel Rojo, appeared to have given a negative answer to this question when on 24 February he warned that cutting Spanish interest rates would mean having to leave the ERM. He knew, of course, that being forced out of the ERM would be a tremendous psychological blow to the Socialists, one that would, as it had done in Italy, signal the collapse of the country's 'European' strategy. The threat was enough to calm the markets: they reasoned that Gonzalez would do anything to keep the peseta in the

---

24 After Solchaga's eventual departure, it became clear that the budgetary position had been deteriorating very substantially. But the extent of the deterioration was not known by markets before the elections.

ERM at least until the election, even if defeat at the polls looked likely. But the threat of further attacks on the peseta was merely suspended, not lifted. As in France, everyone was waiting for the elections.

# SNAFU

The French elections were to usher in a new and culminating phase in the crisis of the ERM, but by a totally unexpected route. The final denouement would shatteringly reveal the full intensity of the bitterness in intra-Community monetary relations. Meanwhile, however, the monetary mandarins were hard at work, in Brussels and Basle, on proving that everything was going swimmingly. The public message they were about to deliver was that John Major's foray into monetary geology showed him to be a clueless amateur: there were no fault lines in the ERM. The two reports commissioned by the Birmingham summit, one by the Monetary Committee, the other by the Committee of Central Bank Governors, would be published shortly after the French elections. But to understand their relevance, or lack of it, to the sequence of events set in train by those elections, the time to reflect on the reports is now.

## Unions that divide us

Tietmeyer, as usual, had been the most loquacious of the participants in the debate. Following up his speech of 25 February, he took the occasion of a trip to Chile, to address the UN Economic Commission for Latin America, to hammer home his views. His address was long – over 6,000 words – and its first half was a review of the political background to economic and monetary integration in Europe of a kind more to be expected from a foreign minister or head of government than from a central banker. This part of the speech was particularly notable in insisting that if the Maastricht Treaty was not ratified – a prospect still uncertain when he spoke – then a smaller group of states would conclude an alternative treaty. This, like the gruesome imaginings of Leon Brittan, was no doubt a threat aimed at the Danish voters and the British Parliament rather than a defensible forecast. And it was a threat that gave further credence to the view that if the Vice-President of the Bundesbank showed his speeches to anyone for clearance, it was less likely to be the President of the Bundesbank than the Chancellor of the Federal Republic. The second major theme of the political part of Tietmeyer's speech was his statement of the view that monetary union in Europe necessarily implied political union, an implicit warning to France that there could be no monetary union before a new treaty revision.

Turning to the ERM crisis, Tietmeyer reiterated a number of constant themes: accumulated divergences in cost and prices in Italy, the United Kingdom and Spain had been the real causes of ERM tensions. In addition, the post-unification challenges to monetary policy in Germany meant that most other countries 'had to adjust their own monetary policies to this stance, unless they wanted to put their respective currencies' exchange rates vis-à-vis the DM at risk'.[1] But the exchange-rate movements since September and 'the provisional floating of the lira and the pound sterling' had eliminated cost and price divergences and put the ERM on a firmer footing. And the difficulties provoked by the 'overburdening' of German monetary policy were not cause for great concern as long as the Bundesbank continued to give the highest priority to price stability in its monetary policy. Finally, the ERM turbulence had had the healthy effect that: 'The illusion often entertained over the past few years that the EMS countries were already a *de facto* monetary union has dissolved into thin air.'[2]

Tietmeyer's Chile speech reprised his familiar public positions: the ERM could work if everyone followed the rules, if the system was not used as a disinflationary tool in its own right, and if no one complained too loudly about Bundesbank policy. A few days earlier, the man who sat at the head of the Bundesbank's Council table had reiterated his markedly different view of the EMS. In the one sentence of his speech that showed convergence with his deputy, Schlesinger bemoaned the fact that 'an illusion had been fed' that the EMS was already a '*de facto* currency union'. But then Schlesinger launched yet another fierce attack on his personal *bête noire*: the intervention mechanisms of the ERM. Intervention was 'the Achilles' heel of any fixed-rate system', and the ERM would become 'an inflationary

---

1 It is interesting to see how Tietmeyer and Schlesinger could use *almost* identical words to convey totally opposite meanings. Schlesinger had previously said that other countries had to follow Bundesbank interest rates only if they insisted on tying their currencies' exchange rates to the DM.

2 This 'illusion' had been Tietmeyer's line in the face of Schlesinger's realignment campaign in 1989–90; and as late as 25 May 1992 he was saying: 'We have to recognize that the EMS is developing into a system of *de facto* fixed exchange rates, with its benefits and constraints at the same time.'

dead-end' if German monetary policy was designed simply to promote exchange-rate stability. In fact, said Schlesinger, 'the EMS still requires the acceptance of a timely change to currency parities if necessary.' With sterling and the lira out of the ERM, and with Spain and Portugal already having devalued their currencies enough to have earned the implicit disapprobation of Tietmeyer, there could be little doubt about who Schlesinger's barbs were aimed at. It was the French sweetheart deal that potentially threatened German monetary stability, and everyone knew it. Of all the conflicts to which testimony was given by the March parade of speeches and press briefings, none was more piquant than that between the President and the Vice-President of the Bundesbank.

## Tacit misunderstanding

The authorities of France itself fell unwontedly silent during their period of jockeying for position on the future of the ERM. Trichet's main concern was not to rock the boat. Thus, while he continued to insist on the responsibility of all countries to give priority to the 'common good', he rather obviously interpreted this 'common good' as an obligation for Germany to adapt its policies to French needs and for all other countries to avoid exchange-rate developments that affected French competitiveness adversely.

There was one implication of the French position, however, that could not be masked yet was unacceptable to the Bundesbank. The French government's determination to avoid a franc devaluation, come what may, signalled that it considered the ERM a fixed-rate régime, the *de facto* monetary union now condemned as dangerous illusion by both Tietmeyer and Schlesinger. For the Bundesbank, monetary union could proceed *only* if the conditions laid down by the Maastricht Treaty were satisfied *and* the degree of political union required to create a 'community of solidarity' achieved. Schlesinger may well have hoped that this meant never, perhaps preferring instead a DM-zone, probably along the lines of the 1941 Economics Ministry plan. For Tietmeyer, the problem was that a *de facto* monetary union would imply a *de facto* political union. But a *de facto* union would be one within an unchanged institutional structure. It would therefore be unacceptable to German political and public opinion. Kohl could support the franc only as long as it was not too politically costly – in terms either of his own European aims or of public opinion – to do so. The point of defending the franc was to avoid derailing a process whose momentum would lead to the right sort of political union: one whose institutional structure would enshrine German dominance in the Community, thus allowing it to pursue its objectives in Central and Eastern Europe by leading Western Europe.[3] Conceding *de facto* monetary union to France now would totally alter the dynamics of the integration process. It would allow France to avoid the institutional change both desired by Kohl and demanded by German public opinion as a quid pro quo for relinquishing German monetary authority.

The sweetheart deal did not represent an outpouring by Germany of selfless love for France, and still less by Tietmeyer of devotion for characters such as Trichet, Sapin and Mitterrand. Tietmeyer could advocate and defend the deal in the Bundesbank Council as long as it helped to keep France on the conveyor belt to political union on German terms – but not if the French overplayed their hand by depicting it as a *substitute* for that model of political union. Tietmeyer, was, in the nature of things, not in a position to make this clear to the French, who as a result grossly overestimated their bargaining power vis-à-vis the Bundesbank, with the consequences we shall discover in chapter 12.

## Horses and rhinoceroses

So deep and apparently unbridgeable were the clefts between the positions of the EMS members that the reports of the two committees would have to be banal if they were to be produced at all. Yet, when they were finally released, following discussion at an informal Ecofin on 22 May, they were fatuous even beyond expectation. The ERM had produced so much misery; it was some small consolation that the two reports on the mechanism should at least have been good for a laugh. The main thrust of the Governors' report, as prefigured to an expectant press a month earlier by its Chairman, Wim Duisenberg of the Dutch central bank, was that everything was marvellous. 'We have looked at the system with a magnifying glass,' he said, 'and we have been unable to find any "fault lines".' Perhaps one should not have been surprised that, if Duisenberg's only

3 Tietmeyer had given a remarkable insight into his own preoccupations as early as the end of 1989, shortly after Kohl had put forward his ten-point plan – soon overtaken by events – for eventual German unification. At an international gathering of monetary officials, when someone said that the DDR would soon be known as 'eastern Germany' rather than 'East Germany', Tietmeyer tartly remarked that many Germans regarded the DDR as 'central' Germany (at that time, Kohl was showing signs of being one of the many apparently reluctant to accept the German–Polish frontier as definitive).

seismological instrument was a magnifying glass, he was unable to detect the ominous movement of tectonic plates. At all events, no changes to the rule were needed, it seemed: rather, the rules should be followed more rigorously than in the past.

The Monetary Committee had evident difficulty even in deciding what the system was.[4] In a section hilariously entitled 'The vigour of the EMS policy consensus', the report offered to the world a sentence as linguistically barbarous as it was economically obfuscating: 'The EMS is a system of fixed but adjustable exchange rates, which requires timely adjustments in response to trend divergence but the system must not be allowed to develop into a "crawling peg system".' The use of inverted commas marked the fact that the committee was not even sure what a crawling peg system *was* that the ERM was *not*. Its authors perhaps encouraged by its daring exploration of logical regress, the report rose magnificently to the challenge of constructing a *reductio ad absurdum*: price stability was reaffirmed as the essential determinant of stability in the ERM, implying the need for timely adjustments of policies to macroeconomic difficulties or shocks. What the report did not acknowledge was that the 'adjustments of policies' required to maintain the price stability needed to *avoid* adjustments of exchange rates (readers may pause here for breath) in the 'system of fixed but adjustable rates' would necessarily *involve* adjustments of exchange rates.

Having so bravely defied logic, the report went on to deny the arguments of all the deluded supporters of the system. After ten years of rhetoric according to which 'tying one's hands' via the ERM constraint was supposed to discipline wage bargainers and enhance the credibility of monetary policy, the Monetary Committee now concluded that the 'hard-currency option' had 'limitations as an anti-inflationary strategy' and was 'a substitute neither for appropriate adjustment in other policies nor for moderation in domestic costs'. So no one knew what the system *was* and no one knew what the system was *for*. It was not, it was now admitted, for

---

4 This is not a happy omen for the future of the Maastricht Treaty. The formal rules of the EMS, as laid down in 1979 and modified in 1985 and 1987, were written in language that was undeniably turgid but nonetheless comprehensible to the initiated. No one understands what on earth the Maastricht Treaty is supposed to mean (not even, or perhaps one should rather say 'least of all', the head of the Commission's legal service, who in evidence to the German Constitutional Court gave an interpretation of the procedures for entering Stage Three entirely at odds with every previous or subsequent Commission pronouncement on the subject: partly as a result of his evidence, the German court produced its own version of what Maastricht meant that immediately brought a welter of conflicting interpretations from German academic lawyers . . . and so on).

producing price stability or inflation convergence. So was it still a 'zone of monetary stability' in an unstable world monetary environment? Apparently not, since both reports concluded that currencies with 'sound fundamentals' could experience speculative attacks – with all their disruptive effects on monetary stability – 'as a consequence of external developments'.

What about coming clean and admitting that the EMS was a political tool, intended to start the Community moving along a conveyor belt to political union? Duisenberg instead bemoaned the fact that there had been a clash between the monetary goals of central bankers and the political considerations of governments: political considerations affecting realignments had, he said, hampered a quick adjustment of exchange rates. Evidently suffering contagion from the epidemic of self-contradiction in the Monetary Committee, he added that 'if central banks are independent then they can take interest-rate decisions purely on exchange-rate grounds' – so as to avoid adjustment of exchange rates! Perhaps the truth of the matter is that while central bankers did not want *governments* to defend exchange rates for political reasons, some of them, including a number of would-be central bankers, were quite prepared, in the pursuit of greater unaccountable power for themselves, to make use of politicians' desire for fixed exchange rates.

## I'm in charge!

There was a still more fundamental reason why it proved impossible to come to a common view of the system in terms of agreed economic principles and desirable economic results. Quite simply, many of the system's managers and defenders appeared to show an almost total lack of interest in economic performance.[5] The rules of the system were, from the outset, more important than its results, for the framing and interpretation of the rules determined the distribution of power between and within – and perhaps even over – the Community countries. Thus the two committees could content themselves with writing twaddle about the economic purpose of the system. That was stuff for the children, so why not suspend the laws of logic as in all the best fairy tales? What the grown-ups cared about was

---

5 It is illuminating that Peter Ludlow, that 'federalist and functionalist', could write three hundred well-informed and painstakingly researched pages on *The Making of the European Monetary System* without once asking what economic results the system was supposed to produce. Ludlow, like the politicians and mandarins whose manoeuvrings, conspiracies, alliances and betrayals he chronicles, is interested in his book in one thing: who won?

something else. But 'not in front of the children': if the committee's report looked like the outcome of a vicious power struggle, then the illusion would be threatened. The power struggles were about the rules of the system, so it was natural that the two committees, quite ready to write nonsense about the *purpose* of the system, could essay no definition or clarification of its rules. The reports were agreed that greater respect of the rules was needed, not changes in the rules. The battles – many of them made public beforehand – about symmetry and asymmetry, about intervention obligations, about the decision procedures for realignments, found no echo in the published deliberations of the committees. Each phrase that might have addressed these issues was the result of numberless numbing hours of sucking out any content, leaving an empty shell.

The nearest either report came to saying something meaningful was the Monetary Committee's recommendation of a regular review of parities on the basis of a set of indicators. But the committee evidently could not agree either on what indicators should be used or on how a negative assessment of the sustainability of a parity should be given effect.

It *is* possible to put forward a sensible definition of an appropriate exchange rate, but it is not one that could have commended itself to the members of the two committees. An exchange rate is appropriate if the degree of departure from internal balance (i.e. between inflation and recession) that it implies, given the requirement of a sound budgetary position and the prospects for domestic demand, is politically acceptable. This definition gives the right result in all circumstances, setting competitiveness and current-account indicators, among others, in context. Thus, for instance, sterling was too low in 1987–88. Domestic demand was so strong that capping the currency against the DM created more inflation than was politically desired. To maintain the desired internal balance, competitiveness should have been worse and the current-account deficit bigger. By 1992, in contrast, domestic demand was so weak – and would have had to get even weaker once an inescapable budgetary tightening took place – that sterling's ERM parity carried the threat of outright deflation in conditions of unbearable economic distress. To restore an acceptable degree of internal balance, competitiveness needed to improve and the current-account deficit to shrink and ultimately turn into surplus.

The application of the definition to France is even more interesting. *Given* domestic demand, which was depressed in 1992–93 by a collective loss of confidence among French households and companies, French competitiveness was not strong enough, and the current-account surplus not big enough, to prevent recession and the threat of deflation: a depreciation of the franc would be needed if the political pain of recession became too great. *Without* the ERM constraint, however, the *morosité* induced by cripplingly high interest rates and an impression of governmental helplessness – particularly disturbing to the Gallic mind – would have been absent. Outside the narrow-band ERM, then, the franc might in early 1993 have been a candidate for appreciation against the DM. Thus the application of the definition could help reconcile the conflicting arguments put forward by market analysts about the strength of French 'fundamentals'. But it would also imply that the ERM constraint was *of itself* creating downward pressure on the franc. Once again, Trichet's doctrine of *'désinflation compétitive'* within the ERM would be turned on its head.

However, there is nothing to suggest that Trichet properly grasped this implication. We must look elsewhere to explain the two committees' rejection by omission of the internal balance approach. One eminently plausible explanation is that the Continental central bankers as a group were horrified by its implications. It implied that monetary policy should be the servant of the economy, not its master, striving to maintain inflation (and thus output and employment) in a range determined by governments (and thus ultimately by voters) and subject to forces of 'animal spirits' and budgetary policy uncontrollable by central bankers. The internal-balance approach to assessing exchange rates was the corollary of inflation targeting, the greatest – because the most rational and well founded – threat yet devised to the powers, privileges and immunities of central banks. 'Hard-core' Continental central bankers exhibit towards it the fear and loathing that the unreformed British trade unions felt for Norman Tebbit in the early 1980s.

In sum, the reports of the two committees left the ERM as disorganized, dishevelled and rickety as the shocked heads of government had found it when they handed down their mandate at Birmingham the previous autumn. If anything, the unmistakable clues provided by the reports that highly intelligent and politically aware central bankers and Treasury officials became, as a collective, squabbling half-wits, should have encouraged further attacks by the markets. Market operators were at times strangely afraid of the imagined cunning, intellectual superiority and capacity for collective action of 'the authorities'. The two fatuous reports must surely have had some impact in causing the markets to reassess the strengths and weaknesses of their official opponents, but by the time the reports were presented to the informal Ecofin meeting of 22 May, and thereby made public, the markets were not interested in them. Events, rather than reports, were again the focus of attention. Events in France had positioned the pieces on the ERM chess board for the endgame. Events in Spain had pointed to the way the unbearable tensions of the ERM would have to be resolved. It is to those events that we now turn.

# Schlesinger's Triumph

## Straitjacket, but no padded cell

Thé defeat suffered by the Socialists in the French parliamentary elections of March 1993 was a massive one: many members of Bérégovoy's government failed to hold their seats; the right-wing parties captured four-fifths of the lower house. Within the Right, the Gaullist RPR led by Jacques Chirac outdistanced the strongly pro-European UDF of Giscard. But in French political life the presidency is the focus of all ambition, and Chirac was a very ambitious man. In 1988 he had fought the presidential election as Prime Minister of a 'cohabitation' government. The cards would have been stacked against him then even if the Socialist incumbent had been someone less wily and consumingly egoistic than Mitterrand. With that Florentine character in the Elysée, Chirac found himself outmanoeuvred at every turn. In the end, the margin of his election defeat was the biggest in any conventional Left/Right contest in the Fifth Republic. Mitterrand, taking advantage of this impetus, dissolved parliament and new elections reinstalled a Socialist government. Five years later, Chirac was determined not to repeat this experience. The now elderly Mitterrand would not be his opponent in 1995. It looked probable that Jacques Delors, having laid the ground in Brussels for a European superstate, would want to take command of the Elysée to ensure that the 'European construction' favoured France and corporatism. Delors would have the great advantage of being outside French politics – formally at least – in the pre-election period. If Chirac became Prime Minister again he would be in the political firing-line, and again in no-win conflict with the sitting President, while Delors would be largely immune from attack.

For his part, Mitterrand had announced in 1988 that his second term would be consecrated to 'Europe'. At the end of March 1993 he announced that he would not appoint as Prime Minister anyone not committed to the *franc fort* and the Franco-German 'couple'. In theory, the Right could have voted down the President's prime ministerial nominee, but a row on this particular issue would have split the majority.[1] It might even have given Mitterrand the chance to call new parliamentary elections. But a right-wing government that did not have the freedom to adopt a more rational monetary policy would find itself hamstrung. If Chirac stayed out of the government, he would be able to campaign two years later as the candidate of change, in some undefined sense.[2] Thus he was happy to see the premiership accorded to his political friend and ally, the man who had been his Finance Minister in 1986–88 – Edouard Balladur.

Balladur himself had been only a reluctant supporter of Maastricht, even though he had been the first to suggest, in January 1988, something called a 'European Central Bank'. His own proposal had been much more inclined towards creating a symmetrical sharing of the adjustment burden via, in effect, Franco-German political bargaining. This was rather different from the independent, supposedly European-minded but in practice German-dominated institution that so many French people thought they saw in the Maastricht Treaty.[3] In immediate, practical terms there was little difference between the implications of the two conceptions. Intellectual orthodoxy and political expediency both demanded a continuation of the *franc fort* policy.[4]

1 Giscard, for instance, had been jibing that anyone who questioned the *franc fort* was a member of the 'foreigners' party', a charge that he himself had had laid against him in 1978 by Chirac for accepting, while President, the direct election of the European Parliament.

2 Chirac's strategy worked in personal terms, even if at the cost of a further fundamental weakening of the French economy and of French civil and political society during the two years of Mitterrandism pursued by Balladur.

3 As we have seen, it was partly reaction to the pressure for greater politically decided 'symmetry' embodied in Balladur's 1988 plan that led some – but by no means all – Bundesbank Council members to go along with the idea of a Maastricht-style ECB. The strongly expressed fears of some Bundesbank figures after Maastricht were, at least on the surface, more to do with what they saw as the primacy of 'irreversible' dates over economic convergence and the imbalance between monetary and political integration than with the nature and role of the ECB itself.

4 In the past two years, several accounts, written from very different political viewpoints but concurring in their essential analysis, have attempted to explain the deficiencies in French intellectual and political culture that have allowed France to be caught in the *franc fort* trap. Particularly worthy of attention are: *The Death of Politics* (London, 1994) by John Laughland, a British Thatcherite political scientist working at the Institute of Political Science in Paris, one of the training-grounds of the French élite; *Deux ministres trop tranquilles* (Paris, 1994) by Philippe Bauchard, a veteran and extremely well-connected Socialist journalist; 'La Tragédie du Franc Fort' (*Revue des Deux Mondes*, September 1993) and 'La Tragédie du Franc Fort: Suite' (*Revue des Deux Mondes*, March 1994) by a pseudonymous group of French economists with clear liberal leanings; and *Le Débat interdit* (Paris, 1995) by Jean-Paul Fitoussi, a left-leaning academic economist, leading light of an influential policy research institute, and well known in French political circles.

The strategy chosen by the Balladur team condemned France to a further deterioration in the public finances, a further retreat from market-oriented policies and a further step away from the convergence of economic culture that monetary – and hence political – union would require. It made a mockery of the process of elections: once Mitterrand had insisted that he would only appoint a prime minister for whom monetary union was the Holy Grail, economic policy was trapped in a straitjacket. The distortions imposed on the French economy by the ERM constraint meant unemployment. Unemployment, if it continued to rise unchecked, would mean defeat for the Gaullists in the 1995 presidential elections as surely as it had meant defeat for the Socialists in the parliamentary elections.

Every lever of policy, then, except the right one, monetary policy, would have to be directed towards stemming the tide of unemployment: state spending and the public deficit would increase; subsidies would be doled out; government interference in the vast quasi-state economy would be ever more pervasive; industrial restructuring would be made more difficult; vociferous and violent pressure groups would find it all the easier to rule the government; protectionism would look ever more tempting. The newly elected centre-right government would, privatization promises notwithstanding, have to pursue the most interventionist, 'Keynesian', left-wing policies seen in France since the defeat of 'Socialism in One Country' in 1983. Mitterrand's glee must have been huge: when Balladur bound himself to the *franc fort*, he shackled his government to the worst traditions of the French bureaucratic state.

## In the beginning was ENA . . .

The continuity of the *franc fort* policy after the 1993 elections thus had little to do with a rational assessment of its economic merits and demerits. The defence of the franc–DM parity had become a true shibboleth: those who could not readily mouth deference to it had their heads cut off. Ephraimites either kept their mouths shut or went into hiding. In September 1993, the French periodical *La Revue des Deux Mondes* published an article entitled 'La Tragédie du Franc Fort', an analysis of the havoc wrought by that policy and a plea for a '*politique à l'anglaise*'. The article, published under a pseudonym, is widely believed to have been the work of a group of dissidents within the Banque de France. They chose to call themselves Galilée (Galileo), thereby proclaiming their belief that the

Earth revolved around the Sun[5] and at the same time confessing that, having been shown the instruments of torture, they sought refuge in pseudonymity.

The article ironized on the theme of '*l'exception culturelle française*' then being developed by the authorities as justification for the ultimately successful attempt to exclude 'cultural activities' from the domain of GATT and to prepare the ground for Jacques Toubon's comical efforts to defend the language of Racine from Anglo-Saxon root surgery. To preach such cultural and linguistic irredentism is perhaps not consistent with the Euroracism of a Jacques Delors, but it is wholly consistent with the substitution of sloganizing for analysis that underlay the *franc fort* policy. For 'Galilée', the true '*exception culturelle française*' was an inability to understand economics. The article was scathing in its denunciation of the economic illiteracy of the *énarchie*, and of the *énarque* High Priest, Trichet, in particular. As we have seen, great scepticism about Trichet's competence to engage in economic discussion was manifested by a number of his foreign 'homologues', but 'Galilée' saw similar failings as the distinguishing mark of the whole ENA caste.[6]

Perhaps a charge of mere incompetence is too kind to the *énarque* state in France. One respected non-*énarque* French official, now working outside France, was recently a member of the 'jury' (examining board) responsible for ranking ENA students (or 'pupils', as they are revealingly known) in their final exams. Out of the eighty graduates that year, he complained that he could imagine, as a potential employer, hiring only two. But was it not at least a great honour to have been invited on to the jury? Not really, he replied; ranking *énarques* on their way out was not regarded as important – they had *all* been shaped and moulded into the

5 This allusion was to prove so uncannily relevant to the French position in July 1993, described in chapter 12 below, as to invite a distinctly un-Galilean belief in the paranormal.
6 ENA is not well loved in France. Edith Cresson, it is said, did only two popular things in her spectacularly short period as Châtelaine of the Matignon: having failed to turn heads in a London street no doubt unwittingly, she accused half British manhood of homosexuality; and she proposed, in the process committing political suicide despite the popularity of the idea, to take ENA down a peg by banishing it to Strasbourg. Characteristically, however, while *les français* do not like *énarques*, a majority of them appear to think the ENA state necessary for their well-being. The French Revolution, it seemed, changed very little – in France at least.

form required of them.[7] The prestigious thing was to be a member of the really important jury – the one that decided who was going to be invited *into* the caste in the first place, who was to take the high road to a ministerial portfolio, the headship of a government department, an Ambassador's residence, or the top seat in the boardroom of a nationalized industry, a bank or a 'private' monopoly company.

One writer, an expert on the relationship between culture and the state in Nazi Germany, was indeed a member of such an entrance jury. He has recently written of the experience, one he found depressing, chilling, frightening. He writes that: 'In the spirit of the would-be *énarque* . . . the State is and always has been, like the Word in St John's Gospel: "All that is made was made by it and without it nothing was made" . . . In their fetishistic attachment to the State (to the State, not the Republic) and in their belief in its power and goodness, certain candidates are close to delirious . . . most candidates brush questions aside with a religious, almost hallucinatory affirmation of the excellence of the State.'

What is most disturbing about many *énarques* is not that they do not understand economics but that their incomprehension leaves them unabashed. For them, economics is not only a subject invented and developed *by* Anglo-Saxons, it is a subject fit only *for* Anglo-Saxons and their decadent liberal democratic societies.[8] The servant of the *énarque* state have no need of economics: they possess power instead. When Trichet, at a meeting of top international monetary officials, defended the *franc fort* policy against North American critics by telling them that they did not understand 'Europe', one of his antagonists declared of himself that he might not understand 'Europe' but he did understand economics. Trichet did not deign to make any rejoinder. Who in his right mind could ever have thought that the *franc fort* was anything to do with economics? It was about power. Like Hitler, like Stalin, the *énarque* believes that power will always prevail over economics. In a sense, and for a time, the *énarque* is right: the

7 The ranking is important for the *énarques* themselves, of course. An inkling of the fiercely competitive atmosphere inside this school is given by no less an alumnus than Jacques Chirac, who records that pupils, having read the key pages of a text for examination, then tear them out so that none of their classmates can read them. It is easy to imagine – at least for anyone who has encountered ENA graduates at work – that the French authorities encourage this ruthless selfishness as the best possible training for the country's future rulers.

8 In this respect, as in a number of others, some *énarques* were akin to the officials of the Nazi *Deutsches Ahnenerbe*, whose activities included the promotion of a specifically *German* science of meteorology so that German weather could be freed from the physical laws that determined everyone else's weather.

ordinary people of France suffer unemployment and insecurity; the principles of the Republic are corrupted by the creation, to please Germany, of an unaccountable central bank; the independence of the nation is traduced by the drive to a European federation; but the empire of the *énarques* in the ministries, the Banque de France and Brussels waxes greater.

If the *énarques* did not understand the markets, the markets did not understand the *énarques*. Market operators had reasoned that, while there would be no point in the Socialist government's abandoning the franc–DM parity when electoral defeat was almost certain, the incoming administration could afford to take a more rational view. Once Balladur had restated the primacy of the *franc fort*, however, there had to be a rethink: the expiring short positions in francs were not renewed. Having missed a golden opportunity of shedding the albatross of the 3.35 parity, Balladur would make a fool of himself and severely damage his presidential ambitions if he were to perform a U-turn a few months later. That much was obvious to markets. They doubted whether the new Prime Minister could keep his promise of stabilizing unemployment by the end of the year, but were prepared to guess that the promise would have to be seen to have been broken before exchange-rate policy could be changed. So there was no point in holding short positions in francs and paying high rates of interest for the privilege. From the beginning of April, money began to flow back into France, at a rate fast enough to avoid the previous dilemma as to whether rebuilding the reserves and reducing interest rates should have priority over a strengthening in the franc: this time, everything could be done at once.

## Politics begins at home

By the middle of April, Schlesinger was moved to comment that France was now in a much better position than before to reduce the interest-rate differential with Germany. Such a reduction would not, he insisted, require prior moves by the Bundesbank: what the new French government had said about its *own* policy was the important factor.

What Schlesinger had in mind was no doubt threefold. First, it was important to dismiss what Alain Juppé, now confirmed as Foreign Minister, had said immediately before the election: that French support for a German seat on the UN Security Council could buy reductions in German interest rates. Even if the tariff proposed by Juppé was less unfavourable to

the Bundesbank than the EMU-for-German-unification trade that Mitterrand and Kohl had agreed three years earlier, Schlesinger had had
enough of using interest rates to support foreign policy objectives – the
*government's* foreign policy objectives at any rate.

The second aim of his comments was to pronounce his blessing on
Balladur's intention to create an independent central bank in France. Here,
Schlesinger may have been at one with the markets in misjudging the
motivation of the French élite. Steeped in the traditions of the Bundesbank,
he must have believed that an 'independent' central bank would be more
likely to put price stability, perhaps achieved through monetary targeting,
ahead of the political imperative of the fixed franc–DM parity. At least, an
independent Banque de France would support the Bundesbank in its
mission to ensure that an ECB, if in a worst-case scenario it came into
being, could resist attempts at interference by governments.

Third, he could deflect the criticism in Germany of pandering to the
French that might be engendered if the Bundesbank now accelerated the
process of cutting interest rates. For even Schlesinger was beginning, it
would seem, to have doubts about the self-righting properties of the
German economy. Throughout March and April, increasingly dire warnings were sounded by industrialists that the German recession could turn
into a slump. And, whereas at the beginning of the year Schlesinger was still
dismissing any prospect of a significant fall in GDP in 1993, by April the
Economics Ministry was forecasting a fall of 2% in output in the west of the
country. According to Bundesbank insiders, even the Bundesbank Directorate member responsible for economic studies, Professor Otmar Issing,
usually regarded as a hawk, was pleading with Schlesinger to cut rates.[9] By
the beginning of May, Schlesinger had gone so far, in an interview in the
*International Herald Tribune*, as to suggest that the new scale of Germany's
post-unification problems was such as to call for 'new answers', and he
staggered many observers by saying that some of those who in the past had
been called hawks might now become doves. Actions spoke even louder
than soft words, and during April and May the Bundesbank, most
unusually, more than once surprised the market with the size or timing of
interest-rate reductions.

It is not difficult to surmise that Schlesinger, watching the inflows into
France, the strengthening of the Banque de France's reserves and the

9 In principle, Issing had just as many votes – one – in the Bundesbank Council as Schlesinger.
But, except in the most unusual circumstances, the members of the Directorate traditionally do
not vote against the President in Council meetings.

increasingly rapid reduction in the differential between French money-market rates and those in Germany (by mid-May, the differential had disappeared), felt there was little short-term prospect of driving the franc from the ERM. By the end of the year, rising French unemployment might again put pressure on Balladur to relax monetary policy, but before the end of the year Schlesinger himself would have retired, to be replaced by Tietmeyer, a man whose objectives were not at all the same. In the meantime, there was little point in holding up German interest rates in the face of a deep recession.

This argument had all the more force as general elections in Germany were only eighteen months away. Monetary policy in Germany has traditionally been used to influence the result of the elections in favour of the party whose supporters are in a majority in the Bundesbank Council.[10] In 1993 that party was the CDU/CSU. If an economic recovery were to be sparked in time to boost its chances in October 1994, then, given the lags in the effect of monetary policy, faster interest-rate reductions would have to start in the spring of 1993. That is exactly what happened.

All this meant that, from the French government's point of view, everything was going very nicely indeed. The market had given up its short franc positions; the German recession was looking even deeper than the French; economists, financial market analysts and German businessmen were increasingly questioning whether DM strength, particularly against the dollar and the yen but also against sterling, the lira and the peseta, was sustainable; and there seemed to have been a perceptible softening of the Bundesbank's stance. The French authorities profited from these conditions to reduce interest rates time and again until, by mid-May, the differential with short-term German rates disappeared and even turned slightly negative. In fact, *all* the narrow-band ERM countries, with the

---

10 The Federal government is responsible for appointing the eight members of the Directorate, the *Länder* governments for appointing the regional central bank chairmen – probably the most sought-after jobs in Germany for their combination of power, prestige, income and almost total lack of genuine work – who, together with the Directorate members, make up the central bank council. CDU/CSU supporters enjoyed a clear majority from 1990 onwards. The clear political motivation in the Bundesbank's timing of interest-rate cycles has recently been brought out by the highly respected German economist Roland Vaubel, no left-winger himself. He demonstrates that there is a political cycle in monetary policy in Germany, with loosenings timed to support the government when its supporters are in the majority in the Bundesbank Council. The only time the Bundesbank has tightened policy in the crucial period ahead of general elections was in 1975, when CDU/CSU supporters were in a majority in the Council and the incumbent government was led by the SPD. The government survived.

exception of Denmark, found themselves in that position by mid-May. And all the narrow-band currencies were clustered within 1% of each other in the ERM band. Everything seemed calm. Perhaps Duisenberg had been right after all, and there really were no fault lines in the ERM.

## Floating an idea

On Wednesday, 13 May, a routine meeting of the Monetary Committee was taking place in Brussels. About an hour into the meeting, it seems, the Spanish Treasury member was called out of the room. When he returned a few minutes later he went up to the chairman, Trichet, and whispered in his ear. The Frenchman must have raised his eyes as if to Heaven. Could ever Job have been so sorely tried? He had just been told that the Banco de España, after vainly attempting to counter massive flows out of the peseta that morning, was about to suspend its intervention obligations in the ERM. Some market participants, in the way that politicians find so upsetting to their timetables, had begun to anticipate the universally predicted post-election devaluation and were starting to protect themselves ahead of time. The Spanish authorities could see little point in raising interest rates: that would only bring the markets in for the kill. Once the outflows started, however, they rapidly snowballed. On 12 May the Spanish authorities decided, it seems, that they would take advantage of next day's scheduled Monetary Committee to ask for a realignment, which would be announced after the close of trading. But the markets knew that a meeting was scheduled. It was not difficult to guess what the authorities might be up to.[11] Early the next morning the Banco de España was rocked by unstoppable waves of peseta sales.

When Trichet heard the unwelcome news from Madrid, the Monetary Committee went into realignment session. The procedure was unprecedented; but the Spanish were determined not to lose large amounts of money – and no doubt earn instead the disapprobation of the Bundesbank, which might be forced into obligatory intervention – in defending the peseta for a few more hours just to follow the rules: not for them John Major's po-faced attempts at face-saving rectitude of 16 September 1992. The members of the committee were clearly in no mood to start squabbling among themselves just a few days before their

---

11 This experience led Trichet to cancel another scheduled meeting of the committee two months later when the franc and the Danish krone were facing selling pressure.

ERM whitewashing report was to be published. A devaluation of the peseta was quickly accorded; blessing was also given to Portugal to follow the move. France would feel the competitive pinch, of course, but with the franc in an apparently comfortable position in the ERM, any suggestion that Iberian devaluations – clearly a *fait accompli* – were important enough to be resisted could only have been unsettling to the market. However, press accounts following the meeting reported rumours that Tietmeyer had told the Spanish members in private that this devaluation was to be the last: if Spain came back to the meeting in similar circumstances they would have to leave the ERM. It is not clear where these rumours came from or if they were true. It is readily imaginable, however, that the Banco de España would find such rumours to its advantage. The devaluation of 13 May, unlike those of September and November of the previous year, was arguably inappropriate from the point of view of the Spanish economy. Growth was likely to pick up as a result of the competitiveness improvement already obtained. There was no obvious anti-inflationary anchor since the 'no-realignment' assumption had had to be abandoned. The bank was anxious to put one in place, but the ERM, with its ongoing incentives for markets to engage in periodic devaluation panics, stood in the way. Gonzalez was obstinately refusing to countenance withdrawal from the system. If the markets could be brought to believe that there would *not* be a further devaluation but a float instead, then future pressure on the peseta might be avoided: speculative sales might provoke a withdrawal from the system enforced by the Bundesbank. In other words, the one-way bet would be eliminated and people who sold the peseta would have to face the risk that the currency might actually *rise*.

The bank may well have been encouraged in this thinking by what actually happened on 13 May after intervention was suspended but before the devaluation was announced. With the markets exposed to considerable uncertainty about what was coming next, the peseta was remarkably steady and remained within its pre-existing band. And, after the rumours about the Bundesbank attitude got into the market, the peseta remained stable in succeeding weeks, confounding expectations that pressure would re-emerge almost immediately. In short, the lesson of the Spanish devaluation was that the ERM was destabilizing, as Schlesinger had been arguing for some time. Within three months, the lesson was to be learnt more generally – but not before renewed strains on the franc brought a bitter row between France and Germany.

# Anchor rancour

Yet, by the end of May, the doubts that began to be raised in some minds were about the credibility of the Bundesbank and the strength of the DM. Some significant personalities began to voice those doubts in a way that was bound to anger Schlesinger. As early as 5 April, shortly after the incoming Balladur government had announced its intention to make the Banque de France 'independent', its Governor, de Larosière, had spoken of a reinforced role for the franc in the EMS. 'There is room, it seems to me,' said de Larosière, 'for a tight Franco-German cooperation that would go beyond the simple question of managing currency crises. Healthy fundamental data put France in a favourable position to take part with the mark in anchoring the EMS.' The 'healthy fundamental data' about which de Larosière was preening himself were France's current-account surplus (perhaps always the most important economic indicator of all for the Colbertist French) and its low inflation. Both, of course, were the result of '*désinflation compétitive*'. Together, they reflected the *morosité* of the French people and the depression of the French economy. In the Looking-Glass World of de Larosière and Trichet, they were signs of potential vigour, not the symptoms of a wasting disease, but this further evidence of economic illiteracy among the managers of French economic policy was not the most significant aspect of the Governor's words. Rather, it was his return to the theme of co-anchoring the system that was to have the loudest reverberations.

Every time the undisputed dominance of the DM had come under threat, there had been fireworks in or from the Bundesbank. In 1981, DM weakness allowed Schlesinger, then Vice-President of the bank, to force through an increase in interest rates to unprecedented levels, killing two birds with one stone: the DM immediately regained its leadership role in the ERM and Helmut Schmidt's political stock was so damaged that his FDP coalition partners next year found an excuse to ditch him and install Kohl in his place. Also in 1981, with Schmidt rendered politically impotent, the Bundesbank sank, with just four words, '*wir wollen das nicht*', the counter-attack, led by the French and the Commission, to reduce the power of the strongest currency in the system. In the autumn of 1987, when the Louvre Accords and the Basle–Nyborg agreements again threatened to weaken the Bundesbank's hold, Schlesinger's authority again persuaded the Council to raise rates, dynamiting the US stock market, and with it the Accords. In 1989, the publication of the Delors Report was greeted by the Bundesbank with a rise in interest rates.

In 1990, the weakness of the DM after the Bundesbank's reunification defeat allowed Trichet to coin the phrase '*l'ancre du système, c'est le système lui-même*'. For the Bundesbank, this mantra was not just hot air, it was the most disgusting flatulence. The stench clung to Pöhl, whose resignation in May 1991 gave Schlesinger the chance to refill Frankfurt lungs with the sweet air of his beloved Bavarian mountains – he raised interest rates. In December 1991, the Bundesbank voiced its disapproval of the Maastricht Treaty by raising interest rates at its meeting immediately after the European Council. In May 1992 the French franc rose briefly above the DM in the ERM band, and even the Governor's Committee in Basle began discussing 'co-anchoring' the system; in June, the Bundesbank profited from the Danish 'no' to increase its interest rates yet again, forcing the French to follow, showing the world who was boss and unleashing waves of exchange-market turbulence. In July 1992, the benighted John Major displayed his ability – later to be shown in its full glory in 'back to basics' – to induce the world to fall in on his head when he claimed that sterling would soon be the leader of the ERM; two months later, comments from Jochimsen and Schlesinger himself had blown sterling out of the system altogether. On 3 September 1992, Mitterrand's television interview questioning the independence of a future ECB, followed two days later by the fractious Bath Ecofin, led the Bundesbank to propose a general realignment and Schlesinger to fire off his letter prescribing that the ECB must be the Bundesbank, the whole of the Bundesbank and nothing but the Bundesbank.

Now, in the spring and early summer of 1993, the evil spirits of co-anchoring were again about in the land. One of them was George Soros, master practitioner of the 'casino economics' so detested by the Bundesbank, sage of the markets and proponent of European Union. On 9 June, *The Times* published a long open letter from Soros. In it, he bitterly complained of what he saw as the Bundesbank's domineering behaviour, 'the flaw in the ERM', and criticized the bank for not having cut interest rates soon enough. He predicted that the mark would fall against all major currencies, particularly the French franc, that French bond prices would rise (i.e. French long-term interest rates would fall) more than German bond prices, but that even German bond prices would rise when, as it inevitably would be forced to do, the Bundesbank bowed to the inevitable, already being discounted by the markets, and capitulated. This capitulation (a word full of historical resonance in both France and Germany) would not, Soros predicted, come as long as Schlesinger remained at the helm, but his retirement was only a few months away. Soros freely admitted that he was 'talking his book', that is, he was advancing arguments that supported the positions in financial markets he had already taken.

According to Frankfurt sources, the Soros article had an electrifying effect on Schlesinger. Every argument in it was totally contrary to Bundesbank – or at least Schlesingerian – philosophy. The DM was being derided as, at least in prospect, the world's weakest currency and the Bundesbank as both stupid and a bully. Its leading role in anchoring the ERM was a malignancy in the system and it needed to be replaced by a European Central Bank. The Bundesbank would ultimately cave in to the pressures exerted by the market, and the resulting 'forced' reductions in short-term interest rates would produce reductions in long-term rates. Schlesinger could not prevent the inevitable, but merely delay it for the few months until Tietmeyer took over.

Schlesinger, however, was no fatalist. He had an invulnerable belief that his strategy was right, and an indomitable will to win. The Soros article presented him with a deadly threat, but also with a glittering opportunity. The threat was clear: the markets were going to push the Bundesbank around. The opportunity was that precisely such a threat from one enemy, the 'casino' Anglo-Saxon markets, could, if it could be combined with a threat from another enemy, the Jacobin French government, transform the short-term political position of the Bundesbank. The bank could again be seen in Germany, not as a propagator of unnecessary domestic recession, but as a beacon for the Germanic virtues of steadfastness and discipline, as a defender of *'Kultur'* against the decadence of 'civilization'.[12] But for that to happen, there had to be one more market attack on the franc – if there were such an attack, both the markets *and* the French would be demanding interest-rate cuts from the Bundesbank.

What Schlesinger needed to do from his side was to counter the domestic economic arguments – an overvalued DM and a deepening recession – for cutting rates. This was essential if the bank was to garner enough support from public opinion to enable it to resist the huge pressure that Kohl would undoubtedly exert in any new franc crisis. From early June onwards, then, Bundesbank officials and spokesmen (notably not including

12 The 1920s battle between the 'Westerners', proponents of 'civilization', and the 'Easterners', defenders of 'culture', was one of the fiercest that eventually ripped the Weimar Republic apart.

Tietmeyer) began 'talking up' the German economy, and with it the DM, claiming output would rise sharply in the second half of the year. Such efforts in other countries rarely, if ever, worked. But so great remained the myth of the Bundesbank that, at least for a while and within Germany, the gloom about German economic prospects lifted just a little – just enough to make the man in the street care more about the defence of the Bundesbank's status than about a half-point reduction in short-term interest rates.

But Schlesinger also needed the French government to show signs of weakness. On the face of it, this would not be easy when the French central bank, and along with it several other Continental central banks, were apparently able to trim their own interest rates as they pleased, without reference to the Bundesbank. Indeed, as June wore on, short-term rates in all the narrow-band countries except Denmark edged below German rates – and even Danish rates looked set to follow the trend.

## Chicken or crow?

The great men of the French Treasury and the Banque de France were in a quandary. On 21 June the Banque de France had once more cut its official interest rates, one of a series of cuts following the defeat of the Socialists. They now stood clearly below corresponding German rates. The market, to judge from analysts' comments and the prices of interest-rate futures, were expecting a further cut, one that would put even more clear blue water between French and German rates. The French economy certainly needed lower rates: the latest figures showed a 5.2% fall in industrial output, and while the disappearance of the Socialists had cheered financial markets it had showed no sign of dispelling the *morosité* of French firms and consumers.

Yet Edmond Alphandéry, the Finance Minister, Trichet, de Larosière and their acolytes hesitated. To cut interest rates yet again, independently of the Bundesbank, would look like a bid for the anchor role. Could it succeed when, as Issing was stressing, French long rates were still marginally above German rates? The French authorities habitually spoke and acted as if short rates and long rates were citizens of two different universes with no concourse possible between them. In trying to still the clamour of industrial voices for interest rates lower than those in Germany, they had sought to deny both the importance of short rates (hence the suppression of Icard's article) and the possibility that cutting short rates might lead to a reduction in long rates. But if a bold cut now succeeded in wresting the ERM anchor from the Bundesbank, long rates would fall, and fall below those in Germany. The franc could even rise rather than fall against the DM, and Soros would have been proved right.

But there were risks. What happened if the markets did not give up their allegiance to the Bundesbank but instead saw a cut in French rates as a sign of weakness, of readiness to let the franc fall? Whatever Soros said, the franc was, along with the Danish krone, the lowest currency in the ERM. And what if a cut provoked a last, enraged response from Schlesinger and an open battle of wills between the single-minded Bavarian and the vacillating Frenchmen? Raymond Barre, Prime Minister under Giscard when the EMS was created and still a respected, if not exactly popular, political figure, was warning that France had already 'gone too fast and too far' in cutting French interest rates so often since the elections: 'risks had already been taken with the Germans'. It was necessary, he said, to steer a course between 'the Charybdis of excessive rigour and the Scylla of a laxity that would become uncontrollable'.

As so often, the hand ultimately on the tiller seems to have been Trichet's.[13] In private, he railed against the structure of the Bundesbank Council: 'It is absurd for the Bundesbank's stance to be fixed by the representatives of the German *Länder*, who only care about local preoccupations and do not take account of the greater interests of Europe and of a Christian Democrat Chancellor doubtless more open to a certain form of Socialism than was François Mitterrand.' That seemed to amount to a lament that Tietmeyer, so closely associated with the Christian Democrat Chancellor, could not always prevail in a Bundesbank Council where he had to confront not only Schlesinger but also the regional central bank chairmen, most of them appointed by SPD-led *Land* governments and tending to sympathize with the SPD. The true road to Socialism, Trichet seemed to be implying, was via Kohl's vision of European Union, not through allegiance to the SPD within Germany.

To complete the picture, a highly placed French official who saw both Trichet and Tietmeyer from close quarters during the ERM turmoil described the Directeur du Trésor as '*fasciné*' by the Bundesbank Vice-

---

13 According to Bauchard, '*Au nom de l'Europe et d'une Europe ouverte, les défenseurs du franc fort vont se battre autour de la direction du Trésor pour convaincre Balladur, espérant toujours que la baisse des taux d'intérêt allemands entraînera une baisse correlative des taux d'intérêt français.*' – 'In the name of Europe – and an open Europe – the defenders of the *franc fort*, still hoping that the fall in German rates would bring a corresponding fall in French rates, did battle around the Treasury to convince Balladur.'

President. The French word conveys more than just 'fascinated': 'held in thrall' would be nearer the mark in this case. Tietmeyer was worried for all sorts of reasons by the prospect of sharp, unilateral cuts in French interest rates (some have already been mentioned, and Tietmeyer's side of the story will be explored more fully a little later). There can be no doubt that Tietmeyer warned Trichet very forcefully to head off such a course of action by the French government. And the same source says with deliberate emphasis: '*Trichet* obéit *à Tietmeyer* – *tout simplement il lui* obéit.'[14] What Trichet was being told by Tietmeyer, it seems, was that some form of co-anchoring might be possible – but only if the French kept quiet about it in public, for Schlesinger and German public opinion would go off at the deep end, with unpredictable consequences, if they saw the French cock crowing. Wait a few more months and I'll see you all right.

At all events, the élite of the French élite were persuaded that the market would react badly to a cut in French rates, seeing it not as a successful takeover bid for the ERM anchor role but instead as a sign that France was prepared to let the franc fall. For most of June, French short rates continued to hover just below German. Tietmeyer must have been on tenterhooks. If this state of affairs persisted, *he* might win: Germany would still be seen as the anchor of the system and the French might just be able to hold on without a new wave of speculation against the franc. But if the French somehow let the market know that they were still hurting, Schlesinger would finish them off.

That the French *were* hurting is clear enough. Balladur was already preparing his first U-turn. After taking contractionary fiscal measures (including a highly unpopular rise in social security taxes) in his first few days, by June he was having to plan increases in public spending and subsidies. A bond issue (the so-called 'Balladur bond') was launched to bring money into the government's coffers ahead of planned privatizations (holders of the bond were promised privileged purchases of privatization shares if and when the flotation went ahead). The issue brought in a vast sum – 110 billion francs, or more than 1% of GDP – and was very quickly to be spent, without being included in calculations of the budget deficit.

But this swing back to Keynesian fiscal expansion looked as though it would not be enough. Balladur was and is a *Colbertiste*, a typical Continental right-winger believing in state regulation and control. He differed from the Socialists only in that the intended beneficiaries of his policies were not the

14 '*Trichet* obeys Tietmeyer – quite simply, he *obeys* him.'

same classes or individuals favoured by the Left. He has been well described (admittedly by a Socialist) as seeking to return France to the age of Louis-Philippe, when a façade of liberalism hid a reality of *dirigisme*.

Balladur's *dirigisme* worked through the personal influence of the government over a network of financiers and big businessmen. Throughout the early summer, he engaged in a round of private meetings with the *grosses légumes* of French industry and finance. The message that came through to him was always the same: 'We can't wait for ever in the hope that an economic pickup in the US will pull Europe along with it; we can't cope with competition from the depreciating countries such as Britain, Spain, Italy and the Nordics while we are burdened with real interest rates of 5%[15] – British firms have to face real rates of only 1.5%, and even German firms 3.5%– as against our 5%; with our inflation rate, we need nominal short rates at US and Japanese levels of 3%; concluding the GATT round will make things even worse for us – you can't have both the GATT and the *franc fort*!'

The last threat hit home particularly hard with Balladur. This instinctive Colbertian's reaction was to prefer the *franc fort* to free trade. But the Germans wanted the GATT to succeed. Rows with them about trade might spook the markets, who were still impressed by the 'sweetheart deal'. To make things worse, the new Gaullist Foreign Minister, Juppé, was as yet getting on less well with the Germans – despite his pre-election UN Security Council seat enticements – than had his Socialist predecessor, Roland Dumas. Bosnia could produce a rift. So too could the remarks of the French Ambassador to Bonn, who had haughtily reproved Germany for pursuing its own contact with Yeltsin – the Rapallo complex at work yet again!

Balladur suffered a further blow in mid-June. It was delivered by Philippe Séguin, the ultra-Gaullist, at once courteous and pugnacious, who had spearheaded the anti-Maastricht campaign in France and was now President of the lower house of the French Parliament. On 16 June, Séguin launched a fierce attack on the failure of the French government, and indeed of all governments, to stay the scourge of unemployment. In a deliberately provocative phrase, he denounced the 'social Munich' of French economic policy. The government, he implied, was appeasing Germany on two fronts at once: GATT and the *franc fort*. The combination of the two would, it was easy to deduce from Séguin's words, have a

15 By June, French short-term rates had come down to around 7%. But inflation was only 2%.

result in the economic field similar to the disastrous political consequences of 1938.[16] Balladur immediately and publicly asked Chirac, as leader of the Gaullist RPR, to disown Séguin. Chirac declined.

Some of these problems were known to the financial markets, but no one was prepared to analyse them in research publications or take short positions in francs themselves: the long arm of the French state could reach out and hurt them, just as Goldman Sachs had, it seems, been 'punished' by the Italian government the previous year and the Danish banks had had to take their beating behind the bicycle shed in January. Analysts who spoke their minds too openly could find themselves getting sacked.[17] This was especially true if they were French: on one occasion Trichet vituperated about an analyst who had criticized the policy stance – he was a *Frenchman* working for a *French* bank. This, he seemed to imply, was what happened to people when they were based in London. Tietmeyer was irritated enough to enquire if for a French analyst to do the job he was paid to do was to be regarded as equivalent to treason. But in this respect, if in no other, it was Trichet who mattered, not Tietmeyer.

Something more, then, was going to be needed if Schlesinger was to triumph: there would have to be an open admission from the French government itself that it could not live with the current level of German interest rates. That admission came more dramatically than anyone could have expected. Schlesinger, one can very reasonably presume, must hardly have been able to believe his luck. But he made the most of it.

## La grande gaffe

Since 1988 there have been twice-yearly bilateral meetings between the French and German finance ministers, their top officials and the two central bank governors. Edmond Alphandéry, Sapin's successor as Finance Minister, was a former university professor of economics. Unlike

16 The irrational and superstitious *idée fixe* of the *énarque* establishment in Paris and Brussels and of their equivalents in other European countries that open markets require fixed exchange rates was discussed in chapter 7.
17 It was not just relatively lowly analysts who had reason to fear retribution if they said the wrong thing in public. 'Galilée' wrote that 'a certain number of people carrying responsibility at the highest level in the [French] financial world disclosed in private that they favoured breaking the franc–DM link. But they did not dare make their opinions known in public, fearing the reactions of the Banque de France or the Treasury. It was all too true that the authorities had ways of exerting pressure very effectively on financial institutions and even on people, if they ran state organizations.'

Schlesinger, he was about to display that he really was a political *ingénu* who did not understand the psychology either of the markets or of the Bundesbank. It was his turn to host the bilateral meetings. One was due to take place in Paris on 25 June. At noon on the preceding day, 24 June, Alphandéry was interviewed on French radio. In just a few seconds, he sealed the fate of the ERM. He was summoning Waigel and Schlesinger, he seemed to say, to Paris the next day to tell them that German interest rates had an importance going far beyond Germany's borders. There were millions of unemployed in France, and the hope of reducing unemployment depended on cuts in German interest rates. '*La gaffe Alphandéry*', as it immediately became known, could not have been more calamitous. One monetary official in Brussels stood looking at the financial news screens as Alphandéry's remarks were reported. To him, the significance of what was being flashed onto the screens was obvious. The official's comment summed it up in admirably lapidary fashion: '*Alors, c'est bien foutu, le système*'.[18]

What had Alphandéry done that caused mouths to gape with horrified surprise? In short, he was The Man Who Told the Truth about the ERM. What Alphandéry did was, by mistake, to state the bleeding obvious, when the whole myth of the ERM, from the very beginning, reposed on a determination to *avoid* stating the bleeding obvious. More specifically, Alphandéry demolished at a stroke the arguments defended by Trichet. He admitted that French unemployment was linked to the level of short-term interest rates – a proposition that Trichet and his minions ridiculed as a symptomatic effusion of 'Anglo-Saxon economics' He then signalled to the markets that Germany was still the boss in the system: there was no more room to reduce French short-term interest rates unless the Bundesbank cut *its* rates first. Next, and perhaps most damaging of all, he gave the impression of issuing summonses and orders to the Bundesbank – an institution whose public image forbade it from appearing, whatever the reality might be, to take orders from the German government, never mind the French.

Within minutes, the phone line between Frankfurt and Bonn must have melted as an incandescent Schlesinger demanded an immediate slapping-down of the presumptuous Frenchman. There was initially a period of some confusion. The Bundesbank press office refused any comment and their Finance Ministry counterparts, apparently asleep, confirmed that

18 'So, the system's well f****d.'

Waigel and Schlesinger were indeed flying to Paris the next day. But by mid-afternoon Waigel's office issued a press statement saying that the scheduled meeting was a routine one and would be postponed indefinitely because the German Finance Minister was 'too busy' (Waigel's drinking habits were notably abstemious by Bavarian standards: 'too tired' would not have rung true as an alternative excuse!). There was no question, the statement added, of any joint decision on interest rates.

Schlesinger may well have been angry, but he also had every reason to be jubilant. The weakness of the French economic position had been revealed to the international markets; the offensiveness of the French political position had been fully revealed to the German public. Schlesinger's position was strengthened immeasurably. He could now be sure of the support of public opinion in any battle of wills with Kohl about supporting the franc. And, without the slightest possible doubt, there *would* now be further attacks on the franc. Alphandéry's ill-judged, unwitting honesty and the rebuff from Bonn shattered any market belief that France could live with the ERM and begat suspicion that the sweetheart deal had indeed gone sour.

In Paris, a damage-limitation exercise was set in motion. Alphandéry's office belatedly emphasized that the bilateral meeting was a long-scheduled affair: neither the meeting nor its postponement had any great significance, it was claimed. There was certainly no question of summoning Waigel and Schlesinger to France. It was very understandable that Waigel's busy schedule prevented him from coming to Paris. After all, everything was going so well in Franco-German economic cooperation, Alphandéry was quoted as telling Waigel over the phone, and the ERM situation was so patently satisfactory to all sides, that there would not have been much to talk about. But, Alphandéry continued, brass-necking in a way that must have driven Schlesinger to even greater fury, France stood ready to support the DM just as Germany had in the past supported the franc. But no 'interpretation' of Alphandéry's remarks and the German snub could put the genie back in the bottle.

A few days after '*la gaffe*' there occurred a quite extraordinary scene. Trichet and Tietmeyer were both to attend one of the many routine international meetings of finance and monetary officials that help keep regulated and protected Continental airlines in business. Trichet arrived in the meeting-room before Tietmeyer. By the time the German entered, the room was almost full. The other participants were treated to an experience that was revealing of the post-gaffe state of Franco-German monetary relations almost to the point of embarrassment. As soon as Trichet saw Tietmeyer, he rushed towards him gasping 'Cher Hans' and, evidently wanting to give physical expression to the celebrated phrase, 'two hearts beating as one',[19] flung his arms around him. Tietmeyer's whole stolid, Westphalian body went rigid, his arms ramrod-straight by his sides. Trichet gazed up, apparently entranced, into Tietmeyer's unwontedly discomposed face, maintaining his embrace so long and so close that onlookers began counting the seconds. Neither party to the embrace, neither the willing nor the unwilling, spoke a word, nor did anyone else in the room. Tension mounted: would Trichet release his grip on Tietmeyer? Would Tietmeyer extricate himself forcibly? Then the door opened; a latecomer entered the room. He stopped dead in his tracks as his eyes fell on the strange tableau before him, giving the relieved spectators the chance to laugh. The tension dissipated, Trichet and Tietmeyer grinned embarrassedly, and the Frenchman's arms fell away from his liege-lord. No one who witnessed this scene could have any doubt about its meaning. The principle of Divine Right was re-established. The monetary courtier Trichet was seeking public forgiveness of his sovereign for an act of attempted rebellion by France.

Not everyone in the world, however, had seen Trichet's antics with Tietmeyer, and not everyone immediately realized the significance of '*la gaffe*'. The day after Alphandéry's fateful radio interview, Count Otto von Lamsdorff,[20] leader of the FDP until he came under a temporary financial cloud and still, in a Germany tolerant of such things, a substantial political figure, remarked that the round of interest-rate reductions by 'follower' central banks earlier in the week clearly showed that the DM was no longer the undisputed anchor of the system. In the early days of the following week, the DM remained weak against almost all currencies. The Bundesbank's propaganda offensive had not been working outside Germany. Markets feared that an over-tight monetary policy would weaken the German economy, aggravate the difficulties of budgetary adjustment and ultimately, perhaps, lead to a much sharper relaxation and a worsened inflation outlook.

Early in the following week Schlesinger argued that competition for the

19 The phase 'two hearts beating as one' had been coined by Sapin to eulogize the Franco-German cooperation in supporting the franc in September 1992.

20 Lamsdorff had not made himself popular with Italian opinion when, dismissing the risk that the former East Germany might become a new Mezzogiorno, he had haughtily remarked that Prussians had been the finest industrial workers in the world before the division of Germany, and they were not to be compared to the workers of southern Italy.

anchor role was healthy but the Bundesbank's credentials remained by far the most impressive. Then, on the Thursday following '*la gaffe Alphandéry*', the Bundesbank surprised the markets by announcing a reduction of 50 basis points in its discount rate (the more relevant of the two official rates when the trend was downwards, since it formed the lower bound of the corridor for money-market rates). The DM strengthened on the announcement: the markets viewed the move as a rational response to the German economy's difficulties.

But *why* did the Bundesbank produce such a large rate reduction out of the blue? No answer to this question can be definitive – each of the 16 members (at the time) of the Bundesbank Council no doubt had his own bundle of prejudices, objectives, arguments and beliefs. And some will have voted against the change. But the cut did two things that were to prove of great importance. First, it took the discount rate far below the repo rate, the main influence on the position of money-market rates within the corridor (the day before the discount rate cut, the Bundesbank's repo rate had fallen by a single basis point, and even this probably reflected a technical mistake by the bank's money market desk). This meant that, for several weeks or even months to come, there would be no 'technical' argument for a further cut in the discount rate. The Bundesbank repeatedly emphasized that the repo rate was the most important in short-term monetary management. If there was enough room in the corridor for the repo rate to move freely, then any change in the discount rate would have to be interpreted as, in effect, the announcement of a policy change – a policy change under foreign pressure. Thus the surprisingly large cut in the rate on 12 July can be seen as preparing the ground for the Bundesbank to resist political pressure when '*la gaffe*' produced the flight from the franc that Schlesinger knew it must. Second, the size of the discount cut re-established that rate as the lowest 'official' rate in the ERM. It was a challenge to France: put your money where your mouth is if you want to be the anchor.

France ducked the challenge: immediately after the announcement of the Bundesbank decision, the Banque de France announced that it would cut its own equivalent of the discount rate the following day – but by 25 basis points, to the same level as the Bundesbank's rate but not below it. In effect, the French were acknowledging that the Bundesbank retained the anchor role. The immediacy of the Banque de France's reaction indicates that the decision had been prepared by the French government – presumably briefed in advance by Tietmeyer on what they should do. Had Alphandéry not given his radio interview a week before, the Bundesbank rate cut and the French reaction would probably have maintained calm in the ERM; Tietmeyer in particular could have been a relaxed man. But after '*la gaffe*', the events of 1 July instead reminded the markets of the vulnerability of the franc.

That vulnerability had been brought to the surface in a highly significant little article, tucked away on the back page of *The Times*, by Anatole Kaletsky on 28 June. In it, he pointed to the incipient tensions in Franco-German relations at both the political and monetary levels, to the insistent moaning and groaning of the captains of French industry, and to the promise Balladur was said to have given them that French short-term rates would be down 4% by the end of the year – something that could now clearly be seen to be impossible without some change in the franc–DM relationship. A number of the most intelligent strategists in the financial markets sat up and quietly took notice. 'We knew these things,' said one, 'but no one was prepared to say them for fear of being accused of an Anglo-Saxon plot. We're all hoping to get our share of the privatization cake in France and don't want to annoy the government. It's important that Kaletsky has brought this out into the open.'

## Meltdown

Events now began to move with ominous rapidity. The impact of '*la gaffe*' and the timidity of the Banque de France response to the Bundesbank rate cut was seen as soon as the markets reopened the following week. To the dismay of the French authorities, French money-market rates began to move up, not down, and the franc began to weaken against the DM. Schlesinger was back in the driving seat, and he was speeding towards the final cataclysmic collision.

On Tuesday, 6 July, the alarming market movements accelerated. The negative differential between French and German short-term interest rates fell from 50 basis points to 18. Then on Thursday came grim news about the French economy. INSEE, the official French forecasting agency, estimated that market-sector GDP would fall by 1.2% in 1993. That would mean a sharp rise in unemployment, falsifying Balladur's promises. The rational response would have been further reductions in interest rates, but the markets now knew that, with the Banque de France once more making formal obeisance to its feudal seigneur in Frankfurt, the required cuts could not come unless France abandoned the narrow-band ERM.

To defend themselves against that prospect, market participants started borrowing francs (driving short-term interest rates up) in order to sell them (driving the franc down). Private information from the banks who were actually carrying out these operations on behalf of their clients makes it clear that there was no Anglo-Saxon plot. Instead, the main sellers of francs were French and German companies whose Treasury departments had built up big holdings of French bonds in the expectations of continued cuts in short-term rates and capital gains on bonds. Interestingly, these corporate holders did not start selling their French bonds. Instead, they began hedging their holdings, borrowing short-term from the banks against the security of their bond holdings and either selling those francs outright or using them to buy put options on francs or call options on DM bonds. Their strategy was straightforward, and it spelled the doom of the ERM. Corporates did not want to sell their French bonds because they knew that the economic situation demanded further cuts in short rates, a positive environment for bonds. But there were three alternative scenarios for such cuts. In one, political pressure from France would force the Bundesbank to reduce its rates, leading to reductions in rates throughout the ERM. In a second scenario, France would itself take the lead in moving rates down within the ERM. But '*la gaffe*' and the consequent restoration of Bundesbank leadership had dimmed the prospects of either of these two scenarios. That left the third: the abandonment of the *franc fort*. It was to cover themselves against that growing possibility that French and German corporates began to hedge their French bonds. By Thursday evening, the franc had weakened sharply. From 3.365 against the DM pre-*gaffe*, it had come close to the 3.40 level for the first time since short positions[21] were unwound at the beginning of April. The short-term interest-rate differential with Germany had become a positive 20 basis points: in the week since the Bundesbank discount rate cut, French money-market rates had *increased* by 40 basis points.

By the following week, the ERM was displaying all the symptoms of fatal malaise: its collapse was now imminent. One important signal was a marked strengthening of 'safe-haven' currencies: the dollar (to a 22-month high of DM 1.73), sterling (which rose 2.5 pfennigs in the second week of July to reach DM 2.572, compared with a low of DM 2.30 in February) and the yen. Within the ERM, in contrast, all currencies weakened against the

---

21 A 'short position' in a particular asset is one in which the player will profit if the price of the asset falls; a 'long position' is one in which a profit will be made if the price of the asset rises. 'Shorting' an asset means taking a short position with respect to it.

DM, except for the Dutch guilder (regarded by markets as a surrogate DM) and the Irish pound (protected by its links with sterling).

The market finally seemed to have learned the lesson of earlier failures to profit from the possibilities for self-enrichment, identified by Schlesinger, that the ERM provided. The franc would not survive unless the Bundesbank, under political pressure, reduced interest rates – but if it did, the ERM currencies as a bloc would move down against the currencies of third countries whose stronger economic performance meant that they did not need interest-rate reductions. So an obvious strategy (and one which again gives the lie to 'Anglo-Saxon plot' theories) was to borrow francs (or other weakening ERM currencies such as the Danish krone) and sell them for 'safe haven' currencies. If the Bundesbank cut rates, the whole ERM would move down, providing a profit on purchases of dollars or sterling. If the Bundesbank did not cut rates, the French franc (and the krone) would have to fall against all other currencies, not only the DM but, again, the dollar and sterling. The effect of these operations was to push French short-term interest rates up (as people wanted to borrow francs to short them) and to weaken the franc's cross-rate with the DM.

By 16 July (exactly a year after the fateful Bundesbank decision to raise its discount rate), the French authorities were having to invoke the sweetheart deal: there was publicly announced intramarginal intervention in favour of the franc by the Bundesbank, and the Banque de France was also reportedly intervening. Yet the franc was pushed near to its lower permitted margin against the DM, and even nearer its margin against the guilder, which was in its accustomed position as the advance-guard of the DM at the top of the band. On the following day, Friday, French three-month interest rates were 46 basis points higher than corresponding German rates; they had risen by a full percentage point in two weeks and now stood at 7.88%, a level likely to incite French industry to despairing mutiny. The rise in interest rates drove Mitterrand to make his first public pronouncement on monetary matters for several months. It was a surprising one, perhaps born of his annoyance with German attitudes on Bosnia, Eastern Europe and GATT: the need to maintain the franc–DM link, he said, had to be finely balanced with the need to give some stimulus to domestic demand in France (but by the middle of the next week he was reiterating, presumably dragged back into line by Kohl, the absolute priority of the link with the DM).

The Danish krone was faring even worse. Unemployment had risen to more than 12% and was still rising. The Social Democrat-led government's known view was that increasing unemployment could not be tolerated. The inevitable result, once the ERM had started to come apart at the seams, was intense selling pressure on the krone. To make things worse, the Swedish krona, after recovering during the spring, was floating downwards again, worsening Danish competitiveness. Several times in the second week of July the Danish currency fell to its lower limit against the guilder. The Nederlandsche Bank had to intervene on several occasions. Danmarks Nationalbank raised its repo rate by 120 basis points and restricted liquidity, with the result that by the end of the week Danish three-month rates were at 9.89%, a crippling level for an economy whose new output data showed sharp falls.

By now, investors were beginning to bet that the Bundesbank would have to cut interest rates to save the ERM. In expectation, they piled into the German bond and stock markets, pushing long-term interest rates down by 15 basis points in the second week of July and sending the German share-price index soaring. Even French long-term rates edged down, despite the rise in short-term rates, and the French Bourse rose by 2.5% over the week: a reaction reminiscent of the leap of joy of the London Stock Market when base rates were raised to 15% on 16 September 1992. The game was clearly up for the ERM.

On Friday, 17 July, the Danish krone again hit its intervention limit within the ERM. As on 4 February, it was supported by concerted intervention by the German, French, Dutch, Spanish and Danish central banks. This time, the Irish too joined in, hoping both to profit from the situation to re-establish their good European name and to avoid being dragged out of the ERM – this time at the top, not the bottom – by the strength of sterling. In mid-afternoon, the Nederlandsche Bank cut interest rates on the guilder, the currency at the top of the system, by 10 basis points in an effort not to exceed the maximum permitted spread of 2.25% against the krone. When the news hit the market screens, there occurred one of the most remarkable and telling episodes of the whole crisis. Before the Dutch rate cut, the Irish pound had been the second strongest currency in the system. As the guilder dipped briefly, the Irish pound replaced it at the top. Within minutes buy orders for the Irish currency pushed it way outside its permitted band against the krone. The Dutch example led the market to bet that the Irish, too, would cut interest rates, thereby raising the price of short-dated Irish bonds; there was a scramble for Irish pounds to buy bonds. When the Irish central bank had recovered from its numbed surprise, it supplied all the Irish pounds – and more – than the market could want, pushing the Irish pound back within the band. But the message had been transmitted loud and clear: Schlesinger had been absolutely right when the previous December he had denounced the ERM as a machine for enriching speculators. The brief flood of money into the Irish pound on 17 July furnished the final proof that Schlesinger needed: maintaining the ERM would mean the destruction of *any* monetary authority in the area; the ERM and its anchor, wherever it might be sited, could not be maintained simultaneously, as even Kohl would have to realize.

On the weekend of 18–19 July, rumours of an imminent krone devaluation began to circulate. But on Monday, 20 July, the Danish central bank reacted by offering liquidity to the market at a rate of 20%, pushing overnight rates to levels that made speculation, in the very short term, prohibitively expensive. For two days, the krone was left in relative peace, though still very close to its lower permitted limit.

On Wednesday, 21 July, the Bundesbank announced the result of its weekly repo allocation: the rate had declined by 13 basis points, leaving it still 40 basis points above the discount rate. With only one Council meeting still to come, on Thursday of the following week, before the summer break, it looked as though only a political crisis would produce a cut in the discount rate in time to save the ERM. To add to the misery of the struggling currencies, Germany's June money-supply figures were announced shortly after the repo result: M3, supposedly the Bundesbank's primary target, had accelerated to an annualized rate of increase of 7.1%, clearly outside the target range. After the previous week's intervention, the July figure was likely to be worse. That apparently gave the Bundesbank little justification for further cuts in rates and provided a backdrop in which the bank could complain about the money-supply effects of any further intervention it might have to undertake.[22]

The market took fright, and began selling the weak ERM currencies. This time, the selling was directly against DM, rather than sterling or the dollar, as operators began to feel that the Bundesbank was not going to bail the ERM out one more time. As a result, the tensions in the system became generalized, spreading from the French franc and Danish krone to the Belgian franc, the peseta and the escudo. The Belgian National Bank was forced to raise its key rates, and by the end of the week Belgian three-

22 In the remaining months of 1993, M3 was to accelerate further. That was not, as we shall see, to prevent a speeding-up of the rhythm of interest-rate cut from October onwards. But by then, of course, Schlesinger was no longer President . . .

month money-market rates had risen by more than a full percentage point compared with a week earlier, threatening to create a vicious circle as markets calculated the impact on the cost of servicing Belgium's huge public debt. On Thursday, the escudo tumbled by 3% in the course of the day, and both Iberian currencies dived deep into the lower half of their bands.

In France, the guns that had been used to impress the market in September 1992 and January 1993 were hauled back into the front line. The 5- to 10-day repo window at the Banque de France, the main source of re-financing for the banks, was closed, to be replaced by a special overnight window intended to restrict speculative borrowing. The rate at which the Banque de France now lent to the market was increased from 7.25% to 10%. By the end of the week, three-month rates were also close to 10%. One-month rates had risen to 12%.

One month was the key period: in a week's time would come the Bundesbank Council meeting that could save the ERM; if salvation did not come, the summer break meant any further hope would be deferred for a month. Yet these French rate rises did not deter selling of francs. With the fixed date of the Bundesbank meeting six days ahead, one-week rates would have had to hit hundreds of per cent to offset the risk of a sharp depreciation of the franc. The measures taken by the Banque de France were merely 'showing willing'. Only the Bundesbank could save the peg. But the Bundesbank had by now realized the nature of the game it was being forced to play. More accurately, Schlesinger had long realized it, but now his most credulous colleagues on the Council had been brought to the same recognition. As for Tietmeyer (only the most credulous of persons would apply the word 'credulous' to the Vice-President), he had to feel uncomfortable when the Bundesbank, which had fought ceaselessly and ruthlessly to hold back the modernization of German financial markets, was called upon to bail out the franc because the Banque de France could not crash its own 'Anglo-Saxon' Paris markets.

## Coup de grâce

By the end of the week of 19–23 July, the feeling that the ERM's death agony had begun was palpable. Even the by now ritual release of a joint Franco-German statement justifying the DM-franc parity had lost its power to calm the markets. Diplomats, officials, commentators, market participants: all had the impression that somehow this communiqué was

318

'weaker' than those issued in September and January. Files were scanned, and the three texts compared word by word. The words, in fact, remained the same, but their almost supernatural power to cow the markets was no longer there.

On Friday evening, the ERM was still breathing – just. But everyone knew that it might have only one more week to live. Everything depended on the outcome of the Bundesbank Council meeting on Thursday, 29 July.

During the weekend, speculation about the intentions of the Bundesbank was frenzied. Rumours flew everywhere: that Kohl had threatened to change the Bundesbank Law if the bank did not save the ERM; that Schlesinger had threatened to resign if Kohl continued to press him; that Alphandéry, Juppé, Balladur and Mitterrand were all ceaselessly cajoling Kohl; that Tietmeyer planned to lead a rebellion within the Bundesbank Council. One report that does appear to have been firmly based on fact is that the Bundesbank had been phoning around the largest market players, asking them how big a reduction it would need to make in its discount rate in order to keep the ERM intact – bigger and bigger as the weekend progressed. On Friday afternoon, market comment called for a half-point cut in the discount rate. Saturday's newspapers spoke of 0.75% as the cost of holding the ERM together. By Sunday, it appeared that only a full point would suffice. To anyone with any insight into Bundesbank thinking, these reports were the final evidence that ERM was going to collapse. Had not Schlesinger made it clear in April that whatever else happened, the Bundesbank would not let the market determine German monetary policy? Yet by the end of the weekend, most commentators had convinced themselves that the Bundesbank would cave in to political pressure from Kohl and cut its discount rate by a full point.

These unrealistic expectations were reflected in the markets when trading restarted on Monday, 26 July. The Frankfurt and Paris stock markets opened strongly and all the 'safe haven' currencies, the dollar, the yen and the Swiss franc rose against the DM. Even the lira appreciated. Several ERM currencies remained close to their lower limits, and short-term interest rates were at unsustainably high levels. But, on Monday and Tuesday, forex trading was relatively subdued. The Belgian franc, however, weakened outside the range of +/−0.3% against the DM which the authorities had been maintaining since the *de facto* link was established in 1990. Belgian money-market rates, which had already been raised on the previous Friday, were hiked again, calming the forex market somewhat – but clearly only temporarily. On Wednesday, both

Denmark and Spain issued data showing a continuing worsening in unemployment situations that were already desperate – to 12% in Denmark and to a massive 22% in Spain. But short-term relief was afforded to the krone and peseta, and to the rest of the ERM grid, by the Bundesbank's repo allocation: the repo rate declined by 20 basis points. Once more, however, the fall is best interpreted as showing a determination by the Bundesbank to be seen as acting normally, sensibly and in line with the needs of the German situation. A cut in the discount rate would be another matter altogether.

The blow fell the next day. As the members of the Bundesbank Council gathered in Frankfurt for their regular fortnightly meeting, markets, officials and politicians throughout Europe were in a state of anguished expectation: the story was everywhere that Kohl had ordered the Bundesbank to cut the discount rate; everyone expected Tietmeyer to lead the case for rate reductions.[23] As the morning wore on, with no news from Frankfurt, tension screwed up another notch. At 2 pm Continental time, New York traders sat in front of their screens earlier than usual, waiting to be first off the mark to sell DM and buy dollars in the first few frantic seconds after the expected announcement of a discount rate cut. Then, at a few minutes after two o'clock, the screens suddenly flashed and beeped: the Bundesbank meeting was over. The Lombard rate, insignificant when rates were falling, had been cut by half a percentage point. But the all-important discount rate was unchanged. There was no full point cut, no three-quarter point, no half point: nothing. For an instant, the professional screen-watchers, reinforced today by gaggles of anxious officials, were frozen in shocked disbelief. But then, not waiting for the Bundesbank spokesman to comment on and explain the decision, they frantically sold French francs, Belgian francs, Danish kroner, pesetas and escudos. The French franc suffered most from the panic, immediately hitting its floor against the DM, despite massive amounts of Banque de France intervention. In his holiday home in France, Commission President Jacques Delors was rung with the bad news by one of his officials in Brussels. Delors was stunned. In an interview with *Der Spiegel* immediately before the Maastricht summit, he had proclaimed: 'I love the Germans without any qualification.' Now, he reverted to his persona of

23 Few details of the meeting have emerged, but it is generally believed that Tietmeyer did argue – and vote – in this direction. Charles Grant, of *The Economist* magazine, states quite baldly in his recent biography of Delors that Tietmeyer did indeed vote for a cut.

March 1983. His reaction was spat out angrily: 'Why have they declared war on us?'

## Eyeball-to-eyeball

On Friday morning, funds continued to flow out of France at a horrifying rate. Just before midday, Reuters news screens announced that the Banque de France had stopped intervening: the franc dipped clearly below its permitted limit against the DM, but did not plunge dramatically. The market was uncertain how to react. What was going on? What seems to have happened is that Balladur, Alphandéry, Trichet and de Larosière were themselves hesitating about how to react to the rebuff from the Bundesbank. The Banque de France could only go on intervening massively by calling on the 'sweetheart deal' and borrowing, borrowing, borrowing from the Bundesbank. Temporarily stopping the intervention could leave the franc in suspended animation for a short time, but if there were no announcements within an hour or two it would be pushed to its lowest permitted level against the DM. Intervention by the Bundesbank would then be marginal and obligatory – any German failure to intervene without limit would be a breach of the EMS rules. Trichet, apparently, still believed that 'Cher Hans' could pull the chestnuts out of the fire and swing the Bundesbank into a reconsideration of what Delors had seen as its act of war. According to the almost preternaturally well-informed Bauchard: *'Jean-Claude Trichet hésite. Il croit encore dans la vertu allemande et dans la fidélité des engagements pris. Il estime que les Allemands ne peuvent en rester là, qu'il faudra bientôt envisager une baisse concertée des taux français et allemands.'*[24] Tietmeyer could not come up with the goods, the ball would still be in the Bundesbank court: Schlesinger might invoke the 'Emminger letter' and, in effect, withdraw from the ERM by refusing to carry out obligatory intervention.

At all events, the French decided to risk an eyeball-to-eyeball confrontation with the Bundesbank. France would resume intervention and force the Bundesbank to do the same. Perhaps Trichet was right, and 'cher Hans' would somehow coax a rate cut out of his colleagues or Kohl would

---

24 'Jean-Claude Trichet hesitated. He still believed in the virtue of the Germans and trusted them to fulfil the commitments they had made. He reckoned the Germans would have to budge, and that an early concerted cut in French and German rates was on the cards.'

bully them into it. Perhaps Schlesinger would invoke the 'Emminger Letter' and turn off the tap of DM credits to France. In the first case, France would have won. In the second, the Bundesbank could be put in the dock, accused of breaking the ERM rules.

When intervention resumed, the Banque de France bought 150 billion francs (about $30 billion) in the single day of Friday – twice the amount poured into the foreign exchange market by the Bank of England on 'Black Wednesday'. The Bundesbank, for its part, fulfilled all its formal obligations to intervene at the margin. Elsewhere in the ERM, the Danish krone was at its lower limit. The peseta, which had been remarkably stable since the 13 May devaluation, had also been sucked into the ERM maelstrom, losing 3% in value in the week of 26–30 July. The Bank of Spain had been impressed by the rock-solid performance of the peseta during the suspension of intervention on 13 May and the stability of the currency during its six weeks of quasi-float. The bank, it seems, was quite prepared to see the peseta float. The Spanish government was alarmed by the squaring-up of France and the Bundesbank. If Kohl put the Franco-German axis above all else, there might be a risk, they thought, of an immediate Franco-German monetary union, extending to the rest of the 'hard core' but freezing Spain out. There had to be some way for the other countries to make their voices heard. If the result was a jointly decided generalized float, or an agreed German withdrawal from a surviving ERM, that would be better than either a Franco-German union or a collapse of the ERM in conditions of bitterness, confrontation and recrimination that might threaten the whole future of EMU. The Spanish government would have liked to request an emergency meeting of the Monetary Committee in Brussels the next day, Saturday, 31 July, but did not dare suggest 'Community' involvement in the private Franco-German squabble.

Ultimately Waigel was prevailed upon by the Bundesbank to request a meeting of the Monetary Committee. But first there was a last attempt at finding a bilateral, Franco-German solution. That evening, Schlesinger and Waigel flew to Paris to confront de Larosière and Alphandéry in person. But this was not the meeting planned for 25 June. The two Bavarians went to Paris in a position of technical and political strength. All Schlesinger's predictions and warnings about the ERM were now clearly seen, by almost everyone in Germany, at any rate, to have been justified. What would happen if the Bundesbank did a volte-face and cut interest rates? The credibility and the supposed independence of the Bundesbank would be irretrievably lost. The DM would slide against the 'safe haven' currencies outside the ERM. Speculators who had sold francs to take positions in these currencies would gain. The ERM would no longer have an anchor, unless the Bundesbank and the Banque de France somehow became a single authority managing a single currency – but that was ruled out by the combination of the German constitution and the Maastricht Treaty. Thus the continuation of the ERM in its present form meant that markets would decide interest rates and monetary policy in Europe. Having won once, what would there be to stop them coming back again and again? Surely the French would like such a situation even less than the Germans?

But the French were unmoved: the Bundesbank must either meet its ERM obligations or the DM must leave the system. The meeting broke up in acrimony.

## Joking apart

The next day, the eyes of the world were on the Borschette Building in Brussels. Throughout the morning, the cafés, bars and friteries of the Place Jourdan, the midtown, rather seedy square close to the immigrant quarter of the Chaussée de Wavre, were packed with pressmen and radio and TV crews. The crisis had been the lead item in every European newspaper, every news bulletin ever since Thursday lunchtime. Even the American media, normally enveloped in an ignorance of European monetary affairs that, it could reasonably be claimed, was truly blissful, were showing an eyelid-flicker of interest in the bust-up.

When the members of the Committee began arriving for the scheduled 2 pm meeting, they were not exactly tight-lipped and ashen-faced as if before a Neasden–Dollis Hill derby, but the bitterness of the Franco-Bundesbank row and the vastness of the issues to be debated certainly made them aware of the historical importance of their gathering. Probably never before had so much been at stake in a Monetary Committee meeting. Any final decision, it was clear, would have to be taken by finance ministers and governors. Yet the meeting of the Committee would be a vitally important preliminary, where the combatants – there was no other way to describe them – would feel out each other's strengths and weaknesses, attempt to attribute blame to others and build alliances to pursue their own objectives, everything cloaked as usual in the sick rhetoric of the 'common good.'.

It was clear from the outset that discussion would be dominated by the confrontation between the two countries that had been the founding fathers of the EMS. The Germans went in to bat first, with Gerd Haller, the State Secretary at the Finance Ministry, taking strike. Haller, an amiable, level-headed but tough character, rather different from the excitable Köhler, whom he had recently replaced, proposed a widening of the ERM bands to 6% for all members. (The idea had been floating around for some time: OECD Chief Economist Kumiharu Shigehara had been suggesting it since the previous autumn; its advocacy was attributed to the Bundesbank by Samuel Brittan in the *Financial Times* on 26 January 1993.)[25]

The French representatives, Arianne Obolensky[26] of the Treasury and Hervé Hannoun, flatly rejected the idea. Instead, they brazenly threw down the gauntlet to their main antagonists. The Bundesbank must respect its obligations under the ERM rules to the letter. On the Monday morning, it must announce to the markets that it was cutting its rates, that it would intervene *without any limit* to buy francs, and – most outrageous of all – that it would purchase those francs outright, taking them into its balance-sheet, rather than merely lending DM to the Banque de France via the VSTF. At this point, it appears, Trichet, as Chairman, attempted a résumé of the opposing positions. In describing the French demands, he referred to three requests. There was shocked surprise as, it seems, Tietmeyer immediately interrupted, in a tone best described as icily emotional. 'Haven't you forgotten a fourth demand?', he growled at Trichet. The Chairman looked perplexed, as did others around the table. Tietmeyer offered to explain, an offer that no one cared – or dared – to reject. 'The fourth demand, Chairman, is that Germany must immediately abandon its monetary sovereignty.'

Tietmeyer was right: what the French were asking for was that the Bundesbank should become a currency board of the Banque de France. If it had done what was asked, the whole backing of the DM money supply would be highly suspect French francs.

But the Bundesbank was not going to let the danger materialize. Perhaps Kohl had indeed threatened to change the Bundesbank Law if the Council did not give in and bale out the French. But everyone in the Bundesbank now knew the threat was a hollow one. Schlesinger had steered events, and Bundesbank policy, so skilfully that Kohl would never have been able to get

---

25 The Bundesbank confirmed, in its Annual Report for 1993 (issued in April 1994), that it had been advocating wider banks in the first half of 1993.

26 A relation of the Prince Obolensky who had scored 'that' try for England in 1936.

a change through the German parliament. Even the public admission that he might be contemplating such a thing would be political and electoral suicide. Kohl had been able to pull the wool over the eyes of someone – either the German people or the French *énarchie* – about the Maastricht Treaty. But there would be no way of finessing the implications of an all-out assault on the Bundesbank intended to assuage Mitterrand, Balladur and the *énarques*.

Tietmeyer must have been enraged by the stupidity of the naked French attack. If only the blithering idiots had done as he had told them and kept their mouths shut over the previous two months, then things might have turned out very differently. Now, faced with the insufferable arrogance of the French ultimatum, one delivered from a position of the utmost weakness, he could do nothing but slap them down hard. He would be lynched if he went back to Germany having agreed to deliver the Bundesbank, bound and humiliated, into the hands of the enemy.

The Portuguese chose to depict the irreconcilability of the French and German positions (by now, Waigel, if not Kohl, had obviously decided that there was politically no choice but to present a united front with the Bundesbank) in particularly stark terms. Taken to the logical conclusion, the opposing contentions implied that there must either be a generalized float or an immediate Franco-German monetary union. Haller, it seems, was shaken out of his habitual calm; he hoped, almost spitting out the words, that the remark about Franco-Germany monetary union was intended as a joke.

The rest of the afternoon was spent, it seems, in inconsequential sparring.[27] The terms of the stand-off were clear. No negotiation would be possible – at least, there could be no negotiation between the French and the Germans in front of the others. The inevitable decision to ask finance ministers and governors to convene the next day was taken. The formal meeting broke up. The members dispersed, although it was clear that the French and Germans would be meeting again in secret conclave that evening.

## Graveness and gravity

The next morning, radio news bulletins everywhere were dominated by speculation about the outcome of the Monetary Committee meeting and prospects for the gathering of ministers and governors – everywhere, that

27  At any rate, the published accounts have nothing much to say.

is, except in the country hosting the meetings. For in Belgium, monetary affairs were overshadowed by the shocking news that King Baudouin had died unexpectedly during the night while holidaying in Spain. Baudouin was a symbol of Belgium as a country – the only substantial symbol. He was a great man, and a good one. His constitutional role was important: his moral authority and the trust in which he was held by all parties and language groups had enabled him to prevent Belgium's recurrent political crises from becoming national crises. His devout Catholic faith and even more his exemplary Christian practice – his concern for the downtrodden and marginalized, prostitutes, drug addicts, immigrants and refugees – were beacons in the flat, bourgeois Belgian moral landscape. For many years, the Belgian political class had fretted about what might happen when Baudouin disappeared from the scene. He and his Spanish wife, Queen Fabiola, were childless, a heavy cross they bore with great fortitude. The heir presumptive, Baudouin's younger brother Albert, was not viewed with any great enthusiasm. A playboy in his youth, he appeared to have none of Baudouin's *sérieux*. Few people expected he would ever be able to play his brother's role successfully. The common assumption had been that Albert's eldest son, Philippe, might be trained up for that role instead. After all, Baudouin was still relatively young, and there was time enough . . .

Thus the King's sudden death was seen in Belgium as a national catastrophe. Fears for the cohesion of the country were immediately aroused. The atmosphere of shock and apprehension impinged in two ways on the monetary melodrama being played out in the Borschette Centre. First, there was the practical problem that the Prime Minister was flying to Spain to accompany the King's body on its journey back to Belgium. An emergency Cabinet meeting was set for 8 o'clock on Sunday evening, the expected time of Dehaene's return, to discuss the question of whether or not Albert should be requested to pass his claim to the throne over to his son. As a result, no definite results could be expected until late at night, since the Belgian monetary emissaries, like many of the rest, would almost certainly need to consult their head of government and perhaps the whole Cabinet before far-reaching decisions on the effective abandonment of the ERM could be taken. Second, the fear of accentuated tension between Flemings and Walloons was to weigh on the Belgian negotiators, ever conscious of the divisive connotations of certain monetary alliances. The importance of this factor was soon to be seen.

The meeting of ministers and governors, scheduled for Sunday afternoon, was preceded by a further session of the Monetary Committee. The bilaterals of Saturday night must have borne fruit, for Trichet was, according to the published accounts, able to put on the table a scheme, apparently proposed by the French and accepted by the Germans, that the DM would temporarily leave the ERM, until Germany's post-reunification problems had worked themselves through. This scheme, too, had been canvassed by the commentators and analysts who were required by TV and radio schedules to say something new every thirty minutes. Peter Jay, BBC Television's economics editor, memorably described the idea as 'the solar system without the Sun'. But the economists who wrote 'La Tragédie du Franc Fort' would not call themselves 'Galilée' just by chance. For the *énarques*, Balladur in the lead, the Sun revolved around the Earth. Only heretics would assert the contrary. The solar system without the Sun was a perfectly imaginable phenomenon. The solar system without the Earth – the French franc – was of course a contradiction of the laws of economic physics. This was something of which the French had long ago managed to convince themselves. It was to be a considerable shock to them to discover how many heretics there were in Church of the ERM.

Trichet was graciously disposed to accept that the Dutch guilder might sink off into the ulterior darkness with the DM. But, as soon as the compromise plan was made known to the other countries, the Luxembourgers announced that if the Dutch followed the Germans, then so too would they. If that meant breaking their link with the Belgian franc, so be it. They had almost done it in 1982, when the Belgian franc last devalued, and now for several months Luxembourg officials had been making snide remarks about the deficiencies of Belgium's economy, its debt problems and its over-generous social security and the abuses it generated. In return, the Belgians had ceaselessly complained about the tax revenues they lost through the notorious 'Belgian dentists' (not to mention Belgian lawyers, architects, businessmen, shopkeepers, car mechanics, train drivers, arms traders, drug dealers and – perhaps above all – politicians) who kept their financial assets in low-tax, no-questions-asked Luxembourg. After 1982, laws had been passed in Luxembourg to ensure that the banks there maintained matched positions in Belgian and Luxembourg francs and would not risk being hurt by a sudden break-up of the currency union. The Luxembourg Monetary Institute was also being prepared as a fully-fledged central bank. Why on earth was one needed within the Belgo-Luxembourg monetary union? It was clear that some influential people in Luxembourg were just waiting for an excuse to change horses (not to mention metaphors) in midstream and hitch themselves to a likelier winner.

Memories of the war meant that the older generation could not accept a peg to the DM; but the Dutch guilder was available as a surrogate DM and had the advantage of being the currency of the third member, along with Belgium and Luxembourg, of the Benelux economic union. And just as Luxembourg officials had recently been increasingly acerbic about Belgium, they had become correspondingly smarmy in the company of their Dutch counterparts.

A breach of the union with Luxembourg would cause problems for Belgium. The Luxembourgers claimed that the much-vaunted Belgian balance-of-payments surplus – in fact the surplus of the BLEU, the Belgo-Luxembourg Economic Union, was attributable to them, via the activities of the disproportionately large financial sector sited in the Grand Duchy, and that in consequence the bulk of the BLEU's foreign exchange reserves belonged to them. If a separate Belgian balance of payments had to be calculated, it would look much less flattering. And if Belgians continued to put their savings into Luxembourg, they would constitute potentially volatile Euro-BEF deposits.

So Belgium clearly had an incentive to avoid a split with Luxembourg. It had an even stronger incentive not to be cut out of an arrangement between Germany, the Netherlands and Luxembourg. Since the BEF had informally pegged to the DM in 1990, the '*franc belge fort*' had been proclaimed as the country's ticket to the supposed Promised Land of EMU, in which Belgian burghers would no longer need to worry about the venality of their ever-revolving, never-evolving governments and in which German taxpayers, rather than Belgians, would shoulder the burden of the country's mountainous debt. But while Walloons were prepared to swallow a DM peg if it was the only way to get to an EMU, they would have choked on Belgium's explicitly joining a DM-zone with France left out.

What was the alternative for Belgium? It was spelled out, perhaps as a piece of deliberate mischief-making, by the Spaniards: Belgium could become part of, in effect, a Latin Monetary Union with France, Spain, Portugal and perhaps an Italy tempted back if the nasty Germans were out of the way. At the very mention of the words 'Latin Monetary Union', the Belgian representatives, it seems, exploded. The Flemish 60 per cent of the country would never accept what might look like a return to the union of 1865–1926, a period in which French-speakers still enjoyed – and exploited – a hegemonic position.

The stone heaved into the millpond by the Spanish created ripples throughout the meeting. The Belgians could not be happy about the prospect of leaving the ERM and following the Germans, Dutch and Luxembourgers (and, it soon became apparent, the Danes, whose astronomical credentials were historically more respectable). But they would be even more unhappy about remaining with the rump. Whether or not there were fault lines in the ERM, the Belgians knew perfectly well that their land remained perched uncomfortably where it had been for a millennium and a half: slap-bang on the fault line between Germanic Europe and Latin Europe. They had always been ardently federalist. If they had been neither dam nor sire of the EMS (Giscard and Schmidt could argue between themselves about which of them was which) they had been its most attentive midwife. They did not want to have to choose between France and Germany. They reluctantly made it clear that if they were forced into a choice, they would follow their northern and eastern neighbours, continuing the recent trend of Belgian history. But they would explore every avenue that could help them avoid the necessity of making that choice.

There was, of course, every reason for the Spanish to have put the cat among the pigeons. They knew, and were a few weeks later to reveal, that Solchaga and his kitchen Cabinet, so recently the darlings of the enthusiastic financial markets, had been presiding over and camouflaging a massive deterioration in Spain's public finances, one that would almost certainly rule Spain out of an EMU in 1997. In the surreal atmosphere created by Maastricht, the Spanish authorities now decided that the obscure object of desire should no longer be 'convergence' in the European context but, rather, the 'competitiveness' of the Spanish economy. The implications of this switch – which, almost inevitably, was subsequently botched – will be looked at later. What is important for now is that Spain had no interest, or so its leaders thought, in allowing a 'hard core' to go on to monetary union with Spain left out. Suggesting a Latin Monetary Union was no more than a piece of calculated impudence. The real aim was undoubtedly that of keeping 'monetary Europe' together in a formal sense – the 'all in the same boat' sense – while making sure that no one was in a position to meet the Maastricht criteria for 1997. If the ERM were dissolved, then everyone would by definition fail the Maastricht test of trouble-free membership of the ERM band in the two years before a decision on Stage Three. Even a widening of the bands would, the Spanish must have thought, create the same effect, since the treaty spoke of two years' membership of the 'normal' bands: everyone knew when the treaty was agreed that 'normal' meant 'narrow' (+/−2.25%) bands.

At this stage, the French were seeing their solar system reduced to one in

329

which the French franc's satellites, no doubt in very irregular orbit, would number just the peseta, the escudo and perhaps the Irish pound. The rival system would see the guilder, the Belgo-Luxembourg franc and the krone clustered around the DM. If that happened, the weekend's meetings would have recreated the German-dominated 'snake' that in 1978 Giscard had wanted to destroy through the creation of the EMS. Anything, from a French point of view, would be preferable to that, even a return to formal floating. At least in a formal float, or quasi-float, the French franc would have some chance of remaining within hailing distance of the DM and France might hope to continue – or return to – exerting some behind-the-scenes influence on German policy.[28]

Thus by the time the Monetary Committee meeting came to an end, it was clear that there was no way to reconcile the conflicting objectives of the various countries within the old ERM. A much greater degree of formal exchange-rate flexibility was the only result that could possibly emerge from the meeting of ministers and governors.

## Laying down the law

What would that mean for the conduct of monetary policies? Tietmeyer was a worried man. Suppose that ERM countries – Spain perhaps, or Portugal, even Belgium, most of all France – might see the evident breakdown of a supposedly cooperative approach to monetary policy as a reason to move to a more domestically oriented policy framework, à l'anglaise. They might cut their interest rates dramatically, taking them far below German rates; their currencies would, initially at least, depreciate against the DM. There would be all sorts of dangers in that from Tietmeyer's point of view. How would Schlesinger react? Would he advise the Bundesbank Council to reduce German interest rates in parallel? Certainly not. Such a cut would imply that Germany was being forced to

---

28 Trichet might even claim that this had been his aim from the outset: that the demands on the Bundesbank, then the suggestion of a DM withdrawal from the system, were merely feints, whose real intention was to bring about a change in the system in which speculators could be outwitted. However, the evidence suggests that Trichet had simply misunderstood the nature of the constraints on 'Cher Hans' and had badly misread the positions of Germany and the other countries. Indeed, Trichet was widely blamed within France for what many saw as a national humiliation. These reproaches led some members of the French Establishment to try to block his appointment as Governor of the Banque de France a few weeks later when de Larosière left to fill the gap in the French domination of international organizations created by the enforced exit of Attali from the marble halls of the EBRD.

follow the monetary policies of others, something Schlesinger would never accept.[29] It would also imply validating the bets taken out by the markets, again something Schlesinger was not prepared to do. So the DM would be in a dangerously over-appreciated position. Tietmeyer could not forget that just a few weeks earlier the markets had been coming to regard the DM as the most overvalued of all the world's major currencies. There had since been a sharp shift in psychology as a result of the ERM crisis and the reassertion of Germany's leadership (or hegemonic) role. That changed psychology might support the DM for a few more weeks. But surely any sharp DM appreciation as a result of introducing more flexibility into intra-European exchange-rate relations could not be sustainable for long. Tietmeyer might find himself taking up his post as President of the Bundesbank in two months' time and being confronted with something that looked nastily like a DM crisis. According to Bundesbank insiders, this was the argument that Tietmeyer had used, in the Bundesbank Council meeting of 29 July, for a cut in the discount rate big enough to defuse the ERM tensions.

Tietmeyer's worries, however, clearly went deeper than this. He had been the person entrusted with ensuring the success of Kohl's European monetary union ambitions. The collapse of the ERM could jeopardize those ambitions. It was up to Tietmeyer to find a way of limiting the damage. He also had to worry not just about how to rescue EMU but also about how to safeguard the role of the Bundesbank and any future ECB. His Chile speech in March had already shown, between the lines, how afraid he was of the inflation-targeting approach adopted by Britain. If the other ERM countries now started running their monetary policies in the interests of their own, real-world economies rather than in the pursuit of a vision of EMU, some of them, too, might start targeting inflation, the surest route to increased accountability of the monetary authorities and to reduced political power for independent central banks.[30]

Tietmeyer thus issued a solemn warning to the other ERM members:

---

29 The situation would be different from one in which the other currencies devalued within the ERM. Then – as Schlesinger had made clear in September 1992 – the Bundesbank would be prepared to cut rates, allowing the others to follow.

30 One should recall here the qualification that when there is a state of Stackelberg warfare between an independent central bank and the government that produces a threat of debt repudiation via inflation, not even an explicit inflation target is enough to restrain an unaccountable central bank. In such circumstances – now faced by Sweden and Italy – only the restoration of government control over monetary policy can allow the government to make the political choices necessary to avoid even more serious damage to the economy.

do not think you can use the dissolution of the ERM, the widening of the bands or whatever other loosening of the ERM constraints comes out of the meeting of ministers and governors; in particular, do not dare to implement sharp cuts in interest rates to levels below those prevailing before the crisis blew up.

No one, it seems, argued with Tietmeyer, who was clearly casting himself as monetary dictator of Europe. This was a role to which Schlesinger had never aspired: if countries such as France, which did not fit naturally into a DM-zone on economic grounds,[31] nonetheless chose to peg to the DM, that was their business. Schlesinger would not tell them what to do with their interest rates – as long as they did not pretend that their interest rates determined German ones. Tietmeyer, in contrast, had always been much more prescriptive in his approach to other countries. The ERM constraint, whatever its form, was for him a fixed point of reference. Other countries' interest-rate policies must be tailored to meet that constraint. But he knew that he could not impose his will on everyone else simply through the force of his own personality. It seems clear that he must have offered, either on 1 August or later, some assurance that once he had taken over from Schlesinger he would steer Bundesbank policy in a way that took account of the needs of other countries.[32] Specifically, the Bundesbank would have to assuage France, since the aspirants to DM-zone status would do what they were told in any case, Ireland was now fairly clearly part of a sterling bloc, and Spain and Portugal had interest rates far above German levels.

It was thus that Tietmeyer combined his unavoidable role as 'the hard man of the meeting', slapping down the open, unacceptable demands of the French, with the maintenance of his reputation as 'the representative of the Banque de France in the Bundesbank Council'. Tietmeyer was monarch of all he surveyed, but his dictatorship could not be absolute: his vassals, regional commissars such as Trichet, would do what he told them but might themselves be vulnerable to revolt if the dictates from the top made life unbearably harsh for their own proles ('constituencies' would obviously be an inappropriate word). Tietmeyer had no interest in seeing the direction of French economic policy fall into the hands of someone like

31 As made clear by Issing, 'economic grounds' for membership of a DM-zone would be stronger if the countries concerned could also be regarded as having strong 'cultural' or historical affinities with Germany and were not likely to contest its monetary leadership role.
32 Bauchard speaks of an '*assez vague promesse*' given by Tietmeyer to the French.

Chirac or Séguin: they might not accept his rule, but instead run policy with French interests to the fore.

Once Tietmeyer had laid down the law on 1 August, and his fellow members and titular equals in the Monetary Committee had, apparently, signalled cowed assent by their silence, there was little left for the ministers and governors except to decide the precise clothing, with its political overtones, of what looked like the effective end of the ERM as a formal constraint on monetary policy.

## Fat man on a Eurobicycle

The meeting of ministers and governors must have begun in an atmosphere in which everyone seemed resigned to – and some even enthusiastic about – the prospect of some form of formal float. Of all the countries involved, only the two that had formal 'opt-outs' from Stage Three – Denmark and the United Kingdom – were reluctant to share this consensus. More accurately, Denmark and Kenneth Clarke were reluctant to share it. Clarke's role turned out to be an important one, but appears to have reflected his personal prejudices rather than a clear domestic consensus about Britain's interests.

The Danish case was different. The country had suffered ten years of macroeconomic instability, including the six most recent years of recession and rising unemployment, as a result of fixed exchange rates. Yet the great men of Copenhagen, proving that they could outdo Nelson when it came to turning a blind eye – to experience, not orders, in this case – remained fixated upon the idea that they must not run their own monetary policy in Danish interests. They chose not to look at New Zealand, a country just as small and now considerably more open than Denmark, which has instituted an inflation-targeting framework with great success, necessitating a clear renunciation of fixed exchange rates.

But it was not clear that Danish public opinion, always fearful of German domination, would tolerate a link between the krone and the DM similar to that between the guilder and the DM – even if the Danish representatives in the Monetary Committee had been willing to countenance one if the DM left the ERM. In any case, it was quite clear that the French would not tolerate any such pegging of the krone to the DM. So the Danish political class needed the retention of at least the formal shell of the ERM as an excuse for a continued rejection of monetary policy independence.

It is thus not surprising that, according to the press reports, the Dane

Henning Christophersen, representing the Commission at the meeting,[33] argued strongly against the complete dissolution of the ERM. More surprisingly, to most participants, it was Kenneth Clarke who rushed to support Christophersen. It seems that the British Chancellor had up to that point taken no active part in the meeting. Press reports portray him as having spent the plane journey to Brussels with the newly installed Governor of the Bank of England, Eddie George, discussing really weighty matters – the likely inadequacy of the catering arrangements for the meeting ahead of them. No doubt this small-talk avoided any awkwardness about the ERM between the two men. George had recently publicly rediscovered a strong dislike for the mechanism, while in Clarke's case political exigency had drawn only the flimsiest veil over a panting lust for membership.

Once in the Borschette, Clarke is believed to have said nothing in the first, short session of the meeting of ministers and governors. During the subsequent long hours of waiting in the ante-chamber and delegation rooms while the Belgian Cabinet was assembling to decide the succession to King Baudouin, other finance ministers huddled in little groups, intriguing amongst themselves, or phoned their capitals, intriguing with – or against – their governments. Clarke apparently had no need of argument or advice. He was a man so sure that the thrust of everything Brussels wanted to do was right that he did not even bother to read the Maastricht Treaty before forcing it down the throats of gagging MPs (and he was subsequently to acquiesce in the retrospective pardoning of Italian CAP illegality in order not to spare the British people the burden of coughing up yet more money for the Brussels bureaucrats to waste on their behalf).

Clarke clearly knew in advance what he was going to do. After Christophersen had made his plea, the British Minister swung the meeting by asking those who thought generalized floating the best solution to declare themselves. No one did. The Spanish, who really did want a float, were afraid of being openly identified as Euro-wreckers, preferring instead to play the role of *agents provocateurs*. Schlesinger and Waigel, for their part, knew that they could not overplay their hand in provoking Kohl too far. Diplomats say that Kohl was constantly phoning Waigel in the Borschette Centre, bellowing that a generalized float must be avoided 'at all costs'. All

33 Delors, to his frustration, was still sciatica-bound in Burgundy. Apparently, he was still fiercely angry with the nation that he had previously 'loved without any reservation': interviewed on French television while the meeting was going on, he demanded that Germany should leave the ERM, since it was the country that had caused all the problems.

the evidence points to Waigel's being prepared to flout his Chancellor's wishes, but only as party to consensus, not as someone who could be pointed to as the leading proponent of a float. Schlesinger would get what he most wanted – the effective freeing of the Bundesbank from the obligations of the ERM – with drastically widened bands. The formal dissolution of the system would be nice, but he, too, could not be the one to suggest it: everyone would then claim that the Bundesbank's tactics over recent weeks had been deliberately aimed at destroying the ERM and, with it, EMU.

Another factor was also coming into play. Tokyo foreign exchange markets would open at 2 am Brussels time, on Monday morning. It was imperative that some decision, any decision, came out of the Borschette before the markets took the decision themselves. The Bundesbank was not formally obliged by the rules of the ERM to intervene to support the franc in Tokyo. In the present circumstances, the sweetheart deal replaced by a vicious tiff, it clearly would not do so voluntarily. If the franc and other currencies fell sharply in Tokyo, say to 3.50 or beyond against the DM, as it might well do if the markets interpreted the absence of a decision as evidence of unresolvable conflict, commercial banks could present huge amounts of francs at the Bundesbank and the Banque de France at 9 am the next morning and demand DM at 3.4305, the formal ERM limit. That would produce chaos and renewed conflict between France and the Bundesbank.

## . . . And the band played on

At all events, after the interventions of Christophersen and Clarke, it seemed to be agreed that some formal, but not practically binding, limits on the movements of currencies would have to be maintained. Ten per cent seemed a nice round number for new, widened bands – to apply to all ERM members. But dealers, economists and analysts had made the journey into their City dealing-rooms at dead of night. As rumours of the 10% bank leaked out of the Borschette, analysts predicted that those bands would be blown apart within minutes – only quasi-floating would restore any sort of calm.

Amazingly, the Borschette Centre does not possess any financial news screens, but presumably the watchers in the central banks, Treasuries and the Commission were constantly faxing or phoning the news both from the Tokyo market – which had now opened, the franc dropping to 3.47 against

335

the DM – and the London analysts. At any rate, within minutes of those first reported reactions, the meeting of the ministers and governors was over and a communiqué was issued: the ERM, bands would be 'temporarily' widened to +/-15%, and the situation would be reviewed by the end of the year; the central rates of the participating currencies would remain unchanged. The commitment of all the Community countries to the Maastricht convergence criteria was reaffirmed.

A rash of press conferences broke out. Naturally, nothing was said at any of them of the rows, plots, subterfuges and confusions that had taken place over the previous two days. Instead, the line put together in the last few minutes of the meeting in conditions of near panic, when no other solution could find agreement, was peddled to a credulous world. Speculative turbulence, it was claimed, had been creating problems for the harmonious working of the ERM. The ministers and governors had decided, as the outcome of a deep and friendly process of cooperation, to reduce the role of speculation by temporarily widening the bands, with the effect of reintroducing two-way risk (a concept of which few of the ministers had heard half an hour earlier) into the system. In short, the heroic ministers had outwitted the malevolent markets.

As we shall see below, the widening of the bands did indeed reintroduce two-way risk, and many market operators did not make the killing they had anticipated. But the ministers' line of reasoning raised some awkward questions (not, unfortunately, in the press conferences, where the journalists appeared as exhausted as the ministers and officials). Most obviously, did not the decision both vindicate Major's assertion, however self-contradictory, that there had been fault lines in the ERM and show the reports of the Monetary Committee and the Governors' Committee to have been nothing more than codswallop? If the decision sealed the fault lines, why were Britain and Italy not rejoining the system? If wide bands were needed to avoid disturbances that were merely speculative in nature and unrelated to 'fundamentals', how could the widening be only temporary? Where did the decision leave the ERM 'normal bands' criterion for Stage Three of EMU? It would, of course, have been impossible for ministers to answer any of these questions convincingly, and it is therefore all the more disappointing that none of them were put.

The faces of the main protagonists may have reflected the course of the meeting more truly than their words. Alphandéry looked dazed. It seems that throughout the frequent breaks in the session over the previous ten hours, while the likes of the shirt-sleeved Clarke contentedly tore at one

French sandwich after another, helping them down with the occasional glass of red wine and adding to the general fug by puffing a large cigar, the French Minister had stood as if with an albatross round his neck, perhaps pondering the terrible mistake that had sparked the whole crisis.[34]

The demeanour of the three German participants in the press conference was revealing (apparently it had not changed throughout the meetings). Tietmeyer was grim-faced, his massive brow furrowed. Waigel was cheerful, chortling and apparently unconcerned. Schlesinger was transfigured. As he moved between the pressmen to the podium he seemed to float – appositely in the circumstances – rather than walk; a beatific smile played on his lips; his grandfatherly features were suffused with a warm glow, a radiance almost.

Tietmeyer's grim mood was easy to understand. His strategy had failed, and Kohl could not be pleased with him. To limit the damage he had issued his solemn warning to the other countries, but would that be enough to keep them in line? At the very best, he would move into Schlesinger's seat in October with his credit already mortgaged: would he be able to swing the Council into granting him the interest-rate reductions he must have promised to the French and the rest? Waigel's cheery, relaxed mien also required little explanation. He had been prepared to face down the Chancellor. The 15% bands had provided a face-saving formula for some of the other countries; Waigel was quite happy to accept it, but he had not needed it. He knew he could bask in glory with Schlesinger in the German press reaction to the outcome.[35] He was on the side of the angels (and literally at the side of someone who at this moment looked very much like an Archangel, even without the benefit of harp and wings). Being able to give Kohl one in the eye, with no risk, at least in the short term, that the bullying Chancellor could hit back, was enough to bring a smile to the lips of any minister who had the dubious pleasure of serving under the overbearing 'Bismarck in a cardigan'.

As for Schlesinger, this was his moment of justification, the moment he knew that he could retire having rid the Bundesbank of the albatross so

34 The next day, after the meeting of French and German finance ministers postponed from 25 June as a result of '*la gaffe*', Alphandéry was attempting a brave face. The effect of his words, however, was just as comical as his efforts at damage-limitation on that earlier occasion. 'I want,' he said, 'to lay to rest all these rumours about the so-called deterioration in Franco-German relations. I can testify that during this period of tension on the markets, the Franco-German couple once again proved its solidity.'

35 The mood was, as so often, best captured by the mass-circulation *Bild*, which exulted in the outcome in a front-page lead on 3 August headlined 'Hurra, die Mark bleibt'.

disgracefully and disloyally hung around its neck by Schmidt. Schlesinger was the man most widely credited with – or blamed for – the monetary policy insurgency in 1981 that contributed to Schmidt's own political demise in 1982. Now, having got rid of Frankenstein eleven years ago, Schlesinger could feel that he had also destroyed Frankenstein's Monster – the ERM. He had long ago grasped the key strategic fact that the ERM and the ERM anchor could not survive simultaneously. It was the ERM, not the Bundesbank's leadership role, that had to go. He had judged his consequent tactics to perfection, preserving as much as possible of his own freedom of manoeuvre under the twin constraints of the German recession and Kohl's demonic attachment to the franc. His understanding and orchestration of German public opinion was superb – and unsurprising, since he seemed to be closer to public opinion than any other German actor. And he had seized on every mistake, every sign of weakness from his opponents. He had won the day. But, switching Gothic horror metaphors, had he driven a stake through the heart of the system, or would the monster rise again from its coffin when dusk next fell?

# PART THREE

# 13

# False Dawn?

## Travelling hopefully

A few days after the widening of the ERM bands, there took place a
meeting of the EC Commission whose circumstances were extraordinary in
every sense of the word. It was almost unheard-of for Commissioners to be
summoned by their President to assemble in Brussels in August. At one
point, it looked as though a quorum would not be reached. Delors himself
was prepared not only to dispense with the boring inconvenience of
holidays but to suffer a long car journey while in severe pain from sciatica.
But several of his colleagues took a different view, displaying extreme
reluctance to abandon the beaches or the mountains. Perhaps they were
taking Christophersen at his word. The previous Friday, as the storm raged
in financial markets, the laid-back Dane had informed the world that there
was no crisis and that 'everyone can go to the beach'. If there had been no
crisis, then what on earth was the point of coming to Brussels now and
pretending there was anything the Commission could do? The two German
Commissioners had additional reason to ignore the summons from Delors.
The choleric Frenchman had publicly put the blame for the crisis on
Germany, the country he had professed to love without qualification. Peter
Schmidhuber and Martin Bangemann could not forget – they had never
shown any sign of trying to forget – that they were German first and
'European' second.

In the end, the pressure exerted by 'Delors's Exocet', his *chef de cabinet*,
Pascal Lamy,[1] was enough to bring the required number of Commissioners, but not the two Germans, to Brussels. The meeting was supposed
to deliberate on how the Commission should react to the ERM's collapse.
According to diplomats, Delors was prepared to declare that with the

---

1 Lamy has a fearsome reputation as an enforcer. A few months before, he had failed to be elected
  as a Socialist MP in France. A few months later he was sent by the government to Paris as the
  number two in the disgraced Socialist-run bank, Crédit Lyonnais. An important part of his job in
  Paris is undoubtedly that of using his knowledge of the pressure points in the Commission to
  help ensure that institution's approval for a state bail-out of Crédit Lyonnais.

mechanism destroyed by German selfishness, other countries should immediately cut interest rates. The result would be to create a new, informal bloc clustered around France. But, the sources say, he was held back by Christophersen.

The part played by Christophersen is easy enough to understand. It was he who, along with Clarke, had put the case for retaining the ERM shell. Denmark, with its fanatical attachment to the concept of fixed exchange rates, would be put in a very difficult position if countries did what Delors was bursting to say they should. Delors is an angry man, and for a few days at the beginning of August his anger with the Germans was apparently fierce enough for him to favour the adoption by France and others of the *politique à l'anglaise* he had previously denounced as anti-communautaire.

The Commission meeting itself was a damp squib. Delors's anger subsided and he acquiesced in the production of a communiqué, drafted by Christophersen's aides, of the utmost banality. Even if it had not been issued in the holiday month of August it would not have caused an eyelid to flicker. The Commission was out of the ERM game, and over the next two years was to concentrate instead on fudging the so-called 'convergence criteria' for entry into EMU. Tietmeyer was the man who counted, and he had expressed his views with unmistakable menace.[2]

The other Continental central banks did as they were told.[3] In the first few weeks following the collapse of the old ERM, there were significant but not dramatic movements in exchange rates. The French franc, for instance, depreciated in the early autumn to as low as 3.55 to the DM, a fall of more than 5% from its ERM central rate. For the Danish krone, the corresponding fall was 7% – a large amount for a small economy such as Denmark's – and for the Belgian franc 5.5%. What is important, however, is that none of the central banks concerned attempted a *politique à l'anglaise* of cutting interest rates below German levels. Their most important reason for not doing so was that they did not want to cross Tietmeyer. But there were other reasons, too. The loss of face involved in accepting the rationality of independent national monetary policies, after all the effort

2 Tietmeyer was to go public on his warning in a speech made shortly after taking over from Schlesinger.
3 A year later Tietmeyer would be able to look back with undisguised and unabashed satisfaction at the results of his diktat, saying that: 'so far the greater room for manoeuvre in monetary policy has not been abused by any ERM country for an expansionary monetary policy. In order to avoid depreciation against the D-Mark, which is still the monetary anchor of the system, the monetary authorities for the currencies participating in the system have continued to gear their policies largely to that of the Bundesbank.'

expended on trying to keep the ERM together, would have been hard for politicians, bureaucrats and central bankers to bear. Some of them may also have believed the anti-economic imprecations ritually hurled at anyone engaging in so-called 'competitive devaluations'. One or two may even have believed the neo-functionalist fallacy that monetary 'progress' was required to prevent back-sliding on the Single Market. All of them were determined that 'speculators' should not profit: immediate reductions in interest rates, to the more sensible levels prevailing in Britain and the United States, were to be denied because the authorities had had their noses put out of joint. Thus the Continental monetary 'Masters of the World' were briefly united by a detestation of financial markets and their *lèse-majesté*. But it did not take long for the scheming, sniping and back-stabbing to resume.

The cross-currents produced in Belgium are in some ways the most intriguing, for they shed the greatest light on the development of European monetary politics in the weeks and months after the collapse. Within days of the band-widening, 'senior official sources' in Luxembourg were being cited as predicting, or advocating, that Belgium would quickly seek an arrangement for the Belgian franc similar to that obtained by the Dutch authorities for the guilder. In other words, a mini-'snake' would be re-created, involving the DM, the guilder, and the Belgian and Luxembourg francs. Such an arrangement was politically impossible. It would amount to a retraction of the desperate compromise agreed by the ministers and governors in the early hours of 2 August. It would leave France on the outside looking in. While it is quite likely Schlesinger would have welcomed such an arrangement, Tietmeyer would have been horrified. More important, the French would have felt betrayed by the scheme and Kohl would quite simply have vetoed it. With no possibility of invoking market-pressure threats to the Bundesbank's money-market control, Schlesinger would be unable to contest such a veto. So why was the idea floated? The most appealing explanation is that, once floated, its non-implementation would be taken by the financial markets as a *Bundesbank* rebuff to Belgium, an indication that the Belgian franc was *not* under Frankfurt's wing. That, in turn, might create pressures on the Belgian franc strong enough to force a devaluation, thus providing the hoped-for pretext for the Luxembourg franc to break its link with the Belgian franc and throw in its lot instead with the DM or its more psychologically acceptable surrogate, the guilder.

Sure enough, the Belgian franc did weaken significantly soon after the band-widening, falling by 5.5% against its ERM central rate. In mid-

August, a group of fourteen eminent Belgian – indeed Flemish – economists published the 'Louvain Manifesto' calling for the abandonment of the DM link and the establishment of an independent, national monetary policy. But Tietmeyer immediately denounced the 'lions of Louvain' as he contemptuously called them. And the Belgian authorities obeyed the instruction Tietmeyer had given them and everyone else on 31 July. Far from attempting to cut interest rates *below* German levels, the Belgian National Bank actually *raised* rates to 'defend' the currency.

The response of markets was initially fear that an irrational monetary policy would weaken the economy, add to the costs of servicing the vast public debt and perhaps even force an eventual repudiation of debt. For once, markets and *énarques* were on the same wavelength. At this time, Trichet himself was in a nervous limbo, his expected translation to the Banque de France contested by certain politicians who rightly saw the events of late July as a defeat for France and blamed him for it, not least after the *Financial Times*, in mid-August, reported the sharp rebuff he had received from Tietmeyer. While Trichet was keeping his head below the parapet, French Treasury and Banque de France officials commented in private that the Belgian policy was 'suicidal'. They knew full well that it would be economically and politically dangerous for them to do the same thing, particularly with the 'sweetheart deal' no longer operative.

But the Belgian government feared that if they tried to follow a 'British' policy they would be signalling they no longer considered themselves part of a DM-zone. The market perception that Belgium was under the wing of the Bundesbank and that its debt was ultimately guaranteed by Germany would change. In *those* circumstances, markets might consider the debt situation unsustainable and the Belgian franc might be driven down as much as the lira had been, inflicting losses on the bond-holding bourgeoisie whose interests all Belgian governments of the past decade have had so close to their hearts. Those governments preferred – and the current government still prefers – to make Belgium '*le paradis du rentier mais l'enfer de l'entrepreneur*', heaven for the rentier, hell for the entrepreneur. To pursue this policy, so destructive of the health of the Belgian economy and of Belgian society, something had to be done to stabilize the Belgian franc. There seemed only two options available. One, favoured it seems by the central bank Governor, Alfons Verplaetse, was to tie Belgium monetarily ever closer to Germany. The other, much more palatable to French-speaking opinion, was to try to recreate a functioning ERM, but one with more account taken of the needs of 'satellite' countries.

It was in pursuing this second option that a group of civil servants and academics gathered around the Finance Minister, Philippe Maystadt (a French-speaker), came up with a plan that appears to have had much in common with the ill-fated Commission proposal of late 1990. The plan foresaw a key role for the European Monetary Institute (EMI) that was due to come into existence on 1 January 1994, amid much debate about its function. Maystadt was president of the Ecofin in the second half of 1993. He was keen to 'make a success' out of the Belgian presidency by securing agreement on a beefy role for Maastricht's first-born child.

What became of the scheme is still rather murky. One source close to Maystadt maintains that when informal soundings were made of the Bundesbank, the response was 'warmer than usual'. Schlesinger was still Bundesbank president at the time. He would certainly have dismissed any such scheme out of hand.[4] More likely, the Belgians will have approached the man due to succeed him at the beginning of October, a man thought to be facing up to the consequences of Schlesinger's triumph with some apprehension. Yet that man, Tietmeyer, had previously been scathing about proposals for a 'symmetrical' solution to the ERM's problems. He may simply have been stringing the Belgians along, anxious to steer them away either from abandoning their *de facto* DM link (as urged in the Louvain Manifesto) or from asking the Bundesbank for a bilateral arrangement as hinted at from Luxembourg. The other possibility, more intriguing, is that Tietmeyer may have seen the scheme as a way of starting out down the road to a tighter ERM, one dominated by the Bundesbank but taking the needs of others, notably France, into account.

Thus the Belgian source also insists that it was the Italians, not the Bundesbank, who scuppered the scheme. If this is true, it is revealing about Maystadt's attitudes as well as Italy's. Italy had long been the sole open supporter, among the Community's member states, of an explicitly symmetrical operation of the ERM. If, in the early autumn of 1993, it turned down just such a proposal, it must have been because the debt problems it faced would have made *any* form of exchange-rate commitment untenable. Being bounced out of the old, asymmetric ERM was a bad enough blow to Italian Euro-aspirations, but the big bad Bundesbank could be blamed. To enter into a new ERM sculpted along the lines the Italians themselves had always found most alluring, and then fail to measure up to

4 The German Finance Ministry had apparently been thinking about a similar scheme in the early months of 1993, but Schlesinger, it seems, had made his opposition clear.

its requirements, would be much worse: better to carp about the ERM from the sidelines. And for Maystadt to require Italian as well as Bundesbank approval for his scheme betrayed his uneasiness about the 'hard-core' approach to a monetary union that was bound to be German-dominated and that leading Flemish governmental and central bank personalities found only too attractive.

Whatever the real inside story of the Maystadt plan, nothing came of it. By October, Tietmeyer, now enthroned as Bundesbank President, started making a series of speeches downplaying the role of the EMI and pouring scorn on 'schemes coming out of Brussels'. Now when 'Brussels' is used as a pejorative term, its reference is almost invariably (outside institutional dining-halls) the Commission. Yet there is no evidence that the Commission was doing anything other than lie very low on the ERM in the autumn of 1993, reflecting internal divisions.

In all likelihood, Tietmeyer's typically dark and allusive animadversions were directed to the capital of Belgium as well as to 'the capital of Europe'. By this time, the Belgian franc had recovered much of the bright-eyed bloom of the consumptive as the feared collapse of the country into two linguistic halves failed to happen. The new King, for all the doubts about his temperament and abilities expressed beforehand, was visibly growing into his role as symbol of Belgian unity. Federalization had, as yet, avoided the clashes about social security finance and debt service that would have been that unity's death-blow. Most important of all, the pro-German faction within the national government was by now holding largely unchallenged sway, and markets were again convinced of Belgium's fealty to the DM. Perhaps even more important, the worst seemed to be over – temporarily at least – for the French franc. There was no longer any need for Tietmeyer to be 'unusually warm' to Maystadt's overtures. He had his own feats of intellectual legerdemain to perform, and even the greatest of conjurors finds it difficult to perform two spectacular illusions at the same time.

No one without Tietmeyer's vast experience in the 'Black-is-White' school of ERM political utterance would have dared undertake the task he now set himself: to operate the Bundesbank as a 'central bank for Europe' while simultaneously issuing public denunciations of any such wickedness. The peg on which he hung his public outbursts was the idea being floated by the economic research unit of the Committee of Governors and soon to be transformed into the EMI, that an asymmetric ERM, with the Bundesbank as leader, could operate to everyone's satisfaction if the

Bundesbank targeted the ERM-wide money supply rather than the German money supply.[5] To most members of the Bundesbank Council, and to German public opinion, such an idea was anathema. The Bundesbank would be taking on responsibility for monetary policy not only *in* the area as a whole (that was nothing new) but also *for* it. Such a responsibility would be contrary both to the Bundesbank Law in Germany and to the Maastricht compromise Stage Two of EMU. Yet to retain leadership, the Bundesbank would have to act as 'the central bank for Europe'. Tietmeyer had to deliver on his promise of lower interest rates.

## Soft soap and bubbles

This is what he proceeded to do once he became President – within the limits imposed by majority voting in his Council.

There were three obstacles in the way of rapid reductions in rates. The money supply was yet again outside its target range, and accelerating further away. Tietmeyer had little faith in the money supply as an economic indicator. But money-supply targeting provided the central bank with cover for a great deal of unaccountable manoeuvring, whether economic or political in inspiration. The second problem was that a sharp reduction in interest rates would prompt the obvious question: if it was right for Tietmeyer to slash rates early in October, why had Schlesinger not done so two months earlier? The equally obvious answer might be that Schlesinger had been unconcerned, or even positively enthusiastic, about a break-up of the ERM. However exasperated Tietmeyer may have been with his predecessor,[6] he could not afford to provide evidence to the Bundesbank's European detractors.

Finally, whatever was happening to the money supply, a sharp cut in German interest rates would send the DM, and its satellites, sliding against the dollar and other non-ERM currencies. That might be exactly what France wanted and what French monetary officials in the Commission were advocating (as were Spanish government officials). Yet by following such a course, Tietmeyer might expose himself to charges of 'competitive

---

5 As compared with the Commission–Maystadt ideas, this proposal would maintain the Bundesbank's leadership role. It had the additional requirement that currency substitution must be an important phenomenon. Both plans wrongly implied that fixed exchange rates among the members of the scheme were optimal.

6 Schlesinger once told central bankers, just before his retirement that: 'In professional life, one's most difficult relations are with one's predecessor and one's successor.'

devaluation' against the US. Any such charge would have been nonsense,[7] but it was a charge that Tietmeyer himself had found, and was to find again in future, a useful one against Britain, Italy and Spain. Adapting his reasoning to suit the circumstances was not something he was averse to engaging in – but one illusion at a time! In addition, a sharp cut in rates and a sudden depreciation against the dollar might well have halted the decline in German long-term interest rates through increasing bond markets' inflation expectations. Implicitly, that would be the purpose of the cut in short rates – to avoid more unemployment-induced disinflation than was required or desired. Therein lies the rub. Such a strategy could be perfectly consistent with maintaining, or even enhancing, the credibility of monetary policy if it were embedded in an explicit inflation-targeting framework. But Tietmeyer feared inflation targeting as vampires fear a crucifix – nothing else so highlighted the limits of monetary policy and so tied an independent central bank to accountability.

Faced with these aims and objectives, the chosen route had to be that of gradual, step-by-step reductions in interest rates, each one justified by market indicators of 'credibility' – the exchange rate against the dollar, and the movement of long-term interest rates in Germany – while firmly signalling the downward trend in advance to the audience of clients.

This programme, carried out in a series of reductions in the repo rate from October to early December, constituted ideal conditions for a 'bubble' in European bond markets. American bond prices started falling gently in October, as markets finally became convinced of the reality of the strong US recovery. But the prospect of cuts in European short-term interest rates, stretching as far as the eye could see, tempted the European bond markets into more and more and more extravagant price rises. Those rises (falls in long-term interest rates) could be taken by the Bundesbank as a token of the 'credibility' of its policy.[8] But suddenly, in early December, the gradual easing-down of the repo rate stopped. It was not to resume until early March. Why?

Yet again, politics played the key role. Some of the more hawkish members of the Bundesbank Council scented success in their battle – for which, of course, they had no mandate, however worthy the cause – to tame the unions, granted an additional access of power by unification. They wanted to keep pressure on the wage-round that was beginning. Certain

7 See chapter 7.
8 Tietmeyer went so far as to claim explicitly that it was only by a policy of gradual, rather than 'forced', reductions in short rates that 'bubbles' could be avoided.

other members of the Council who were close to the SPD were unhappy with what could be seen as a Bundesbank policy based in part on boosting Kohl's re-election chances. In January and February, SPD spokesmen launched a series of attacks on what they claimed was the Bundesbank's abuse of its independence. Tietmeyer himself was a particular target – accused of being too close to Kohl for his power to be acceptable. The SPD suggested that, if it came to power, the Bundesbank would be reminded of its duty, stated in the law, to support the general economic policy of the government – which included an SPD government, if there should be one.

Members of the Directorate are said to have confirmed in private that Tietmeyer lost his majority on the Council during this period. Of course, no Bundesbank President was ever going to admit to that, or to the reasons for it. He had to find a cover story for the freeze in interest-rate reductions. A convenient one presented itself: the dollar was strengthening along with the US economy. That was precisely what France and Spain, and probably Tietmeyer himself, wanted. But with no other obvious excuses, Tietmeyer began to emphasize 'stability' of the DM against the dollar as the key factor conditioning Bundesbank interest-rate policy. Doubts began to be sown in the minds of bond-market professionals. Since December, in Germany at least, the man in the street had come to the conclusion that long-term interest rates had gone so low that the only way they could go from then on was up. Everyone except the professionals started selling bonds and taking out long-term fixed-rate loans from the banks. But the professionals, most of all German banks, continued to hope for further gains in the market. They were prepared to buy all the bonds the non-professionals were selling. In December and January, there was an uneasy calm in bond prices, reflecting this balance of bears and bulls.

But, at the beginning of February 1994, the bubble was pricked. The Fed slightly raised US short-term interest rates. This was a move that had been widely anticipated, given the strength of the American economy, but US bond prices nonetheless fell back further. So, too, did bond prices in European countries, as markets believed, given what Tietmeyer had been saying about the dollar–DM rate, that the previous assumption of ongoing falls in German short-term interest rates would have to be revised. All bets were off.

Normally, the discomfiture of the 'bond-market professionals' would have produced unalloyed pleasure in the Bundesbank. This time, however, *Schadenfreude* was tinged with concern: the German banks had been among the biggest buyers of bonds, and were now facing heavy losses. At around the same time, German money-supply figures for January appeared. They showed an annual rate of increase of more than 20% – the result of the desire of non-banks, at the turn of the year, to borrow long and deposit short, a desire that the banks, still betting on further falls in short- and long-term interest rates, had been all too willing to accommodate.

By now, things were also stirring in the German economy. The US was booming. So too were 'emerging countries' in Latin America and Asia. Their demand for imports, and particularly for imports of capital goods, was manna from heaven for the order-starved exporting giants of German industry. On top of that, the pricking of the bond-market bubble meant that German firms and households had won, and won big, on their bets with the banks. Having rushed to take out long-term credits at rates they were sure represented a once-in-a-lifetime opportunity (German long-term rates around the turn of the year were, as a result of the 'bubble', an unsustainably low 5.5%), they now started to use those credits.

Business *and* consumer confidence began to turn up in February. The economic factors just mentioned played a role, but so did politics. Faced with a big SPD lead in the opinion polls, the Kohl coalition began soft-pedalling on the 'need for sacrifice' rhetoric that had been so prominent a feature of ministerial speeches for the previous eighteen months. Budgetary austerity went on hold for the duration of the election campaign. German big business and the three big banks with whom they were so closely intertwined, worried by the prospect of an SPD-led government, began 'talking the economy up'.[9] Indeed, they did more than that, and began increasing output exceptionally early in the orders cycle.[10] This upturn enabled the government to point to a pre-election economic recovery without having to stimulate one themselves through Keynesian fiscal expansion of the sort by then being practised in France and Denmark.

## What is 'street cred' in German?

Thus, by early spring, everything was beginning to suggest that the freeze in Bundesbank interest-rate reductions should continue: the speed of money-supply growth was making the target range look ridiculous; though inflation

---

9 One of the SPD proposals that created most anguish in the banking-industrial complex involved reducing the power of the big banks and limiting their involvement in industry.

10 Much of the increase in GDP in Germany in the first half of 1994, it could subsequently be seen, came from a change in stock-building behaviour by industry.

was coming down, it was still considerably above what the Bundesbank publicly considered acceptable and was now beginning to look sticky; long-term interest rates were going up (something that should have indicated, according to the Bundesbank theology of late 1993, that cuts in short rates had already gone too far); most market participants expected the dollar to rise against the DM; and business surveys were indicating that the trough of the German recession might have been passed.

Yet, in mid-March, the Bundesbank began edging the repo rate down again, Why? A member of the Bundesbank Directorate made it known to the ´other 'hard-core' ERM countries that Tietmeyer had regained a majority in the central bank Council. It is difficult to be sure which Council members had switched and why – the Bundesbank is the most secretive of all the major central banks, never publishing records of Council meetings and votes, precisely because it is so political and politicized an institution. One clue is that Gerd Haller was confidently telling bureaucrats in other countries that the discount rate would be down to 4.5% by the time of the elections in October. This suggests that the swing votes in the Council were union-bashing 'hawks' who had come to the conclusion that they should hold what they had. The alternative might be to risk the election of an SPD-led government that would, so campaign statements threatened, institute a national planning framework in which the Bundesbank would be expected to listen to the government and unions rather than simply telling them what to do.

Trichet was also appealing to Tietmeyer for help: the newly independent Banque de France was under a lot of pressure within France. Its attempt at establishing a monetary framework was, as we shall see below, nothing more than a cover for shadowing Bundesbank interest-rate decisions. With the French recovery at that stage almost totally dependent on government fiscal incentives to housing and to car purchases, rumblings about Trichet's subservience to Tietmeyer were growing in volume. Trichet needed 'Cher Hans' to come up with the goods.

The biggest problem the Bundesbank faced, went the new spin, was the vast overshoot of the money-supply target in the early months of 1994. The cause of the overshoot, it was argued, was a 'liquidity logjam' created because German households and companies were reluctant to buy bonds: the interest rates on short-term bank deposits, which made up the bulk of the money supply, were too attractive. Reducing short-term interest rates would encourage people to move out of deposits into bonds, thereby pegging back the money supply. The argument made a nonsense of the theory underlying the Bundesbank's money-supply targeting procedures. In its simplest form, that theory said that *increasing* short-term interest rates raised the cost of holding money and therefore *reduced* the demand for money to be supplied by the banking system. The new Bundesbank argument not only had the tail wagging the dog, but had the dog chasing its own tail at the same time.

Below the still waters of the Bundesbank's primitive-monetarist[11] pond lay the turbulent deeps of market expectations.[12] It is undoubtedly true that the surge in money supply had been created by Bundesbank policy – but only because German banks were participants in the bond-market bubble while non-banks were not. Banks thought bond prices would go up, non-banks that they would go down. So how could the Bundesbank be 'credible' if the two elements of its domestic constituency had diametrically opposed sets of expectations? How could such a divergence arise? The answer, like everything else in this book, lies in the distortion of economic reason by the struggle for political power uncontrolled by any democratic process.

Tietmeyer was not paranoid either about markets or about 'Anglo-Saxons', and, unlike Trichet, was in general favourable to market rather than technocratic solutions. But he was, and is, determined that the Bundesbank should not have its political wings clipped, its freedom of action restricted, by accountability to financial markets any more than by formal accountability to governments (helping Kohl from behind a mask of impartiality was another matter altogether).

The problem faced by the Bundesbank would appear even starker to a European Central Bank, and is worth looking at. The Bundesbank has traditionally been said to enjoy a good deal of 'credibility' as it is known in academic, central banking and market discussion. In essence, this means that the market believes the monetary authorities will deliver what they say

11 Milton Friedman, the father of postwar monetarism, would deny that the Bundesbank was monetarist even in principle – the Bundesbank has never attempted to control the supply of money. Instead, it attempts to steer the demand for money by setting its price (the short-term interest rate). A central bank that controlled the money supply, via controlling the amount of bank reserves, would let the short-term interest go up or down as a function of money demand relative to the predetermined supply.

12 The Bundesbank argument actually recalled Keynes, a hate figure in Frankfurt, in implying that the money supply was being swollen by speculative balances, not transactions balances, and had therefore lost relevance as a policy target. This naturally provoked considerable intellectual discomfort, gloriously apparent on the first day of June when three members of the Bundesbank Council, speaking in three different German cities, made totally contradictory, indeed impenetrable, statements about the usefulness of money targets and the relationship between money supply and interest rates.

they will deliver in terms of low and stable inflation. The Bundesbank believes that a major element in its acquisition and retention of 'credibility' has been its independence of governments. More likely, it comes from a deep-rooted aversion to inflation among the German people, the result of the two German hyper-inflation episodes of this century (this aversion cannot be transposed to other countries without first subjecting them to the ravages of hyper-inflation themselves – but this is not an aversion therapy that any monetary psychiatrist is likely to propose).

At all events, in concrete financial-market terms 'credibility' implies that markets expect the monetary authority to deliver the future sequence of short-term interest rates (the main policy tool of all central banks) that will be consistent with the desired degree of price stability in conditions of reasonable economic equilibrium. In turn, since long-term interest rates are essentially an average of expected future short-term rates, the slope of the yield curve – the difference between *current* short rates and long rates – indicates the direction in which short rates must move and how fast they must move if 'credibility' is to be maintained.[13] Unfortunately, the Bundesbank does not see things this way, for this way of seeing things depicts bond-market traders as 'bond-market vigilantes' constantly monitoring the behaviour not only of budgetary policy but also of monetary policy. If these 'vigilantes' take decisions that result in a move in long-term rates, then they appear to be giving directions to the monetary authorities on the future course of short-term rates. In fact, what they are doing is forecasting, on the basis of the information available to them, what the credible monetary authority will have to do to achieve its advertised objectives. The Bundesbank, however, seems to view its 'credibility' in this sense, which implicitly ties it, at least in market expectations, to a particular sequence of actions, as a threat to its own 'independence' or freedom for unaccountable political manoeuvring. It therefore faces a deep paradox: 'independence' (from governments) is supposedly a precondition for 'credibility', but 'credibility' destroys 'independence' from markets.

13 Cutting corners somewhat, one can say that the central bank should move short rates sharply when it becomes aware of a disturbance to the economy, thus steepening the yield curve in one direction or another. Gradual, pre-programmed movements in short rates should take place only when the economy is subsequently gradually returning to its pre-disturbance equilibrium, thus flattening the yield curve. At the beginning of 1994 the German yield curve was already flat. If the Bundesbank had been credible, markets could not have expected further gradual reductions in short rates. That they did have such expectations, as shown by the futures market, implies that the Bundesbank was not credible.

*This* is why the Bundesbank is so opposed to the development of financial markets on the New York/London model, why it disparagingly refers to Wall Street and the City as 'casinos', and why Tietmeyer rails against 'bond-market professionals'. Another member of the Bundesbank Directorate, Gerd Häusler, has recently said that competition in financial markets has given rise to 'central bank watchers' and that the central bank is regarded as villain if the market is surprised by policy moves and thereby suffers losses. In fact, the emergence of 'central bank watchers' implies that markets do not know what decision rules are being used by the central banks and have to try to deduce these uncertain rules from their actions and, perhaps even more important, their pronouncements. If central banks were fully 'credible', their governing Councils could be replaced by computers. Thus just as one can see that independent central banks *require* 'bad' behaviour from governments and private-sector agents in order to justify that independence, so also one can see that those banks must deliberately eschew real credibility if they are to enjoy the discretion that they seem to value above all else.

A desire *not* to do what the financial market indicators were suggesting should be done (reduce short-term interest rates sharply and quickly) in the autumn of 1993 was, ERM considerations aside, a major constraint on the Bundesbank. It contributed directly to the bond-market 'bubble' that Bundesbank spokesmen, from Tietmeyer downwards, so piously said they wanted to avoid.[14] When the bubble eventually burst, as inevitably it had to, in early 1994, hypocritical Continental central bankers led by the Bundesbank and the Banque de France immediately blamed bond-market 'speculators'. In truth, the bubble was created by the Continental central banks and the big *losers* were the dreaded 'hedge funds'. The hedge funds were in effect forced out of the market, leaving 'technical' traders in command; this was a major reason for the rises in long-term interest rates,

14 Professional economists will notice that I am using the term 'bubble' loosely. It would be more precise to talk of an endogenous bubble, in which markets imputed to the Bundesbank, on the basis of that institution's own actions and pronouncements, a decision rule for the setting of short-term interest rates that was inconsistent with financial-market equilibrium. At some point, that false decision rule would have to be changed, but the timing of the change would depend on the uncertain political currents within the Bundesbank Council. Bond-market professionals presumably believed they could get out in time when the fact of a change in the decision rule became apparent. In other words, they suffered from the so-called 'illusion of liquidity', and when the time to get out of the bond market did eventually announce itself, price falls were exacerbated by liquidity problems.

so damaging to claims of central-bank credibility, during the rest of 1994. Clearly, the Bundesbank Council was prepared, in order to 'show the markets who is boss', to let Tietmeyer pursue his geopolitical strategy at the cost of financial market instability and damage to the Bundesbank's own 'credibility'.[15]

The episode is instructive about what might happen in EMU. For most of its history, the Bundesbank has simply not had to cope with an integrated, deregulated and innovated world financial market. It has fought to keep German banking provincial, with its huge network of small, regional savings banks, and to keep Frankfurt dominated by the three huge German 'universal banks' (Deutsche, Dresdner and Commerz), susceptible to 'moral suasion'. In 1974, when a Cologne bank, Herstatt, got into difficulty as a result of unauthorized dealing by junior staff, followed by increasingly wild speculation in attempts to recoup losses, the Bundesbank was so concerned to 'punish' speculators that it failed to act as lender of last resort to the then relatively new international inter-bank market, causing a chain reaction that led to the temporary suspension of the US inter-bank payments system and to a serious risk of global banking difficulties.[16] Nonetheless, the Bundesbank was not able to prevent the growth of a global inter-bank market.

A global capital market has posed an even greater threat to it. It is only in the past few years that the German capital market has been of significant interest to foreign investors, and the Bundesbank has not liked the experience. It therefore sees an ECB operating in Frankfurt and on the Bundesbank model as presenting certain advantages. The ECB would be able to strengthen the grip on European financial markets, particularly if

---

15 Central bankers tried to cover their embarrassment about bond-market developments by putting the blame on public-sector deficits for creating a world 'savings shortage'. Of course, deficits were too large in several 'emerging market' countries. But there is no evidence that the 1994 bond-market collapse had its origin in generalized worries about public finance – high-debt countries such as Sweden and Italy were cases apart. Similarly, the sharp recovery in bond markets in the first half of 1995, led by the US, had nothing to do with greater optimism about public finance – there was none (Tietmeyer even attributed the weakness of the dollar over that period to the failure of the balanced-budget amendment to pass the US Congress, ignoring the fact that long-term interest rates were *falling* rapidly).

16 The Bundesbank's behaviour in the Herstatt affair contrasts unfavourably with the Bank of England's response to the Barings collapse in 1995. The 'Old Lady' declined to bail out Barings' managers and shareholders but provided the London market with whatever liquidity was required to avoid systemic risk.

Britain were part of an EMU,[17] and it might be able to extend Frankfurt's relative financial backwardness to the whole of Europe, enabling it to give the finger to the bond-market professionals. An ECB operating along Bundesbank lines would also protect the German universal banks from competition from foreign banks. The Bundesbank wants to preserve minimum reserve requirements in Germany because they are an essential feature, along with the discount lending facility, in the patron/client relationship through which the Bundesbank exercises 'moral suasion' on the German banks. But in certain other important banking centres, notably Britain and Luxembourg, there are no reserve requirements, exposing German banks, or at least their domestic branches, to foreign competition for deposits. Thus the Bundesbank is determined that if there is ever an ECB it must be dominated by Germany and must impose reserve requirements throughout Europe. Häusler, no doubt predicting and fearing a British decision to stay out of EMU, has even suggested the *worldwide* imposition of reserve requirements.

French technocrats see in 'Europe' a way of preserving their power against the free world market in which competition, not state diktat, decides what gets produced, where and by whom. They are prepared to give the appearance of ceding some degree of French national sovereignty to do this, confident that their expertise and ruthlessness will ensure French *international* sovereignty instead (their recent successes in the bail-outs of Bull, Air France and Crédit Lyonnais, and their frustration of a single market in electricity, give their view some credence). Similarly, the Bundesbank under Tietmeyer might in the end be prepared to give the impression of sacrificing its own national monetary policy autonomy via the creation of an ECB, in order to protect central-bank prerogatives from the encroachment of globalized 'Anglo-Saxon' *financial* markets – *if* the ECB is set up to behave exactly like the Bundesbank.

Tietmeyer is indeed confident that he can shape the ECB in the way he wants – as long as Trichet is kept on board[18] – making it a Bundesbank

17 On 9 March 1995, in a British television interview, Tietmeyer expressed a preference for Britain's participation in EMU. In part, he was trying to downplay the German 'hard-core' concept of European union that was hurting Balladur in the French presidential race. But probably more important was his understanding that the power of an ECB would be undermined by the maintenance of free, deregulated financial markets in London.

18 At least one member of the EMI Council habitually refers to the Governor of the Banque de France – except to his face – as 'Hans Trichet'. Lower down, no word of dissent from Bundesbank thinking is ever heard from Banque de France representatives in the committees and working groups of the EMI.

clone. In terms of its philosophy, its operating procedures and its instruments it would to all intents and purposes also be a Bundesbank vassal (results would be a catastrophically different matter, as we shall argue in the final chapter). But he is almost certainly wrong in thinking that it could resist the march of financial markets and of the fund managers who have to put their money where their mouth is. An ECB might succeed in destroying London as a financial centre if Britain joined an EMU, but it would not succeed in solving the credibility/independence paradox in the face of global bond markets in New York and the Far Eastern centres. The Bundesbank and the *énarques* do not like the modern world. They cannot hold back the tide, but they will do a lot of damage in trying to.

## Heads above water

As 1994 progressed, the hopes of the EMU enthusiasts, so damped by the acrimonious collapse of the old ERM, began to revive. The turbulence in the bond markets seemed to leave ERM exchange rates intact. A recovery in the European economies became more and more evident. In those countries whose currencies had depreciated sharply since the ERM crisis began in mid-1992, that was only to be expected (by any open-minded economist at any rate). Unexpectedly, the 'core' economies began to pick up as well. It was this precocious recovery that made it possible for exchange rates to remain within a fairly tight band throughout 1994, even if there were very few days in the year when all the former narrow-band currencies were actually within the old 2.25% of each other. The collapse of the old ERM was in itself a psychologically helpful factor, however much its former priests might hate to admit it: the atmosphere of permanent conflict and crisis seemed to have gone. The prophets of EMU proclaimed a new dawn: economic recovery would still any voices raised against monetary union. And by easing the burden of recession-fighting that had fallen on fiscal policy, it would make it easier for countries to reduce budget deficits to the limit of 3% of GDP laid down in the 'convergence criteria' for entry into EMU in the Maastricht Treaty. But as so often before, this optimism was based on a misreading, whether cynical or merely illiterate, of what was actually happening and why. Not for the first time, Denmark provides a *locus classicus* of economic misunderstanding by the EMU enthusiasts.

The Danish economy, which had seemed out for the count in mid-1993, began to recover in spectacular fashion by the end of the year. One element of the government's tactics in the second referendum campaign had been a straightforward bribe: there would be large-scale tax cuts if there were a 'yes' vote. In fact, the cuts would probably have gone ahead whatever the referendum result. The Socialists (in power since February 1993) were rightly worried about the structural damage that would be done to the Danish economy by the prevailing unemployment rate of 12.5%, the legacy of ten years of 'the hard-currency option'. But, still anxious to double-cross the electorate by forcing Denmark into EMU at some stage in the future, they continued to deprive themselves of any possibility of independent monetary action, even after the widening of the bands to 15%. The only remaining option was fiscal expansion, one they embraced with some enthusiasm.

The results confounded all those pundits who had seen previous Danish experience as proof that *reducing* the budget deficit *increased* demand and output (we analysed this experience in chapter 10 above). From the beginning of the 1990s, Denmark had, along with France and Ireland, been caught in an ERM-imposed version of a Keynesian liquidity trap: a depressed economy was driving inflation down, but nominal interest rates could not go significantly below the floor set by German rates, so real rates rose, further depressing the economy, and so on. In such a Keynesian setting, 'Keynesian' fiscal expansion was bound to have a powerful effect. Conventional macroeconomic models suggest that the stimulatory impact of fiscal expansion is small and that it very rapidly fades away as higher interest rates, the result of higher government borrowing, start to 'crowd out' private-sector investment and consumer spending. What the models ignore, however, is that for an economy in a liquidity trap or its ERM equivalent, fiscal expansion not only has a direct effect on spending (as people's disposable income goes up via tax cuts), but actually 'crowds *in*' additional spending. The immediate effects of the fiscal expansion arrest the forces of price deflation in the economy and, with nominal interest rates set outside the country, *real* interest rates *fall*. Thus fiscal expansion has a powerfully favourable impact on demand, output and employment. This was clearly seen to be the case in Denmark from the second half of 1993 onwards (it was also, as we shall see in a moment or two, the case in France).

In Keynes's mind, focused on the problems of the early 1930s, the fiscal expansion could be withdrawn after a short time, once the conditions of depressed confidence that created the 'liquidity trap' were remedied. In the ERM, however, the analogy is not complete, since the liquidity trap will remain as long as inflation in the country afflicted is lower than inflation in Germany, the country where nominal short-term interest rates are set. But if inflation is *not* lower than in Germany, the afflicted country can never improve its competitiveness. In short, *any* negative disturbance in a 'satellite' country in the ERM will set in motion what Norman Tebbit has perspicuously called the 'Eternal Recession Mechanism'.[19] Fixed exchange rates are extremely destabilizing. What is worse, the fiscal expansion which is the only way to treat the problem has to be *permanent*: withdrawing an initial expansion will, because the liquidity-trap conditions still exist, plunge the economy back into a down phase of the cycle. But a permanent fiscal expansion implies a permanently rising ratio of government debt to national output, and ultimately a financial crisis.

In passing, one can note immediately that the Maastricht Treaty's so-called 'convergence criteria' for deciding whether a country is fit to enter EMU are powerfully deflationary in the circumstances described here. It is also immediately obvious – and this is something that Tietmeyer, to his credit, has made clear – that the problems would be aggravated, not eliminated, by moving from an ERM to EMU. This is an important point, since some of the more blinkered proponents of EMU aver that the ERM experience, in which market loss of confidence in an ERM currency leads to the imposition of devastatingly high rates of interest to 'defend' it, would not carry over into EMU: there could be no speculative attacks on currencies and thus no extravagant interest-rate differentials.[20]

What these purveyors of piffle ignore, or choose to ignore, is that even if there is a single interest rate in the monetary union, with no differentials, a disturbance will ultimately end up creating either permanent recession or financial instability or both. In the ERM, once anything like this happened, markets began to suspect, hope, fear, or whatever, that the exchange-rate peg would have to go. As a result, pressures built up on interest rates and in

---

19 Strictly speaking, *any* disturbance will have this effect. As we have seen in chapter 3 and *passim*, even an initially positive disturbance will, because it creates cycles, at some point produce an economic downturn in a fixed-exchange-rate setting.

20 One of the most enthusiastic propagators of this mistake is Leon Brittan. But it is instructive to compare what he now says about EMU, and particularly British participation in it, with what he said when arguing in 1989 for British participation in the ERM. The arguments he now uses are exactly the same, almost word for word, as those he adduced in 1989. One might have thought that he would be rather abashed, given what happened when his advice was followed and Britain did embark on its calamitous, but mercifully brief, period of ERM membership.

the end the ERM *did* go, to everyone's benefit. The interest-rate and exchange-rate stresses and strains were not the result of a political conspiracy by markets. Instead, they were a clear signal from markets concerned only with money that politicians and bureaucrats were playing silly buggers with their economies. In EMU, those market signals would not be able to operate. Instead, the strain would have to be taken by employment, wages, migration, budgetary transfers among member countries and unsustainable fiscal expansion. As Eddie George has recently emphasized in his highly significant and highly EMU-sceptical speech in Luxembourg, a direct riposte to Kenneth Clarke's characteristic obfuscation of the EMU debate, none of these alternatives is in the least attractive. They would create, in George's diplomatic understatement, 'political disharmony' in Europe as well as economic under-performance.

What George did not point to openly, but Tietmeyer stresses repeatedly, is what is shown by the experience of existing monetary unions such as the United States. The economic risks can be rendered acceptable only if, as we argued in chapter 3, the 'economic culture' is basically the same in all regions of the union. For this to happen, there has to be a union-wide harmonization of many aspects of political, economic, social and educational life. In turn, this requires a central government with significant power relative to the regions. But even if all this (which already implies a federal system, and one weighted towards the centre) is in place, the economic damage can never be entirely eliminated,[21] as is shown by the long-term depression of, say, West Virginia within the US or Newfoundland within Canada, or by the shorter-term disturbances in recent years to the economies of New England, Texas or California. It remains the case that 'the degree of solidarity characteristic of a nation' (to use a phrase characteristic of the Bundesbank) is necessary if there is ever to be political

---

21 As we argued in chapter 3, a 'satellite' economy that is small relative to, and very highly integrated with, a hegemonic neighbour may judge the residual risks worth taking for the benefit of reduced transactions costs and reduced exchange-rate uncertainty. The monetary unions between Luxembourg and Belgium and Ireland and Britain are two such examples. But we have seen in this book that the first of these unions is fragile and that the second was ended in 1979 partly because it was considered inconsistent with Ireland's political independence from Britain. In the Irish–British case, while it lasted, the adjustment mechanism of migratory flows had been available because of a shared language and close family links; but there was no 'national' solidarity between Ireland and Britain – quite the opposite – and so no possibility of redistributive budget flows. Such flows *have* existed, of course, between Great Britain and Northern Ireland within the political nation of the United Kingdom.

acceptability for adjustment mechanisms such as large-scale migratory flows and heavy redistributive budgetary transfers between regions, decided on by the centre. In other words, the economics of monetary union can never be separated from its politics: in for a penny, in for a pound, or rather for an ECU, a Euromark or a Eurofranc. It is highly unlikely – let us avoid absolute determinism – that this 'solidarity characteristic of a nation' will ever be created in Europe; and it is even more unlikely that it will ever be created *by* 'Europe'.

What makes up a nation is something we shall look at in the concluding chapter of this book. For now, it is time, after this long but important general parenthesis, to return to the specific case of Denmark. The country's fiscal expansion gave a starting jolt to an economy whose engine had stalled in the ERM permafrost. And as soon as the engine sparked into life, private-sector demand pressed down hard on the accelerator. Thanks to a quirk of Denmark's financial system, the Bundesbank-induced bubble in European bond markets meant that most of Denmark's families could feel they had won the national lottery. House purchase in Denmark is financed through the issue of mortgage bonds (as a result, tiny Denmark had one of the ten largest bond markets in the world in the mid-1980s). The rapid fall in long-term interest rates in the months after the ERM collapse, combined with a technical legal change, gave Danish households a not-to-be-missed chance to refinance their mortgages and lock them in at very much lower cost.

The resulting boost to disposable incomes immediately led to higher spending in the economy. The outlook further brightened when the Danish authorities to all intents and purposes devalued the krone. The Danish krone remained consistently outside its old narrow ERM band after the August decisions, and it settled until very recently at a rate implying, in effect, a devaluation of around 3% from the central rate. A modest shift, but combined with the strengthening of sterling and the Swedish krona, both important for Danish trade, during the course of 1993 it provided some competitive relief to Denmark.

Taking all this together, it is not surprising that the Danish economy went up like a rocket. It will not escape the ERM gravitational field and once the rocket has run out of the fuel of fiscal expansion it will begin to fall again, but the period of heady, near-vertical ascent produced a new bout of giddiness in the Danish authorities. At the beginning of 1994, the Economics Minister, Marianne Jelved, had the temerity to suggest to an Ecofin meeting that the time was ripe to take the 2 August communiqué at its word and end the 'temporary' widening of the ERM bands.[22] To her disappointment, made clear in her press comments after the meeting, the previously zealous defenders of the narrow-band ERM parity in other countries had become distinctly Augustinian in their thoughts on the timing of a return to a state of Grace.

Erik Hoffmeyer, the crusty Governor of the Danish central bank, lost patience with the politicians. According to a report in a Danish financial newspaper he did what certain Luxembourgers had six months earlier suggested Belgium should do: he appealed to the Bundesbank to grant the krone a reciprocal $+/-2.25\%$ band arrangement like the guilder's. Asked to react, the Bundesbank press office said a very great deal, but between the lines: 'We cannot comment. This is a political question and can only be decided at the highest level.' Copenhagen sources say that the Danish government was enraged by the reports: the politicians might have their agenda for cheating the electorate on their EMU intentions, but joining a DM-zone was – at least before the October elections – politically unthinkable: fear of German domination had been the main reason for the 'no' vote in the first Maastricht referendum. Hoffmeyer, it seems, was hauled over the coals and ordered to issue a denial of the report. This he duly did, but the terms of his denial amounted, to keen observers, to a *confirmation* both that the approach had been made and that it had been rejected by Germany for political reasons. For the krone to have got the arrangement allegedly asked for, said Hoffmeyer, 'would have been a political slap in the face to France'. Indeed it would. It would also have reopened an agonized debate in Belgium. And it would have moved European monetary relations in the direction sketched in the 1941 blueprint, probably favoured by Schlesinger but insufficiently grandiose for Kohl. As for Tietmeyer, his strategy had been aimed above all else at

---

22  Mrs Jelved continues to agitate for Denmark to give up its opt-out from a single currency. In February 1995 she claimed in a press interview that the opt-out kept Danish interest rates higher than in the 'hard-core' since, she said, the markets interpreted the opt-out as Denmark's wanting to retain the right to devalue. As long as Denmark pursues an exchange-rate objective, yet keeps the krone low in its band, as was the case for nearly all the period since August 1993, she is right: the market is highly unlikely to believe that the krone will, in such a setting, ever appreciate substantially against the DM but sees a risk that it might depreciate. That would change, however, if Denmark pursued an inflation target instead of an exchange-rate target: appreciations would then be as likely as depreciations, and there would be no interest-rate premium, in real terms at least. There seems recently to have been some government acceptance of this: the krone has been allowed to appreciate to mid-1993 levels in order to forestall an inflation risk.

keeping France on board. As always, France was the key. And in France, Trichet was treading on eggshells.

## Do as I say, not as I do

The Maastricht Treaty had laid down that all countries wishing to take part in EMU must first make their central banks independent of the government. Mitterrand's true views on the question of central-bank independence, or at least the independence of the ECB, had been disclosed on 3 September 1992, with the results we have seen. But it is clear that in return for the subsequent 'sweetheart deal', France had to display virtue to its German sugar daddy by promising independence to the Banque de France. A bill was introduced under Bérégovoy and taken up, little changed, by Balladur. The resulting law came into effect at the beginning of 1994, by which time Trichet had been installed as Governor. The ceding, supported by all the major parties, of the government's monetary authority to an unaccountable quango represented an enormous departure from French republican tradition. It was further confirmation of the death of democratic politics in France under Mitterrand. As Raymond Barre has recently put it: 'A financial, political and administrative oligarchy is claiming to be the sole embodiment of the well-being of the nation . . . Our very conception of the democratic state is being thrown into question.'[23]

Jean-Claude Trichet presents his bank as independent of the Bundesbank as well as of the French government and himself as an equal partner of Tietmeyer. It was to this end that the Banque de France engaged in January 1994 in the meaningless exercise of defining a framework for monetary policy decisions. An inflation ceiling was set (inflation was below the ceiling and showed no sign, at the time, of going anywhere but down, flirting with absolute deflation), but there was no floor. A monetary target was also specified (to please the Bundesbank, even though Tietmeyer himself saw monetary targets as simply a cover for unaccountable manoeuvring).[24]

23 Barre's concerns sit uneasily with his fervent support of the Maastricht Treaty, but he did make his comments when thinking about entering the presidential race.
24 In March 1994 Trichet made a speech, entitled 'The Importance of Franco-German Cooperation in the Construction of EMU', in Frankfurt (Tietmeyer also spoke on the same occasion) that will forever be treasured by collectors of Trichetobilia. Trichet's apologia for its independence had much in common with Balladur's more recent defence of illegitimate wire taps: 'The independent Banque de France fits easily into the democratic life of our country. Its relations with the President of the Republic and the government as well as with Parliament are set out in the law. And, like all independent central banks, it must tirelessly listen, meditate,

Since the French money supply was actually *falling*, however, the target was set for an undefined medium-term period. Both the asymmetrical inflation ceiling and the vague money target were intended to give the impression that monetary policy was somehow related to French needs without triggering the independent French interest-rate reductions that Tietmeyer had forbidden.

Nothing was farther from the case. For the first few months of his reign Trichet therefore had to contend with sharp public criticism that French monetary subservience to Germany was strangling the recovery in output and, especially, fall in unemployment that France so desperately needed – hence his appeals to Tietmeyer for support. But as 1994 wore on, the lagged expansionary effects of German rate cuts, followed by France, of the bond-market boom in late 1993 and of Bérégovoy's and Balladur's budgetary expansion, together with new government fiscal incentives to housing and car sales and the boom in world trade, generated considerable momentum in the French economy. Criticism of Trichet subsided. The franc remained close to the old ERM band for much of the year (though rarely, contrary to imprecise official statements with an eye on the Maastricht convergence criteria, within it).

But it was impossible to ignore the fact that French growth, like growth in Denmark, was underpinned by a degree of fiscal expansion that could not be maintained indefinitely (in 1990 the budget deficit had been 1.5% of GDP; 6.1% is currently admitted to for 1994, and the true figure may be even more). France, with a floor to its nominal interest rates set in Germany, was caught like Denmark in a liquidity trap. As in Denmark, fiscal expansion had thus crowded spending *in* rather than *out*. The problem was, and is, that the fiscal expansion would sometime have to be put into reverse, particularly if the Maastricht criteria were to be met. At that point, unless France began, as Britain had done from the autumn of 1992 onwards, to operate an independent, *national* monetary policy, there would be a risk of a renewed economic downturn.

In late 1993 one observer had warned European central bankers that by the end of 1994 the Banque de France would be using the size of the budget deficit as an excuse for maintaining inappropriately high levels of French interest rates. So it turned out. At the end of 1994 Trichet pontificated that, while his bank had been behaving omnisciently and

decide, explain and convince.' Trichet also boldly claimed that: 'Franco-German cooperation permitted the monetary tensions of 1992 and 1993 to be overcome.'

impeccably, the government was letting the side down by failing to control the deficit. This was doubly rich. First, it was Trichet's own *franc fort* policy that had forced desperate governments to swell the deficit so as to ease the squeeze on the economy. Second, while still *directeur du Trésor* Trichet had exceeded the formal limits of his role and personally meddled in budgetary policy with, according to French officials, disastrous results.

Trichet's comments were received badly by the market: French long-term interest-rate differentials with Germany rose and the franc weakened against the DM.[25] Since then it has (at the time of writing) hardly stopped weakening and French short-term rates have had to be moved up to prevent it weakening even more. Of course, franc weakness in early 1995 (in mid-March it was 6.5% below the strongest ERM currency) has been compounded by the fall of the dollar in the first half of 1995 and by political uncertainty ahead of the presidential elections. And several other European currencies have been suffering as much as, or more than, the franc. But the markets have been giving signals about the incompatibility of French fiscal retrenchment with continued monetary-policy subservience to Germany, an incompatability just as evident after the election as before it. Unemployment in France is officially put at 12.5%. Youth unemployment is double that. Many people in their twenties have never had a job and will soon have exhausted their entitlement to unemployment benefit. When they do, the sporadic rioting of 1994 might turn into a nightmare of urban alienation and violence.

The path to Maastricht's monetary union could be barred by social breakdown in France even if it were reconcilable with *la gloire de la France*. But markets are in addition increasingly aware of other political realities to which politicians shut their eyes. They have gradually detached the franc from a true politically believable 'hard core' around the DM comprising the guilder, the Austrian schilling and (perhaps rather dubiously) the Belgian franc. The markets have thus been signalling their recognition of what Schlesinger, and even the monetary planners of the Third Reich, had long understood but Tietmeyer has fought to ignore – that there is no true community of monetary interest between France and Germany. If the likes of Trichet continued a Vichy policy there would eventually be a French

---

25  Trichet had said that the 'the franc has a potential for appreciation', a formula he repeated on a number of occasions in the months that followed: one French current affairs magazine commented that 'the formula delighted the market professionals, who don't have all that many chances to laugh'.

popular reaction in protest. But if instead the *énarchie* attempted a monetary takeover of Germany it would receive a shattering rebuff – yet again.

It is this impossibility theorem of a viable EMU that must occupy us in the final chapter of this book. But is not EMU supposed to be about more than just an inner core? The continuing travails of Spain suggest not. Indeed, the way that country has recently been treated by France and Germany indicates a degree of selfishness and contempt that the Spanish politicians may well have brought on themselves yet still shows up the hollowness of idealism about 'Europe'.

## Sabotaging Spain

The history of Spain's involvement in the ERM and the EMU process is one of a shifting balance between political opportunism and economic pragmatism. In this continuing struggle the Banco de España has generally been on the side of the angels, guided by, if not an angel, then a man of wisdom, conviction and integrity, Luis Angel Rojo, first as Deputy Governor and then Governor, and his band of very capable lieutenants. The Banco de España is itself an important institution in post-Franco Spanish democratic life, for reasons similar to those that led the Western Occupation Powers to create the forerunner of the Bundesbank in post-Nazi Germany. (It is worth a parenthesis to note once again the shocking lack of historical sensitivity of those who think that the Bundesbank model can be transposed to 'Europe' via an ECB: the Bundesbank, at conception if not always in practice, and the Banco de España have been successful buttresses of democratic pluralism in societies scarred by Fascism, necessary, if perhaps temporary, adjuncts to the process of learning to live with democracy – an ECB would be a totally anti-democratic institution that hastened the decaying of political life in 'Europe' and a probable precursor of an authoritarian reaction to mounting chaos.) While Gonzalez was all too ready to engage in the political opportunism of a European strategy, the economic pragmatism of the Banco de España had always made it hesitant about the ERM. It was certainly not on the advice of the Banco de España that the peseta was stuffed into the ERM in 1989. And, as we saw in earlier chapters, the bank chafed under the ERM constraints that first prevented a deceleration in Spain's damagingly high inflation rate and then turned boom into bust.

Thus when the ERM bands were widened to $+/-15\%$ in August 1993, the Banco de España saw an opportunity to put in place a more rational, domestically-oriented monetary policy along the lines adopted by Britain after sterling's ERM exit. As in Britain, the centrepiece of the new strategy would be an explicit target for inflation. But the announcement of the new framework was fatally delayed. Britain had had no choice after September 1992, but in Spain the mirage of EMU and its expected handouts still bewitched too many people. In the weeks and months following the band-widening, it became evident, to the frustration of the Banco de España, that France and the German satellite countries were going to obey Tietmeyer's orders not to act independently. Senior Banco de España officials railed against the pusillanimity of the French – if France did not move, there was no way the still-prevailing Spanish political fascination with 'Europe' would allow Spain to move. As 1994 progressed, the Spanish economy began to recover, noticeably if not strongly, under the influence of Solchaga's fiscal loosening the previous year, the pickup in the world economy and, of course, the massive depreciation of the peseta since June 1992. Yet because the deflationary forces operating on the economy in 1992 had been so intense, the inflation rate, sharply down in 1993, did not pick up. Nonetheless, accelerating recovery would be likely to put upward pressure on inflation at some point.

By the autumn of 1994 the Banco de España judged that the time was right to announce an explicit forward-looking inflation framework. It would allow them to raise interest rates modestly, a decision that would otherwise be quite hard to sell to the Spanish public. It would also make it clear that Spain was not going to pursue a policy of continuous 'competitive devaluation'. Yet they had trepidation in their hearts. Tietmeyer had had wind of what was going to happen via discussions in the EMI. In late September, in a speech in Kiel, he intensified his attacks on inflation-targeting. The Banco de España had every reason to worry about what might happen to them if they disregarded Tietmeyer's warnings. But Rojo, not a man to be bullied easily, gave the go-ahead. In December, the bank announced its new framework, downgrading the exchange rate and setting explicit medium-term inflation targets. The gods were not with Rojo. The monetary announcement coincided with the eruption of a new wave of political scandal in Spain, implicating Gonzalez's government in killings of separatist terrorists in the early 1980s. To the frustration of the bank, the peseta weakened on the political worries. In line with its new policy framework, the bank did nothing: politically driven and probably temporary turbulence in the exchange rate did not affect the medium-term inflation outlook, so there was no reason to raise interest rates on that account.

Indeed, raising rates would be a perverse reaction, since it would convince the markets that the bank was not serious about its new framework. The same applied to intervention.

The Banco de España, as the authorities repeatedly insisted, did not spend a penny – or any other currency unit – in support of the peseta in December. Yet the forex markets, both in Madrid and London, were full of strange talk of heavy and repeated intervention. Where did this talk originate? At the beginning of January, rumours began to circulate that the Bundesbank was 'worried' that Spain might be thinking of taking advantage of the widely anticipated entry of the Austrian schilling into the ERM by asking for a devaluation. On 4 January, after two days in which the peseta stabilized and even strengthened marginally in the market, the Banco de España raised its key short-term interest rate, by 65 basis points. There can be little doubt that the bank had wanted to raise the rate at the time of its monetary policy announcement in December, to show that inflation-targeting was no 'soft option' and to make it clear that a rise in VAT, to take effect in January, should not pass through into wage costs.[26] It had earlier held back the rate rise for fear that it would be interpreted as a measure to 'defend' the peseta: the stabilization of the currency on 2 and 3 January would, the bank hoped, make such an interpretation untenable. Sadly, the markets had been primed to believe in a peseta crisis. The interest-rate rise backfired badly, confirming markets in their belief that the currency was in big trouble. And while a 65 basis points rise was in fact an assertive move in the context of adjusting medium-term inflation prospects, it looked outright wimpish when (wrongly) interpreted as a peseta-defence measure. Pressure on the currency immediately reappeared, taking it within a week to an all-time low in the ERM and taking the spread between the peseta and the strongest ERM currency (the guilder, as usual) to 11%, against a permitted maximum of 15%. No one, in Madrid or anywhere else, believed for a moment that the Bundesbank would let itself be forced to provide intervention help for the peseta at the official limit: there was some spread short of 15% at which Spain would have to devalue or leave the ERM.

The government regarded both options as unattractive on grounds of political face and of residual unwise hopes of Spanish participation in EMU. The Finance Minister, Pedro Solbes, was saying that 1997 looked unlikely for EMU but that Spain would be eligible if it did happen. The

---

26 It may be better to have an inflation target that excludes the impact of indirect tax increases; ideally, the government should decide this question on political grounds.

bank was clearly opposed to a devaluation – which would increase inflationary pressure and damage the new monetary policy framework – and, it must be presumed, would have favoured a withdrawal from the ERM. In the absence of government approval for such a move it had no choice but to start intervening to head off a devaluation.

For a while, in late January and into February, the peseta benefited from reaffirmation of Catalan party support for Gonzalez, allowing the discredited Prime Minister to hang on and avoiding an early election campaign. But at the end of February a downward drift in the dollar (begun at the end of 1994 as the impact of the Mexican crisis sank in) accelerated. As has traditionally been the case, dollar weakness created ERM strains – the hoped-for 'zone of monetary stability' was quite the opposite for Germany's partners: their efforts not to be dragged down against the DM helped preserve German competitiveness sure enough, but created unnecessary stresses within their own economies. On this occasion, weakness in the peseta reappeared, but the French franc also became increasingly wobbly, giving the Spanish authorities a face-saving excuse for a devaluation. At the beginning of March, public statements from Madrid pointed to dollar weakness, DM overvaluation and generalized ERM strains. Rumours swept Madrid that there would be a devaluation. Given all this, it was hardly surprising that the markets rushed to get out of the peseta. It was equally not surprising, after the Banco de España had been forced into very heavy intervention in the late afternoon of Friday, 3 March, that the Spanish government requested a meeting of the Monetary Committee to decide a devaluation. After eleven hours of weekend discussion, the peseta was devalued by 7%, its fourth devaluation since September 1992, and the escudo by 3.5%, the third devaluation since November 1992.

Reports of the meeting, and especially Iberian reports, leave no doubt that it was, as diplomats put these things, 'difficult'. The Spanish Finance Minister was unusually open and explicit about the nature and extent of this 'difficulty' when he reported back to the Spanish Parliament a few days later. Spain, he said, had rejected a suggestion made at the meeting that the peseta's bands should be temporarily widened to +/–25%. Although the Spanish authorities had considered the peseta already undervalued, they had asked for a bigger devaluation than the one they obtained (Spanish press comment had already blamed French fears about competitiveness for the scaling-down of the devaluation) simply in order to give themselves a more comfortable margin within the system. Spain had asked for the realignment, Solbes said, when the peseta had dropped into the lower third of its +/–15%. Solbes's revelations implied that support from Spain's 'partners' in the ERM would not be forthcoming and that the effective band for the currency was 10%, not 15%, since the Bundesbank would not allow any test of whether or not intervention obligations at the margin still existed for the strong currency. Solbes even made it clear that the half-point increase in interest rates introduced by a reluctant Banco de España on the Monday following the devaluation had nothing to do with inflation prospects but had been exacted by the other ERM members as an earnest of Spanish determination to defend the new parity – a meaningless and indeed counterproductive gesture. So the net result of the operation was a higher level of interest rates and a lower value of the peseta than the Spanish economy needed, together with the near-certainty of yet another crisis in the ERM at some point in the future. Yet, said Solbes, in one of the great classics of ERM doubletalk, an example of illogicality worthy of Trichet himself, Spain had never dreamt of leaving the system, because 'the ERM helps stabilize the Spanish economy'.

As for the Banco de España, it must have been close to despair. The devaluation was totally unnecessary. Indeed, the bank must have been hoping in early December that the long decline of the peseta, since June 1992, was nearly over and that it would even start to recover as the economy strengthened and an inflation-targeting framework gave the opportunity for limited, measured, appropriate and – above all – domestically-oriented interest-rate rises. Instead, the new inflation-targeting framework had, within three months of its inception, been severely damaged by a combination of Bundesbank ill-will and Gonzalez's apparent concern for his own face. The only consolation there could have been for the bank was the recognition that the episode, so typical of the whole ERM story, might bring the final, irreversible collapse of the perverse and perverting system. But there was to be yet another twist in the tortuous course of exchange-rate relations in Europe.

For strategically placed analysts, the clear implication of Bundesbank attitudes at the end of December and beginning of January was that the Bundesbank was preparing to ease Spain out of the ERM altogether. If Spain left, there would be a good chance that Portugal would leave too. Then only Ireland would remain to get rid of – that would be easy enough, given that for several months the Irish pound had been tied as if with a restored umbilical cord to sterling. At that point the ERM would consist only of Germany's own satellites plus France. Tietmeyer would be able to go on running the Bundesbank as the 'Bank for Europe', in effect re-creating the 1983–86 ERM as a viable alternative to, or at least antecedent of, an eventual 'hard-core' Maastricht monetary union of countries that, in Tietmeyer's view, were suitable for the necessary step of comprehensive political union.

At some point before March, however, Tietmeyer seemed to take a step back from the DM-zone. Why? One problem for Tietmeyer was that the French franc was weakening in the market and Balladur in the opinion polls. The point was nearing at which Trichet would have to raise French interest rates to defend the franc's link with the DM. That would not be easy for French public opinion to swallow – it would become almost impossible if it were thought that the DM link was simply leading to a 'hard-core' monetary union in which France would cut a lonely figure among the German satellites. France would be trapped in nothing more than the expanded snake that its monetary diplomacy had been trying avoid ever since 1978. The risk would start to grow exponentially – especially if Chirac won the presidential election and made Philippe Séguin Finance Minister or even Prime Minister – that Trichet would finally be put in his place, the 'independence' of the Banque de France rescinded, and a truly independent, *French*, monetary policy implemented instead. That was exactly what Tietmeyer had spent the whole of his five years at the Bundesbank trying to prevent. So it became his short-term tactical priority, as opposed to his underlying strategy, not to frighten the horses with the prospect of a DM-zone.

As a result, the Bundesbank switched from preparing to escort the peseta out of the system to persuading the French to accept a peseta devaluation instead, despite the damaging effect it would have on French competitiveness. In return Tietmeyer would at least hint at German interest-rate reductions, for the sake both of Trichet and of a Germany economy itself becoming uncomfortably vulnerable to the effects of currency overvaluation. He was being forced back to his tactics of 1993.

## Plus ça change

Tietmeyer's own concerns about the DM exchange rate, never far from the surface, were given increasingly open expression in the wake of the March turbulence. Waigel had declared immediately before the peseta realignment that the surge in the DM reflected a strong economy benefiting from good policies. Tietmeyer felt impelled instead to comment shortly afterwards that the DM had gone further than the fundamentals warranted – a judgement soon supported by a marked downturn in German industrial confidence indicators. But, as always with Tietmeyer, the German economy was not his only concern. With the French presidential elections looming and French industrialists and farmers flooding Bercy with complaints about 'unfair' competition from Italy, Spain and Britain, the Bundesbank President had to reduce the risk, seen from his perspective, that France might pursue an independent monetary policy. Thus it was that in late March the Bundesbank caught the markets wrong-footed, cutting its discount rate when only a couple of weeks earlier all the market talk had been of a rise in German interest rates to counter incipient inflation pressures.

The discount cut came as relief not only to French industry but – by stabilizing the French franc, the peseta and the lira – also to Trichet, perhaps emboldening him sufficiently to enter the French presidential debate, in effect, by using the Banque de France's annual report to warn against the budgetary and wage policies being advocated by candidate Chirac.

When Chirac finally entered the Elysée, at the third time of asking, he appears to have adopted a twin-track strategy: make implied threats to Germany that France would follow a looser exchange-rate policy in the absence of sufficient German 'understanding' on interest rates; and threaten Spain, Italy and Britain with unspecified horrors if those countries did not implement *tighter* exchange-rate policies aimed at improving French competitiveness.

The first track suggested that some, but not all, of the lessons of summer 1993 had been absorbed in Paris. Despite Trichet's bluster, no one was any longer prepared to give credence to a French takeover of the anchor role for German monetary policy. In any case, such talk had merely angered the Schlesinger-run Bundesbank. Much better, it now seemed in Paris, to play instead on a Tietmeyer-run Bundesbank's fears, the fears that Tietmeyer had himself expressed, while still Schlesinger's number two, in the fateful Bundesbank Council meeting of 29 July 1993.

Tietmeyer himself appears to have reacted in the way the French would have hoped, the need to prevent DM appreciation evidently carrying ever greater weight in his thinking. By the early summer of 1995, with the German economy slowing after its election-year spurt in 1994, he had reason enough to be looking for opportunities for further interest-rate reductions. Yet the resulting shift in market expectations about German interest-rate prospects was not enough, even combined with a sharp downtrend in long-term interest rates across the world as the US economy, too, visibly slowed to provide the new French government with much comfort. Still everyone could see that the required cutback in the French budget deficit would bring a need for interest rates to be significantly *lower* in France than in Germany – something that could be achieved only if the franc first floated much further down against the DM.

To make things worse, the franc had in fact been appreciating steadily in effective terms since the end of 1994. Before Christmas, the French Treasury was already being swamped with complaints from industrialists finding themselves having to fight for markets with Italian, British and Spanish rivals no longer burdened by the hopelessly overvalued currencies of the early 1990s. For France (as for Germany), a 'level playing field' in the Single Market had always meant a slope steeply in their favour – the result of the ERM and Social Charter impositions, both intended to keep the 'peripheral' countries of the Community in a state of economic weakness and political dependency. With one of these crutches now kicked away, French industry and agriculture began to scream loudly. Within the walls of the Banque de France Trichet vituperated about the lira above all, calling down the wrath of heaven on the unfortunate Italians. At one international gathering, Trichet, breaching normal protocol, voiced his concern about the lira directly and in prescriptive terms to Lamberto Dini. Dini, installed as 'technocratic' Prime Minister in Italy, did not lose his cool. He had the large ears, sad eyes and lugubrious expression of a basset hound, but he had used his sharp mind and quick tongue to good effect against Trichet and others in the past. With studied affability, according to Italian diplomats, he told Trichet he quite agreed the lira was too low, but there was nothing he could do about it: if Trichet was worried, all he had to do was to tell his forex dealers to sell francs and buy lire.

Dini's advice was undoubtedly sound. But accepting it would have meant a deliberate further loosening of the DM–franc link. And, just as in the summer of 1993, the French bigwigs were not prepared to go for broke in the poker game they were playing with Germany. They would have to make do with Tietmeyer's efforts to ease German monetary policy. There is little doubt that Kohl had laid down the law to Chirac during their VE celebration meeting in Berlin two days after the French presidential elections. And Alain Juppé, virtually Kohl's appointee as French Prime Minister, soon made it plain that he was at least as attached to the *franc fort* as Bérégovoy, Balladur or Trichet.

With the first track of the dual strategy pushed as far as the French authorities dared to take it in the face of their political subservience to Germany, the second track had to be pursued more vigorously. Even if it brought no practical economic results, it would at least provide politically useful scapegoats.

Even before the French elections, Balladur had been exerting pressure on the Commission to 'defend' the Single Market against 'competitive devaluation'. Juppé followed the same line. According to diplomats, the new French government began demanding that Brussels should issue threats to make EC transfers to countries such as Spain and Italy conditional on 'good behaviour' on the exchange rate and permit France to grant subsidies, contrary to Single Market rules, to its own producers. Initially at least, these efforts made little headway; other countries' Commissioners in Brussels were unwilling to start dismantling the Single Market for the sake of France's state industrial complex.

But the danger to the Community created by the poisonous obsession was there for all to see. That did not mean, of course, that everyone saw the danger. For the Community Establishment, the problem was not the *franc fort* but the risk of 'competitive devaluation' – a frequent theme of the new Commission President, Jacques Santer. More important than Santer's ruminations, the French and German governments seem to have decided in May 1995 that Italy must rejoin the ERM, whether it liked it or not. In April, Tietmeyer had already 'discussed the possibility' with Dini in Rome: the wheel had turned almost full circle, back to 1978. The 'snake' in effect recreated after the ERM band-widening was not enough to provide German industry with a protected, quietly profitable life. Yet France could not openly join a narrowly defined snake. For both countries, Italy, at least, and preferably Spain and Britain too, had to be suborned into abandoning their own interests in the name of the 'common good' of European exchange-rate fixity.

Spain, of course, was an easy nut to crack. Gonzalez had shown himself time and time again to be prepared to accept any distortion of the Spanish economy, every confirmation of a servant–master relationship between Spain and the Franco-German 'motor'. Italy is a different matter: as long as doubts remain about the ability of the government to avoid debt unsustainability, the lira will remain highly volatile. Putting the currency back in the ERM, even with +/–15% bands, would bring the risk of renewed destabilization of the economy and make the task of budgetary adjustment that much harder. Yet Italy's financial and political weakness leaves it open to pressure from France and Germany.

The pressure was made public after the first talks, on 19 May 1995, between Kohl and Chirac after the latter took office as French President. The two men, say diplomatic sources, discussed bringing the lira back into the ERM, since both countries were concerned by the impact of lira depreciation on the competitiveness of their own industrial sectors. It would take complex negotiations, said the same sources, to set a new pivot rate for the lira in the ERM grid. Italy, it seemed, was to have no say in the decision – the Italians would simply have to do what they were told, just as in 1978 and just as in 1981! Once more, the 'common good' of the ERM could be seen as an expression of Franco-German determination that other countries should order their economic affairs for the perceived benefit of France and Germany, not their own countries. By June, Dini showed signs of bending to the Franco-German pressure, despite the fact that Antonio Fazio, Banca d'Italia Governor since April 1993, made no mention whatsoever of the ERM in his speech introducing the bank's annual report at the end of May (instead, the bank moved very clearly in the direction of an inflation target – something totally incompatible with exchange-rate rigidity in an economy so far from full equilibrium as Italy's). In early June, Dini stated that the question of the lira's re-entry would have to be considered in the autumn. The proposed timing was significant. For some months, German officials had apparently been telling their French counterparts that a decision on moving to a single currency by the latest date set in the Maastricht Treaty, 1 January 1999, could not possibly be taken in 1998. General elections in Germany would be held in 1998, and the single-currency question would thus actually have to be raised in public, political debate, something that had never before happened in a German general election campaign. In such highly regrettable circum-stances, the German people might insist on their government's saying 'no'. To forestall this danger, the decision would have to be taken late in 1997. This timetable suits the French. They want monetary union without the political union demanded by Wolfgang Schäuble, Kohl's right-hand man and heir presumptive. They believe that they have a chance of obtaining that from Kohl, who has promised his party he will step down in sufficient time before the 1998 elections for his successor to bed himself in, but from no other German politician. Dini was presumably well aware of these calculations – and of the implied need for the lira to be back in the ERM by the autumn of 1995 at the latest to meet the two-year qualifying period condition for EMU membership. The Italian 'technocratic' government, whatever its merits, and particularly those of its head, was clearly still so distrustful of Italy's inability to stand on its own feet politically that it still hankered after the prospect of what they thought would be rule from Brussels – or from Berlin.

The final target of the Franco-German (and particularly French) offensive is, of course, Britain. On 10 June, after a summit meeting between Chirac and Major, the French President, professing knowledge of and understanding for the British position (thereby displaying an extra-ordinary talent for mind-reading), announced that, at the request of the two leaders, the Commission would conduct an urgent study of exchange-rate relationships between future participants and non-participants in EMU. Major spoke of a 'breath of fresh air'. To informed observers, however, there was a smell of rotting fish. The suspicion must be that Chirac was offering to rescue Major from isolation, which he has been taught by the Foreign Office to fear, on such questions as veto rights and the relative powers of national parliaments and the European Parliament,[27] in exchange for 'cooperation' in some new, perhaps unannounced, incar-nation of the ERM. Major has shown himself time and again to be a keen supporter of the ERM – he used Mrs Thatcher's political weakness to force Britain into the system in 1990; he attempted in the Maastricht negotiations to make membership a legally binding obligation; he was prepared to take the country to the brink of bankruptcy to stay in the system in September 1992. His Chancellor and Foreign Secretary are even more convinced of the system's merits. Instead of playing on Chirac's fears of a German-dominated political union and of increasing British economic success if Britain stayed well clear both of EMU and the ERM, Major may be prepared to accept the bait when the Commission reports in the autumn – if his party will let him. Chirac is proud to proclaim himself a Gaullist. Major may yet prove himself to be closer to the Bourbons – who remembered everything and learnt nothing.

The deadly serious monetary games being played in Europe in the first half of 1995 made one thing obvious: even the panic widening of the ERM bands to +/–15% in August 1993 had not succeeded in depoliticizing European exchange-rate relations. Only a clear commitment to floating exchange rates and to the pursuit of truly independent, nationally-oriented

27 Significantly, Commission President Jacques Santer had the day before issued a 'warning' to Britain that, despite the unambiguous provisions of the Treaty of Rome, Britain must not attempt to use its veto in certain key areas. Two days earlier, Santer had had a long meeting with Chirac in Paris, at which, it seems, a 'hard man, soft man' approach to the British 'problem' may have been agreed.

monetary policies by the major European countries could do that. But that would mean destroying the EMU project – the rotten heart of Europe that so many people, misguided or cynical, held so dear.

# 14

# The Rotten Heart of Europe

## One nation, one money

The central aspiration of the Treaty of Rome was 'an ever closer union of the peoples of Europe'. By a strange chance, the acronym of 'ever closer union', ECU, is also that of the European currency unit, destined by Maastricht to become the single currency of the European Union. Would the adoption of the ECU single currency lead to the ECU of friendship, trust and fellow-feeling among the citizens of the neighbouring countries of Europe?

The ERM was always intended as the locomotive that would carry Europe to one ECU or the other. Sadly, the history of the ERM suggests that, far from being two sides of the same ECU coin, monetary union and harmonious relations in Europe are as far apart as dross and gold. The true story of the ERM has been one of duplicity, skulduggery, conflict; of economic harm done to every country in the caste interests of the élite; of the distortion of economic logic and the dilution of political accountability. The contrast between ERM reality and ERM myth should of itself be warning enough against accepting the even more dangerous myths of EMU and European 'union'. But just as, in Britain, Lawson saw the failure of his ERM-shadowing policy as a reason for embracing the ERM itself, so now the propagandists portray the failures of the ERM as the cost of 'non-Europe'. This book has already pointed to the economic harm that would be done by monetary union – it would work only if it were not necessary, as the example of monetary relations between Germany and the Netherlands shows. This final chapter will look closely at the *politics* of European monetary and political union – the two go together – and argue that 'Europe' is a dangerous fantasy.

The true lesson of the ERM story is that a Europe, even a Rhenish Europe, built on its money would be a Europe sitting atop the fault lines of an earthquake zone. Those fault lines correspond with the borders of nation-states, for the Commission slogan 'One Market, One Money' is no more than a prediction of discredited 'neo-functionalist' theory. In contrast, the counter-cry of 'One Nation, One Money' is the product of psychological, political and historical reality. Could 'Europe' ever be a nation? What kind of nation would it be?

## Death of the nation-state?

The obituary of the nation-state has been written many times in recent years, most recently and most aggressively in the Lamers report from the CDU parliamentary group dealing with European affairs. Whether one likes it or not, the argument often goes, increasing globalization of economic activity and the mobility of factors of production have already destroyed the nation-state as a meaningful entity in economic terms.

What does it mean to say that the nation-state is no longer an economically viable unit? What implications might there be for 'Europe'? The most careful historical research into the development of the EC shows that the Community has, up to now, been a mechanism for preserving those features of regulatory state power that liberals find objectionable. It is this feature of Europe that has made it attractive to Socialists and corporatists in national governments and the Commission. Only their insistent propaganda has created the myth that 'Europe' is about 'an ever closer union of peoples'.

The French élite have very distinctive views on these questions. They certainly do not believe that the *nation* is dead, at least not the French nation. Their fear is that the nation is no longer so clearly identifiable as an economic unit as to provide a basis for the power of a regulatory, interventionist, technocractic state.[1] Liberals will rejoice that the globalization of the world economy, combined with the technological revolution, is making many aspects of the state redundant and enhancing individual freedom. French technocrats are appalled at the inroads into their power being made by the world (that is, 'Anglo-Saxon') market.[2] A choice has to be made, in their minds, between '*le désordre anglo-saxon et l'état républicain*'. Only by extending the borders of the state from the French nation to 'Europe' can that state hope to retain its domestic power. And only through

---

1 In Britain, Denis Healey has recently expressed this view in almost identical terms.

2 One of the most influential proponents of this view is the man who is the identikit 'intellectual' *de nos jours*, Alain Minc, *énarque* himself, consultant to Balladur and author of a report commissioned by Balladur, *La France de l'an 2000*. Debating with Philippe Séguin, Minc makes no bones about it: 'I prefer the power of an independent central bank to the dictatorship of the jittery people in the markets.'

such an extension can France 'stand up' to the American and Japanese ogres. One of the most lasting images of the Maastricht referendum campaign in France is that of the posters and press adverts put out by the 'yes' side (that is, in effect, the government) of a paunchy cowboy and a gross sumo wrestler sitting astride the globe. Only through 'Europe', the posters screamed, can the French soul escape the domination of the barbarians.[3]

Yet this route of 'escape' poses a problem for France: escaping the yoke of Anglo-Saxon and Japanese barbarians must involve embracing the German demons. The solution, seen from Paris, is the European Union, in which the *énarques*, the true inheritors in Europe of the Prussian state tradition, would 'tie down' and tame Germany. The 'yes' campaign in France thus developed a double theme: confront the outside world via the creation of a European economic, political and military mammoth; and, within this new 'Europe', ensure French control over Germany by the extension of the French technocracy.[4]

In essence, the French technocratic dream was to be able to present European union as a move from the nation-state to the state-nation. The nation-state (identified by many French political theorists with the concept, which they attribute to Germany, of *jus sanguinis* – 'where there are Germans, there German soil is') can be represented as a destructive, selfish and dangerous excrescence of tribalism. The state-nation, on the other hand (identified with the French concept of *jus solis* – 'where there is French soil, there Frenchmen are'), is depicted as the creation of feelings of unity among many different 'tribes' through common fealty to a state whose principles and functions offer material, social and even spiritual advantages to all those who choose to accept them.

3 Sadly, these ideas not confined to the French élite. There has long been an unwholesome strand of thinking among Tory 'toffs' (whether born to that status or, like Edward Heath, still hoping to attain it), that resents the fact that America took over world leadership from Britain. In the national (and world) crisis of May 1940, for instance, Rab Butler (one of the arch-appeasers of Hitler) reacted to the news of Churchill's appointment as Prime Minister by sneering his contempt for 'that American half-breed'. Edward Heath is notably unsympathetic to America, of course. And, very recently, Tim Renton, Chief Whip during the Tory leadership election of 1990 when he was at odds with his leader on Europe, let the cat out of the bag when he told a television audience: 'We need a strong Europe to maintain our independence from the United States and the Pacific Rim.'

4 Delors was perhaps the most explicit of all in his period of almost unrestrained Euro-ambition in 1991, stating without any ambiguity whatsoever that 'Europe' must become a superstate and a military superpower, even advocating the handing-over of the French nuclear strike-force to the armed forces of 'Europe'.

Of course, the two great historical examples of the creation of state-nations other than by military subjugation are the forging of the United Kingdom in the eighteenth century and the transformation of the United States by immigration in the final quarter of the nineteenth century and the early years of the twentieth. It is no coincidence that the 'functionalist' and 'neo-functionalist' theories of European integration were born in America, where the US State Department has been a tireless patron of the idea of 'Europe'. If America could become a state-nation, why not Europe?

What the integrationist gurus of the State Department closed their eyes to (despite repeated warnings from the US Treasury and the Fed) was that the sort of 'Europe' that was being planned within the old Continent was, from the very first, a technocratic one (how else could it be, given the role of Jean Monnet in building the foundation of 'Europe'?) imposed from above instead of being built from below by people voting with their feet. The United States had been a meeting-point of many nationalities, all of them fleeing poverty, economic oppression, ethnic discrimination or political tyranny in their countries of origin, and all of them prepared to become 'Americans' and speak the Americans' language in the pursuit of personal freedom and economic opportunity.[5] Europe (that is to say, the democracies of Western Europe) was a collection of states all of which not only had their own linguistic and cultural identities but, after the short period of postwar reconstruction, enjoyed reasonable economic prosperity and political legitimacy.[6] For them to surrender sovereignty to 'Europe' could only happen as a reaction to external pressure that threatened that happy state of affairs.

For forty years after the war, the greater peceived external threat was to political legitimacy, and it came from the Soviet Union. That threat was

5 The more recent trend towards encouraging linguistic pluralism in the United States may ultimately cause great political strain. If it does, it is hard to imagine that the United States could remain a monetary union.

6 The two partial exceptions – disregarding the southern latecomers to 'Europe', Spain, Portugal and Greece – are interesting. Southern Italy remained very poor for long after the war. One of . the prime objectives of Italian policy in the European Community, and one of the main reasons for Italy to join, was to ensure the acceptance by other European countries of substantial migration from the South. Belgium's political legitimacy has been questioned by the rivalries between the country's two 'nations', Walloons and Flemings. Belgium is not a nation-state, but nor is it a state-nation. It is an artificial and failed political entity. Euroenthusiasm is presently taken for granted there, but this is an expression of intra-Belgian xenophobia, not of genuine internationalism. If ever Flanders and Wallonia become quasi-independent regions within 'Europe', they will become perhaps the most nationalistic and inward-looking areas of the Continent.

countered by the combination of the North Atlantic Alliance and the increasingly liberal, multilateral world economic system. The distinctive feature of the arrangements for postwar European security was that they avoided non-trivial interference by any country with the rights of any other to order its own domestic affairs. The limiting of free-world sovereignty-pooling to the defence policy arena was crucial to its success. Further, the willingness of the members of NATO to put forestalling Soviet expansion-ism above all other foreign policy aims was, except perhaps in France, absolute.

It is also worth recalling, given the deliberate misuse so often made of it, the circumstances in which Churchill's 1946 call for a united Europe was made.[7] Like his offer of joint citizenship to France in the summer of 1940 (an offer rejected in favour of the defeatism that led, via Vichy, along the long road to 'common citizenship' in the European Union), Churchill's Zurich speech was a reaction to the most miserable of prospects in which avoiding the worst was more important than achieving the best. Europe in 1946 was an economic catastrophe area, totally dislocated. It was also militarily denuded, with the American withdrawing, Britain close to bankrupt, German rearmament – indeed the recreation of Germany – still almost unthinkable, and a restoration of French power likely to bring a risk of revanchism. Mass starvation, internal Communist takeovers or Soviet pressure were all real fears. Some sort of economic and political union in Europe seemed to Churchill to offer at least the hope of avoiding the most immediate dangers, whatever problems it might bring with it. It was, even so, not Churchill's intention that Britain should form part of a European Union. Clearly, Britain would, in the world of 1946, have had to play a major part in shaping a union. But there was no suggestion that Britain should be at its heart, even though the country had much more chance of playing such a role than it does now. In the event, the happy combination of Harry Truman and Ernie Bevin[8] produced Marshall Aid and NATO instead, allowing Europe to prosper in a world of interdependent, cooperating, separate democratic countries. Schemes for union, with a very different motivation, were taken over by technocrats and corporatists instead.

7 A recent blatant example was given by Michael Heseltine, who misinterpreted Churchill's 1946 speech as supporting his own views and then had the cheek, befitting a Euroenthusiast, to write: 'The Tory party, as so often in the past, would be wise to listen to his words.'

8 Bevin is one of very few British foreign secretaries – perhaps the only one – neither to be overawed by his mandarins nor to share their hereditary attitudes and prejudices.

The contrast between French technocratic vision of 'Europe' as a state-nation on the one hand and either the emergence of the multi-ethnic American nation or the success of the North Atlantic Alliance on the other could hardly be more marked. In some important respects, the French vision corresponds more closely with the Anglo-Scottish Union of the eighteenth century. England and Scotland (Lowland, Protestant Scotland at any rate) had sufficiently strong religious and commercial interests in common, particularly among élites, to justify a fusion of the two Parliaments. France played an important role in this acceptance of fusion. Its existence across the Channel represented religious antagonism, colonial competition and – in a mercantilist world – commercial rivalry. In the same way, French perceptions, still rooted in mercantilist thinking, see 'Europe' as a way of increasing muscle in a series of struggles, primarily against the United States, over culture, economic philosophy, 'spheres of influence' and economic hegemony.

But the conditions that allowed the successful development of the United Kingdom, after centuries of war between England and Scotland, do not exist in Europe.[9] The Union, via the British Navy, allowed Britain's technological leadership and private sector capitalist spirit to dominate the world economy. The Union was *not* an attempt to buttress and extend the power of a state technocracy – since next to none existed[10] – and would have failed if it had been. Europe does not have technological leadership

9  One economic reason why these conditions may now be less evident within Britain than in the eighteenth century is precisely that monetary union between England and Scotland intervened. Between 1750 and 1850 Scotland's per capita income went from around 50% of England's to around 100% in a context of internal free trade without monetary union of the Maastricht type. This period, which also not uncoincidentally saw the flowering of the Scottish Enlightenment, was marked by the existence of a successful and stable free banking system in Scotland, with private money issue. In England, in contrast, the dominant role of the Bank of England held back the growth of commerce. In 1844 the Bank Charter Act enshrined the Bank of England as a central bank, the sole producer of cash, south of the border. English businessmen complained that this gave an unfair competitive advantage to the Scots, and in 1845 the Act was extended to Scotland, ending free banking and subjecting the country to the depredations of a monopoly central bank. Scotland's relative economic decline soon began, gradually reducing attachment to the political union. The spread of external Free Trade, at around the same period, was another economic factor *reducing* the economic need for Scotland to form part of a political union with England. In all, the waxing and waning of the British union is a powerful counter-example to the intellectually lazy arguments of those like Heseltine who claim that economic integration and a single market will 'open the floodgates to demands for political union'.

10  It is true of course that there was a large number of sinecures in the gift of government, but it is in the nature of sinecures that, while they are clearly unfair and sometimes corrupt, they do not do a great deal of harm in other ways – except, since most sinecures were in the Admiralty or the War Office, during wars!

and 'Europe', if it came into being along lines shaped by French thinking, would certainly not have a private-sector capitalist spirit. Moreover, France would be neither willing nor able to play the role of Scotland in the eighteenth-century United Kingdom. Nor would Germany allow France to play the role of England – apart from anything else, the economic philosophies of the two countries are, despite the protestations of the prophets of 'Rhenish capitalism', still far apart. Moreover, the world really has changed, and French attempts to recreate the global mercantilism of the eighteenth century will fail. The opening-up of the world economy leads not to the hegemony of one country but to a reduced economic role for the state. Next, as we argued in chapter 3, the attempt by the French technocratic élite and their allies to opt out of world capitalism would lead to the economic decay of the whole of Europe. And, perhaps most important of all, 'Europe' does not, except in the eyes of the French technocracy and griping Tory 'toffs', now have an enemy to unite against as Scotland and England had France. The attempt of certain Euroenthusiasts to create such an enemy in the shape of the US and Japan smells nastily of *1984*.

How does this intellectual excursion tie in with the story of the ERM and EMU? EMU as seen by the French élite would be the single most important step in the attempt to construct a European state-nation in the furtherance of their interests in the world as a whole. But the ERM shows how the second great French preoccupation – the perceived risk of Germany hegemony *within* Europe – would be tackled. The ERM experience hardly went unnoticed in Germany. During the turbulence of early 1993, when the Bundesbank was under constant pressure from the French government to cut interest rates, German resentment and suspicion were voiced in explicit terms in an article in *The European* by Klaus Engelen, the editor of *Handelsblatt*. The occasion, the author and the vehicle were all significant. The article was written to mark the thirtieth anniversary of the Elysée Treaty between France and Germany. It is worth quoting at length:

Many Germans, particularly the older generation, want to avoid sounding nationalistic at almost any price. So they keep their uneasiness and doubts about the troubling aspects of Franco-German relations under wraps . . .

French Prime Minister Pierre Bérégovoy has made it clear that the overriding French goal of monetary union is to end France's politically embarrassing dependence on the Bundesbank. The implication is that the Germans must sacrifice their currency so as not to damage Franco-German relations . . .

There is now French rejection and distancing when it comes to keeping the world trading system open. France would rather wreck GATT than make further concessions at the expense of its farmers. This stance spells disaster for export-orientated Germany and is an ominous sign of where the EC is going under French domination. There are many Germans who have not forgotten France's attempts to jeopardize German unification. As some said at the time: 'With friends like this, who needs enemies?'

There is no doubt that Bérégovoy's *franc fort* policy gives the French additional bargaining leverage in the development of the structures of the EMU. He knows how to mobilize France's capitalist system – managed by a tight-knit, highly motivated *grande école* élite – towards a policy of containing the new Germany.[11] The aim is to bind Germany to a politically, economically, administratively and monetarily French-dominated EC. It is through a strategy of German containment that France's *grande école* élite hopes to run and represent the new and larger Europe . . .

Professor Günther Ammon, an expert on Franco-German relations, explains: 'In the mid-1980s, the French *grande école* state élite put forward a new political and economic order for Europe under the slogan of "European Single Market by 1992".' He concludes: 'With the fall of the Berlin Wall, the political concept of EC '92 – which was basically the projection of the French idea of nation-state to all of Europe – became obsolete.'

France's strategy of containing Germany within the new Europe is perhaps their last chance to save what is left of the original plans. The Germans are left dwelling on the illusion that, by exporting the Bundesbank model through the Maastricht Treaty to all of Europe, they will have protected their legitimate interests. There are many open-minded Germans who will have an uneasy feeling this week.

## Exporting the Bundesbank

Engelen was right to question the idea that setting up a Bundesbank look-alike and calling it the ECB would protect legitimate German interests – although it might further *illegitimate* interests. Quite simply, it would be impossible either to export the Bundesbank to the rest of Europe or to import the ECB into Germany. The place of the Bundesbank in German federalism is a very idiosyncratic one. Recall that its forerunner was set up by the Allied occupation authorities *not* primarily to prevent hyperin-flation[12] but to prevent the formation of a strong central government in Germany.[13] Of course, a strong central government *did* emerge. Nonethe-

---

11  It would probably be more accurate to say that the tight-knit highly motivated *grande école* élite knew how to mobilize Bérégovoy.

12  As we saw, the devastating inflation of the 1920s came immediately after an independent Reichsbank was set up; the monetary reform of 1948 came after a second inflation in which there was no German government at all.

13  The independent Bank deutscher Länder was a compromise between the Americans, who wanted to forbid any central monetary authority at all, and the British, who favoured a central bank covering the whole of the Western occupation zones but were in the process of nationalizing the Bank of England at home.

less, the Bundesbank's independence and its regional representation have subsequently been a source of considerable irritation to the French, as witnessed by Mitterrand's ill-starred declarations during the referendum campaign and by Trichet's fulminations against those members of the Bundesbank Council who were allegedly unsympathetic to Kohl's 'certain kind of Socialism'.

Over the past forty-seven years the Bundesbank has often abused its independence. There has also been a steady drift away from regionalism towards increased influence from central government. Both of these trends seem to be accelerating under Tietmeyer, yet the Bundesbank still comes in for very little public criticism in Germany. The SPD campaign against it, and against Tietmeyer in particular, in 1994 may have been electorally counterproductive. The unusual, almost unique, status of the Bundesbank reflects the particular historical and political circumstances of postwar Germany. It has been run by Germans, usually for Germany, and gave the country monetary leadership in Europe in a period when many Germans felt inhibited from being proud of their country in other ways. All that made it worth putting up with the central bank's not infrequent excesses. The Federal Republic was and is still a state in which Germans managed their own domestic affairs, including monetary affairs. The Bank deutscher Länder would clearly have been much less popular if its decision-making bodies had been composed mainly of British and Americans with just one token German. And an ECB with only one or two Germans on a Council of perhaps twenty would also drastically reduce political legitimacy in Germany.

It has been exactly what makes the Bundesbank so revered in Germany that makes the French élite so determined to eliminate it. As Engelen's article showed, many Germans are quite aware of this; it is hardly a secret. In September 1992, David Marsh, author of an informative and entertaining book on the Bundesbank, wrote in the *Financial Times* that:

Although ensconced on Europe's monetary throne, the Bundesbank is not without rivals who seek to pull it down. The EC's plan for economic union is not, as Lord Ridley, then UK secretary of state for industry, remarked with grandiose failure of perception in 1990, 'a German racket designed to take over the whole of Europe'. Rather, it is an attempt, led by France and Italy, to emasculate the Bundesbank by subsuming the D-Mark into a single European currency.

But Nicholas Ridley was a man of unfailingly acute perception. He would have no need to be told what France and Italy were up to. He was soon to see the Rome ambush of his friend and leader. Helmut Kohl, too, is hardly a political *ingénu*. What Ridley was doing was to give one possible answer to the vexing question of *why* Kohl has been willing to go along with scarcely concealed French plans to rob Germany of its most treasured institution.

## A European Germany or a German Europe?

The idea of 'Europe' has long been politically correct in Germany. Germany's experience as a nation-state of sorts was an unhappy one: from Prussian-dominated authoritarianism through Weimar chaos and Nazi barbarism, culminating in catastrophic defeat and dismemberment, the history of the German nation-state was punctuated by revolution, hyperinflation, mass unemployment and deliberate acceptance of the likelihood of war. The Federal Republic's forty-year life as a state before reunification, however, was one of economic prosperity, political stability and international ultra-respectability (with the significant exception of its shady dealings with Moscow and East Berlin). But there are many Germans, and foreigners, who treat that period, not the seventy-five years of nation-statehood, as the historical aberration – Germany must be saved from itself, they say. Before 1989, the Yalta agreement and the Cold War operated to 'tie Germany down'. With the break-up of the Yalta settlement and the removal of the Soviet threat to Western Europe, Germany will revert to type unless it commits itself to a new set of constraints: the European Union. Parroting the dictum first uttered by Thomas Mann, they cry: 'Better a European Germany than a German Europe.'

Presumably, what is meant by this is that everyone will feel happier if Germany continues to behave as it did from 1949 to 1989, striving to advance its own interests within the constraints imposed by mutual acceptability within a multilateral framework, rather than imposing *its* will on its neighbours. The step from this unobjectionable statement to the proposition that Germany can and should 'tie itself down' in 'Europe' is a very big one indeed. For as long as Germany remains a state-nation, Germans will have an interest in keeping Germany 'European' in this rather special sense: it will *need* partners if it is to advance its interests in an interdependent world. While as soon as there is a 'Europe', Germans will have an interest in making it German.

It has been pointed out for instance that German diplomatic tactics concerning the Helsinki process and the setting up of the Conference on Security and Cooperation in Europe were a classic example of what

Helmut Schmidt himself described as the 'attempt to cover our actions multilaterally'. 'Genscherism' as it evolved in the 1980s was based on the same premises. But in the multilateral context, Germany could not attempt to impose its will on its interlocutors: it was subject to constraints. In contrast, one of the first acts of German diplomacy after the signing of the Maastricht Treaty was to bounce the rest of the EC into recognition of Croatia and Slovenia by declaring unilaterally that the conditions reluctantly laid down by the EC had been met. However right or wrong German views may have been in this particular instance, the episode gives at the very least an indication of how much German sensitivity to the feelings and (self-perceived) interests of other European countries will be reduced in a 'Europe' of political union. It may even indicate a reason for Kohl's obsession with 'Europe' very different from the self-denying ordinance embraced by so many idealistic Germans. Kohl is hardly the man to believe that Germany needs to be 'saved from itself': 'Europe' may be precisely the way he hopes to legitimize a 'German Europe' including not only *Frankenreich* but also the lands to the east of Germany.

At all events, credulity really is strained beyond breaking-point by the suggestion implicit in much 'analysis' of Kohl's position that he is prepared to give up the Bundesbank and the DM so that its partners might consent to arrangements for tying Germany down![14] Instead, German prescriptivism about European Union is increasingly overt, and reflects one characteristic of many Germans that their neighbours find offensive: an insistence that what Germans do is right for Germans and must therefore be right for everyone else. German prescriptivism is a twentieth-century version of 'the white man's burden'. While the French élite vision of Europe can reasonably be called imperialist, the German *popular* vision, in contrast to Kohl's dream of a new *Frankenreich*, is missionary-colonialist.

The recent instance most notoriously unsettling to Germany's neighbours was the paper produced in September 1994 by the CDU's

14 Some political scientists produce a naive calculus along the following lines: France desperately wants monetary union and is mildly opposed to political union; Germany is very keen on political union and will not object too strongly to monetary union if an ECB looks like the Bundesbank; moving to monetary and political union simultaneously would therefore be in the interests of both countries. Even if the assumptions were descriptively accurate, the conclusion would not hold. Monetary union and political union interact with each other in a way that invalidates the static argument since monetary union is seen in both France and Germany not as an economic issue but as a way of altering the balance of political force between the two countries. Monetary and political union are two sides of the same coin and cannot be traded off against each other.

Parliamentary Committee on European Affairs under its chairman, Karl Lamers. This document, apparently approved by Kohl, insisted that France must abandon its 'obsession' with the 'empty shell of the nation-state' and that monetary and political union must proceed via a 'hard core' of Germany, France, the Benelux and Denmark. It also contained a naked threat: 'Never again must there be a destabilizing vacuum of power in central Europe. If European integration were not to progress, Germany might be called upon, or tempted by its own security constraints, to try to effect the stabilization [a word full of unpleasant historical echoes] on its own and in the traditional way.' Naturally, the 'peripheral' countries reacted unfavourably to the report (as, it needs to be said, did the SPD and FDP in Germany). But French reactions were the most significant.

## Torching the Republic

Just as Germans are justifiably more and more disinclined to allow France to create a technocratic state-nation out of 'Europe', most ordinary French people are aghast at the ideas in the CDU report. They are uneasy about being told by Germany not only what they must do but also what they must think. They suspect that the 'hard core' would become a '*Grosswirtschafts-raum Deutschlands*'. Unlike the Nazi blueprint, the DM area would include France, but France would have to conform to the German model. Even worse, the CDU hard men are insisting on a 'European army' as the inevitable complement to a single currency. Even for Delors to *advocate* such a thing produced worry in ordinary Frenchmen; for German politicians to *insist* on it produced fear.

The Maastricht referendum in France was a preview of the much fiercer debate that will take place when French people stir from the torpor that Mitterrand and Balladur induced in them. But until then the technocratic élite, encouraged by Klasen and Engelen in a belief in its own supremacy, will continue to press for the earliest possible monetary union, hoping to finesse the political and military quid pro quo that Kohl and the CDU may demand. As one highly placed *énarque* has recently put it: 'Of course we want monetary union. Ninety per cent of the élite want it. There is a little danger because the people do not want it: but we will take care of that.'

Is the French élite so determined to press on because its members really fear that the alternative is the reawakening of 'old demons' in Germany? The disinclination of the French élite to take decisive steps to *political* union in the wake of Germany's increased weight after unification and the arrival in the Community of three new members who show every sign of following Germany's lead (with more to come) still suggests that for them the important thing is to preserve and extend their own power. As Klaus Engelen stated so explicitly, the French idea of monetary union can only damage the 'ever closer union' of the *peoples* of Europe. What he might also have said, however, is that the same is true of the German idea. Maastricht, with monetary union at its heart, is *not* the natural completion of the Treaty of Rome; instead it is a manifesto for division and conflict in Europe.

As we have seen, German monetary leadership in Europe has been simultaneously embraced in France, if only by the Vichy tendency in the French élite, as necessary expiation for past sins (suffering being inflicted on ordinary people, who do not matter, not on the élite themselves) and bitterly resented. By hamstringing the ability of French governments to act in the interests of the French people – or, to put it more realistically, by giving them an excuse for not so acting – that embrace has destroyed political legitimacy in France. It has contributed to a contempt for democratic politics so profound, among both rulers and ruled, that the survival of the Fifth Republic may be brought into doubt in the next few years, 'Europe' or no 'Europe'.

The monetary union now so fervently wished for by the French élite would not restore legitimacy in France. Instead it would be the one thing *most* likely to reawaken 'old demons' in Germany because, if it were run to suit France, however unlikely that seems, it would interfere in the ordering by Germans of their own domestic affairs. In other words, it would destroy political legitimacy in Germany, just as the *franc fort* policy and the drive to 'Europe' have done in France.

Mitterrand, Balladur, Chirac, Juppé and Trichet have important differences, but they also have one hugely important thing in common – a belief in the primacy of the 'General Will'. For most people in Britain, politics is seen as providing a framework within which the constant balancing of the interests of different groups, or for that matter of different regions or countries, can proceed in legitimacy and reasonable harmony. Three hundred years of constitutional continuity from 1688 to 1972, without civil wars, revolutions, *coups d'état* or foreign occupation were testimony to the strength of that framework. That idea of politics is, literally, foreign to French technocrats. What they are interested in is power – first imposing *their* will on France and then imposing their conception of France's will on everyone else. Where they differ among themselves is in their idea of who should decided the General Will. Trichet clearly wants to be the arbiter by virtue of his appointment as Governor of the Banque de France and, he probably hopes, as first President of the ECB. Mitterrand, in his time, and most of the rest of the French politicians deem themselves entitled to that role, by virtue of their appointment by the élite.

The French public has no choice and, as yet, little interest in the matter. France has had foisted on it an 'independent' central bank totally incompatible either with republican tradition or with nostalgia for monarchy and totally inappropriate to France's historical and economic circumstances. It has happened with barely a murmur of protest other than from genuine Gaullists such as Philippe Séguin and Philippe de Villiers (the latter's anti-Maastricht party was the surprise packet of the 1994 European elections), who are then themselves branded 'Jacobin' for their trouble. This remarkable aberration is testimony to how much the fixation on 'Europe' has enfeebled political discourse. Governments in France have become hardly more accountable to the public than the independent central bank itself. The 'Socialist'–Mitterrandist government introduced legislation to create such a bank before its thumping electoral defeat; the 'Gaullist'–Mitterrandist government of Balladur reintroduced the same legislation in its essential details.

All supporters of an independent central bank in France have informed the electorate that it is necesary because the Governor of the Banque de France is at least a Frenchman, while the members of the Bundesbank Council are not: only the independence of the Banque de France will permit the construction of the ECB which will also, it is implied, have a French President and thus free France from Germany monetary domination. But if the ECB *is* ever created, it will certainly not act in a disinterested way in the interest of the Community as a whole, simply because there is no such thing as the Community interest. Either it will act in French interests or it will not. If it does, then Germany will destroy it, putting an end to fifty years of a 'European Germany'. If it does not, then it might well destroy France. There has been a revolution of one sort or another in France every generation since 1789 (only the First World War provided sufficient diversion to break this pattern). The decadence of French politics and the devastating unemployment together brought by 'Europe' provide the setting for the next upheaval. The trigger for it could turn out to be a realization that the pain of the *franc fort* and the near-abandonment of democratic principles had brought only the enthronement not of a new Frankish emperor but of an unaccountable monetary oligarchy in Frankfurt.

The technocrats have a contempt both for history and for democracy so total that the present tactic of the French administration seems nonetheless to be to go hell for leather for monetary union. The 'grandoise failure of perception' seems likely to be theirs. Once again, illusion will be more important than reality. Once again, all will be left to play for. Once again, economic perversity will go hand-in-hand with political perversion. Once again, the prosperity, legitimacy and stability of the European countries and amity among their peoples will be put gravely at risk. The history of the ERM is one of repeated rejection of the basic requirement of monetary union – that the people in every country should be prepared to let governments and central banks care more about economic conditions in the Community as a whole than about economic conditions in their own country. In short, the ERM story showed that 'Europe' is *not* a nation.

Jacques Delors was a federalist for less than totally praiseworthy reasons – a desire to confront the Anglo-Saxon world and 'Anglo-Saxon' market economics combined with a compulsion to expiate the French shame of 1940 and 1983 – but at least he saw what federalism implied. His decision not to run for the French presidency, and his last, defeated speech to the European Parliament as Commission President, expressed his realization that the requirements for a federal Europe could not be met. But that will not stop people trying. Still the cynicism of the French technocrats, traitors to their own people, and the arrogant, overbearing, menacing zeal of the German federalists, not to mention the grandiose ambitions of Helmut Kohl, remain on a collision course. The result of this clash of forces cannot yet be predicted with any precision. But it will be extremely unpleasant for the peoples of Europe.

## Offshore island?

Jacques Rueff, fierce 1950s critic of American monetary hegemony, once said; 'Europe will be built through a currency or it will not be built at all.' What the ERM story shows is quite the opposite: trying to lock countries like France and Germany together via their currencies does not forge one nation; instead it turns domestic monetary questions into international political conflicts. It damages the economic and political well-being of every country involved in it. Yet despite that clear evidence, even countries that were never part of the first Frankish Empire are drawn towards EMU like moths to the flame. One whole chapter of this book and substantial sections of several others have been devoted to one such country – Britain.

Despite the attention I have given to British problems, I suspect most readers will view those problems as essentially peripheral to what the ERM was really about: to repeat a phrase I used earlier, Britain is not at the heart of Europe, it never has been and it never will be. To the extent that the heart of Europe is found in its currency relations, Britain has every reason to be thankful for its present distancing. Neither John Major nor Tony Blair, however, refuses to rule out future British participation in a single currency. Why? Even Euroenthusiasts rarely if ever even attempt to adduce *positive* arguments for Britain to join a monetary union. Instead the anti-reason of fear is employed: the supposed costs of peripherality are played up. This dreadful monetary union is going to happen whether we like it or not, and we will be penalized if we don't close our eyes, say a few prayers, brace ourselves and walk into it.

The first and, in some ways most important, thing the British Euro-enthusiasts have neglected is that within a European shell Britain, like Mercia in the eighth and ninth centuries, would be an offshore island, but with considerably less independence. It would be influenced by the Continent, forced to obey its laws and to pay tribute to it, but would have no influence on it. Britain's 'peripheral' status would be *confirmed*, not miraculously transformed, by participation in 'Europe'.[15]

Some Euroenthusiasts, many of them Tory 'toffs', would prefer that tributary status for the sake of 'independence' from the United States. They hold these views despite the fact that the United States has three times this century – even if late on each occasion – helped Britain preserve its independence (on each occasion, the threat has come from the European Continent). And they hold them even though since the 1950s, American influence has, by re-establishing the 'Anglo-Saxon world system' so hated by the Nazis and by Mitterrand, Kohl and Delors, helped give both Britain and the Continent their greatest material prosperity ever.

Perhaps the clue to the real thinking of these people is given by Roy Jenkins, who made the claim, during the ERM turbulence of 1993, that Britain would have to be part of a single currency because otherwise it would be easier for the Continentals to bully us in currency terms – as if

15 The same is true for the other 'peripheral' countries – Italy, Spain, Portugal, Greece, Ireland and probably Finland – although the 1941 blueprint suggests Sweden might be invited in at some point, despite its public finance problems. It goes without saying of course that the 'cohesion countries' and Italy are being courted – and will probably be bribed and/or threatened – by France and Germany to give their assent at the 1996 Inter-Governmental Conference, just as they were bribed, to the tune of 15 billion ECUs, to give their assent to Maastricht.

Britain had experienced anything other than bullying since it joined the Community, and as if one British seat on an ECB Council taking majority decisions on a one-man, one-vote basis would change anything! In contrast, Britain's monetary independence, restored since September 1992, has, it is universally agreed, provided the best macroeconomic conditions for national success since Nigel Lawson went off the rails in his enthusiasm for the ERM.

A variant of the argument that if we do not give in to Continental bully boys they will take it out on us has recently been expressed by one of the most Euroenthusiastic of British banking figures, Christopher Johnson, of Lloyds Bank, who is also Chairman of the Association for the Monetary Union of Europe. Suppose there is a single currency and Britain stays out. Then, the argument goes, sterling will depreciate and our partners will accuse us of 'competitive devaluation' and find some way of restricting British access to their markets. Therefore Britain should join the single currency.

There are many things wrong with this argument, so revealing not only of the bad economics of the Euroenthusiasts but also of their underlying lack of backbone.

First, there is no reason to believe that sterling would depreciate rather than appreciate if it remained outside a single currency. The Swiss franc *appreciated* at the end of the 1992 when the people of Switzerland voted against their country's incorporation into the European Economic Area, ante-room to the European Union. Long-term interest rates in Switzerland fell, and consumer confidence started to improve, more than a year ahead of any improvement elsewhere in Continental Europe.[16] And something similar happened when the people of Norway rejected the European Union at the end of 1994. The Norwegian krone remained rock-solid during the currency tremors around the turn of the year, avoiding the weakness of other Nordic currencies.

What happens to sterling if Britain decides to stay out of a single currency will depend in part on market perceptions of whether Britain or 'Europe' is a more convincing economic and political area. The British side of the equation is in British hands. It is up to the people of Britain and their political leaders to decide how strong Britain is going to be. If defeatists prevail, if Britain decides to follow the Vichy example, then the country can be weakened enough to make the argument self-justifying. But Britain will

16 Despite all this, it is still the intention of Swiss politicians to push the country into 'Europe' at some point in the future. This, like the contempt of Danish politicians for the views of their own people, is depressing evidence of the permanent threat to democracy posed by 'Europe'.

surely see Churchill, not the Pétain of 1940, as the better historical model.[17]

As for 'Europe', a monetary union cannot survive without a political union, as the Bundesbank has said time without number.[18] But there will *not* be a political union cohesive enough for everyone to put 'Union' interests above national interests. That, too, has been made abundantly clear by the history of the ERM. It follows that the single European currency will certainly be weaker than the DM and probably weaker than *any* of the currencies of the *Frankenreich* bloc presently are. This will be true even if, as seems close to certain, Spain, Portugal, Greece, Italy and perhaps Ireland, are kept out. Even leaving aside the lack of political cohesion that will make running monetary policy a thankless and ultimately impossible task within a hard-core EMU, the political agenda of its most fervent proponents – France and the European Commission – would transfer French corporatism, and thus France's increasingly evident structural economic weakness, to the EMU area as a whole.[19] The EMU

17 Clearly, the analogy between present circumstances in Europe and those in 1940 should not be overplayed. Kohl, Mitterrand, Delors and their supporters and successors do not *intend* the abominable, pagan barbarism of Nazism; they are not threatening recalcitrant countries with military annihilation; they do not intend to unleash racial pogroms or establish death camps. But their ambitions, if realized, would create the conditions of economic decline, political illegitimacy and resentment among 'regions' in Europe in which xenophobic, as opposed to liberal, nationalism would flourish, and military superpower status would, as in Wilhelmine Germany, produce a temptation to engage in 'adventurism' on the world stage as a distraction from intractable domestic problems. Three years ago, who would have dreamt that the world would again be confronted with pictures from Europe of emaciated, broken men staring numbly out from behind the barbed wire of a concentration camp? Bosnia should be a dreadful warning to all those who want to destroy the political structures in Western Europe that have kept its countries in peace, friendship and prosperity for half a century.

18 The Bundesbank's basic argument is that the degree of 'solidarity' characteristic of nations would be required if a monetary union were to hold together in the face of disturbances inevitable once the exchange-rate shock-absorber was abolished. Kenneth Clarke has recently stated that monetary union would not necessarily require political union. It is true that monetary union would not create major macroeconomic disturbances if *all* the conditions described in chapter 3 were fulfilled first, but fulfilling all those conditions would take decades. More important, in the context of Clarke's contention, such fulfilment would, as we argued in chapter 3, in itself amount to a thoroughgoing *political* union. Moreover, while monetary union might not do any significant harm in such circumstances, it would bring only trivial benefits: there would be no significant *economic* reason for wanting it and only a *desire* for *political* union could explain a continued, fervent insistence on monetary union. Either Clarke has not thought the logic of his argument through, or he has simply chosen to continue the Euroenthusiast policy of deliberate obfuscation and deception.

19 Recall that this is a major reason why thinking Germans do not want a monetary union and why there will be very negative economic repercussions for Germany if there is one.

currency would thus need to *depreciate* in real terms against the currencies of countries fortunate enough to be outside it.

Whatever might happen at the point the decision was taken, sterling would inevitably – and appropriately – fluctuate against the single currency over the course of subsequent economic cycles. This book has shown what economic and political damage has been done – throughout Europe – by attempting to prevent appropriate currency fluctuations. And if foreign politicians' anger at failing to impose their will on Britain did ever overwhelm economic self-interest, those politicians would be revealing themselves as so hostile and irrational that Britain would surely count some trade difficulties a small price for keeping out of their clutches in other areas.

The argument put forward by Johnson and his ilk poses the question: what were first the Common Market and subsequently the Single Market *for*? 'Neo-functionalist' theorists see them as having little value in themselves but instead as being merely Trojan Horses for federalism and the European superstate.[20] It is undoubtedly the case that 'conveyor-belt' federalists have played a large role in the development of the European Community. Yet the creation of the Community itself was the product of its member states' desire to advance their *national* economic interests. At the point at which the Community, the Union or whatever, stops being an arrangement for the mutual advancement of national interests and instead becomes a vehicle for the imposition by 'neo-functionalists' of their idea of the 'interests of the Union', it will break down in conflict and chaos, for the neo-functionalists have next to no popular support and no legitimacy. The single currency would be the point of no return for the European Community.

At the risk of being boringly and annoyingly repetitive – some risks are worth taking – it has to be stressed yet again that the story of the ERM is totally at odds with neo-functionalist theory: it shows a fierce, ruthless struggle for *national* interests. But unlike the establishment of relatively unhindered trade within the Community – a development that made it possible for *everyone's* national interest to be advanced simultaneously – the ERM could not profit one country without simultaneously harming others. Ultimately, it hurt everyone. Fixed exchange rates transform domestic policy questions from 'low politics' (what gets done?) to 'high politics' (who

---

20 Many politicians in Germany try to draw a distinction between federalism and the European superstate; yet these are often exactly the same people who claim to be afraid that only a federal Europe can prevent federal Germany from acting as an aggressive superpower!

THE ROTTEN HEART OF EUROPE

decides what gets done?). The struggle for control of monetary policy becomes all-important, to the enormous detriment of economic and political health. The single currency will simply institutionalize that conflict, however 'independent' the ECB is supposed to be. It would certainly be best for everyone if it did not happen. But if it did, it would certainly be best for Britain not to be part of it.

The Euroenthusiasts – perhaps better described as British defeatists – have other arguments. The claim is made that foreign investment in Britain will dry up if Britain is 'left out' of a single currency. And it is said that London's importance as a financial centre will be jeopardized in such an event. These arguments too are wrong. Britain is the most attractive site in Europe for foreign direct investment for the same reasons that most *British* direct investment goes to parts of the world other than Europe: relative to the rest of Europe, Britain provides a market-friendly, outward-looking, non-protectionist, politically stable environment.[21] Compared to the rest of the world, Europe looks corporatist, inflexible, protectionist and inward-looking. Britain's advantages compared to the rest of Europe would be acentuated, not diminished, by the creation of a single currency with sterling outside, since the single-currency area would be economically hobbled and politically unstable. Of course, in an interdependent world, Britain, like everyone else, would suffer some harm from the self-inflicted folly of an EMU; but the advantages of staying out, once such an EMU was formed, would be considerable. Delors himself complained that Britain would be 'a paradise for foreign investors' with its Social Chapter opt-out and its floating currency. For once, he was right.

What are Britain's minus points from the point of view of potential overseas investors? Thanks to the Thatcher revolution, the risk of a return to the Socialism/corporatism of 1940–79 is much reduced – as long as Britain keeps its distance from 'Europe'. But the country does have a record of macroeconomic instability. The 1979–81 recession was painful, but may have been necessary and unavoidable. The 1987–92 boom/bust was unnecessary, avoidable and damaging. It was caused by ERM-shadowing and ERM membership. The lesson should be clear: allow sterling's exchange rate to adjust to economic circumstances if Britain is to become more stable in terms of the things that matter to overseas investors: output,

---

21 One of Mrs Thatcher's ambitions was for Britain to have both its major parties support the capitalist economy. The conversion of Tony Blair to so many of Mrs Thatcher's policies means that her ambition is on the way to being realized – as long as Blair himself can be rescued from his infatuation with 'Europe'.

the inflation rate, the public finances, tax rates, the cost of capital relative to the prospective return on it. The irony of Mrs Thatcher's legacy is that some of the most dangerous politicians, those who ignore this lesson because they distrust market capitalism, are, for the time being at least, big beasts of a Tory Party in precipitate decline.

What about the City? The answer is obvious. London is such a successful financial centre because it provides the right environment for the markets it hosts. Those markets are the epitome of capitalism red in tooth and claw – whether one likes that or not.[22] They would be suffocated in a single-currency area.

A single currency would be managed by the ECB. However much it looked like the Bundesbank and however much it were dominated by Germany, it would not, of course, *be* the Bundesbank. The ECB would enjoy neither market credibility nor political legitimacy (the absence of the second being enough on its own to ensure the absence of the first). One could make the ECB *look* like the Bundesbank, but one could not – even if one wanted – make 'Europe' like Germany. But it is unquestionable that the ECB would try to mimic the Bundesbank *in the way it interacts with financial markets in its area*. The Bundesbank's operating techniques both shape and reflect the nature of German financial markets: dominated by 'universal banks', they are conservative, heavy-footed and clannish. This suits the Bundesbank, which sees financial markets as being as much of a threat to its autonomy as governments are. It has characterized London financial markets – lightly regulated, securitized, disintermediated, internationally oriented and innovative – as a 'casino', over which a central bank can have little control.

---

22 One aspect of global capitalism proves particularly objectionable to protectionist 'Europeans' such as Delors. They argue that Asian workers are paid wages so low that competition from them would force European wages down catastrophically in the absence of protection. This fallacy has been a constant in French economic thinking for centuries and crops up from time to time even among 'Anglo-Saxon' commentators. It betrays not only a failure of economic reasoning but a selfish and insulting attitude to the poor of the world. In reality, the combination of global capital flows and free trade *raises* the wages of workers in poor countries rather than *lowering* the wages of workers in rich countries. As output rises in the poor countries (reducing, *ceteris paribus*, the output of rich countries), poor-country incomes also rise, *increasing* demand for rich-country output. Of course, incomes and spending will not remain exactly in step in any particular year, but the consequences of this are questions of short-term macroeconomic stabilization; in no circumstances do they provide a justification for limiting the free flow of capital or trade. The changes in the world pattern of production also require structural flexibility in the rich countries – something that always makes defensive, negative thinkers uncomfortable. But that is their problem, and it should not be made a burden for the backs of the poor.

The Bundesbank's current president, Tietmeyer, can be seen throughout the Continent, at one of his 'client' central banks after another, wagging
his massive index finger, giving his menacing teeth-bared half-smile, half-
snarl, and warning his audience grimly that they must beware of financial
market professionals. The Bundesbank has a reputation for liking to
'surprise' the international markets, that is, to remind them who is boss by
inflicting losses on them. At the same time, it is very concerned to keep the
German domestic banks sweet so that it can exert 'moral suasion' over
them. And it does all this while maintaining a holier-than-thou disdain for
the lender-of-last-resort function of the traditional central bank. As a result
of this patron–client relationship, Frankfurt has remained a financial
market backwater in which the large German banks enjoy economic rent.
An ECB will be able to behave in the same way *only* if the culture, structure
and behaviour of financial markets in its area conform to the present
German model. London financial markets decidedly do not.

If Britain became part of the domain of an ECB, London would have to
transform itself into a Frankfurt clone – yet the real Frankfurt would benefit
from its geographical, linguistic and cultural proximity to the ECB and
London would lose its existing advantages. In global terms, the whole of
Europe would be the financial-market backwater. And within Europe,
London would – if imprisoned in EMU – inevitably be discriminated against
by the ECB and the European Council (that is, by Continental authorities).
The temptation to introduce regulations and controls that would cripple
London and cut it off from world financial markets would be hard to resist.[23]

London is essentially a *global* financial centre. It is vital for it to be able to
compete with New York and Tokyo – and, increasingly, with Singapore and
Hong Kong and even Seoul. To do that it needs to remain innovative,
deregulated, securitized and disintermediated. And to do *that* it needs to
operate with a central bank that, like the Fed and the Bank of England, does
not display antipathy towards financial markets but instead has financial-
market stability as its *raison d'être*. Within a single-currency area ruled by a
would-be Bundesbank, it simply could not do that. An EMU with Britain
in it would mean terminal decline for London. But if EMU happened and
Britain stayed out, London would be perfectly placed to cash in on the
inevitable decline of Paris and Amsterdam within 'Europe' and of 'Europe'
as a whole versus the rest of the world.

23 The question here is not one of trade, where to some extent Germany shares British instincts,
but of regulation of domestic financial activities, where Bundesbank ideas are not at all the
same as those of Britain.

Many of the single-currency zealots in Europe know all this perfectly well. This is why so much of the Commission's propaganda effort has been directed – via its contacts with and subventions to organizations like Christopher Johnson's AMUE – towards fooling people into believing exactly the opposite. On this question, as on every other question about the ERM and monetary union, the propaganda steamroller attempts to flatten analysis. For analysis can only mean dissent. And dissent cannot be tolerated.

# References

## Introduction

xii Schapiro, writing of Stalin: *The Communist Party of the Soviet Union* (2nd ed., London, 1970), p. 477, quoted in Alan Bullock, *Hitler and Stalin: Parallel Lives* (London, 1991).

xiii thoughts of John Pinder: 'From Milan to Maastricht: Fifty Years of Federalist Struggle for the Uniting of Europe', essay prepared for the convention 'Europe called to account: federalism or nationalism', Milan, 26 November 1993.
   The head of the Commission's . . . ceaseless denigration: See Geoffrey Martin, 'Migrants: How about some more facts?', letter to *Sunday Times*, 26 February 1995, and 'Euroscepticism, The New British Disease', in *European Brief*, vol. 2 no. 6, March/April 1995, pp. 20–2.
   'The two . . . without borders': Gabriel Robin, *Un monde sans maître* (Paris, 1995).

xiv 'the KBG . . . shoulder': Quoted in Charles Grant, *Delors: Inside the House that Jacques Built*, (London, 1994), p. 209.

xv 'the pitch-black distrust': *Süddeutsche Zeitung*, 28 March 1994.


## Chapter 1

5  (note 2) Kenneth Clarke opined: See *The Times*, 16 January 1995.

6  Schmidt wanted political union: See David Marsh, *The Bundesbank: the Bank that Rules Europe*, (London, 1993), p. 232.

7  'The EEC . . . coachman': Quoted in Andrew Tyrie, 'Political economy of economic and monetary union', *Rivista di Politica Economica*, 81, no. 5, May 1991, pp. 411–42.

7  (note 5) '*Par la guerre*': Quoted in Henry Kissinger, *Diplomacy*, (New York, 1995), p. 604.

8  The Bundesbank had been set up: The early years of the Bundesbank are related, along with much else, in Marsh, *Bundesbank*.

9  'We had to use brute force': Interview in Leo Brawand, *Wohin steuert die deutsche Wirtschaft*, (1970), quoted in Marsh, p. 187.
   one reason for Schmidt to conduct his initial negotiations: The negotiations on the setting-up of the EMS are described in some detail in Peter Ludlow, *The Making of the European Monetary System* (London, 1982).

12 the Catholic élite in Ireland: See D. Keogh, 'Ireland, the Vatican and Catholic Europe 1916–1939', doctoral thesis, European University Institute, Florence, 1982, cited in Ludlow.

ambition that he himself eagerly supported: See Ludlow, p. 256.

13 (note 10) Euroenthusiasm and the idea of 'Christendom': A useful review of French Catholic attitudes in the key years of the early 1950s is Yvon Tranvouez, 'Europe, chrétienté et catholiques français en marge du MRP', in Serge Berstein, Jean-Marie Mayeur et Pierre Milza (eds), *Le MRP et la construction européenne*, (Paris, 1994).

'Lotharingian' origins: Joseph Hours, 'L'Europe à ne pas faire', in *La Vie Intellectuelle*, October 1950; quoted in Tranvouez.

attempts to create a 'European' Catholic identity: See François Perroux, *Europe sans rivages* (Paris, 1954); quoted in Tranvouez.

French Catholic thinking . . . German Catholicism: See Joseph Rovan, 'Catholiques de France, Catholiques d'Allemagne, in *La Nef*, January 1954; quoted in Tranvouez.

14 'a Community of Inflation': See Ludlow, p. 136.

'we would not be dealing with M. Giscard d'Estaing': Interview in *Die Zeit*, 14 July 1978, quoted in Ludlow, p. 137.

15 relaunched the previous autumn by . . . Roy Jenkins: Roy Jenkins, 'Europe's Present Challenge and Future Opportunity, First Jean Monnet Lecture, Florence, 27 October 1977.

17 'the spirit of Charlemagne brooded over us': Quoted in *Corriere Della Serra*, 16 September 1978, as reported in Ludlow, p. 182.

## Chapter 2

19 Schmidt actually threatened to revoke its independence: See Marsh, p. 194.

21 (note 1) they did not bother with euphemisms: See Michel Winock, *Nationalisme, antisémitisme et fascisme en France* (Paris, 1990), chapter 3 ('L'antiaméricanisme français').

'post-fascist' Minister . . . accused 'New York Jews': As reported in *La Repubblica*, 12 August 1994.

'exchange-rate stability cannot be imposed on the system': US Treasury Press Releases, B.905, 15 May 1978, quoted in Ludlow, p. 119.

EC Commission in its 'convergence report': Published as Commission of the European Communities, *European Economy*, no. 53, 1994.

28 'There is an international conspiracy against France': Quoted in Jacques Attali, *Verbatim, Tome 1, 1981–1986* (Paris, 1993), p. 350.

29 The pressures on the franc . . . battle in Paris: For accounts of these events see, for instance, Philippe Bauchard, *La guerre des deux roses: du rêve à la réalité, 1981–1985* (Paris, 1986).

Kohl was . . . battle in Paris: See Grant, p. 53.

30 'arrogant and uncomprehending people': See Grant, pp. 52–3.

31 'tutelage of the victorious Nazis: John Laughland, *The Death of Politics: France under Mitterrand* (London, 1994), p. 227.

33 'modern-day Gold Standard': Speech at IMF meeting in Washington, 24 September 1990.

41 Kohl and Gorbachev had already come to an agreement: See *International*

*Currency Review*, Occasional Paper No. 4, World Reports Limited, London, September 1993, p. 20.

42 Balladur would present . . . a proposal: Edouard Balladur, 'The Monetary construction of Europe', Memorandum from Minister of Finance to Ecofin, January 1988.

## Chapter 3

43 'The Memoirs of a Tory Radical': Nigel Lawson, *The View from No. 11: the Memoirs of a Tory Radical* (London, 1992).

49 'Walters Critique': Set out in Alan Walters, *Britain's Economic Renaissance* (London, 1986).

62 Lawson quite rightly insisted . . .: Nigel Lawson, 'The State of the Market', Institute of Economic Affairs, London 1988.
The former Chancellor himself has recently claimed: 'The Conduct of Economic Policy', *Bank of England Quarterly Bulletin*, May 1994, vol. 34, no. 2, pp. 175–80.
Kenneth Clarke . . . preventing a recrudescence: Mansion House speech, 15 June 1994. Lawson immediately attacked Clarke's analysis: see 'Lawson scorns plan to avoid boom-bust cycle', *Financial Times*, 24 June 1994.

64 'It may well be . . .: Lawson, *View from No. 11*, p. 994.
tears of a Clown: The most comprehensive statement of Brown's thinking on these issues was given in a speech in London on 17 May 1995.

65 [Lawson] excoriated the Delorsian view: The best example, quoted approvingly by Mrs Thatcher in her memoirs, is in Lawson's speech at Chatham House, 25 January 1989.

66 Howe – subsequently identified: See Grant, p. 279.

67 Mrs Thatcher . . . direct public criticism of Lawson: See Lawson, *View from No. 11*, p. 919, and Margaret Thatcher, *The Downing Street Years* (London, 1993), p. 710.
she had to apologize to Lawson in private: Lawson, *View from No. 11*, p. 920.

68 Howe . . . intimations from Spain: See Lawson, *View from No. 11*, p. 929.
Grant, p. 279, seems to imply that Howe and Gonzalez may have been in cahoots on certain issues.

70 (note 19) 'One Market, One Money': Commission of the European Communities, 'One Market, One Money, in *European Economy*, 44, Brussels, October 1990.

71 Mrs Thatcher . . . majority voting: See Thatcher, p. 56.

72 'Nigel Lawson was a very clever man': Interview in 'The Downing Street Years', BBC Television, October 1993.

## Chapter 4

74 (note 2) Michael Portillo made the point: 'A [single currency] would mean giving up the government of the UK.' Remarks of 1 May 1994, quoted in *The Times*, 2 May 1994.

# THE ROTTEN HEART OF EUROPE

75 the construction of an 'imagined community': The idea was popularized by
Benedict Anderson, *Imagined Communities: Reflections on the Origin and Spread of
Nationalism* (New York, 1983).

Delors was thrown back on generalizations: See Delors's article 'Calendrier
pour l'Europe', in *Belvedere*, October/November 1991, and his interview 'Wir
müssen Grossmacht werden', in *Der Spiegel*, 14 October 1991. Delors does not
speak more than rudimentary German, and the *Spiegel* interview must have been
conducted in French and translated into German. However, Delors's archives
claim that the French 'translation' they hold is 'unreliable' and cannot be made
available – perhaps suggesting a desire for the views he expressed in the article
not to be too widely known in France.

packed the Commission with French Socialists: See Grant, especially
chapter 6.

(note 3) the idea of 'Europe' . . . simply absent: Alan S. Milward,
'Conclusions: the value of history', in Alan S. Milward, Frances M.B. Lynch,
Ruggero Ranieri, Federico Romero and Vibeke Sorense, *The Frontier of
National Sovereignty: History and Theory 1945–1992* (London, 1993), p. 185.

77 *Bild* spilled the beans: 'Das Ende der Mark', *Bild-Zeitung*, 11 December 1991.
79 the committee's report: Report on Economic and Monetary Union: (Delors
Report), EC Publications Office, Luxembourg, 1989.

Lawson . . . with Pöhl: Lawson, *View from No. II*, p. 908.
85 campaign . . . in favour of a DM realignment: See, for instance, Karl Otto
Pöhl, 'Aktuelle Fragen der Währungspolik', speech to Banking Federation in
Bonn, 6 October 1989; Lothar Müller, Bundesbank Council, 'Europa braucht
eine Stabilitätsgemeinschaft', speech to French Banking Association, Munich,
24 November 1989.

'Pöhl . . . speech to a banking association: Pöhl, cited above.
86 Bérégovoy confirmed French obduracy: Speech to French National Assembly,
17 October 1989.

(note 13) Pöhl . . . contradicted the Lawson argument: Pöhl, cited above.
88 Tietmeyer . . . stated quite categorically: Speech to German savings banks
association, Garmisch-Partenkirchen, 7 November 1989.
89 'Something of a rough diamond for an official': Lawson, *View from No. II*,
p. 500.

(note 15) Hesse . . . : quoted in David Marsh's book Marsh, p. 76.
91 (note 18) stability policy was 'possible only if the exchange-rate instrument is
available': 'Aktuelle geld-und währings politische Fragen – Auf den Weg zur
Währungsunion', lecture to Statistics and Economics Association, Basle, 11
December 1989.
92 Pöhl had described the idea of monetary union as 'fantastic': Interview in *Die
Zeit*, 26 January 1990, quoted in Marsh, p. 205.

Schlesinger as 'very unrealistic': Quoted in Marsh, p. 208.
93 members of the Bundesbank Council . . . public statements: See Wilhelm
Nölling, member of Bundesbank Council, interview with *Hamburger Abendblatt*,
23 May 1991, quoted in Marsh, p. 218.
98 Wilhelm Nölling put it very clearly: Remarks to US–German economic policy

404

group, 7 March 1991, quoted in Marsh, p. 236. He repeated these remarks word for word shortly after his retirement in an address to Cityforum Ltd, Durham, 1 December 1992, when he also expressed very strong opposition to the Maastricht Treaty.

Its existence was revealed: 'Axes pour sortir de la crise du SME', Marcel Letelier (pseudonym), *De Pecunia*, Brussels, August 1993.

99 'all for one and one for all': Statement by the Bundesbank in its *Monthly Report*, February 1992.

the member states dismissed the scheme: This was confirmed by Erik Hoffmeyer, Governor of the Danish central bank, in a speech at the conference on 'Denmark and the European Union', Luxembourg, 9 February 1994.

102 'I could not help noticing. . .': Lawson, *View from No. 11*, p. 1011.

The Bundesbank . . . unsustainable rate: Remarks by Karl-Otto Pöhl in September 1990, reported in Marsh, p. 336, note 71.

104 an even sillier hare: See Grant, p. 169.

The announcement . . . angered him: See the 'Observer' column of the *Financial Times*, 7 October 1990. Mrs Thatcher recalls in her memoirs (p. 710) that Leon Brittan had told her in 1989 that Delors had said to him: 'If she joins, she wins.' Brittan seems to have given the impression that Delors meant she would win against her European 'partners'; it is much more likely that what Delors was afraid of was a victory over those Tories who wanted to get rid of her.

(note 33) a valedictory utterance: Speech to European Parliament, December 1994.

106 (note 38) Hunt . . . told Eurofanatic conservatives: BBC TV, 'On the Record', January 1995.

'Delors . . . stamped his foot: Press conference after European Council, Rome, 15 December 1990.

108 [Pöhl] described unification as a 'disaster': Comments to economic committee of the European Parliament, 19 March 1991.

109 Marsh . . . surprisingly says: Marsh, p. 4.

113 The Banco de España . . . French franc: See interview given by Mariano Rubio, Governor of the Banco de España, in *Le Figaro*, 18 June 1991.

Some academic commentators . . . absurd fashion: Daniel Gros and Niels Thygesen, *European Monetary Integration: From the European Montary System to European Monetary Union* (London, 1992), p. 197.

114 (note 45) 'The present . . . EMS': Gros and Thygesen, cited above.

## Chapter 5

117 Pöhl . . . said in an interview: Quoted in Marsh, p. 235.

118 Kohl told the Bundestag: Statement to Bundestag of 13 December 1991 on results of the Maastricht European Council.

What would happen, asked Nölling: Presidential address, Landeszentralbank of Hamburg, 15 January 1992.

119 (note 1) Kohl's agreement to the 'irrevocable' final date . . .: See Wayne

Sandholz, 'Monetary bargains: the Treaty of EMU', in Alan Cafruny and Glenda Rosenthal (eds), *The State of the European Community* (Boulder, Colorado, 1993), pp. 125–42.

root-and-branch attack on monetary union: 'Economic and Political Aspects of European Monetary Union, lecture to council meeting of the Southern Economic Association, November 1991; translated in *Deutsche Bundesbank: Auszüge aus Presseartikeln*', no. 6, 23 January 1992.

interview given to a French newspaper by Jacques de Larosière: Interview with *Le Figaro*, 14 January 1992, translated in *Deutsche Bundesbank: Auszüge aus Presseartikeln*, no. 7, 28 January 1992.

120 (note 2) Horst Köhler said in April 1992: Interview with *Der Spiegel*, April 1992. Quoted in Marsh, p. 253.

121 'a German hatchet-job' . . . 'victory of German selfishness over international solidarity': Quoted in speech by Lothar Müller, 'Währungspolitik im Spannungsverhältnis zwischen europäischer Union und deutscher Wiedervereinigung', Augsburg, 14 January 1992.

(note 5) Padoa-Schioppa himself has expressed disgust: Lorenzo Bini-Smaghi, Tommaso Padoa-Schioppa and Francesco Papadia, 'The Transition to EMU in the Maastricht Treaty', *Essays in International Finance*, no. 194, November 1994.

126 Press reports of the meeting: In for instance *Publico* and *Diario dos Noticias* of 6 April 1992, and also the *Financial Times* of the same date.

127 Braga told the Portuguese press: *Publico*, 24 November 1992.

## Chapter 6

129 Delor's plans . . . revealed in the press: An article by Boris Johnson, 'Delors plan to rule Europe', in the *Sunday Telegraph* of 4 May 1992 was widely reprinted in the Danish press.

130 [Pinheiro] was particularly savage: See *Financial Times*, 5 June 1992.

'Something is rotten . . .': Quoted in *Financial Times*, 4 June 1992.

The Treaty of Rome be damned: On 3 June, Mitterrand was quoted by a French government spokesman as saying that no revision of Maastricht would be necessary, despite the Danish rejection, because 'Eleven of us will do what twelve cannot.' See *Financial Times*, 4 June 1992.

No, they implied . . . crisis for Denmark!: See David Buchan, 'Partners leave Danes to ponder their fate', in *Financial Times*, 5 June 1992.

a judge of the European Court . . . joined in: Paul Kapteyn, article in *Het Nederlandse Juristenblad*, June 1992, as reported by AP-Dow Jones, 22 June 1992.

133 influential article by David Walton: David Walton and Paola Bergamaschi, 'Italy under pressure', in *The International Economics Analyst*, Goldman Sachs, London, June 1992.

Pöhl's throwaway lines: Quoted in Marsh, p. 24.

137 Major made a quite staggering statement: Remarks quoted in *Sunday Times*, 7 July 1992.

140 Norman Lamont . . . steps of the Treasury: The text of the statement can be found in *Financial Times*, 27 August 1992.
speech to be made by Reimut Jochimsen: Remarks contained in version, released in advance, of speech to be delivered in Düsseldorf, 26 August 1992. The speech as actually delivered did not contain these remarks, enabling the Bundesbank to issue a statement (26 August) denying that it was seeking a realignment. As on the occasion, three weeks later, of the advance release of remarks by Schlesinger that were said not to have been 'cleared for publication' (p. 155 of the text), the markets were much more impressed with the unexpurgated version as revealing the Bundesbank's true thinking.
EC finance ministers issued a statement: Communiqué issued by the Monetary Committee of the European Communities, Brussels, 28 August 1992.

141 What the treaty meant, said Mitterrand: Remarks in televised referendum debate, 'Aujourd'hui l'Europe', TF 1, 3 September 1992.

142 next edition of the *Auszüge*: *Auszüge aus Presseartikeln*, no. 61, 9 September 1992.
German newspapers . . . complaining: See, for instance, Lothar Rühl, 'Paris und die Dämonen', in *Die Welt*, 4 September 1992. For French criticism of statements by leading politicians, see Eric le Boucher, 'Bonn: l'exploitation de la "peur de l'Allemagne" dans la campagne irrite beaucoup. . .', in *Le Monde*, 4 September 1992. For an analysis by a newspaper from a 'non-combatant' country see 'With Friends Like These. . .', in *Wall Street Journal*, Brussels, 2 September 1992.

143 (note 17) Schlesinger had referred to the Bundesbank's fears: 'After Maastricht: European Monetary Integration in the 1990s', address to the Stockholm School of Economics, 31 January 1993.
(note 18) Schlesinger made his own feelings plain: Speech in Amsterdam, 5 November 1992.
'Interest rates are at unbearable levels': Quoted in *Financial Times*, 5 September 1992.

146 finance ministers' statement . . . 'confirmed': The communiqué of the finance ministers and governors of the EMS countries was issued on 5 September 1992. It and the comments by Lamont and Sapin were quoted in the *Financial Times* of 7 September 1992.

147 Schlesinger declined to support: Interview on 'The World This Weekend', BBC Radio 4, 6 September 1992.
(note 21) It is already clear from Lamont himself: Interview on BBC TV 'On the Record', February 1995.

148 'candidates for devaluation': Report by AFX news agency, Frankfurt, 9 September 1992, summarized by ITV Oracle teletext service, same day.
Ciampi defied the rules: Quoted in *Financial Times*, 11 September 1992.
Major . . . destroy his credibility: Speech to Scottish CBI, Glasgow, 10 September 1992.

149 Previous accounts . . . portray him as having misled: See, notably, Peter Norman and Lionel Barber, 'The monetary tragedy of errors that led to currency chaos', in *Financial Times*, 11 December 1992.

story was publicly recounted . . . by Schlesinger: 'Fortschritte der monetären Integration in Westeuropa', speech at Institut für Weltwirtschaft, Kiel, 14 September 1992.

150 Kohl had paid a secret visit:  See Peter Norman, 'The day Germany planted a currency time bomb', in *Financial Times*, 12/13 December 1992.

they travelled to Paris:  See Norman, cited above.

document that fuelled a bitter row:  'Comments made by Bundesbank President Professor Dr Helmut Schlesinger on reproaches made by some members of the British government', statement released by the German Embassy in London, 30 September 1992. The same evening, the British Treasury issued a counter-statement denying that a realignment request had been put to Britain during the period 11–13 September; see 'the UK Treasury again denies Frankfurt's version of events', in *Financial Times*, 1 October 1992.

(note 25) Nölling . . . reported:  Wilhelm Nölling, address at Cityforum Ltd, Durham, 1 December 1992.

151 'sweetheart deal' (a term first coined . . . Bertie Ahern):  See *Financial Times*, 6 January 1993.

155 newspaper interview to be published the next day:  Report by German news agency, DPA, on 15 September of interview to be published in *Handelsblatt* the next day.

156 British ministers ordered Leigh-Pemberton:  See Norman, cited above.

(note 30) 'The ironic thing':  Quoted in *Financial Times*, 18 September 1992.

'hole in the head':  Quoted in *Financial Times*, 17 September 1992.

157 It was Major himself . . . wanted reassurance:  Philip Stephens, 'Smiling through the tears', *Financial Times*, 18 September 1992.

158 surprising facet of the suspension call:  See Andrew Hill, 'British effort to suspend mechanism quickly rebuffed', *Financial Times*, 18 September 1992.

(note 31) Major . . . blaming Germany . . . Tietmeyer . . . haughtily declared: Ivo Dawnay and Robert Graham, 'Major calls for ERM reform', *Financial Times*, 19/20 September 1992.

162 Treasury . . . economists . . . had come to the conclusion:  These concerns were voiced publicly by officials, to the distress of ERM supporters such as Sam Brittan, on the margins of the IMF meetings in Washington a few days after White Wednesday; see Sam Brittan, 'Anatomy of the UK defeat', *Financial Times*, 24 September 1992.

163 'singing in the bath':  Remarks by Norman Lamont to journalists at IMF/ World Bank meetings, Washington, 20 September 1992.

'Clearly, it is not imminent':  Quoted in *Financial Times*, 19/20 September 1992.

164 Lamont had claimed:  Norman Lamont, speech to European Policy Forum, London, 10 July 1992; Norman Lamont, 'Yes, it hurts but I won't change tack', article in *Daily Mail*, 16 August 1992.

(note 34) Sam Brittan . . . declared:  'Early end to puerile joy', in *Financial Times*, 5 October 1992.

Eddie George was later to point out:  Speech at the Annual Dinner of the 100 Group of Finance Directors, London, 3 November 1993.

(note 35) Lamont . . . changed the line: See Philip Stephens, 'The note on ERM that could produce discord', *Financial Times*, 25 September 1992.
165 Lamont . . . said with justifiable satisfaction: Interview on the 'Today' pogramme, BBC Radio 4, 18 September 1992.
(note 36) pointed out by Anatole Kaletsky: Anatole Kaletsky, 'Economic View: Labour should be grateful for Major's 1992 victory', *The Times*, 25 May 1995. Sam Brittan, himself writing: Sam Brittan, 'Economic Viewpoint', *Financial Times*, 17 September 1992.
(note 37) appeal to the spurious notion: Philip Stephens, 'Smiling through the tears', *Financial Times*, 19/20 September 1992.

## Chapter 7

167 '*Réalignements? Il n'y en aura plus*': The doctrine that there would never be any change in the Franc–DM parity even if other countries realigned had already been publicly enunciated by Bérégovoy at a meeting of the Franco-German Economic and Finance Council on 24 August 1989.
the two authors concluded: Gros and Thygesen, *European Monetary Integration*, p. 166.
169 The 'fault lines' . . . Major belatedly discovered: Interview on 18 September 1992, quoted in *Financial Times*, 19/20 September.
170 Keynes could write: Preface to French edition of *A Tract on Monetary Reform* (London, 1924).
176 (note 8) a German newspaper . . . derided French fears: Karl Jetter, 'Deflation – eine Chiffre der Besorgnis: Zur Wirtschaftsdebatte in Frankreich', in *Frankfurter Allgemeine Zeitung*, 4 September 1992.
177 Schlesinger . . . speech describing the French franc: Quoted in *Financial Times*, 22 September 1992.
179 speculators had been beheaded: Quoted in *Financial Times*, 24 September 1992.
181 Delors had insinuated: Quoted in *Financial Times*, 25 September 1992.
182 a monetary mini-union *immediately*: Quoted in *Financial Times*, 26/27 September 1992.
get his retaliation in first: Quoted in *Financial Times*, 23 September 1992.
(note 12) 'no place in a democracy': Speech in Quimper, 28 August 1992, cited in Grant, p. 223.
'short-term satisfaction of their public opinion': Remarks to press, Brussels, 24 September 1992, quoted in *Financial Times*, 25 September 1992.

## Chapter 8

188 Spain began insinuating: See, for instance, remarks to reporters outside a meeting of the Monetary Committee in Berlin, 23 October 1992, apparently attributed to Manuel Conthe, Director-General of the Spanish Treasury, and quoted by Reuter. Similar remarks were made by Solchaga in a *New York Times* interview on 5 November 1992, quoted in the *Financial Times* of 6 November.

He had earlier called for an 'urgent reordering' of ERM parities (quoted in *Financial Times*, 26/27 September 1992).

189 (note 6) Mrs Anne Wibble had asked: See *Financial Times*, 6 January 1993.
Schlesinger . . . went out of his way: 'After Maastricht: European monetary integration in 1990s', address to the Stockholm School of Economics, 31 January 1993.
'a currency that doesn't really exist': See *Wall Street Journal*, 23 November 1992.

190 Issing had raised the spectre: Speech quoted in *Financial Times*, 11 November 1992.

191 insinuated . . . that the ERM had been 'hijacked': See Peter Bruce and Andrew Gowers, 'A testing of Spanish mettle', interview with Gonzalez and Solchaga, *Financial Times*, 5 October 1992.

193 Braz, told reporters: Reuter, 22 November 1992.
(note 8) Italian newspaper accounts: See, for instance, *Il Sole-24 Ore*, 24 November 1992.

194 According to Spanish and Portuguese newspaper accounts: See, for instance, *El Pais*, 23 November 1992.

196 explosive last sentence: Communiqué of Finance Ministers and Central Bank Governors of EMS countries, 22 November 1992.

197 Barucci made it clear . . . unnamed Banca d'Italia officials: See *Il Sole-24 Ore*, 24 November 1992.

199 rescuing the Irish Micawber: The strategy of hoping for a realignment involving the French franc and Danish krone was subsequently admitted to publicly, by the Finance Minister, Bertie Ahern: see 'Dublin voices anger as punt is devalued', in *Financial Times*, 1 February 1993.
rumours were circulating . . . Kohl had told Tietmeyer: These rumours later surfaced in the *Financial Times* of 16 August 1993.

201 'Dix ans de désinflation compétitive': *Les notes Bleues de Bercy*, Direction du Trésor, 16–31 October 1992.

## Chapter 9

206 machine for enriching speculators: Speech at Cologne University, 1 December 1992, quoted in *Financial Times*, 2 December 1992.

208 pointed out with his usual bluntness by Helmut Kohl: See his article, 'An anchor in an unstable Europe', in *Financial Times*, 4 January 1993.

212 Schlesinger thus declared: News conference in Brussels, quoted by Reuter, 28 January 1993.

213 According to the left-wing daily, *Libération*: 14 January 1993.
provoked . . . Ray MacSharry to attack Delors openly: See *Financial Times*, 6 November 1992.
(note 4) 'report, which has since been deeply buried': Reuter, 29 January 1993.

215 (note 7) André Icard had submitted an article: 'The transmission of monetary policy in an environment of deregulation and exchange rate stability: the French experience', *Journal of Monetary Economics*, 33 (1994), pp. 87–103.

216 (note 8) This was revealed . . . parliamentary investigations: See *Le Figaro*, 13 July 1994.

Juppé . . . made thinly veiled criticisms: See *Le Figaro*, 16 March 1995.

220 Irish press reports indicated: Sean Flynn, 'Long, hard battle for the pound', in *Irish Times*, 23 January 1993.

[Schlesinger] conspicuously praised the Irish authorities: News conference in Brussels, quoted by Reuter, 28 January 1993.

(note 14) 'We are like fair-weather friends': Flynn, cited above.

223 Irish officials pleaded with Trichet: See Sean Flynn, 'Ahern tells his side of devaluation fight', in *Irish Times*, 16 February 1993.

224 One Catholic bishop . . . intoned: Quoted by Reuter, 29 January 1993.

225 'too little, too late': Flynn, cited above, 16 February 1993.

226 'indicative of Britain's whole attitude': Reuter, 30 January 1993.

'Doesn't have the right to try to solve': AP-Dow Jones, 1 February 1993.

227 'a paradise for foreign investment': Quoted in *Financial Times*, 1 February 1993.

(note 22) directors . . . had warned Trichet and Sapin: See Philippe Bauchard, *Deux ministres trop tranquilles* (Paris, 1994), p. 60.

231 'Europe is much . . . the past': See Heinrich Hunke (ed), 'Europäische Wirtschaftgemeinschaft' (Berlin, 1942), quoted in *International Currency Review*, Occasional Paper no. 4, September 1993, p. 9.

237 'The statements . . . Dehaene . . . Verplaetse . . . Van Miert: See *Financial Times*, 18 January 1993.

(note 35) 'Franco-German cooperation is very close': Remarks by Sapin at dinner of G-7 Council, quoted in *Financial Times*, 13 January 1993.

239 he went on to list the countries: AP-Dow Jones, 3 February 1993.

241 'pressure . . . made explicit by Köhler: Reuter, 1 February 1993.

242 (note 37) Köhler had made similar remarks: See *Financial Times* of 9 December 1992 and 14 January 1993.

243 'This is is the signal we've been waiting for': Quoted in *Financial Times*, 5 February 1993.

'The supertanker has changed course': Quoted in *Financial Times*, 5 February 1993.

'good political signal': Quoted in *Financial Times*, 5 February 1993.

244 'politicians have the last word': Quoted in *Financial Times*, 5 February 1993.

245 'We hope this unfriendly game sometimes called dominoes': Quoted in *Financial Times*, 5 February 1993.

Bertie Ahern gave a grudging welcome: Quoted in *Financial Times*, 5 February 1993.

## Chapter 10

250 Tietmeyer gave warnings to Britain and Italy: See his speech 'Aktuelle Fragen der Geldpolitik aus deutscher und europäischer Sicht', Hamburg, 25 February 1993.

258 Political scientists consider: See, for instance, John Goodman, *Monetary*

*Sovereignty: the politics of central banking in Western Europe* (Ithaca, N.Y., 1992).

260 Padoa-Schioppa . . . 'the inconsistent quartet': See Tommaso Padoa-Schioppa et al., 'Equity, efficiency and growth', Commission of the European Communities, Luxembourg, 1985.

262 (note 12) article on the negotiations: See Bini-Smaghi, Padoa-Schioppa and Papadia, 'Transition to EMU', cited above.

269 (note 17) Fabrizio Saccomani . . . went public: Quoted in J. Frieden, 'Making commitments: France and Italy in the EMS, 1975–1985', in Eichengreen and Frieden (eds), *The Political Economy of European Monetary Unification* (Boulder, Colorado, and Oxford, 1994), p. 42.

271 (note 19) Delors . . . told . . . European Parliament: Quoted in *Agence Europe*, Brussels, no. 6430 (new series), 1 March 1995.

275 Braga made a fierce attack: Quoted by AP-Dow Jones, 5 March 1993.

279 Delors had warned: Quoted by AP-Dow Jones, 17 February 1993.

## Chapter 11

282 [Tietmeyer] took the occasion of a trip to Chile: Speech to the UN Economic Commission (CEPAL) in Santiago de Chile, 23 March 1993.
gruesome imaginings of Leon Brittan: See Lionel Barber, 'Ailing ERM handed a new lease of life', in *Financial Times*, 5 February 1993.

283 'Achilles' heel': Speech prepared for delivery by Helmut Schlesinger, Bocconi University, Milan, 15 March 1993.
(note 1) Schlesinger had previously said: See, for instance, his speech 'Current issues of German economic and monetary policy', American Council on Germany, New York, 15 January 1992.
(note 2) 'the EMS . . . fixed exchange rates': Hans Tietmeyer, speech to World ACI Conference, Sydney, 25 May 1992.

285 the reports of the two committees: *Lessons to be drawn from the disturbances on the foreign exchange markets*, Monetary Committee of the European Communities, Brussels, May 1993; *The implications and lessons to be drawn from the recent exchange-rate crisis*. Committee of Governors of the Central Banks of the Member States of the European Communities, Basle, May 1993.
'We have looked . . . magnifying glass': Remarks to the press by Wim Duisenberg following meeting of Central Bank Governors Committee, Basle, 20 April 1993.

286 (note 4) the head of the Commission's legal service . . . gave an interpretation: Reported in *Frankfurter Allgemeine Zeitung*, 3 July 1993.

287 (note 5) Ludlow: See full citation for p. 9 above.

## Chapter 12

295 'All that is made . . . excellence of the state': Philippe Meyer, *Dans mon pays lui-même* (Paris: 1994).
(note 7) no less an alumnus than Jacques Chirac: Quoted in Tony Allen-Mills, 'School for Scandal', in *Sunday Times* magazine, 22 January 1995, p. 24.

## REFERENCES

(note 8 ) German weather: See Jonathan Meades, 'The Devil's Work, *The Times*, 20 October 1994.

296 Schlesinger was moved to comment: Interview in *New York Times*, 6 April 1993.
Alain Juppé . . . immediately before the election: Interviewed in *Le Monde*, 5 March 1993.

297 Schlesinger . . . interview in *International Herald Tribune*: 26 May 1993.

298 (note 10) clear political motivation . . . has recently been brought out: See Roland Vaubel, 'Eine Public-Choice Analyse der Deutschen Bundesbank und ihre Implikationen für die Europäische Währungsunion', in Dieter Duwendag and Jürgen Siebke (eds), *Europa vor dem Eintritt in die Wirtschafts- und Währungsunion*, (Berlin, 1993). See also Susanne Lohmann, 'Federalism and Central Bank Autonomy: the Politics of German Monetary Policy, 1957–92', mimeo, University of California at Los Angeles, October 1994.

301 de Larosière had spoken of a reinforced role for the franc: Interview in newsletter of the French banking association (AFB), 5 March 1993.

305 Raymond Barre . . . was warning: Quoted in Bauchard, *Deux ministres*, p. 146.
he railed against the structure of the Bundesbank Council: Quoted in Bauchard, p. 22.
(note 13) '*Les défenseurs du franc fort vont se battre autour de la direction du Trésor*': Bauchard, p. 152.

307 He has been well described . . . as seeking to return France: Bauchard, p. 213.
round of private meetings with the *grosses légumes* of French industry and finance: The flavour of these meetings is given, with an extensive cast list, in Bauchard.

308 (note 17) the authorities had ways of exerting pressure: 'Galilée' (pseudonym), 'La Tragédie du Franc Fort', *Revue Des Deux Mondes*, September 1993, p. 23.

309 Alphandéry was interviewed on French radio: Reported by Reuter, 24 June 1993.

310 Alphandéry . . . told Waigel over the phone: Reported in *Frankfurter Allgemeine Zeitung*, 25 June 1993.

311 Count Otto von Lamsdorff . . . remarked: Quoted by Reuter, 25 June 1993.
Schlesinger argued that competition . . . was healthy: Quoted in *Financial Times*, 29 June 1993.

315 drove Mitterrand to make his first public pronouncement: Quoted by Reuter, 17 July 1993.

320 everyone expected Tietmeyer: Grant, p. 263, states unequivocally that Tietmeyer voted for a cut in the discount rate.
interview with *Der Spiegel* 14 October 1991.

321 '*Jean-Claude Trichet hésite*': Bauchard, p. 164.
France would resume intervention: See *Libération*, 6 August 1993.

322 Waigel too had been prevailed upon . . . to request a meeting: See *The Economist*, 7 August 1993, p. 22.
Schlesinger and Waigel flew to Paris: See Bauchard, p. 164.

324 The Germans went in to bat first: Several accounts of the facts of the weekend's meetings were published shortly afterwards. In English, the first

(which brought out the nature of the Franco-German confrontation on continued interventions) was in the *Financial Times* of 3 August 1993; fuller accounts appeared in *The Times* of 12 August 1993 and the *Financial Times* of 17 August 1993.

327 Trichet was graciously disposed: Details of this part of the meeting were revealed, in the BBC television 'Newsnight' programme, as early as Monday, 2 August 1993, and further elaborated in *The Economist*, 7 August 1993. In France, key points of the meeting were revealed in *Le Figaro* of 3 and *Libération* of 6 August 1993. In Germany the conflicts in the meetings are brought out in some detail in 'High noon um zwei Uhr nachts' (an account apparently based largely on quotes from the Dutch Finance Minister, Wim Kok), in *Süddeutsche Zeitung*, 3 August 1993. The French proposal was also commented on extensively in *Die Welt* of 6 August 1993. Balladur told journalists on 2 August 1993 that France would have preferred a DM withdrawal from the ERM to the widening of the bands: see *Le Monde*, 3 August 1993.

332 (note 32) an *'assez vague promesse'* given by Tietmeyer:  See Bauchard, p. 166.

334 (note 33) Alphandéry was attempting a brave face:  Press conference following meeting of Franco-German Economic and Financial Council, Paris, 3 August 1993.

337 (note 34) 'a blow for freedom':  Press conference in Bonn, 2 August 1993.


## Chapter 13

341 'everyone can go to the beach':  AP-Dow Jones, 30 July 1993.

342 (note 2) Tietmeyer was to go public:  Hans Tietmeyer, 'Interest rate policy and political interest rates: stabilization policy versus business cycle policy?', speech to the 39th monetary policy conference organized by the 'Zeitschrift für das Gesamte Kreditwesen', Frankfurt, 27 October 1993.
(note 3) Tietmeyer . . . unabashed satisfaction:  Speech to the Association for the Monetary Union of Europe, Frankfurt, 20 September 1994.

343 'senior official sources' in Luxembourg . . . cited as predicting:  Reuter, 5 August 1993. Commenting to a Belgian financial newspaper on the Reuters report, the Luxembourg Finance Minister, Jean-Claude Juncker, said: 'It would not be surprising if an agreement of this sort could be conceded but it would not be welcome for a finance minister, in present circumstances, to give any indication of the date or the modalities of such an agreement.' Quoted in *L'Echo de la Bourse*, 6 August 1993.

344 fourteen eminent Belgian . . . economists published the 'Louvain Manifesto':  Filip Abraham *et al.*, 'Manifeste pour une politique favorable à l'emploi', Katolische Universiteit Leuven, 24 August 1993.

345 He was keen . . . beefy role for Maastricht's first-born child:  Maystadt's fullest public statement of his views on the EMI was subsequently given in his address on 'Prospects for EMU on the Eve of Stage II' at the European Finance Convention, Brussels, 29 November 1993.

346 'central bank for Europe' . . . if the Bundesbank targeted the ERM-wide money supply:  The most forthright statement of Tietmeyer's public views on

these questions is perhaps to be found in his Frankfurt address, of 27 October 1993.

idea being floated by the economic research unit: Carlo Monticelli, 'Monetary policy coordination under an exchange-rate agreement and the optimal monetary policy instrument', Committee of Central Bank Governors, Basle, 1993.

349 SPD spokesmen launched a series of attacks: The most explicit questioning of Tietmeyer's links with Kohl came from SPD economics spokesman Uwe Jensen at a news conference in Bonn on 26 January 1994, when Jensen also presented a 10-point 'national pact' involving the Bundesbank as well as the government and the two sides of industry.

351 'liquidity logjam': Speech by Olaf Sievert, Leipzig, 1 June 1994.
(note 12) three members of the Bundesbank Council . . . made totally contradictory . . . statements: Olaf Sievert, speech presenting first annual report of Landeszentralbank of Saxony and Thüringia, Leipzig, 1 June 1994; Günther Palm, radio interview in Saarbrucken, 1 June 1994, quoted by AP-Dow Jones and Knight-Ridder Financial Services; Reimut Jochimsen, radio interview in Hamburg, 1 June 1994, quoted by AP-Dow Jones and Knight-Ridder Financial Services.

354 Gerd Häusler has recently said: Speech on 3 February 1995.

356 Häusler . . . has even suggested the *worldwide* imposition of reserve requirements: Gerd Häusler, speech on 3 February 1995.
(note 17) Tietmeyer expressed a preference for Britain's participation in EMU: 'Newsnight', BBC TV, 9 March 1995.

359 (note 20) The arguments he now uses . . . adduced in 1989: A characteristic expression of Brittan's views on EMU can be found in a speech to a business conference in London, 17 November 1994; for his 1989 advocacy of the ERM, see his speech to a Swiss bank conference in London on 15 June 1989, extensively quoted in *The Times*, 16 June 1989.

360 Eddie George has recently emphasized: Sir Winston Churchill Memorial Lecture, 'The Economics of EMU', Fondation J.-P. Pescatore, Luxembourg, 21 February 1995. He repeated his warnings in a speech to the Ramon Areces Foundation in Madrid on 19 May 1995.
Kenneth Clarke's characteristic obfuscation of the EMU debate: Speech to the European Movement, London, 9 February 1995.

361 Marianne Jelved had the temerity to suggest: Quoted by Reuter, 12 January 1994.

362 According to a report in a Danish financial newspaper: *Börsen*, 7 February 1994.
'This is a political question': *Börsen*, 7 February 1994.
(note 22) she claimed . . . that the opt-out kept Danish interest rates higher: Interview in *Okonomisk Ugebrev*, 27 February 1994, quoted by AP-Dow Jones.
'a political slap in the face to France': Interview in *Börsen*, 14 February 1994; the interview was picked up and quoted by Reuter.

363 Raymond Barre has recently put it: Quoted in *The Times*, 25 February 1995.
(note 24) Trichet made a speech in Frankfurt: 'Importance de la coopération

franco-allemande dans la construction de l'UEM', speech at conference 'Rencontres Financières Paris-Europlace', Frankfurt, 25 March 1994.

364 Trichet pontificated: Press conference to present the Banque de France's monetary policy for 1995, Paris, 21 December 1994.
Trichet had exceeded the formal limits of his role: See Bauchard, p. 179.

365 (note 25) 'French current affairs magazine commented: Philippe Durupt, 'Le franc à la baisse', in *Valeurs Actuelles*, 4 March 1995.

367 In late September . . . he intensified his attacks: Address to Kieler Konjunktur Gesprach, Institut für Weltwirtschaft, Kiel, October 1994.

368 Solbes was saying that 1997 looked unlikely for EMU: Remarks to Spanish Parliament, 15 February 1995, quoted by Reuter.

369 The Spanish Finance Minister was unusually open and explicit: Remarks to the Spanish Parliament, 8 March 1995, quoted by Knight-Ridder agency.

371 Waigel had declared: Quoted in *Financial Times*, 2 March 1995.
Tietmeyer felt impelled: Quoted in *Financial Times*, 8 March 1995.

375 That pressure was made public: Diplomatic sources quoted by Reuter, 19 May 1995.
the bank moved . . . inflation target: See Guido Tabellini, 'Bankitalia o si dà un target', *Il Sole-24 Ore*, 8 June 1995.
In early June, Dini stated: See *Financial Times*, 10/11 June 1995.

## Chapter 14

379 the Lamers report from the CDU parliamentary group: 'Überlegungen zur europäischen Politik' (Reflections on European Policy'), CDU/CSU faction in the Bundestag, Bonn, 1 September 1994.
(note 1) Denis Healey has recently expressed this view: Denis Healey, 'Not a very solid state', article in the *Sunday Times*, 5 March 1995, section 10, p. 10.
(note 2) *La France de l'an 2000*: Paris, 1994.
'I prefer . . . markets': Alain Minc and Philippe Séguin, *Deux Frances?* (Paris, 1995), p. 65.

380 (note 3) Tim Renton . . . told a television audience: 'On the Record', BBC TV, February 1995.
(note 4) Delors was perhaps the most explicit of all: See references for p. 75.

382 not Churchill's intention that Britain should form part of a European Union: The relevant section of Churchill's September 1946 speech at Zurich University is quoted in Norman Rose, *Churchill: An Unruly Life* (London, 1995), p. 332.
(note 7) Heseltine . . . had the cheek: See Michael Heseltine, 'Britain must march behind Churchill into Europe', article in the *Sunday Times*, 5 February 1995.

383 (note 9) intellectually lazy arguments of . . . Heseltine: See Heseltine, cited above.

384 German resentment and suspicion was voiced: Klaus Engelen, *The European*, 21–24 February 1993.

386 David Marsh . . . wrote in the *Financial Times*: David Marsh, 'A hard act to follow', in *Financial Times*, 23 September 1992, p. 16.

387 It has been pointed out . . . German diplomatic tactics . . . 'Genscherism' . . . recognition of Croatia and Slovenia: See Timothy Garton Ash, *In Europe's Name: Germany and the Divided Continent* (London, 1994), esp. pp. 262 and 395–6.

392 his last, defeated speech: Speech to European Parliament, Strasbourg, 19 January 1995.

393 Roy Jenkins . . . made the claim: Quoted in David Marsh and Lionel Barber, 'Shoot-out at the currency coral', in *Financial Times*, 6/7 February 1993.

394 A variant of the argument . . . expressed by one of the most Euroenthusiastic of British banking figures: Christopher Johnson interviewed on the 'Today' programme, BBC Radio 4, 7 February 1995.

395 (note 18) Kenneth Clarke has recently stated that monetary union would not necessarily require political union: Speech to the European Movement, London, 9 February 1995.

# Index

Aachen agreement, 15, 17
Ahern, Bertie, 218n, 245
Alphandéry, Edmond, 308–9, 313, 336–7
Amato, Giulio, 132
AMUE (Association for the Monetary Union of Europe), 394, 400
Andreotti, Giulio, 12, 105, 132, 260
Anglo-Scottish Union, 383
asymmetry: definition, 33
Austrian schilling, 368
*Auszüge*, 119, 142
Aznar, Jose-Maria, 279

Baker, James: conflict with Schlesinger, 40–1
Balladur, Edouard, 35, 37, 374; and ECB proposal, 42, 73; U-turn in policy, 306–7
Banca d'Italia, 133, 184, 376; 'divorce' from government, 258–9; and ERM crisis, 155; on monetary union, 259–60, 261; raising of discount rate, 136, 143; relations with Bundesbank, 144, 148, 149, 271; reluctance to cut interest rates after ERM exit, 185; *see also* Dini, Lamberto
Banco de España (Bank of Spain), 111; on devaluation (March 94), 370–1; inflation-targeting policy after ERM widening, 367–9; introduction of tough exchange controls (Sept 92), 187; response to overheating of economy at ERM entry, 83–4; suspension of intervention obligations, 299, 300; trimming of interest rates (1991)
Bank deutscher Länder, 8, 386
Bank of England, 79, 156, 399
Bank of Portugal, 274; attack on by Braga de Macedo, 275–6; and ERM, 124, 125, 126
Banque de France, 24, 36, 177, 211; cut in interest rates (June 92), 304; De Larosiere on Maastricht, 119–20; establishment of monetary framework, 351, 363–4; independence, 371, 363, 390, 391; intervention in franc crisis: (Jan 87), 37;

(Sept 92), 178, 179, 181, 204; (Jan 93), 209; (July 93), 318, 321, 322; market methods of monetary control, 36; preferential rates for lending banks, 215; response to Bundesbank rate cut (July 93), 312, 313; unable to re-build reserves, 211; *see also* Trichet, Jean-Claude
Barings collapse, 355n
Barre, Raymond, 21, 24, 305, 363
Barucci, Piero, 197
Basle-Nyborg agreement, 39–40, 41, 42, 73, 131
Bath: informal Ecofin meeting, 144–7
Baudouin, King, 326
Beleza, Miguel, 276
Belgian franc, 16, 235, 236, 250, 257, 319, 343; weakening of after ERM collapse, 344, 345, 346
Belgian National Bank (BNB), 235, 317–18
Belgium, 26, 33, 328–9; death of King Baudouin, 326; deceleration in inflation, 257; and DM zone, 234–7, 328, 344; history, 16–17; and Luxembourg, 327–8; Maystadt plan, 345–6; monetary policy after ERM collapse, 343–5; prospect of leaving ERM, 328–9; *see also* Belgian franc
Belgo-Luxembourg Economic Union (BLEU), 328
Benelux Treaty (1947), 16, 26
Benning, Dr Bernhard, 231
Bérégovoy, Pierre, 29, 35, 86, 121, 214, 243, 385
Berlin Wall: impact of fall of, 87
Bildt, Carl, 190
Black Wednesday, 154–7
Blessing, Karl, 9
BLEU (Belgo-Luxembourg Economic Union), 328
Blum, Léon, 7
Boissonat, Jean, 224n
bond-markets:'bubble' in, 348–50, 354–5, 357, 361